15th International Conference on Cognition and Exploratory Learning in Digital Age (CELDA 2018)

Budapest, Hungary
21-23 October 2018

Editors:

Demetrios G. Sampson
Dirk Ifenthaler
Pedro Isaias

ISBN: 978-1-5108-7539-5

Printed from e-media with permission by:

Curran Associates, Inc.
57 Morehouse Lane
Red Hook, NY 12571

Some format issues inherent in the e-media version may also appear in this print version.

Printed by Curran Associates, Inc. (2019)

International Association for Development of the Information Society (IADIS)
Rua Sao Sebastiao Da Pedreira
No. 100, 30, 1050-209
Lisbon, Portugal

Phone: 351 21 3151373
Fax: 351 21 3151244

secretariat@iadis.org

Additional copies of this publication are available from:

Curran Associates, Inc.
57 Morehouse Lane
Red Hook, NY 12571 USA
Phone: 845-758-0400
Fax: 845-758-2633
Email: curran@proceedings.com
Web: www.proceedings.com

15th INTERNATIONAL CONFERENCE
on

COGNITION AND EXPLORATORY LEARNING IN THE DIGITAL AGE (CELDA 2018)

PROCEEDINGS OF THE 15th INTERNATIONAL CONFERENCE on

COGNITION AND EXPLORATORY LEARNING IN THE DIGITAL AGE (CELDA 2018)

BUDAPEST, HUNGARY

OCTOBER 21-23, 2018

Organised by

IADIS
International Association for Development of the Information Society

Edited by Demetrios G. Sampson, Dirk Ifenthaler and Pedro Isaías

Associate Editor: Luís Rodrigues

TABLE OF CONTENTS

FULL PAPERS

SHORT PAPERS

REFLECTION PAPERS

FOREWORD

These proceedings contain the papers of the 15th International Conference on Cognition and Exploratory Learning in the Digital Age (CELDA 2018), held during 21 to 23 October 2018, which has been organized by the International Association for Development of the Information Society (IADIS).

The CELDA conference aims to address the main issues concerned with evolving learning processes and supporting pedagogies and applications in the digital age. There have been advances in both cognitive psychology and computing that have affected the educational arena. The convergence of these two disciplines is increasing at a fast pace and affecting academia and professional practice in many ways.

Paradigms such as just-in-time learning, constructivism, student-centered learning and collaborative approaches have emerged and are being supported by technological advancements such as simulations, virtual reality and multi-agent systems. These developments have created both opportunities and areas of serious concerns. This conference aims to cover both technological as well as pedagogical issues related to these developments. Main tracks have been identified. However innovative contributions that do not easily fit into these areas will also be considered as long as they are directly related to the overall theme of the conference – cognition and exploratory learning in the digital age.

The following areas are represented in the submissions for CELDA 2018:

- Acquisition of Expertise
- Assessing Progress of Learning in Complex Domains
- Assessment of Exploratory Learning Approaches
- Assessment of Exploratory Technologies
- Cognition in Education
- Collaborative Learning
- Educational Psychology
- Exploratory Technologies (Simulations, VR, i-TV, etc.)
- Just-in-time and Learning-on-Demand
- Learner Communities and Peer-Support
- Learning Communities & Web Service Technologies Pedagogical issues related with Learning Objects
- Learning Paradigms in Academia
- Learning Paradigms in the Corporate Sector
- Life-long Learning
- Student-centered Learning
- Technology and Mental Models
- Technology
- Learning and Expertise
- Virtual University

The CELDA 2018 Conference received 85 submissions from more than 31 countries. Each submission was reviewed in a double-blind review process by at least two independent reviewers to ensure quality and maintain high standards. Out of the papers submitted, 37 were accepted as full papers for an acceptance rate of 44%; 20 were accepted as short papers and 5 were accepted as reflection papers. Authors of the best published papers in the CELDA 2018 proceedings will be invited to publish extended versions of their papers in a book from Springer.

In addition to the presentation of full, short and reflection papers, the conference also includes one keynote presentation from an internationally distinguished researcher. We would therefore like to express our gratitude to this year keynote speaker: Professor Tobias Ley, Professor for Learning Analytics and Educational Innovation, Head of the Center of Excellence in Educational Innovation, Tallinn University, Estonia.

A successful conference requires the effort of many individuals. We would like to thank the members of the Program Committee for their hard work in reviewing and selecting the papers that appear in this book. We are especially grateful to the authors who submitted their papers to this conference and to the presenters who provided the substance of this meeting. We wish to thank all members of our organizing committee.

Last but not least, we hope that participants enjoy Budapest and their time with colleagues from all over the world.

Pedro Isaías, The University of Queensland, Australia
Conference Chair

Demetrios G. Sampson, University of Piraeus, Greece & Curtin University, Australia
Dirk Ifenthaler, University of Mannheim, Germany & Curtin University, Australia
Program Co-Chairs

Budapest, Hungary
October 2018

PROGRAM COMMITTEE

CONFERENCE CHAIR

Pedro Isaías, The University of Queensland, Australia

PROGRAM CO-CHAIRS

Demetrios G Sampson, University of Piraeus, Greece & Curtin University, Australia
Dirk Ifenthaler, University of Mannheim, Germany & Curtin University, Australia

COMMITTEE MEMBERS

Ah-Choo Koo, Multimedia Univerisity, Malaysia
Alke Martens, University of Rostock, Germany
Anthony Y. H. Liao, Asia University, Taiwan
Aparna Lalingkar, International Institute of Information Technology, India
Arif Altun, Hacettepe University, Turkey
Barbara Lockee, Virginia Tech, USA
Carol H.C Chu, Soochow University, Taiwan
Charalampos Karagiannidis, University of Thessaly, Greece
Chien Sing Lee, Sunway University, Malaysia
Chung Hsien Lan, Nanya Institute of Technology, Taiwan
Chun-Wang Wei, Kaohsiung Medical University, Taiwan
Clark Quinn , Quinnovation.com, USA
Davinia Hernandez-leo, Universitat Pompeu Fabra, Spain
Farshad Badie, Aalborg University, Denmark
Flavio Manganello, National Research Council, Italy
Giuliana Dettori, National Research Council, Italy
Giuliana Guazzaroni, University Politecnica Delle Marche, Italy
I-fang Liu, National Central University, Taiwan
Imran Zualkernan, American University of Sharjah, United Arab Emirates
Jay Loftus, Schulich School of Medicine & Dentistry, Canada
Jie-Chi Yang, National Central University, Taiwan
Jirarat Sitthiworachart, Walailak University, Thailand
John Brine, The University of Aizu, Japan
Jon Dron, Athabasca University, Canada
Jose Janssen, Open University of the Netherlands, Netherlands
Juan Felipe Calderon, Universidad Andres Bello, Chile
Julie-Ann Sime, Lancaster University, United Kingdom
Katherine Sinitsa, International Research and Training Center of Information Technologies and Systems, Ukraine
Kuo-Liang Ou, National Hsin-chu University of Education, Taiwan
Kyparisia Papanikolaou, School of Pedagogical and Technological Education, Greece
Lence Miloseva, Goce Delcev University, Macedonia
Maiga Chang, Athabasca University, Canada
Michael Verhaart, New Zealand
Min Kyu Kim, Georgia State University, USA
Ming-Chi Liu, Feng Chia University, Taiwan

KEYNOTE LECTURE

LEARNING AS REFLECTIVE SEARCH: MODELING CONVERGENT AND DIVERGENT PROCESSES IN SOCIAL EXPLORATORY SEARCH

Professor Tobias Ley, Professor for Learning Analytics and Educational Innovation, Head of the Center of Excellence in Educational Innovation, Tallinn University, Estonia

Abstract

When people learn by exploring information online, we regard this as an iterative process of reflective search. Finding and reading sources online reflects on the learner's memory, and this in turn guides future search behavior. In social information spaces (as the Web), reflective search is also influenced by interpretations of other learners. For example, our research shows that individual learning is to some extent dependent on convergent processes that happen in the group (i.e. agreement that individuals reach about the meaning of particular terms). I then propose a computational cognitive model that models search processes and reflections on memory. The model explains convergence in the group as well as individual learning processes. In a final step, we have turned the computational model into a recommender service for a social information environment. I report results from an online study that shows the recommender balances convergence in a creative group work setting by promoting divergence (i.e. helping individuals stay fluent in generating ideas). The reflective search framework is based on a validated cognitive model of memory and learning. By employing the research strategy discussed in this talk, it is possible to extend the range of application of this model from the laboratory to more realistic learning settings with a large number of learners.

Full Papers

GET OUT! - HELPING TEACHERS ORCHESTRATE OUTDOOR GAME-BASED LEARNING ACTIVITIES

Kadri Mettis and Terje Väljataga
Tallinn University, Narva mnt 25, 10120 Tallinn, Estonia

ABSTRACT

Outdoor learning activities are very time consuming for teachers to prepare and difficult to manage, especially when the activity takes place in a non familiar environment for instance zoos. M-learning could help teachers to conduct outdoor education by involving learners in the creation and orchestration of artefacts (game). For that it is necessary to know how to arrange, orchestrate and monitor such diversified forms of learning in a systematic and technical manner. In pursuit of these goals to reduce teachers workload and share part of the orchestration load to students a case study was conducted where 9 students and 3 teachers participated. Together with the teachers and the Zoological Gardens pedagogues, the activities were planned, where the learner could acquire the knowledge through playing and creating the tracks, consisted of location points with assignments. The created activities were also tested in practice to determine their suitability for use in real life learning conditions. For creating activities and learning at the Zoo, SmartZoos app was used. It is a game based learning app where users move from one location to another with the guidance of their phone and in specific location points tasks open that learners need to fill. Students were divided to groups and every group was followed by an observer who took notes about occurring problems and time spent using the phone. Students and teachers evaluated their experience by answering questionnaires, additional interviews were conducted with the teachers to get a deeper understanding of their perspective to sharing orchestration load with students and how they managed the groups at the zoo. The results of this case study show that students were successfully engaged in the planning and creating learning artifacts stage, reducing teachers workload and planning time for this outdoor learning activity. The main issues that teachers brought out were group managing, communication with students for example following students movement, having access to students work or results and assessment.

KEYWORDS

Outdoor Learning, Game-Based Learning, Orchestration, Mobile Learning

1. INTRODUCTION

Educational institutions can provide resources for teachers to plan, orchestrate, and support co-operation and creativity. For example, computer technology has several functions for helping orchestration (Kollar et al., 2011), although the use of technology always challenges a teacher's work (Arvaja et al., 2009). The effectiveness of m-learning in outdoor learning has been studied previously, various ways have been proposed to reduce the burden of orchestration (Lai et al., 2015; Munoz-Cristobal, 2017), but in all of these studies, the main creator and designer of the learning process is a teacher. Crompton et al. (2017) points out that in most m-learning studies students are ready-made consumers of knowledge and are not exploiting the full potential of mobile devices. Ishtaiwa et al. (2015) survey showed that m-learning has different uses, but tends to focus on certain activities. Crompton and others (2017) have further pointed out that a large proportion of m-learning studies have been conducted in a formal education environment, that is, in a classroom or school district. The use of m-learning in a non-formal environment (Crompton et al., 2017), for example, in a park, a zoo, and a botanical garden, should be explored. Goal of this study is to explore the challenges of orchestration while outdoor learning and how the used SmartZoos app is supporting teachers to orchestrate the activities.

2.1 Orchestration

Several intellectuals have used the word "orchestration" to design and manage real-time classroom activities, learning processes and teaching activities (Gravier et al., 2006; Dillenbourg & Fischer, 2007). An orchestration does not indicate that the lecture is more intense or that the teacher has to make a show. Orchestration is more like the meaning of "teacher's central constructivism". Students need to learn through activities, but teachers have a role as manager in the whole scenario (Dillenbourg & Jermann, 2010). Prieto et al. (2011) has suggested 5+3 aspects in his literature review about orchestration that have emerged from different studies. These aspects are planning/design, management, awareness/assessment, adaption, roles, theory, pragmatism and synergy. These aspects can be helpful for planning evaluation for orchestration process and tools (Prieto et al., 2011). Due to the high workload of teachers, it is difficult to put in place new methods and tools that would be needed to implement the new learning pathway. The solution would be to reduce the burden on teachers' orchestration, for example by allowing for applications where a large proportion of the planning would be distributed to students.

2.2 Instrumental Orchestration

Instrumental orchestration is defined as the intentional and systematic organization of various digital artefacts by the teacher to guide students (Drijvers et al., 2010). In instrumental orchestration, three elements can be distinguished: didactic design or how different means are related to the environment; the way in which the teacher decides to use the didactic design and the didactic presentation, or how the selected didactic design and presentation are actually used, such as how to link student questions to the context or how to cope with emerging problems (Drijvers et al., 2010).

Coordinating the academic environment of an IT environment in recent years has been a source of interest in research communities engaged in studying technology learning (Dillenbourg, Järvelä & & Fischer, 2009; Roschelle, Dimitriadis & Hoppe, 2013). Since the first problem faced by teachers in carrying out such activities is the creation and preparation of a scenario, several studies have recommended the use of a special environment that allows linking all other tools in one place (Munoz-Cristobal et al., 2014; Ternier et al., 2012) . In these environments, however, there are restrictions on orchestration: 1) most variants have limited or even no opportunity to regulate the flexibility of students' work; this is especially important in the case of the use of librarianship environments that may require partial orchestration burden for students (Sharples, 2013); 2) many environments do not allow the integration of technologies that teachers already use, which reduces the use of these methods by teachers (Cuendet et al., 2013; Prieto et al., 2014); 3) most environments do not allow the use of surrounding or context where learning takes place which is an important factor in achieving unobtrusive learning (Milrad et al., 2013).

In addition to the limitations described above, in the case of out-of-school education, the real dispersal of students must also be taken into account, which makes it very difficult for the teacher to monitor and support the learning process. In order to solve this problem, it would be wise to develop a technological solution that helps orchestrate learners in dispersed environments.

2.3 SmartZoos Learning App

M-learning could help teachers to conduct outdoor education by involving learners in the creation and orchestration of artefacts (game). For that it is necessary to know how to arrange, orchestrate and monitor such diversified forms of learning in a systematic and technical manner. In pursuit of the goal to reduce teachers workload and share part of the orchestration load (in this case planning) to students, a game/based outdoor learning app was used. That solution is still in the development process and the case study describes the first piloting of the app called SmartZoos. SmartZoos is location based game developed for the use at the Tallinn, Helsinki and Stockholm Zoos. It is a game based learning app where users move from one location to another with the guidance of their phone and in specific location points tasks open that learners need to fill. Users can create activity items themselves. In the creation process it is possible to choose from different types of questions like information, one correct answer, multiple correct answers, freeform answer, match pairs, make an embedded content question or photo task. It is possible to set also other parameters like language, distance from location point from how far the task opens, location of the task.

SmartZoos app was used in this pilot as a support tool for orchestrating outdoor learning. It provides a frame and a structure for activities conducted outside and helps to set learning goals and sequence of the activities (Figure 1).

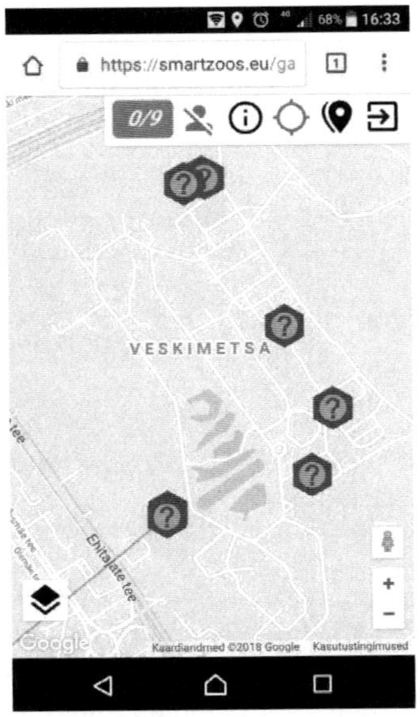

Figure 1. Screenshot from SmartZoos app of one track created in the TallinnZoo. Questionmarks mark the location of different tasks

2.4 Method

Conducted case study is part of a research which follows design-based research. Current paper describes one piloting under investigation. This piloting session focused on testing the suitability of the SmartZoos app for outdoor learning, investigating participators attitudes and experience and what are the future possibilities for developing this app. For the data collection both quantitative and qualitative methods were used. Students attitudes and experience were measured with questionnaires which contained open-ended questions, Likert-type scale questions for the attitude and multiple answers questions for background and experience questions. Observers followed student groups and gathered information about occurring problems and time spent using the phone by filling in questionnaire as often as needed. Teachers were interviewed to study their attitude and experience using SmartZoos game for outdoor learning. In pursuit of these goals a case study was conducted where 9 students and 3 teachers participated. Together with the teachers and the Zoological Gardens pedagogues, activities were planned, where the learner could acquire the knowledge through playing and creation of the tracks.

Participators were 9 10th graders from one Tallinn school and three biology teachers who had experience in using SmartZoos. The activities took place in two days. On the first day students came to the Zoo and were instructed how to use SmartZoos app and how to play. Students were divided into 3 groups. Groups were followed by observers, who filled in forms about group engagement to the phone and problems they faced during the activity. Students completed the tracks and afterwards gathered at the last point to fill in the feedback form and to get instructions for a homework task. As a homework, every group had to design one track for the next. They were instructed that they have to create some questions themselves but they also can use already existing questions. The next time they came to the zoo all groups had managed to create one track. Before going to play they filled in feedback form about creating a track. As they were already familiar with the game they only chose tracks and didn't need any more instructing. Students met after finishing the tracks and gave each other feedback and shared their experiences about other students created tracks (Figure 2).

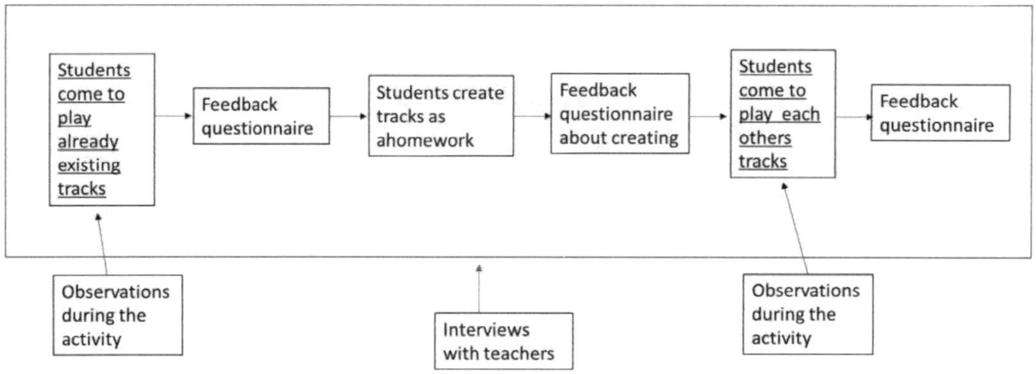

Figure 2. Case study design conducted at the Zoo

2.5 Results

2.5.1 Students Feedback

From 9 students who participated in this case study 3 were girls and 6 were boys with age 16-17 years. 3 of the students used Samsung smartphones, 4 iPhones and 2 did not use their own device for game but teamed up with somebody else. Most used browsers for the game were Safari and Chrome, one student used Explorer. Many students faced technical challenges while using SmartZoos. 4 students stated that their phones showed wrong location, 3 of the students marked that they had problems while opening the game and only 2 students stated that they had no problems with using the app. 4 students who had problems tried to find the solution on their own and 3 of them just ignored the problem and continued the game.

Students attitudes to the first activity where they played tracks created by Zoo pedagogues, were mostly positive. 7 students marked that they liked the game, 1 was neutral and 1 didn't like the game. The students would like to use the game again (6 would use again, 2 neutral and 1 wouldn't use again) but were satisfied with the game itself (5 satisfied, 4 neutral). Some students were excited to use this game but others were more neutral (exited 4, neutral 4, not exited 1). 8 out of 9 students found that used app was helpful for learning. Most of the students found that the game was easy (easy 6, neutral 1, complicated 2) and interesting (interesting 7, neutral 1, boring 1) and that they had enough time to observe the animals (had enough time to observe 5, neutral 3, did not have enough time to observe 1). But not so many students marked that app was easy to use (easy 4, neutral 5).

Students also had some problems while creating the tracks as a homework. Most problematic for them was to mark the location for activity items, because they didn't know the Zoo very well. Overall the attitude for creating tracks activity was positive. Students thought that creating tracks was easy and that they liked to create tracks themselves. All the participating students stated that they have gained knew knowledge during this activity. They also didn't think that creating the tracks would have been very time consuming.

In general we can say that students enjoyed using the SmartZoos and found it interesting. Also it was good to note that students didn't mind creating tracks themselves and that they found they learned while using SmartZoos.

2.5.2 Interviews with Teachers

Interviews were conducted with 3 teachers who had experience with using SmartZoos with their students for both: playing and creating. The answers were grouped and categorized into 8 categories based on orchestration aspects Prieto (2011) defines in his 5+3 orchestration framework (Prieto et al., 2011). The formed categories were planning/design (planning, often referred to as learning design), regulation/management (issues related to class, time, workflow and group management), adaptation/flexibility/intervention (changing and adapting the design/plan to both the local context of the classroom and the emergent occurrences during the enactment of learning activities), awareness/assessment (awareness of what is happening in the classroom and within the learners' minds, assessment), roles of the teacher and other actors, pragmatism/practice, alignment/synergy and models/theories. The aim of conducting the interviews was to get a deeper understanding of what is teachers attitude to using this kind of outdoor learning game, what kind of support would teachers need to reduce the orchestration load and what are the challenges for teacher in every orchestration aspect.

At the beginning of the interview some questions were asked about their attitude and previous experience in using technology for learning. Teachers have same goals for using mobile devices in their lessons. They want to make use of already existing students devices, make lessons more interactive or making students to self-study. Schools have more equipment than before which is giving more possibilities.

Teacher 3: *"There are new tablet sets at the school, we only had one laptop set before. Two tablets sets and WiFi router. And it goes well, I use much more this year. We also have technical support at school who checks if everything is okay, batteries full and programs installed. If the technological side is okay, then it goes nicely."*

They all use smartphones in their lessons for example electronic tests, searching for information. They also have used mobile devices in outdoor learning, for example plant and lichen determinants and Avastusrada (location based game similar to SmartZoos) to make discovery tracks around the schoolhouse or park. There exists big motivation to use more technology in outdoor settings but there are certain limitations for example location, weather and a lot of work with preparation.

Design: Time allocation for preparing outdoor learning activities is time consuming. Teachers point out that preparing outdoor activity at the Zoo is even more time consuming, because teacher needs to visit the Zoo, needs to find the animals and study what information is available at that location and then prepare the questions. They also mention that the time expenditure depends on how well the teacher knows the Zoo. If you are more familiar than it takes less time.

Teacher 3: *"Teachers will need 2 days for preparation. One day for walk and planning at the zoo, the other day for completing the track. Teachers would prefer already composed tracks most likely."*

Teachers suggest that the questions and tasks should already exist beforehand to make the preparation easier. Questions should contain meta-info about the grade and topic to make the finding easier, so it would be possible to filter. They also suggest that there is a need for a place where to change experiences and ideas with other teachers like a forum or the possibility to evaluate tracks so that other users would know what kind of tracks to choose. They refer to similarity in social media, that good rating is trusted. Teachers point out that it is necessary to give a possibility for students to create the questions and tracks. On the one hand that takes away the need to prepare and on the other hand it gives students the chance to be creative.

Teacher 3: *"Good that students create, but the question is how correct these tasks are."*

As a best design for this kind of outdoor learning activity teachers suggest a project day type of solution where students create the questions and tracks directly at the zoo and play each others tracks later. The activity would be longer for students but at the same time it would free teacher from preparing the tracks and questions.

Management: In outdoor learning activities it is difficult to keep track on students progress and especially in very dispersed settings it is difficult to support and help students. From the group management perspective teachers liked the possibility to track students activity. The other feature that they all mentioned but at the moment is missing from the SmartZoos app was communication. Teachers would like to have the possibility to contact students easily on the field.

Teacher 2: *"I'm responsible, I have to know that they are safe. It is very important. Would be good to see where they are.*

Teachers note that completing the track takes students at least 1-2 hours. Also they added that before starting the activity there is a need to explain how to use the app which adds 15-30 minutes.

Adaption: Under adaption category were gathered teachers experiences with adapting with the sudden changes while outdoor learning. For example some conditions change, or teacher wants to add some relevant information or activity. It is important that environments that support orchestration would enable fast changes. Teachers mentioned that in SmartZoo it is easy to change questions, so teacher can interrupt and change tasks or information quickly which helps to adapt the activity to the current situation.

Teacher 2: *"Once I was too busy to go there and I used only website. And they didn't find the answers. You have to put much effort into it, but you can change questions here easily."*

Awareness/assessment: Teachers answered questions about being aware of student's progress in outdoor learning activities while using SmartZoos. Came out that they don't have overview of what students are doing but in their opinion it is important to monitor students work progress. They also want to give feedback to students while they are in the creating process to support and guide them. But one teacher also notes that it is not good to monitor too much, students creativity and joy will be restricted.

Teacher 1: *"I have no idea what students are doing, and if they are doing at all. "*

Teachers found that SmartZoos at the moment is not supporting assessment because teachers don't have overview nor access to students work. They also mention that it is not important to know where the students are more important is the possibility to give feedback and assess. This goes for both playing and creating. Teachers want to be able to interrupt students for guidance and support to avoid misconceptions.

Teacher 3: *"Right now it is not supporting assessment. I don't see summary report. I don't know how students performed. It is not possible to grade. They can play and complete... well.. they played...so? nice? How did you like? liked! What did you learn? I only get to know if I ask them afterwards. "*

Roles: Sharing orchestration load to students and by that also giving the role of a teacher partly to students, is is greatly supported by teachers. They see it as a more effective way of learning. But at the same time they also note the risks with the quality of the information provided by students and the possibility of students not taking the task seriously.

Teacher 1: *"If students make the questions then it is much more effective learning."*

Pragmatism/practice: One of the biggest questions while arranging outdoor learning with mobile devices is either to use students or school/institutions devices. Teachers admit that when using students devices there should be someone helping, because there will be many technical questions with different device models and settings. They also emphasize that students age is important to keep in mind. There are more possibilities for older students. Mostly because they already have better phones and access to unlimited data. Younger students often don't have those possibilities so in that case it would be important to look for other options, for example it would be good if Zoo or some other institution would offer their own digital devices or if possible use school equipment. This would give teachers more confidence, because they will know that everything works.

Teacher 3: *"At least you know that battery is full and everything works. GPS works, browser is updated."*

At the same time they also note that it can be tricky to use school devices, because it is not possible to borrow the tablets for a long time or there is no possibility to use mobile internet. Goals related with using technology in the lessons are mostly derived from curricula. Developing students digital competences were mentioned several times by all teachers. Teachers see it as a very important part of learning and try to find different ways to use digital technology in the classroom.

Teacher 3: *"Nowadays the digital competences development is very important. when students can create games on their own then that is a big plus."*

Theory: Under theory category are assembled attitude and belief regarding using mobile devices in outdoor education. Teachers attitude is positive and supportive. They mention that best place to learn nature is in nature and it is important to emphasize using different senses, discussions and discovery while learning. As a positive side to using mobile devices they point out motivating, support for students natural need to discover and purposeful use of device.

Teacher 3: *"It is a very big plus that students can investigate and try themselves."*

They also agree that creativity is something that students should do more, but for what they don't have very many possibilities. Same is with playing, they say it keeps students motivated, so it is good to have possibilities where fun and learning go together.

Allignment/synergy: From the orchestration perspective it is very important that different environments and activities would be combined smoothly and would support each other. From the interviews we can say that SmartZoos enabled the combining of physical and virtual space, helping students to learn and engage more. Teachers liked that the SmartZoos activity was fun and engaging and that there was a possibility for competition.

Teacher 2: *"I like that students are active and need to show initial. Guys were engaged. I was surprised. One was facetiming with boyfriend but others were engaged... It was fun, like Pokemon Go. Boys liked it. Even though there were problems with GPS, it was still fun for them. It was like catching the Pokemon. "*

3. CONCLUSION

The goal of this case study was to explore the challenges of orchestration while outdoor learning and how the used SmartZoos app is supporting teachers to orchestrate the activities. Students feedback for the activities conducted were positive. Most of the students claimed that they liked the game, would like to use this kind game again and were engaged in the activities.

Teachers were positively minded about using this kind of learning tool and setting. They provided important insight to what kind of support they would need while orchestrating outdoor mobile activity. All the teachers agreed that planning and designing the outdoor learning activity takes a lot of time, even days if teacher is planning to go to some new location. Puzzle piece like task items that teachers can combine themselves was suggested. The other idea was to plan the activity so that the students would create the tracks on the location. That design would minimize planning but then teachers would like to have the possibility to access students creating process. Teachers would like to have access to finished student works for assessment. Neither of those features were provided in the used app. Teachers admitted that they would like to have a possibility to communicate directly through the app to students that are dispersed around on a big area.

The results from this case study showed that pedagogical design needs to be reconsidered. The choice of methods should be analyzed and rearranged keeping in mind already existing studies (Drijvers, 2010; Lai, 2015; Munoz-Cristobal, 2017). Design where students visit the Zoo on two separate days and create the tracks at home is not practical from time, money and teaching perspective. Technical solution needs to be completed and supplemented with functionalities that would support the orchestration from teachers perspective and students learning and creation process. If this tool could successfully be used in activities where more responsibilities are given to students(Munoz-Cristobal, 2014). From awareness, assessment and management perspectives it is necessary to add learning analytics features for teachers.

The aim of this case study was exploratory and the idea was to explore and illustrate the problem of orchestrating outdoor learning. Because of the small sample size, there is no possibility to generalize the results. These findings are good start for developing a tool that would support teachers while planning, conducting and sharing orchestration load in outdoor learning.

ACKNOWLEDGEMENT

This project is partially funded by SmartZoos, CB64, Central Baltic Programme 2014-2020; and the European Union's Horizon 2020 Research and Innovation Programme, grant agreement No. 669074.

REFERENCES

Arvaja, M., Hämäläinen, R., & Rasku-Puttonen, H. (2009). Challenges for the teacher's role in promoting productive knowledge construction in computer-supported collaborative learning contexts. In J. O. Lindberg & A. D. Olofsson (Eds.), Online learning communities and teacher professional development: Methods for improved education delivery (pp. 263–280). Hersey: IGI Global.

Crompton, H., Burke, D., Kristen H., Gregory, K. H., (2017). The use of mobile learning in PK-12 education: A systematic review. Computers & Education, 110(51-63)

Cuendet, S., Bonnard, Q., Do-Lenh, S., & Dillenbourg, P. (2013). Designing augmented reality for the classroom. Computers & Education, 68, 557-569.

Dillenbourg, P., Jermann, P. (2010). Technology for Classroom Orchestration. New Science of Learning, 525-552.

Dillenbourg, P., Järvelä, S., & Fischer, F. (2009). The evolution of research on computer-supported collaborative learning. In N. Balacheff, S. Ludvigsen, T. Jong, A. Lazonder, & S. Barnes (Eds.), Technology-enhanced learning (pp. 3e19). Dordrecht: Springer Netherlands.

Dillenbourg, P. & Fischer, F. (2007). Basics of Computer-Supported Collaborative Learning. Zeitschrift für Berufs- und Wirtschaftspädagogik. 21, pp. 111-130.

Drijvers, P., Doorman, M., Boon, P., Reed, H., Gravemeijer, K. (2010). The teacher and the tool: instrumental orchestrations in the technology-rich mathematics classroom. Educ Stud Math,75, 213–234

Gravier, C., Fayolle, J., Noyel, G., Leleve, A. & Benmohamed, H. (2006). Distance Learning: Closing the Gap between Remote Labs and Learning Management Systems, Proceedings of IEEE First International Conference on E-Learning in Industrial Electronics , Hammamet , Tunisie , December 18-20, pp. 130-.134.

Ishtaiwa, F. F., Khaled, A., Dukmak, S. (2015). Faculty Members' Perceptions of the Integration, Affordances, and Challenges of Mobile Learning. International Journal of E-learning & Distance Education, 30(2)

Kollar, I., Hämäläinen, R., Evans, M., De Wever, B., & Perrotta, C. (2011). Orchestrating CSCL – More than a metaphor? In H. Spada, G. Stahl, N. Miyake, & N. Law (Eds.), Connecting computer-supported collaborative learning to policy and practice: CSCL2011 conference proceedings. Volume II (pp. 946-947). International Society of the Learning Sciences.

Lai, A., Lai, H.-Y., Wei-Hsiang Chuang, W.-H. & Wu, Z.-H. (2015). Developing a mobile learning management system for outdoors nature science activities based on 5e learning cycle. International Conference e-Learning 2015 Juan A. Munoz-Cristobal, Vanesa Gallego-Lema, Higinio F. Arribas-Cubero, Alejandra Martínez-Mones-, Juan I. Asensio-Perez (2017). Using virtual learning environments in bricolage mode for orchestrating learning situations across physical and virtual spaces. Computers & Education, 109, 233–252

Milrad, M., Wong, L.-H., Sharples, M., Hwang, G.-J., Looi, C.-K., & Ogata, H. (2013). Seamless learning: An international perspective on next-generation technology-enhanced learning. In Z. L. Berge, & L. Y. Muilenburg (Eds.), Handbook of mobile learning (pp. 95e108). Abingdon: Routledge.

Munoz-Cristobal, J. A., Gallego-Lema, V., Arribas-Cubero, H. F., Martínez-Mones, A., Asensio-Perez, J. I. (2017). Using virtual learning environments in bricolage mode for orchestrating learning situations across physical and virtual spaces. Computers & Education, 109, 233–252

Munoz-Cristobal, J. A., Prieto, L. P., Asensio-P erez, J. I., Martínez-Mones, A., Jorrín-Abell an, I. M., & Dimitriadis, Y. (2014). Deploying learning designs across physical and web spaces: Making pervasive learning affordable for teachers. Pervasive and Mobile Computing, 14, 31e46.

Prieto, L. P., Wen, Y., Caballero, D., & Dillenbourg, P. (2014). Review of augmented paper systems in education: An orchestration perspective. Journal of Educational Technology & Society, 17(4), 169e185.

Prieto, L. P., Dlab, M. H., Gutiérrez, I., Abdulwahed, M., & Balid, W. (2011). Orchestrating technology enhanced learning: a literature review and a conceptual framework. International Journal of Technology Enhanced Learning, 3(6), 583–598. Inderscience.

Roschelle, J., Dimitriadis, Y., & Hoppe, U. (2013). Classroom orchestration: Synthesis. Computers & Education, 69, 523e526.

Sharples, M. (2013). Shared orchestration within and beyond the classroom. Computers & Education, 69, 504e506.

Ternier, S., Klemke, R., Kalz, M., van Ulzen, P., & Specht, M. (2012). ARLearn: Augmented reality meets augmented virtuality. Journal of Universal Computer Science, 18(15), 2143-2164.

USABILITY EVALUATION OF A VIRTUAL LEARNING ENVIRONMENT: A UNIVERSITY CASE STUDY

Attila Vertesi[1], Huseyin Dogan[2], Angelos Stefanidis[2], Giles Ashton[2] and Wendy Drake[2]
[1]*Bournemouth & Poole College, North Rd. Poole, BH14 0LS, United Kingdom*
[2]*Bournemouth University, Talbot Campus, Fern Barrow, Poole, BH12 5BB, United Kingdom*

ABSTRACT

As part of educational technology developments in Higher Education, every university has adopted a Virtual Learning Environment (VLE) that facilitates online methods of delivery by enabling the submission of course materials, course management system and computer-mediated communication. VLE is regarded as technology which is either accepted or rejected by its users such as students, academics and administrators. Perceived usefulness and ease of use play an important role in user acceptance and satisfaction. This paper provides quantitative results of usability evaluations i.e., the System Usability Scale (SUS) scores from different user groups including students (n=137), academics (n=23), administrators (n=19) and learning technologist (n=3). The qualitative element of the VLE evaluation comprised the utilization of an approach called Interactive Management (IM) (n=13). The results showed that the newly implemented VLE performed under the average usability expectation (SUS score of 58.6). Students on average evaluated the usability of the VLE higher than the staff. The usability scores of the students from different courses showed remarkable differences. The ranked and categorised feedback from the IM session highlights the importance of planning, training and communication before and during the implementation, as well as the aspect of usability and learnability of the VLE.

KEYWORDS

Virtual Learning Environment (VLE), Learning Management System (LMS), Usability Evaluation, System Usability Scale (SUS), Interactive Management (IM), Technology Acceptance Model (TAM)

1. INTRODUCTION

Information technology is an essential component of the educational technology in Higher Education. Virtual Learning Environment (VLE) and Learning Management System (LMS) are often used as synonyms (Paulsen, 2002, p.6) describing a complex information technology system that integrates course management tools for the course administrators, online accessibility of learning materials and assignments; as well as a communication and collaboration platform for the students and lecturers (Ryan et al, 2013). The quality and usability of a VLE are the key features for its success by influencing user satisfaction and acceptance (Babić, 2012). Usability is the extent to which users can use a product or service to achieve specified goals efficiently and effectively while promoting feelings of satisfaction in a given context of use (ISO 9241-11). There are two aspects of usability in educational technology: technical usability and pedagogical usability (Melis et al, 2003). Technical usability refers to the Human-Computer Interaction (HCI), while pedagogical usability aims at supporting the learning process. Perceived usefulness and perceived ease of use represent usability as main factors in the Technology Acceptance Model (TAM) (Davis et al, 1989). TAM tries to predict the acceptability of a new technology.

The university has dedicated VLEs have been in operation for more than 12 years, currently used by over 20,000 students and 2,000 staff. Under EU regulations, the university was required to go out to tender for a new VLE at the end of the contract with the current VLE supplier. In total, 250 students and staff members, representing ten departments participated in the selection of the new VLE. More than 50 staff worked on the preparation and implementation of the new VLE for 8 months before it was introduced in September 2017 in a phased implementation. During phase 1, 40% of the students were transferred to the new system. The university moves towards, the full rollout from September 2018. The new VLE offers a personalised learning experience with learning analytics capabilities, integrated social media, chat, video features and game-based learning for the students. Staff can benefit from the customisable course development, program management, account management, training, and end-user help desk support. In order to support the decision making for selecting the most appropriate VLE for the university, a preliminary usability evaluation has been carried out in 2016 on the three VLEs remaining in contention during the final stages of a rigorous procurement process.

In this research, a follow-up usability examination has been carried out on the implemented new VLE utilising the same methodology (SUS) in April 2018, six months after its launch. The result contributes to the next phase of the implementation process and provides feedback to the implementation team.

System Usability Scale (SUS) (Brooke, 1996) was utilised to carry out a general quantitative usability evaluation. The SUS scores from different user groups were analysed and compared. More detailed, factor analysis was applied where the low usability scores demanded it.

Interactive Management (IM) (Broome and Keever, 1986) methodology was applied to facilitate effective group communication to receive detailed feedback about the usability and the implementation of the new VLE.

The aim of this paper is twofold: (a) to provide reliable quantitative and qualitative feedback of the usability and the implementation of the new VLE (b) to offer a proposal on how to apply different evaluation methods to assess the usability of an educational technology system, e.g., VLE by the combined application of SUS and IM methodology.

In section 2, related usability studies are discussed in, especially SUS application on VLEs. Section 3 introduces the methodologies used, SUS and IM. The results are discussed and interpreted in section 4 and conclusions presented in section 5.

2. USABILITY STUDIES ON VIRTUAL LEARNING ENVIRONMENTS

A growing number of studies examine the usability of the VLE by utilizing SUS as a methodology. In 2006, a web-based e-learning platform called SPIRAL was developed and evaluated (Renaut et al., 2006) at University Claude Bernard Lyon 1. Although the SUS ratings have not been published, 72% of the professors found the system usable, according to the paper.

Three different e-learning platforms were measured using SUS by Ayad and Rigas (2010). User performance, learning effectiveness and satisfaction were examined to explore the usability aspects of the system. The three platforms were Virtual Classroom, Game-based and Storytelling. The SUS scores for the three platforms were 75.3, 73.4 and 64.5 respectively. The Storytelling scored a little behind the other two.

An interesting comparative research article was published (Gallud et al., 2013) regarding the usability enhancement of the Moodle LMS. The study examined the performance of the system in remote collaboration. The SUS score of the original Moodle system in these features was 46.75, which indicates serious usability problems. Using a different collaborative tool called Drag&Share within Moodle, the usability of the LMS enhanced dramatically. The SUS score increased significantly to 89.5 after the implementation of Drag&Share, which indicates a very good usability in the remote collaboration feature.

There is a very rare longitudinal study about a simulation-based learning system (Luo et al., 2014), that measured the perceived usability of the students after the first semester and after the second semester. Initially, the SUS score was 58.1, suggesting that the system needed improvement. Based on the collected data, the system had been modified, and after the second semester, the score rose to 65.9. Following another development for teachers, they evaluated the new module to 74.45, showing their satisfaction. This research also highlights the perceived usability of different user groups (e.g., teachers and students) may vary.

The above-mentioned divergence between the perceived usability of students and teachers is discussed by Emelyanova and Voronina (2014). The various aspects of the VLE and the difference between the perception of the usability should be considered when making a decision about the improvement of the system.

A comprehensive usability study was conducted in nine European secondary schools, all using UNITE e-learning platform, with the participation of 23 teachers and 47 students (Granic and Cukusic, 2011). Teachers evaluated the system at 53.15 and students gave 59.36 in average using the SUS questionnaire. The difference between the perception of the usability is also noticeable in this study. However, in this case, the students scored the system higher than the teachers.

3. METHODOLOGY

3.1 System Usability Scale (SUS)

Usability evaluation consists of methodologies for measuring the usability aspects of a system's user interface and identifying specific problems (Nielsen, 1993). There are numerous methods available for assessing the usability of a product (Brooke, 1996; Lewis, 1991, 1995; Tullis and Albert, 2008). System Usability Scale (SUS) is one of the most widely adopted methods (Brooke, 1996) due to its shortness, simplicity, comprehensiveness and reliability even with a small sample size (Tullis and Stetson, 2004).

SUS, developed by Brooke (1996), is a 10-item scale (Fig. 1). The ten statements can be rated on a five-point (Likert-type) scale ranging from 'strongly disagree' to 'strongly agree'. The SUS score, calculated from the answers, is a number between 1 and 100 which can easily be compared to the SUS scores of other similar or different systems and products. This methodology provides a reliable quantitative result of the usability of the VLE (Orfanou et al., 2015) that can highlight potential usability issues but does not identify them or give in-depth analysis about the possible causes.

1. I think that I would like to use this system frequently.
2. I found the system unnecessarily complex.
3. I thought the system was easy to use.
4. I think that I would need the support of a technical person to be able to use this system.
5. I found the various functions in this system were well integrated.
6. I thought there was too much inconsistency in this system.
7. I would imagine that most people would learn to use this system very quickly.
8. I found the system very cumbersome to use.
9. I felt very confident using the system.
10. I needed to learn a lot of things before I could get going with this system.

Figure 1. SUS questionnaire

3.2 Interactive Management (IM)

Interactive Management (IM) is a methodology designed to manage complex or new organisational or technical problems associated with multiple disciplines, involving different departments (Broome and Keever, 1986). IM offers methods to facilitate effective communications, promotes consensus-based decision making through idea generation, structuring and design. IM methods can be used to gather the requirements, needs, demands and ideas of the stakeholders for a better understanding of the problem space (Dogan and Henshaw 2010). IM tools are utilised to obtain feedback from the users about the implementation of the new VLE system. IM involves three phases: Planning, Workshop and Followup (Warfield and Cárdenas 1994). During the workshop, Trigger Questions, Idea Writing (IW) and Nominal Group Technique (NGT) were applied. The outcome of the Workshop is a list of ranked and organised statements reflecting the implementation phase of the new VLE, addressing positive and negative usability issues.

A three-hour meeting was organised by the authors in April 2018 at the university for academics (n=4), administrators (n=8) and learning technologists (n=1). The participation was voluntary. The aim of the IM session was to collect feedback, discuss questions, problems and capture ideas in connection with the implementation and usability of the new VLE.

3.2.1 Idea Writing

At the beginning of the IM session, the facilitator (one of the author) introduced the methods and the Trigger Questions for the Idea Writing (IW):

Trigger Question 1: What are the **positive** aspects of the implementation of the new VLE?

Trigger Question 2: What are the **negative** aspects of the implementation of the new VLE?

The participants formed two mixed groups (n=6, n=7) and without discussing the question, every participant, focusing on *Trigger Question 1*, wrote one positive aspect of the implementation of the new VLE on his/her paper then passed the A4 sheet to the next member of the group in the circle. After reading the previously listed statements on the new A4 sheet, members wrote another positive statement and circulated the A4 sheets until the original sheets arrived back. The same practice was followed with the *Trigger Question 2*.

3.2.2 Nominal Group Technique

Following the Idea Writing phase, the members of the groups discussed, clarified and edited the positive and negative statements for the preliminary ranking. Each participant selected the five most important statements from the whole list and ranked them by associating numbers from one to five for each statement, five being the most important. Single Transferable Vote technique was utilised to minimise discarded votes during the ranking process.

4. THE RESULTS

4.1 System Usability Scale

4.1.1 The Participants

The quantitative usability evaluation was conducted by utilising the SUS methodology. The total number of participants is n=182 including students (n=137), academics (n=23), learning technologists (n=3) and faculty administrative teams (n=19). Printed (paper) and online questionnaires were offered. N=13 SUS questionnaires arrived on paper evaluated by learning technologists (n=1), academics (n=4) and administrators (n=8). The online questionnaire was submitted by 169 users including learning technologists (n=2), students (n=137), academics (n=19) and administrators (n=11). The evaluation was based on the general experience gained during the first phase of the implementation (from September 2017 to April 2018) of the new VLE by using the features needed for the different user groups. The questions were derived from the original SUS questions (Brooke, 1996) with a slight change in the wording. Unfortunately, a small error slipped into the online student questionnaire. One of the questions was repeated twice and as a result, the last question was left out. This small discrepancy does not affect the result significantly as the structure of the SUS questions and the methodology make the evaluation robust and flexible to small errors and changes (Sauro and Lewis 2011). The standard error is within 0.25 regarding the final SUS score. The accuracy is higher than 99.5 %.

4.1.2 The Interpretation of the SUS Result

The overall SUS score of the new VLE measured after 7 months (April 2018) of the implementation (first phase) is **58.6** out of 100. This is the mean result of the evaluation of n=182 users including students (n=137), administrators (n=19), academics (n=23) and learning technologists (n=3).

There is a well-accepted adjective scale based on the benchmarks set up by Bangor et. al. (2009). A SUS score over 80 suggests a very good, highly usable system, between 68 and 80 is still OK but could be improved, between 51 and 68 means "Fair", it still works but should be improved, below 51 is poor and below 36 is unusable. The SUS score 68 corresponds to 50% which means that the average score of more than 2300 different systems and products is around 68.

The final score (58.6) is in the range of 51-68 which is below the average usability expectation (68) but still suggest a usable system with scope for improvement.

4.1.3 The Comparison of the User Group Evaluations

A more detailed picture can be seen by analysing and comparing the evaluation of the different user groups. The largest number of users participating in this evaluation are the students (n=137) scored 61.1 opposed to all members of staff (n=45) 49.4. Students' SUS score weighted more in the overall score and resulted 58.6 for the total average. If the two user groups formed by the students and the staff are weighted equally, the mean SUS score is 55.6, lower than the average score 58.6 calculated with all users as one group. The following chart (Fig. 2) displays the SUS score in respect to the two main user groups, the group average and the total average.

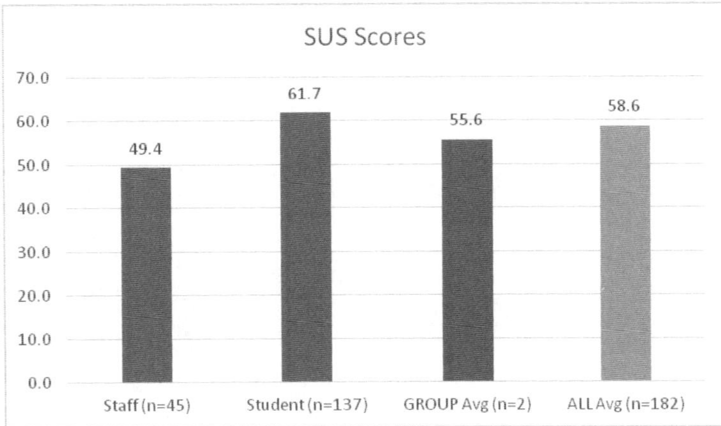

Figure 2. SUS scores of students and staff

4.1.4 Student Group Evaluations

Starting the analysis with the largest user group, the students (n=137), it is interesting to see the comparison of the SUS scores of the different sub-groups within the students.

Student Groups by Levels

Undergraduate (n=127) and postgraduate (n=10) students filled in the online form.

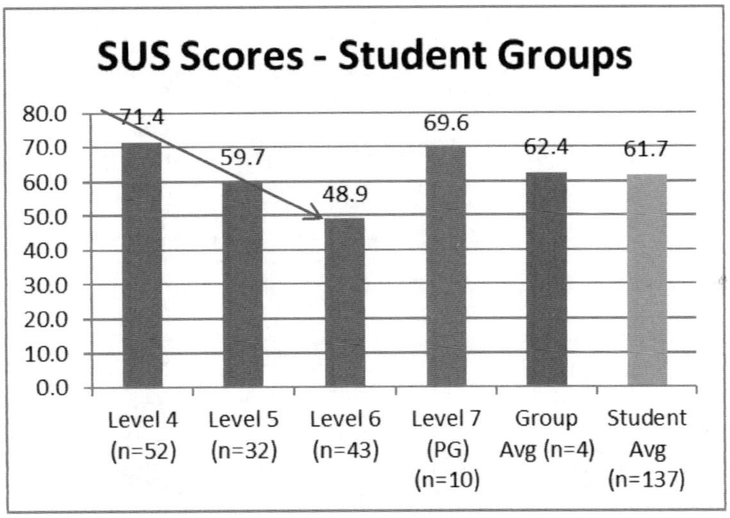

Figure 3. SUS scores of student groups by level

There is a falling trend can which be seen in the graph (Fig. 3) by the undergraduate student groups from 71.4 (Level 4) through 59.7 (Level 5) to 48.9 (Level 6). The first year (Level 4) students evaluated the new VLE slightly above the average expectation. They seem to be satisfied with the new system, unlike the Level 6 students who have higher expectations. The postgraduate students (level 7), however, gave 69.6 for usability (Figure 3) which is near to the generally accepted average (68) for SUS scores.

Student Groups by Frameworks/Courses

The results of six different groups of students can be seen in Figure 4. The groups were formed based on frameworks and courses. The students are from different levels/years in each group. The largest group is the nursing students (n=66). Their average SUS score is 60.3 which is very close to the average score of the six groups (60.2). The difference between the lowest (43.9) and highest SUS score (74.7) is more than 30 (30.8).

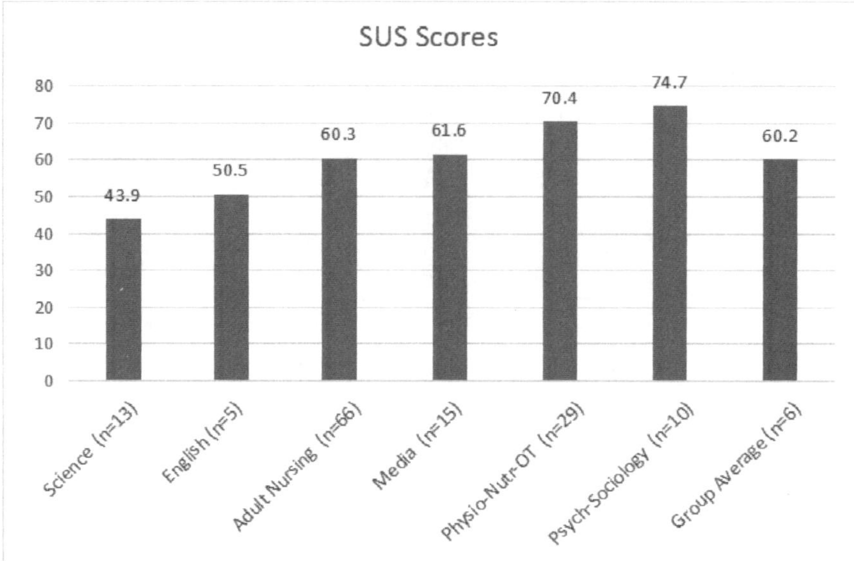

Figure 4. SUS scores of student groups by frameworks/courses

4.1.5 Staff Group Evaluation

N=45 evaluation derived from staff members either online (n=32) or on paper (n=13). The following groups are created: academics (n=23), administrators (n=20), learning technologists (n=3). Figure 5 shows the results graphically. It is conspicuous that academics gave very low usability score (37.8) to the new VLE since administrators and learning technologists scores suggest that the VLE is close to an average system with respect to the usability. The mean value of the groups' SUS scores is 55.4 which is acceptable but the total average falls below 50 (49.4) which is on the borderline of the usability.

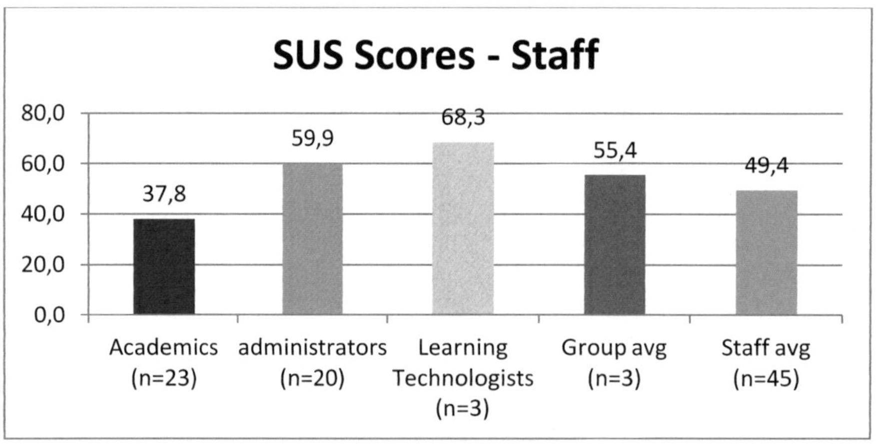

Figure 5. SUS scores of staff groups

The result of the academics (SUS = 37.8) highlights some usability issues. For further analysis, Figure 6 chart shows the individual scores in the academics group (n=23). Blue bars (n=19) shows the online result, yellow bars (n=4) relate to the paper-based questionnaire.

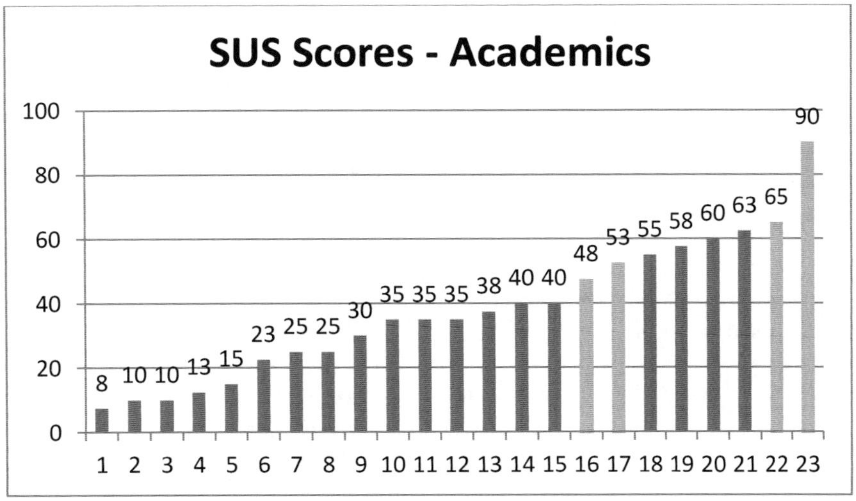

Figure 6. SUS scores of academics

Half of the group of academics (n=12) evaluated the new VLE below 38 which indicate serious usability issues. Interestingly, the paper-based results (n=4) are significantly higher (SUS avg = 64) than the online scores (SUS avg = 32). However, the overall standard deviation is not high (21), the range and distribution of the scores are unusual.

4.1.6 Factor Analysis

A more detailed analysis can reveal the weak areas of the new VLE according to the academics (n=15) who evaluated the system lower than 41. Figure 7 shows the result of each factor (the scores given to each question) of the evaluations which have the total SUS score under 41. These are the first 15 scores from the left on the bar chart in Figure 7.

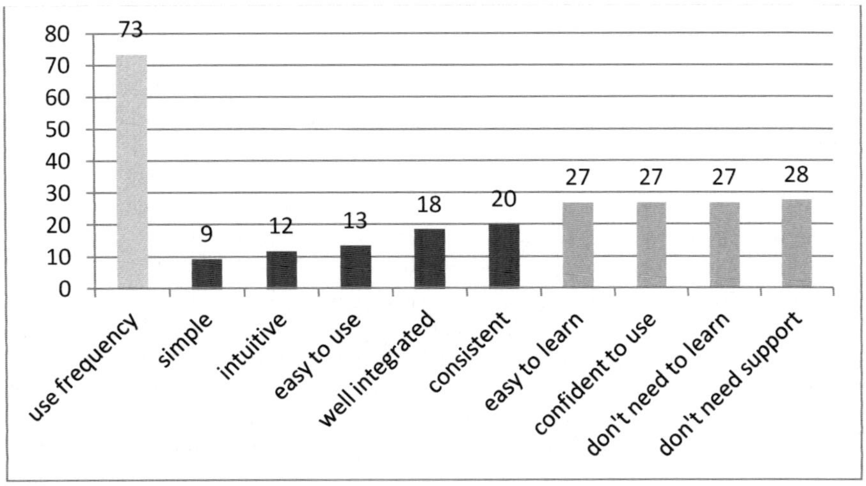

Figure 7. Factor analysis of the weakest evaluations (SUS < 41)

The weakest areas, scored from 9 to 20, are highlighted in red on the bar chart. These academics (n=15 out of 23) did not find the new VLE simple, intuitive, easy to use, well integrated or consistent.

4.2 Interactive Management Session

By the end of the IM session, four lists of ranked statements were produced for the two trigger questions by the two groups. The two positive and two negative lists were merged into one positive and one negative list. The extract of usability related statements are grouped into categories (see Table 1 and Table 2).

Table 1. *Trigger Question 1* Statements

Positive Statements Grouped into Categories
Usability
Clean and fresh, works good, better user interface
Functionalities for staff/students
Programme Support help area now a lot cleaner
Allows students to hand in late submissions in same area, lateness is clearly marked
Learnability
Access to Sandbox to mess around without worrying about breaking the system.
Training organise and run in plenty of time
Advantage in piloting is confidence in year 2
Help section divided for academics/professional support
Support
Able to contact trainers
On-demand help from Learning Tech, contact directly
Programme Support help area now a lot cleaner
Learning technologists were very helpful
Training organised and run in plenty of time
Help section divided for academics/professional support

Table 2. *Trigger Question 2* Statements

Negative Statements Grouped into Categories
Support
No LT support
Training too general
No personal training for unique faculty needs
Too many ways of accessing the same thing
Sandbox can't simulate everything
Usability
Current VLE and new VLE not always linked up
Systems not talking to each other as well as advertised
A lot of things shown were not useful in terms of usability for teaching
No template for structure of unit
Software lacks consistency in interface
Who was consulted regarding large file submission
Communication
Systems not talking to each other as well as advertised
Who was consulted regarding large file submission
Lack of info prior to rolling out
More communication required about Implementation

The positive and negative statements are grouped into categories based on similarities which makes the problem domain clearer and easier to recognise structure and pattern. The order of the statements follows the scores in ranking. The list starts with the most important statements. Some statements are listed in more than one categories if it was required. The categories refer to usability, learnability, support and communication. The individual statements specify the area and nature of the usability issues. IM offers a valuable feedback by supporting the general evaluation of the SUS with specific comments.

5. CONCLUSION

The usability evaluation of the new VLE at this stage provided a reliable and meaningful feedback. The overall SUS score (58.6) suggest a usable system in general but also indicate some usability issues in particular areas. As the implementation is in its early stage (phase 1), this score should not be considered as the SUS score of the fully implemented and fine-tuned system. The analysis of the evaluation of the different user groups and individual users discloses more details and differences within and between the usability perception of the user groups. The VLE is a complex system with numerous features. Each user group evaluates a slightly or significantly different part of the VLE. The divergence between the SUS scores hints that (a) the system is not uniform regarding the usability (b) the expectation and perception are different. The detailed analysis of the low SUS scores (37.8) given by the academics identified five problematic areas: simplicity, intuitiveness, ease of use, integration, consistency. Students are mostly satisfied with the new VLE, although, interesting trends can be seen in the undergraduate results (see Figure 3). Academics and administrators are not always fully satisfied. The IM workshop offered a great opportunity to identify, communicate and resolve some serious usability issues. The feedback captured during the workshop was useful and valuable. The usability evaluation provided a realistic picture of the new VLE at the end of the first phase of the implementation. The case study offers an example of a feasible usability evaluation of a VLE combining SUS and IM methodologies.

The feedback captured in the IM session give some explanation of the SUS scores. There are more negative statements (n=29) in the ranked lists than positive ones (n=19). The categories refer to the areas that need attention either from the usability perspective or regarding the implementation process. The high importance of support, training, communication is well recognized by the team that manages the implementation and confirmed by the result of this study as well.

The implication of the research:

a) The implementation team gained an overall picture (SUS score) of the usability of the new VLE.
b) The SUS score can be compared to the preliminary and subsequent results.
c) The implementation team could identify usability related issues during the first phase of the implementation and address them at this early stage.

The research has the following limitations. The different user groups were not represented in equal number. Three times more student completed the online evaluation, but no students participated in the IM session. The SUS score comparison of the user groups gives an equal weighting to every user group.

The online SUS questionnaire for students had an error. Question 5 (Fig. 1) was repeated so, question 5 and 6 were the same and the further questions (6-9) were scrolled down to 7 to 10. As a result, the last question (10) has been left out. As the SUS questions were designed with some redundancy for robustness (Bangor et al., 2008), this error did not cause a significant difference in the SUS result of the student evaluation. The phrasing of the first question was modified from 'I think that I would like to use this system frequently' to 'I use this VLE frequently'. The reason behind this change is that there was no choice of using other VLE for these users. The impact of this change is that the SUS scores given to the first question are relatively high compared to the average scores. It slightly raises the mean SUS score.

REFERENCES

Albert, W. and Tullis, T., 2013. *Measuring the user experience: collecting, analyzing, and presenting usability metrics*. Newnes.

Ayad, K. and Rigas, D., 2010. Comparing virtual classroom, game-based learning and storytelling teachings in e-learning. *International Journal of Education and Information Technologies*, *4*(1), pp.15-23.

Babić, S., 2012. Factors that influence academic teacher's acceptance of e-learning technology in blended learning environment. In *E-learning-organizational infrastructure and tools for specific areas*. InTech.

Bangor, A., Kortum, P. and Miller, J., 2009. Determining what individual SUS scores mean: Adding an adjective rating scale. *Journal of usability studies*, *4*(3), pp.114-123.

Bangor, A., Kortum, P.T. and Miller, J.T., 2008. An empirical evaluation of the system usability scale. *Intl. Journal of Human–Computer Interaction*, *24*(6), pp.574-594.

Brooke, J., 1996. SUS-A quick and dirty usability scale. *Usability evaluation in industry*, *189*(194), pp.4-7.

Broome, B.J. and Keever, D.B., 1986. Facilitating Group Communication: The Interactive Management Approach.

Davis, F.D., Bagozzi, R.P. and Warshaw, P.R., 1989. User acceptance of computer technology: a comparison of two theoretical models. *Management science*, *35*(8), pp.982-1003.

Dogan, H. and Henshaw, M.J.D., 2010. Transition from soft systems to an enterprise knowledge management architecture. In: International Conference on Contemporary Ergonomics and Human Factors 13-15 April 2010 Keele University, UK.

Emelyanova, N. and Voronina, E., 2014. Introducing a learning management system at a Russian university: Students' and teachers' perceptions. *The International Review of Research in Open and Distributed Learning*, *15*(1).

Gallud Lazaro, J.A., Albertos Marco, F. and Ruiz Penichet, V.M., 2013. Collaborative e-learning through drag & share in synchronous shared workspaces.

Granic, A. and Cukusic, M., 2011. Usability testing and expert inspections complemented by educational evaluation: A case study of an e-learning platform. *Journal of Educational Technology & Society*, *14*(2), p.107.

Lewis, J.R., 1991. Psychometric evaluation of an after-scenario questionnaire for computer usability studies: the ASQ. *ACM Sigchi Bulletin*, *23*(1), pp.78-81.

Lewis, J.R., 1995. IBM computer usability satisfaction questionnaires: psychometric evaluation and instructions for use. *International Journal of Human-Computer Interaction*, *7*(1), pp.57-78.

Luo, G.H., Liu, E.Z.F., Kuo, H.W. and Yuan, S.M., 2014. Design and implementation of a simulation-based learning system for international trade. *The International Review of Research in Open and Distributed Learning*, *15*(1).

Melis, E., Weber, M. and Andrès, E., 2003. Lessons for (pedagogic) usability of eLearning systems. In *E-Learn: World Conference on E-Learning in Corporate, Government, Healthcare, and Higher Education* (pp. 281-284). Association for the Advancement of Computing in Education (AACE).

Nielsen, J. and Phillips, V.L., 1993, May. Estimating the relative usability of two interfaces: heuristic, formal, and empirical methods compared. In *Proceedings of the INTERACT'93 and CHI'93 conference on Human factors in computing systems* (pp. 214-221). ACM.

Orfanou, K., Tselios, N. and Katsanos, C., 2015. Perceived usability evaluation of learning management systems: Empirical evaluation of the System Usability Scale. *The International Review of Research in Open and Distributed Learning*, *16*(2).

Paulsen, M.F., 2002. Online education systems: Discussion and definition of terms. *NKI Distance Education*, *202*.

Renaut, C., Batier, C., Flory, L. and Heyde, M., 2006. Improving web site usability for a better e-learning experience. *Current developments in technology-assisted education*, pp.891-896.

Ryan, S., Scott, B., Freeman, H. and Patel, D., 2013. *The virtual university: The internet and resource-based learning.* Routledge.

Tullis, T.S. and Stetson, J.N., 2004, June. A comparison of questionnaires for assessing website usability. In *Usability professional association conference* (Vol. 1). (pp. 7–11).

Venkatesh, V. and Davis, F.D., 2000. A theoretical extension of the technology acceptance model: Four longitudinal field studies. *Management science*, *46*(2), pp.186-204.

Warfield, J.N. and Cárdenas, A.R., 1994. *A handbook of interactive management* (p. 338). Ames: Iowa State University Press.

NET BENEFITS OF FACE-TO-FACE VERSUS ONLINE INSTRUCTION AT SCHOOL: A REPETITIVE FACTORAL EXPERIMENT IN AN ECOLOGICAL SETTING

Stephan Poelmans, Katie Goeman and Yves Wautelet
Department of Information Management, Modeling and Simulation, KU Leuven, campus Brussel, Warmoesberg 26, 1000 Brussel, Belgium

ABSTRACT

Within the field of e-learning, numerous studies focus on the benefits of online delivery systems and tools for learners. Nevertheless, there is still limited understanding of why learners perform better or worse and experiments are only rarely the method of inquiry. This study reports on findings of a repetitive factoral experiment in an ecological setting with 151 secondary school pupils in order to scrutinize crucial determinants for perceived and observed benefits of two delivery modes: face-to-face versus online instruction. For these purposes, the study incorporates the DeLone and McLean's information systems success model, extended to cover perceptions of enjoyment. The findings show that pupils' performance in the e-learning condition is significantly poorer than in the face-to-face condition. The results further point to the dominant position of perceived enjoyment as a determinant of satisfaction and e-learning preference. By examining system and individual antecedents of learning performance in an experimental design, we contribute to the body of knowledge regarding online learning effectiveness. The study's limitations and opportunities for further study are discussed.

KEYWORDS

Learning Performance, Online Instruction, Secondary Education, Delone & Mclean, Factoral Experiment

1. INTRODUCTION

In the past decade a lot of research effort has been put in explaining e-learning success in terms of learning performance and (continued) deployment of systems by individuals and organizations. Despite the increasing attention, there is limited understanding of why learners, especially pupils within secondary schools, perform better or worse, or how their personal preference for online or offline approaches is affected.

In this paper we describe an experimental study focused on the beneficial outcomes of a particular e-learning (EL) approach in a secondary school, as compared to a more traditional offline approach, and on assessing potential influencing variables related to the EL system and individual characteristics. The study was initiated by a group of Belgian secondary schools, searching for evidence about the benefits and drawbacks of the EL system they had been using for several years. In order to keep up with the fast pace of technological change and to better adapt to the learning needs of the 'millennium learners' (Ananiadou & Claro, 2009) the headmaster conveyed a sense of urgency to employ the wide range of tools available at the schools in order to create a more attractive and effective learning environment. A comparative perspective of delivery formats was preferred: face-to-face (F2F) versus online (EL). Despite existing publications on such comparisons (e.g. Abdous & Yoshimura, 2010; Jang et al, 2016), none of them give sufficient information on how to design e-learning, using the available tools in the virtual learning environment (VLE) Smartschool, with the purpose of improving or at least not reducing pupils' learning outcomes and satisfaction. In addition, there is a shortage of relevant experiments in real-life school settings in studies regarding the impact of educational technology, due to organizational complexity (Grubišić et al, 2009) or ethical issues.

For the purpose of understanding individual differences in benefits of using an e-learning application, Delone and Mclean's Information System's success model (ISSM) offers a well-established approach, suited to be used to evaluate both mandatory and voluntary use of a multitude of information systems in various types of organizations and contexts. Contrary to a behavioral model like the Technology Acceptance Model (TAM), the ISSM concentrates on the evaluation of actionable system and information characteristics (Wixom & Todd, 2005). The model corroborates that the system, information, and service quality of an information system are the key dimensions affecting users' intentions or actual behavior and their satisfaction. In their latest model (Delone & McLean, 2003), the construct of 'net benefits' is proposed as a key dependent factor, influenced by intention to use and satisfaction (Figure 1).

Although the ISSM has been deployed to study a plethoria of ISs (including enterprise systems, and e-commerce and e-government systems), some studies also used the ISSM in an e-learning context (e.g. Aparicio et al, 2017; Daghan & Akkoyun, 2016; Wang et al, 2007; etc.). The findings indicate the importance of system and information quality and learners' satisfaction as drivers of e-learning success.

However, most of these reports target higher education students and analyze learners' perceptions by means of a cross-sectional survey. In addition to a shortage of experiments in real-life school settings, we further observed a limited understanding of the objective and subjective nature of the net benefits related to EL system usage. To our knowledge, previous contributions did not scrutinize antecedents of both learners' performance (objective measure) and learners' perceived benefits (subjective measure), and their interrelationships. We therefore propose to extend the ISSM with particular components and to apply it an experiment in an ecological setting, using a comparative approach.

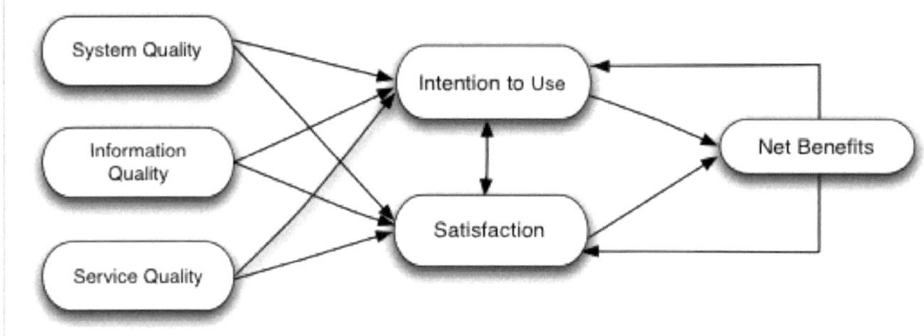

Figure 1. The Information Systems Success Model (DeLone and McLean, 2003)

In the following, we address 2 main research questions: 1) Do secondary school pupils benefit from online instruction when compared to face-face instruction? And 2) Which factors contribute to individual differences between pupils in terms of net benefits?

2. METHOD

2.1 Research Design

We conducted an experiment in a mid-sized secondary school in Belgium as a first iteration in design-based research, 'a methodology (...) that seeks to increase the impact, transfer and translation of education research into improved practice' (Anderson and Shattuck, 2012: 16). Following Grubišić et al. (2009), we opted for a factoral experimental design in which two or more parallel groups and two or more cycles are created (Figure 2). Each teacher taught the same course content using two delivery methods: online and face-to-face. So pupils followed two lessons, one online and one face-to-face. Immediately after instruction, their learning performance was assessed by means of a written test.

We strongly advocate the use of the factoral experiment with two parallel groups and two cycles in order to overcome typical biases due to undesired group or topic effects. As Grubišic´et al. (p. 595) pointed out: '*If we find that in each cycle one and the same factor is more efficient than the other, then we can conclude that a certain factor is better regardless of a difference between taught domain knowledge. In the same way, if the same factor is more efficient in each cycle, in spite of the groups that it has been introduced in, then we can conclude that a certain factor is better regardless of a difference between the groups.*' A repetition of such a factoral approach, in several classes and grades in the underlying study, strengthens the reliability of the findings. Because our factoral design is reiterated 6 times with different teachers and subjects, potential biases due to teacher and subject effects are minimized.

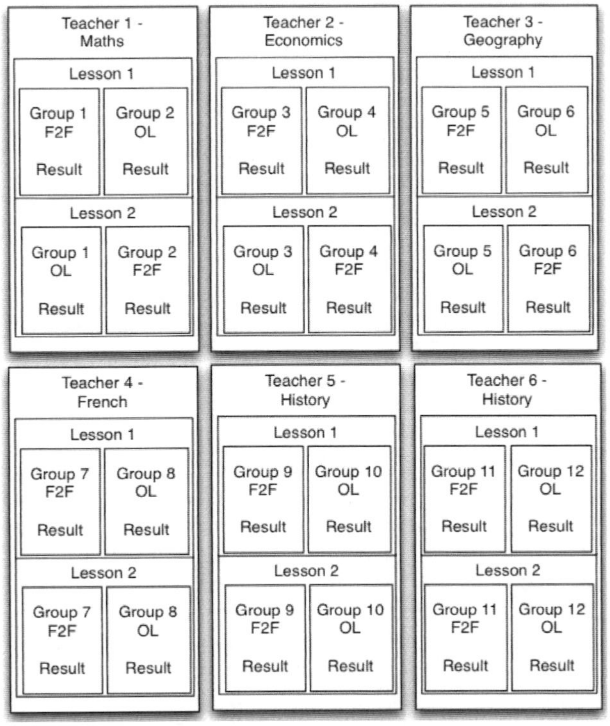

Figure 2. The Repeated Factoral design

2.2 Participants

The full sample consisted of 151 pupils between 12 and 18 years old, from the 7th until the 12th grade of secondary education. 70% are male. 39.7% of the participants were enrolled in a general secondary education program, 32.5% in technical secondary education, 19% in a vocational program, and 9% in a secondary arts program. Within a class, 10 to 15 pupils were randomly assigned to one of the test conditions (EL or F2F). In the course of one week, one group received a F2F lesson and the other group received the digital equivalent. The next week, the order was reversed. For example, a pupil belonging to group 1 received a history lesson in EL mode. In that same week, group 2 received the F2F version of that lesson, by the same teacher. In the following week group 1 received F2F a subsequent history lesson, whereas group 2 received the EL equivalent. As a result, each pupil followed one F2F and one EL lesson. After each lesson, all pupils took the same closed book tests which were constructed in accordance with the regular school procedures and regulations. Test scores ranged from 0 to 10. In total, 24 lessons were organized, covering 5 subjects and 12 different groups. The subjects were: Mathematics, History, Geography, French and Economics (see Figure 2).

Each of the 6 involved teachers prepared 2 lessons for their subject. The learning contents were part of the regular curriculum. Each lesson in the EL condition was developed as a digital 'learning path', a number of pre-ordered learning activities which offer 'a road map to learners' (De Smet et al, 2014). Each path contained multiple learning objects including online text materials, pictures, online exercises and hyperlinks to external websites and video clips. A pupil worked individually on a desktop computer, using a headphone. Teachers were present in the classroom, they assisted pupils in the event of a technical problem.

2.3 Research Model

The research model incorporats the original constructs of the ISSM, extended by using variables related to perceived enjoyment, and redefines the concept of 'net benefits' (Figure 3). In the following, we elaborate on the rationale behind the model and its hypotheses.

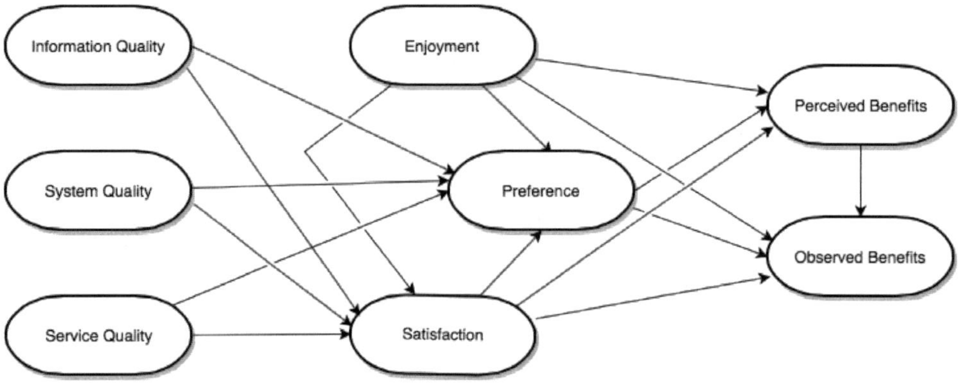

Figure 3. The Research Model

The observed benefits are conceived as differences in learning performance between the EL and F2F conditions. The latent construct of perceived benefits is defined as the 'perceived usefulness of the EL system for learning, as compared to the conventional way of teaching'. In this regard, we assume that learners evaluate previous experiences with ICT and make a total judgment as to whether the benefits outweigh disadvantages (Kirkman, 2000). In line with this stance, we ascertain the value of perceived benefits and consider it to be a real proxy and predictor of observed (tested) benefits. The model further posits that net benefits are dependent on three primary beliefs: preference, satisfaction and enjoyment.

Within a secondary school context 'voluntary (intention to) use' is restricted, since educational institutions or teachers decide on when and how to use EL tools. As a consequence, we included the concept of 'preference' as a replacement for the ISSM's 'intention to use', as proposed by Bourgonjon et al (2009). Preference is defined as 'the positive and preferred choice for the continued use of e-learning systems in the classroom'. We contend that preference for a system will affect pupils' learning experiences positively and thus lead to better results, i.e. improved net benefits. Satisfaction is another principal determinant, expressed as 'the feelings and attitudes that stem from aggregating a user's efforts and benefits from using an information system' (Wixom and Todd, 2005). As such, satisfaction is conceived as an aggregated attitude that positively influences the system's net benefits (as proposed by DeLone and McLean, 2003). Perceived enjoyment is defined as 'the extent to which using technology is perceived to be enjoyable in its own right, independent of any performance consequences' (Cheng, 2011). Sufficient evidence validates perceived enjoyment as a significant driver of intention to use, usage and ease of use of EL systems (e.g., Cheng, 2011; Teo & Noyes, 2011). We argue that an increase in perceived enjoyment stimulates pupils to make use of the EL course materials.

The ISSM further distinguishes between the system quality, the quality of the information that is provided by the system, and the quality of the service that is provided to use the system. In our context, we defined information quality as 'the level of difficulty of the EL system, the multimedia components and the related learning activities'. System quality was, in line with the ISSM literature, conceived as 'the degree to which the system is easy to manipulate and interact with'.

Pupils were not trained beforehand; if necessary they received technical support by a teacher during the lesson. Thus, in this study service quality is conceived as the degree to which support was available and sufficient. Congruent with the ISSM, we propose system, information and service quality as determinants of preference and satisfaction.

In the literature, enjoyment has been established as a direct determinant of the use of learning systems (or the usage intention) (cf. Saade et al, 2008). Using preference instead of (intention to) use, it is plausible to contend that if a pupil enjoys the sheer use of the EL environment, s/he will likely prefer its further use and be more satisfied with it. Consequently, we propose perceived enjoyment as a determinant of both use preference and satisfaction.

2.4 Measures and Analyses

Several previously validated instruments were employed (cf. Wang et al, 2007). Both self-reported (perceived) and objectively measured (observed) gauges were used to evaluate the pupils' learning performance. The observed benefits were calculated as differences in test performance between pupils in the EL and F2F condition, resulting in a differential score between -10 and 10. Perceptions were measured as latent constructs, using multiple items (see the appendix).

Table 1 shows the factor loadings and internal consistency measures for every latent construct. All constructs show sufficient internal consistency with Cronbach's alphas of higher than 0.7. The composite reliability and average variance extracted (AVE) are both above the expected thresholds of 0.7 and 0.5 for all the constructs, suggesting adequate convergent validity (Hair et al, 2006). While omitting the display of all item cross-loadings in the interest of brevity, we confirm that discriminant validity is established and that all items loaded on their constructs as expected. In the case of multiple determinants, the variance inflation factor was below 2.0 level, excluding collinearity issues.

Table 1. Internal consistency of the measures

Construct	*Items & their Factor Loadings*	*Composite Reliability*	*Cronbach's Alpha*	*AVE*
Perceived Benefits	PB1: 0.79; PB2: 0.86; PB3: 0.76	0.85	0.73	0.65
Preference	Pref1: 0.90; Pref2: 0.94; Pref3: 0.90; Pref4: 0.92	0.95	0.93	0.83
Satisfaction	Sat1: 0.88; Sat2: 0.72; Sat3: 0.88	0.87	0.78	0.69
Perceived Enjoyment	PE1: 0.90; PE2: 0.94; PE3: 0.92	0.95	0.91	0.85
Information Quality	IQ1: 0.68; IQ2: 0.81; IQ3: 0.80; IQ4: 0.83; IQ5:0.83	0.89	0.85	0.63
System Quality	SQ1: 0.77; SQ2: 0.67; SQ3: 0.88; SQ4: 0.73	0.83	0.72	0.55
Service Quality	SeQ1: 0.91; SeQ2: 0.96	0.93	0.86	0.87

We tested the measurement and research model by applying a partial least square (PLS) modelling approach using the SmartPLS application (Ringle et al, 2005).

3. RESULTS

3.1 Descriptives

On average, the EL instruction was modestly accepted (see Table 2). The information, system and service quality received rather positive scores between 3.30 and 3.55 (on a scale of 1 to 5); with a mean score for satisfaction of 3.09. Perceived benefits, perceived enjoyment, and in particular preference, however, received scores below the neutral point (3). Remarkably, pupils' performance in the EL condition was significantly poorer compared to the F2F instruction mode (with test scores of 75.7% for the F2F versus 56.8% in the EL condition). It seems pupils appreciated the quality of the system and the EL materials but were not in favour of it and would not choose it if it were optional.

Table 2. Global Descriptives

	Mean	*Std. D.*	*Min*	*Max*
Test Results F2F	7.57	2.25	0	10
Test Results EL	5.68	2.75	0	10
Test Results Difference	-1.89	3.34	-10.0	10.00
Perceived Benefits	2.63	0.82	1.00	5.00
Preference	2.24	1.05	1.00	5.00
Satisfaction	3.09	0.86	1.00	5.00
Perceived Enjoyment	2.61	1.02	1.00	5.00
Information Quality	3.30	0.68	1.00	5.00
System Quality	3.55	0.66	1.00	5.00
Service Quality	3.49	0.98	1.00	5.00

The most salient outcomes of a comparative analysis considering grade, subject and programme type (see Table 3), can be summarised as follows:

(1) The observed benefits' score, i.e. the differences in test results among respondents from the 7th grade, is -4.96, which is significantly lower than the scores of the pupils in other grades.

(2) The observed and perceived benefits' score of the pupils enrolled in general secondary education (-3.43 and 2.29) is significantly lower than that of vocational, technical and arts pupils.

(3) The observed benefits' score for maths is significantly lower than that for other course subjects. The 'perceived benefits' scores are the highest for French.

Table 3. Mean scores according to grade, subject and programme type

School grade[a]	**7th gr.**	**9th gr.**	**10th gr.**	**11th gr.**	**12th gr.**
N	24	49	28	21	29
Observed Benefits	**-4.96***	-1.86	-0.25	-0.71	-1.83
Perceived Benefits	2.31	2.65	2.90	2.43	2.74
[a] There were no students of the 8th grade					
Subjects	**Geography**	**Economics**	**French**	**History**	**Mathematics**
N	30	28	30	39	24
Observed Benefits	-1.97	-2	-0.03	-1.44	**-4.71***
Perceived Benefits	2.79	2.79	**2.96***	2.39	2.22
Education Type	**General**	**Vocational**	**Arts**	**Technical**	
N	49	28	14	60	
Observed Benefits	**-3.43***	-1.68	-0.64	-0.25	
Perceived Benefits	**2.29***	2.79	2.55	2.90	
** : Significance is based on Kruskal-Wallis or 1-way Anova*					

3.2 The Tested Structural Model

The tested model is depicted in Figure 4. Enjoyment plays a key role in explaining satisfaction and use preference. System and service quality have no significant impact. Information quality and satisfaction are significantly related (β=0.20; p<0.05). The impact of enjoyment on the net benefits is fully mediated via satisfaction and preference. Preference has a strong impact on perceived benefits (β=0.47, p<0,001) but a negative impact on observed benefits (β=-0.29, p<0.05). Thus, the data suggest that pupils who are in favour of EL system usage are not the pupils with the best test results. Satisfaction is only weakly related to perceived benefits. It has no impact on the observed benefits, but a considerable effect on preference. A strong relationship exists between perceived and observed benefits (β=0.45; p<0.001).

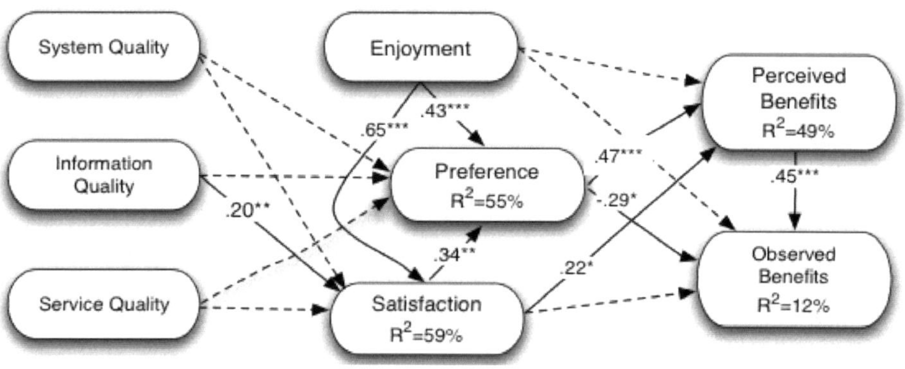

Figure 4. The Tested Structural Model

4. DISCUSSION

4.1 Findings

Our experiment reveals that secondary school pupils have better test results in a face-to-face instructional situation. The pattern is consistent across subject, grade and educational type (despite some differences (see table 3)). This finding is also strengthened by rather low overall scores on the perceived benefits (M=2.63) and on pupils' preference for using the system (M=2.24). Given the radical nature of the EL approach, where pupils had to deal with the online contents without further assistance, and the novelty of it in secondary education in Belgium, these results are understandable. The explanatory model, built upon the ISSM that we tested, helps to explain why the EL instruction mode resulted in lower scores on perceived and observed benefits.

The model includes both instrumental and emotional determinants of preference and satisfaction. It is clear that the emotional variable, perceived enjoyment, is the most important determinant of satisfaction and preference, the latter being a dominant predictor of net benefits. Perceived enjoyment has a modest mean of 2.61 and its impact on user preference and satisfaction is strong and significant. In other words, if pupils think they (will) enjoy working with an EL system, they really prefer its use and are satisfied with it.

The instrumental determinants that focus on observable qualities of the deployed system, i.e. service, system and information quality, are not the reason for the lack of preference for the EL instruction mode. Only information quality impacts satisfaction significantly, indicating that a higher level of appreciation of the EL contents slightly increases satisfaction.

4.2 Contributions and Limitations

Our approach not only targets the less-studied group of secondary education learners, but also integrates a research model with an experimental design in an ecological setting. Moreover, it includes both perceived and objectively measured learning outcomes, and the construct of 'preference' as a substitute for 'intention to use'. The latter is particularly pertinent in a context of non-voluntary usage, which is common in secondary education. The resulting validated model is re-usable for future research endeavors in- and outside the context of secondary education research, and it can be applied within an experimental design or in a mere survey-based investigation.

On a methodological level, by applying the factoral approach we have been able to minimize typical biases due to undesired group or topic effects. The repetition of the design (in several classes and), only strengthens the findings.

A first plausible limitation of the study is the fact that teachers were only allowed to intervene in the event of technical problems. In other words, a quite radical EL approach was introduced. A second limitation is related to the limited number of cycles employed within the larger framework of a design-based research (DBR) approach. The quest for sound, validated sets of guidelines for educational design, adapted to one's organization, preferably involves multiple iterations in a longitudinal set-up (Anderson and Shattuck, 2012) and multiple methods (Wang et al., 2011).

4.3 Implications

At first glance, our findings are somewhat contradictory to the current body of research findings that stress the importance and beneficial contributions of e-learning. However, our results should not be regarded as being opposed to such a stance. In essence, we have explored the limits of EL in secondary education and our results primarily point to aspects and considerations that need to be addressed when introducing EL systems in schools.

In particular, when following new trends in education, such as 'flipping the classroom' (FtC), one should take into account the nature of the materials and learner characteristics. In a context where pupils are used to conventional classroom teaching, the transition to more EL instruction is not evident, not even for millennials (the subjects of the underlying study). We contend that pupils today may be technology-oriented but when it comes to learning, they have limited proficiencies. Reading and comprehending learning materials independently and on-screen, without outside guidance, seems less fruitful than conventional F2F lessons. In the light of FtC, where pupils are provided with EL artefacts they need to process themselves, our findings clearly mark a warning. Teaching should not be confined to providing learning materials and follow-up class-based activities, as pupils need to be scaffolded in their knowledge acquisition process as well. A principal consequence of this stance implies a shift of focus to frameworks such as 'self-regulated learning' (e.g., Lee and Lee, 2008), explaining learners' cognitive strategies and control of their efforts; and/or the self-determination theory, a theory of motivation that taps into our natural tendencies during a task-achievement process (e.g. Jang et al, 2016).

5. CONCLUSIONS

This study contributes to EL research by assessing the antecedents of perceived and observed benefits of EL instruction as compared to F2F teaching, in secondary education. 151 pupils and 6 teachers from a secondary school participated in a repetitive factoral experimental design in an ecological setting. This design facilitated the comparison of instructional formats in an empirical sound way, while yielding interesting information for practitioners. The DeLone and McLean's ISSM underpins the experimental approach. The model was extended with three factors: perceived enjoyment, and perceived and observed net benefits.

Overall, both the observed test results and the perceived benefits are determinants for lower effectiveness rates of EL as compared to F2F classes. This finding was confirmed across subjects, educational levels and types. Our results show the importance of perceived enjoyment. However, pupils who preferred and enjoyed the system are not necessarily the best performing ones. This finding is very important. It indicates that a shift towards EL to achieve better learning results should not be taken for granted. We assume that the particular EL approach we opted for - in close cooperation with the school's headmaster and his team of teachers - requires from pupils that they master self-regulated learning skills. In short, schools should preferably try to find the optimal equilibrium between F2F and EL instruction, while focusing on both enjoyment and performance.

Follow-up studies could further extend the proposed model with context and individual characteristics related to teaching and cognitive presence (Joo et al, 2011), alongside self-regulated learning (Lee & Lee, 2008).

REFERENCES

Abdous, M., and Yoshimura, M., 2010. Learner outcomes and satisfaction: A comparison of live video-streamed instruction, satellite broadcast instruction, and face-to-face instruction. *Computers & Education*,Vol. 55,pp. 733–741.

Ananiadou, K., and Claro, M., 2009. 21st Century Skills and Competences for New Millennium Learners in OECD Countries. *OECD Education Working Papers*. Paris: OECD Publishing.

Anderson, T., and Shattuck, J., 2012. Design-Based Research: A Decade of Progress in Education Research? *Educational Researcher,* Vol. 41(Jan/Feb.), pp. 16-25.

Aparicio, M., et al, 2017. Grit in the path to e-learning success. *Computers in Human Behavior*, Vol. 66, pp. 388–399.

Bourgonjon, J., et al, 2009. Students' perceptions about the use of video games in the classroom. *Computers & Education*, Vol. 54, No. 4, pp. 1145-1156.

Cheng, Y.-M., 2011. Antecedents and consequences of e-learning acceptance. *Information Systems Journal*, Vol. 21, No. 3, pp. 269-299.

DeLone, W., and McLean, E., 2003. The DeLone and McLean Model of Information Systems Success: A Ten-Year Update. *Journal of Management Information Systems*, Vol. 19, No. 4, pp. 9-30.

De Smet, C., et al, 2014. The design and implementation of learning paths in a learning management system. *Interactive Learning Environments*, Vol. 24, No. 6, pp. 1076-1096.

Grubišić, A., et al, 2009. Controlled experiment replication in evaluation of e-learning system's educational influence. *Computers & Education.* Vol. 53, No. 3, pp. 591-602.

Hair, J., et al, 2006. *Multivariate Data Analysis*. New Jersey: Prentice Hall. USA.

Jang, H., et al, 2016. A new autonomy-supportive way of teaching that increases conceptual learning: Teaching in students' preferred ways. *The Journal of Experimental Education*. Vol. 84, No. 4, pp. 686-701.

Joo, Y.J., et al, 2011. Online university students' satisfaction and persistence: Examining perceived level of presence, usefulness and ease of use as predictors in a structural model. *Computers & Education,* Vol. 57, No. 2, pp. 1654–1664.

Kirkman, C., 2000. A model for the effective management of information and communications technology development in schools derived from six contrasting case studies. *Journal of Information Techology for Teacher Education,* Vol. 9, No. 1, pp. 37-52.

Lee, J.-K., and Lee, W.-K., 2008. The relationship of e-Learner's self-regulatory efficacy and perception of e-Learning environmental quality. *Computers in Human Behavior,* Vol. 24, No. 1, pp. 32–47.

Ringle, C. M., et al, 2005. SmartPLS 2.0 (beta). Germany, University of Hamburg. Germany.

Saade, R., et al, 2008. Impact of Motivation on Intentions in Online Learning: Canada vs China. *Issues in Informing Science and Information Technology,* Vol. 5, pp. 137-147.

Teo, T., and Noyes, J., 2011. An assessment of the influence of perceived enjoyment and attitude on the intention to use technology among pre-service teachers: A structural equation modeling approach. *Computers & Education.* Vol. 57, No. 2, pp. 1645-1653.

Wang, M., et al, 2011. Creating a performance-oriented e-learning environment: A design science approach. *Information & Management,* Vol. 48, pp. 260-269.

Wang, Y., et al, 2007. Measuring e-learning system success in an organizational context: Scale development and validation. *Computers in Human Behavior,* Vol. 23, No. 4, pp. 1792-1808.

Wixom B.H., and Todd, P.A., 2005. A Theoretical Integration of User Satisfaction and Technology Acceptance. *Information Systems Research,* Vol. 16, No. 1, pp. 85-102.

APPENDIX. QUESTIONNAIRE ITEMS

Constructs	*Item*
Perceived Benefits	PB1 To what extent is a learning in Smartschool better than a conventional class (given by a teacher) PB2 By using Smartschool, I can understand the course material PB3 By using Smartschool, I could study my lesson
Satisfaction	Sat1 To what extent are you satisfied with the lesson in Smartschool? Sat2 Are you satisfied with this way of teaching? Sat3 Are you satisfied with the use of Smartschool within the school?
Preference	Pref1 If I had to choose between a learning path in Smartschool and a conventional class, I would choose a learning path in Smartschool Pref2 I prefer to use Smartschool Pref3 If it was up to me, Smartschool would be used more frequently Pref4 In the future, I would like work more with Smartschool in the classroom
Perceived Enjoyment	PE1 I find the use of Smartschool enjoyable PE2 Learning via Smartschool is pleasant PE3 I find it pleasurable to learn via Smartschool
System Quality	SQ1 Smartschool is easy to use SQ2 To what extent did you experience technical problems during the class SQ3 Did you find it easy to work with Smartschool SQ4 How responsive was the system (the pages shown on the screen)
Information Quality	IQ1 Was the learning path (with its components) clear and understandable IQ2 How much do you appreciate the contents presented (text, video's, pictures) IQ3 Were the presented assignments in the system clear IQ4 Could you understand the topic with the available information IQ5 The topic was well presented in the learning environment
Service Quality	SeQ1 If I needed help from the teacher I received valuable help SeQ2 The support I got was sufficient

INTEGRATION OF CHILDREN WITH SPECIAL NEEDS IN MATHEMATICS THROUGH VIRTUAL REALITY

Thomas Keller, Andreas Hebeisen and Elke Brucker-Kley
Zurich University of Applied Sciences, School of Management and Law
St.-Georgen-Platz 2, 8401 Winterthur, Switzerland

ABSTRACT

Students with special needs in mathematics lessons can be specifically supported through virtual reality (VR) if they are offered virtual learning environments that offer real benefits through their implementation in VR. In addition to learning by doing, the visualization of mathematical facts in 3D for the training of imagination can offer added value in relation to the tasks themselves or that content can be experienced in class for which this is otherwise not simply possible. The evaluation of the developed learning environments with learners has shown that possible advantages of an immersive learning environment compared to classical teaching aids can be a positive effect on motivation, concentration and learning success.

KEYWORDS

Virtual Reality, Education, Integration of Children with Special Needs

1. INTRODUCTION

The possibilities and benefits of the use of new media in teaching at elementary schools have been discussed for some time. In the context of computer use in schools, the terms media pedagogy and media didactics are often used (cf. (Krauthausen 2012), p. 1). In the context of the present work, however, "new media" primarily means the use of so-called learning or exercise programs. With the use of IT resources, specific knowledge can be imparted in many subjects. New teaching concepts are possible. Especially VR and augmented reality (AR) bring completely new possibilities into the classroom. Simple examples are Google Expeditions and the Google Cardboard. A study by Samsung in Germany in 2017 shows: "More than three-quarters of teachers (79%) agree with the statement that thanks to VR, students have the opportunity to make experiences that they would never otherwise have. [...] In addition, the majority of teachers believe that the use of VR in class can increase the motivation of students (74%) and improve their learning success (62%). According to the teachers (58%), the use of the technology can also help in understanding learning concepts. The greatest potential benefits of VR are attributed to the subjects geography/geography (80%), history (74%) and science (62%)" ((Samsung Studie: Lehrer Sehen Großes Potenzial Für Die Nutzung von Virtual Reality Im Unterricht 2017)).

Interestingly, however, digital media are only used hesitantly in elementary schools. There may be many reasons for this. On the one hand, on the side of teachers, on the other hand in pedagogy and in very new media such as virtual reality, the lack of pedagogical content for use in the classroom.

What Confucius (551-479 B.C.) already knew still applies to today's school teaching: "Tell me, and I will forget. Show me, and I may remember. Involve me, and I will understand." This guideline is not only perfectly suited to the topic of virtual reality, it is also often quoted in connection with competence-oriented learning in the context of Lehrplan 21 (d-edk 2016) (Swiss curriculum for primary and secondary schools), where the focus is on the actions of learners. The aim of this work is therefore to develop and implement concrete learning units for mathematical learning in VR that exhibit a degree of interaction that comes close to doing in the sense of Confucius. The learning units are to be designed with a mathematical-didactic view in the context of integration of children with special needs into regular schools. Integration of children with special needs into regular schools often focuses on students with learning difficulties. In the context of this work, however, the term should be viewed holistically and potential for students with special talents should also be pointed out.

2. STATE-OF-THE-ART

In the following, important principles and guiding ideas of integration of children with special needs into regular schools as well as mathematics didactics are examined in order to subsequently deal with immersive learning in the context of VR.

2.1 Integration of Children with Special Needs into Regular Schools

"Less efficient learners bring with them serious deficits from primary education due to cumulative backlogs, so that performance heterogeneity at lower secondary level is particularly high and will increase" ((Affolter and Walt 2017), p. 6).

According to ((Affolter and Walt 2017), p. 7), teaching and learning processes must be arranged in such a way that learners are cognitively activated, i.e. stimulated to think. Good means of doing this is to encourage learners to discover, analyse, justify and explain. "While the learners work on the assignments, the teacher actively observes their learning activities. The teacher deals with the learners, talks to them and asks them for insights into their ways of thinking and strategies. Because a look at learning outcomes alone often offers too little information to identify any misconceptions and make them manageable" ((Affolter and Walt 2017), p. 7).

The integration consciously involves children and young people with disabilities in the regular school and ensures specific support through appropriate measures. Inclusion means that the school accepts all students from its perimeter. It focuses its offer on possible impairments and special needs (cf. (Eckhart 2016), p. 16 f.). According to Schaumburg ((Schaumburg 2015), p. 65), the basic aim is to adapt the lessons to the individual learning requirements of the students. Since the adoption of the UN Convention on the Rights of Persons with Disabilities in 2008, the focus has once again been on the ideal of inclusive teaching, as it focuses on the heterogeneity of pupils as a central principle on which all didactic considerations must be oriented.

2.2 Didactics of Mathematics

Krauthausen ((Krauthausen 2012), p. 3 f.) criticises the fact that computer-assisted learning programs in mathematics that are well-known and widespread on the market today pay too little attention to the current state of research and knowledge in mathematics didactics. The focus is too much on technology instead of content (the subject-specific content) and the programs thus contribute much to the media competence of learners but little to mathematics skills.

Burrill ((Burrill 2017), p. 316) mentions mathematical accuracy (fidelity) and user experience as central mathematics didactic principles. The mathematical accuracy means that the software should always be mathematically correct, the user experience should not hinder the work with the mathematical task and should promote mathematical thinking.

Learners need to be able to make decisions to expand their thinking. This possibility is also closely related to the complexity of a task, which does not necessarily require complex mathematical requirements (cf. (Geiger 2017), p. 289). According to Joubert ((Joubert 2017), p. 20 ff.), while working on a mathematical task, students use means from the so-called "Modes of Production". These include acting (usually in the sense of indicating a solution), formulating (developing hypotheses, solution strategies, etc.) and validating (checking based on evidence, theorems or explanations). Formulation and validation almost always have to be initiated by the teacher.

For the motivation of learners, mathematics itself should increasingly be presented in a way that makes them exciting and captivating themselves, rather than motivating them with other means in the learning programs (cf. (Krauthausen 2012), p. 20): "Effective learning processes are characterized by a high degree of motivation and joy, which however arise from the matter and not from its packaging" ((Krauthausen 2012), p. 21).

Mathematical learning is an important pedagogical task. Mathematical tasks are intended to encourage learners to do something mathematical and thus experience mathematics in the broadest sense (cf. (Joubert 2017), p. 4). All tasks should always contain pragmatic and epistemological aspects. The epistemological aspects refer to the insights to be conveyed to learners while working on a task (cf. (Sinclair and Zazkis

2017), p. 177), whereby the pragmatic value of a task is almost always equated with solving the task (cf. (Sinclair and Zazkis 2017), p. 190). Laborde ((Laborde 2011), p. 82) supplements cognitive aspects (what kind of learning the task triggers in the learner at the current state of knowledge), didactic aspects (with what means the task is set) and instrumental aspects (which instruments the learner needs to solve the task).

2.3 Immersive Learning

Learning in virtual worlds is often called "immersive learning". According to Höntzsch et al. ((Höntzsch et al. 2013), p. 3), immersion describes the degree to which individuals perceive that they interact more with their virtual than with their real environment (individual sense of being there). In a virtual reality, immersion seems to be determined by the degree of representation of the learners, their presence and their possibilities of interaction.

Höntzsch et al. ((Höntzsch et al. 2013), p. 3) describe with reference to Burdea and Coiffet ((Burdea and Coiffet 2003), p. 3) the three "I" of learning with virtual realities: Imagination, immersion and interaction. "Imagination describes the imaginative power of learners to put themselves in the position of a simulation. Real-time visualizations and reactions of the system provide users with immediate feedback on their inputs (interaction). The information is also recorded multimodally [...], i.e. with several senses. This creates a feeling of immersion, i.e. of being directly involved in the simulated world" ((Höntzsch et al. 2013), p. 3). Imagination, immersion and interaction seem to be important factors for immersive learning.

With regard to pedagogy, Geiger ((Geiger 2017), p. 288 f.) points out in the context of mathematics how eminently important it is to select, adapt and implement the tasks in the learning environments. In this context, he points out the importance of cooperation between teachers and researchers in order to anchor well-designed tasks with pedagogically correct approaches in the learning environments and thus improve learning.

A sufficient degree of challenge is important for the learning process (cf. (Geiger 2017), p. 289). Höntzsch et al. ((Höntzsch et al. 2013), p. 4) list the following measures as necessary to avoid overburdening learners in immersive learning environments:

- clear learning objectives, work orders and instructions,
- permanently available background information,
- hints and exercises that stimulate reflection (for example, setting a specific state of the simulation)

Höntzsch et al. ((Höntzsch et al. 2013), p. 3) list the possible support of immersion on learning processes in connection with flow and presence experience as a thesis when using three-dimensional virtual worlds. However, with reference to Grunewald (2009), they point out that these effects are also mentioned in the context of computer game addiction. Chen ((Chen 2016), p. 644) also shows a positive effect on the learning (in the context of language learning) of such environments.

According to Höntzsch et al. ((Höntzsch et al. 2013), p. 4), discovering learning leads to an expansion of personal experience space and to the generation and examination of hypotheses, since knowledge in these learning environments is not predetermined but explorative. It is pointed out that the learning environments must be simulated as truthfully as possible in order for the findings to be successfully transferred into reality. It also describes advantages in the depth of information processing, learning success and motivation, the latter not per se resulting in a higher quality or quantity of cognitive processing and skill acquisition.

3. INTRODUCTION OF THE LEARNING UNITS

The following three learning environments from the "mathbuch IF" (Affolter and Walt 2017) were selected for implementation in VR. The selection was based on interviews with teachers and taking into account the characteristics of a VR environment.

For all virtual learning environments there are the roles learner (works with the virtual learning environment), supervisor (also "coach"), supports learners with errors and problems and asks them to discover, analyse, justify and explain as well as the virtual learning environment (system). The concept is based on the "Game Design Outline" according to Olbrish ((Olbrish 2014), p. 51).

The learning environments are accessible at http://neuelehrkonzepte.ch/ for HTC Vive.

3.1 Virtual Learning Environment 1: Introduction to Virtual Reality

The first virtual learning environment serves to introduce learners to virtual reality. The virtual reality is to be experienced for the first time and the basic operating concepts for the other learning environments are to be learned. This should be done to a degree that allows learners to concentrate fully on the task in the subsequent learning environments and not be distracted because of the controls.

At the beginning, various geometric bodies are stacked on a glass shelf a few meters away. The first task is displayed with a text in the room: The learner must teleport to the shopping cart and slider using the controller. Once there, you can change your position by walking around in real space. The next task is displayed: The objects should become accessible by tilting the tray using the slider. The handle of the slider can be gripped and moved for this purpose. As soon as an angle of approx. 45° is reached, all objects fall to the floor or onto the table and the next subtask, collecting all objects and placing them in the shopping cart, is displayed. Once all items have been placed in the shopping cart, the task can be completed by selecting the button that is now displayed ("Done"). The learner remains in the virtual room and discusses the developed solution and the learned operating elements with the supervisor in virtual reality.

3.2 Virtual Learning Environment 2: Base Area Times Height

Virtual reality should make it possible "that learners know units of length, area and space with the corresponding support concepts" ((Affolter and Walt 2017), p. 175). The learning unit should be "built up experimentally and action-oriented, in that the learners can get to know different models of prisms and cylinders" ((Affolter and Walt 2017), p. 175) in virtual reality and interact with them. "The learners gain so many basic geometric experiences and train their spatial perception" ((Affolter and Walt 2017), p. 175).

The starting position in the learning environment is close to the table. On the table is a geometric body (a cube), whose volume can be calculated by means of base area times height. The first task is to achieve a volume of 1000 cm^3 for the cube. This can be achieved by changing the side length with a slider. If the solution is correct, after a short delay (to prevent random solutions) the next body appears on the table (lying on the surface). As an intermediate task, this body's base must now be placed on the table, as this often causes problems for the learners. When the body is on its base, the sliders for base area and height are displayed and a volume of 1000 cm^3 can be achieved again. Subsequently, the subtasks are repeated for the remaining three bodies.

The difficulty of the subtasks is increased in three steps: The first body is the cube for which only the side length can be changed by a slider. For the next three bodies (circular cylinder, triangular prism, hexagonal prism) a slider is available for the base area and the height. This corresponds to the focus of the task and is therefore realized for the majority of bodies. The cuboid as the last body can be changed individually in three dimensions. The base area can therefore be specifically set with width and length. Since a volume of exactly 1000 cm3 cannot be achieved for the three middle bodies (circular cylinder, triangular prism, hexagonal prism) with steps of exactly 1 cm for base area and height, a tolerance of a few cubic centimeters is provided. This tolerance was increased from 3 to 30 cm in two steps. The reasons for this were not to demotivate the learners with their tendency to perfection if they make an effort but still cannot find a solution, as well as the solubility of the task in practice. The circle number Pi is simplified with the value 3, as is often common for use in integration of children with special needs into regular schools.

If the volume for the cuboid (for this exactly 1000 cm^3) was also reached correctly, a button appears to leave the learning environment. The learner remains in the virtual room and discusses the solution with the teacher. The solution for all subtasks must also be explained in consultation with the supervisor.

3.3 Virtual Learning Environment 3: So Small! So Big!

"Dealing with sizes and masses is very demanding for many learners. Lack of sizing [...] and insufficient knowledge of kilo-, deci-, centi-, milli- and the relationships between units of measurement (e.g. 1 kg = 1000g) are also not rare at secondary level" (Affolter and Walt 2017). It is precisely at these points that the virtual learning environment is intended to build on and provide learners with opportunities to compare sizes: "What is e.g., heavier, shorter, higher, has less content? " (Affolter and Walt 2017).

In order to enhance the learning effect and immersion, the learning environment must be realized with extensive possibilities for interaction with objects and sizes. This learning environment consists of four scenes.

Scene 1: In the start menu you can select from a series of different units of measurement and start the respective scene by selecting one of the buttons. The principle for the individual scenes is identical.

Scene 2 is described using the task for the measure of capacity. However, this is realized identically for the other units of measurement. Six objects of different sizes are displayed in random order (e.g. a cube of 1 m^3 filled with water, an aquarium, a trophy). However, these are all displayed in the same size. The appropriate unit of measurement (e.g. hectoliter for the aquarium) must now be assigned to each object from the position panel. If a unit of measurement has been assigned to each object, the button for displaying the solution becomes active. If the solution is requested, the objects are sorted according to the place value chart and displayed in their original size. The different sizes make misconceptions immediately apparent to learners. In addition, a reference of the sizes to suitable objects can be produced in original size.

Scene 3 for learning assurance is similar in structure to scene 2. Six objects are displayed. This time, however, not only the appropriate unit of measurement but also the appropriate dimension and a ratio factor must be assigned.

As scene 4, a task for sorting objects according to size, weight, etc. is optionally implemented. Six objects are displayed in random order (optically identically large). Instead of assigning units of measurement, the objects must be sorted by size (or weight, etc.) using buttons. If the solution is activated, the order is retained, but the objects are displayed in real size.

4. RESULTS

In order to gain further insights into the learning environments developed, these were played through at four different schools in the form of a controlled experiment with 20 learners with special needs after completion of development. The objectives, structure and results of this evaluation are described below.

The aim of the evaluation is not a scientific study on the measurement of impact. Primarily, factors such as the fun or motivation of the students to learn in a virtual environment, the learners' personal feelings about learning success, the didactic correctness and the quality of the implementation (especially usability) of the learning units themselves should be evaluated. In this way, a first indicator of possible effectiveness and the potential for improvements in learning environments is to be shown.

4.1 Choice of Sample

In mathematics lessons in particular, diagnoses for isolated learning disorders (dyscalculia) are no longer often issued. Instead, there is talk of a partial weakness in mathematics. Discussions with the teachers of the selected schools have shown that the idea of inclusion by Eckhart ((Eckhart 2016)) has been lived here for about a year and that the affected learners have been integrated into regular classes. The lessons are therefore distributed to the system and not to individual students. As a result, the field for the evaluation was opened a little bit. Students with special needs in mathematics were selected as participants, but who do not necessarily (diagnosed) suffer from an isolated learning disorder. The decision as to who would participate in the evaluation was made by the teachers. Table 1 shows the number of participants by class and gender.

Table 1. Summary of participants

Class	Age	Sex	Number
7	13–15	female	1
		male	7
8	14–16	female	3
		male	3
9	15	female	1
		male	5
Total number of participants			**20**

4.2 Procedure

The evaluation sessions at one school lasted between half a day and a full day (depending on the number of participants and other interested parties). If possible, a room was reserved for the entire duration of the evaluation and the test set-up started approximately one hour before the start of the evaluation. This consists of a complete PC system with sufficient graphic performance including a screen for observation by the supervisor and the "HTC Vive" system consisting of Head-Mounted Display (HMD, "glasses"), the two controllers and the base stations (also "Lighthouses") for tracking. For details on the technical operation and installation of the system, refer to the "HTC Vive" manual.

The learners were taken out of class individually or in pairs and completed the various learning environments in a maximum of 45 minutes. Before entering the virtual world, the instructions including rules and rights were discussed and the most important operating elements explained. The coaching during the stay in the virtual learning environments was also carried out by the author as a supervisor.

Finally, all learners completed an anonymous questionnaire for the evaluation.

4.3 Survey Results

The questionnaire with 24 questions was submitted to the learners on paper. For three questions a text answer is expected, 21 questions contain a scale on which the degree of approval is marked. Questions 1 and 2 ask about the previous experience with virtual reality and video games. Questions 3 to 5 examine the operation and clarity of the tasks. The learning environments 2 and 3 are evaluated more precisely with questions 6 to 14 (some questions appear duplicated because they refer to learning unit 2 and 3). The introduction is not addressed with specific questions, as it is not the main focus of the evaluation and to keep the questionnaire short. The remaining 10 questions deal with the general learning experience.

Table 2. Compilation of survey results

#	Age	Class	Sex	Learning unit 1 (VLU1)	Learning unit 2 (VLU2)	Learning unit 3a (VLU3)	Learning unit 3b (VLU3)	1. Do you have already experience with VR?		2. How often are you gaming?		3. How easy was the user interface to learn?		4. How clear were the tasks?		5. How much were you dependent on the support of the supervisor (coaching)?		6. How well known were the tasks? Have you already solved similar tasks?		7. How much did you like the learning environment?		8.! How difficult were the tasks for you? (inverse scale)		9. How did you solve your tasks?	
1	15	9	male	X		X	X	0,0	0,0%	9,9	64,7%	14,8	96,7%	15,3	100,0%	0,0	0,0%	14,6	95,4%						
2	14	8	male	X		X	X	0,2	1,3%	10,6	69,3%	7,6	49,7%	14,9	97,4%	7,5	49,0%	7,7	50,3%						
3	15	9	male	X	X	X	X	0,2	1,3%	2,6	17,0%	13,9	90,8%	14,9	97,4%	10,2	66,7%	14,7	96,1%	14,2	92,8%	1,7	11,1%	7,2	47,1%
4	15	9	female	X	X	X	X	0,0	0,0%	0,0	0,0%	7,4	49,0%	14,3	94,7%	7,2	47,7%	7,5	49,7%	13,2	87,4%	10,0	66,2%	8,7	57,6%
5	15	8	female	X	X	X	X	0,2	1,3%	4,1	27,2%	11,1	73,5%	12,9	85,4%	7,6	50,3%	14,2	94,0%	12,4	82,1%			5,5	36,4%
6	14	8	male	X	X	X	X	7,5	49,7%	8,0	53,0%	12,7	84,1%	4,1	27,2%	7,5	49,7%	7,7	51,0%	9,2	60,9%	3,9	25,8%	5,3	35,1%
7	15	9	male	X	X	X	X	0,0	0,0%	9,6	63,6%	12,6	83,4%	11,3	74,8%	6,5	43,0%	6,4	42,4%	11,4	75,5%	1,7	11,3%	11,8	78,1%
8	15	9	male	X	X	X	X	7,5	49,7%			7,5	49,7%	11,6	76,8%	9,7	64,2%	0,0	0,0%	11,3	74,8%	2,4	15,9%	15,0	99,3%
9	15	9	male	X		X	X	7,5	49,7%	5,6	37,1%	13,8	91,4%	15,1	100,0%	11,2	74,2%	15,1	100,0%						
10	13	7	female	X	X	X	X	7,0	48,3%	5,6	38,6%	12,7	87,6%	7,2	49,7%	7,2	49,7%	7,2	49,7%	14,5	100,0%	6,3	43,4%	9,3	64,1%
11	13	7	male	X	X	X	X	0,0	0,0%	11,8	81,4%	8,7	60,0%	14,5	100,0%	3,6	24,8%	6,6	45,5%	13,0	89,7%	5,1	35,2%	11,2	77,2%
12	13	7	male	X	X	X	X	7,2	49,7%	11,7	80,7%	14,3	98,6%	14,4	99,3%	7,4	51,0%	10,3	71,0%	8,1	55,9%	6,1	42,1%	11,1	76,6%
13	14	8	female	X	X	X	X	0,0	0,0%	10,1	69,7%	7,2	49,7%	10,5	72,4%	7,2	49,7%	9,7	66,9%	11,5	79,3%	6,2	42,8%	9,8	67,6%
14	16	8	male	X			X	6,2	42,8%	1,4	9,7%	6,1	42,1%	7,0	48,3%	6,8	46,9%	7,7	53,1%						
15	15	8	female	X	X	X	X	0,0	0,0%	2,1	14,5%	10,0	69,0%	13,9	95,9%	7,4	51,0%	10,5	72,4%	8,8	60,7%	7,8	53,8%	0,0	0,0%
16	14	7	male	X	X	X	X	14,1	97,2%	5,6	38,6%	11,2	77,2%	13,9	95,9%			0,7	4,8%	11,7	80,7%	3,5	24,1%		
17	13	7	male	X	X	X	X	6,1	42,1%	4,1	28,3%	8,4	57,9%	7,2	49,7%	7,3	50,3%	13,9	95,9%	11,5	79,3%	3,5	24,1%	14,3	98,6%
18	15	7	male	X	X	X	X	1,3	9,0%	10,1	69,7%	11,3	77,9%	11,8	81,4%	8,3	57,2%	14,1	97,2%	13,7	94,5%	3,8	26,2%	8,9	61,4%
19	13	7	male	X	X	X	X	0,2	1,4%	2,3	15,9%	13,8	95,2%	14,1	97,2%	9,0	62,1%	9,5	65,5%	13,0	89,7%	0,3	2,1%	10,5	72,4%
20	13	7	male	X	X	X	X	3,0	20,7%	7,4	51,0%	14,5	100,0%	9,9	68,3%	9,5	65,5%	11,4	78,6%	14,3	98,6%	1,0	6,9%	7,2	49,7%
N									20		19		20		20		19		20		16		15		15
Max									97,2%		81,4%		100,0%		100,0%		74,2%		100,0%		100,0%		66,2%		99,3%
Min									0,0%		0,0%		42,1%		27,2%		0,0%		0,0%		55,9%		2,1%		0,0%
Average									23,2%		43,7%		74,2%		80,6%		50,2%		64,0%		81,4%		28,7%		61,4%
Median									5,2%		38,6%		77,6%		90,1%		50,3%		66,2%		81,4%		25,8%		64,1%
Variance									7,9%		6,5%		3,8%		4,8%		2,6%		8,4%		1,8%		3,4%		6,6%
Standard deviation									28,1%		25,6%		19,4%		21,9%		16,2%		29,0%		13,4%		18,3%		25,6%

#	10. How much did you like the learning environment?		11.! How difficult were the tasks for you? (inverse scale)		12. Did you know the "Stellentafel" before?		13. How easily did you recognize the objects?		14. How much did it help you to see the items in full size to imagine the sizes?		15.! How was it for you in the virtual environment? (inverse scale)		16. How concentrated were you in the virtual environment compared to normal lessons?		17. How well could you concentrate on the instructions of the supervisor?		18. Wie sehr hat sich das Lernen nach Schule angefühlt?		19. Did the awards in the main menu motivate you to solve further tasks or to repeat a task?		20. How much do you think you have learned?		21. Would you like to have classes in virtual reality again?	
1	15,3	100,0%	6,2	40,5%	12,3	80,4%	11,5	75,2%	7,5	49,0%	0,0	0,0%	10,3	67,3%	15,3	100,0%	5,5	35,9%	10,5	68,6%	11,5	75,2%	13,1	85,6%
2	14,9	97,4%	6,7	43,8%	7,2	47,1%	12,6	82,4%	11,8	77,1%	0,2	1,3%	12,6	82,4%	14,7	96,1%	0,6	3,9%	7,3	47,7%	4,2	27,5%	14,9	97,4%
3	13,9	90,8%	2,0	13,1%	12,4	81,0%	12,4	81,0%	15,3	100,0%	0,0	0,0%	15,2	99,3%	12,3	80,4%	3,0	19,6%	15,3	100,0%	11,4	74,5%	15,3	100,0%
4	11,9	78,8%	7,1	47,0%	12,8	84,8%	11,0	72,8%	13,4	88,7%	4,1	27,2%	12,5	82,8%	12,5	82,8%	5,4	35,8%	13,8	91,4%	10,7	70,9%	11,7	77,5%
5	11,0	72,8%	6,8	45,0%	1,2	7,9%	11,1	73,5%	14,0	92,7%	5,0	33,1%	11,5	76,2%	12,2	80,8%	12,9	85,4%	11,7	77,5%	10,4	68,9%	12,3	81,5%
6	8,7	57,6%	3,8	25,2%	11,2	74,2%	5,6	37,1%	13,2	87,4%	1,3	8,6%	11,0	72,8%	12,0	79,5%	13,0	86,1%	10,6	70,2%	7,7	51,0%	14,7	97,4%
7	10,2	67,5%	2,6	17,2%	0,6	4,0%	14,5	96,0%	7,1	47,0%	6,5	43,0%	7,1	47,0%	13,3	88,1%	11,3	74,8%	13,0	86,1%	10,1	66,9%	13,9	92,1%
8	11,3	74,8%	2,4	15,9%	15,0	99,3%	11,3	74,8%	15,1	100,0%	10,2	67,5%	0,0	0,0%	14,9	98,7%	3,5	23,2%	13,6	90,1%	7,5	49,7%	11,5	76,2%
9	12,1	80,1%	2,1	13,9%	13,8	91,4%	14,4	95,4%	14,8	98,0%	3,5	23,2%	4,1	27,2%	12,1	80,1%	8,2	54,3%	12,3	81,5%	3,0	19,9%	12,5	82,8%
10	14,5	100,0%	6,3	43,4%	6,6	45,5%	7,1	49,0%	10,7	73,8%	0,0	0,0%	14,5	100,0%	11,2	77,2%	11,5	79,3%	14,5	100,0%	10,6	73,1%	14,4	99,3%
11	13,1	90,3%	6,2	42,8%	0,1	0,7%	7,8	53,8%	10,2	70,3%	7,2	49,7%	14,4	99,3%	14,5	100,0%	5,6	38,6%	12,8	88,3%	6,8	46,9%	14,5	100,0%
12	14,3	98,6%	3,9	26,9%	10,9	75,2%	14,3	98,6%	10,7	73,8%	0,4	2,8%	13,5	93,1%	14,3	98,6%	7,0	48,3%	14,4	99,3%	8,0	55,2%	14,5	100,0%
13	8,8	60,7%	6,2	42,8%	6,8	46,9%	10,7	73,8%	9,5	65,5%	6,3	43,4%	12,7	87,6%	6,8	46,9%	12,5	86,2%	9,3	64,1%	9,4	64,8%	14,5	100,0%
14	11,5	79,3%	6,2	42,8%	13,3	91,7%	7,4	51,0%	13,3	91,7%	0,4	2,8%	13,3	91,7%	13,1	90,3%	13,3	91,7%	13,6	93,8%	13,9	95,9%	13,1	90,3%
15	6,4	44,1%	4,9	33,8%	12,5	86,2%	14,5	100,0%	11,4	78,6%	0,0	0,0%	12,2	84,1%	12,5	86,2%	2,5	17,2%	6,9	47,6%	8,4	57,9%	14,5	100,0%
16	11,8	81,4%	3,9	26,9%			13,7	94,5%	13,8	95,2%	0,5	3,4%	13,5	93,1%	14,0	96,6%	13,8	95,2%	7,2	49,7%	14,1	97,2%	14,0	96,6%
17	11,6	80,0%	3,5	24,1%	13,5	93,1%	13,6	93,8%	6,7	46,2%	0,2	1,4%	14,3	98,6%	10,8	74,5%	6,9	47,6%	7,0	48,3%	9,5	65,5%	14,3	98,6%
18	14,2	97,9%	6,1	42,1%	8,4	57,9%	8,4	57,9%	6,7	46,2%	0,2	1,4%	13,0	89,7%	12,1	83,4%	3,0	20,7%	11,2	77,2%	10,2	70,3%	14,0	96,6%
19	13,1	90,3%	1,3	9,0%	13,2	91,0%	13,7	94,5%	10,1	69,7%	0,3	2,1%	12,4	85,5%	8,5	58,6%	12,8	88,3%	0,6	4,1%	12,3	84,8%	13,4	92,4%
20	12,4	85,5%	0,1	0,7%	6,6	45,5%	10,0	69,0%	10,2	70,3%	0,3	2,1%	13,8	95,2%	11,6	80,0%	13,4	92,4%	13,9	95,9%	10,8	74,5%	14,4	99,3%
N		20		20		19		20		20		20		20		20		20		20		20		20
Max		100,0%		47,0%		99,3%		100,0%		100,0%		67,5%		100,0%		100,0%		95,2%		100,0%		97,2%		100,0%
Min		44,1%		0,7%		0,7%		37,1%		46,2%		0,0%		0,0%		46,9%		3,9%		4,1%		19,9%		76,2%
Average		81,4%		29,8%		63,4%		76,2%		76,1%		15,6%		78,6%		83,9%		56,2%		74,1%		64,5%		93,2%
Median		80,8%		30,3%		75,2%		75,0%		75,5%		2,8%		86,6%		83,1%		51,3%		79,5%		67,9%		97,0%
Variance		2,4%		2,1%		10,1%		3,5%		3,4%		4,4%		6,8%		1,9%		9,4%		6,1%		3,8%		0,7%
Standard deviation		15,4%		14,4%		31,7%		18,8%		18,4%		21,0%		26,0%		13,6%		30,7%		24,6%		19,4%		8,1%

5. DISCUSSION

Only two participants stated in question 6 (N=20) that they had never seen the tasks before. According to them, however, this has no noticeable effect on the understanding of the task (cf. question 4) or on the difficulty of the task (cf. questions 8 and 11). The others had already seen the tasks (7), they were familiar with them (5) or very familiar (6). As a result, the majority of the test persons recognized the tasks from the "math book".

For questions 7 and 10, all of them stated that they liked the learning environments up to perfect (median 81.4% and 80.8%, respectively; N=16 and N=20). Almost all of them indicate the level of difficulty (questions 8 and 11) between easy and medium. Only two indicate this (about both questions together) with rather difficult (N=15 and N=20 respectively). The observations have shown that few were able to solve the tasks (especially learning environment 3) directly without having to think and correct their first solution. For learners who have succeeded in doing so, there is a small tendency for them to assess their concentration (Question 16) and their learning success (Question 20) lower.

For learning environment 2 (base area times height), the first two learning and performance goals set out in the concept have been met by all learners from an external perspective: The geometric bodies have been perceived as such virtually and in 3D, they have been interacted with and changed characteristics of the bodies have been visible and tangible for the learners. The aspects of the targeted change of properties in order to achieve the given volume and to recognize under which circumstances the volumes of the bodies are the same, however, could rarely be observed. Although 2 learners state (question 9, N=15) only to calculate, mostly (7) or at least in half (3) to solve the task, experimental solving subjectively outweighed calculating.

The place value chart (question 12, N=19) from virtual learning environment 3 did not know 3 learners according to their statements. The others had already seen it, with a tendency to know it well. This didactic material is therefore also well recognized in its virtual form of presentation. Only 9 immediately recognized the objects (question 13, N=20). The others did not recognize them immediately. According to the observations, this particularly affects the child's 3D models of the lengths (1 m, often thought to be a doll) and the syringe and ink cartridge of the hollow masses (even in original size the difference in size was often not recognized). Replacing or resizing some 3D models could help here. Scales have therefore been added as supporting aids during the implementation.

Seeing the objects in their original size has helped all (mostly a lot) (question 14, N=20). It therefore seems to have succeeded in making it possible to experience orders of magnitude that are difficult to comprehend on paper and to point out errors simply, comprehensibly and impressively.

According to the learners (question 16, N=20), learning in the virtual learning environment has a positive influence on concentration. 3 learners state to have been more concentrated than in class, a full 14 that they have even been very concentrated. The 3 test participants (all from the 9th grade), who stated lower values, had the subjective impression that the tasks were rather too easy for them. This is also confirmed by their answers on the level of difficulty and subjectively perceived learning success. In question 5, many stated that they were dependent on the support of the supervisor. It is therefore also important to know whether they were able to concentrate on their instructions, while at the same time they had to focus on the task and the operation and had quiet music in the background. In answer to question 17 (N=20), 14 say that they were able to concentrate very well on the instructions, 4 state well and 2 that they at least understood some instructions.

What is surprising is the effect of the trophies in the main menu as a minimal form of gamification on the motivation of the learners. This was observed during the evaluation and is also clearly reflected in the questionnaire in the answers to question 19 (N=19) (median 79.5%). Only one person states that the awards hardly motivated him. 10, on the other hand, have been very motivated, 5 also indicate a strong positive influence on motivation and the remaining 4 have at least been somewhat motivated.

With an overwhelmingly high value, all participants state that they would very much like to have lessons in virtual reality again (question 21, N=20, median 97.0%, minimum 76.2%). The positive effect of the new medium on motivation seems to be confirmed. The fact that half of all learners say that learning in the virtual environment felt more than half (or even completely) like school (question 18, N=20), and that everyone claims to have learned something (mostly much, median 67.9%) (question 20, N=20) also points out that the interest in teaching virtual reality is not just an escape from school. The observations confirm the impression of learning success. Many participants seemed to have gained a decisive insight at a certain point in one of the learning environments.

6. CONCLUSION

The positive effect on motivation and possible new experiences mentioned in the literature was confirmed by the evaluation. Almost all learners have worked in a very concentrated manner and state this in the questionnaire. The potential for addiction quickly became apparent during the evaluation. Questions were quickly asked about the possible use of the technology for video games and many stated in the answers to the questionnaire that they already spend a lot of time with video games every day. In the context of the school, contact with questionable content can be largely controlled by a suitable selection. However, a constructive discussion with the learners about addictive behavior and content in private use appears to be sensible and, alongside clear rules of conduct, the only possible means against problematic media behavior.

The learning environments largely follow the principles of immersive learning. Coaching is also considered important for immersive learning. The findings of the evaluation have confirmed this. Most learners say that they were dependent on the support of the supervisor and were able to concentrate on them. According to these data, most of the subjects could be kept in the flow channel (Olbrish 2014) during the evaluation, as the observations also confirm. The correctness of the model can also be guessed by the minor correlation that has been recognized in the answers on task difficulty, concentration and learning success. The positive effect on learning success and motivation mentioned in the literature can be supported. With a few exceptions, all learners indicated a positive learning success in the responses to the questionnaire. Many learners were able to observe how they could expand their personal experience space (eureka moment). However, empirical proof is still lacking.

Ultimately, virtual reality is seen in mathematics as a good complementary tool that can also be used without any problems for children with special needs into regular schools and which gives an idea of its strengths in the area of motivation, concentration and learning success of learners. The actual effect would have to be measured precisely in further studies. Before a broad use of virtual reality is possible at elementary school, the medium must develop further and further tasks must be provided in dialogue with experts from pedagogy.

REFERENCES

Affolter, W. and Walt, M. (2017).Mathbuch IF: Begleitband Für Die Integrative Förderung Klassen 7 - 9. 1. Auflage. Klett und Balmer Verlag.

Burdea, G. C, and Coiffet, P. (2003).Virtual Reality Technology. 2nd Edition. New Jersey: John Wiley & Sons.

Burrill, G. (2017).Designing Interactive Dynamic Technology Activities to Support the Development of Conceptual Understanding. *In* Digital Technologies in Designing Mathematics Education Tasks: Potential and Pitfalls. Allen Leung and Anna Baccaglini-Frank, eds. Pp. 303–328. Mathematics Education in the Digital Era. Switzerland: Springer.

Chen, Yu-Li (2016). The Effects of Virtual Reality Learning Environment on Student Cognitive and Linguistic Development. The Asia-Pacific Education Researcher 25(4): 637–646.

d-edk (2016).Lehrplan 21: Gesamtausgabe. InternetDocument. https://v-ef.lehrplan.ch/lehrplan_printout.php?e=1&k=1.

Eckhart, M. (2016). Eine Schule Für Alle: Integration: Begriffe, Grundlagen, Herausforderungen Und Konkrete Umsetzung. 4 Bis 8 8/2016: 28–29.

Geiger, V. (2017). Designing for Mathematical Applications and Modelling Tasks in Technology Rich Environments. *In* Digital Technologies in Designing Mathematics Education Tasks: Potential and Pitfalls. Allen Leung and Anna Baccaglini-Frank, eds. Pp. 285–302. Mathematics Education in the Digital Era. Switzerland: Springer.

Höntzsch, S., Katzky, U., Bredl, K., Kappe, F. ,and Krause, D. (2013).Simulationen Und Simulierte Welten: Lernen in Immersiven Lernumgebungen. InternetDocument. http://l3t.tugraz.at/index.php/LehrbuchEbner10/article/download/102/108.

Joubert, M. (2017). Revisiting Theory for the Design of Tasks: Special Considerations for Digital Environments. *In* Digital Technologies in Designing Mathematics Education Tasks: Potential and Pitfalls. Allen Leung and Anna Baccaglini-Frank, eds. Pp. 17–40. Mathematics Education in the Digital Era. Switzerland: Springer.

Krauthausen, G. (2012).Digitale Medien Im Mathematikunterricht Der Grundschule. Heidelberg: Spektrum Akademischer Verlag.

Laborde, C. (2011).Designing Substantial Tasks to Utilize ICT in Mathematics Lessons. *In* Mathematics Education with Digital Technology. Adrian Oldknow and Carol Knights, eds. Pp. 75–83. New York: Continuum International Publishing Group.

Olbrish, K. (2014).Immersive Learning: Designing for Authentic Practice. Alexandria, VA: ASTD Press.

Samsung Studie: Lehrer Sehen Großes Potenzial Für Die Nutzung von Virtual Reality Im Unterricht (2017). PressRelease. Schwalbach/Ts. https://news.samsung.com/de/wp-content/themes/sw_newsroom/download.php?id=NfO684PPbcmccJ0mMOmjsg%3D%3D.

Schaumburg, H. (2015). Individuell Fördern Mit Digitalen Medien: Chancen, Risiken, Erfolgsfaktoren. Bertelsmann Stiftung, ed. 1. Auflage. Gütersloh: Verlag Bertelsmann Stiftung.

Sinclair, N., and Zazkis, R. (2017). Everybody Counts: Designing Tasks for TouchCounts. *In* Digital Technologies in Designing Mathematics Education Tasks: Potential and Pitfalls. Allen Leung and Anna Baccaglini-Frank, eds. pp. 175–192. Mathematics Education in the Digital Era. Switzerland: Springer.

ONLINE LEARNERS' READINESS AND LEARNING INTERACTIONS: A SEQUENTIAL ANALYSIS

Muhittin Şahin[1] , Sinan Keskin[2] and Halil Yurdugül[3]
[1]*Ege University, İzmir-Turkey*
[2]*Van Yuzuncu Yil University, Van-Turkey*
[3]*Hacettepe University , Ankara-Turkey*

ABSTRACT

An important advantage of e-learning environments is the numerical observation of the learning behaviors of students. The use of e-learning environments by students creates a learner data. From these learner data, the navigation patterns obtained by using educational data mining have a very important place in learning and teaching design. Studies have shown that learners' learning behaviors in online learning environments may vary according to the characteristics of learners. Studies on the differentiation of the navigation patterns according to the psycho-educational characteristics of the learners provide very strong inputs to the design of the learning environment appropriate to the characteristics of the students which is named as adaptive learning environments. According to these inputs, learning environment designs can be developed according to the individual characteristics of the students. Online learners' readiness (OLR) for e-learning is an important psycho-educational structure. The aim of this study is to investigate students' navigations in the e-learning environment according to the level of readiness for e-learning. Lag sequential analysis was used when students' system interactions were analyzed sequentially. According to the results of the analysis, it has been found that the sequential navigation patterns of the students differ according to the OLR structure. The findings of this research are expected to provide important information and suggestions to online learning environment designers.

KEYWORDS

Online Learners' Readiness, Log Data, e-Learning, Lag Sequential Analysis

1. INTRODUCTION

Nowadays, e-learning and distance learning are offered to learners by many educational institutions. E-learning is rapidly being adopted by learners as it has many advantages such as ease of access to the learning environment, convenience to individual pace and flexibility. However, the level of readiness of learners as an important psycho-educational structure for e-learning directly affects the learning process. Online learners' readiness (OLR) is a complex structure that encompasses students' competence in using learning technologies, autonomous learning skills and some affective structures. The most important of the sub-constructs of OLR are self-directed learning, learner control, motivation etc. According to the level of having these skills, learners' online learning behaviors may also differ (which is the hypothesis of this research). If these learning behaviors can be determined in advance, changes can be made in the learning, instructional design and even in the design of the learning environment.

The way in which learners learn in relatively new e-learning environments, the learning behavior patterns that are implemented here, are one of the areas of research that are currently unexplained and curious. Data mining, descriptive statistics, inferential statistics etc. methods are used for determining of behavioral patterns in the e-learning environment. There is significant number of researches which aims to explain the navigational behavior patterns of students according to their personal characteristics (Abdullah, Daffa, Bashmail, Alzahrani, & Sadik, 2015, Keskin, Şahin, Özgür, Yurdugul, 2016).

In the scope of this research, the navigation patterns of the students are studied using sequential analysis. Sequential analyzes were performed according to two different levels of OLR, both low and high. In this study; OLR is addressed in the context of self-directed learning, learner control, motivation towards e-learning. The interaction of the students with the e-learning system is covered under three sub-themes as learner-content, learner-assessment and learner-learner proposed by Moore (1989). The learner-content theme was derived from interactions with written materials, SCORM packages, and videos. The learner-learner theme is based on the interaction data in the forum pages. The interactions with the assessment materials in the e-learning environment are considered as the learner-assessment theme. Interactions with content can be considered as a stage of information acquisition. After this phase, the interaction between the other learners in the forum pages can be named as the constructing knowledge. Finally, the interaction with assessment the can be said to be the reflection phase of the e-learning.

1.1 Lag Sequential Analysis

Lag sequential analysis (LSA) (Bakeman & Gottman, 1997) is one of the widely used methods to reveal the consecutive model of human behavior and communication patterns. Consecutive analyzes have emerged, considering that sequential and conditional examination of behavioral probabilities will provide more information rather than simple probabilities. Because in sequential measurements, results of measurements are not independent of each other. Subsequent measurements are influenced by the results of previous measurements (Gottman, & Roy, 1990).

In lag sequential analysis, firstly, a transitional frequency matrix, which shows the transitions between the behaviors, is created. Transition probabilities are calculated using matrix values. The Z-statistics are used to test the significance of transitions between behaviors. The following formula is used in the calculation of the Z score (Bakeman, 1991). The Z score is calculated by using the conditional probabilities which we express as the transition probabilities of the behaviors. If the z score greater than 1.96, we can say that transition is significant at the 0.05 significance level.

$$z = \frac{f_{rc} - f_r p_c}{\sqrt{f_r p_c (1-p_c)(1-p_r)}} \text{ (Bakeman, 1991)}$$

2. METHOD

The aim of this study is to investigate students' navigations in the e-learning environment according to the level of readiness for e-learning. Lag sequential analysis was used when students' system interactions were analyzed sequentially. Log and self-report data were used in the research. The data sources are explained in detail in the next subtitle.

2.1 Data Collection

The log records used in this study were collected from learners who had a 16-week learning experience at Moodle LMS. Self-report was obtained using "undergraduate students' e-learning readiness scale" developed by Demir and Yurdugül (2016). The scale form was rated on a 7-point likert type. Self-directed learning, learner control, motivation sub-dimensions were used in this study. The research also deals with learning approaches that are closely related to autonomous learning. "Biggs' Revised Two Factor Learning Approaches Scale" was used for gathering data about learning approaches. The scale was developed by Biggs, Kember and Leung (2001) and adapted to Turkish by West, Tetik and Gürpınar (2010). The scale is structured in the 5-point likert type.

2.2 E-Learning Environment Design

Moodle LMS was used as e-learning environment in the research. 59 students participated in the research and students had a 16-week learning experience in the e-learning environment. Students interact with the content, discussion and assessment tasks in the system. The learner-content theme was derived from interactions with written materials, SCORM packages, and videos. The learner-learner theme is based on the interaction data in the forum pages. Students interact with their friends and teachers on the forum pages. The interactions with the assessment materials in the e-learning environment are considered as the learner-assessment theme. The system has assessment tasks that are configured separately for each course chapter.

3. FINDINGS

Each of the psycho-educational structures was handled separately and sequential analyzes related to them were carried out. In this section, the transitional frequency matrix and sequential patterns related to the sequential navigations of the students are given. Firstly, in Table 1 transitional probability matrices for OLR structures are given.

Table 1. Transitional probability matrices for OLR structures

High Self Directed					Low Self Directed				
Frequency	*C*	*D*	*A*	*Total*	Frequency	*C*	*D*	*A*	*Total*
Content (C)	0.64	0.19	0.17	0.49	*Content (C)*	0.59	0.13	0.28	0.48
Discussion (D)	0.47	0.41	0.13	0.18	*Discussion (D)*	0.56	0.28	0.17	0.11
Assessment (A)	0.27	0.07	0.67	0.33	*Assessment (A)*	0.31	0.04	0.65	0.41
Total	0.49	0.19	0.33	1.00	*Total*	0.47	0.11	0.42	1.00

High Learner Control					Low Learner Control				
Frequency	*C*	*D*	*A*	*Total*	Frequency	*C*	*D*	*A*	*Total*
Content (C)	0.62	0.19	0.19	0.47	*Content (C)*	0.61	0.14	0.26	0.50
Discussion (D)	0.51	0.35	0.14	0.17	*Discussion (D)*	0.52	0.31	0.18	0.12
Assessment (A)	0.27	0.06	0.67	0.35	*Assessment (A)*	0.31	0.05	0.64	0.39
Total	0.48	0.17	0.35	1.00	*Total*	0.48	0.12	0.40	1.00

High Motivation Towards E-Learning					Low Motivation Towards E-Learning				
Frequency	*C*	*D*	*A*	*Total*	Frequency	*C*	*D*	*A*	*Total*
Content (C)	0.58	0.16	0.25	0.47	*Content (C)*	0.63	0.18	0.18	0.46
Discussion (D)	0.47	0.37	0.16	0.15	*Discussion (D)*	0.51	0.34	0.15	0.16
Assessment (A)	0.33	0.06	0.61	0.38	*Assessment (A)*	0.22	0.05	0.74	0.38
Total	0.47	0.16	0.37	1.00	*Total*	0.46	0.16	0.39	1.00

This research also examined the learning approaches of the students which are highly related to the sub-structures of online readiness. Students' learning approaches are dealt with in two categories as deep and surface approach. Transitional probability matrices for learning approaches is presented in Table 2.

Table 2. Transitional probability matrices for deep and surface learning approaches

Deep Approach					Surface Approach				
Frequency	*C*	*D*	*A*	*Total*	Frequency	*C*	*D*	*A*	*Total*
Content (C)	0.66	0.18	0.16	0.51	*Content (C)*	0.63	0.18	0.18	0.46
Discussion (D)	0.49	0.40	0.11	0.18	*Discussion (D)*	0.51	0.34	0.15	0.16
Assessment (A)	0.26	0.07	0.67	0.31	*Assessment (A)*	0.22	0.05	0.74	0.38
Total	0.50	0.19	0.31	1.00	*Total*	0.46	0.16	0.39	1.00

The statistical significance of the transitions in the sequential navigations of the students was examined by calculating the z-score. As a result of these calculations, statistically significant patterns are presented based on psycho-educational characteristics. In this section, only statistically significant transitions are present. Firstly, sub-dimensions of OLR are discussed. The results of the lag sequential analysis were then studied according to the learning approach of the students.

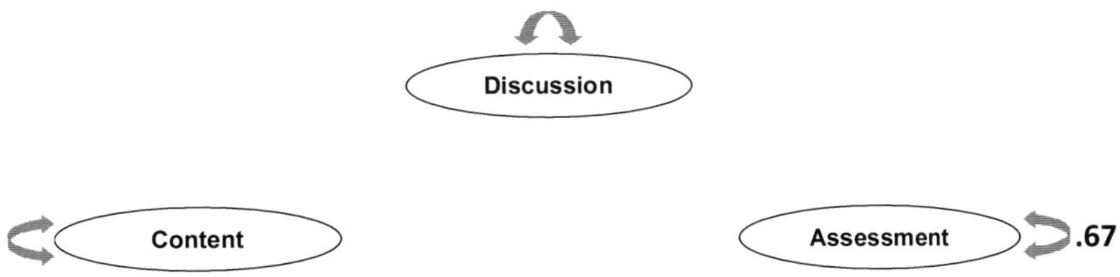

Figure 1. High-level self-directed learner group results

As can be seen in Figure 1, it is possible to say that the students in the high-level self-directed learner group have a persistent navigation pattern. While there was no significant transition between all three themes, the themes seemed to provide statistically significant loop within themselves. The cyclical transition was found to be significant P^{tr}=0.64 in content (z=13.00; p<.05), P^{tr}=0.41 in discussion (z=11.32; p<.05) and P^{tr}=0.67 in assesment (z = 21.65; p <.05).

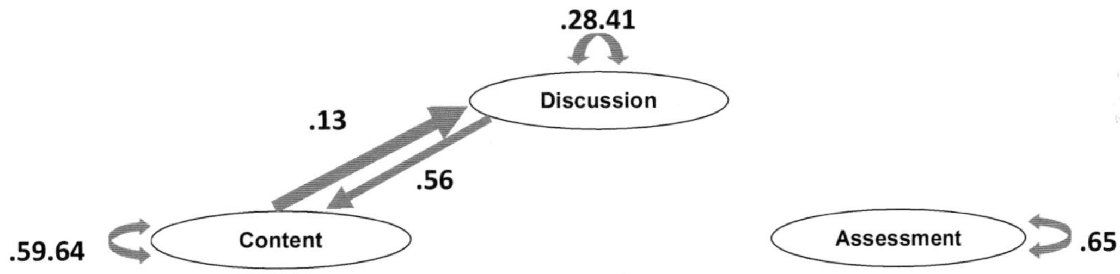

Figure 2. Low-level self-directed learner group results

As can be seen in Figure 2, it is possible to say that the students in the low-level self-directed learner group have a transitional pattern between the themes. The cyclical transition was found to be significant P^{tr}=0.59 in content (z=9.78; p<.05), P^{tr}=0.28 in discussion (z=11.73; p<.05) and P^{tr}=0.65 in assessment (z = 17.75; p <.05). Besides, for low-level self-directed learner group, the transitions from content to discussion (P^{tr}=0.13, z = 3.21) and discussion to content (P^{tr}=0.56, z = 2.51) was found to be statistically significant.

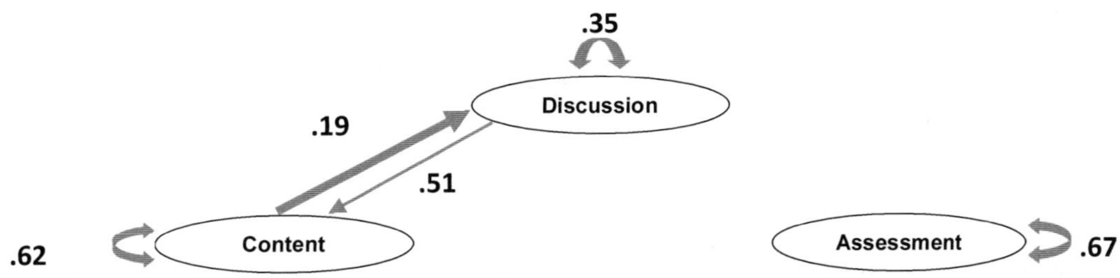

Figure 3. High-level learner control group results

As can be seen in Figure 3, it is possible to say that the students in the high-level learner control group have a transitional pattern between the themes. The cyclical transition was found to be significant P^{tr}=0.62 in content (z=15.29; p<.05), P^{tr}=0.35 in discussion (z=12.21; p<.05) and P^{tr}=0.67 in assessment (z = 28.07; p <.05). Besides, for high-level learner control group, the transitions from content to discussion (P^{tr}=0.19, z = 2.53) was found to be statistically significant. It was determined that there was a transition from discussion to content at a significance level of 0.10.

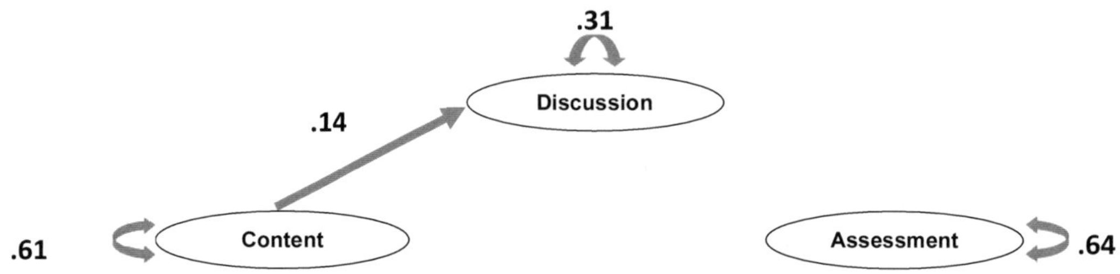

Figure 4. Low-level learner control group results

As can be seen in Figure 4, it is possible to say that the students in the low-level learner control group have a transitional pattern between the themes. The cyclical transition was found to be significant P^{tr}=0.61 in content (z=12.65; p<.05), P^{tr}=0.31 in discussion (z=10.52; p<.05) and P^{tr}=0.64 in assessment (z = 20.25; p <.05). Besides, for low-level learner control group, the transitions from content to discussion (P^{tr}=0.14, z = 2.35) was found to be statistically significant.

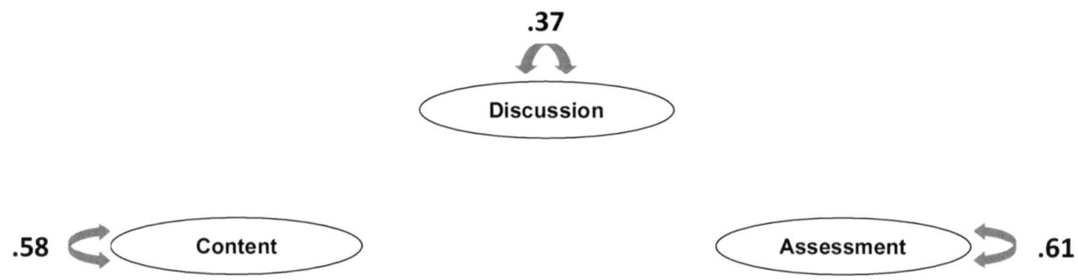

Figure 5. Navigational patterns of students with high motivation towards e-learning

In Figure 5, navigational patterns of students with high motivation towards e-learning was given. Accordingly, it can be said that there is a persistent navigational pattern. While there was no significant transition between all three themes, the themes seemed to provide statistically significant loop within themselves. The cyclical transition was found to be significant P^{tr}=0.58 in content (z=9.78; p<.05), P^{tr}=0.37 in discussion (z=11.73; p<.05) and P^{tr}=0.61 in assessment (z = 17.75; p <.05).

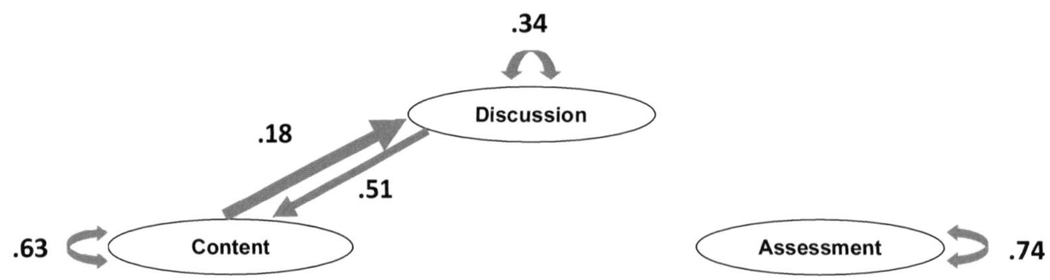

Figure 6. Navigational patterns of students with low motivation towards e-learning

In Figure 6, navigational patterns of students with low motivation towards e-learning was given. Accordingly, it can be said that there is a transitional pattern between the themes. While there was only two significant transition between content and discussion theme, the themes seemed to provide statistically significant loop within themselves. The cyclical transition was found to be P^{tr}=0.63 in content (z=15.65; p<.05), P^{tr}=0.34 in discussion (z=10.50; p<.05) and P^{tr}=0.38 in assessment (z = 26.52; p <.05).

In addition to OLR, sequential navigations based on students' learning approaches have been examined in this research. Findings according to students' learning approaches are presented in Figures 7 and 8.

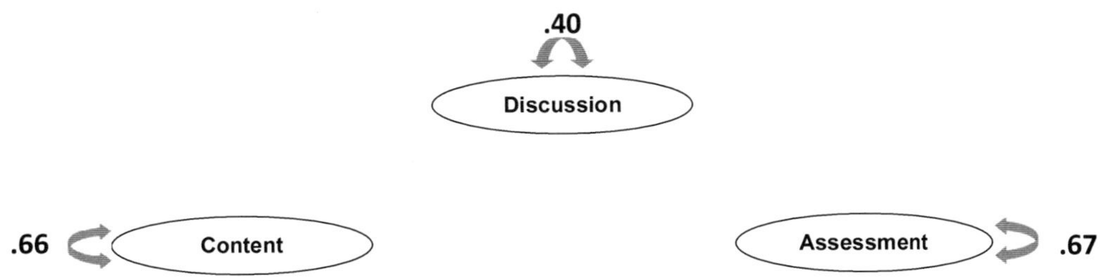

Figure 7. Navigational patterns of students with deep learning approach towards e-learning

When we examine navigational patterns of students with deep learning approach, it is seen that only cyclic transitions are statistically significant (Figure 7). The cyclical transition was found to be significant P^{tr}=0.67 in content (z=13.88; p<.05), P^{tr}=0.40 in discussion (z=11.55; p<.05) and P^{tr}=0.41 in assessment (z = 23.40; p <.05).

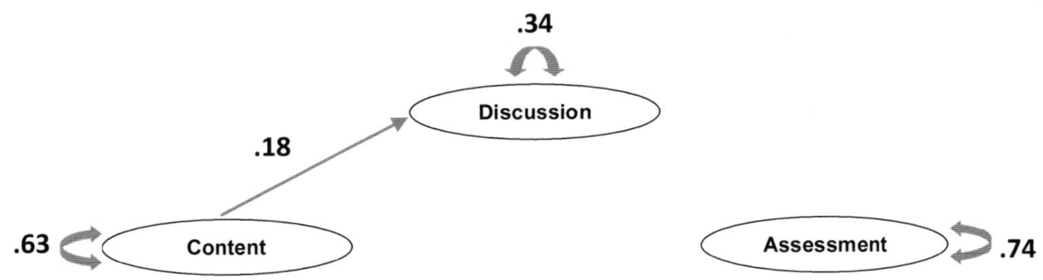

Figure 8. Navigational patterns of students with surface learning approach towards e-learning

In Figure 8, navigational patterns of students with surface learning approach towards e-learning was given. Accordingly, it can be said that there is a transitional pattern between the themes. The cyclical transition was found to be significant P^{tr}=0.57 in content (z=9.54; p<.05), P^{tr}=0.33 in discussion (z=9.17; p<.05) and P^{tr}=0.64 in assessment (z = 16.88; p <.05). Besides, for students with surface learning approach, the transitions from content to discussion (P^{tr}=0.17, z = 3.24) was found to be statistically significant.

4. CONCLUSION

In this study, OLR and the learners' navigation (interaction) sequences in e-learning environments are examined. According to findings, students who have high levels of self-directed learning, learning control, and learning motivation tend to have a consistent interaction in interaction types. On the other hand, it has been observed that students who have these psycho-educational structures low level prefer non-persistent interaction rather than persistent interaction. These students' interactions with content and other themes were intertwine. Because the behaviors expected by students in an LMS environment respectively; a) knowledge acquisition via interaction with content, b) knowledge construct via interaction with learner and finally c) reflection and examining themselves via interaction with assessment. Another pattern observed in the findings is students' interactions were intertwining that have low-level psycho-educational structures. This situation reveals that students need mentoring and scaffolding in e-learning environments.

Readiness is perhaps the first step in learning. Readiness consists two basic skills. One of these is the using instructional technology (computer using, internet using) and the other is autonomous learning skills. Students with high self-directed learning and motivation levels, which are considered to be autonomous learning skills, are consistent in online interactions, while those who are at low levels are more likely to cross between themes. According to this, it can be said that these learners are weak about online learning skills. Because these students have continuously transitioned to discussion and to content without completing a learning task. The behavior of these students was observed to be deep-learner behaviors because of the high level of readiness is typical of deep learning behavior. The instruction designer and environment designer should consider this study and this type study's finding.

REFERENCES

Abdullah, M., Daffa, W. H., Bashmail, R. M., Alzahrani, M., & Sadik, M. (2015). The Impact of Learning Styles on Learner's Performance in E-Learning Environment. International Journal of Advanced Computer Science and Applications, 6(9), 24-31.

Bakeman, R. (1991). From lags to logs: Advances in sequential analysis. *Revista Mexicana de Análisis de la Conducta/Mexican Journal of Behavior Analysis*, *17*(3), 65-83.

Batı, A. H., Tetik, C. & Gürpınar, E. (2010). Assessment of the Validity and Reliability of the Turkish Adaptation of the Study Process Questionnaire (R-SPQ-2F). *Turkiye Klinikleri Journal of Medical Sciences, 30*(5), 1639-1646.

Gottman, J. M., & Roy, A. K. (1990). Sequential analysis: a guide for behavorial researchers. Cambridge University Press.

Keskin, S., Şahin, M., Özgür, A. & Yurdugül, H. (2016). Online learners' navigational patterns based on data mining in terms of learning achievement. 13th International Conference on Cognition and Exploratory Learning in Digital Age 2016 (CELDA 2016), 28-30 September, Mannheim, Germany.

Moore, M. G. (1989). Three types of interaction. American Journal of Distance Education, 3(2), 1-6.

Yurdugül, H., & Demir, Ö. (2016). An investigation of Pre-service Teachers' Readiness for E-learning at Undergraduate Level Teacher Training Programs: The Case of Hacettepe University. *H. U. Journal of Education 32*(4): 896-915.

MOBILE LEARNING: APPLICATION OF WHATSAPP MESSENGER AS A LEARNING TOOL IN A UNIVERSITY DISTANCE LEARNING PROGRAM IN GHANA

William Kofi Koomson
PhD, Valley View University, Oyibi, Off Adenta-Dodowa Rd. Ghana

ABSTRACT

This paper describes an ongoing research study, which began in January 2017, about how to create an effective distance learning program in a hybrid mode that integrates WhatsApp Messenger as the learning platform for students who live in Ghana's remote areas where Internet connectivity and electrical power supply are limited. Qualitative approach was employed with a total sample size of 807 students, composed of 58 percent male and 42 percent female. The results from the demographics report fit traditional adult learners as described in the literature. About 89 percent of the students indicated that they work, while 54 percent of them were engaged in full time employment. I concluded that using WhatsApp Messenger in a blended mobile learning context is not nuisance to students, rather it is a 'helpmate' to help resolve many of the contextual difficulties that plague them in distance learning situation in Ghana.

KEYWORDS

Blended Learning, Connectivity, Mobile-Learning

1. INTRODUCTION

Mobile technologies with cellular connectivity continue to dominate the information communication technology market in sub-Saharan Africa. According to the Pew Research Center (2015), cell phone usage in Africa pales in comparison to that of developed countries like the United States of America. However, there has been a dramatic surge in the growth of smartphone usage in sub-Saharan Africa. As of 2014, the following countries recorded high percentages of cell phone usage; Uganda 65%, Tanzania 73%, Kenya 82%, Ghana 83%, and South Africa, 89%. In the same year, the United States' cell phone usage was 89%, the same as in South Africa and only in single-digits, higher than Ghana and Kenya. Among the many uses of cell phones in Africa for a twelve-month period, texting was the most (Pew Research Center, 2015).

Joy Online (2013) reported that Ghana was ranked by the International Telecoms Union Report as number one in Africa with more people using or connected to mobile broadband. Laary (2016) stated that for the period ending December 2015, Ghana's mobile phone voice penetration rate surged to 128%, far above earlier projections by telecommunication experts. The adoption of mobile technology with its diverse apps can serve as a conduit for mobile learning.

2. RELATED WORK

Motlik (2008) suggested that, mobile learning will pave the way for online learning as the internet is not stable and is unavailable in many parts of rural areas in developing nations. Also mobile learning is more affordable to less developed nations and financially constrained groups (Gronlund & Islam, 2010). UNESCO (2013) defines mobile learning (m-Learning) as involving; "the use of mobile technology, either alone or in combination with other information and communication technology (ICT), to enable learning anytime and anywhere. Learning can unfold in a variety of ways: people can use mobile devices to access educational resources, connect with others, or create content, both inside and outside classrooms (p. 6).

Notwithstanding these positive developments, some, including academics in higher education in sub-Saharan Africa, refuse to accept the fact that online learning can be done through mobile devices. They still believe that because of the unstableness of Internet connectivity, few institutions of formal learning can successfully go online in sub-Saharan Africa, including Ghana (Yeboah & Ewur, 2014). However, with mobile learning technologies like "WhatsApp Messenger," developing countries have no excuses as to why they are not able to adopt online learning in the remotest parts of the country where connectivity is a major setback. Everywhere a mobile phone is used, whether for WhatsApp, Email, SMS, video or photo sharing, online learning is possible. In the academic environments, just as in the community, households and business places, WhatsApp Messenger has been used to create group chats for work teams, social networking, and learning.

In Ghana, the most common format adopted in Distance Learning is the tutorial format, where very few online interactions occur; in most instances, there are no online interactions. The universities that enroll their students through the distance learning mode, rely heavily on print materials in the form of course modules and students meet regularly during weekends in tutorial centers throughout the nation where they receive face-to-face instructions. Very few programs include videos and voice presentations in their distance learning pedagogy (Larkai, et al, 2016; Yeboah & Ewur, 2014).

2.1 WhatsApp Messenger for m-Learning

Research on the application of WhatsApp Messenger in the classroom is new and developing, however, its usage as a social media tool on smartphones is widespread (Cetinkaya, 2017; Bouhnik & Deshen, 2014; Yeboah & Ewur, 2014; Church & de-Oliviera, 2013). WhatsApp is the most popular mobile messaging application widely used worldwide and is ranked as the number one in terms of monthly active users, based on a study of over 22,500 sources worldwide (Statista, 2018).

WhatsApp features include;

- Text – simple and reliable;
- Group Chat – keeping in touch with love ones, people in your network, business partners, and parishioners;
- On the Web and Desktop – keeping the conversation going anytime, anyplace, anywhere;
- Voice and Video Calls – free face-to-face conversation, when voice and text are not enough;
- End-to-End Encryption – provides security by default;
- Photos and Videos – opportunity to share moments that matter;
- Voice Messaging – using the voice messaging system to convey emotional moments; and
- Documents – attaching and sharing documents including PDFs, spreadsheets, slideshows, photos, and Word documents (http://www.whatsapp.com/features/).

WhatsApp Messenger features make it easy for teaching and learning. The app uses phone internet connections (4G/3G/2G/EDGE of Wi-Fi) of users to send and receive messages. That is, as long as there is data on users' phones, sending and receiving messages are free. (https://faq. whatsapp.com/en/android/20965922/). WhatsApp announced in May 2018 at its F8 developer conference in San Jose, California, that over 65 billion messages have been sent by users with more than 2 billion minutes of voice and video calls made everyday on the app platform, and about 1 billion people uses this messaging app each day (Al-Heeti, 2018).

2.2 Key Players of the Ontology

According to Kent Löfgren's (2013) introduction to the word and the concept of ontology, the word ontology is used in two different contexts; philosophical and non-philosophical. At the philosophical context, the word is used to study what is real and what exist. However, at the non-philosophical context, Löfgren explained that the word is used more narrowly to describe what exists within a determined field. He further posited that, under the non-philosophical context, researchers focus on identifying important key players in a particular field and investigate the inter-relationships that brings them together (Carson, et al, 2001; Barry, 1992; Löfgren, 2013). For example, an effective distance learning program requires inter-relationships among key players. This section identifies four important key players, which include: students, faculty, support staff, and administrators (Barry, 1992):

2.2.1 Students

Students' engagement in an online learning has taken a new shape. Brian Kathman (2017) posited that, higher education institutions are engaging students more and more through text messaging and fostering of one-to-one relationships. In the past, distance learning students were not as able to freely interact with each other to share their backgrounds and interests. However, new technologies are bringing students together and helping to build communities of learners through distance education (Barry, 1992, pp. 30-32).

2.2.2 Faculty

The success of an effective distance education program depends on the faculty. Bernard Bull (2013), list faculty roles of an effective online teacher as: the tour guide, the cheerleader, learning coach, individual and group mirror, social butterfly, big brother, valve control, and co-learner (www.facultyfocus.com).

2.2.3 Support Staff

Willis Barry (1992) described the support staff as "silent heroes of a successful distance education program" (p. 37). The support staff assist in promoting persistence and participation to avoid students' dropout. Their services include academic, administrative, and technological support. In most institutions, the support staffs' services are offered through extended hours (Moisey & Hughes, 2008).

2.2.4 Administrators

Administrators are entrusted to ensure that a strategic plan is in place that promotes effective teaching and learning. Their duties include, planning for technological resources, deploying manpower resources, financial and the necessary capital expenditures to enhance the institution's online learning mission. They also "lead and inspire faculty and staff in overcoming obstacles that arise. Most importantly, they maintain an academic focus, realizing that meeting the instructional needs of distant students is their ultimate responsibility" (Barry, 1992, p. 38).

3. THE CONTEXT

This paper used qualitative approach, framed under the paradigm which postulates that reality is relative and depends on multiple systems for meaning. *On-to-logy*, a Greek word, relates to the nature of reality as seen in the lens of a person in his experiences, this experience may lead the individual to seek meaning. There are two schools of thoughts: the objectivist and subjectivist. The objectivist approach correlates with a quantitative research paradigm, while the subjectivist approach sees the world as socially constructed – a qualitative paradigm (Hudson & Ozanne, 1988; Lincoln & Guba, 1985; Neuman, 2000).

Qualitative ontological researchers believe that the researcher and the researched are not mutually exclusive and that the context, background, cultural setting, and values of the researcher can influence the observation. Qualitative researchers seek to create theory and new meaning in specific settings, while quantitative researchers test objective theories as they do examine the relationship between and among variables. In a qualitative study, the researcher observes why events occur and what those events mean to the population being studied (Bogdan & Biklen, 2006; Corbin & Strauss, 2008; Creswell, 2014).

The study was based in a university in Ghana with three campuses and two learning centers with total student population of about 10,000. A sampled total of 807 students from three campuses and two learning centres of the university adopted the use of WhatsApp Messenger in a blended online learning mode.

4. ANALYSIS OF THE ONTOLOGY

Total sample size for the study was 807, composed of 58 percent males and 42 percent females. Students above the age of 25 formed the dominant age group for the study, scoring a total of 83 percent. Sixty percent of the students were married with about 44 percent indicating that about 4 persons depend on them for their sustenance. About 51 percent of the students indicated that they entered the university with other qualifications apart from associate degree or high school diploma. Concerning commitment to study, about 89 percent of the students indicated that they work, while about 54 percent of them were engaged in full time employment. Forty-three percent of the students in the study were committed to study for about ten hours a week.

4.1 Blended Mobile Learning Structure

I present in Table 1, a mobile learning structure indicating a summary comparison between a typical Learning Management System (LMS) and the proper application of the use of WhatsApp as mobile learning platform in a Ghanaian context. The following assumptions were made to explain table 2 above:

Assumption # 1

Why it will not work

a) WhatsApp Messenger as a social media tool is not fit for the classroom – for learning purposes.
b) A typical LMS delivers courseware over the internet – lack of internet connectivity and prolonged power outages in Ghana, especially, in the countryside makes it impossible to sustain online learning. Therefore, LMS will not work for students in Ghana who live far away from the cities.

Assumption # 2

How it will work

a) For WhatsApp to function properly in online learning environment, the features must be properly integrated to fit the purpose of teaching and learning in a mobile learning context.
b) WhatsApp Messenger uses phone internet connections of users to send and receive messages. That is, as long as there is data on users' phones, sending and receiving messages are free. Therefore, students in Ghana, who live far away from the cities can also access online learning benefits through their mobile devices.

Jurado, et al, (2014), classified learning management systems features into four different tool groups, namely: distribution, communication, interaction, and administration.

1. **Tools for distribution** allow lecturers to upload documents, available to students. Earlier it was mainly text documents and today it may also be different kinds of media files. Nevertheless, the process is still one-way, that is, teacher-to-learner distribution of information.
2. **Tools for communication** allow information to go either way as well as from student-to-student. The most common example is E-mail.
3. **Tools for interaction** call for reaction and feedback. Discussion boards are the most typical example. These tools are of great interest since they may promote student activity and cooperation, hence enhancing the learning experience.
4. **Tools for course administration** are used to monitor and document the educational process, rather than to facilitate teaching or learning (p.4).

Table 1. Mobile Learning Structure Using WhatsApp Messenger – Ghanaian Context

Application: Online learning tools. Jurado, et al., (2014)	**Key Players:** Students/faculty/ support staff/ administrators	**Purpose:** Teaching and learning using blended mode of online learning	**Learning Management System (LMS):** Why LMS will not work in Ghana due to lack of Internet Access	**WhatsApp Messenger for Learning:** How WhatsApp will work despite lack of Internet Access in Ghana
Distribution	1. Faculty 2. Student Interaction flows from teacher to student	One-way: from teacher to student – one way process	1. Teacher sends course information to students via the course management system 2. Students retrieve course information 3. LMS delivers courseware over the internet 4. Students lack access to retrieve and view course content via the internet.	1. Teacher sends course information via PDFs or Word document attachments to students 2. Students sign their name (forum signature) before each WhatsApp post; 3. Students retrieve course information 4. WhatsApp Messenger uses phone internet connections 5. As long as there is data on students' phones, viewing course content is possible.

Communication	1. Faculty 2. Student Interaction flows both ways	Information go either way. Teacher to student, student to teacher	1. Students respond to teacher via the course management system 2. Teacher grades students work and post comments on course management system	1. Students post completed assignments in more than one format via: a. PDF or Word attachments b. Direct text message 2. Teacher grades students work and post comments via WhatsApp Messenger 3. Teacher sends transcripts of WhatsApp communication to course administrators.
Interaction	1. Students Peer interactions. Student to student	Discussion boards, students reactions and feedbacks.	1. Student to student interaction through LMS discussion forums 2. Teacher as facilitator guides students	1. Students to student interaction through: a. WhatsApp 'group-chat' b. Possible video and voice calls 2. Teacher as facilitator guides students
Course Administration	1. Support Staff 2. Administrators Back-end interaction	Course monitoring, management, documentation, and evaluation.	1. Teacher setup the courses via the LMS 2. Teacher post course syllabus and assignments for class discussions 3. Teacher grades students work and post grades online 4. Students perform teacher and course evaluations online	1. Support staffs create WhatsApp groups for students and faculty 2. Support staff monitors students and faculty interactions through WhatsApp transcripts 3. Support staff receives transcripts from teachers regularly and monitors for course content and interactions 4. Teacher sends WhatsApp transcripts to program office for archival purposes. 5. Support staff archives course materials for quality control purposes.

Table 2 describes how students preferred the use of the WhatsApp Messenger in a blended mobile learning due to ease of use, convenience, cost, and accessibility.

Table 2. Results from Selected Campuses/Centre Surveys: Social Media and Mobile Learning

SURVEY QUESTIONS	CAMPUSES/CENTRES*			MOSTLY CHECKED ITEM
	Campus 1	Campus 2	Centre 1	
1. Which communication method do you prefer for social and business networking? Please check all that apply.	Phone calls; WhatsApp; Email	Phone calls; WhatsApp; Email	Phone calls; WhatsApp; Email	Phone calls; WhatsApp; Email; and Facebook
1. Do you own a computer with an internet connection?	58% = Yes	54% = Yes	57% = Yes	About 56% answered Yes
2. Do you own a mobile phone?	100% = Yes	100% = Yes	100% = Yes	Everyone answered Yes
3. How often do you have your mobile phone with you?	100% = Always	100% = Always	66% = Always 34% = Sometimes	Students keep phones Always
4. Do you have internet access through a Wi-Fi connection on your mobile phone?	8% = Yes	5% = Yes	2% = Yes	About 5% have Wi-Fi Connections
5. Do you have internet access through a cellular network on your mobile phone?	100% = Yes	98% = Yes	94% = Yes	Students have access thru Cellular network
6. Which activities do you most often engage in on your mobile phone? Please check all that apply.	Phone calls; WhatsApp; Facebook	Phone calls; WhatsApp; Facebook	Phone calls; WhatsApp; Facebook	Phone calls; WhatsApp; Facebook; Email
7. Would you be comfortable allowing your lecturer to contact you through your mobile phone?	100% = Yes	95% = Yes	100% = Yes	Students will Allow lecturer contact thru cell phones
8. Would you be comfortable receiving your grade report through text messaging?	100% = Yes	98% = Yes	68% = Yes	Students are ok receiving grade report thru text
9. Would you agree that having course materials such as lecture notes, practice quizzes, videos, and PowerPoints available on your mobile phone would be beneficial to your study process?	100% = Agree	90% = Agree	100% = Yes	Students prefer course materials available thru mobile phones
10. Would you be willing to purchase a new mobile device if you thought it would improve your performance at school?	87% = Yes	90% = Yes	80% = Yes	Students willing to purchase mobile device for learning
11. Would you agree that the use of some kind of mobile learning software would improve overall success in your courses?	100% = Yes	95% = Yes	82% = Yes	Student willing to adopt Moodle LMS

*(Selected Campuses/Centre with more than 100 students)

When the question was asked about students' willingness to purchase a new mobile device if they thought it would improve their performance at school; 87 percent indicated "yes." All the students indicated that having course materials such as lecture notes, practice quizzes, videos, and PowerPoints available on their mobile phones would be beneficial for their study process.

Students indicated that they would be comfortable to allow their lectures to contact them through their mobile phones. When the question was asked that "which communication method do you prefer for social and business networking?" Students checked phone calls as number one, followed by WhatsApp Messenger. Students also indicated that, apart from using their mobile phones to make and receive calls, WhatsApp texting was the activities they often engaged in with their mobile phones.

5. DISCUSSION AND CONCLUSION

5.1 Discussion

This paper depicted an ontology of an ongoing research study. The purpose of the research was to better understand the application of WhatsApp Messenger by using its features to construct meaning for learners and instructors in a blended mobile online learning context. The study was based in a university in Ghana with three campuses and two learning centers with total student population of about 10,000. A sampled total of 807 students from three campuses and two learning centres of the university adopted the use of WhatsApp Messenger in a blended online learning mode.

Total sample size for the study was 807, composed of 58 percent male and 42 percent female. Students above the age of 25 formed the dominant age group for the study, scoring a total of 83 percent. Sixty percent of the students were married with about 44 percent indicating that about 4 persons depend on them for their sustenance. About 51 percent of the students indicated that they entered the university with other qualifications apart from associate degree or high school diploma.

Concerning commitment to study, about 89 percent of the students indicated that they work, while about 54 percent of them were engaged in full time employment. Forty-three percent of the students in the study were committed to study for about ten hours a week. The results from the demographics report fit traditional adult learners as described in the literature. According to Ross-Gordon (2011), adult students, referred to as – non-traditional students form sizeable presence on university campuses and also constitute a substantial share of the undergraduate student body. Choy (2002) cited the 2002 NCES statistics that defined seven characteristics of non-traditional students as follows:

1. Entry to college delayed by at least one year following high school,
2. Having dependents,
3. Being a single parent,
4. Being employed full time,
5. Being financially independent,
6. Attending part time, and
7. Not having a high school diploma.

Ross-Gordon (2011) described characteristics that separate re-entry adults from other traditional university students to be; "the high likelihood that they are juggling other life roles while attending school, including those of worker, spouse or partner, parent, caregiver, and community member" (p. 27).

5.2 Conclusion

In designing the blended mobile learning structure, I applied agile methodologies using WhatsApp Messenger as a learning platform, that meets the current infrastructural conditions in Ghana.

Seth Earley (2017), stated that, there must be the need to interpret user signals accurately to "enable the system to present the right content for the user's context," this may "require not only that our customer data is clean, properly structured, and integrated across multiple systems and processes but also that the system understand the relationship between the user, his or her specific task, the product, and the content needed" (pp. 58-64).

According to Yeboah and Ewur (2014), the adoption of WhatsApp in the classroom is anathema. To them, the technology is nuisance to university students. They concluded that, "if students bring their mobile phones to class, they get bored of the lesson and find their way onto WhatsApp. These detracts their attention from the main lesson, and are not able to fully understand what is going on, hindering participation and drawing them even further into WhatsApp making it more difficult for them at the end of the day" (p. 162).

Contrary to Yeboah and Ewur's, assertions, the current paper has proven otherwise. In this study, I made several assertions that, for WhatsApp to work properly in any classroom in Ghana, there must be intentional designs and step-by-step approach to teach both the faculty and the students how to use the application to achieve the utmost outcomes. Because, I believe that, "seemingly intractable problems have been solved by advances in processing power and capabilities. Not long ago, autonomous vehicles were considered technologically infeasible due to the volume of data that needed to be processed in real time. Speech recognition was unreliable and required extensive speaker-dependent training sessions. Mobile phones were once "auto-mobile" phones, requiring a car trunk full of equipment" (Earley, 2017, pp. 58-64).

REFERENCES

Al-Heeti, A, 2018. *WhatsApp: 65B messages sent each day, and more than 2B minutes of calls.* C/net News. Retrieved on July 14, 2018, from: https://www.cnet.com/news/whatsapp-65-billion-messages-sent-each-day-and-more-than-2-billion-minutes- of-calls/

Barry, W, 1992. *Effective distance education: A primer for faculty and administrators.* Monograph Series in Distance Education No. 2. Fairbanks, Alaska.

Bogdan, R. & Biklen, S.K, 2006. *Qualitative Research for Education: An Introduction to Theories and Methods*. 5th ed. London, UK: Pearson.

Bouhnik, D. & Deshen, M, 2014. WhatsApp goes to school: Mobile instant messaging between teachers and students. *Journal of Information Technology Education: Research,* Vol. 13. pp. 217-231.

Bull, B, 2013. *Eight roles of an effective online teacher.* Higher Education Teaching Strategies from Magna Publications:

Faculty Focus. Retrieved on July 18, 2018, from: https://www.facultyfocus.com/articles/online-education/eight-roles-of-an-effective-online-teacher/

Carson, et al, 2001. *Qualitative Marketing Research.* London: Sage.

Cetinkaya, L, 2017. The impact of WhatsApp use on success in education process. *The International Review of Research in Open and Distributed Learning.* Vol. 18, No. 7. pp. 10.19173/irrodl.v18i7.3279.

Church, K. & de Oliveira, R, 2013. *"What's up with WhatsApp? Comparing mobile instant messaging behaviors with traditional SMS."* In Proceedings of the 15th International Conference on Human-Computer Interaction with Mobile Devices and Services (MobileHCI), Munich, Germany, pp. 352–361.

Choy, S, 2002. *Findings from the Condition of Education 2002: Nontraditional Undergraduates.* Washington, DC: National Center for Education Statistics. http://nces.ed.gov/programs/coe/2002/analyses/nontraditional/index.asp

Corbin J, Strauss A, 2008. *Basics of Qualitative Research: Techniques and Procedures for Developing Grounded Theory.* 3rd ed. Thousand Oaks, CA: SAGE Publications; eds.

Creswell, J. W, 2014. *Research design: Qualitative, quantitative, and mixed methods approaches* (4rd ed.). Los Angles:Sage.

Earley, S, 2017. There's no AI (artificial intelligence) without IA (information architecture). *IT Professionals* Vol. 18, No. 3. pp. 58–64. Doi: 10.1109/MITP.2016.43

Gronlund, Å., & Islam, Y, 2010. A mobile e-learning environment for developing countries: The Bangladesh virtual interactive classroom. *Information Technology for Development,* Vol. 16, No. 4. pp. 244-259. doi:10.1080/02681101003746490

Hudson, L. & Ozanne, J, 1988. Alternative Ways of Seeking Knowledge in Consumer Research. *Journal of Consumer Research*, Vol. 14, No. 4. pp. 508–521.

Joy Online, 2013. Increase use of smartphones made Ghana No-1in mobile broadband penetration. Retrieved from: business.myjoyonline.com/pages/news/201301/99976.php

Jurado, et al, 2014. Classification of the feature in learning management systems. *XVII Scientific Convention on Engineering and Architecture*, Havana City, Cuba, Nov 24th – 28. Conference Paper.

Kathman, B, 2017. *3 biggest trends impacting higher education communication this year.* Higher Education Technology: SignalVine. Retrieved on July 18, 2018, from: https://www.signalvine.com/higher-education-communication-trends/

Laary, D, 2016. *Ghana: Mobile phone penetration soars to 128%.* The Africa Report. Retrieved from: www.theafricareport.com/West-Africa/ghana-mobile-phone-penetration-soars-to-128.html

Larkai, et al, 2016. Distance education in Ghana: An overview of enrolment and programme patterns. *Proceedings of INCEDI 2016 Conference*, Accra, Ghana; 184 – 190.

Lincoln, Y., and Guba, E, 1985. *Naturalistic Inquiry*. London: Sage.

Löfgren, K, 2013. *What is ontology? Introduction to the word and the concept.* Examily. Retreived on July 14, 2018, from: https://examily.com/article/what-is-ontology-introduction-to-the-word-and-the-concept-10090

Moisey, S. & Hughes, J, 2008. *Supporting the Online Learner.* In: Anderson, T. (Ed.), The Theory and Practice of Online Learning, 2nd ed., AU Press: Athabasca, Alberta, 419–432, 2008.

Motlik, S, 2008. Mobile learning in developing nations. Technical Evaluation Report. *The International Review of Research in Open and Distance Learning,* Vol. 63, No. 9. p. 2. Retrieved from

Neuman, L. W, 2000. *Social research methods: Qualitative and quantitative approaches (4th Ed.)*, USA: Allyn and Bacon.

Pew Research Center Surveys (2015). *Spring 2014 global attitudes survey:* Q68. Retrieved from: www.pewglobal.org/2015/04/15/cell-phones-in-africa-communication-lifeline/

Ross-Gordon, J.M, 2011. Research on adult learners: Supporting the needs of a student population that is no longer nontraditional. *Peer Review,* Vol. 13, No. 1. pp. 26-29.

Statista, 2018. *Most popular mobile messaging apps worldwide as of April 2018, based on number of monthly active users (in millions).* The Statistics Portal. Available at: https://www.statista.com/statistics/258749/most-popular-global-mobile-messenger-apps/

UNESCO (2013). UNESCO policy guidelines for mobile learning. Paris, France. ISBN 978-92-3-001143-7

Yeboah, J. & Ewur, G. D, 2014. The impact of WhatsApp Messenger usage on students' performance in tertiary institutions in Ghana. *Journal of Education and Practice.* Vol. 5, No. 6. pp. 157–164.

VIRTUAL REALITY AT SECONDARY SCHOOL – FIRST RESULTS

Thomas Keller, Philipp Glauser, Nico Ebert and Elke Brucker-Kley
Zurich University of Applied Sciences, School of Management and Law
St.-Georgen-Platz 2, 8401 Winterthur, Switzerland

ABSTRACT

This paper examines the use of Virtual Reality (VR) at Swiss secondary schools. Despite many years of research, no well-founded data are available on the effects of the technology on children's learning success. It is assumed that VR is compatible with the learning theory of constructivism through the possibility of immersion, interaction, 3D representation and the possibility of adopting several perspectives.

To investigate the topic, a vision has been developed for a learning unit within the competence area Nature and Technology on the subject "Plastics and its effects on the environment". Divided into five learning blocks, the learning unit provides the students with knowledge about the structure, production, recycling and environmental consequences with possible approaches to solutions. Ideas for possible VR applications were developed for each of these blocks. The vision was discussed in four interviews with teachers. The VR applications were commented and evaluated by 20 students of the same class. The topic "Environmental Problem Microplastics" selected for implementation is topical, fits into curriculum and is compatible with the specialist areas suitable for VR.

In summary, it can be said that VR is still a long way from a nationwide deployment at the Swiss elementary school. Nevertheless, the educational institutions should observe the technology and develop an understanding of its possibilities through pilot tests.

KEYWORDS

Virtual Reality, Education, K-12, Secondary School

1. INTRODUCTION

VR has received a great deal of media attention since the technological developments of the last three years. Currently, it is mainly private consumers who are in the virtual world for personal entertainment. In the future, however, the technology could increasingly be used in companies and public institutions. According to technology analysts, Virtual Reality will enter the classroom in five to ten years.

This paper examines the practical application of VR at a Swiss elementary school. For this purpose, a prototype of a VR learning environment has been developed for the Nature and Technology 3.3 competence area from Lehrplan 21 (Deutschschweizer Erziehungsdirektoren-Konferenz (D-EDK) 2016), a Swiss curriculum for primary and secondary school, and tested as part of a pilot project. The aim of this work is to examine whether VR can bring didactic added value to the Swiss primary school system.

Despite the subject's long research history, no scientific data is available on the long-term effects of VR learning environments on competence development and student motivation. Research to date has shown that scientific fields in particular are suitable for the use of VR.

The research paradigm is based on design science (Hevner et al. 2004). At the beginning, a learning unit on "Plastics and its effects on the environment", consisting of five learning blocks, was designed. Different ideas for VR applications could be developed for each of these blocks. The vision created in this way was discussed with four teachers with regards to its didactic compatibility and the use cases were evaluated. The proposal "Environmental Problem Microplastics" selected for implementation not only fits well into curriculum 21, but has a high social relevance and is in line with the requirements for a VR learning environment defined in the literature.

2. VIRTUAL REALITY IN THE EDUCATION DOMAIN

Using VR in schools is not a recent idea. The topic has been researched since the 1990s, especially in Anglo-Saxon countries. The field of research has its origin in the field of flight simulation.

Since the 1990s, various authors have been analysing the possibilities of VR and deriving potential benefits for training. In the following, a selection of relevant publications for Education is presented and briefly summarized.

Wickens (Wickens 1992) justifies the use of VR at school with four factors. At first he mentions the possibility that thanks to the interaction with the learning environment a higher intrinsic motivation can be achieved. Secondly, the presentation of real learning situations should allow an improvement in knowledge transfer. The third point is the property of taking on different perspectives and thus discovering certain scenarios in context. As a fourth factor, he mentions the chance to interact with the world in a natural way.

Winn (Winn 1993) argues in his work that the principles of constructivist learning theories and the characteristics of VR are compatible with each other. He sees the key to this compatibility in immersion, in particular in VR's ability to gain experience from the first person's perspective. Dede, Salzmann and others (Dede 2009), (Salzman et al. 1999) mention four factors of VR in addition to immersion which are highly compatible with constructivist learning methods. The three-dimensional presentation of content in different reference frameworks promotes in-depth learning, in which it enables different, complementary perspectives on a topic. VR controllers enable interaction that addresses the multisensory stimuli of users. This promotes in-depth learning and supports the safeguarding of knowledge. Furthermore, well-designed immersive worlds increase motivation, which leads to more time and concentration being allocated to the individual tasks in a VR environment. The last point is the possibility of telepresence, which allows shared experiences regardless of location.

Dede (Dede 2009) published a much-noticed work on the subject of immersion in 2009, in which he points out three ways how it can improve education. The study overlaps to a large extent with the findings of Wickens and Winn (Wickens 1992) described above. First, he mentions the opportunity to take both the egocentric and the exocentric perspective and thus better depict complex phenomena (enabling muliple perspectives). While he regards the exocentric view as suitable for abstract and symbolic insights, the egocentric perspective should increase the interaction and motivation of the learner. The second reason he cites is the possibility of putting the learner in a certain situation (situated learning). According to Dede, situational learning can improve commitment and academic performance. The third possibility is that the transfer of knowledge for learners is simplified by the representation of real situations (transfer).

Table 1 summarizes the findings regarding the benefits of VR for training in relation to the functions of VR in a simplified form. The authors' statements overlap at various points. In addition, the analysis reveals that functions and benefits are often mixed and that the distinction between immersion and the other possibilities of VR does not follow a clear pattern.

Table 1. Summarized benefits of VR for Education

	Benefits for Education					
VR Functions		Motivation / engagement	Knowledge transfer	Deep learning	Knowledge assurance	Location independent Learning
	Immersion	X	X	X	X	
	Interaction	X	X		X	
	Multiple Perspectives			X	X	
	3D-Visualization	X	X	X	X	
	Telepresence					X

Whether the benefits hoped for by VR can be achieved for training has been investigated since the beginnings of this research area. The results of various meta-studies are presented below.

Youngblut's meta-study (Youngblut 1998) includes the analysis of 20 VR learning units. The evaluation of the results was divided into the categories of effectiveness and user-friendliness. Despite positive results, the results are no longer relevant today for two reasons: Firstly, under the term VR, Youngblut also examined studies that were carried out with virtual desktop environments and secondly, fully immersive systems were not technologically mature at that time.

The work of Mikropoulos et al (Mikropoulos and Natsis 2011) examines 53 scientific papers on VR in education published between 1999-2009. Of the 53 studies, 16 used a fully immersive solution with head mounted displays (HMD). For the rest, a desktop-based solution was used. One finding of this work is that the combination of technological characteristics of VR and the individual prerequisites and needs of the learning person must be put in relation to learning success. It was also found that the students and teachers accepted the new technology with a positive attitude. No statement could be made as to whether learners with VR would retain their knowledge for longer. An important conclusion of the work is that every virtual learning environment must be oriented to the didactic goals of the application area.

The meta-study by Merchant et al (Merchant et al. 2014) examines the effectiveness of desktop-based VR applications in the areas of games, simulations and virtual worlds for primary and secondary school education. The authors analysed a total of 67 papers. Since the studies are based on desktop-based VR applications, a statement is only possible to a limited extent as to what degree the results also apply to fully immersive VR applications. The work has shown that the transfer of knowledge with playful components is much more effective than the other two types of knowledge transfer. The results of knowledge testing of the students shortly after the application of a VR game and at a later time, were at the same level. According to the authors, this is an indication that knowledge is retained for a long time through the use of this technology. Whether this knowledge can be better transferred to other situations by the students was not examined in the study. Another finding is that students learn less well in collaborative learning environments than in non-collaborative ones. The authors were able to prove that the novelty of the technology has a positive effect and that the performance of the students decreases when used several times.

Liu et al. (Dix 2009) summarize the challenges that should be solved for a successful use of VR in the training sector (Table 2).

Table 2. Challenges of VR for education ((Dix 2009), S. 123)

Category	Challenges
Technology	The costs of VR hardware need to decrease and the portability must improve.
	The simulation of the environment must improve thereby improving the degree of immersion.
	The human – machine interaction must become more natural and intuitive.
VR Learning Unit	Adequate learning units, tested by pedagogues, must be created.
	Cognitive overload of students needs be avoided.
	The monitoring and evaluation of learning effects must be researched in depth.
Experience of Students	The technology must be user friendly and easy to use.
	A VR identity (avatar), which can be used in the environments, is to be established.
	Privacy protection and security must be ensured.
Integration	VR learning environments must be easily integrated into existing learning environments.

Despite the interesting characteristics of VR in the context of education, the areas of application should be specifically selected. For a complete list of the conditions under which the use of VR makes sense, please refer to the publication "Reasons to Use Virtual Reality in Education and Training Courses and a Model to Determine When to Use Virtual Reality" by Pantelidis (Pantelidis 2009). It can be emphasized that VR can always be used when a situation is difficult to represent in the real world and a simulation serves the better understanding.

Merchant (Merchant et al. 2014) examined 25 papers on VR for primary and secondary education (K-12) as part of her meta-study. More than 50% of the surveys are in the field of natural sciences and mathematics. Winn (Winn 1993) provides an explanation for this focus: This highlights the possibility that any size comparisons are possible in the virtual world. For example, learners can move within an atom and replace electrons in orbitals or take intergalactic excursions into space. According to Salzman et al. (Salzman et al. 1999), VR has the potential to complement model-based science teaching.

3. VR ENHANCED LEARNING UNIT

As part of the project a VR enhanced learning unit has been designed, implemented as a prototype and evaluated by students.

As a project partner the secondary school in Meilen was selected. Based on curriculum 21 and the features of VR the potential areas of highest impact have been identified and discussed with experienced teachers from the circle of acquaintances. Following Table 3 summarizes the relevant features of the chosen learning unit. In a next step the prototype for the learning unit has been designed. As a platform for the VR application the Unity engine with HTC Vive as the HMD has been selected. The prototype was then tried out with students on 19. April 2018 at the Meilen secondary school. Of the 16 participants, 10 were female and 6 male. The majority of the students were 14 years old at the time of the study. Around 60% had already gained experience with VR. Of these, 80 % tried out VR systems at one event. 100% of male participants and 20% of female participants said they played video games. During 120 minutes, the students were able to test the VR learning environment on two systems in succession. Directly after each student had experienced the learning unit the student had to fill out a survey. The survey asked questions about usability, learning experience and comprehensibility. The evaluation of the learning success was not the aim of the study.

Table 3. Tabular representation of the learning unit

Learning unit	**Environmental problems and challenges**
Reference to Curriculum 21	NT.3.3 c / BNE / MI
Learning outcomes according taxonomy levels of Bloom	K1: Students can describe environmental problems caused by the use of plastic. K4: The students analyse how microplastic enters the food cycle.
Learning contents	What impact does the use of plastic have on the environment? • How and where do environmental problems arise? • What impact does plastic have on the environment? • What is microplastics? • Toxicity of plastics and influence on the hormonal balance of living organisms.
Knowledge assurance	Poster - Showing the plastic cycle and the impact on the environment and me personally. Learning documentation - analysis of the products at my home, where could microplastics occur.
VR use cases	• Students are in a place contaminated with plastic waste. • Problem of microplastic: What is microplastic? Size comparison based on living organisms in waters.

The VR prototype consists of the following three scenes: «below the water", «microworld", and "enjoy your meal". The prototype is available for download at http://neuelehrkonzepte.ch/.

3.1 Scene 1 – Below the Water

At the start of the learning environment, the student is underwater. The underwater landscape is decorated with plants, rocks, fish, a car wreck and a boat. The student receives an order to search for illegally disposed waste via an audio output. Orders can be displayed in all scenes at any time at the push of a button. As the student approaches the rubbish heap, the task becomes more specific. He should look for the bottle with the sauce he normally eats with french fries. The ketchup bottle is hidden in the middle of a bush of blades of seaweed and emits microplastic. This is represented by pink dots which radiate from the bottle body. An audio output explains to the student that the particles are absorbed by the carp eating in the sea grass. Next, the student has to pick up the bottle and bring it to the laboratory. He walks past the car wreck and the boat to the surface. The scenery on land resembles the shore of a mountain lake. Birds circle in the sky, a hare and a deer are feeding and in the middle of the square there is a wooden hut, which is prominently labeled "Laboratory". The acoustics have changed in the meantime. While the student has heard underwater diving noises, the birds now chirp ashore. With the ketchup bottle stretched out, the student enters the laboratory and the "Microworld" scene is loaded.

Figure 1. Impressions of scene 1

3.2 Scene 2 – Microworld

The student is inside the hut and stands in front of a blackboard. In front of it are a pike, a perch and the ketchup bottle. A robot voice tells him that within the laboratory the fish and the ketchup bottle are displayed in their original size. The sizes are displayed on the blackboard. After the student has looked at the objects, he should go outside into the micro world. He goes through the door for it. Outside he sees a perch enlarged 1000 times and an equally large ketchup bottle. Four microplastic particles lie on a base. Now the student should compare the particles with the fish and the ketchup bottle to get a feeling of how small microplastic is. Next, the student should dispose of a microplastic particle in the trash can. As soon as the particle touches the bottom of the trash can, a screen and a button appear. The student is asked to press it. Now a three-minute film starts about plastic and its consequences for the environment. After the film, the student is asked to look for the exit. As soon as he walks through the door, the scene "Enjoy your meal" starts.

Figure 2. Impressions of scene 2

3.3 Scene 3 – "Enjoy your Meal"

The student sits at a camping table, which has been set up in the initial scene in the meantime. The table is set. On the student's plate lie two fish. The student's family is also present. The father sits on the chair, the mother is by the fire and the brother dances to the music that sounds from the loudspeaker. The student is given the task of eating the "right" fish via an audio output. One of the fish is marked with the pink dots representing the microplastic particles. The other fish looks normal. After the student has brought the fish to his mouth without microplastic, he is congratulated on the successful conclusion. He is asked to turn around. The instruction to take off the VR-glasses is now written on a blackboard.

Figure 3. Impressions of scene 3

4. RESULTS

In the following, the results of the survey are presented according to the VR functions in Table 1.

4.1 Immersion

Nearly 70% of the participants stated that the world depicted looks realistic. The remaining 30% assessed the question as neutral or negative. This result is not surprising and can probably be traced back to various reasons. The resolution of the used HTC Vive is 1080*1200 pixels per eye. Raja Koduri was CEO of chip manufacturer AMD until 2017. He said in an interview in 2016 that for a VR experience that looks real, a resolution of 15360*8640 (16k) per eye is required (AMD's Graphics Boss Says VR Needs 16K at 240Hz for "True Immersion" 2016). On the hardware side, VR is therefore still far from the optimum properties. A second aspect is the 3D models used. Various compromises had to be made in the work. For example, objects with a low number of polygons were sometimes used due to a lack of alternatives.

Nevertheless, the experience felt realistic for 95% of the participants. The detailed decoration of the landscape, the audio effects and the possibility of interacting with the world could have played a role in this. It is advisable to collect the exact reasons for this in a further survey.

Furthermore, 95% of the students stated that they were more concentrated than in normal class. This is certainly due to the fact that this was their first experience with VR in the school context and the pilot experiment was a special, unusual event for the test persons. In addition, the students were under observation of the two system supervisors. Reliable data should be collected by means of long-term studies. An interesting approach could be the measurement of body functions, such as heart rate. Such an experiment was carried out by the Universita` della Svizzera italiana in Lugano with a VR application in the tourism sector (Marchiori, Niforatos, and Preto 2018). It was found that the presentation of content from special perspectives and the interaction with animated objects have the potential to be remembered in the long term.

Three participants felt uncomfortable during their stay in the VR environment, one person had to abort early. This result is not surprising, as many users complain about a weak stomach during the first experience in a VR environment. Cobb et al. (Cobb et al. 1999) describe as a possible cause the user's urge to discover everything the first time and thus execute very fast movements. In fact, there are also users who are uncomfortable with multiple use of a VR environment.

4.2 Interaction

Nearly 90% of the participants said they would welcome learning together with a classmate in the virtual world. Liu describes this possibility as Social Learning (Liu et al. 2017).

For most of the participants it was clear how they should operate the controllers. This is certainly due to the high technological affinity of this generation. Over 85% of the students understood the instructions. Only half stated that the number of instructions was sufficient. The nervousness of the students could have played a role in this assessment. The first time in the immersive world, many users are focused on environmental impressions and control. In doing so, they cannot follow the orders conveyed via the soundtrack. Few people have used the option of displaying instructions at the touch of a button. The interaction with the objects was considered simple and logical by most of the students.

4.3 Learning

The majority of the students stated that the VR learning environment was helpful in understanding the topic of microplastics. In analyzing this question, it is noticeable that 8 subjects said it was true, but did not select the maximum evaluation. This may be an indication of how far the students have understood the content. The same applies to the result of the question whether size comparison in the micro-world was helpful for understanding. More than 95% of the students realized that microplastic enters our food chain.

Both the possibility to move and research freely, as well as the audio comments and the video were rated by the students as conducive to understanding. The video received the highest number of ratings with the maximum number of points.

4.4 Motivation

A good 95% of students say that VR could increase their interest and motivation to learn. Only one person has marked this as inapplicable. One reason for this assessment could be the participant's comment that the VR glasses were too heavy. All students would like to learn again in a virtual learning environment.

5. CONCLUSION

Although the results of previous research and this work partly point to a positive effect of VR on training, they should be treated with caution due to various limitations. Most previous studies are not based on fully immersive systems as they have been available since technological development in recent years. Another problem is the lack of long-term studies. This means that the effect of novelty comes into play with every evaluation, which can lead to improved results. As a result, there are only assumptions and indications of potential added value. However, no scientifically founded statement can be made in this respect. Dede and Richards (Liu et al. 2017) underline that it requires strategic planning and research collaboration to obtain reliable data on the effects of VR on the school development of students. Specifically, joint research laboratories, design heuristics, terminologies and process models are required. The statements of the two researchers coincide with our own findings from this work.

Furthermore, the effects of social learning, i.e. joint learning in the virtual world, should be investigated. Most of the students surveyed would welcome to study together with a classmate in the VR. The possibility of telepresence could play an important role here in the future. For example, it would be possible for a student from a class in Geneva to work together with a student from a class in Zurich in the VR learning environment.

An important point for practical use is the manageability of a fully immersive VR system. The installation takes up a considerable physical area. It is unlikely to be available in many schools today. Here we would like to introduce the idea of making the systems mobile and setting them up, for example, in rooms that are not used very often. The auditorium was used for this purpose in the pilot experiment. On the hardware side, the investment has meanwhile fallen to an affordable level for end consumers, which certainly lowers the entry hurdle. Since the fully immersive systems have only been on the market for a few years, the software range is still small.

The way VR is integrated into the classroom and the role of the teacher are important factors for the success of the technology in the classroom. Integration should be viewed from an organisational and didactic perspective. During the pilot test it became clear that system support takes a lot of time. In addition, no complete class can currently study together in the VR environment These limitations must be taken into account when using the technology in everyday school life. From a didactic perspective, VR should be optimally integrated into the classroom. During the pilot test, not the entire learning unit was carried out. The students were given a reading assignment as preparation. The learning assignment after the test attempt, which should have ensured the transfer of knowledge according to the model of De Freitas and Neumann (de Freitas and Neumann 2009), could not be carried out for time reasons. Simplicity in operation is important for the success of VR learning units. If the systems are designed too complicated and can only be operated with extended IT knowledge, the technology will hardly be able to establish itself.

In this work, the added value of VR for the Swiss secondary school could not be conclusively evaluated. There are various signs that indicate positive effects. Fully immersive VR systems are still little known to the general public. The prototype created can make an important contribution to presenting VR's possibilities for training in a practical way. It will be the starting point for conducting medium to long-term studies on the assurance of learning.

REFERENCES

AMD's Graphics Boss Says VR Needs 16K at 240Hz for "True Immersion" (2016) https://www.tweaktown.com/news/49693/amds-graphics-boss-vr-needs-16k-240hz-true-immersion/index.html, accessed May 17, 2018.

Cobb, S. V. G., S. Nichols, A. Ramsey, and J. R. Wilson (1999). Virtual Reality-Induced Symptoms and Effects (VRISE). Presence 8(2): 169–186.

Dede, C. (2009). Immersive Interfaces for Engagement and Learning. Science (New York, N.Y.) 323(5910): 66–69.

Deutschschweizer Erziehungsdirektoren-Konferenz (D-EDK) (2016). Lehrplan 21 - Gesamtausgabe. http://v-ef.lehrplan.ch/container/V_EF_DE_Gesamtausgabe.pdf, accessed October 31, 2017.

Dix, A. (2009). Human-Computer Interaction. *In* Encyclopedia of Database Systems. LING LIU and M. TAMER ÖZSU, eds. Pp. 1327–1331. Springer US. http://link.springer.com/referenceworkentry/10.1007/978-0-387-39940-9_192, accessed October 3, 2017.

de Freitas, S., and Neumann, T. (2009). The Use of 'Exploratory Learning' for Supporting Immersive Learning in Virtual Environments. Computers & Education 52(2): 343–352.

Hevner, Alan R., Salvatore T. March, Jinsoo Park, and Sudha Ram (2004). Design Science in Information Systems Research. MIS Q. 28(1): 75–105.

Liu, Dejian, Chris Dede, Ronghuai Huang, and John Richards, eds. (2017). Virtual, Augmented, and Mixed Realities in Education. Smart Computing and Intelligence. Springer Singapore. //www.springer.com/gb/book/9789811054891, accessed May 17, 2018.

Marchiori, Elena, Evangelos Niforatos, and Luca Preto (2018).Analysis of Users' Heart Rate Data and Self-Reported Perceptions to Understand Effective Virtual Reality Characteristics. Information Technology & Tourism 18(1–4): 133–155.

Merchant, Zahira, Ernest T. Goetz, Lauren Cifuentes, Wendy Keeney-Kennicutt, and Trina J. Davis (2014). Effectiveness of Virtual Reality-Based Instruction on Students' Learning Outcomes in K-12 and Higher Education: A Meta-Analysis. Computers & Education 70: 29–40.

Mikropoulos, Tassos A., and Antonis Natsis (2011). Educational Virtual Environments: A Ten-Year Review of Empirical Research (1999–2009). Computers & Education 56(3): 769–780.

Pantelidis, Veronica S. (2009). Reasons to Use Virtual Reality in Education and Training Courses and a Model to Determine When to Use Virtual Reality. Themes in Science and Technology Education 2: 59–70.

Salzman, Marilyn C., Chris Dede, R. Bowen Loftin, and Jim Chen (1999). A Model for Understanding How Virtual Reality Aids Complex Conceptual Learning. Massachusetts Institute of Technology 8(3): 293–316.

Wickens, Christopher D. (1992). Virtual Reality and Education. *In* Systems, Man and Cybernetics, 1992., IEEE International Conference On Pp. 842–847. IEEE.

Winn, William (1993). A Conceptual Basis for Educational Applications. University of Washington. http://www.hitl.washington.edu/research/education/winn/winn-paper.html~, accessed December 2, 2017.

Youngblut, Christine (1998). Educational Uses of Virtual Reality. Institute for Defense Analysis.

AUTODIDACT: INTRODUCING THE CONCEPT OF MUTUAL LEARNING INTO A SMART FACTORY INDUSTRY 4.0

Fazel Ansari*, Philipp Hold*, Walter Mayrhofer**, Sebastian Schlund** and Wilfried Sihn*
**TU Wien, Institute of Management Science, Research Group of Smart & Knowledge-Based Maintenance*
***TU Wien, Institute of Management Science, Research Group of Human-Machine Interaction*
Theresianumgasse 27, 1040 Vienna, Austria

ABSTRACT

This paper explores the concept of mutual (reciprocal) learning as an enabler of the emergence of a collective human-machine intelligence across a smart factory. The interlinking of digital profiles of humans and machines permits the identification and measurement of learning outcomes through participating in and performing of (shared) tasks. To achieve this goal and ultimately to transform today's smart factory into a self-learning factory, the concept model of AUTODIDACT, underlying objectives and research questions related to mutual (reciprocal) learning are outlined.

KEYWORDS

Human Learning, Machine Learning, Human-Machine Interaction, Hybrid Learning, Industry 4.0, Collective Intelligence

1. INTRODUCTION

A trendy topic in the research area of human-technology interaction at the workplace is job automation. Modern factories and the vision of Industry 4.0 inevitably lead to higher automation and a decreasing number of direct personnel in factories. However, the recent European skills and jobs survey (Cedefop, 2018), which comprises a large body of studies, doubts the significance of the predictions with regard to the robotization of the labor market. The main reason for imperfect predictions is grounded in the market, industry sector or technology specificity of the hypotheses, which affects the formulation of theory and accordingly proper explanation and interpretation of a set of phenomena. At the same time, the survey reveals that the march of technological progress may widen inequality, e.g. with regard to wages and contribute to the polarization of jobs in the labor market (Cedefop, 2018). Evidently, the automation of jobs and firms reliance on robots are highly correlated (Acemoglu & Restrepo, 2017).

Over the past decades, the reliance of European companies on robots has been increasing from 0.6 robots per 1,000 workers in 1990s to 2.6 robots per 1,000 workers in the late 2000s (Acemoglu & Restrepo, 2017), where robots have primarily replaced low-medium skilled workers carrying out manual and repetitive tasks rather than critical, non-routine or decision-making tasks. As a result, there is less opportunity for human learning, in particular for low-medium skilled workers, resulting in decreasing tacit knowledge about processes and systems. This effect was described 35 years ago as one of the "ironies of automation" (Bainbridge, 1983) and "recent technological developments may have some new ironies in store for us" (Baxter et al., 2012). Such recent technological developments include robotics and (intelligent) assistance systems as well as the possibilities of distributed Internet of Things (IoT)-applications, artificial intelligence and machine learning, which are some of the driving forces behind Industry 4.0. However, in all the excitement about the new technological potential with respect to automation and digitalization, human capabilities are often considered as a given, almost static variable. In an extension of the "human-in-the-loop" approach, this paper presents a mutual (reciprocal) learning methodology to human-machine learning with the goal, to improve the capabilities of both humans and machines simultaneously in order to raise their "Collective Intelligence" (Levy, 1994; Glenn, 2013).

Reframing the risks of automation as an opportunity, the key research question is "How to build an integrated human-machine collaboration framework for mutual learning in smart factories?", based on the definition of mutual learning (also known as human-machine reciprocal learning) given by (Ansari et. al., 2018a). Foresight involves future-oriented awareness in order to enable today's smart factories to transform into human-centered self-learning factories. To this end, Section 2 discusses learning in smart factories under consideration of background terminologies, challenges and requirements from both technological and non-technological perspectives. Furthermore, it discusses the concept of mutual learning and introduces related terms such as "human and machine as a learner" in smart factories. Accordingly, Section 3 presents the AUTODIDACT concept for building a mutual learning platform in TU Wien's Pilot Factory Industry 4.0. Finally, Section 4 concludes the discussion and elaborates on a future research agenda.

2. REQUIREMENTS AND CHALLENGES FOR LEARNING IN SMART FACTORIES

2.1 Smart Factories: Terminology and Background

Advances in collaborative robotics and data science are expected to lift factory automation to a new level (IFR, 2017; Bauer et al. 2016; Monostori et al. 2016). Together with the widespread use of IoT technologies within manufacturing facilities, their implementation is widely referred to as "smart factory" (Zühlke 2008, Kagermann et al. 2013; Wagner et al., 2017). The vision of Industry 4.0 advocates the realization of smart factory technologies to connect humans, machines and intelligent objects in order to create high-performance processes and products (Spath, 2013; Liao et al., 2017).

Traditionally, automation and Industry 4.0 tend to emphasize technological opportunities and focus less on the organizational setting and socio-technical environment. In order to tap the full potential of Industry 4.0 and to create a conducive environment to test new approaches in human-machine learning, it is necessary to employ a comprehensive approach that takes well-known interdependencies of factories, as socio-technical entities with strong interdependencies between technological and organizational changes, into account.

It is already visible, that the transformation with regard to the integration of new technologies will have significant effects on the way manufacturing is organized. The increasing degree of autonomy of intelligent robots and assistance systems poses a major challenge to the traditional organization of factories. Collaborative and mobile robotics will carry out manual routine tasks, while digital assistance systems take over cognitive routine tasks and provide support in non-routine situations. Consequently, the organization of work will inevitably change and autonomous systems increasingly require human work that is more flexible. The required competences of factory workers as well as those of support functions such as maintenance and quality assurance staff, are expected to change significantly (Jaeger et al. 2012; Erol et al. 2016; Lanza et al. 2016).

2.2 Learning Matters in Smart Factories

As the expected changes in competency development due to Industry 4.0 are widely discussed, there is a need to establish processes to adapt learning in a factory environment to those changes, in order to retain and improve learning curves for blue-collar and white-collar employees. Due to increased automation in smart factories, the challenges of learning grow on various levels. The barriers (challenges) to learning in smart factories comprise the following:

- **Larger scope:** Due to higher automation and increasingly autonomous technical systems, the average staffing per machine decreases. Hence, the number of processes, to be mastered by the remaining employees, is increasing.
- **Fewer learning opportunities:** Due to the fact, that machines take over routine tasks and the resulting focus of humans is put on non-routine tasks, less learning opportunities with respect to routine processes exist for human operators (Baxter et al., 2012).
- **Uncertain role of human work in hybrid (human-machine) settings:** Due to collaborative tasks with machines and algorithms, additional requirements in terms of learning emerge. Especially the

"reciprocal learning approach" will become necessary in hybrid (man-machine) settings in a smart factory. This approach uses human experience and tacit knowledge to train machine data sets (machines learn from humans) and on the other hand employs data-based learning that is guided by smart algorithms (humans learn from machines) (Goldberg, 2017).

Besides the challenges mentioned above, learning in a smart factory also changes its perspective with regard to different periodicity.

- **Short-term:** The need for process optimization, operational excellence and quick results usually drives learning in the short-term. To learn how to carry out one or several work tasks more efficiently, usually follows a learning curve (Zangwill, 1998) and short-term learning goals translate into a steepening of the learning curve during the ramp-up phase.
- **Mid-term:** With the emergence of hybrid settings of mixed man-machine teams, there is a need for an optimal assignment of tasks in order to guarantee a good fit with the team members. The assignment of tasks depends on the individual capabilities and the needed effort to train each team member for a specific task. Moreover, task assignment is most likely not static and will change over time as the capability level of workers and machines evolves. Hence, there will be a constant need for training and retraining and task assignment will be evaluated with respect to relevant parameters such as economic and organizational goals, but also regarding competency development and learning.
- **Long-term:** Learning about and gaining an understanding of a manufacturing process usually contributes to process and product innovations. Mistakes, mishandling and unplanned events regularly offer room for small improvements or even novel ideas. Furthermore, the tacit knowledge of processes and their interconnections and eventual impacts provide a competitive advantage that is often hard to copy. Therefore, the optimal ratio of automated and human decision-making is essential in maintaining an organization's ability to improve and adapt to unplanned and to some extent unforeseeable changes.

2.3 Human and (Intelligent) Machines as a Learner in Smart Factories

Considering the technological advancements in smart factories, the division of tasks between human workforces and machines is changing from distinctive roles and tasks into hybrid (collaborative) roles and task schemes. The latter divides the entire pool of tasks into three clusters, namely; i) tasks assigned to the human workforce, ii) tasks assigned to (intelligent) machines, and iii) shared tasks assigned to both human workforce and intelligent machines (including robots in particular collaborative robots (cobots), virtual assistance systems, etc.) (cf. Figure 1).

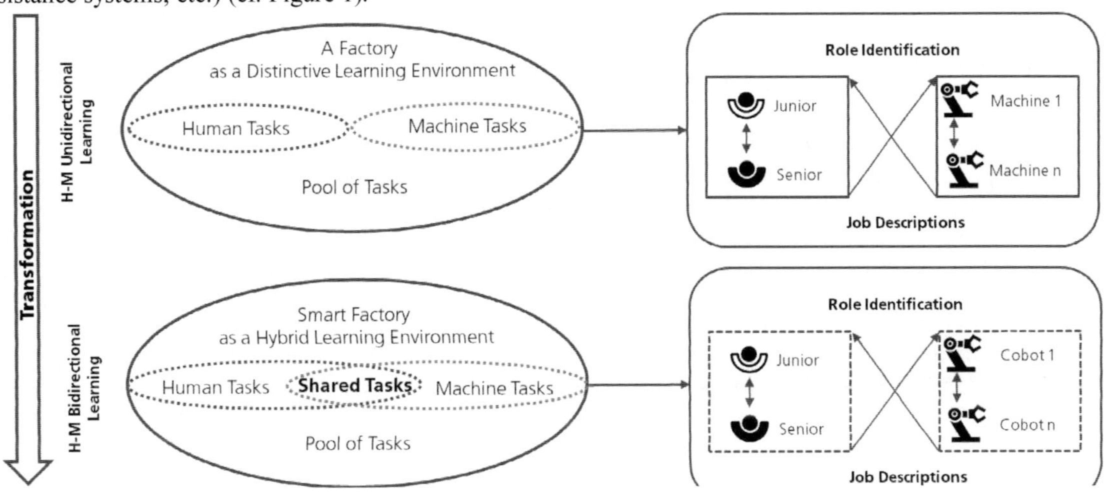

Figure 1. Division of tasks and its impact on human-machine learning

Participation in the shared tasks necessitates the learning capabilities of human workforce and machines (i.e. humans and machines as a learner) and further combines them into a new boundary system in which mutual learning takes place. Here, we slightly modify the definition of human-machine mutual learning given earlier by (Ansari et al., 2018a) as follows: «*Mutual learning is a bidirectional process involving reciprocal exchange, dependence, action or influence within human and machine collaboration on performing shared tasks, which results in creating a new meaning or concept, enriching the existing ones or improving skills and abilities in (symmetric or asymmetric) associated with each group of learners*».

Creating digital profile of the aforementioned group of learners facilitates modeling, estimating and evaluating the exact magnitude and significance of the learning effectiveness and outcomes resulting from mutual learning in smart factories. Furthermore, digital profiles of human workforces and machines provide possibilities to collect data, construct distinct learning profiles and identify mutual learning in a consistent, dynamic and realistic way. A digital profile typically comprises all basic information, i.e. personal or professional information of a human workforce or technical specifications of a machine. It also contains on-the-job performance data collected by means of sensors and condition monitoring systems for the target human workforce or machine as well as feedback collected e.g. via a 360°-feedback (multi-source feedback) approach, or via a customer or end-user questionnaire survey. Such a continuously growing database provides opportunities for identification and prediction of learning trajectories for both human and machine workforces over time.

The machine's digital profile can be quantified based upon the determination of the degree of autonomy of the individual machine functions. The degree of autonomy of a machine specifies its technical ability to autonomously adapt to dynamically changing production conditions, without endangering the efficiency and effectiveness of the production process. In order to define the degree of autonomy of a machine, a descriptive basis for a corresponding comparison must first be determined. There are various possibilities for this corresponding comparison, e.g. as proposed by (Gronau & H. Theuer, 2016):

i) [Number of autonomous functions / number of all functions],
ii) [Number of autonomous controlling systems / number of all controlling systems],
iii) [Number of autonomous actuator systems / number of all controlling actuators],
iv) [Number of autonomous resource supply systems / number of all resource supply systems],
v) [Number of autonomous mobility systems / number of all mobility systems], and
vi) [Autonomous quantity of data / total quantity of data].

The degree of autonomy shall be determined for each machine function. A summation of the corresponding quantified degrees via Likert scaling enables the definition of a specific machine's digital profile, which can be described in the form of a vector representation.

Furthermore, the concept of machine's digital profile may resemble the virtual representation, monitoring and configuration of a machine's components and functions in a dynamic manner. Therefore, the term Digital Twin is defined as an evolving digital profile of a production system (Brenner & Hummel, 2017). It establishes an interface between the physical and digital world through streaming and linking the status data of all physical objects in the production system to their virtual models (Uhlemann et al., 2017). Using intelligent data analytic methods, learning accomplishments can be recorded and corresponding implementation decisions can be directed to operators and technical systems (Mussomeli et al., 2017). In the proposed concept of AUTODIDACT, the term Machine Digital Twin is used to address the digital profile of a machine workforce (cf. Section 3).

The definition and characteristics of the Human Digital Profile are based on descriptive parameters consisting of different determinants, which enable a human workforce to perform a task in a work system. According to (Schlick et al., 2010) these determinants include i) human constituent characteristics, ii) human disposition characteristics, iii) human qualification and competency characteristics, and iv) human adaptation characteristics. Employing "Performance Shape Factors 3" (PSF 3) introduced by (Bubb, 2005), it is possible to build a quantified human digital profile as discussed in (Ansari et al., 2018b).

Human- and machine's digital profiles are the core building blocks for realizing an integrated human-machine collaborative framework for mutual learning in smart factories, which is discussed in Section 3.

3. AUTODIDACT - TOWARDS MUTUAL LEARNING IN TU WIEN'S PILOT FACTORY INDUSTRY 4.0

The TU Wien Pilot Factory Industry 4.0 (PFI4.0) is a research lab and demonstration factory for promoting the realization of smart factory technologies – tailored to the future-oriented solutions for manufacturing industries (PFI40, 2018; Ansari et al., 2018a). Human-technology collaboration is one of the main problem areas in which the current focus is on realizing innovative solutions for human and technology interactions, including human-robot collaboration, digital assistance systems, etc. Such solutions aim at enhancing workplace productivity and efficiency, and improving working conditions and safety. As discussed earlier, learning is the key to innovation. In particular, mutual learning is essential to develop and enhance synergistic innovation capability in the PFI4.0. Hence, the concept of "AUTODIDACT" envisages an integrated human-machine collaboration framework for mutual learning in the PFI4.0 (cf. Figure 2).

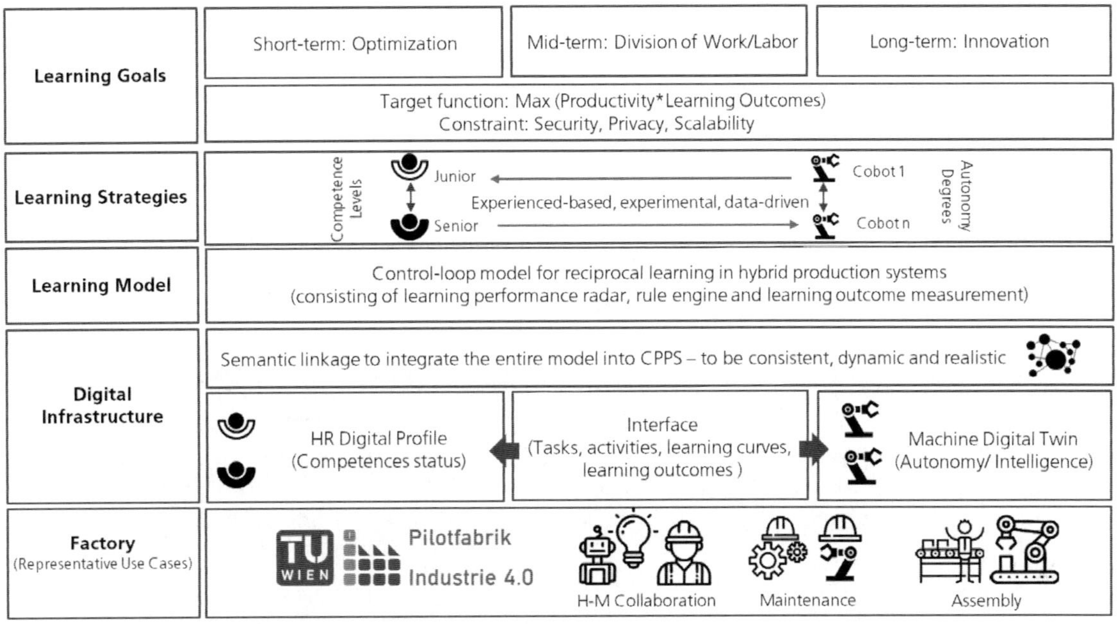

Figure 2. AUTODIDACT – An integrated human-machine collaboration framework for mutual learning

From a design perspective, AUTODIDACT consists of four functional layers, excluding the factory layer, consisting of representative use-cases in manufacturing and assembly units. These layers are introduced in the followings:

- ***Digital infrastructure*** consists of human workforces and machine's digital profiles, known as HR Digital Profile and Machine Digital Twin, respectively. In addition, it features taxonomies of tasks, domain ontologies, and associated statistical models and indicators for estimating learning curves and measuring learning outcomes. The entire digital profiles are semantically linked to the existing cyber physical production systems (CPPS) for dynamic acquisition and exchange of knowledge.
- ***Learning model*** is a control-loop model that assists in building learning profiles and trajectories for each group of learners as well as identifying and measuring the mutual learning outcomes. It includes a learning performance radar and rule engine to facilitate monitoring and assessing the learning outcomes.
- ***Learning strategies*** refer to experience-based, experimental and data-driven strategies enhanced by machine learning and statistical learning methods for both groups of learners, i.e. human or cobots in various competency and autonomy level, respectively. It mainly deals with various learning strategies to improve not only unidirectional learning ($Human_i \rightarrow Machine_j$, $Machine_j \rightarrow Human_i$, $Human_i \rightarrow Human_h$, $Machine_j \rightarrow Machine_k$) but also bidirectional ($Human_i \leftrightarrow Human_h$, $Machine_j \leftrightarrow Machine_k$, $Human_i \leftrightarrow Machine_j$).

- ***Learning goals*** feature the target function that should link productivity to learning outcomes under certain constraints and boundary conditions such as security, privacy, scalability, etc.. The outcome is used for progressing towards the factory goals, i.e. i) short-term: optimization of tasks and processes, ii) mid-term: new division of works between human and machine workforce, and iii) long-term: innovation in products and services.

Human-robot collaboration (cf. Figure 3) is one of the typical use-cases in smart factories, which represents certain characteristics of mutual learning, i.e. participation of two groups of learners in performing tasks, including shared tasks, and at the same time the acquisition of (new) knowledge within a dynamic and changeable environment. In this case, the teacher and learner role (i.e. senior and junior) can be identified depending on the human competences and performance determinants (e.g. constitutional, disposition, adaptation, qualification and competence characteristics) as well as the machine's (robot's) intelligence and technical functions/conditions represented by the associated digital profiles, respectively (Hold et al., 2016; Ansari et al., 2018b).

Figure 3 schematically represents the human-robot collaboration in an assembly cell, consisting of two human workforces and two cobots. The mutual learning between human workforce (e.g. operator) and cobot occurs by fulfilling the four steps of a so-called questioning, controlling and summarizing, clarification, and prediction, as originally proposed by (Hacker and Tenent, 2002) in the context of reciprocal teaching. The four steps are as follows:

a) To check the counterpart with regard to learning success (questioning),
b) To change the execution of the activity among them (controlling and summarizing),
c) To experimentally transfer the performance of a similar activity to each other (clarification); and
d) To allow the other party to make a prediction for the execution of a new task and finally to perform the predicted task execution (prediction)

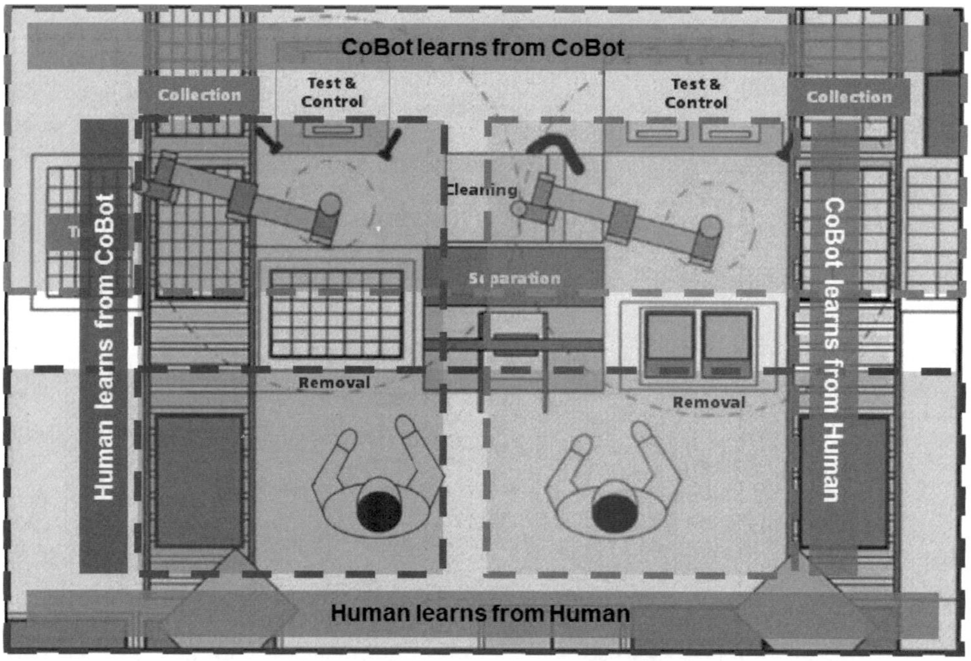

Figure 3. Schematic Representation of Human-Robot Collaboration

For this purpose, the control loop model of mutual learning illustrated in Figure 2 is set into direct interaction with the human workforces and cobots. Based on a fundamental and prospectively planned task distribution between the human workforces and cobots, the success of a corresponding task execution along a learning process is measured (questioning) via different sensor systems. The task execution between human workforces and cobots is changeable and comparable with regard to the learning success (summarizing) via different control logics. Corresponding decisions for a new distribution of activities between them can be carried out by means of data analysis (clarification). This provides possibilities to dynamically switch between human workforces and cobots in relation to comparable activities (prediction). In this way, new types of learning logic are identified and will be taken into account with regard to an improved distribution of tasks in the forthcoming planning period.

4. FUTURE RESEARCH AGENDA

Naturally, the proposed concept of mutual learning has a dual character affected by human cognitive capabilities and machine's intelligence (i.e. cognitive computing capabilities). Hence, building AUTODIDACT in various smart factories is tied to theoretical and application-oriented research in both human- and machine specific learning domains. In particular, the following steps should be foreseen:

1) To define learning profiles and trajectories for both human and machine workforce e.g. in TU Wien's Pilot Factory Industry 4.0, considering specific use-cases in three areas of human-robot collaboration, maintenance and assembly.
2) To define AUTODIDACT's system specifications for modeling and measuring mutual learning, including technological and non-technological requirements and constraints.
3) To build up AUTODIDACT's ontological knowledge-base, which specifies the shared conceptualization of tasks and associated domain knowledge between human and machine workforce.
4) To define AUTODIDACT's control-loop, consisting a rule-engine (set of rules) for inferring optimal task sharing and measuring learning outcomes in relation to key performance indicators (KPIs) used in production management.

ACKNOWLEDGEMENT

The authors would like to express their sincere gratitude to the Austrian Research Promotion Agency (FFG) and several private industrial firms that co-finance the TU Wien Pilot Factory Industry 4.0.

REFERENCES

Acemoglu, D.; Restrepo, P., 2017. Robots and jobs: evidence from US labour markets. Cambridge, MA: National Bureau of Economics Research (NBER). Working paper; No 23285.

Ansari, F., Erol, S., Sihn, W., 2018a. Rethinking Human-Machine Learning in Industry 4.0: How does the Paradigm Shift Treat the Role of Human Learning? *Procedia Manufacturing*, Vol. 23C, 2018, pp. 117-122.

Ansari, F., Hold, P., Sihn, W., 2018b. Human-Centered Cyber Physical Production System: How Does Industry 4.0 Impact on Decision-Making Tasks?, 2018 IEEE Technology and Engineering Management Society Conference, 27 June-1 July 2018, IL, USA.

Bainbridge L., 1983. Ironies of automation, *Automatica*, Vol. 19, pp. 775-780.

Bauer W., Bender M., Braun M., Rally P., Scholtz O., 2016. Lightweight robots in manual assembly – best to start simply. Examining companies' initial experiences with lightweight robots, Stuttgart, pp. 1-32.

Baxter, G., Rooksby, J., Wang, Y., Khajeh-Hosseini, A., 2012. The ironies of automation … still going strong at 30?. in Turner, P., Turner S. , *Proceedings of the 30th European Conference on Cognitive Ergonomics,* New York, USA, pp. 65-71.

Brenner, B., Hummel, V., 2017. Digital Twin as Enabler for an Innovative Digital Shopfloor Management System in the ESB Logistics Learning Factory at Reutlingen - University,Procedia Manufacturing, Vol. 9, pp. 198–205.

Bubb, H., 2005. Human reliability: A Key to Improved Quality in Manufacturing, Hum. Factors Ergon. Manuf., Vol. 15, No. 4, pp. 353-368.

Cedefop, 2018. Insights into skill shortages and skill mismatch: learning from Cedefop's European skills and jobs survey, Luxembourg: Publications Office, Cedefop reference series; No 106.

Erol, S., Jäger, A., Hold, P., Ott, K., Sihn, W., 2016. Tangible Industry 4.0: a scenario-based approach to learning for the future of production. *Procedia CIRP 54, 6th CIRP Conference on Learning Factories, Gjøvik, Norway*, pp. 13 - 18.

Glenn, J. C., 2013. Collective Intelligence and an Application by the Millennium Project, *World Futures Review,* Vol: 5 Issue 3, pp. 235-243.

Goldberg, J., 2017. The Robot-Human Alliance: Call it Multiplicity: diverse groups of people and machines working together. *The Wall Street Journal*, June 11, 2017.

Gronau, N., Theuer, H., 2016. Determination of the Optimal Degree of Autonomy in a Cyber-Physical Production System, *Procedia CIRP*, Vol. 57, pp. 110–115.

Hacker, D. J., Tenent, A., 2002. Implementing reciprocal teaching in the classroom: Overcoming obstacles and making modifications, J. Educ. Psychol., Vol. 94, No. 4, pp. 699–718.

Hold, P., Ranz, F., Sihn, W., Hummel, V., 2016. Planning Operator Support in Cyber-Physical Assembly Systems, IFAC-Pap., Vol. 49, No. 32, pp. 60–65.

Jäger, A., Mayrhofer, W., Kuhlang, P., Matyas, K., Sihn, W., 2012. Total Immersion: Hands and Heads-On Training in a Learning Factory for Comprehensive Industrial Engineering Education, *International Journal of Engineering Education*, Vol. 29/No. 1; pp. 23 - 32.

International Federation of Robotics (IFR), 2017. How robots conquer industry worldwide, Presentation IFR Press Conference, September 27 2017.

Kagermann H., Wahlster W., Helbig J., 2013. Recommendations for implementing the strategic initiative INDUSTRIE 4.0. Final report of the Industrie 4.0 Working Group, Ed. By Forschungsunion Wirtschaft – Wissenschaft und acatech – Deutsche Akademie der Technikwissenschaften e.V.

Lanza, G., Minges, S., Stoll, J., Moser, E., Haefner, B., 2016. Integrated and Modular Didactic and Methodological Concept for a Learning Factory. *Procedia CIRP 54, 6th CIRP Conference on Learning Factories, Gjøvik, Norway*, pp. 136-140.

Levey P., 1994. *L'intelligence collective. Pour une anthropologie du cyberspace*, La De´couverte, Paris.

Liao, Y., Deschamps, F., Rocha Loures, E. F., Ramos, L. P. P., 2017. Past, present and future of Industry 4.0 - a systematic literature review and research agenda proposal, International Journal of Production Research, 55:12, pp. 3609-3629.

Monostori, L., Kádár, B., Bauernhansl, T., Kondoh, S., Kumara, S., Reinhart, G., Sauer, O., Schuh, G., Sihn, W., Ueda, K., 2016. Cyber-physical systems in manufacturing. *CIRP Annals - Manufacturing Technology 65 (2)*, pp. 621-641.

Mussomeli, A., Cotteleer, M., Parrott, A., 2017. Industry 4.0 and the digital twin - Manufacturing meets its match, Deloitte University Press.

PFI40, Website of TU Wien Pilot Factory Industrie 4.0, Retrieved from: http://pilotfabrik.tuwien.ac.at, Accessed on 31.07.2018

Schlick, C. M, Bruder, R., Luczak, H., 2010. *Arbeitswissenschaft*. Berlin, Heidelberg: Springer Berlin Heidelberg.

Spath, D. (Ed.); Ganschar, O., Gerlach, S., Hämmerle, M., Krause, T., Schlund, S., 2013. Produktionsarbeit der Zukunft – Industrie 4.0. Fraunhofer-Verlag, Stuttgart.

Uhlemann, T. H.-J., Lehmann, C., Steinhilper, R., 2017. The Digital Twin: Realizing the Cyber-Physical Production System for Industry 4.0, Procedia CIRP, Vol. 61, pp. 335–340.

Wagner, T., Herrmann, C., Thiede, S., 2017. Industry 4.0 impacts on lean production systems, *Procedia CIRP 63, 50th CIRP Conference on, Taichung City, Taiwan,* pp. 125-131.

Zangwill, W. I., Kantor, P. B., 1998. Toward a Theory of Continuous Improvement and the Learning Curve, *Management Science,* Vol. 44, No. 7, pp. 910-920.

Zühlke, D., 2008. SmartFactory – A Vision becomes Reality. In: Proceedings of the 17thWorld Congress IFAC'08, pp. 14101–14108.

IMPLEMENTATION OF AN ADAPTIVE INSTRUCTIONAL DESIGN FOR A PHYSICS MODULE IN A LEARNING MANAGEMENT SYSTEM

Christof Imhof, Per Bergamin, Ivan Moser and Matthias Holthaus
UNESCO chair on personalized and adaptive distance education, Swiss Distance University of Applied Sciences (FFHS)
Überlandstrasse 12, Brig, Switzerland

ABSTRACT

This article demonstrates how an adaptive instructional design for a physics module can be realized in a standard learning management system. We implemented a didactic design with physics-specific online exercises that were accompanied by either detailed or non-detailed instructions, depending on the results of the previous task (or a prior knowledge test for the very first exercise). This was realized by use of simple technological tools within the framework of a straightforward recommender system with four components. Consequently, students with less prior knowledge and/or lower learning achievements received more and different teaching assistance than those with high levels of prior knowledge or performance. This was done in the form of recommendations embedded within task feedback, suggesting which task to tackle next. We present first results which show that prior knowledge and online activity contribute to the learning progress in different ways depending on the type of task that was chosen. The detailed versions of the tasks were beneficial only to the students with lower or medium prior knowledge test scores while the students with higher levels of prior knowledge had less learning progress. In the future, our simple recommender system may serve as the basis for a more complex adaptive system, further closing the gap between research and practice in the field of technology-based adaptive learning.

KEYWORDS

Technology-based Learning, Adaptive Learning, Cognitive Load, Expertise Reversal Effect, Learning Management System, Log Files

1. INTRODUCTION

As countless aspects of our lives have become more and more digitalized in the past few decades, so has learning. Accordingly, new forms of learning such as distance learning or technology-based learning have emerged and have been gaining in importance ever since (Bergamin et al. 2012). Due to their flexible nature, these new forms of learning allow learners independence and autonomy, offer freedom of choice and break space-time barriers, thus granting many people the opportunity to pursue academic studies in circumstances that do not commonly allow for that to occur (e.g. full-/part-time employment or parenthood). In addition, such flexibility allows for individual requirements and contexts to be taken into account, which can vary substantially between learners and which can then determine the appropriate instructional design. In university education, learners are usually expected to develop the same competences over the course of their studies despite differing in key characteristics such as different prior knowledge or experience in relation to certain topics or learning skills. One way to achieve the goal of comparable learning success despite heterogeneous preconditions is through adaptation of the learning process, replacing the classic "one-size-fits-all" approach.

The importance of adapting the learning process to the needs of the learner can be demonstrated by the finding that instructional techniques (e.g. guidance by a tutor or detailed instructions) that prove beneficial for novices in a given field can lose their effectiveness or even be counterproductive when applied to experts; a phenomenon known as the Expertise Reversal Effect (Kalyuga et al. 2003). On a technical level, adaptive learning environments may be provided through Learning Management Systems (LMS), which are increasingly accessible due to the raise of technology-based learning.

Despite the popularity of studies on adaptive educational hypermedia, actual practical implementations of adaptive technology-based learning are still scarce (Somyürek 2015). Scanlon et al. (2013) found "a surprising failure" (p. 4) to translate research results in the field of technology-based learning (e.g. prototypes) into commercial applications, due to the so-called "valley of death" (i.e. failure due to lack of funding amongst other factors). According to Price et al. (2017), this gap between research and practice in technology-based learning appears to be systemic in nature, requiring change on multiple levels, including institutional change. Murray and Pérez (2015) claim that intelligent technology-based learning environments are still "years away", in spite of the advances that have been made, and appeal for pedagogy rather than technology to "drive the evolution of advanced learning systems" (p. 124). Oxman and Wong (2014) also identify the challenges of (further) implementation of technology-based learning systems as structural (e.g. term length) and operational rather than technological. Therefore, bridging the gap between research and practice requires an interdisciplinary approach that involves large-scale field studies in appropriate contexts as well as well-founded instructional designs (cf. Scanlon et al. 2015). This study seeks to narrow the gap between experimental research and its practical application by addressing the question whether an adaptive learning system can be implemented in a traditional learning environment without the use of high-end technology (such as deep neural networks). In this paper, we demonstrate how adaptive learning can be implemented in practice on a university level by applying it to a physics module within the learning management system "Moodle". Our approach utilises a fairly simple rule-based instructional design. We further explore to what extent adaptive instruction design, online activity and prior knowledge are related and how much they contribute to the learning progress. Finally, we discuss the potential and limitations of rule-based adaptive learning systems within the boundaries of a standard LMS.

2. THEORETICAL BACKGROUND

As explained above, the Expertise Reversal Effect – the phenomenon that teaching support which is beneficial for novices can turn out to be superfluous or even detrimental to experts and vice versa – may obstruct learning success in many learning scenarios, especially in classic settings where all learners receive the same instructions or guidance (Kalyuga 2007b). "Reversal" refers to the circumstance that the effectiveness of didactical aspects may be reversed for different levels of learners' expertise (Lee & Kalyuga 2014). The most common explanation for this effect is the Cognitive Load Theory (Sweller 1988), which focusses on the interactions between long-term and working memory. According to this theory, the former is used to store knowledge and has an unlimited storing capacity while the latter is involved in consciously processing novel information, but is limited in its capacity of storing it, both in terms of amount and duration (van Merriënboer & Sweller 2005). Recent accounts of the theory differentiate between (at least) two kinds of cognitive load, the intrinsic load and the extraneous load. Intrinsic load concerns cognitive processes that are required for processing learning materials and may be affected by the (perceived) complexity or difficulty of the material. In contrast, extraneous load refers to cognitive processes caused by factors that are not directly related to the learning task but are nevertheless crucial for the learning process, for instance convoluted instructional design or unfavourable presentation of the learning material (Kalyuga 2009a).

The basis of the Cognitive Load Theory is the notion that the intrinsic and extraneous loads combined cannot exceed the limitations of the working memory (Paas et al. 2003). If high extrinsic load results from an unnecessary processing of design or presentation aspects, less capacity can be made available for the processing of the actual learning tasks (i.e. intrinsic load). Consequently, learning is impaired if the learning activities require too much cognitive capacity, resulting in overload.

Importantly, the current cognitive load of a learner is not only determined by objective factors (such as difficulty of the learning content and instructional design), but also by characteristics of the learner. In parts, human expertise results from cognitive schemata with varying degrees of complexity and automation housed by the long-term memory (van Merriënboer & Sweller 2005). Knowledge is stored in and organized by these schemata, which may become automated through training, thus freeing space in the working memory, thereby reducing the intrinsic load and leaving more cognitive capacity for the processing of new content (Kalyuga 2009a). Put differently, the level of available knowledge exerts considerable influence on the cognitive load (Kalyuga 2007b). This implies that optimal teaching of complex learning content needs to take learners' cognitive load into account and actively manage it though instructional interventions (Somyürek,

2015; Rey & Buchwald, 2011). In the case of the Expertise Reversal Effect, this concerns the degree of instructional guidance: On the one hand, a lack of sufficient guidance during a complex task may result in the application of poor problem-solving strategies or arbitrary trial-and-error behaviour. On the other hand, vast amounts of instructional guidance may lead learners to squandering their resources by comparing and contrasting their prior knowledge with the incoming information, thus inflating their intrinsic load (Kalyuga 2007b).

Consequently, at the start of the learning process, novices should be provided with instructional guidance (e.g. step-by-step instruction) in order to help them with their tasks and optimise their cognitive load. As the learners gain more expertise over time, this guidance can then gradually be reduced (cf. the concept of fading scaffolds; van Merriënboer & Sluijsmans 2009). The educational implications of the Cognitive Load Theory in general and the Expertise Reversal Effect in particular have been confirmed by numerous studies (e.g. Rey & Buchwald 2011). However, it should also be noted that the cognitive load approach is limited to the acquisition of subject-specific knowledge as the learning goal (Kalyuga & Singh, 2016) and is less applicable to other learning objectives such as the acquisition of self-regulated learning skills or the increase of learning motivation. Moreover, learners may feel overburdened with the necessary monitoring and adaptation of the learning process (Kirschner & van Merriënboer 2013). Technology-based adaptive learning can assist these processes, thus reducing the extrinsic load and increasing the effectiveness of learning.

In contrast to traditional technology-based approaches, adaptive learning allows learning aspects (contents, navigation, support) to be presented in a dynamic environment that continually changes in response to information collected in the course of learning. This raises the question, which sources of a learning scenario are most suitable as a basis for adaptation processes in a course module (cf. Nakić et al. 2015, for an overview). Principally, three main groups of characteristics can be identified: (1) stable or situational personal characteristics of the learners such as gender, culture, learning style, prior knowledge or emotional state, (2) specific characteristics of the content such as topics or task difficulty and (3) characteristics of the context such as learning time or self-regulation (Wauters et al. 2010). The learning process itself can then be adapted by means of altering the instructional design regarding the relevant learning objects in accordance with the needs of an individual or a group of learners.

3. INSTRUCTIONAL DESIGN AND SYSTEM IMPLEMENTATION

In our instructional design, we focus on task difficulty as the adaptive factor, similar to Brunstein et al. (2009); Hsu et al. (2015); and van Der Kleij et al. (2015). Distance students in general and the students at our university in particular tend to have significantly different levels of background knowledge and learning strategies (mostly due to different educational and/or professional careers). Therefore, we implemented an adaptive instruction design in the learning management system used by our university (Moodle), which recommended tasks with step-by-step detailed or non-detailed instructions and thus varied the task difficulty accordingly. In the context of self-regulated learning, students could either follow the recommendation or choose an alternative learning path. Aiming to reduce the cognitive load, less proficient students were given instructions that offered more support and assistance while more proficient students received less support, thus increasing the task difficulty. The recommendations and interventions were each embedded in the feedback of the previously processed task. Our framework for processing and linking learning data with adaptive learning instructions was inspired by a model by Zimmermann et al. (2005). Conceptually, the system was based on four components that together formed the adaptation mechanism. The first component was the sensors, which were linked to the task data (specifically if a task has been solved correctly or not). The second component was the analyser, which collected the data measured by the sensors. This information was then transferred to the third component, the controller, which determined whether a certain threshold had been met. Depending on the outcome, the controller determined if the learning object (for example a task) was to be adjusted. The last component was the presenter, which then displayed objects of learning support (such as recommendations). As an entry point, we used the data from a prior knowledge test that was administered at the beginning of the course and assessed the level of expertise with which the students started the course. In the course of the semester, further tests and assessments were then fed to the sensor component data base. Consequently, students received instructions and learning support adapted to their learning performance and behaviour. The learning support focused on three different elements: the initial sensor, the step loop and the task loop.

The initial sensor was an assessment of prior knowledge in physics in the form of a set of standard exercises solved at the very start of the course. Based on their performance, the students were then divided into two groups, "novices" (less than 50% correct answers) and "experts" (more than 50% of the answers were correct). Depending on the score, the first proper task in the module appeared in a detailed (high learning support) or a standard form (low learning support). The second element, the step loop, measured the current level of knowledge within a task and accordingly determined the appropriate learning support. Based on the correctness of the answer, the students received feedback which was provided after each step in the task and changed depending on how often the same question was answered incorrectly. This served the purpose of clarifying possible misunderstandings the students might have had as quickly as possible, e.g. by reminding them of forgotten information (Durlach & Ray 2011). The third element, the task loop, consisted of two kinds of tasks, namely standard tasks and transfer tasks. The former assessed the ability to solve a particular physics problem, while the latter had two objectives: On the one hand, the transfer task checked whether a student had understood a particular problem and was thus able to solve the task in its standard form (see "vertical transfer", van Eck & Dempsey 2002), and on the other hand, it evaluated whether the student was able to apply the now acquired problem-solving knowledge to a similar task in a different topic (see "horizontal transfer", van Eck & Dempsey 2002). Within each set of tasks, the system recommended which task the student should tackle next and in what form (detailed or standard). The detailed version featured numerous small solution steps, while the standard version was composed of few solving steps. We chose a rule-based adaptive learning system with a fixed set of rules. The reason for this decision was two-fold: On the one hand, the sensors in our learning scenario do not generate enough data for a complex self-learning system and on the other hand, we wanted to keep the adaptation mechanisms transparent for our students in the sense of an "open learner model".

Starting in the autumn semester of 2015/16, we carried out a two-year field study that implemented our adaptive learning approach into one of our university's study modules. The chosen bachelor module was part of the course of studies in industrial engineering and featured three main physics topics (thermodynamics, optics and microphysics). The module was organized in a blended learning format, which means there was a mixture of face-to-face sessions (20% of the overall expected effort) and both on- and off-line self-study (80%). In order to promote the acceptance of our system among students, we chose a mixed control approach between the system (adaptation) and the learner (adaptability). In their feedback, the students thus received recommendations as to which tasks they should ideally complete and in which form they should choose it. As previously stated, compliance with these recommendations was always optional. The sensor data (i.e. the current state of knowledge) was made available to students in a transparent and concise way to foster their self-assessment skills as well as their acceptance of the recommendations (see open learning models, e.g. Long & Aleven 2017; Suleman et al. 2016).

4. ANALYSIS

4.1 Object of Investigation, Subjects, Procedure and Hypotheses

As previously stated, the students attending a physics module in the semesters 2015/16 and 2016/17 served as the participants in our investigation. The module is offered each autumn semester and was chosen for its reputation as a "problem module", due to its above-average failure rate. Each semester, the students are divided into seven or eight classes, split among different lecturers. Considering the high degrees of employment of our students, the class division was based on the students' preferences in terms of optimal time and location for the five face-to-face events (with four options to choose from in terms of location), which had no bearing on the module content or the online part of the course. In the autumn semester 2015/16, 105 students were enlisted in the course while 106 students participated in the course the following year (2016/17). In both years, the data of several students had to be excluded for our main analyses since they either didn't complete the prior knowledge test (11 in the 2015/16 semester) or the final exam at the end of the semester (7 in the first and 16 in the second year). There were no missing prior knowledge test scores in the second year since the test was not optional anymore. The course offered 43 adaptive tasks not all of which had to be completed by the students. More proficient students for example may only need to solve a fraction of the task array after having successfully completed the first assessment (initial sensor) in order to succeed at the final test at the end of the semester while less proficient students may have to complete a larger portion of the task set in order to achieve the same goal (following the recommendations).

As for the procedure, we first evaluated the distributions of the prior knowledge test scores and three different indicators of online activity (sum of daily clicks, sum of completed standard tasks and sum of completed detailed tasks) based on the students' log files. The sum of daily clicks was used as a general online activity measure, while the other two were specific for engagement with either detailed or non-detailed tasks. In order to investigate how our instruction design impacted the learning progress of our participants, we then explored the relationship between online activity, prior knowledge and the learning progress by calculating several regression models. We formulated four hypotheses for this exploratory study: H_1: prior knowledge is negatively related with learning progress (the less one knows, the more one can learn, i.e. a ceiling effect); H_2: general online activity (in the form of the sum of daily clicks) and learning progress are positively related; H_3: engagement with the tasks (be it detailed or standard tasks) is positively related with learning progress;

H_4: There is a negative interaction between online activity (all three forms thereof) and prior knowledge (more online activity benefits less knowledgeable students more than it does those with high levels of prior knowledge). The whole procedure was done separately for both semesters since the second semester served as a replication and expansion of the first. All statistical analyses were performed with R (R Core Team 2013).

4.2 Distributions of the Prior Knowledge Test Scores and Online Activity Measures

Before examining the distribution of the prior knowledge test scores, the scores in the separate three topics (microphysics, thermodynamics and optics) were added and standardised to an index of 100. Using the R psych package (Revelle 2017), we calculated the mean scores of the prior knowledge test and the mean sums for the online activity measures, as well as the skewness and kurtosis of the distributions (see *Table 1* for an overview). The normality of the distributions was then tested using the Shapiro-Wilk normality test. In the 2015/16 semester, the null hypothesis that the data was normally distributed wasn't rejected ($W = 0.99$, $p = .59$) while it clearly was in the 2016/17 semester ($W = 0.94$, $p < .001$). Thus, for the semester of 2015/16, the test scores were found to be approximately normally distributed while in the 2016/17 semester, the data was not normally distributed but instead skewed to the left due to overall low test scores (not a single person reached a score higher than 45 out of 100) and a high proportion of test scores of 0.

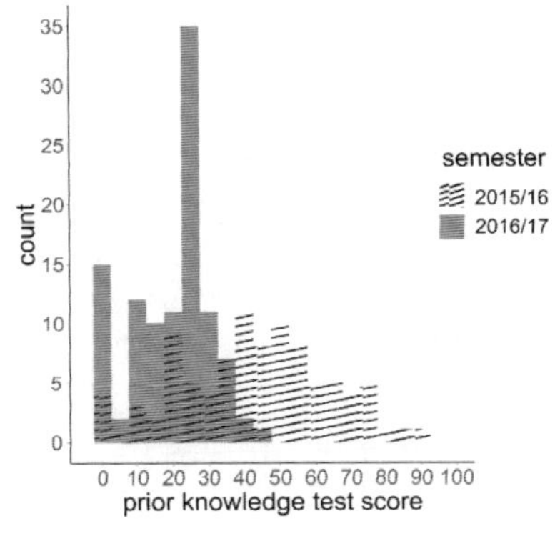

Figure 1. Two overlapping histograms showing the distributions of the prior knowledge test scores in both semesters. The frequencies of the scores did not differ from a normal distribution in year 1 (2015/16) but were left-skewed in year 2 (2016/17)

As for the online activity measures, only completed tasks were accounted for since the recommendation in the task loop was only given after having completed a task; aborted tasks were not counted. All six online measure distributions were clearly left-skewed due to the high frequencies of low levels of activity.

Table 1. Distribution of the prior knowledge test scores and three online activity measures in the two semesters, including the number of participants, means, standard deviations, the Shapiro-Wilk test statistic W and the according p-value

Measure	Mean (*SD*)	Skewness	Kurtosis	W (*p*)
	Semester 2015/16			
Prior knowledge test score (n=94)	42.88.0 (20.93)	-0.06	-0.53	0.99 (.59)
Sum of daily clicks (n=87)	831.56 (693.19)	1.25	1.77	0.89 (<.001)
Sum of completed standard tasks (n=87)	7.03 (8.72)	1.40	1.26	0.80 (<.001)
Sum of completed detailed tasks (n=87)	9.25 (8.30)	0.65	-0.72	0.90 (<.001)
	Semester 2016/17			
Prior knowledge test score (n=106)	19.71 (11.02)	-0.36	-0.67	0.94 (<.001)
Sum of daily clicks (n=90)	860.75 (626.45)	0.61	-0.07	0.95 (<.001)
Sum of completed standard tasks (n=90)	11.10 (9.55)	0.75	0.11	0.92 (<.001)
Sum of completed detailed tasks (n=90)	7.85 (7.32)	0.76	-0.10	0.90 (<.001)

4.3 Prior Knowledge, Online Activity and Learning Progress

In the following section, we report the relationship between prior knowledge, online activity and the learning progress within the adaptive module. For this purpose, the learning progress for each student was defined as the difference between the results of the prior knowledge test and the final test, both standardized to 100. We explored the relationship between the prior knowledge, the students' online activity and their learning progress by calculating three regression models for each of the three online activity measures ("OA" models 1 to 3) as well as a regression model solely containing prior knowledge (the "PK" model), all of which was done separately for both semesters. We used the R package ggplot2 (Wickham 2009) for the regression plots. The first OA model included only the online activity measure as a predictor. The second OA model added a second predictor in the form of the prior knowledge test score and the third and final OA model added the interaction between the online activity measure and the prior knowledge test score (see *Figure 2*). In all instances, the three models were supposed to predict the learning progress.

4.3.1 Prior Knowledge

For both semesters, the PK model yielded a significant regression with an adjusted R^2 of 0.29 for the 2015/16 semester ($F(1, 85) = 36.01$, $p < .001$) and an adjusted R^2 of 0.03 for the 2016/17 semester ($F(1,85) = 4.02$, $p = .047$). In line with our hypothesis H_1, there was a significant negative relationship between prior knowledge test score and predicted learning progress ($b = -0.61$, $p < .001$) for the 2015/16 semester, i.e. students with higher prior knowledge showed less learning progress. A similar relationship was found for the 2016/17 semester ($b = -0.31$, $p = .048$).

4.3.2 Sum of Daily Clicks and Prior Knowledge

For the 2015/16 data, two significant regression models were found, namely OA models 2 ($F(2, 84) = 21.8$, $p < .001$) with an adjusted R^2 of 0.33 and model 3 ($F(3, 83) = 15.82$, $p < .001$) with an adjusted R^2 of 0.34. In model 2, there was a positive relationship between sums of daily clicks and predicted learning progress ($b = 0.01$, $p = .02$) and a negative relation between prior knowledge and learning progress ($b = -0.67$, $p < .001$), supporting H_2 and H_1 respectively. Contrary to H_4, the interaction between the two predictors (model 3, see *Figure 2*) was not significant ($b = -0.0003$, $p = .09$). Model 2 significantly improved model fit compared to model 1 ($F(1, 84) = 43.96$, $p < .001$), while model 3 did not did not improve model fit compared to model 2 ($F(1, 83) = 2.88$, $p = .09$). In contrast, none of the regression models were significant for the 2016/17 data.

4.3.3 Sum of Completed Standard Tasks and Prior Knowledge

We again found two significant regression models in the 2015/16 semester, namely for OA models 2 ($F(2, 84) = 29.07$, $p < .001$) and 3 ($F(3, 83) = 19.18$, $p < .001$), both with an R^2 of 0.39. In model 2, both factors were significant predictors of learning progress. As before, participants' predicted learning progress was positively related to the sum of completed standard tasks (b = 1.08, $p < .001$) and negatively related to the prior knowledge test score (b = -0.91, $p < .001$). In model 3 (see *Figure 2*), the interaction between the two predictors again did not reach significance (b = -0.003, $p = .80$). Thus, the results supported hypotheses H_1 and H_3 but not H_4. As before, model 2 provided a better model fit ($F(1, 84) = 56.51$, $p < .001$) compared to model 1. The same could not be said about model 3 ($F(1, 83) = 0.06$, $p = .80$). Again, none of the regression equations were significant in case of the 2016/17 data.

4.3.4 Sum of Completed Detailed Tasks and Prior Knowledge

In the 2015/16 semester, all three models were significant, with OA model 1 ($F(1, 85) = 6.54$, $p = .01$) having an R^2 of 0.06, model 2 ($F(2, 84) = 21.2$, $p < .001$) an R^2 of 0.32 and model 3 ($F(3, 83) = 17.67$, $p < .001$) an R^2 of 0.37. In model 1, the predicted learning progress was positively related to the sum of completed detailed tasks (b = 0.75, $p = .01$). This was also in the case in model 2 (b = 0.55, $p = .03$). Like before, the relationship between predicted learning progress and prior knowledge test was negative (b = -0.58, $p < .001$). Unlike before, the interaction between online activity and prior knowledge (see *Figure 2*) was significant (b = -0.04, $p = .01$). Hence, hypotheses H_1, H_3 and H_4 were all supported by the data. A simple slope analysis (using the R package jtools, Long 2018) revealed that the slope of the sum of completed detailed tasks was only significantly different from zero when the prior knowledge test score was either medium (b = 0.52, $p = .04$) or low (b = 1.28, $p < .001$). As before, model 2 ($F(1, 84) = 35.92$, $p < .001$) was an improvement over model 1 in terms of model fit. Unlike before, model 3 further improved upon model 2 in this case ($F(1, 83) = 7.39$, $p = .01$). However, none of the regression models were significant for the 2016/17 data.

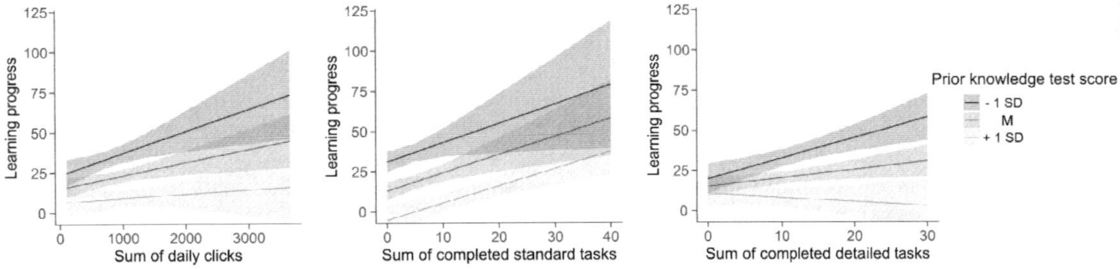

Figure 2. Regression model 3 for all three measures of online activity separately. All models are based on 2015/2016 data exclusively. In model 3, learning progress is predicted by *prior knowledge test score*, *online activity* and the interaction between the two. That interaction was significant only when using sum of completed detailed task as the measure of online activity. In order to illustrate the interaction, we plotted the predicted effect of online activity on learning progress using simple slopes for students that scored one standard deviation below the mean (-1 SD), students that scored one SD above the mean (+1 SD) and students with mean prior knowledge test scores (M)

5. DISCUSSION

The purpose of this article was to demonstrate how an adaptive instruction design could be implemented in a standard learning management system. On a theoretical level, the instruction design was based on the Cognitive Load Theory in general and the Expertise Reversal Effect in particular. We developed an adaptive task set which was then combined with a rule-based recommendation system within the learning management system Moodle. Our adaptive system was applied to a physics module during two semesters (2015/16 and 2016/17) with the respective enlisted students of our university serving as our participants.

The results for the 2015/16 semester reveal that the prior knowledge test score and the level of online activity are both important predictors of learning progress. As hypothesized, the relationship between online activity (be it the sum of daily clicks or the amount of standard tasks solved) and learning progress was positive (the higher the level of online activity, the larger the learning progress), while the relationship between prior knowledge test scores and learning gain was negative (the higher the initial score, the smaller the learning gain). Contrary to our hypotheses, this effect was independent from the level of online activity in most cases with the detailed tasks being the exception, where we found the expected negative interaction: the amount of tasks solved was positively related with learning gains when the prior knowledge test score was low and negatively related when the score was high. This means the less proficient students (i.e. the "novices") benefitted from the detailed tasks more than the advanced students (i.e. the "experts"). Even though this result suggests a presence of the Expertise Reversal Effect (Kalyuga et al. 2003), an according conclusion cannot be drawn unless we know whether the students followed the recommendations. Moreover, the ceiling effect we found could also account for that result, especially when considering that classic exams always have a maximum score that cannot be exceeded.

Surprisingly, neither the prior knowledge test scores nor the levels of online activity predicted the learning progress in the 2016/17 semester, neither separately nor in interaction. We argue that this result was found due to the peculiar distribution of the prior knowledge test scores. As stated before, the scores in that semester were very low with not even a single student reaching 50 points out of a 100. The test was exactly the same as the year before, where it showed no floor or ceiling effects and yielded a mean slightly below what one would expect for a test of medium difficulty (in this case, 50). Since the test itself was identical, the difference between the semesters must have a different explanation. Even though the distributions of the online activity levels were also left-skewed, this could not explain the difference since those distributions were similar in both semesters. As previously stated, what differed between the semesters was the circumstance that the prior knowledge test was mandatory in the 2016/17 while it was not the year before. Motivational aspects thus may factor into a possible explanation or a potential homogeneity within the particular group of students, which has yet to be investigated (e.g. similar previous education that was light on physics).

A major limitation of the study is the lack of a control group. Control groups are hard to achieve in contexts like the one this field study was conducted in since the grades the students receive at the end of the semester are real, thus posing ethical problems comparable to withholding of treatment in clinical studies. In this particular case, there was no non-adaptive past version of the course available to compare to the adaptive one, and even if there was, comparisons might not be all that conclusive given the difference in key factors we witnessed between the 2015/16 and 2016/17 semesters. As of the time of this writing, the adaptive system is still being used in the 2017/18 semester, the results of which will be available soon. Another limitation is the lack of information concerning whether the students actually complied with the recommendations (rather than making their choice either at random or as they saw fit). However, the students' compliance with the recommendations will be analysed soon as well.

6. CONCLUSION

We demonstrated that a simple rule-based adaptive system can be implemented in a common learning management system, getting one step closer to bridging the gap between theory and practice of implementing adaptive systems. As our results show, the implementation of the task-difficulty based adaption process was successful (to an extent), even though we (expectedly) encountered a ceiling effect concerning the learning progress of the students with higher levels of prior knowledge. Our results also demonstrate the importance of reliable assessments serving as the sources of adaption (e.g. well-balanced tests). Future studies in this line of research could grant insight into the transfer tasks, which were very rarely solved by the students and thus could not be analysed properly. Despite the limitations of this study, this line of research holds potential since the successful implementation of simple rules can serve as the basis for a more complex adaptive system, for instance by expanding the sources for adaption (e.g. mood) or by refining the instruction design (e.g. by adding more levels of difficulty). In the near future, research in the field of learning analytics (see e.g. Bannert et al. 2017) may result in the development of more holistic sensors that measure several metrics relevant to learning at once, providing multiple sources for adaption, potentially even allowing implementations within common LMS. Such improvements could result in adaptive systems with more intelligent and complex algorithms at their core, which could then lead to more accurate prognoses, higher efficiency of the adaptive process and more suitable recommendations for the students, which in turn may enhance the acceptance of such systems among students and lecturers.

ACKNOWLEDGEMENT

We would like to thank the many students who participated in the course as well as Dr. Stéphanie McGarrity for proofreading this manuscript and giving us invaluable advice.

REFERENCES

Bannert, M. et al., 2017. Relevance of Learning Analytics to Measure and Support Students' Learning in Adaptive Educational Technologies. In *LAK'17 Proceedings of the Seventh International Learning Analytics & Knowledge Conference*. Vancouver, BC, Canada: ACM New York, NY, USA, pp. 568–569.

Bergamin, P.B. et al., 2012. The Relationship between Flexible and Self-Regulated Learning in Open and Distance Universities. *International Review of Research in Open and Distance Learning*, 13(2), pp.101–123.

Brunstein, A., Betts, S. & Anderson, J.R., 2009. Practice Enables Successful Learning Under Minimal Guidance. *Journal of Educational Psychology*, 101(4), pp.790–802.

Durlach, P.J. & Ray, J.M., 2011. *Designing adaptive instructional environments: Insights from empirical evidence (Technical Report 1297)*, Arlington, VA: U. S. Army Research Institute for the Behavioral Social Sciences.

van Eck, R. & Dempsey, J., 2002. The Effect of Competition and Contextualized Advisement on the Transfer of Mathematics Skills in a Computer-Based Instructional Simulation Game. *Educational Technology Research & Development*, 50(3), pp.23–41.

Hsu, Y. et al., 2015. Interactions Between Levels of Instructional Detail and Expertise When Learning with Computer Simulations. *Journal of Educational Technology & Society*, 18, pp.113–127.

Kalyuga, S., 2007b. Expertise Reversal Effect and Its Implications for Learner-Tailored Instruction. *Educational Psychology Review*, 19(4), pp.509–539.

Kalyuga, S., 2009. Managing cognitive load in adaptive ICT-based learning. *Journal of Systemics, Cybernetics and Informatics*, 7(5), pp.16–21.

Kalyuga, S. et al., 2003. The Expertise Reversal Effect. *Educational Psychologist*, 38(1), pp.23–31.

Kalyuga, S. & Singh, A.-M., 2016. Rethinking the Boundaries of Cognitive Load Theory in Complex Learning. *Educational Psychology Review*, 28(4), pp.831–852.

van der Kleij, F.M., Feskens, R.C.W. & Eggen, T.J.H.M., 2015. Effects of Feedback in a Computer-Based Learning Environment on Students' Learning Outcomes: A Meta-Analysis. *Review of Educational Research*, 85(4), pp.475–511.

Lee, C.H. & Kalyuga, S., 2014. Expertise reversal effect and its instructional implications. In *Applying science of learning in education: Infusing psychological science into the curriculum*. Washington, DC: Society for the Teaching of Psychology, pp. 32–44.

Long, J.A., 2018. *jtools: Analysis and Presentation of Social Scientific Data*, R package version 1.0.0, https://cran.r-project.org/package=jtools.

Long, Y. & Aleven, V., 2017. Enhancing learning outcomes through self-regulated learning support with an Open Learner Model. *User Modeling and User-Adapted Interaction*, 27(1), pp.55–88.

van Merriënboer, J.J.G. & Sluijsmans, D.M.A., 2009. Toward a Synthesis of Cognitive Load Theory, Four-Component Instructional Design, and Self-Directed Learning. *Educational Psychology Review*, 21(1), pp.55–66.

van Merriënboer, J.J.G. & Sweller, J., 2005. Cognitive Load Theory and Complex Learning: Recent Developments and Future Directions. *Educational Psychology Review*, 17(2), pp.147–177.

Murray, M.C. & Pérez, J., 2015. Informing and performing: A study comparing adaptive learning to traditional learning. *Informing Science*, 18(1), pp.111–125.

Nakić, J., Granić, A. & Glavinić, V., 2015. Anatomy of student models in adaptive learning systems: A systematic literature review of individual differences from 2001 to 2013. *Journal of Educational Computing Research*, 51(4), pp.459–489.

Oxman, S. & Wong, W., 2014. White Paper: Adaptive Learning Systems. *DV X Innovations DeVry Education Group.*

Paas, F., Renkl, A. & Sweller, J., 2003. Cognitive Load Theory and Instructional Design: Recent Developments. *EDUCATIONAL PSYCHOLOGIST*, 38(1), pp.1–4.

Price, L., Casanova, D. & Orwell, S., 2017. Modeling an institutional approach to developing Technology Enabled Learning: Closing the gap between research and practice. *INTED2017 Proceedings*, pp.5009–5018.

R Core Team, 2013. R: a language and environment for statistical computing. *R Foundation for Statistical Computing, Vienna, Austria.*

Revelle, W.R., 2017. psych: Procedures for Personality and Psychological Research.

Rey, G.D. & Buchwald, F., 2011. The expertise reversal effect: Cognitive load and motivational explanations. *Journal of Experimental Psychology: Applied*, 17(1), pp.33–48.

Scanlon, E. et al., 2013. *Beyond prototypes: Enabling innovation in technology-enhanced learning*, Open University, Milton Keynes.

Scanlon, E., O'Shea, T. & McAndrew, P., 2015. Technology-Enhanced Learning : Evidence-based Improvement. In *L@S '15 Proceedings of the Second (2015) ACM Conference on Learning @ Scale*. Vancouver, BC, Canada: ACM New York, NY, USA, pp. 229–232.

Somyürek, S., 2015. The new trends in adaptive educational hypermedia systems. *International Review of Research in Open and Distributed Learning*, 16(1), pp.221–241.

Suleman, R.M., Mizoguchi, R. & Ikeda, M., 2016. A New Perspective of Negotiation-Based Dialog to Enhance Metacognitive Skills in the Context of Open Learner Models. *International Journal of Artificial Intelligence in Education*, 26(4), pp.1069–1115.

Sweller, J., 1988. Cognitive Load During Problem Solving: Effects on Learning. *Cognitive Science*, 12, pp.257–285.

Wauters, K., Desmet, P. & Van den Noortgate, W., 2010. Adaptive item-based learning environments based on the item response theory: possibilities and challenges. *Journal of Computer Assisted Learning*, 26, pp.549–562.

Wickham, H., 2009. *Ggplot2 : elegant graphics for data analysis*, Springer.

VALIDITY AND RELIABILITY OF THE TEACHER LEADERSHIP INVENTORY IN MALAYSIAN EDUCATIONAL CONTEXT

Mahaliza Mansor, Jamal Nordin Yunus and Fanny Kho Chee Yuet
Sultan Idris Education University, Tanjung Malim, Perak, Malaysia

ABSTRACT

The aim of this article is to report the validity and reliability of Teacher Leadership Inventory (TLI). The sample of the study consists of 244-trained teachers who are chosen using random sampling technique from 19 secondary schools in Perak. The content validity, criterion validity and construct validity analyses have been carried out by using this set of data. The findings of this study using exploratory factor analysis through orthogonal rotation with varimax method has formed three factors, consisted of 15 items of TLI with factor loadings range from .54 - .84. The reliability Cronbach Alpha coefficient for the overall item is .85, meanwhile for each factors developed ranged from .66 to .91. As the conclusion, these analyses have generated a new pool of TLI item to measure the construct of Teacher Leadership elements in Malaysian Educational context.

KEYWORDS

Teacher Leadership, Factor Analysis, Validity and Reliability

1. INTRODUCTION

Teaching is creative, complex and requires high skills. Hence, teachers must constantly deepen their knowledge, skills and value to be effective leader throughout their careers. In recent studies, teacher leadership has been defined as it is centered on a vision of a teacher who is able to build influence and interaction, rather than power and authority (Poekert, 2012). According to Fairman and Mackenzie (2012), teacher leadership emerged within many different contexts, such as individual and collective efforts; informal and formal actions; narrowly focused and broader school-wide improvement efforts; a school climate of isolation and mistrust or one of collegiality, shared vision and trust. Whereas, Hunzicker (2012) reported that, teacher leadership roles and responsibilities are closely related to student-focused concerns. However, their self-efficacy increase when the teacher actively pursued leadership skills and positively influence their self-conceptions of teacher leadership.

Meanwhile, according to Danielson (2006), the leadership of teacher is the activities carried out by individuals who have knowledge and skills to influence other individuals inside and outside the organization. This in line with A. Ghani, Mohd Rashid, Marzuki, and Faisol (2011) and Fairman and Mackenzie (2014), where teacher leadership concept refers to teachers who make a difference whether within or outside the organization through knowledge and skill and style that affects colleagues. Therefore, it is shown that teachers use the knowledge, skills and value to influence colleagues in adopting best practices in school. There are at least three major elements need to be considered in enhancing teacher leadership, which is knowledge, skill (Fairman & Mackenzie, 2012; Katzenmeyer & Moller, 2009; Phelps, 2008; York-Barr & Duke, 2004) and value (MOE, 2009), of the teacher, which are going to discussed further.

1.1 Knowledge

According to Green (2005), knowledge is what teachers know in order to promote the success of all students. Furthermore, with adequate knowledge; they can identify an appropriate and acceptable process for the schools' success. Knowledge in this study refers to teachers' understanding on teacher leadership concept, where teachers tend to use their content knowledge on teachers' leadership and apply it in the school and community in order to strive for schools' excellence. Therefore, according to Tamuri, Mahmud, and Bari, (2005), teachers require extensive knowledge about students' physical, psychological, the theory of pedagogy and andragogy to facilitate knowledge to be pass on students more effectively.

Leadership knowledge also can be enhanced through practicing teachers` professional learning for continuous improvement (Fairman & Mackenzie, 2014). In this context, teachers will be able to voice their opinions to achieve the shared vision and mission of the school improvement. Meanwhile, novice teachers who are still lack of knowledge about the school systems and teacher leadership skills (Muijs, Chapman, & Armstrong, 2013) can use this platform to enhance their knowledge. According to Lead (2013), teacher leadership also provides spaces for teachers to share knowledge across borders. This can be done through the involvement of teachers in teacher leadership programs at the ministry level, where teachers have been given opportunity to express their views in policy making and share their best practices. In conclusion, teachers should be exposed with leadership skills since at early stage at teacher`s training colleges so that they can face the challenges in the process of improving the teaching and learning (Moller & Katzenmeyer, 1996).

1.2 Skill

Teacher leadership skill is closely relate to good teamwork skill. Teachers can lead by engaging, inspiring and motivating others to improve through their actions. They are able to lead by effectively communicate with colleagues and inform them of their goals in ways that can garner support of their vision for the school improvement (Danielson, 2007). However, the teachers can only acquire this leadership skill by practice. According to Katzenmeyer and Moller (2009) teachers who have the leadership skills to influence other teachers or students can act as facilitators, mentors, counselors, curriculum specialists and able to lead the study group. Every teacher should have leadership skills and attributes (Danielson, 2007). According to Danielson (2007), there are some skills and characteristics that can be adopt by individuals as teacher. Effective teachers must be open-minded and respect others' views. They also should show confidence, assertive, flexible and willing to try a different approach if their efforts failed, as well as willing to encounter a variety of risks such as time constraints in their daily job. Meanwhile, Grant, Gardner, Kajee, Moodley and Somaroo (2010), and Elsabe and SG (2011), emphasis that teacher leadership occurs in four setting which is in the classrooms, working with other teacher outside the classrooms, extra-curricular activities, and school development and leadership practices among schools community. However, their study concluded that most of the leadership practices happen in the classroom, during teaching and learning improvement. Therefore, teachers must learn to lead a group, listen, use the data and identify other needs to acquire a strong set of skills to be use in the school daily routines (Katzenmeyer dan Moller, 2009).

Research done by Angelle, Nixon, Norton and Niles (2011), showed that teacher leadership skills imposed high impact on school development through shared responsibility among teachers. This can be achieve through collaborative relationship and school culture based on trust. To achieve collaborative relationship and trusted culture, Jackson, Burrus, Basset and Roberts (2010) suggested teachers should learn in groups. According to, Roberts and Pruitt, (2009), group learning refers to the learning process that takes place among teachers to discuss on important issues in schools in identifying students' learning. This professional learning community and collaboration has led to changes in pedagogy through shared goals, relationships and trust as well as support continuous learning give a positive impact on student achievement, improve teacher effectiveness (Harris & Jones, 2010; Sharratt & Fullan, 2009; Rovere 2013) and as an effort to help other colleagues (A. Ghani, & Crow, 2013).

Therefore, Teacher Leadership Exploratory Consortium, (2011) suggests that teachers need to understand the family, culture, and society as they give a big impact to the educational process and student learning. Teacher needs to work with colleagues to establish a good continuous relationship with families, communities, and other stakeholders to improve the education system and student learning opportunities. Finally, teachers also can play a vital role as a reference leader to guide students, lead and guide himself or herself and their colleagues to the shared purposive goals without being autocratic (Idris & Hamzah, 2012). In conclusion, these studies clearly shown that a teacher who has leadership skills can be the role model and referral leader to students, colleagues, parents and the community. Indirectly, it showed that leadership skills can be applied in each and every teacher as individual.

1.3 Value

The value is defined as beliefs about what is the right and wrong way for people to behave and it is also known as moral principles (MOE, 2009). The term value in this study has been defined as a set of beliefs that teachers have towards the school and community and could give a great impact in schools transformation process. Teachers have an important responsibility to nurture students who will constantly practice good values in their daily lives. Teachers also need to instill professionalism of teaching practices in them, while being a guidance and role model to the students. According to MOE (2009), the practice of the professionalism will be a platform for teachers to develop good characters to fulfill the function of the school as a place of national establishment to develop human capital. This in line with the Malaysian National Education Philosophy and Philosophy of Teacher Education aspirations. The practice of professionalism in teaching is an initiative to develop a teacher who has a towering personality in becoming an excellent teacher (MOE, 2009).

Teachers also must have a high cognitive skills and a good personality. According to Mohd. Kassim (2008), teachers who have values and high self-esteem should be aware that the dignity of the teaching profession lies in their hands and teachers also should highlight the positive values in them because the students often refer them as the role models. In line with the philosophy of Malaysian Teacher Education, teachers must be honorable, have a progressive and scientific vision, ready to uphold the aspirations of the country, ensuring the development of individuals as well as preserve the unity, democratic, and progressive community (Mok, 2010). In order to meet the current education challenges, teachers should have a strong values and self-esteem in them. According to Mat Som (2009), the main aspects to be address in promoting the teaching profession is a teacher's own personality. This is because the personal quality of the teacher is a source of knowledge and able to emulate the formation of good character (Abas, 2007). In other words, the teacher is acting as `value developer` (MacBeath, Pedder & Swaffield, 2007). Therefore, teachers need to show good personal values to the students, schools and communities. These good personal qualities can guide and educate students to develop their personal character. In conclusion, the core values that a teacher must have are honest, discipline, responsibility, timeliness and a commitment to work (MOE, 2009).

Thus, according to the literature, teacher leadership can be classifed into three dimensions as suggested by Katzenmeyer and Moller (2009), Phelps (2008), Fairman and Mackenzie (2012; 2014) and MOE (2009): knowledge, skills and values in practice, which are used in our model. However, currently, there are still not many suitable instruments to measure secondary school teachers` perception toward teacher leadership. Most of the previous studies have been carried in Western countries, such as Teacher Leadership Self-Assessment (TLSA) developed by Katzenmeyer dan Moller (2009) and the measurement is not really suitable with Malaysian context as well as less has been reviewed by previous researcher. Secondly, is the use of suitable statistical procedure in developing and validating items. The exploratory factor analysis has been well suggested by experts if there are less research have been carried out regarding the observe factor structure (Bandalos & Finney, 2010). Given these various constraints and limitations of existing instrument reviewed, it was therefore necessary to develop an empirically validated TLI specifically in measuring perceptions, for Malaysian secondary school teachers. The use of EFA, criterion validity and, content validity as well as internal consistency are more suitable in developing and validating items.

2. METHOD

This section will discuss about questionnaire design sampling procedure, factor analyses, validity and reliability.

2.1 Questionnaire Design

The questionnaire is composed of three parts, 15 items including: knowledge, skill and value. The instrument used has been adopted from Niche-Research Grant Scheme (NRGS) 2014 Project 4: Teacher Leadership. The questionnaire items were answered using a four-point scale anchoring at 1, 2, 3, and 4 (strongly disagree, disagree, agree, strongly agree). The comparative analysis of teacher leadership models such as Katzenmeyer and Moller (2009), Phelps (2008), York-Barr and Duke (2004), Fairman and Mackenzie (2012; 2014), Malaysian Education Development Plan, Malaysian National Policy of Education, Malaysian Teacher Standard (2009) as well as through key informants and survey of lecturers and teachers from schools and higher learning institutions in Malaysia has been done to develop these items.

2.2 Sampling Procedure

The data used in this research was obtained from 19 regular secondary schools in Batang Padang district in Perak. This set of data was used in preliminary study as to perform exploratory factor analysis. 15 sets of questionnaires were distributed to each of these 19 regular secondary schools. A total of 285 survey forms were circulated, of which 244 surveys were return and valid for analysis.

2.3 Factor Analysis, Validity and Reliability

The Cronbach Alpha coefficient is used to measure the internal consistency of these scales (Nunnally & Bernstein, 1994). In this study, the constructs which had Cronbach Alpha coefficients greater than .70 have been retained for further analysis (Hair, Black, Babin, Anderson &Tatham, 2010). Furthermore, measures with item-to-total correlation larger than .3 are considered to have criterion validity (Hair et al, 2010). The item-to-total correlation of each measure was more than .3, therefore we consider the criterion validity of each scale to be satisfactory. The items are reviewed by a panel of Sultan Idris Education University lecturers to ensure the translation of meaning and terminology met the theoretical background as the technique. The panel consists of an assessment and measurement expert, a human resource development expert and an educational leadership expert.

Then, the questionnaires have been administered to six trained teachers to identify if there were any confusion regarding the items and record it in the space provided for improvements or been dropped out (Flowers, 2006). The purpose was to improve the items and to ensure it was suitable for Malaysian context. Furthermore, it was important to get feedback on quality of each items, as it was easy to understand and used the appropriate language and terminology. The samples were asked to evaluate about the clarity of each items by using the scale given (Flowers, 2006). A scale of 1 to 10 is used to determine the validity coefficient for each items. According to Tuckman and Waheed (1981) in SidekMohd Noah and Jamaludin Ahmad (2005) if the total of the score obtained from the experts is 70% or above, it means that the item has a high score for the content validity aspect. Otherwise, the item will be dropped from the questionnaires. The results of content validity are presented in Table 1 below.

Table 1. Content validity scores

Panel	Panel 1	Panel 2	Panel 3	Panel 4	Panel 5	Panel 6	Cum Score
Percentage (%)	92.72	91.51	88.48	82.42	82.42	80.00	86.84

Meanwhile, to ensure the instrument has reasonable construct validity, exploratory factor analysis was used. The exploratory factor analysis (EFA) through orthogonal rotation with varimax method had been used on these 15 items. The EFA applied the following rules as suggested by Hair et al. (2010):

i. Bartlett's Test of Sphericity had to be significant ($p < .05$);
ii. Kaiser-Meyer-Olkin measure of sampling index $\geq .5$;
iii. Eigenvalue > 1;
iv. Items with the factor loading $> .5$ were retained;
v. Factors building are based on teacher leadership models and previous studies.

The results of exploratory factor analysis are presented in Table 2.

Table 2. Exploratory factor analysis and internal consistency values for the questionnaires

Construct	Number of Factor	Number of item per construct	Factor loading	% of variance	Cum. percentage	Cronbach's α
Teacher Leadership	3	15	.54-84	15.80	67.69	.85
Knowledge		7		46.11		.91
Value		4		12.85		.70
Skill		4		8.73		.66

3. DISCUSSION AND CONCLUSION

The purpose of this study is to develop and validate teacher leadership inventory used to measure secondary teachers` perception in Malaysian setting. This study used statistical approach to identify fifth teen-items in developing new TLI. The Egien values showed that there are three factors which score more than one and the total cumulative percentage is 67.69%. All fifth teen-items have been accepted and pooled to form TLI final version. The factor analysis of 15 items shown that there are three major factors have been formed. The factors are knowledge, skill and value, as suggested by previous literatures mentioned by Katzenmeyer and Moller (2009), Phelps (2008), York-Barr and Duke (2004), Fairman and Mackenzie (2012; 2014), Malaysian Education Development Plan, Malaysian National Policy of Education, and Malaysian Teacher Standard (2009). Results from this study suggested that TLI and its constructs shown the good internal consistency values to measure teachers` perception toward teacher leadership model. The overall internal consistency value is .85, meanwhile the values of factor loading of each constructs range from .54 to .84. Therefore, these items are suitable to use in exploratory research.

This study has a few weakness, such as the comparison of the values of internal consistency among the studies cannot be done extensively because less of reviewed inventory. Secondly, the sample only consisted of secondary schools, therefore the next study should be extended to primary school teachers. Thirdly, the use of confirmatory factor analysis (CFA), is more suitable in developing and validating items. As the CFA can be used as a basis for a final determination regarding an underlying construct, because this analysis is designed to maximize the amount of variance within the current variable set, and subsequent analyses with other data sets may not reproduce the same factor structure. Furthermore, EFA only focus on statistical and not according to the theory in determining the measurement structure scale as well as not enough to measure error. Fourthly, the comparison between research findings cannot be done because this inventory is the newly developed one. Further study also should be explored on the perception of the teachers on the existence of other teacher leadership models. However, hopefully the findings are valuable for the researchers, ministry of education, school-based professional learning developers` and teacher educator references, who are interested more in exploring teacher leadership.

ACKNOWLEDGEMENT

This research is funded by University Research Grant (2017- 0166 -106-01).

REFERENCES

A. Ghani, M., F. & Crow, G., M. (2013). Amalan Komuniti Pembelajaran Profesional:Perspektif Pemimpin Sekolah Cemerlang Negara Maju. *Jurnal Kurikulum dan Pengajaran Asia Pasifik.* 1 (3), 10 - 27.

A. Ghani, M., F., Mohd. Rashid., N., Marzuki., S., & Faisol, E. (2011). Pengenalan kepada Amalan Kepimpinan Guru di Malaysia: Cabaran dan Cadangan. *Management Research Journal*, 3, 71–92.

Abas., I. (2007). Peranan Guru Membina Murid Menghadapi Cabaran Wawasan 2020. *Jurnal Penyelidikan Pendidikan Institut Perguruan Islam,* Selangor, Jilid 10.

Angelle, P. S., Nixon, T. J., Norton, E. M., Niles.C.A. (2011). *Increasing organizational effectiveness: An examination of teacher leadership, collective efficacy, and trust in schools*. Paper presented at the annual meeting of the University Council for Educational Administration, Pittsburgh, 19 Nov. 2011.

Bandalos, D. L. & Finney, S. J. (2010) Factor analysis: Exploratory and confirmatory . In G. R. Hancock and R. O. Mueller (Eds.), *The reviewer's guide to quantitative methods in the social sciences* (pg. 94-114). New York: Routledge

Danielson, C. (2006). *Teacher leadership that strengthens professional practice.* Alexandria, VA: Association for Supervision and Curriculum Development.

Danielson, C. (2007). The many faces of leadership. *Educational Leadership.* 65(1), 14 - 19.

Elsabé de Villiers & SG (Fanie) Pretorius. (2011). Democracy in schools: are educators ready forteacher leadership? *South African Journal of Education,* Vol 31:574-58

Fairman, J. C., & Mackenzie, S. V. (2012). Spheres of teacher leadership action for learning. *Professional Development in Education.* 38(2), 267-286.

Fairman, J. C., & Mackenzie, S. V. (2014). How teacher leaders influence others and understand their leadership. *International Journal of Leadership in Education*, (August), 1–27.

Flowers, C. (2006). Confirmatory factor analysis of scores on the clinical experience rubric: A measure of dispositions for pre service teachers. *Educational and Psychological Measurement*, 66(3), 478-488.

Grant, C., Gardner, K., Kajee, F., Moodley, R., & Somaroo, S.(2010). Teacher leadership: a survey analysis of KwaZulu-Natal teachers' perceptions. *South African Journal of Education*, 30:401-419.

Green, R. L. (2005). *Practicing the Art of Leadership: A Problem-based Approach to Implementing the ISLLC Standards*. Ohio: Pearson

Hair, J. F., Black, W. C., Babin, B. J., Anderson, R. E., & Tatham R., L. (2010). *Multivariate data analysis*. New Jersey: Pearson Prentice Hall.

Harris, A., & Jones, M. (2010). Professional learning communities and system improvement. *Improving schools, 13*(2), 172-181.

Hunzicker, J. (2013). Attitude has a lot to do with it: dispositions of emerging teacher leadership. *Teacher Development*, 17(4), 538–561. doi:10.1080/13664530.2013.849614

Idris, N., H., & Hamzah, R.(2012). *Nilai Profesionalisme Bakal Guru Berteraskan Indikator Standard Guru Malaysia (SGM).*

Jackson, T., Burrus, J., Bassett, K. and Roberts, R. D. (2010), *Teacher Leadership: An Assessment Framework for an Emerging Area of Professional Practice*. ETS Research Report Series, 2010: i–41. doi:10.1002/j.2333-8504.2010.tb02234.x

Katzenmeyer, M., & Moller, G. (2009). *Awakening the sleeping giant: Helping teachers develop as leaders*. Corwin Press.

Lead, T. T. H. E. (2013). YourGoals. *Instructor*, 7–10.

MacBeath, J., Pedder, D., & Swaffield, S. (2007) *Improving learning how to learn : Classroom, schools and networks*. Routledge: New York

Mat Som,H., & Megat Daud, M., A., K. (2008). Globalisasi dan Cabaran Pendidikan di Malaysia [Globalization Educational Challenges in Malaysia]. *Masalah Pendidikan*, 31(1). ms. 91-101.

Ministry of Education. (2009) *Malaysia Teacher Standard.* Putrajaya: Kementerian Pelajaran Malaysia.

Mohd. Kassim, A. (2008). Pengaruh personaliti terhadap kepuasan kerja dan stress kerja guru. Jurnal Teknologi.

Mohd Noah, S. & Ahmad, J. (2005). *Pembinaan modul: Bagaimana membina modul latihan dan modul akademik.* Serdang: Penerbit UPM.

Mok, S, S. (2010). *Psikologi Pendidikan dan Pedagogi Murid dan Alam Belajar*. Kuala Lumpur. Penerbitan Multimedia Sdn. Bhd.

Moller, G. & Katzenmeyer, M.(1996). *Every teacher as a leader*. Jossey-Bass: San Farancisco.

Muijs, D., Chapman, C., &Armstrong, P. (2013). Can Early Careers Teachers Be Teacher Leaders? A Study of Second-year Trainees in the Teach First Alternative Certification Programme. *Educational Management Administration & Leadership, 41*(6), 767–781.

Nunnally, J.C. & Bernstein, I. H. (1994). *Psychometric theory*. New York: McGraw-Hill.

Phelps, P.,H. (2008*)* Helping Teachers Become Leaders. *The Clearing House: A Journal Of Educational Strategies, Issues And Ideas*, 81,(3)

Poekert, P. (2012). Teacher leadership and professional development: examining links between two concepts central to school improvement. *Professional Development in Education*, 38(2) ms. 169-188.

Roberts, S. M., & Pruitt, E. Z. (2009). *Schools as professional learning communities: Collaborative activities and strategies for professional development*. Thousand Oaks: Corwin Press.

Rovere (2013). *Teacher Leadership in Professional Learning Communities such as Networks*,York Region District School Board

Sharratt, L., and Fullan, M. (2009). Realization -*The Change Imperative for Deepening District-Wide Reform*.California: Corwin Press.

Tamuri, A., H., Mahmud, Z., & Bari, S. (2005). Permasalahan pelajar-pelajar fakir miskin di daerah Sabak Bernam. *Journal Pendidikan Malaysia*, *30*, 21-33.

Teacher Leadership Exploratory Consortium (2011). *Teacher leader model standards* [online].Available from: http://www.teacherleaderstandards.org [Accessed 10 February 2012].

York-Barr, J., & Duke, K. (2004*). What do we know about teacher leadership? Findings from two decades of scholarship*. Review of Educational Research, 74,255–316.

THE COMMUNICATION PREFERENCES OF COLLEGIATE STUDENTS

Joan Ann Swanson[1], Susan L. Renes[2] and Anthony T. Strange[3]
[1]*Skidmore College, Saratoga Springs, NY, USA*
[2]*University of Alaska Fairbanks, Fairbanks, Alaska, USA*
[3]*Wayland Baptist University, Plainview, Texas, USA*

ABSTRACT

This paper presents findings on communication preferences of college students (N=1986) related to academic and non-academic purposes. This study also examines the use of technological tools which influence student communication preferences. Findings indicate a preference for face-to-face interactions despite the heavy utilization of technological devices. Educational implications are shared which challenge educators to incorporate communication involving not only reading or hearing others, but using tools for technological interactions to also view others, thus creating situations utilizing face-to-face encounters via those tools.

KEYWORDS

Communication, College Students, Preferences, Technology

1. INTRODUCTION

An estimated 20.6 million students will enter degree-granting postsecondary institutions in the United States in the fall of 2018 (National Center for Education Statistics, 2017). Each of these individuals will communicate in some fashion for academic related purposes with educational administrators, faculty and students, and as well as communicating with many others for personal purposes. A majority of these students in institutions of higher education today were born into a generation immersed in technology and thus are referred to as digital natives, digital learners, and digital residents (Gutiérrez-Porlán et al, 2018; White & Le Cornu, 2011; Prensky, 2001).

Today's technological environment has not only greatly influenced how our society communicates; technology has also redefined learning and educational opportunities in many ways. In the academic realm, it is of immense importance to recognize and reconcile college student communication needs and preferences, and how they should impact corresponding educational practices.

For the purposes of this paper, communication is defined as the collaborative transmission of information between individuals through a common verbal or nonverbal system based upon an understanding of their strengths and limitations (Munodawafa, 2008). This collaborative process can be accomplished in a multitude of ways and may be enhanced through the use of technological tools. For the sake of learning situations, communication is the key venue with which messages are disseminated, whether written, spoken, or through non-verbal means. With the rapid proliferation of technological communication tools, colleges and instructors can potentially connect with students anytime and anywhere. Colleges need to stay abreast of the most effective ways to communicate with today's college students.

2. LITERATURE REVIEW

With the onslaught of potential ways to communicate, administrators and instructors struggle to know the most effect means by which to relay messages and important details to collegiate students. These students represent individuals who most likely own and use mobile devices, yet utilize a multitude of platforms from which messages could potentially be disseminated. Collegiate communication specialists state that relying on only one method of communication to college students can result in messages not being received; thus a growing trend now is to additionally utilize Facebook, Twitter, Pinterest, and other forms of social media (Mangan, 2012).

Additionally, preferences and patterns for use of communication devices may vary a great deal among college students. Even though most have grown up in a digital age, their competencies may vary. As this study seeks to understand communication preferences and patterns of college students, it also acknowledges that not all students are the same, and adjustments may be needed for varied levels of competence related to communication tools and methods.

2.1 Communication and Technology

The use of technological tools has become so wide spread that these tools permeate daily functioning. The Pew Research Center reports (2018) that 95% of American adults own a cellphone and 77% own a smartphone. This trend of mobile device ownership has become a key factor in communication modes today, not only for simple conversation, but as a means to access the Internet and its accompanying vast variety of communication avenues including social media outlets. Perrin and Duggan (2015) report 96% of 18-29 year olds use the Internet daily. Additionally, Pew reports three quarters of adults in the United States own desktop or laptop computers.

In 2010 and then again in 2013, Cassidy and colleagues (2014) investigated the trends in higher education student usage of emerging technologies, they noted the increasing variety in technological tools as well as the utilization and dependence on technology in education. These technologies expand the options for choosing modes of communication.

2.2 Communication Competence and Purpose

Communication often occurs in contexts that may overlap. There are also ramifications when communication is unsuccessful, such as embarrassment, disruption in a relationship, and misunderstandings. When technological tools enter the communication equation, Conole and colleagues (2008) found students select technologies they feel comfortable with to meet their learning needs and rely upon those technologies for their interactions as well. This supports the concept that personalization and a sense of control build toward communication competence while using familiar tools for communication purposes.

Often communication choices, even if they are influenced by available tools, are also dependent upon the purpose for such communication. In an educational setting, the way a course is delivered (face-to-face, blended, or online) happens through some form of communication (speaking in a classroom, on-line with live videos or chat, or through information disseminated via a computer). In each of these instructional situations, communication between the instructor and the students is a key element in the learning process. Conole et al, (2008) remark about the extent to which students are now capitalizing on the social affordances of technology to communicate and build peer support. Students may have an opportunity to choose how to interact and communicate in these situations or it may be dictated to them by the instructor.

2.2.1 Academic Situations

Recent technological developments provide students with a rich variety of alternatives for interaction and communication in relation to learning; and a flexibility of use which enables them to take control of their learning (Conole et al, 2008). However, the purpose of the communication may impact the preferred method of communicating. When examining communication preferences of students involved in Massive Open Online Courses (MOOCs), Zhang et al, (2016) found students overwhelmingly preferred asynchronous text-based posts (45%) to text-based chats which were synchronous (38%) or video- and audio- based conversations (15%). Chang and colleagues (2015) additionally sought to understand student preferences related to instructor communication in online courses in light of new technological developments. They found 97% of their study participants preferred communication through email and secondly (77%) through a course learning management system. These studies demonstrate students preferred communication in computer-mediated courses to be more distant, and they especially valued communication with the instructor the most. However, these studies reflect investigation involving online course delivery. There seems to be a lack of such investigation for blended and traditional course formats.

2.2.2 Non-Academic Situations

After completing a systematic review of communication technology, Hessel and Dworkin (2017) note research gaps in the study of the manner in which emerging adults communicate. However, there is no argument or lack of evidence that today's college student is operating in a fast-paced, media saturated environment with unlimited options for communication. Research conducted by Chang and colleagues (2015) revealed that many collegiate students do communicate frequently via social media but more frequently check email. Regardless of the mode, one outstanding finding concerning college students is that staying connected is central (Robinson, Stubberud, & Anton, 2012). Mobile devices are a key part of that connection, however, the mode for the communication may vary (e.g. texting, messaging, talking, chat, social networking, emailing). Communication methods have now been found to be influenced by immediacy and mobility (Baskin & Barker, 2004; Robinson, 2011) with the most preference given to modes where communication can be accomplished quickly. Despite being in a technologically rich environment, when surveyed, researchers report many college students indicate a preference for face-to-face communication especially involving personal relationships (Morreale et al, 2015).

2.3 Theory for Communication Preferences and Choices

The construction of communication preferences and communication choices can be viewed from several theoretical lenses. According to Hoeffler & Ariely (1999), two aspects of experience impact preferences – their intensiveness and extensiveness. As college students have an increased amount and breadth of experience with any given mode of communication they will naturally have a propensity to prefer that mode. However, Glasser (1999) contends that our behavioral choices are based upon meeting certain needs (power, love and belonging, freedom, fun, and survival). In this sense, students will choose to communicate in manners that will accomplish what they need given that particular situation. Often times this looks differently in academic and non-academic situations because the purpose for the communication differs. Learning is often socially mediated (Vygotsky et al, 1980). Communication is a key part of social interactions and occurs within multiple cultural contexts. Communication is additionally influenced by opportunities afforded by choice (Glasser, 1999) such as a technological tool. Individuals can then choose how they communicate in any given situation. In summary, preferences for communication will be chosen because they align with a particular purpose within a given context, and will be based upon experiences and needs, as well as involve social mediation (Figure 1).

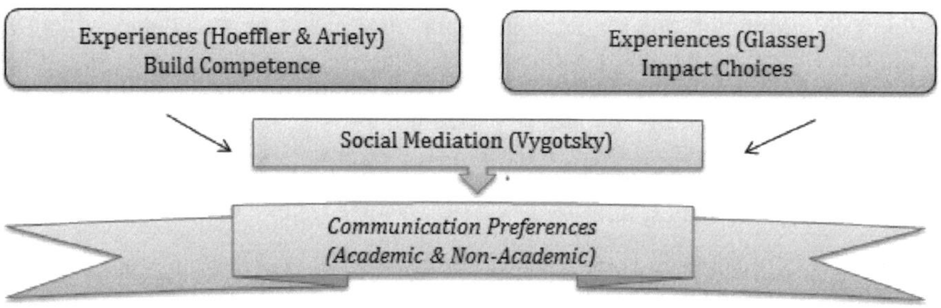

Figure 1. Theoretical lenses for communication preferences

The purpose of this study is to better understand the communication-related preferences of collegiate students and how those preferences and use patterns are affected by student interactions with technological tools. The importance of this understanding of student communication is to then provide awareness to educators of preferred and enhanced communication and learning opportunities. The following research questions guided this study:

1) What are the patterns for preferred communication for college students?
2) Do the technological preferences of college students affect their communication preferences and practices?

3. METHOD

This study was descriptive comparative and utilized survey methodology in which a sampling of the college student population in the United States was gathered through a cross-sectional design (Shaughnessy, Zechmeister, & Jeanne, 2011) to study the prevalence of college student communication patterns and preferences. This paper is part of a larger study that expanded upon previous work comparing college students' academic and non-academic technology use (Swanson & Walker, 2015). The study follows survey methodology suggestions of Busha and Harter (1980) seeking representative samples of collegiate experiences but also had the goal of increased demographic data enhancing comparative analysis.

3.1 Participants

Participants in this study included a cross section of college students (N=1,986) from four coeducational institutions in the northeastern, southeastern, southwestern, and northwestern regions of the United States (Table 1). One of the institutions was a private college only serving undergraduates with the other three institutions enrolling students in undergraduate through doctoral programs. Of the latter three institutions, one was private and the other two public. Males in this study represented 31% of the total participants while females made up 65% and another 4% indicated other or preferred not to answer. The participant age range in years varied from students under 18 years (1%), 18-26 years (53%), to over 27 years (44%), and an additional 2% preferred not to answer. While most traditional undergraduate institutions target emerging adults who are considered to be 18-26 years of age, many institutions serve students well beyond the defined emerging adult age range.

Table 1. Comparison of survey respondents' enrollment by percent

Institution	Gender		International	Emer. Adult	Coursework			
	M	F			Traditional	Blended	Online	Other
A - private	25.5	72.8	**	100 99	1		0	0
B – public	21.1	75.7	2*	74	73.9	30.9	14.1	5.9
C - private	40.7	58.7	2*	22	31.5	40.4	35.4	0.6
D - public	32.2	65.7	5*	48	48.4	28.7	31.9	4.8
Total	31	65	≥9	53	63.2	25.3	81.4	2.8

Note: *Estimate as some preferred not to answer this;**Citizenship was not asked for at this institution.

The cultural and ethnic diversity of these participants was broadly composed of African American (8%), Asian (5 %), European American (68%), Hispanic (11%), American Indian/Alaskan Native (8%), other (4%), and 6% preferring not to answer. Students reported citizenship representing 40 difference countries; however 89% were from the United States, 3% international, 2% of dual citizenship and 5% preferring not to answer. Lastly, students identified 33 languages as their first language, in addition to English, but 54 students, 3% of the total respondents, did not choose to share their first language.

3.2 Survey

The data collection instrument for this project was a self-report, anonymous Internet survey administered using Survey Monkey following approval of Internal Review Boards from all four institutions. Email invitations to participate in the survey were sent to students at all four institutions with a 9% return, providing a yield of 1,986 participants. The survey was comprised of 21 questions which sought both demographic information about the students as well as their technological preferences and use patterns. Students were asked to indicate time spent using technological devices and for what purpose. They were also asked specifically to rank their preferences for academic and non-academic communication. The format of these questions included check-off boxes, ranking for Likert-typed scaled responses, and open-ended response boxes.

4. RESULTS

Based upon the survey results of a cross sectional sample of college students in the United States, the following research questions were addressed regarding communication preferences and patterns. A more precise analysis was achieved by collecting data about communication preferences separately from technological tool use. These are related but different points of analysis.

4.1 What are the Patterns of Preferred Communication for College Students?

The survey results indicated that collegiate students preferred the following technological devices: the mobile/cell phone, the personal computer, an institutional computer, and an iPad/tablet (Figure 2). The use of these devices was then broken down into segments and analyzed for frequency of use: daily, weekly, and never used. Additionally, presentation and storage or sharing tools were used almost exclusively for academics. YouTube, online news, and TED talks were frequently used both academically and non-academically. Social media, blogs, Google Maps and games were utilized mostly for non-academic purposes.

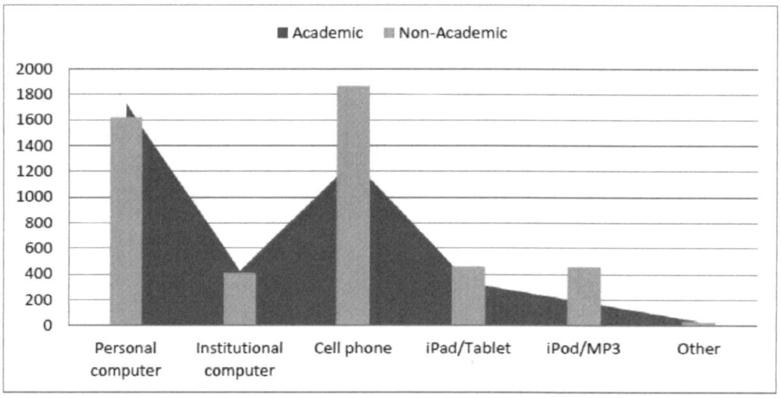

Figure 2. Preferred technological tools by collegiate students

One factor that impacts both academic and non-academic related communication is the comfort level students have using technology. When experiences increase in breadth with a particular technological tool, their comfort level and competence is likely to increase. The more students use a tool, which meets their specific needs, the more likely they are to frequently turn to that tool and will be able to transfer communication skills between academic and non-academic situations. Students in this study reported between 25 and 100% of their non-academic time involves technology, and 50 to 100% of their time related to academics involves technology.

4.2 Do the Technological Preferences of College Students affect their Communication Preferences and Practices?

Academic and non-academic communication preferences patterns in college students can first be understood by analyzing the modes of communication most frequently utilized by this population. Individuals in this study who rated traditional landline phone use high for academic communication were 64% more likely to rate landline use high for non-academic communication, 40% less likely to refrain from texting for non-academic communication, 25% less likely to use social media for academic communication, 15% less likely to use social media personally, and 24% more likely to use postal communication. The use of a traditional landline phone likely reflects the varied demographic of the ages of today's college students.

Most participants in this study indicated daily use of a personal computer as well as a mobile phone for both academic and non-academic use. A large number of students report using institutional owned computers on a weekly basis for academic use, while half of the respondents never reported using an iPad or tablet. Communication involving a computer or mobile phone would then be supported naturally as a communication preference for either academic or non-academic use because of the depth and breadth that comes from using that tool daily and it can serve to fulfil both academic and non-academic needs. Communication then utilizing these devices supports the most preferred academic mode of communication; email since email can be accessed with these devices.

However, as indicated in the survey results, students across all four institutions and regions of the United States highly prefer in-person communication for both academic and non-academic purposes (Figure 3). The collegiate student demographics did have some additional impact on communication choices. For example, emerging adults were 13.8% less likely to want to use a landline for communicating academic purposes. Modes of communication involving the digital technology may be assumed to be preferred or favored by digital natives, yet, emerging adults who were 18-25 years of age, had a positive correlation with preference for in-person communication $r(1893) = .227$, $p < .01$, $R2=.052$.

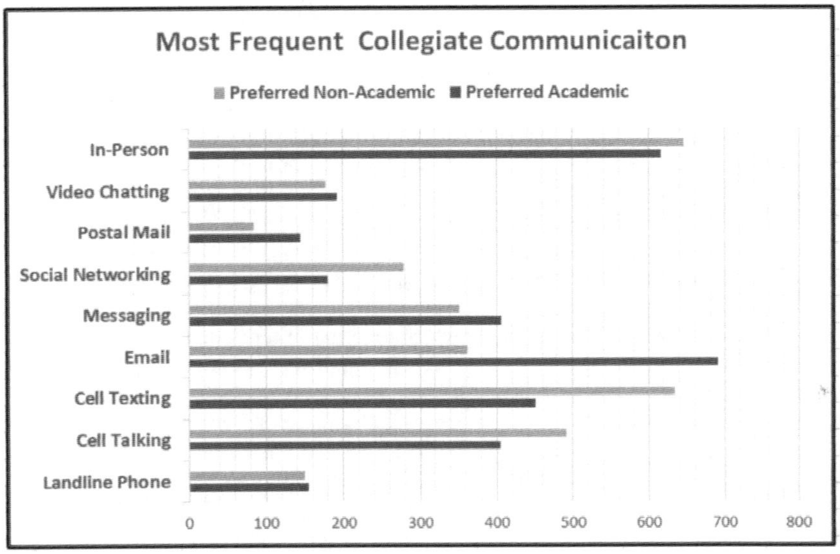

Figure 3. Most frequently used collegiate communication disaggregated by academic and non-academic purposes

5. DISCUSSION AND CONCLUSION

These results support previous work which found that collegiate students prefer face-to-face communication in most situations (Morreale et al. 2015). However, most college students heavily use technological tools to communicate. For example, academic communication is most preferred via email (Figure 3), followed by cell texting and messaging. Although many campuses are using Facebook, Twitter, and other modes of social media, these are not as highly preferred modes to receive message for academic purposes. The communication modes involving email, texting, talking, messaging, and social networking can all be accomplished via a mobile phone and often personal computer if it is a laptop. This explains why the computer, personal and institutional, ranked in the top three for most used technological devices.

The purpose of this study was to investigate college student communication preferences and one significant and unexpected finding relates to the hesitancy of students in sharing information that communicates ethnicity and country of origin. This finding may reflect a hesitancy to communicate for fear of repercussions surrounding the current political state in the United States relating to immigration. This finding reinforces the socio-cultural role in interactions impacting student communication preferences and the role that the purpose for such communication may hold.

With the understanding of how heavily mobile phones and mobile devices are being utilized by college students, it makes sense to consider more innovative ways to communicate and instruct using these tools. However, it also makes sense to establish an understanding that there are preferred types of communication associated with such tools.

The reported lack of innovative academic uses of varied technological resources may relate to collegiate instructor's lack of incorporation of such technology into their courses. Similarly, students may not indicate a preference for certain tools or modes of communication in academic realms simply because of a not having experienced the use of such tools for academic communication.

Students across all four institutions and regions of the United States who participated in this survey overwhelmingly indicated a preference for face-to-face communication. While there are some advantages of electronic communication, such being able to correspond from a distance, and the communication being immediate, accessible and affordable; however there are also communicative disadvantages such as missing face-to-face cues like body language and voice tone (Carter & Werts, 2015).

Many factors need to be considered when choosing communication modes involving college students. Traditional educational settings, where students and instructors are face-to face, are not always feasible or optimal. However, because of technological developments, there are alternatives and possibilities involving bringing face-to-face types of experiences to academic communication. Students and instructors can communicate via a screen and still view the other person they are speaking with. This can be accomplished by web conferencing types of communication or even using applications that provide face-time with a mobile device. Understanding the importance of this type of communication to learners should influence how courses, including on-line courses, incorporate elements where face-to-face conversation can occur.

Understanding that communication is an essential, socially mediated process for collegiate students should provide the impetus for instructors to seek to explore and understand communication preferences within the context of academic and non-academic realms. Students indicate daily and weekly use for online resources yet still highly value face-to-face communication. Technology is here to stay and is continuously evolving. Educators and researchers need to value the importance of accessing and disseminating information yet understand the significance and role of in-person communications. Additionally, educators need to choose modes of communication with students and technology that best meets the educational skills, competencies and needs of their students Preferences for both academic and non-academic communications will be impacted by those students' breadth of experience, the competence they have built with particular modes of communication and additionally the purposes for specific communications. Student communication preferences will continue to develop thus making continued investigation significant.

REFERENCES

Baskin, C. and Barker, M., 2004. Scoping social presence and social context cues to support knowledge construction in an ICT rich environment. *Proceedings of 2004 AARE Conference*. Melbourne, Victoria. Retrieved from http://www.aare.edu.au/04pap/bas04434.pdf

Busha, C. H. and Harter, S. P., 1980. *Research methods in librarianship: Techniques and interpretation*. Orlando, FL: Academic Press.

Carter, L. C., and Werts, N., 2015. Intimacy in the Electronic Age. *Journal of Health Education Teaching Techniques, 2*(1), 16-24.

Cassidy, E. D. et al, 2014. Higher education and emerging technologies: Shifting trends in student usage. *The Journal of Academic Librarianship, 40*, 124-133. doi.org/10.1080/03634523.2014.978799

Chang, C. et al, 2015. You've got mail: Student preferences of instructor communication in online courses in an age of advancing technologies. *Journal of Educational Technology Development and Exchange, 8*(1), 39-37. doi.org/10.18785/jetde.0801.03

Conole, G. et al, 2008. 'Disruptive technologies', 'pedagogical innovation': What's new? Findings from an in-depth study of students' use and perception of technology. *Computers & Education, 50*, 511-524.

Glasser, W. 1999. *Choice theory: A new psychology of personal freedom.* New York, NY: HarperPerennial.

Gutiérrez-Porlán, I. et al, 2018. Strategies for the communication and collaborative online work by university students. *Comunicar, 26*(54), 91-99. doi:10.3916/C54-2018-09

Hessel, H. and Dworkin, J., 2017. Emerging adults' use of communication technology with family members: a systematic review. *Adolescent Research Review.* doi: 10.1007/s40894-017-0064-1

Hoeffler S. and Ariely, D. 1999. Constructing stable preferences: A look into dimensions of experience and their impact on preference stability. *Journal of Consumer Psychology 8*(2),113-139. doi: 10.1207/s15327663jcp0802_01

Mangan, K., 2012. As students scatter online, colleges try to keep up. *The Chronicle of Higher Education*. Retrieved from: https://www.chronicle.com/article/Digitally-Savvy-Students-Play/134224

Morreale, S. et al, 2015. First-year college students' attitudes toward communication technologies and their perceptions of communication competence in the 21st Century, *Communication Education, 64*(1), 107-131. doi:10.1080/03634523.2014.978799

Munodawafa, D. 2008. Communication: Concepts, practice and challenges. *Health Education Research, 23*(1), 369-370. doi.org/10.1093/her/cyn024

National Center for Education Statistics, 2017. Enrollment in elementary, secondary, and degree-granting postsecondary institutions, by level and control of institution, enrollment level, and attendance status and sex of student: Selected years, fall 1990 through fall 2026. *Digest of Education Statistics, Table 105.20.* Retrieved from https://nces.ed.gov/programs/digest/d16/tables/dt16_105.20.asp?current=yes

Perrin, A. and Duggan, M., 2015. *Americans' internet access: 2000-2015.* Pew Research Center. Retrieved from http://www.pewinternet.org/files/2015/06/2015-06-26_internet-usage-across-demographics-discover_FINAL.pdf

Pew Research Center, 2018. *Mobile fact sheet.* Retrieved from http://www.pewinternet.org/fact-sheet/mobile/

Prensky, M., 2001. Digital natives, digital immigrants. *On the Horizon, 9*(5), 1-6. doi.org/10.1108/10748120110424816

Robinson, S., 2011. *MAT2R model.* Retrieved from https://blogs.psu.edu/mt4/mt.cgi? mode=view& type=entry&id=357413&blog id=l 1032

Robinson, S. and Stubberud, H. A., 2012. Communication preferences among university students. *Academy of Educational Leadership Journal, 16*(2), 105-113. Retrieved from https://search.proquest.com/docview/1037692095?accountid=13894

Shaughnessy, J. et al, 2011. *Research methods in psychology (9th ed.).* pp. 161–175. New York, NY: McGraw Hill.

Small, F. et al, 2012. Teacher communication preferred over peer interaction. *Journal of International Education in Business, 5*(2), 114-128. doi. 10.1108/18363261211281735

Survey Monkey Inc. 1999. Retrieved from www.surveymonkey.com

Swanson, J. A. and Walker, E., 2015. Academic versus non-academic emerging adult college student technology use. *Technology, Knowledge, and Learning, 20*(2), 147-158.

Vygotsky, L. S. et al, 1980. *Mind in society: Development of higher psychological processes*. Cambridge, MA: Harvard University Press.

White, D. and Le-Cornu, A., 2011. Visitors and residents: A new typology for online engagement. *First Monday, 16*(9). doi.org/10.5210/fm.v16i9.3171

Zhang, Q. et al, 2016. Exploring the communication preferences of MOOC learners and the value of preference-based groups: Is grouping enough? *Educational Technology Research & Development, 64*(4), 809-837.

ONLINE PROFESSIONAL LEARNING COMMUNITIES FOR DEVELOPING TEACHERS' DIGITAL COMPETENCES

Sabine Seufert, Josef Guggemos and Eric Tarantini
University of St.Gallen, Guisanstr 1a, 9010 St.Gallen, Switzerland

ABSTRACT

Digital transformation shapes the educational system in many ways. It has also far-reaching implications for teachers as their job description may fundamentally change in the future. In this light, it is important 1) to identify necessary digital competences of teachers and 2) to find ways to foster those competences in an efficient way. By means of a literature review and expert interviews, we developed a framework of teachers' digital competences. In line with Baumert and Kunter (2006) as well as Koehler and Mishra (2009), it comprises content knowledge, pedagogical content knowledge, and pedagogical knowledge. However, these facets have extended meaning in the context of digital transformation. Moreover, our framework considers the official EU competence framework (Carretero et al., 2017) and hence covers instrumental skills and knowledge in handling digital media. We successfully validated our framework by means of structural equation modelling with a sample of 215 Swiss teachers. Utilising an Importance Performance Map Analysis, we identified competence facets that show the highest effects on the (self-reported) use of digital media and content. For efficiently fostering those facets, we will establish online professional learning communities consisting of a communication platform, webinar series, and blended learning courses.

KEYWORDS

Digital Competence, Online Professional Learning Communities

1. INTRODUCTION

One would be hard pressed to find a topic of current debate in education policy and educational practice that is as exhaustively discussed as the (proper) handling of the digital transformation (e.g. 'standing conference of the ministers of education and cultural Affairs' [KMK], 2016). A widely shared perception is that a more intensive use of digital media in the classroom will improve learning effectiveness, facilitate greater orientation to the future needs of learners, and support accompanied personality development in a digital society. The sweeping pressure to make changes is marked with a high degree of uncertainty regarding the use and benefits of digital media in schools (Bach, 2016).

Teachers addressing digital skills, such as the competent handling of online information, are often entering uncharted territory in their respective fields (media education). In this context, teachers are increasingly asking for inclusion of media-specific qualification objectives. However, the kind of competences teachers need to acquire remains somewhat vague and is largely limited to the use and operation of computer applications and digital content media (Blömeke, 2003; Blömeke, 2005). Furthermore, it is obvious that formal seminars, such as one-day training workshops on how to use ICT, are neither sufficient nor effective for developing teachers' digital competences. On the contrary, successful support initiatives to develop teachers' competence will have to be rooted in their particular context and simultaneously embedded in innovation strategies and quality development processes in their respective schools (Schneider & Mahs, 2003). The conceptualisation and design of suitable training measures for teachers requires a systematic approach to the professional development of teachers at vocational schools. Developing professional communities among teachers to underpin the benefit of learning together and from each other is of central importance (Hord, 1997). Learning communities that make use of the potential of digital information and communication are becoming increasingly important as a means of continuously fostering teachers' digital competences. However, there is a research gap in the promotion of digital competences for teachers (Büsser, 2017, p. 15). In this light, this paper focuses on two research questions:

1) How can digital competences of teachers be defined and measured?
2) How can measures and interventions to foster online professional learning communities (online PLCs) be designed and evaluated for a systematic development of teachers' digital competences?

The paper consists of three parts. In the first part, we consolidate relevant theoretical considerations. The second part outlines the research methodology and the results of the research conducted. The third and final section discusses the results of the study, implications for designing online PLCs and presents a perspective for further research.

2. REVIEW OF THE LITERATURE

2.1 Digital Competences of Teachers

Baumert and Kunter (2006) and Kunter et al. (2009, 2011) presented a highly regarded model of professional teaching competence, which comprises professional knowledge, convictions in the sense of personally biased basic orientations, values, motivational orientations, and self-regulation (for empirical findings on professional knowledge in the commercial sector, cf. Seifried and Wuttke [2015]). Professional knowledge consists of content knowledge, pedagogical content knowledge and pedagogical knowledge. This division can be traced back to Shulman (1986, 1987). Koehler and Mishra (2009) added technological aspects to these facets of professional knowledge. They include technological knowledge as a new, disparate type of knowledge.

Current technological developments, such as artificial intelligence and cognitive computing, are flanked by fundamental questions about which digital competences teachers need to possess.

Moreover, approaches for developing media skills (Tulodziecki, 1995; Baake, 1999; Aufenanger, 2008; Schorb, 2009; Mayrberger, 2012) might be taken into account. In this vein, Blömeke's (2003) model is an approach that refers to teacher training. It distinguishes five areas of competence: 'didactic media competence', 'educational media competence', 'socialisation-related competence', 'school development competence', and 'personal media competence'. The demands faced by a vocational school in the light of ever-increasing digitalisation cannot be tackled through the efforts of single individuals. In such a case, the individual teachers would quickly feel overworked (Seufert & Scheffler, 2016). In the light of digital transformation, appropriate advisory and organisational knowledge regarding cooperation in teams and networks can thus be regarded as a relevant facet of competence for the joint development of teaching and schools.

For vocational education and training, the official EU competence framework (Carretero et al., 2017) is leading the way because it defines cross-vocational digital competences (in the sense of "digital literacies"), which can be specified in the Europass European Skills Passport[1] in the form of self-evaluations. The KMK Strategy 2016 follows a similar path, identifying six areas of competence for education in the digital world – comparable to the EU competence framework (KMK, 2016). However, the implications for professional teaching skills have remained (as yet) ambiguous.

Empirical findings on technology-mediated learning (TML) indicate that affective-motivational characteristics of the instructor are a decisive factor influencing the educationally effective use of digital media in the classroom (Gupta & Bostorm, 2009). Teachers have widely divergent views regarding the extent to which the lessons themselves should undergo digital change (Schmid, Goetz, & Behrens, 2017).

In sum, professional competence can be conceptualised as a "bundle of occupation-related characteristics" (Voss et al., 2015, p. 4), which are central prerequisites for observable professional behaviour or ability (Shavelson, 2013; Blömeke et al., 2015). Professional knowledge is thereby acknowledged as a key aspect of professional competence (Baumert & Kunter, 2006; Voss et al., 2015). In addition, digital competences must encompass skills in the competent use of digital media and tools as well as attitudes toward digitalisation (fostering digital skills of students, digital content and use of digital media in education).

[1]The Europass aims to provide a way to present qualifications and competences in a way that is transparent and understandable throughout Europe, cf. https://europass.cedefop.europa.eu/de.

2.2 Online PLCs for the Professional Development of Teachers

Teacher training and its effectiveness is a field of research that has great untapped potential (Terhart et al., 2014; Garet et al., 2001). Currently, there are virtually no studies that demonstrate the effectiveness of measures for digital competence development (Lipowski, 2010; Lorenz et al., 2017, p. 228). According to Terhart et al. (2014, p. 517ff.), the efficacy of training measures must be considered on a case-by-case basis. Since this can be influenced by countless variables and contextual factors (class, teacher, setting, quality of training content, diverse and challenging learning opportunities for teachers, etc.), Terhart (2014) proposes that it is practically impossible to distinguish generally applicable quality standards.

Multiple studies have shown that teachers develop their skills mainly in the informal context of their professional practice, i.e. in exchange with colleagues or through individual, critical reflection (Hoekstra et al., 2009; Meirink, Meijer, Verloop, & Bergen, 2009; Jurasaite-Harbison, 2009). As a result, international research literature on teacher education and training is especially focused on "integrated learning at the workplace", which is increasingly aimed at informal learning and reflective dialogue among the teaching staff (Meirink et al., 2009). For this reason, strong learning environments are based on design principles from a socio-constructivist perspective in the context of informal learning theories. Team and community-based learning may be considered one of the most effective and predominant learning methods in this context and it is against this backdrop that the construct of the professional learning community (PLC) should be mentioned. According to Hord (1997), PLCs involve groups of teachers or the entire teaching staff at a school that are jointly and constantly seeking ways to increase the effectiveness of their teaching, sharing what they have learned, attempting to put new ideas into actual practice, systematically testing these ideas, and reflecting on them (Höfer, 2006). New competence requirements in the wake of increasing digitalisation necessitate ongoing (further) education that is marked by a high degree of speed and innovation dynamic. Teachers can no longer implement these changes individually and in isolation from one another in their day-to-day school routine. Bonsen and Rolff (2006, p. 170) therefore propose "the combination of community and professionalism" in times of turbulent change. In general, experimental testing of new approaches is risky. Hence, it requires continuity and a stable framework for developing common value patterns (Bonsen & Rolff, 2006, p. 170). Effectiveness studies on PLCs have produced key success factors: shared practice (Hord, 2004, p. 7), reflective dialogue, deprivatisation of teaching (teaching is a personal, but not a private matter), common focus on students' learning (shifting the focus from teaching to learning), and fundamentally reinforced cooperation (Newmann, 1994).

Learning communities that make use of the potential of digital information and communication media are becoming increasingly important as a means of fostering teachers' digital competences. In this regard, the relevance of virtual and online learning communities has become apparent. The conditions for their success (such as coherence, transparency, and quality of moderator performance) have been examined in numerous studies (particularly noteworthy is the meta study [comparison of 64 studies] by Wegener & Leimeister, 2012, cf. also Carlén, 2010, Hew, 2009; Carlén, 2007; Arnold, 2005; Dückert, 2003; Lazar & Preece, 2002; Seufert et al., 2002). Similar results have been obtained in studies that investigate professional learning community for the teaching profession supported by digital media (Huffman et al., 2003). The advantages of online support are clear, especially in terms of time and location flexibility for cooperation as well as the availability of knowledge gained through specific experience.

3. METHOD

3.1 Design

First, it is necessary to delineate professional competences of teachers in the context of the digital transformation. The resulting framework concept must then be systematically differentiated. For the subsequent test development phase, it is imperative to take into account the purpose of the measurement and the intended use of the results (AERA, APA, & NCME, 2014, p. 75f.). The purpose of the measurement is to assess teachers' digital skills for formative purposes. The results should serve to identify potential for improvements and to design appropriate support measures. With this in mind, we have designed a self-assessment tool that has been validated using confirmatory factor analyses. Since the aim of our research is to identify adequate professional development measures, which is within teachers' own interest, we regard a self-assessment instrument as suitable.

In collaboration with five partner schools from German-speaking Switzerland, we have developed items that capture the constructs described in section 2.1, cf. table 1. The items are measured on a 7-point rating scale. We have validated the instrument by means of 12 expert interviews. The experts show a diverse background: training representatives of companies, researcher in the field of digitalization, school principals, educational policy makers, and federation representatives. Moreover, we carried out five focus group discussions with teachers at every partner school.

We utilised an importance-performance map analysis (IPMA) (Ringle & Sarstedt, 2016) to assess teachers' competences and promising fields for improvement. This method, though not yet widely used in the PLS-SEM context, enables a clear and theoretically justified presentation of the results for a baseline evaluation. The first dimension (Importance [I]) of the importance-performance map depicts for each construct, cf. table 1, or item its impact on a previously specified construct. In our case, we utilize frequency of use (measured on a 5-point rating scale) as the target construct, cf. table 2. For instance, a value of 0.1 for "pedagogical knowledge" would indicate that an increase in this construct by one unit on the rating scale increases the expected frequency of digital media use by 0.1 units. IPMA also considers indirect effects. This enables us to identify measures that are potentially most beneficial in terms of increasing the frequency of use of digital media. The second dimension (Performance [P]) places each construct or item on a scale from 1 to 100, indicating how pronounced the construct or item is among the teachers studied. A value that is low compared to other constructs or in absolute terms may indicate a potential for improvement. When selecting interventions, the focus should be on constructs that have a comparatively strong impact on the target construct and are not (yet) close to the maximum. We discuss IPMA-results in focus group interviews with school administrations and specialist representatives from pilot schools, and focal points for fostering digital competences within the framework of an online PLC.

3.2 Instruments and Data Analysis

The final instrument for capturing teachers' digital competence consists of 86 items covering 11 constructs (10 facets of digital competences, cf. table 1 and frequency of use, cf. table 2). 215 teachers at nine Swiss vocational schools act as a sample. 50 % of them are female. On average, they are aged 45 (SD = 6) and have 18 (SD = 10) years of teaching experience. The lack of normal distribution for all items is noteworthy (Shapiro-Wilk test: $p < .05$). Overall, 3.9% missing values occurred. The absence of values does not follow any specific pattern. A Little's MCAR test performed taking into account all context variables was not significant ($\chi^2 = 3616$, $df = 3297$, $p = 1$). We also checked for outliers using Mahalanobis distances. However, we did not exclude any observation.

Table 1 provides an overview of the 10 competence facets measured by a seven-point rating scale: from "very low" to "very high" (content knowledge, pedagogical content knowledge) and from "does not apply at all" to "applies very strongly" for all other facets (see table 1):

Table 1. Facets of teachers' digital competences including sample questions

Professional knowledge (classroom level, school level) with respect to digitalisation	Instrumental skills and knowledge in handling digital media	Affective-motivational characteristics related to digitalisation
Classroom-oriented professional knowledge *Content knowledge:* 1) General knowledge about digitalisation (e.g. "My basic knowledge about decisive principles of digitalization is…") 2) Business knowledge about digitalisation (e.g. "My knowledge about digital value chains is…")	8) Digital skills: - handling digital information (e.g. "I can efficiently use search strategies to find online information"); - creating digital content (e.g. "I can create learning videos"); digital collaboration (e.g. "I can efficiently use digital communication tools"); - ensuring digital security (e.g. "I regularly check my	9) Positive attitudes (e.g. "I like using digital media/tools in my instruction") 10) Negative attitudes (e.g. "I am afraid of making mistakes when using digital media/ tools in my instruction")

Pedagogical Content knowledge: 3) Knowledge about digitalisation as a school subject (e.g. "My knowledge about teaching digital value chains is…") *Pedagogical knowledge:* 4) General knowledge of digital media (e.g. "I am able to use digital assessment tools for students' summative assessment") 5) Promoting students' interdisciplinary digital skills (e.g. "I am able to foster my students' digital skills to use online information") 6) Media didactics (e.g. "I am able to select adequate learning videos for students' knowledge creation") Professional knowledge at the school level: 7) advisory and organisational knowledge (e.g. "I am able to support my colleagues to improve professional practice in terms of digital content and digital media use")	security settings of my digital devices and/or applications"), - digital problem solving (e.g. "I can regularly keep up-to-date my skills in handling digital media/ tools); - specific applications (e.g. "I can use profession-specific applications (e.g. Office applications)"

Table 2. shows the three elements of the target construct "frequency of use". They are measured on a 5-point rating scale: never, infrequently (1-2 times per semester), occasionally (3-5 times per semester), frequently (every month), very frequently (every week).

Table 2. Target construct 'frequency of use' including sample items.

Frequency of use	Sample Items
digitalisation as a class subject (professional, interdisciplinary);	How often do you consider digital related topics in your instruction? How often do you foster students' competences when dealing with digital media (e.g. dealing with online information)?
Use of digital media for individualisation;	How often do you practice individualisation of your teaching according to the learning progress supported by digital media? How often do you practice individualisation of your teaching according to learning preferences supported by digital media?
General use of digital media	How often do you use blended learning scenarios (e.g. flipped classroom)? How often do you use digital learning arrangements in your instruction?

Overall, we consider our instrument suitable for a comprehensive and valid formative assessment of digital competences as well as for competence development among teachers.

4. RESULTS

4.1 Instruments and Data Analysis

Test validations by means of confirmatory factor analyses generally yielded good values for all eleven constructs (CFI > .980, TLI > .969, RMSEA < .093, SRMR < .036). Moreover, the measures are reliable, indicated by Cronbach's alpha and composite reliability above .80. Convergent validity is established as all standardized factor loadings exceed .7. Hence, for every construct, the average variance extracted (AVE) is greater than .5, which indicates convergent validity. Discriminant validity is ensured because the square roots of AVE are always higher than the correlations among the constructs (Fornell-Larcker criterion). Measurement invariance analyses demonstrate the instrument's suitability for assessing competence development as well as group comparisons in terms of gender, age, and teaching expertise. The findings on the prognostic validity of the instrument are positive: Frequency of use can be adequately explained using the facets of digital competence (.36 > R2 > .26).

The results of the structural equation models show that, in general, all competence facets are important for the use of digitalisation and digital media in teaching. "Negative attitudes" are the exception. This may indicate that it is not necessary to address "negative attitudes". Rather, the affective aspect of "positive attitudes" may be put into focus.

It is important to view the facets of competence in context, and to systematically foster all of them. However, developing all facets of competence at the same time would likely overtax the teaching personnel. Therefore, the next step will be to concentrate on selected competence facets within the framework of an online PLC. In line with the IPMA (baseline evaluation), these would primarily encompass the following:

- Media didactics: This facet of competence exhibits both a low self-assessment and a high level of effect on the frequency of use of digitalisation and on teaching with digital media; the findings show that digital media is primarily used for instructional knowledge acquisition (e.g. use of learning videos), but less for constructivist and cognitive processes, such as for discussion, reflection, or for forms of action-oriented teaching and learning (e.g. simulations, multimedia applications).
- Pedagogical knowledge: General, interdisciplinary knowledge of digital media also shows a rather high importance and a moderate performance. In this area, competence diagnostics with digital media in particular constitutes a knowledge gap for many teachers (this is accompanied by the relatively low values for formative and summative self-assessments in the competence facet of media didactics, which basically represents the concrete implementation level);
- Fostering students' digital skills: Teachers give the lowest rating to their ability to promote their students' knowledge acquisition of digital media. Against the requirements in vocational education and training, this finding is alarming and illustrates how pressing the need for action to develop the skills of teachers in this area is.
- Instrumental skills and knowledge in handling digital media: This competence facet also has a relatively strong effect on the use of digital content and digital media. The importance of the inclusion of digitalisation related topics in the classroom is even higher than that of the use of digital media in the classroom. A teacher who seems to be more active in the 'digital world' is more likely to recognise the necessity and become familiar with concrete application possibilities in order to integrate digitalisation topics into the classroom in a didactic manner.

In sum, media didactics has a particularly positive influence on the use of digital learning arrangements. There is potential for improvement, particularly in the digital assessment of learners' competences (summative and formative).

4.2 Developing Teachers' Digital Competences in Online PLCs

The results of the study were discussed with the school administrators of the nine schools in the sample. In this process, we addressed focal points for the ongoing promotion of digital competences within the framework of cross-school online PLCs. The design of the online PLC as a social construct for a continuous set of measures was conceptually established and access to the technological platform was regulated. Table 3 describes the online PLCs.

Table 3. Interventions for developing digital competences within online PLCs

Online PLC	Objectives	Implementation
Communication platform (continuously expanded)	Theme-based channel for digitalisation (blog with comment functionality);	Portal structure with access to online PLC
	Collection of good practices (webinar recordings, teaching materials)	Wordpress platform
"Good Practices" webinar series, approx. 2 hours per session	Moderated good practice sessions in an online setting: 5 webinars within one year; each participating school hosts one webinar	Teacher input, moderated reflection; virtual classroom (with ZOOM software)
Blended learning courses over 8 weeks	One blended learning course in one year (per intervention study), with three course components:	Three-phase concept:
	Learning with digital media (subject area "Interdisciplinary Competences")	Preparation phase (building on existing experience, providing new impetus);
	Testing with digital media (subject areas "Economy and Society", "Consolidating and Networking")	Presence phase (experimenting) and;
	Digital school development (everyday school life: joint cooperation among different places of learning)	Transfer phase with learning assignment Moodle platform (access via portal website)

5. CONCLUSION AND OUTLOOK

Our research project has produced a framework for the conceptualisation of digital competences of VET teachers in the field of business. In terms of professional knowledge, there are two building blocks of digital competences: 1) Instructional level: designing classroom situations, and 2) School level: shaping school development. Drawing on this framework model, we were able to operationalise the ten facets of digital competence in an instrument that we tested empirically in a pilot study with 215 teachers. The quality criteria of the instrument are high, allowing the results of the pilot study to be used as a baseline evaluation for subsequent research projects.

Furthermore, it was possible to acquire insight into how these digital competences can be continuously and effectively fostered among teachers by means of online PLCs. The aim is not only to examine the effectiveness of the support models, but also to explore which factors influence teachers' use of digital learning opportunities. In this way, it will also be possible to ascertain potential ways to increase the effectiveness of the support models.

For one thing, the significance of reflected documentation of effective learning episodes in the form of interactive knowledge among the faculty became evident (in which the descriptions of knowledge are differentiated into the dimensions of content knowledge, pedagogical content knowledge, and media didactics) (Mishra & Koehler, 2005; Fried, 2003). This interactive knowledge seems to be of particular relevance for restructuring and innovating teaching development in terms of self-produced knowledge coupling in the area of practice (Fried, 2003). Since the questionnaire for the framework model of digital competences of teachers in the field of business is already very extensive, the open questions for the qualitative survey of interactive knowledge in the following three contexts were not yet included: 1) Any teacher in any subject, 2) A colleague teaching the same subject and 3) An individual learning episode. These areas of knowledge are to be included in a follow-up project as a further facet of competence based on a qualitative research design. This also offers the advantage that institutional framework conditions (e.g. support structures, cultural development at schools) can be analysed using a qualitative evaluation design.

The main limitation of our study is the reliance on self-assessments. This could result in two different types of bias: Teachers deliberately give inaccurate answers or are not able to make a valid assessment. We regard the first bias as unlikely because the survey was voluntary and anonymous. Irrespective of this, based on the impressions gained during the qualitative phase of the research project, we can attest that the teachers are highly self-reflective. This indicates that the second type of bias may also be inapplicable.

The results of the empirically validated instrument for assessing the digital competences of VET teachers and the baseline evaluation involving 215 teachers provide a very good basis for the follow-up project. In this context, we intend to assess the online PLGs in a longitudinal study.

REFERENCES

AERA, APA, & NCME (2014). Standards for educational and psychological testing. Washington D.C.: American Educational Research Association.

Arnold, P. (2005). Kooperative Lerngemeinschaften. Gestaltungsdimensionen und -prinzipien. In Burkhard, L. & Bloh, E. (Hrsg.). *Online-Pädagogik, Band 3: Referenzmodelle und Praxisbeispiele.* Baltmannsweiler: Schneider-Verlag Hohengehren, S. 98–107.

Aufenanger, S. (1997). Medienpädagogik und Medienkompetenz. Eine Bestandsaufnahme. In: Bonn: Deutscher Bundestag (Hrsg.). *Medienkompetenz im Informationszeitalter* (S. 15-22). Bonn: Deutscher Bundestag.

Baacke, D., Kornblum, S., Lauffer, J., Mikos, L. & Thiele, G. A. (Hrsg.) (1999). *Handbuch Medien. Medienkompetenz - Modelle und Projekte.* Bonn: Bundeszentrale für Politische Bildung.

Bach, A. (2016). Nutzung von digitalen Medien an berufsbildenden Schulen – Notwendigkeit, Rahmenbedingungen, Akzeptanz und Wirkungen. In: J. Seifried, J., S. Seeber, S. & B. Ziegler, B. (Hrsg.), *Jahrbuch der berufs- und wirtschaftspädagogischen Forschung 2016* (S. 107-123). Opladen: Verlag Barbara Budrich.

Baumert, J. & Kunter, M. (2006). Stichwort: Professionelle Kompetenz von Lehrkräften. *Zeitschrift für Erziehungswissenschaft, 9*(4), 469-520.

Blömeke, S. (2003). Neue Medien in der Lehrerausbildung. Zu angemessenen (und unangemessenen) Zielen und Inhalten des Lehramtsstudiums. *Zeitschrift für Theorie und Praxis der Medienbildung.* 1-29.

Blömeke, S. (2005). Medienpädagogische Kompetenz. In A. Frey, R. S. Jäger, & U. Renold (Eds.), *Berufspädagogik: Bd. 5. Kompetenzdiagnostik. Theorien und Methoden zur Erfassung und Bewertung von beruflichen Kompetenzen* (S.76–97). Landau: Empirische Pädagogik e.V.

Blömeke, S., Gustafsson, J.-E., & Shavelson, R. J. (2015). Beyond dichotomies: Competence viewed as a continuum. *Zeitschrift für Psychologie, 223*(1), 3–13.

Bonsen, M. & Rolff, H. (2006). Professionelle Lerngemeinschaften von Lehrerinnen und Lehrern. *Zeitschrift für Pädagogik*, 52(2), 167-184.

Büsser, B. (2017). Zwischen digital und analog. In*: Bildungsdirektion Kanton Zürich (Hrsg.) (2017). Schulblatt 6/2017 - Digitalisierung. Wo stehen Schulen.* Zürich: Staempfli.

Carlén, U. & Jobring, O. (2007). Perspectives on the sustainability of activities within online learning communities. In: *International Journal of Web Based Communities 3 (1)*, 100–113.

Carlén, U. (2010). *A professional community goes online. A study of an online learning community in medicine* (Doctoral Dissertation, Department of Applied Information Technology). Gothenburg: University of Gothenburg.

Carretero, S., Vuorikari, R.. & Punie, Y. (2017). *DigComp 2.1: The Digital Competence Framework for Citizens with eight proficiency levels and examples of use.* Luxembourg: European Union (EU).

Dückert, S. (2003). Treffpunkt Wissensnetzwerk. In: *Wissensmanagement 8*, S. 20–22.

Fried, L. (2003). Pädagogisches Professionswissen als Form und Medium der Lehrerbildungskommunikation - empirische Suchbewegungen. *Zeitschrift für Pädagogik, 49*(1), 112-126.

Gupta, S. & Bostrom, R. P. (2009). Technology-Mediated Learning. A Comprehensive Theoretical Model. In: *Journal of the Association for Information Systems (Volume 10, Issue 9)*, 686–714.

Hew, K. F. (2009). Determinants of success for online communities. An analysis of three communities in terms of members' perceived professional development. In: *Behaviour & Information Technology 28 (5)*, 433–445.

Hoekstra, A., Korthagen, F., Brekelmans, M., Beijaard, D., & Imants, J. (2009). Experienced teachers' informal workplace learning and perceptions of workplace conditions. *Journal of Workplace Learning, 21*(4), 276-298.

Höfer, C. (2006). Unterrichtsentwicklung als Schulentwicklung. In H. Buchen & H.-G. Rolff (Eds.), Professionswissen Schulleitung (S. 752-788).

Hord, S. M. (1997). Professional learning communities. Communities of continuous inquiry and improvement. Austin: Southwest Educational Development Laboratory.

Huffman, J. B. & Hipp, K. K. (2003). *Restructuring schools as professional learning communities.* Lanham, MD: Scarecrow Education.

Jurasaite-Harbison, E. (2009). Teachers' workplace learning within informal contexts of school cultures in the United States and Lithuania. *Journal of Workplace Learning, 21(4),* 299-321.

KMK (2016). *Strategie der Kultusministerkonferenz „Bildung in der digitalen Welt".* Abgerufen unter http://www.kmk.org/fileadmin/Dateien/pdf/PresseUndAktuelles/2016/Entwurf_KMK-Strategie_Bildung_in_der_digitalen_Welt.pdf.

Koehler, M. J. & Mishra, P. (2009). What Is Technological Pedagogical Content Knowledge? *Contemporary Issues in Technology and Teacher Education, 9*(1), 60-70.

Kunter, M., Baumert, J., Blum, W., Klusmann, U., Krauss, S. & Neubrand, M. (2011). *Professionelle Kompetenz von Lehrkräften. Ergebnisse des Forschungsprogramms* COACTIV. Münster: Waxmann.

Kunter, M., Klusmann, U., & Baumert, J. (2009). Professionelle Kompetenz von Mathematiklehrkräften: Das COACTIV-Modell. In Zlatkin-Troitschanskaia, O., Beck, K., Sembill, D., Nickolaus, R. & Mulder, R. (Hrsg.), *Lehrprofessionalität. Bedingungen, Genese, Wirkungen und ihre Messung* (S. 153–166). Weinheim: Beltz.

Lazar, J. & Preece, J. (2002). Social considerations in online communities. Usability, sociability, and success factors. In Van Oostendorp, H. (Hrsg.). *Cognition in the digital world.* Mahwah, NJ: Lawrence Earlbaum.

Lipowski, F. (2010). Lernen im Beruf. Empirische Befunde zur Wirksamkeit von Lehrerfortbildung. In: Müller, F. Eichenberger, A., Lüders, M. & Mayr, J. (Hrsg.). *Lehrerinnen und Lehrer lernen. Konzepte und Befunde zur Lehrerfortbildung.* Münster: Waxmann.

Lorenz, R., Bos, W., Endberg, M., Eickelmann, B., Grafe, S. & Vahrenhold, J. (Hrsg.) (2017). Schule digital – der Länderindikator 2017. Schulische Medienbildung in der Sekundarstufe I mit besonderem Fokus auf MINT-Fächer im Bundesländervergleich und Trends von 2015 bis 2017. Münster: Waxmann Verlag.

Mayrberger, K. (2012). Medienpädagogische Kompetenz im Wandel – Vorschlag zur Gestaltung des Übergangs in der Lehrerbildung am Beispiel mediendidaktischer Kompetenz. In: R. Schulz-Zander (Hrsg.), *Jahrbuch Medienpädagogik* (S. 389–412). Wiesbaden: Springer VS.

Meirink, J., Meijer, P., Verloop, N., & Bergen, T. (2009). How do teachers learn in the workplace? An examination of teacher learning activities. *European Journal of Teacher Education, 32*(3), 209-224.

Mishra, P., & Koehler, M. J. (2005). What happens when teachers design educational technology? The development of technological pedagogical content knowledge. *Journal of Educational Computing Research, 32*(2), 131-152.

Newmann, F. M. (1994). School-wide Professional Community. *Issues in Restructuring Schools, 6*, 1-3.

Ringle, C. M., & Sarstedt, M. (2016). Gain more insight from your PLS-SEM results. *Industrial Management & Data Systems, 116*(9), 1865–1886.

Schmid, U., Goertz, L., Behrens, J. (2017) *Monitor Digitale Bildung. Die Schulen im digitalen Zeitalter*. Gütersloh: Bertelsmann Stiftung. Abgerufen unter http://www.bertelsmann-stiftung.de/digi-monitor.

Schneider, P. & Mahs, C. (2003). Kontinuierliche und Kooperative Selbstqualifikation und Selbstorganisation (KoKoSS) der Ausbilder. In: Euler, D. (2003). *Handbuch der Lernortkooperation. Band 2: Praktische Erfahrungen* (S. 298-312). Bielefeld: Bertelsmann.

Schorb, B. (2009). Gebildet und kompetent. Medienbildung statt Medienkompetenz? *merz, 53*(5), 50-56.

Seifried, J. & Wuttke, E. (2015). *Was wissen und können (angehende) Lehrkräfte an kaufmännischen Schulen? – Empirische Befunde zur Modellierung und Messung der professionellen Kompetenz von Lehrkräften.* In: Schumann, S. & Eberle, F. (Hrsg.). Ökonomische Kompetenzen in Schule, Ausbildung und Hochschule. Empirische Pädagogik, 29, H. 1, Themenheft. Landau, 125-145.

Seufert, S. & Scheffler, N. (2016). Developing Digital Competences of Vocational Teachers. *International Journal of Digital Literacy and Digital Competence (ILDLDC), 7*(1), ISSN 1947-3944.

Seufert, S.; Lechner, U. & Stanoevska, K. (2002). A Reference Model for Online Learning Communities. *International Journal on E-Learning (IJEL), 1*(1), 43-54.

Shavelson, R. J. (2013). On an Approach to Testing and Modeling Competence. *Educational Psychologist, 48*(2), 73–86.

Shulman, L. S. (1987). Knowledge and Teaching. Foundations of the New Reform. In: *Harvard Educational Review* 57(1), 1-23.

Shulman, L. S. (1996). *Those Who Understand: Knowledge Growth in Teaching.* In: Educational Researcher, 15(2), 4-14.

Terhart, E., Bennewitz, H. & Rothland, M. (2014). *Handbuch der Forschung zum Lehrerberuf (2. Auflage).* Münster/New York: Waxmann Verlag.

Tuldoziecki, G. (1998). *Entwicklung von Medienkompetenz als Erziehungs- und Bildungsaufgabe.* Pädagogische Rundschau 52 (1998) 6, S. 693-709.

Voss, T., Kunina-Habenicht, O. Hoehne, V., & Kunter, M. (2015). Stichwort Pädagogisches Wissen von Lehrkräften. Empirische Zugänge und Befunde. In: *Zeitschrift für Erziehungswissenschaften*, 18(2), 187–223.

SELF-ORGANIZING MAP ANALYSIS OF EDUCATIONAL SKILLS USING QUESTIONNAIRE TO UNIVERSITY STUDENTS IN COMPUTING CLASSES

Tadanari Taniguchi, Yukiko Maruyama, Daisaku Kurita and Makoto Tanaka
IT Education Center, Tokai University, 4-1-1 Kitakaname, Hiratsuka, Kanagawa 2591292, Japan

ABSTRACT

We propose developing a method to set key educational skills which students need to achieve for each class using a student self-assessment questionnaire in analytical approach. It is difficult to set key academic skills for class since there are little systematic methods to set them. The questionnaire survey with 25 educational skills was conducted to ICT classes in our university using a computer-assisted web-interviewing (CAWI) technique. The questionnaire results are analyzed using self-organizing maps (SOMs). A SOM is used to visualize the similarity relations between educational skills based on student's consciousness. We show that 25 skills were classified into several skill groups of introduction, fundamentals, and advanced courses, respectively.

KEYWORDS

Educational Skills, Self-Organizing Map, Questionnaire Survey, Educational Performance Indicator

1. INTRODUCTION

The skills and attributes to be learned in school education are changing in the 21st century. There are various skills and attributes such as the 21st century skills announced by the United States Department of Education and the key competencies of the DeSeCo project organized by the OECD. Skill and attribute targets including the curricula of various countries are classified into the following three categories. The first is "basic literacy" dealing with languages, mathematics and information, the second is "cognitive skills" dealing with thinking ability and learning way, and the third is "social skills" related to society, relationships with others and independence. In Japan, the National Institute for Educational Policy Research conducted research on curriculum which fostered attributes and skills. This institute conducted integrated and experimental study of educational goals, contents, method and evaluation. In future, it is necessary to advance research on learning method, teaching method and the evaluations.

Tokai University to which we belong has formulated the following four key abilities as a specific evaluation indicator and training for cultivating social practical power since 2009. The first is thinking ability, the second is communication ability with others, the third is challenging ability and the fourth is accomplishment ability. The faculty has denoted the appropriate abilities and evaluation indicators in a syllabus as a skill to train in class. However, the skill setting method is not theoretical or systematic approach. The purpose of this study is to set effective educational skills and educational performance indicators for each class in analytical way.

As a research to evaluate evaluation indexes and skills, there are meta-analyses (Robinson, et al, 2008; Poropat, 2009; Stajkovic and Luthans, 1998), data envelopment analyses (Avkrian, 2001; Abbott, 2003), and mediational analysis (Elliot, 1999). The meta-analyses examined the relative impact of different types of leadership on students' academic and nonacademic outcomes (Robinson, 2008), and the analyses examined the relationship between self-efficacy work-related performance (Stajkovic, 1998). Poropat (2009) reported a meta-analysis of personality-academic performance relationship with cumulative sample sizes ranging to over 70,000. The data envelopment analyses examined the relative efficiency of Australian universities (Avkrian, 2001) and estimated technical and scale efficiency for the population of Australian universities

(Abbott, 2003). The study (Elliot, 1999) examined achievement goals, motivational study strategies and exam performance by a mediational analysis.

We have examined the relationship between students' educational skills using a multidimensional scaling (Taniguchi, 2018). The multidimensional scaling (MDS) is a method of multivariate analysis. It is a method of summarizing the relationships of classification objects in a low dimensional space and visualizing the relation of classification objects. Cano (2002) informed an evaluation of Spanish educational research journals using multidimensional scaling. Pounder (2009) studied an evaluating the relevance of quality to institutional performance assessment. Gatewood (1993) studied the relationship between initial job choice decisions, the corporate images and recruitment images by multidimensional scaling. However, MDS solutions require a high dimensional space to explain the relevance of complicated data.

In this study we survey the self-assessment questionnaire of students' educational skills using a self-organizing map (SOM). SOM (Kohonen, 1995) is an unsupervised neural network method. It is suitable for analyzing complicated data and its calculation is not difficult. The SOM is an efficient tool for visualizing the relationship between multidimensional data. A SOM was used to visualize the similarity relations between educational skills based on student's consciousness.

2. METHODS

2.1 Participants

A questionnaire survey was conducted in the beginning classes of the spring semester in 2018. A questionnaire for students of 19 ICT classes and 13 faculties was surveyed in Tokai University. The classes are classified by difficulty for introduction course, fundamentals course, and advanced course. Students can take these ICT classes regardless of student years or their faculties. Table 1 shows the student years, the genders, the faculties of survey respondents. All participants agreed to participate in the study. A cumulative total of 946 students participated in this study. Table 3 shows the list of ICT class names and the number of students.

Table 1. Survey respondents and legend of symbols in Figures 1 to 3

		Symbol	Introduction	Fundamentals	Advanced
Total			578	273	95
Year	First	1	108	33	0
	Second	2	166	100	6
	Third	3	207	93	49
	Fourth	4	97	47	40
Gender	Female	F	85	58	8
	Male	M	493	215	87
Faculty	Letters	LT	49	41	3
	Cultural and Social Studies	C	7	2	0
	Political Science and Economics	P	69	28	5
	Law	L	22	13	2
	Humanities and Culture	HC	13	9	1
	Physical Education	G	20	6	1
	Health Studies	H	2	2	0
	Science	S	74	22	24
	Information Science and Technology	I	99	43	28
	Engineering	E	220	104	31
	Tourism	T	1	2	0
	Information and Telecommunication	IT	1	1	0
	Biological Science	B	1	0	0

Table 2. Educational skills and the abbreviations

Educational skill	Abbr.
Learning skills	LRN
Thinking skills	THK
Inquiring skills	INQ
Communication skills	COM
Collaboration skills	CLB
Relationship building skills	RB
Self-assessment skills	SA
Evaluating other skills	EO
Problem finding skills	FND
Problem setting skills	SET
Creative thinking skills	CT
Planning skills	PLN
Implementing skills	IMP
Continuity skills	CNT
Accomplishment skills	ACP
Analytical skills	ANL
Modifying and improvement skills	MAI
Collecting information skills	CI
Decision making skills	DM
Logical thinking skills	LT
Problem solving skills	SLV
Artistic skills	ART
Setting goals skills	SG
Constructing knowledge skills	CK

Table 3. ICT classes and the number of students

ICT Class	Abbr.	Course	students
Introduction to ICT	IT	Introduction	180
Information Systems B	B	Introduction	80
Introduction to Internet Technology	N	Introduction	45
Introduction to Computer Programming	P	Introduction	42
Basic Computer Programming	BP	Introduction	102
Introduction to Web Creation	W	Introduction	9
Introduction to Data Analysis	DA	Introduction	64
Interface Design	BD	Introduction	81
Digital Imaging	DI	Fundamentals	18
Applied Computer Programming	AP	Fundamentals	121
Basic Web Creation	BW	Fundamentals	56
Music Creation	M	Fundamentals	31
Movie Creation	MV	Fundamentals	18
Computer Networking	NW	Fundamentals	4
Applied Web Creation	AW	Advanced	2
Computer Algorithm	A	Advanced	40
Computer Graphics	G	Advanced	19
Software Engineering	SE	Advanced	3
Operating System	O	Advanced	31

2.2 Procedure

A computer-assisted web-interviewing (CAWI) technique was used to collect questionnaire data. Participants were asked to complete the online questionnaire containing the educational skills. The questionnaire and the study purpose information were provided for the participants by web pages. All participants joined voluntarily and checked the informed consent terms on the web pages.

2.3 Questionnaire

A questionnaire survey was conducted to analyze the 25 educational skills (Ota, 2016; Miyaji, 2011) in Table 2 that students gained through their lessons. Students declared the educational skills themselves by the questionnaire. All items are rated on a nine-point Likert-type scale from 1 (not at all) to 9 (very high degree).

2.4 Data Analysis

A SOM is an efficient tool for visualization of multidimensional data. The SOM was used to visualize the similarity relations between educational skills based on student's consciousness. We analyze the relations of 25 educational skills, regarding introduction, fundamentals, and advanced courses. In this analysis, 25 educational skills (Table 2) were used as SOM variables. This study used the SOM-Toolbox (Vesanto, 1999) in MATLAB to make and visualize the SOM for datasets. Questionnaire results for introduction, fundamentals, and advanced courses were used as the data sets. These data were normalized such that each variable has unit variance. After the SOMs were initialized and trained by principal component analysis, the SOM results were obtained.

3. RESULT

The visualization results of the SOM are shown in Figures 1 to 3. There are the U-matrices (unified distance matrices) and the label matrices in the upper low of these figures. The other matrices are the component planes. In the U-matrices, the difference of reference vectors (yellow dot sequence) represents the cluster boundary. Each label matrix illustrates the relationship among student years, genders, ICT classes, and faculties, respectively. The label matrices (year, gender, class, and faculty of students) are associated with map units. The component planes illustrate 25 educational skills as SOM variables. In the component planes, yellow means higher skill rating and blue color means lower skill rating. Similar component planes are boxed in these figures then the planes can be classified into four or six educational skill groups.

4. DISCUSSION

The U-matrix of Figure 1 shows two cluster boundaries in the introduction course. The left-top boundary means students have lower educational skill values by self-evaluation and the bottom-center one means they have higher skill values by themselves. Therefore the students at the left-top had lower evaluation for many educational skills and the students at the bottom-center one had higher evaluation for many skills. The U-matrix of Figure 2 shows two cluster boundaries in the fundamentals course. The left-top boundary means students have lower educational skill values by self-evaluation and the bottom-right one means they have higher skill values by themselves. As in the introduction course, the students at the left-top had lower evaluation for many educational skills and the students at the bottom-right one had higher evaluation for many skills. The U-matrix of Figure 3 shows one cluster boundary in the advanced course. The left-top boundary means students have lower educational skill values by self-evaluation. However there is no clear boundary at the bottom. As in the above two courses, the students at the top had lower evaluation for many educational skills. Regarding educational skills, students with high ratings are placed at the bottom-left or at the bottom-right.

The label matrices in Figures 1 to 3 show the educational skill values by self-evaluation does not depend on student years, genders, ICT classes, and faculties. Therefore students' consciousness of 25 educational skills does not depend on these variables.

From Figure 1, the component planes can be classified into four educational groups. Groups 11 to 41 are basic thinking skills, executing skills, communication skills, and creative skills, respectively. In most component planes, the skill evaluation is lower at the top and the evaluation is higher at the bottom. The evaluation values in group 31 are increasing from the left-top to the right-bottom. Meanwhile, the evaluation values in group 41 are increasing from the right-top to the left-bottom. Therefore, communication skills (group 31) are incompatible with creative skills (group 41) under students' consciousness. From Figure 2, the component planes can be also classified into four educational groups. Groups 12 to 42 are basic thinking skills, executing skills, creative skills, and communication skills, respectively. In most component planes, the distributions of skill evaluations in Figure 2 are the same as Figure 1. The evaluation values in groups 12 and 42 are increasing from the left-top to the right-bottom. Meanwhile, the evaluation values in groups 22 and 32 are increasing from the right-top to the left-bottom. Therefore, communication skills (group 42) and basic thinking skills (group 12) are incompatible with creative skills (group 32) and executing skills (group 22) under students' consciousness. The component planes in Figure 3 can be classified into six educational groups. Groups 13 to 63 are learning skills, thinking skills, problem finding skills, accomplishment skills, communication skills, and creative skills, respectively. For advanced course, there are three increasing directions in the component planes. One group is increasing from the right-top to the left-bottom. The appropriate groups are 13 and 23. Second group is increasing from the left-top to the right-bottom. The appropriate groups are 43, 53, and 63. The other group is increasing from the top to the bottom. The appropriate group is 33. The results of component planes for advanced course students are complicated than the other courses. Advanced course students might be seriously considering their educational skills because they had finished many ICT classes.

Similar skills in the SOMs are thought to be highly relevant skills in the student's consciousness. It is difficult to teach many skills in class. Some similar skills might be able to be replaced by a few skills. There is a possibility that an effective lesson can be realized without imposing load to teachers and students. Even now we have set educational goals and performance indicators for each lesson, but they were not analytical methods. Using the SOM results, we try to set more effective educational goals and performance indicators for each lesson.

5. CONCLUSION

We have propose developing a method to set key educational skills which students need to achieve for each class using a student self-assessment questionnaire in analytical approach. It is difficult to set key academic skills for class since there are little systematic methods to set them. The questionnaire survey with 25 educational skills has been conducted to ICT classes in our university using a CAWI technique. The questionnaire results have been analyzed using SOMs. A SOM is used to visualize the similarity relations between educational skills based on student's consciousness. We have showed that 25 skills were classified into several skill groups of introduction, fundamentals, and advanced courses, respectively. Present and Future works focus on the improving class contents, the setting effective educational goals, and performance indicators for each lesson using SOM results.

ACKNOWLEDGEMENT

We would like to thank the ICT class students who cooperated in this questionnaire. Without their participation this paper would not be possible. And we also would like to express our gratitude to our faculty who took time from the busy time schedule to participate in the questionnaire survey.

REFERENCES

Robinson, V. et al, 2008. The impact of leadership on student outcomes: An analysis of the differential effects of leadership types, *Educational Administration Quarterly*; 44: 5, pp. 635-674.

Poropat, A., 2009. A Meta-Analysis of the Five-Factor Model of Personality and Academic Performance, *Psychological bulletin*, pp. 1-68.

Stajkovic, A. and Luthans, F., 1998, Self-efficacy and work-related performance: A meta-analysis, *Psychological bulletin*, 124, 2, pp. 240-261.

Avkiran, N., 2001, Investigating technical and scale efficiencies of Australian universities through data envelopment analysis, *Socio-Economic Planning Sciences*, Elsevier, 35, pp. 57-80.

Abbott, M. and Doucouliagos, C., 2003, The efficiency of Australian universities: a data envelopment analysis, *Economics of Education review, Elsevier*, 22, pp. 89-97.

Elliot, A. et al, 1999, Achievement goals, study strategies, and exam performance: A mediational analysis, *Journal of Educational Psychology*, 91: 3, pp. 549-563.

Pounder, J., 2000, Evaluating the Relevance of Quality to Institutional Performance Assessment in Higher Education, Evaluation, *Sage Publications*, 6: 1, pp. 66-78.

Fernández-Cano, A. and Bueno, A., 2002, Multivariate evaluation of Spanish educational research journals, *Scientometrics, Springer*, 55: 1, pp. 87-102.

Gatewood, R. et al, 1993, Corporate Image, Recruitment Image, and Initial Job Choice Decisions, *Academy of Management Journal*, 36: 2, pp. 414-427.

Kohonen, T., 1995, Self-Organizing Maps, Springer Series in Information Sciences, Vol. 30, Springer.

Ota, G. et al, 2016, The Comparative Survey of Computer Science and Programming Education for Primary and Secondary Schools in the UK, Australia and USA, *Japan Journal of Educational Technology*, 40: 3, pp.197-208 (in Japanese).

Miyaji, I., 2011, Difference in Effects of Creating Digital Story Telling by the Difference of Theme, *IEICE Technical Report*, 3, pp. 83-88, (in Japanese).

Taniguchi, T. et al, 2018, Analysis and Classification of Educational Skills Using Questionnaire to University Students, *In Proceeding of KES 2018*, pp.2021-2029.

Vesanto, J. et al, 2000, Self-organizing map in Matlab: the SOM-Toolbox. Proceedings of the Matlab DSP Conference 1999. Espoo, Finland,35-40.

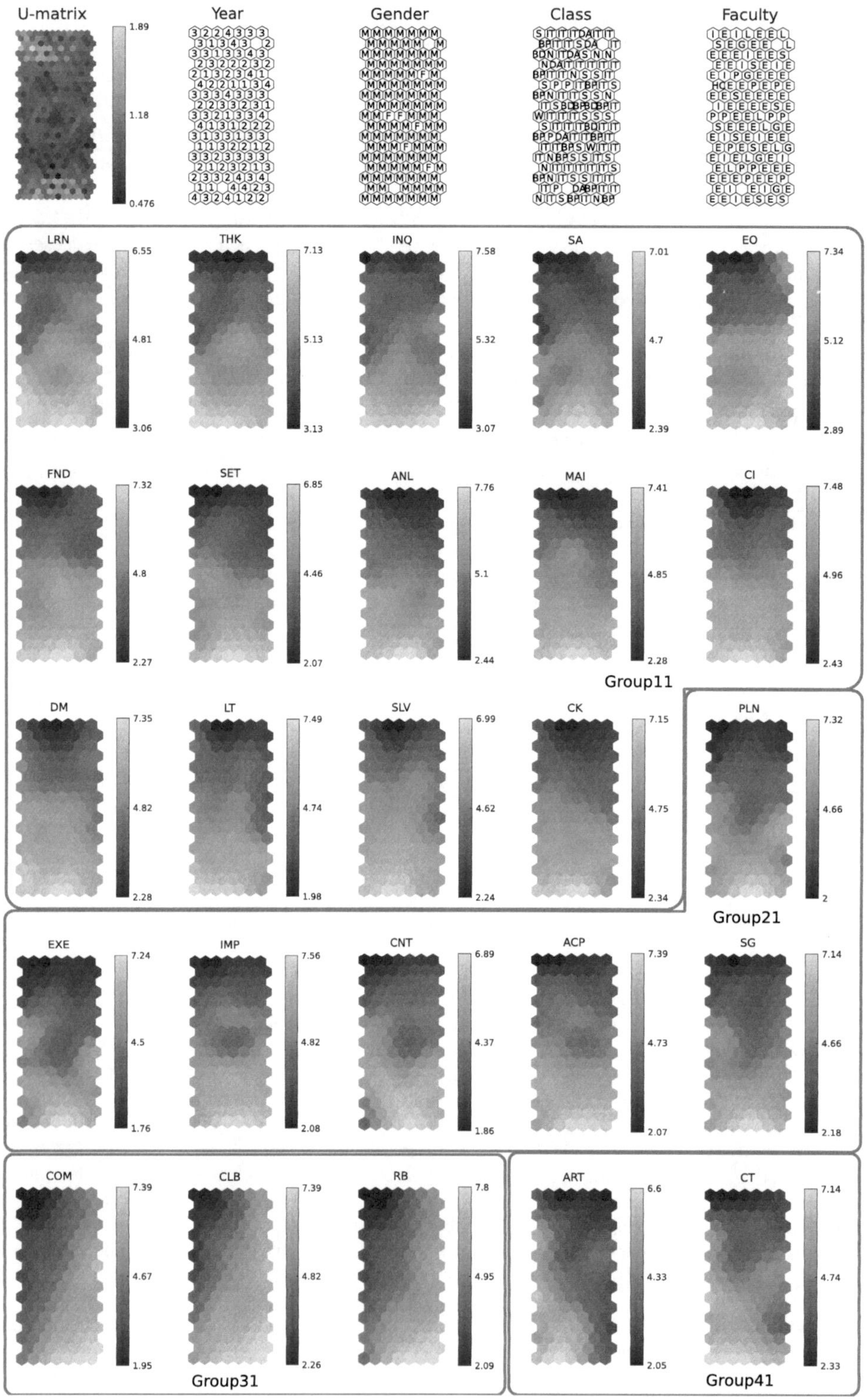

Figure 1. U-matrix, the labels, and the component planes for introduction course

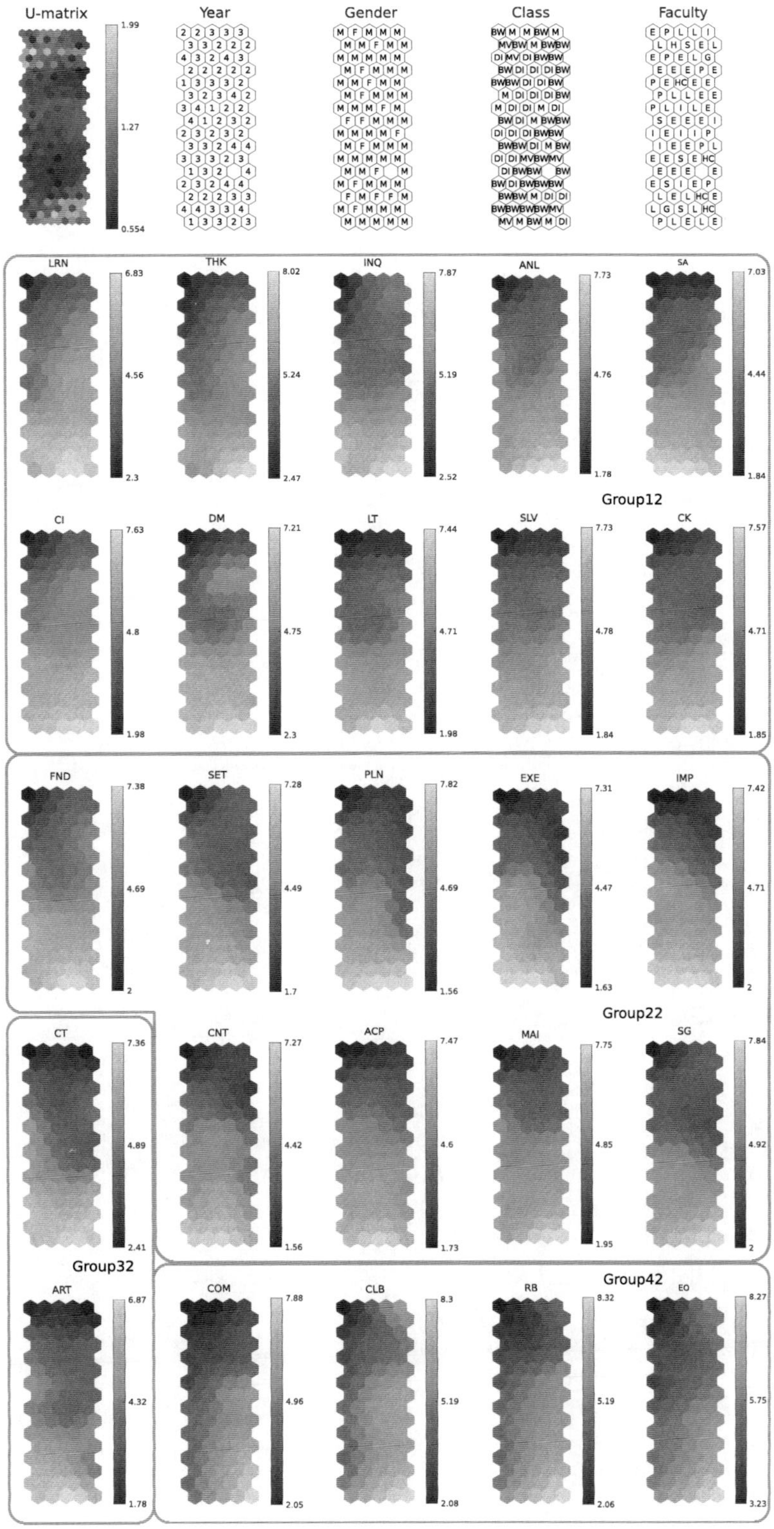

Figure 2. U-matrix, the labels, and the component planes for fundamentals course

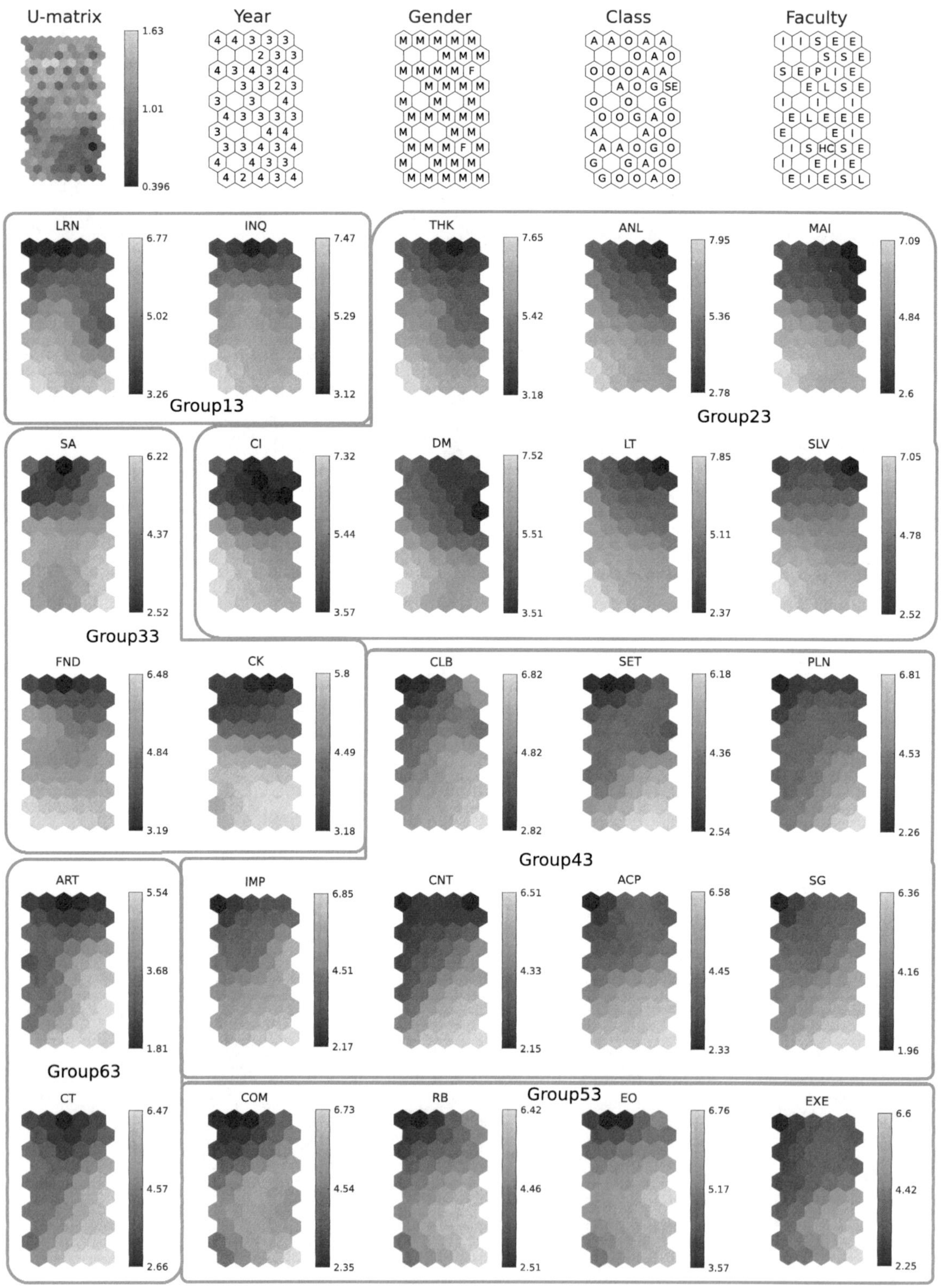

Figure 3. U-matrix, the labels, and the component planes for advanced course

INSIGHTS INTO PERSUASIVE TECHNOLOGY FOR M-LEARNING USING ACTIVITY THEORY

Nhlanhla A. Sibanyoni and Patricia M. Alexander
UNISA, P O Box 392, 0003, South Africa

ABSTRACT

In theory, educational applications that are engaging and motivating should easily persuade learners to use a mobile device for studying. Since this technology is already familiar to learners, mobile learning should be easily accessible; given a suitable m-learning application, learners could practice mathematics anytime or anywhere. LevelUp is an m-learning application, an example of educational persuasive technology that provides learners with educational content to practice mathematics exercises, it offers learners who successfully complete mathematics exercises with rewards, such as airtime or data bundles. The use of rewards is intended to persuade the learners to establish a new, sustained, learning behaviour. However, in the research reported on in this paper the learners were not attracted to and persistent in using the application. The aim of this study was, therefore, to understand the learners' perspective of the LevelUp application as a persuasive technology. This is an explanatory case study where the interpretive paradigm was used for analysis. The analysis used Fogg's Behaviour Model and Activity Theory as a way to understand this complex activity and to highlight the contradictions between LevelUp's intentions as a persuasive technology and the learners' perspective. Focus group interviews, questionnaire and observation were all used to collect data. The study contributes towards designing educational persuasive technologies that are effective and sustainable for use after school time from the learners' perspective.

KEYWORDS

Persuasive Technology, Study Behaviour, Mobile Application, Motivation, m-Learning

1. INTRODUCTION

This study focuses on a particular group of users in a particular context - learners who wait at a particular South African school, after school hours, for transport home. Some stay long after the school has closed without adult supervision, and might get into mischief. The LevelUp application, created by a group of developers that the researchers are not part of, looks for ways to influence learners similar to these to establish a behaviour to study mathematics using a mobile device application and it could be used during this waiting time. The application uses rewards of data bundles or airtime for successfully completing mathematics exercises. This is done to encourage the learners to return regularly to use the application, and to create a long-term study habit.

The designers of the LevelUp application seem to view learning on a mobile device as a simple activity. They make this assumption, in part, because learners use mobile devices continuously after school time for personal purposes and hence the technology is very familiar (Nikou & Economides 2017). Various forms of persuasion to use an application or a web site has become very common and effective. Hence, developers may assume that learners can be equally easily motivated to engage with educational applications (Yordanova 2007). There is indeed extensive research that shows that persuasive mobile technology, when implemented as recommended, has excellent potential to enhance education and to support learning environments (some recent examples are given by (Botha & Herselman 2015; Bray & Tangney 2016; Nikou & Economides 2017).

In the case of the LevelUp mobile application, using rewards to encourage the learners to study regularly was not successful. This study, therefore, aims to answer the question, 'Why were the learners not attracted to and persistent in using this persuasive technology?' The purpose of the study was to understand the learners' perspective of persuasive technology as implemented in the LevelUp application. The study aims to contribute insights into the design of educational persuasive technology by highlighting the learners' perspective.

In order to do this, the Fogg Behaviour Model (FBM) is used to understand learner behaviour (Fogg 2003). This is supplemented by Activity Theory (AT) (Engeström 1987). FBM focuses on the behaviour of the individual, while AT assists the researcher in understanding specific relationships in a complex activity (studying the mathematics) within a social context. Focus groups, questionnaires, observation of learners' after-school behaviour and the LevelUp database were employed as data collection instruments. The paper is organised as follows: First a brief literature review is presented followed by the analysis of data using FBM. Next Activity Theory is applied which leads to the conclusion.

2. LITERATURE REVIEW

2.1 Persuasive Technology

Mobile learning is the use of mobile devices (tablets, smartphones and cell phones) for learning. A persuasive technology application is software or an information system designed to change the behaviour of the targeted group (without using coercion or deception) (Oinas-kukkonen & Harjumaa 2009). Research shows persuasive technology to be effective in encouraging the adoption of a healthy lifestyle, socially responsible driving habits, informal education, reduction in energy consumption and as a means of interactive marketing; however, it is challenging to implement (Kaptein & Kruijswijk 2016).

2.1.1 The Fogg Behaviour Model

The Fogg Behaviour Model (FBM) assists us to understand behaviours related to persuasive technology (Ng et al. 2016). FBM proposes that three elements must exist simultaneously for a behaviour to occur: motivation, ability and a trigger (Figure 1). It is however important to first identify the specific target behaviour that you are aiming to encourage.

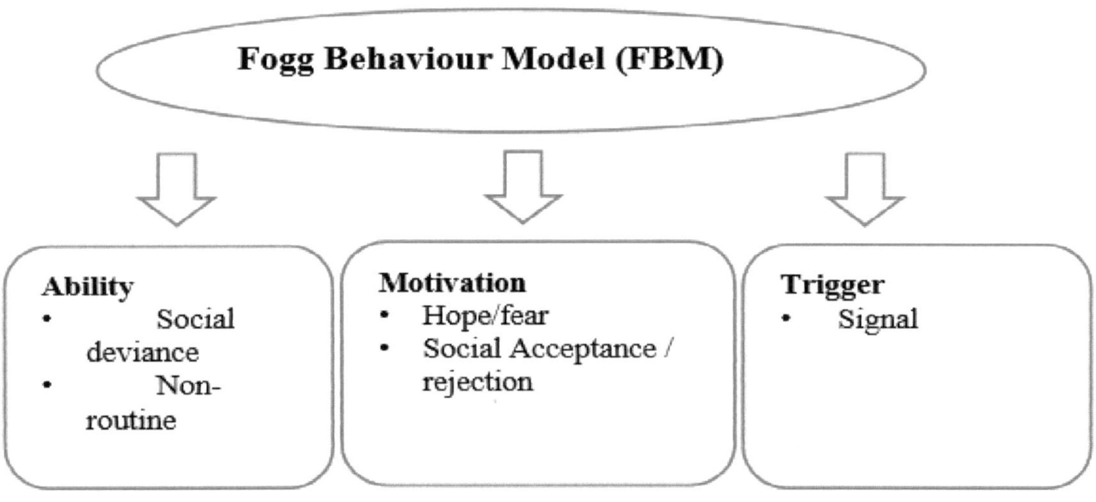

Figure 1. Elements and sub-elements of FBM (Fogg 2009; Ng et al. 2016)

Fogg (2009) also identified an eight-step process for designing persuasive technology (Figure 2). The current study is limited to the evaluation step (Step 3), that is, to finding out whether the persuasive technology effectively encourages the target behaviour; according to FBM, hindrances could be lack of motivation, ability or a well-timed trigger. In this case, the immediate targeted behaviour is the sustained use of the application and not the more complex behaviour of learning mathematics although the application's overall goal is the more complex one.

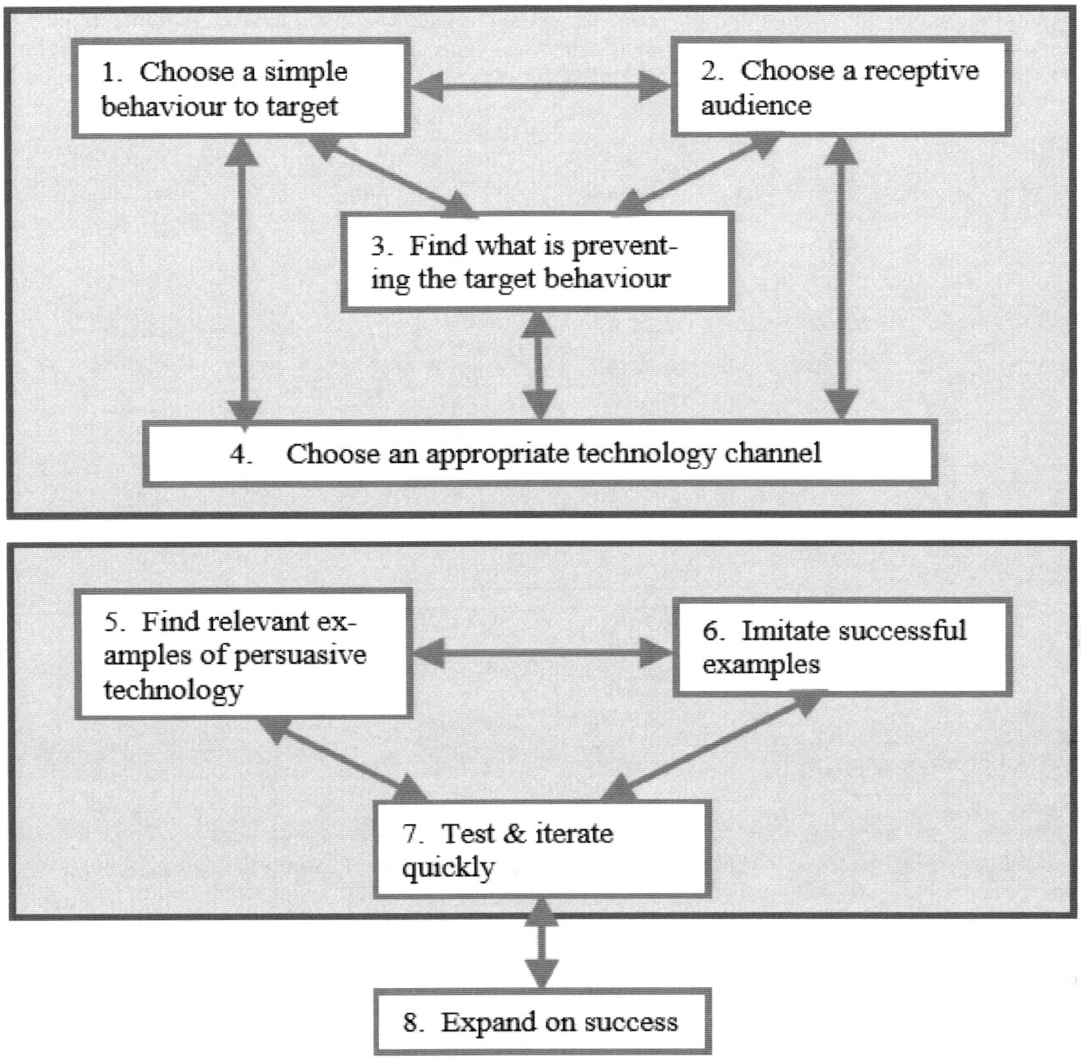

Figure 2. The eight-step process for designing persuasive technology (Fogg 2009)

It is an ongoing concern that developers' attempts to design persuasive technology fail (Fogg 2009). In the South African educational context, Botha & Herselman (2015) report that there is a noticeable failure of ICT in education initiatives and this requires further investigation and research.

2.2 Activity Theory

The major advantage of using Activity Theory (AT) to understand a mobile learning environment is that it emphasizes that learning is an activity, situated in a virtual space and socially mediated, but using tools. Persuasive technology design often does not take complexity sufficiently into consideration (Mintz & Aagaard 2012) and hence AT is a valuable theory. In the case reported on here, it is used to understand the complex environment and context and to highlight contradictions between different stakeholders (in this case the developers and the learners) as reflected in their activities.

In AT, an individual activity is explained as an activity system, which is the basic unit of analysis. The activity system has an object that is shared by a group of people or a community. The activity then, using tools such as computers and mobile devices, transforms that object into an outcome (Hardman 2005). Figure 3, depicts an activity system and shows the relationships between the subject (the person undertaking the activity), tools, object, community, rules and the division of labour (these are the six nodes or elements) (Engeström 1987). An activity is seen as a systemic whole because all the elements are linked. During the activity, the object often changes and manifests itself in different ways.

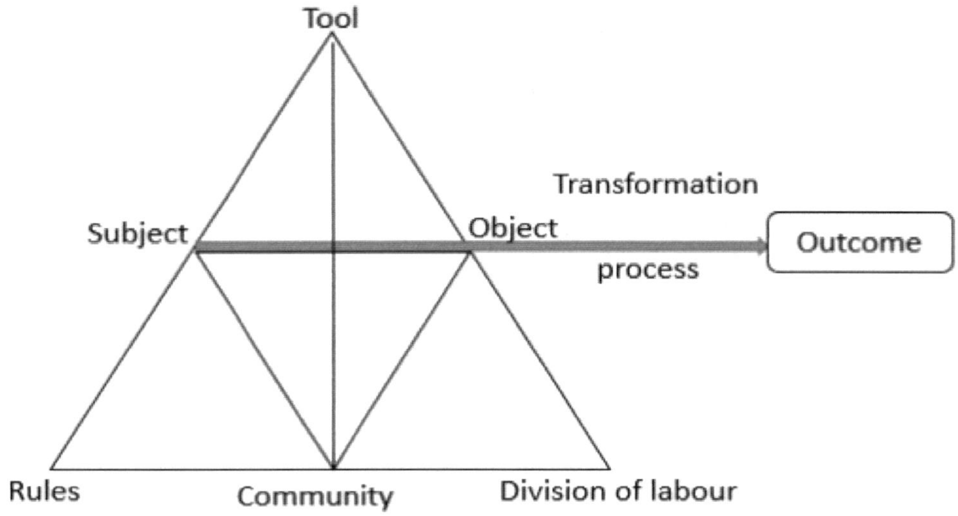

Figure 3. An Activity System (Engeström 1987)

3. METHODOLOGY

This is an explanatory case study where the interpretive paradigm was used for analysis. The interpretation was supported by two theories (FMB and AT). Although the 25 learners who were using the application in this research were all from a single grade in one school, the school is not being studied. The school's authority and parents' consent was obtained before conducting the study and the learners' names were kept confidential. Focus groups, questionnaires and observation were employed to collect data. As noted in the introduction, the main research question is, 'Why were the learners not attracted to and persistent in using the LevelUp application?' The proposition is that persuasive technology as used for informal educational purposes, cannot rely solely on motivating individual learners as the activity that they are engaged in is both complex and social.

4. FINDINGS AND DISCUSSION

To answer the main question of the study, this question was divided into sub-question. Tables 1 and 2 show examples of the data collected for two of the sub-questions – but note, this is not all of the data collected. Learners expected the LevelUp application to assist them to study mathematics in a way similar to a human teacher or peer (Table 1), therefore ideally, the application should leverage the power of social influence to motivate and persuade. Table 2 shows that daily homework set at school is the learners' highest priority. Secondly, parents play an important part in motivating their children to study - there is an expectation that they should study (Table 2). While learners were aware that they would get an immediate tangible reward, they also hoped that their maths marks would improve (see Table 1). The last comment in Table 1, "I feel like people are honestly better" illustrates the importance of human interaction and social influence. Peer pressure, social comparison and group polarization are all types of influence that arise from a social (school) environment. Mobile applications, when designed to act as social actors, will leverage the social influence principle to motivate and persuade (Fogg, 2002).

Table 1. Sub-question 1.
Do you think a person or people are better than technology in encouraging you to study and why?

Learners' responses
… So when you have a study partner you'll achieve more mentally with that person compared to doing it alone, compared to technology, that's my opinion, … I think people are better because people understand they have feelings they know what we go through, they understand the stress. … I agree with her and I think that people are better you'll have a better experience with a person than with a tablet or a phone, they can't tell you what you doing wrong and whether you understand it or not the tablet doesn't really care, so a person is better, …I think a person is better because if you don't understand something a person can try and explain it in a different way whereas a tablet won't be able to, so you'll have a better understanding with a person because they can think of a way you can relate to and understand the topic that's being tested, … I think a person is better because if you actually like the person then you start to have fun with it because not only are you spending time with the person but you learning in a fun way, …I think I agree with everyone that interaction with people is better, you get either a positive or negative feel, like emojis can't really tell a person's feelings, so I think people are better I don't know about the app. If the app can give feedback as though we've done something I think it can be better, …I feel like people are honestly better, I feel like an app is kind of programmed to tell you, it isn't on a one on one level where you can actually share your frustrations an app is more programmed, it doesn't seem realistic to me

Table 2. Sub-question 2. Do you think an App like LevelUp could be designed to encourage people your age to study?

Learners' responses
…Ja it will motivate you because there are rewards and as a teenager I would want airtime to call my girlfriend or something, … With Level up why I think it will even motivate me further is the rewards system, why not study and also get short term rewards such as airtime or data bundles in the process, … We all obviously do homework first because we get it every day, … Parents and teachers wouldn't reward us because studying to them is something that we have to do but to a lot of us we not motivated enough to do things we have to do, …I think it depends on how much homework you have that day. So I go home with transport, if I have a lot of homework then I'll go home first and start my homework and then do everything else I need to do. When I don't have that much homework to do, I go home late. If the app works I'll put some time into my schedule for it if it works for me.

4.1 Data Analysis using Fogg Behaviour Model (FBM)

The three elements in the model (motivation, ability and trigger) were analysed and linked to data collected during two focus groups sessions with the learners and from the semi-structured questionnaire completed by the learners individually to test the views amongst the wider audience of the focus group participants. FMB was used to answer the main study question: 'Why were the learners not attracted to and persistent in using the LevelUp application?'

4.1.1 Element of Motivation

People are influenced to act in a certain way by different factors, for example, hope and or social acceptance or rejection (Fogg 2009; Ryan & Deci 2000).

Motivator #1: Hope is when people anticipate a positive outcome for doing something. In the case study, while learners were aware that they would get an immediate tangible reward (Table 1), they also hoped that their maths marks would improve (this is not as definite an outcome as the immediate reward).

Motivator #2: Social acceptance or rejection – during the observation sessions, all of the learners were seen standing in groups while waiting for their transport. Group formation can result in individual learners seeking social acceptance, wanting to fit in the group or a fear of being rejected (Table 1). One learner explained that the rest of the group would consider it impolite if you were spending an extended period working on a mobile device instead of chatting in the group.

Time #3: The target behaviour requires that the learners have time available to complete the challenges every day after school. Although the learners were short of time for using LevelUp (Table 2), they were not really short of the ability to use the application; for example, they were familiar with the mobile device and had sufficient money to buy airtime or data bundles.

4.1.2 Element of Ability

The aim is to increase the users' ability. In terms of the Fogg Behaviour Model this is neither about the standard learning measure (easy-hard) of the mathematics exercises offered nor about increasing learners' skill in using the technology. It is about the convenience, schedule or feasibility to use the application.

Social Deviance and Non-Routine – LevelUp is not part of the school curriculum, this makes it difficult for the learners to fit additional Maths exercises, using the LevelUp application, into their school daily routine as it requires additional time that deviates from the normal curriculum activities (Table 2).

4.1.3 Element of Trigger

A persuasive technology must have a trigger presented at the right moment for users to recognise and respond to Fogg (2009). LevelUp uses a text notification as a trigger to remind the learners to do their daily mathematics exercises. This trigger just reminds the learner to do the daily challenges as it was assumed that they possess both the motivation and the ability to use a mobile device. The LevelUp application is leveraging the principle of convenience by attempting to present the message to the learners after school at an opportune moment.

4.2 Analysis using Activity Theory

Sub-question 2 ('Do you think an App like LevelUp could be designed to encourage people your age to study?') is a social question. Activity Theory is, therefore, used to answer this question and to analyse the studying mathematics activity using LevelUp as the unit of analysis. Activity Theory holds that an activity must be analysed in the context in which it occurs (Jonassen & Rohrer-Murphy 1999). The analysis examined the entire activity through the activity system (Figure 4). In this case, the study identifies who is engaged in the activity, the tools used and their history (which may shape the way people act and think), the social and context within which the activity system operates, the rules and norms (which may facilitate or limit the use of tools), and the community and its role through the division of labour.

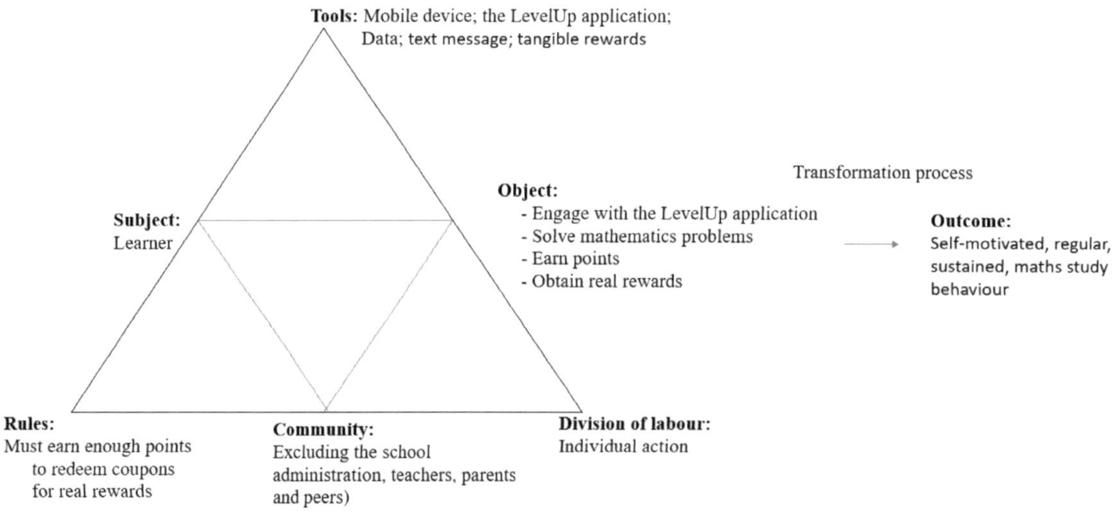

Figure 4. The Activity System for Learners using the LevelUp Application

Activity system: The activity system consists of the subject, tools, rules, community, division of labour, object and outcomes for the learners' activity of completing the LevelUp mathematics daily exercises.

Subject: The learners have been identified as individual subjects who are encouraged to participate and complete the activity, independently and voluntarily after school.

Tools: The LevelUp application is a mobile application tool used; airtime; data bundles; text message and tangible rewards.

Rules: The learners can only obtain the rewards when they have earned enough points.

Object: Although the learners indicated that their object of using a mobile device for more general reasons is convenience as it enables them to communicate, socialise with friends, and search for information and so on (Table 1), the object of the activity is very different (see Figure 4).

Outcome: This is the longer term goal where the extrinsically motivated learner becomes self-motivated. The transformation process takes the Object of the activity to this outcome.

Division of labour: The studying mathematics on a mobile device is an individual action, the application does not leverage aspects of collaboration (Figure 3).

Community: The observation shows that the school administration, teachers, parents or peers are not involved. The LevelUp application is meant to encourage learners to study outside school time.

Identifying contradictions within an activity and between different activities is an important part of analysis using AT. In the research undertaken, other activities, in particular the activity of designing the application, was also analysed. Unfortunately page limits in this paper do not allow these to be explained. The issue of contradictions is discussed therefore only in terms of the learners' activity. The objective of mobile phone activity, is understood by the learners as for communicating with friends and family, Internet surfing, but is not used for LevelUp activity, Hence there is a major contradiction between the learners' other activities and this one. Figure 3 shows only the activity of studying mathematics using a mobile device and LevelUp. So this points to a contradiction between the object of the mobile phone activity and the activity that the App supports. A further contradiction is clear from the division of labour and the community. The application is designed for individual use and hence there is no division of labour or involvement by the other people who usually motivate the learner and assist. These roles have been taken over entirely by the application (tool). However, as AT points out, activities are social.

5. CONCLUSION

The current study has illustrates that FBM and Activity Theory complement one another as a way to assess persuasive technology. Firstly, FBM was applied to understand why the learners' target behaviour would occur or not occur. The analysis of the three elements of FBM, that is, motivation, ability and trigger shows that at least one of the elements are lacking (see Section 4.1.1). This implies that the target behaviour would not occur or persist. Activity Theory was used for the in-depth analysis of the activity systems (only one activity system was discussed in this paper but in the full research others were also analysed) and enabled the study to highlight contradictions. However, Activity Theory does not explicitly talk about persuasive technology and motivation, and therefore the two theories apart could not explain the complexity of studying mathematics using the LevelUp application. This combined use of theories is expected to help the developers of persuasive technology to understand that m-Learning is a complex social activity and, therefore, that they should design systems or applications that are acceptable in the community and continuously (sustainable) used by leveraging the social support of social learning, social comparison, competition, normative influence, social facilitation and cooperation. The study contributes to use of FBM and AT to understand m-learning. Further research is required that will apply these theories after school time for learners studying mathematics.

ACKNOWLEDGEMENT

We appreciate the contribution made by The Reach Trust Organisation of which this work would not have happened without their sincere ingenuousness.

REFERENCES

Botha, A. & Herselman, M., 2015. ICTs in rural education. In *Annual Symposium on Computing for Development - DEV '15*. New York, New York, USA: ACM Press, pp. 105–113.

Bray, A. & Tangney, B., 2016. Enhancing student engagement through the affordances of mobile technology: a 21st century learning perspective on Realistic Mathematics Education. *Mathematics Education Research Journal*, 28(1), pp.173–197.

Engeström, Y., 1987. *Learning by Expanding: An Activity-Theoretical Approach to Developmental Research*, Finland: Orienta-Konsultit.

Fogg, B.J., 2009. A behavior model for persuasive design. In *Proceedings of the 4th International Conference on Persuasive Technology - Persuasive '09:* California: ACM Press, pp. 1–40.

Fogg, B.J., 2003. Computers as Persuasive Social Actors. In *Persuasive Technology: Using Computers to Change what We Think and Do*. San Francisco: Morgan Kaufmann, pp. 89–120.

Hardman, J., 2005. Activity theory as a potential framework for technology research in an unequal terrain. *South African Journal of Education*, 19(2), pp.378–392.

Jonassen, D.H. & Rohrer-Murphy, L., 1999. Activity theory as a framework for designing constructivist learning environments. *Educational Technology Research and Development*, 47(1), pp.61–79.

Kaptein, M. & Kruijswijk, J., 2016. StreamingBandit: A Platform for Developing Adaptive Persuasive Systems. In *Adjunct Proceedings of the 11th International Conference on Persuasive Technology*. Salzburg, Austria.

Mintz, J. & Aagaard, M., 2012. The application of persuasive technology to educational settings. *Educational Technology Research and Development*, 60(3), pp.483–499.

Ng, K.H., Bakri, A. & Rahman, A.A., 2016. Effects of persuasive designed courseware on children with learning difficulties in learning Malay language subject. *Education and Information Technologies*, 21(5), pp.1413–1431.

Nikou, S.A. & Economides, A.A., 2017. Mobile-based assessment: Investigating the factors that influence behavioral intention to use. *Computers & Education*, 109, pp.56–73.

Oinas-kukkonen, H. & Harjumaa, M., 2009. Persuasive Systems Design: Key issues, process model, and system features. *Communications of the Association for Information Systems*, 24(28), pp.485–500.

Ryan, R.M. & Deci, E.L., 2000. Intrinsic and extrinsic motivations: Classic definitions and new directions. *Contemporary Educational Psychology*, 25(1), pp.54–67.

Yordanova, K., 2007. Mobile learning and integration of advanced technologies in education. *Proceedings of the 2007 international conference on Computer systems and technologies - CompSysTech '07*, p.1.

ADULT EDUCATION AS A CONTRIBUTORY FACTOR TO THE INTEGRATION INTO MODERN SOCIO-CULTURAL ENVIRONMENT

Marina Yurtaeva, Natalia Glukhanyuk, Anna Muzafarova and Tatiana Rasskazova
Ural Federal University named after the first president of Russia B.N. Yeltsin
Address 19, Mira Street, Ekaterinburg, 620002 Russia

ABSTRACT

The advent of the so-called "post-literacy" era imposes on an individual the need to master not only various verbal, but also visual, artistic and scientific languages that have been developed in modern culture, which requires an adult to constantly improve their general educational and cultural level and to constantly struggle against functional illiteracy. The authors believe that by engaging in continuous education and lifelong learning, individuals not only increase their adaptive capacities essential for integrating into a dynamically changing socio-professional environment but also satisfy their need for self-actualisation, fulfil their potential, thus also preserving their mental, cognitive and social resources.
Since self-actualisation explains a person's effectiveness in all areas of life, determining its level can serve as the basis for designing the most appropriate educational programmes that would allow an individual to realise their potential and increase their adaptive capacity. The paper presents the results of a study of self-actualisation in adults who seek opportunities for self-development by enrolling in further education programmes and professional development courses. The study revealed that adults who seek opportunities for continuous education do so in the desire to enhance their hidden merits, to use, preserve and enrich their cognitive resources and, thereby self-actualize.
This raises the issue of tailoring further education programmes to specific self-actualisation needs of adult learners, developing new models of lifelong education that would foster the activation of adults' cognitive capabilities, identifying potential resources and modelling modern educational environments that would cater for the operation of self-development mechanisms.

KEYWORDS

Self-Actualisation, Lifelong Learning, Further Education, Cognitive Resources

1. INTRODUCTION

Innovations have always been part of human life. The emergence of any innovation changes the ways we think and act and, as a consequence, the consciousness and self-determination of an individual and of large groups of people.

In this regard, education has a new mission: to promote the innovative model of development in a variety of industries and areas of activity. This will eventually determine the competitiveness of economic, social, cultural projects, and an individual's adaptive capabilities.

The current global problem is the mismatch between a person's ability to adapt to changes in the surrounding world and the pace of these changes. Formal basic education, obtained at the early stages of life, does not keep up with the changes and, fundamentally, cannot provide a person with the knowledge, skills and qualities required to fulfil social and professional roles throughout life. We chronically lag behind the changes, do not have time to comprehend them, to understand their essence, to find a rational way of action (Toffler, 1971.)

A system of continuous lifelong education, with adult education as its main part, can become an instrument for supporting these essential changes. Continuous education can also contribute to strengthening a person's social connections that tend to weaken in later life stages, thus carrying out important social and psychological functions.

1.1 Context and Background: Adult Education in the Modern Reality

Adult education has been the arena for intensive scientific research and international cooperation since 2001 when the Lisbon Strategy defined education as an essential resource for development (European Commission, 2001). The benefits of adult education have been actively discussed by many researchers (Dench and Regan, 2000; Merriam and Kee, 2014).

The Russian educational system with its long history has entered the period of change unprepared for dealing with the new challenges. Nevertheless, over the past decades, a new sphere has established itself in the country - further adult non-professional education. The orientation towards the consumer, the flexibility in the new conditions of relative freedom, the application of not only pedagogical but also social and psychological technologies - all this has become a distinctive feature of Russian educational institutions that offer programmes for the adult population of the country.

This type of education is expected not only to give new knowledge but to preserve mental and social activity, which is an essential condition for achieving and developing success in a dynamically changing socio-professional environment. In the collective sense, they can be referred to as cognitive resources and an individual's potential (Nurgaleyeva, 2015).

Special expectations from adult education are associated with the penetration of information technologies into our daily life, which requires an adult to constantly improve their general educational and cultural level and to constantly struggle against functional illiteracy. The subject matter of adult education consists in a fundamentally new understanding of literacy or "post-literacy", which includes mastering not only various verbal but also visual, artistic and scientific languages that have been developed in modern culture and synthesized by various media.

The difference between adult and youth education is a higher motivation for learning in the former and, hence, the possibility of more effective learning. The learner plays a leading role in the education process, in the interaction with those who teach them, as well as in planning, implementing and evaluating programmes, syllabuses and teaching methods. Science needs to rethink the structural model of lifelong learning, giving a meaningful place to self-education (Litvinova, 2003).

The content of education is determined by the fact that it has two main consumers (stakeholders): organizations and individuals. The individuals' requirements influence the content of education in two ways: first, based on professional specifics, and secondly, on the basis of the qualities that a person needs to possess to effectively integrate into modern professional communities.

A special feature of adult education is the psychological characteristics of the adult learner, which include striving for self-realisation; the leading role in the learning process; life (everyday, social, professional) experience, which can be used as a source of learning; steady motivation. The learning process is also influenced by outdated ideas about the learning process, the formed structure of complexes, a certain deficit type of information processing (perception filters), mental manifestations, resistance mechanisms based on psychological barriers and defences.

Thus, we believe that modern adult education is not only and not so much about the process of developing professional competencies, but, above all, working with cognitive resources, the individual's potential and the opportunity to realize oneself.

A person's awareness and development of their own potential allow them to effectively realize their abilities in personal and professional life, to feel satisfaction from their own achievements. In the conditions of modern social transformations, the role of active attitude to self-development is increasing. A modern individual needs to have not only sufficient professional knowledge and skills but also to be able to build their own life strategy, adapt to changes, integrate into various communities, independently determining their internal potential for development. Adults' self-actualisation deserves special attention and study, and so does the creation of specific educational environments, forms and technologies for its controlled development.

2. METHODS AND RESULTS

2.1 Research Design

Self-actualisation is a phenomenon that manifests itself in all spheres of modern life since it is considered a construct that explains a person's effectiveness in the fields of culture, career, education and life in general. Therefore, we assumed that determining its level will give us the basis for designing the most appropriate educational programmes.

Our study was conducted in a group of Russian teachers and was designed according to the classical rules of the educational experiment with the measurement of the indicators before and after a certain stage. The goal was to establish changes in self-actualisation in comparison with the expression and generalisation of its main indicators as a result of education. The experiment involved 72 people, aged from 32 to 56 (average age 44.6 years), 37% of men and 63% of women. The study of the specifics of self-actualisation was carried out using the Personal Orientation Inventory developed by Everett L. Shostrom to measure the attitudes and values related to the construct of self-actualisation: its Russian-language modification (Shostrom, 1964, 1996; Aleshina et al, 1995).

2.2 Results and Discussion

The research objective was to study the change in the self-actualisation of adults through a special training programme. The study of the features of *self-actualisation* as a person's striving for self-realisation made it possible to obtain the following results (Figure 1).

The relative homogeneity in the level of self-actualisation is established. This fact testifies to the lack of distinctness characteristic of the studied group of subjects in the manifestation of the potential for self-actualisation. The fluctuation of indicators varies within the limits of the average statistical norm (the asymmetry values of all indicators of the methodology do not exceed critical values and are close to zero). It follows that the participants are characterized by an average degree of internalisation (appropriation) of those behavioural and value indicators that characterize the self-actualising personality. This average statistical representation of the self-actualisation phenomenon is observed in all the main spheres of life of the self-improvement of a person - cognition, values, attitudes toward oneself, other people, and life as a whole.

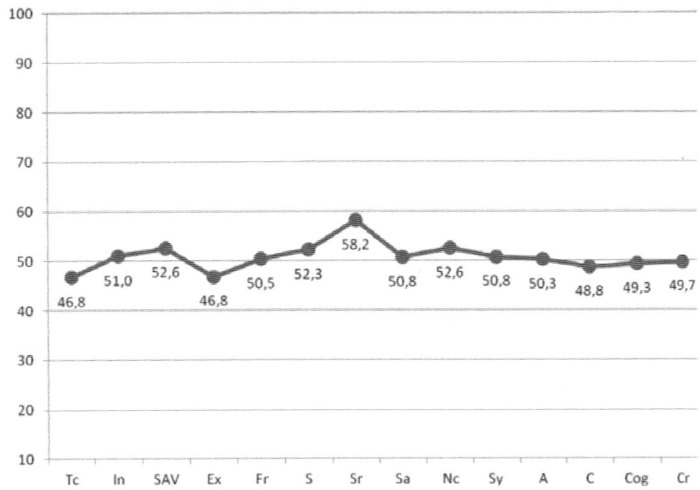

Tc – time competence, In – independence (support), VALUES: SAV – value orientations, Ex – behaviour flexibility, FEELINGS: Fr – sensitivity to one's own needs and feelings, S – spontaneity in expressing feelings behaviorally, SELF-ACCEPTANCE: Sr – self-regard, Sa – self-acceptance, HUMAN CONCEPT: Nc – Nature concept, Sy - synergy, INTERPERSONAL SENSITIVITY: A – acceptance of aggression, C – ability for contact, ATTITUDE TO COGNITION: Cog – cognitive needs, Cr – creativity.

Figure 1. Average values of self-actualisation indicators for the study participants

The measured indicators of self-actualisation appeared to be relatively homogenous. This evidences the lack of pronounced distinction that would characterize the studied group's potential for self-actualisation.

The subsequent analysis of descriptive statistics made it possible to reveal the following features. In terms of "time competence", there is a tendency to prevail in lower than medium and high values in terms of expression (Xsr: Mean = 46.8; standard deviation: std.dev. = 8.03). It was found that 37.33% of the participants are characterized by low values in this indicator, and high ones are expressed in 8.7% of participants. The data show that more than a third of the participants in the study find discrete perception of their life path, focusing only on one of the segments of the time scale (past, present or future). And only a tenth of the participants exhibits the psychological perception of time typical of self-actualising personalities. According to many authors, competence over time positively correlates with the personal development of a person (Kronik, 2008).

According to indicator In "Independence/Support", the basic indicator of self-actualisation, it was found that low values are characteristic of 27.8% of participants and high of 31.7%. The analysis of measures of variability showed a wide range of variation of individual values (excess Ex <0, Ex = -0.78). It follows that the educational programme is attended by quite different people in relation to the inherent locus of control of their behaviour, both "from the outside" and " from within directed "personalities" (following A. Reisman's idea, cited from Aleshina et al., 1995).

Significant differences in the expression and generalization of the measured parameters (Mann-Whitney U test, $p = 0.003$) were identified in the sphere of values (scales SAV – Value orientation, Ex – Behaviour Flexibility, Figure 1). It means that the majority of the participants share and accept the values inherent in a self-actualizing person (scale 3, M = 54.12), but show a lack of willingness to orient to these values in their own behaviour (scale 4, M = 47.98). The declared and actual aspects of value behaviour regulation do not match: the subjects demonstrate they are unprepared for behavioural flexibility in realizing their values.

A similar trend was observed in the sphere of feelings (scales Fr – Sensitivity to one's own needs, S - Spontaneity, Mann-Whitney U test, $p = 0.000$). The study participants tend to highly appreciate their strengths, positive character traits, to respect themselves for these (scale 7, M = 60.4), but on the behavioural level, they are not willing to accept themselves as they are, regardless of the evaluation of their merits and shortcomings.

Another feature of the self-actualisation profile was identified in the sphere of interpersonal sensitivity. The analysis of the central tendency measures showed that most participants are characterized by low, rather than high, capacity for contact (scale Con, Me = 43, Mo = 37). Hence, the subjects demonstrate a weak ability to quickly establish deep and close emotionally intense contacts with other people. It should be noted that the capacity for contact as a self-actualisation indicator is understood as sensitivity and tactfulness in interpersonal relationships, as an indirect indicator of social intelligence. The analysis of the study participants' communicative sphere showed that they are characterized by a high and non-frustrated need for communication, with a tendency for dominance, perversity and conformity. However, the subjects do not demonstrate harmony or ecology in interpersonal communication, that is, their high communicative ability is of an egocentric nature.

Thus, the self-actualisation profile is distinguished by an average level of self-realisation drive, the inconsistency between the declared and behaviorally demonstrated values, the discrepancy between high self-esteem and self-acceptance, and low interpersonal sensitivity.

Comparative analysis (Wilcoxson) dynamics in the process of attending the educational programme of the desire for self-actualisation, measured using the technique "Self-actualisation test" in the adaptation of L.Ya. Gozman et al., led to the following results (Figure 2, Table 1).

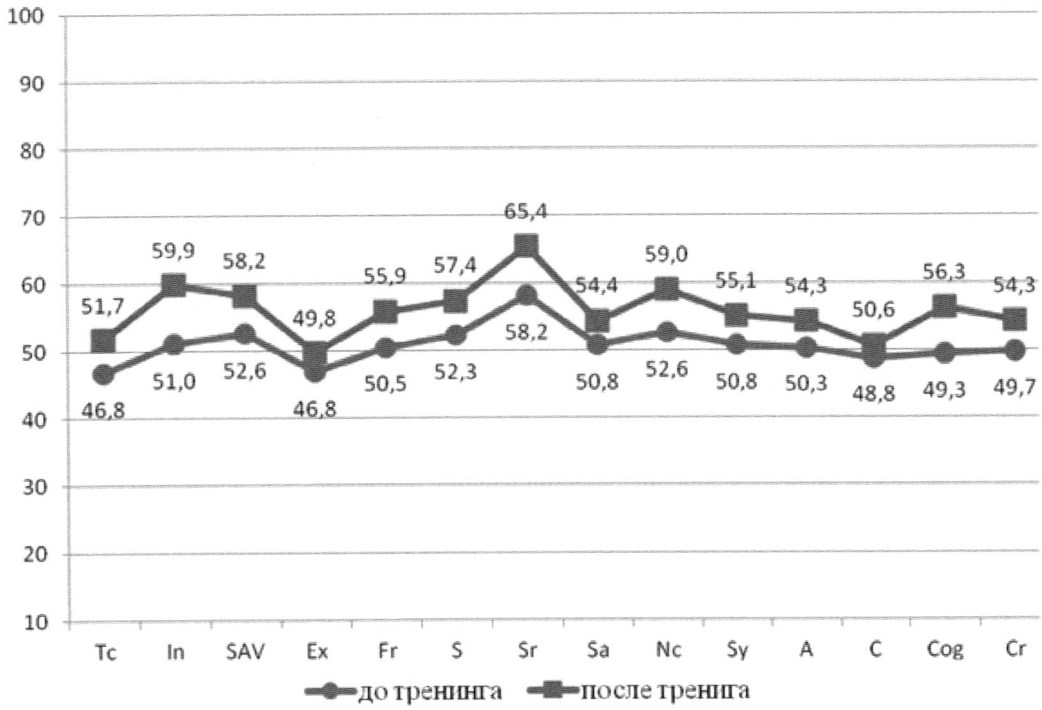

Figure 2. Mean values of self-actualisation indicators before (lower green line) and after (upper red line) the training

The trajectories of two self-actualisation profiles with a visual assessment (Figure 2) show concurrent trends in the expression of the indicators. However, the shift (according to the T-criterion of Wilcoxson) of values of self-actualisation indicators (profile) with respect to the level of their expression was statistically reliable (Table 1). A highly significant shift of all values of self-actualisation indicators towards their increase is established upon repeated measurement after taking the educational programme. An exception was the indicator "ability for contact" (C) from the block of interpersonal sensitivity as the area of self-realisation of a person ($p = 0.177$).

Anticipating the interpretation of established empirical facts, it is necessary to designate the conceptual definition of self-actualisation, which is the basis of the experiment. In the course of the existential-humanistic approach, the phenomenon is treated as a striving for self-realisation, more precisely, the tendency to actualise the potential. This tendency can be called the desire of a person to be as close as possible to whom they can become (Gozman et al., 1995). Indicators of self-actualisation, presented in the form of judgments in the test, were behavioural and value characteristics that distinguish a healthy self-actualising person from a neurotic, as well as a person who manifests marginal forms of behaviour.

It follows that psychological technique, which was the basis of the educational programme, initiated the desire of its participants to realise their potential. An essential feature of this initiated aspiration was not just informing and accepting the values of self-actualisation (the first scales in each of the self-actualisation blocks in the methodology), but also the willingness to realize these values in the behaviour (the second scales in each of the techniques blocks).

Table 1. The results of a comparative analysis of indicators of self-actualisation in the group of participants before and after the passage educational programme

NB. 1. Comparative analysis was performed using the Wilcoxson T-test (Wilcoxson T-test) for dependent samples, n = 72. 2. The table shows the probability of error (p), the sum of the ranks of the negative shifts, the sum of the ranks of the positive shifts

Indicators	Error probability, p; shifts		Change dynamics, ↑ ↓	T-Wilcoxcon
	The sum of negative shifts	The sum of positive shifts		
Time competence (Tc)	p=0,000 116,0	4829,0	↑	-5,541
Independence / support (In)	p=0,000 740,5	5700,5	↑	-7,108
Value orientation (SAV)	p=0,000 1023,0	4333,0	↑	-5,452
Behaviour flexibility (Ex)	p=0,001 1774,0	3897,0	↑	-3,348
sensitivity to one's own needs and feelings (Fr)	p=0,000 794,0	4562,0	↑	-6,206
spontaneity (S)	p=0,000 1212,5	3938,5	↑	-4,623
self-regard (Sr)	p=0,000 1044,0	5397,0	↑	-6,238
self-acceptance (Sa)	p=0,000 1999,5	4441,5	↑	-3,500
Nature concept (Nc)	p=0,000 917,5	4032,5	↑	-5,441
synergy (Sy)	p=0,000 1285 ,5	3274,5	↑	-3,694
acceptance of aggression (A)	p=0,000 1576,0	4310,0	↑	-4,193
ability for contact (C)	p=0,177 2600,0	3505,0	0	-1,350
cognitive needs (Cog)	p=0,000 661,0	4389,0	↑	-6,414
creativity (Cr)	p=0,000 1524,0	4471,0	↑	-4,459

The peculiarity of the dynamics of the self-actualisation profile is that the declared indicators (the first scale in the block) in all spheres of self-realisation revealed a greater shift in expression ($p < 0.01$) than generalized indicators (the second scale in the block), showing the realisation of self-actualisation values in behaviour. Thus, the mean of the Wilcoxson T-test in the group of indicators of self-actualisation values (scales SAV, Fr, Sr, Nc, A, Cog) was Xmean = -5.657, in the group of generalized indicators (Ex, S, Sa, Sy, C, Cr) - Xmean = -3.494. The result of this comparison indicates that the desire for self-realisation among programme participants, the measure of their acceptance of self-actualisation values, is expressed much more intensely than the readiness to implement these values in their own behaviour, attitudes, and activities.

The strongest shifts in the T-criterion (Table 1) in the direction of increasing values are recorded in such spheres of self-actualisation as feelings (self-sensitivity and spontaneity), self-perception (self-esteem and self-acceptance) and attitude to cognition (cognitive needs and creativity). It follows that the impact has led to changes in the sphere of self-reflection, the accuracy and subtlety of self-understanding, respect for oneself and the desire to acquire new knowledge.

Highly significant shifts are also recorded in the values of the basic indicators of self-actualisation - time competence (Tc) and independence (In). This fact can be interpreted as follows: the participants at the end of the programme showed a more harmonious, non-discrete perception of their own time, as well as a greater independence of their values and behaviour from external circumstances, a tendency to internal rather than an external locus of responsibility.

These results can indirectly be considered as indicators of the content validity and the targeted orientation of psychological technique implemented in the educational programme.

3. CONCLUSION

The attempt to study the level of self-actualisation in adults who are seeking opportunities for self-development and self-realisation through further education allows us to draw the following conclusions.

- Those with a strong need to confirm their potential (hidden) personality traits and a low level of cognitive resources search for educational opportunities for personal development.
- The level of self-actualisation according to all indicators has average values and is rather indistinct.
- The level of generalization of self-actualisation indicators for all blocks exceeds their level of expression.
- The desire to actualize reserves is present but does not manifest itself in real behaviour. It is this result that evidences the decision to participate in educational programmes.

Thus, the study revealed that adults who seek opportunities for self-development through enrolling on further education programmes do so in the desire to enhance their hidden merits, to use, preserve and enrich their cognitive resources and, thereby self-actualize.

The practical implications of the study results include, but are not limited to the following: understanding the specifics of self-actualisation of adult learners can facilitate tailoring further education programmes to their needs; by diagnosing self-actualisation in adults educational managers can identify their target audience and select prospective participants for further education programmes.

The development of adult education as a factor of integration into the contemporary reality is inextricably linked with activating the adults' cognitive capabilities, identifying potential resources and modeling modern educational environments that would adequately provide for the operation of self-development mechanisms.

Increasing the adaptive capacity of an adult to ensure a constructive response to socio-cultural changes is essential and can be realized through promoting new models of lifelong education.

ACKNOWLEDGEMENT

The reported study was funded by RFBR according to the research project 17-29-09136.

REFERENCES

Aleshina Yu.E. et al, 1995. *Self-actualisation test*. Moscow: Rossiyskoye pedagogicheskoye agentstvo.

Toffler, A., 1971. *Future shock*. Bantam.

Dench S., Regan J., 2000. Learning in later life: Motivation and impact. Research Report RR183, London: Department for Education and Employment.

European Commission, 2001. *Lisbon Strategy*. Brussels.

Gozman, L.Ya., Kroz, M.V. and Latinskaya, M.V., 1995. Samoaktualiziruyushchiy test. M.: Rossiyskoye ped. agentstvo, 44, p.4.) (Gozman, L.Ya., Croz, M.V. and Latin, MV, 1995. Self-Actualizing Test. M .: Russian ped. agency, 44, p.4.) In Russian

Kronik, A.A., 2008. Psikhologicheskoye vremya lichnosti/Ye.I. Golovakha, A.A. Kronik. M.: Smysl. (Kronik, A.A., 2008. Psychological time of personality / E.I. Golovakha, A.A. Kronik. M .: Sense.) In Russian

Litvinova, N.P., 2003. Sozdaniye optimalnoy modeli upravleniya sistemoy obrazovaniya vzroslykh. (Creation of the optimal model for managing adult education system). In *Obrazovaniye vzroslykh–globalnyy dialog.* Saint Petersburg. In Russian.

Merriam S. B., Kee Y., 2014. Promoting community wellbeing: The case for lifelong learning for older adults. *Adult Education Quarterly,* 64(2): 128-144.

Nurgaleyeva, L.V., 2015. Kognitivnaya integratsiya v kontekste modelirovaniya sovremennykh obrazovatelnykh sred (Cognitive integration in the context of modeling modern educational environments). *Gumanitarnaya informatika*, 9. In Russian.

Shostrom, E.L., 1964. An inventory for the measurement of self-actualisation. *Educational and psychological measurement*, *24*(2), pp.207-218.

Shostrom, E.L., 1996. *Personal orientation inventory*. Educational and Industrial Testing Service.

VISUOSPATIAL WORKING MEMORY AND EARLY MATH SKILLS IN FIRST GRADE CHILDREN

Rachele Fanari, Carla Meloni and Davide Massidda
Department of Education, Psychology, Philosophy, University of Cagliari (Italy)

ABSTRACT

This study aimed to investigate the relationship between different components of active visuospatial working memory and math ability in young children. In a longitudinal study, we compared the contributions of active visual and spatial working memory (WM) tasks in early math performance at two times: the beginning of the first class of primary school (T1) and the end of the first class of primary school (T2). Two tests were conducted with 43 young participants to investigate active visual WM (Imaginative Puzzles) and active spatial WM (Corsi Backward). Measurements related to pre-math ability (BIN 4-6 test) at T1 and math skills (AC-MT 6-11 test) at T2 were accomplished. The relationship between visual and spatial WM and math ability was analyzed using a regression model in which the predictors were identified through a forward selection based on the use of the BIC index (Bayesian Information Criterion). Results show that at the beginning of primary school, basic knowledge of magnitude and numbers is strongly influenced by spatial WM. T1 pre-math performance is the sole predictor of mathematical performance at T2. These results suggest different implications of domain-general and domain-specific variable on early math performance, depending on the child's development period. This finding brings additional evidence to the debate on the relationship between visuospatial WM and math ability in young children.

KEYWORDS

Visual Working Memory, Spatial Working Memory, Early Math, Pre-Math, Longitudinal Study

1. INTRODUCTION

The literature of early math skills development emphasizes that, at the beginning of primary school, this type of learning involves both domain-specific skills related to numerical cognition, such as understanding of quantity, recognition of numbers and counting skills (Geary, Hamson, & Hoard, 2000; Krajewski & Schneider, 2009), and domain-general cognitive skills that predict not only mathematics achievement but also other general learning abilities (De Smedt et al., 2009; Fuchs et al., 2005; Passolunghi, Mammarella, & Altoè, 2008; Passolunghi, Vercelloni, & Schadee, 2007).

Among the domain-general cognitive abilities involved in math learning, the literature assigns a key role to working memory (Hitch, 1978; McLean & Hitch, 1999; Gathercole & Pickering, 2000; Rasmussen & Bisanz, 2005; Bull, Espy, & Wiebe, 2008; Passolunghi et al., 2008) and its visuospatial components (e.g., Krajewski & Schneider, 2009; Passolunghi & Mammarella, 2010; Alloway & Passolunghi, 2011; Passolunghi & Cornoldi, 2008).

Working memory (WM) is a mental space that controls, processes, and maintains relevant information to complete a complex cognitive task. According to the original Baddeley and Hitch model (Baddeley & Hitch, 1974; Baddeley, 1998) WM consists of a unitary central executive (CE), considered to be the heart of the model because it controls and manipulates relevant information, and two sub-components, the phonological loop and the visuospatial sketchpad, that maintain verbal and visuospatial information. Shah and Miyake (1996) questioned whether the CE should be considered a unitary construct, suggesting that, even at the level of higher cognitive processes, it is necessary to make a distinction between the verbal and visuospatial domains. At a lower level of processing, Logie and Pearson (1997) proposed separating the visual and spatial WM maintenance sub-components, with the visual component active in the recall of shapes and textures and the spatial component devoted to the recall of spatial locations and sequences.

The Cornoldi and Vecchi (2003) Continuity Model is a WM model that recognizes both the distinction between storage and processing and the presence of distinct verbal, visual, and spatial components at various levels of cognition. This model has a cone structure characterized by two main dimensions: the horizontal continuum and the vertical continuum. The horizontal continuum defines the type of information used in a given task and, at this level, it is possible to hypothesize the existence of semi-independent systems and, therefore, to identify possible dissociation between specific types of information (e.g., verbal, visual, and spatial codes), while the vertical continuum represents the level of active control associated with a particular cognitive task.

The literature on the relationship between active WM and math skills is mainly related to the Baddeley and Hitch model and highlights how the CE is the WM component that best predicts mathematics performance. The CE involvement results come principally from studies that used verbal, active WM tasks, such as backward digit span, counting recall, and listening span tests (see Raghubar, Barnes, & Hecht, 2010 and Friso-van den Bos, van der Ven, Kroesbergen, & van Luit, 2013 for reviews).

Even though the CE is considered to be the best predictor of mathematics performance, there are few studies on the relationship between the CE (the active WM) and math performance conducted with separation of the active visuospatial domain and the active verbal domain. Instead, most of the works that have investigated the involvement of the CE in math learning have considered verbal and visuospatial active memory task performances together with a unique score (e.g. Passolunghi and Lanfranchi, 2012; Simmons, Willis and Adams, 2012). The results of these studies confirm the involvement of active WM skills in early mathematical performance and learning but do not allow us to identify the presence of a unique contribution of visuospatial active WM abilities in math abilities development.

A clear suggestion about the utility of separating the verbal and visuospatial components of active WM in relation to learning abilities is found in St Clair-Thompson & Gathercole (2006), who explored the influence of active visuospatial WM and active verbal WM on school performance in a sample of adolescents. Their results showed a strong relationship between visuospatial WM and math, while verbal WM was involved only in the English score. Further evidence that active visuospatial WM is individually implied in math learning comes from Cornoldi, Della Vecchia, and Tressoldi (1995) who studied sixth-grade children with low visuospatial ability and observed that these children had greater difficulty in math than in other school disciplines; the children had low scores in both active and passive visuospatial tasks, but the effects were more apparent in active visuospatial tasks. Bull et al. (2008), in a similar vein, observed in a longitudinal study that visuospatial WM, evaluated in first grade through the Corsi Backward test, predicted mathematical performance in the third class of primary school.

These results suggest that active visuospatial abilities are involved in math learning and that the involvement of active visuospatial processing may be different at different ages during math learning processes.

As for the distinction between spatial and visual active WM, to our knowledge, there are no studies that have directly investigated the different contributions of visual and spatial active WM to early numeracy.

In the current study, we investigated the implications of different sub-components of active visuospatial WM (according to the Cornoldi and Vecchi Continuity Model) on the developmental trend of pre- and early math skills. We performed a longitudinal design structured with two pivot times: Time 1 (T1), the beginning of the first class of the primary school; Time 2 (T2), the end of the first class of primary school.

In our work, we have maintained a distinction between visual and spatial active tasks, considering the involvement of the different components of the CE in the very first stage of math learning. We also take into account the relationship between pre-math abilities and later math performance, since recent studies show that early numeracy abilities are important domain-specific predictors for math learning (e.g., Passolunghi et al., 2007).

Our first goal was to observe whether there is a different contribution from the active visual and spatial WM abilities in children's math performance, measured at two different moments. The literature describes research on passive STM visual and spatial processes linked to math learning, but there are no studies that have kept the spatial and visual domain distinct in the active WM. If active processing follows the same path of passive processes, we should expect different contributions from the visual and spatial WM tasks at different development stages; the spatial areas are most involved in the youngest children's performance, while the visual areas are most involved in the subsequent years of schooling (McKenzie, Bull, Gray, 2003; Holmes et al. 2008). Finally, we expect continuity between pre-math competence and early math performance during the first year of primary school.

2. METHOD

2.1 Participants

Forty-three Italian children (23 males and 20 females) were recruited from a public school in Cagliari (Italy). Children were tested at the beginning of the first primary school year (October, time 1; mean age = 77.7 months; SD = 3.32; range: 71-84 months) and at the end of the first primary school year (May, time 2; mean age = 82.7; SD = 3.73). All participants showed typical development as identified by local educational services, and all were native Italian speakers. Both the school and the children's parents agreed to let the students take part in the research study, and all signed informed consent forms. Ethical approval was granted by the ethics committee of the Department of Education, Psychology, Philosophy of the University of Cagliari.

The socioeconomic status of the sample, measured by the Family Affluence Scale (Boyce, Torsheim, Currie, & Zambon, 2006), was middle class.

2.2 Procedure

An experienced psychologist tested children individually in a quiet room of the school in a single session according to the procedure defined for the tests, from Monday to Friday and from 8:30 a.m. to 11:45 a.m. daily. Each session lasted about 30 minutes.

The psychometric tools used to collect data included instruments designed to measure the active visuospatial WM, instruments designed to assess early numerical competence, and instruments to evaluate mathematics achievement. The same tests were presented at T1 (beginning of the first year of primary school) and T2 (end of the first year of primary school).

During the time elapsed between the first and second test sessions the children attended to the learning/teaching activities following the Italian Education Ministry guidelines, which do not include specific visuo-spatial skills training, and which lead to the acquisition of the basic concepts of mathematics through verbal activities integrated with visual ones such as completion games, puzzles and card games.

Active visuospatial working memory tasks. The visuospatial WM skills were tested through the Italian BVS-Corsi test (Battery for Visuo-Spatial Memory; Mammarella, Toso, Pazzaglia, & Cornoldi, 2008), by using two tasks: the Imaginative Puzzles test (identified in the next sections with the term VisWM) to evaluate the active visual WM, and the Corsi Backward test (identified with the term SpWM) to evaluate the active spatial WM.

Early numerical competence assessment. Children's early numeracy skills at T1 were evaluated through the "Battery for the evaluation of Numerical Intelligence from 4 to 6 years of age" (BIN 4–6) (Molin, Poli, Lucangeli, 2007), a standardized test providing norms for pre-school Italian children. The battery is made up of 12 subscales divided into four areas: lexical, which requires knowledge of numerical symbols (numbers recognition task, Arabic digits reading task, and Arabic digits writing task); semantic (comparing two Arabic digits to determine which represents the larger quantity and comparing two arrays of dots to determine which contains more dots); counting (counting forward and backward; ordering Arabic numerals; completing numerical series); and pre-syntactic (matching Arabic numerals with corresponding dots; the one-many task; ordering different objects cards from bigger to smaller and vice versa). The final score of Early Numerical Competence (ENC) is the sum of all the subscales of the battery.

Mathematics achievement. To assess the mathematical performance at T2, the Italian test "AC-MT 6-11 - Test for the evaluation of calculating and problem-solving abilities" (Cornoldi, Lucangeli, & Bellina, 2012) was used. The test was administered collectively to the entire class under the supervision of an experienced psychologist. AC-MT 6-11 is a paper and pencil test comprising five subtests: Operations (child must solve additions and subtractions); Number judgment (evaluates the semantic comprehension of number quantities); Tens and Ones task (evaluates the ability to process the syntactic structure of numbers); Larger to Smaller task and Small to Large task (evaluates the semantic representation of numbers). The final score of Numerical Intelligence (NI) is the sum of the scores of the five subtests.

2.3 Statistical Analyses

Descriptive statistics of variables and measures were calculated (Table 1).

Table 1. Descriptive Statistics of the Variables Considered in the Study for Each Time (n = 43). VisWM = visual WM, measured by the Imaginative Puzzles test; spWM = spatial WM measured by the Corsi Backward test; ENC = Early Numerical Competence measured by BIN 4–6 test; NI = numerical intelligence measured by AC-MT 6-11 test

	Time 1			Time 2		
	Mean	sd	Range	Mean	sd	Range
Age	77.7	3.73	71-84	82.7	3.73	76-89
VisWM	11.19	4.57	2-20	12.12	4.05	2-20
SpWM	2.60	0.66	2-5	2.93	0.67	2-5
ENC	100.05	4.27	88-106	-	-	-
NI	-	-	-	20.28	5.25	4-26

Exploratory correlation analyses were performed to examine the relations between math measures and active VSWM measures. The Pearson's index was used. The analysis showed significant correlations between ENC (T1) and: NI (T2), $r(43) = .50$, $p < .01$, VisWM (T1), $r(43) = .36$, $p < .05$, SpWM (T1), $r(43) = .46$, $p < .01$. Further, significant correlations were found also between NI (T2) and: VisWM (T1), $r(43) = .40$, $p < .01$, SpWM (T1), $r(43) = .35$, $p < .05$, VisWM (T2), $r(43) = .31$, $p < .05$. There was not a significant correlation between SpWM (T2) and NI (T2), $r(43) = .23$, $p > .05$.

Table 2. Pearson's *r* correlation between active VSWM measures and early numerical competence tasks (ENC) at T1 and numerical intelligence (NI) at T2. VisWM: active visual WM; SpWM: active spatial WM

	VisWM (T1)	VisWM (T2)	SpWM (T1)	SpWM (T2)	ENC (T1)	NI (T2)
VisWM (T1)	-					
VisWM (T2)	.40**	-				
SpWM (T1)	.28	.47**	-			
SpWM (T2)	.28	.24	.26	-		
ENC (T1)	.36*	.52***	.46**	.35*	-	
NI (T2)	.40**	.31*	.35*	.23	.50***	-

*** $p < .001$; ** $p < .01$; * $p < .05$.

As second analysis step, we fitted two regression models to study the influence of active VSWM variables both on early numeracy abilities ENC at T1 and on math ability NI at T2. Relevant predictors were identified by a forward selection procedure based on the Bayesian Information Criterion (BIC) index (Schwarz, 1978), which selected the best model from a Bayesian perspective.

Results at T1 showed that ENC was predicted by only the active spatial WM task ($\beta = .46$, $p = .001$), which explained 21% of the variance in early numeracy ability. Results at T2 showed that NI performance was predicted only by the ENC measured at T1 ($\beta = .50$, $p = .0004$), which explained 25% of the variance in Numerical Intelligence.

3. DISCUSSION AND CONCLUSIONS

In the present study, we longitudinally studied the involvement of active VSWM on early numeracy abilities during the first year of primary school, distinguishing between spatial and visual active WM sub-components. In our work, children at the beginning of the first (T1), and at the end (T2) of the first primary school year were given two tasks that investigated active visual WM (Imaginative Puzzle task) and active spatial WM (Corsi Backward task). Moreover, early numeracy competence was measured with a pre-math normed test, (BIN 4-6 - Molin et al., 2007) at the beginning of the first year of primary school, and mathematical skills were measured with a normed math test (AC-MT 6-11 - Cornoldi et al., 2012) at the end of the first year of primary school.

We explore through a correlation analysis the relationship between early numeracy competence (BIN test score at T1) and later math skills (total AC-MT 6-11 test score at T2). Early numeracy abilities significantly correlated over time with later math skills. Children who, before starting school, had best learned how to handle numerical magnitude and numerical symbols, show—at the end of first grade—a better comprehension of the semantic and syntactic structure of numbers and are more able in written calculations. This result was expected, indicating that the first knowledge of magnitude and numbers provides an important foundation that influences the child along the first stage of formal mathematics teaching. It is a well-known phenomenon, in fact, that one of the best predictors of school success in mathematics is the level of early numeracy abilities (Gersten, Jordan, & Flojo, 2005; Jordan, Kaplan, Olàh, & Locuniak, 2006; Passolunghi et al., 2007; Passolunghi et al., 2008; Lyons, Price, Vaessen, Blomert, & Ansari, 2014).

Concerning the involvement of active WM components (visual and spatial) with numerical ability, the correlation analysis shows at T1 a good correlation between WM abilities, both visual and spatial, and pre-math abilities. At T2, instead, the correlation between math abilities and WM abilities is weaker: only the visual WM is significantly correlated with NI, while the spatial WM abilities are not significantly correlated with Numerical Intelligence score. It should be noted that the correlation between NI and earlier T1 WM competences is quite strong. Correlation analysis, so, suggests that, while before starting the formal path of math learning, both visual and spatial active WM abilities are correlated with pre-math knowledge, at the end of first grade the visual WM may be more influential than the spatial one.

To better explore these results, two regression analysis were computed. The first regression model aimed to study the influence of active VSWM variables on early numeracy abilities measured at T1 and showed that spatial working memory ability is the best predictor of mathematical performance; it explains the 21% of variance. However, a second regression analysis, in which all variables measured at the two times have been considered, suggests that at different time steps it is possible to find a different involvement of domain-specific and domain-general variables. In this second regression analysis the math performance measured at T2 is predicted only by the early numerical competence measured at T1, that explains 25% of the variance.

Therefore, at the very beginning of primary school, when there has not yet been a formal math teaching, the construction of basic knowledge about magnitudes and numbers and the first knowledge about the lexical and semantic aspects of numbers are strongly influenced by spatial active WM. Moving to the end of first grade (T2), our results show that at this stage the math performance is mainly based on the already possessed knowledges about magnitude and numbers.

Our exploratory study aimed to cast light on the involvement of visual and spatial active WM in the first phase of math learning, at a developmental stage for which no data are available: the first year of primary school. Even considered the limitation of a relatively scarce sample size, our results show that active VSWM influences early math performance in the very first phases of math learning and that there is a different individual contribution of visual and of spatial components.

At a theoretical level, this preliminary result suggests the importance to distinguish between visual and spatial WM components also at the processing level, following the suggestion coming from the passive WM literature (e.g. McKenzie et al., 2003).

As previously mentioned, the influence of active VSWM and the specific role of its constituent parts (visual and spatial) on math development in very young children has not been studied in the literature; therefore, our expectations for this study were mainly based on passive WM literature.

Our results seem to follow the same trend observed in researches that have studied the influence of the spatial and visual passive memory components on early numerical cognition: both our work and passive memory studies show a greater involvement of the spatial component than the visual one on pre- and early math abilities. For example, McKenzie, Bull & Gray (2003) found that 6-year-olds mainly use a spatial rather than a visual-type strategy to solve arithmetic operations. These results suggest that the link between numbers and space is particularly important for the development of numerical cognition and suggest the idea that the child, prior to math formal teaching, develops a spatial code for numbers probably thanks to a mental number line, as suggested by the Dehaene studies (1992). Accordingly with the number line idea, our data seem to suggest that in very early stage of math learning the spatial WM contributes to the formation of the first, mostly spatial, numerical representations.

In summary, our results show a clear influence of spatial skills on younger children's number and magnitude knowledge, while later, at the end of the first year of primary school, the association between spatial memory and mathematical performance is not significant either in the correlation analysis nor in the Bayesian model. This trend confirms passive WM literature findings and suggests, as for example hypothesize by Holmes and Adams (2006), that initially the child relies mainly on spatial strategies (while in a later stage a verbal strategy emerges) and that spatial WM functions as a workspace to support the transition from early concrete informal knowledge to the nascent formal mathematical knowledge.

Our exploratory longitudinal study showed that both domain-specific knowledge and domain-general variables are implied in the first math learning process, but with different weights along time. Prerequisites confirm themselves as the ground of the first math learning at the end of first grade, while before (beginning first grade) domain-general ability such as spatial active WM is an important variable in the math learning processes.

Our findings, at a theoretical level, suggest that the involvement of general domain abilities in early-math performance can be better understood within the framework of active WM models in which the spatial and the visual components are kept separate, as for instance the WM Continuity Model (Cornoldi & Vecchi, 2003).

The relationships between active VSWM variables and first math learning highlighted in our study are important for a better understanding of the components involved in the first phases of math abilities development and a better identification of strengths and weaknesses in children with early math difficulties. These relationships are worth of further investigation in future longitudinal research that will involve a larger number of subjects and need to be extended over a longer time span to better explore the involvement of active visuospatial working memory abilities along the math learning process.

ACKNOWLEDGEMENT

This study was supported by the University of Cagliari (Italy). The authors want to thank the principal of the school where data collection took place. Special thanks go to the children, families, and teachers who participated in the study.

Declaration of interest: none.

REFERENCES

Alloway, T. P., & Passolunghi, M. C. (2011). The relationship between working memory, IQ, and mathematical skills in children. *Learning and Individual Differences*, *21*(1), 133-137.

Baddeley, A. D., & Hitch, G. (1974). Working memory. *Psychology of Learning and Motivation*, 8, 47-89.

Baddeley, A. (1998). Recent developments in working memory. *Current Opinion in Neurobiology*, 8(2), 234-238.

Boyce, W., Torsheim, T., Currie, C., & Zambon, A. (2006). The family affluence scale as a measure of national wealth: validation of an adolescent self-report measure. Social indicators research, 78(3), 473-487.

Bull, R., Espy, K. A., & Wiebe, S. A. (2008). Short-term memory, working memory, and executive functioning in preschoolers: Longitudinal predictors of mathematical achievement at age 7 years. *Developmental Neuropsychology*, *33*(3), 205-228.

Cornoldi, C., Lucangeli, D., & Bellina, M. (2012). *AC-MT 6-11. Test di valutazione delle abilità di calcolo e soluzione dei problemi [AC-MT 6-11 - Test for the evaluation of calculating and problem solving abilities]*. Gruppo MT. Trento, Italy: Erickson.

Cornoldi, C., & Vecchi, T. (2003). *Visuospatial working memory and individual differences*. Hove, UK: Psychology Press.

Cornoldi, C., Vecchia, R. D., & Tressoldi, P. E. (1995). Visuospatial Working Memory Limitations in Low Visuospatial High Verbal Intelligence Children. *Journal of Child Psychology and Psychiatry*, *36*(6), 1053-1064.

De Smedt, B., Janssen, R., Bouwens, K., Verschaffel, L., Boets, B., & Ghesquière, P. (2009). Working memory and individual differences in mathematics achievement: A longitudinal study from first grade to second grade. *Journal of Experimental Child Psychology*, *103*(2), 186-201.

Dehaene, S. (1992). Varieties of numerical abilities. *Cognition*, 44(1-2), 1-42.

Friso-van den Bos, I., van der Ven, S. H., Kroesbergen, E. H., & van Luit, J. E. (2013). Working memory and mathematics in primary school children: A meta-analysis. *Educational Research Review*, *10*, 29-44.

Fuchs, L. S., Compton, D. L., Fuchs, D., Paulsen, K., Bryant, J. D., & Hamlett, C. L. (2005). The prevention, identification, and cognitive determinants of math difficulty. *Journal of Educational Psychology*, *97*, 493–513.

Gathercole, S. E., & Pickering, S. J. (2000). Working memory deficits in children with low achievements in the national curriculum at 7 years of age. *British Journal of Educational Psychology*, *70*(2), 177-194.

Geary, D. C., Hamson, C. O., & Hoard, M. K. (2000). Numerical and arithmetical cognition: A longitudinal study of process and concept deficits in children with learning disability. *Journal of Experimental Child Psychology*, *77*(3), 236-263.

Gersten, R., Jordan, N. C., & Flojo, J. R. (2005). Early identification and interventions for students with mathematics difficulties. *Journal of Learning Disabilities*, 38(4), 293-304.

Hitch, G. J. (1978). The role of short-term working memory in mental arithmetic. *Cognitive Psychology*, *10*(3), 302-323.

Holmes, J., Adams, J. W., & Hamilton, C. J. (2008). The relationship between visuospatial sketchpad capacity and children's mathematical skills. *European Journal of Cognitive Psychology*, *20*(2), 272-289.

Jordan, N. C., Kaplan, D., Nabors Oláh, L., & Locuniak, M. N. (2006). Number sense growth in kindergarten: A longitudinal investigation of children at risk for mathematics difficulties. *Child Development*, *77*(1), 153-175.

Krajewski, K., & Schneider, W. (2009). Exploring the impact of phonological awareness, visual–spatial working memory, and preschool quantity–number competencies on mathematics achievement in elementary school: Findings from a 3-year longitudinal study. *Journal of Experimental Child Psychology*, *103*(4), 516-531.

Logie, H.R., & Pearson, D. G. (1997). The inner eye and the inner scribe of visuo-spatial working memory: Evidence from developmental fractionation. *European Journal of Cognitive Psychology, 9*(3), 241-257.

Lyons, I. M., Price, G. R., Vaessen, A., Blomert, L., & Ansari, D. (2014). Numerical predictors of arithmetic success in grades 1–6. *Developmental Science*, *17*(5), 714-726.

Mammarella, I. C., Toso, C., Pazzaglia, F., & Cornoldi, C. (2008). *BVS-Corsi. Batteria per la valutazione della memoria visiva e spaziale [Bvs-Corsi – Battery for the evaluation of spatial and visual memory]*. Trento, Italy: Erickson.

McKenzie, B., Bull, R., & Gray, C. (2003). The effects of phonological and visual-spatial interference on children's arithmetical performance. *Educational and Child Psychology*, 20(3), 93-108.

McLean, J. F., & Hitch, G. J. (1999). Working memory impairments in children with specific arithmetic learning difficulties. *Journal of Experimental Child Psychology, 74*(3), 240-260.

Molin, A., Poli, S., & Lucangeli, D. (2007). *BIN 4-6, Batteria per la valutazione della Intelligenza Numerica in bambini dai 4 ai 6 anni [BIN 4-6, Battery for the evaluation of the Numerical Intelligence in children from 4 to 6 years of age]*. Trento, Italy: Erickson.

Passolunghi, M. C., & Cornoldi, C. (2008). Working memory failures in children with arithmetical difficulties. *Child Neuropsychology*, *14*(5), 387-400.

Passolunghi, M. C., & Lanfranchi, S. (2012). Domain- specific and domain- general precursors of mathematical achievement: A longitudinal study from kindergarten to first grade. *British Journal of Educational Psychology*, *82*(1), 42-63.

Passolunghi, M. C., & Mammarella, I. C. (2010). Spatial and visual working memory ability in children with difficulties in arithmetic word problem solving. *European Journal of Cognitive Psychology*, *22*(6), 944-963.

Passolunghi, M. C., Mammarella, I. C., & Altoè, G. (2008). Cognitive abilities as precursors of the early acquisition of mathematical skills during first through second grades. *Developmental Neuropsychology*, *33*(3), 229-250.

Passolunghi, M. C., Vercelloni, B., & Schadee, H. (2007). The precursors of mathematics learning: Working memory, phonological ability and numerical competence. *Cognitive Development*, *22*(2), 165-184.

Raghubar, K. P., Barnes, M. A., & Hecht, S. A. (2010). Working memory and mathematics: A review of developmental, individual difference, and cognitive approaches. *Learning and Individual Differences, 20*(2), 110-122.

Rasmussen, C., & Bisanz, J. (2005). Representation and working memory in early arithmetic. *Journal of Experimental Child Psychology*, *91*(2), 137-157.

Schwarz, G. (1978). Estimating the dimension of a model. *The Annals of Statistics*, 6, 461-464.

Shah, P., & Miyake, A. (1996). The separability of working memory resources for spatial thinking and language processing: an individual differences approach. *Journal of Experimental Psychology: General*, *125*(1), 4.

Simmons, F. R., Willis, C., & Adams, A. M. (2012). Different components of working memory have different relationships with different mathematical skills. *Journal of Experimental Child Psychology*, *111*(2), 139-155.

St Clair-Thompson, H. L., & Gathercole, S. E. (2006). Executive functions and achievements in school: Shifting, updating, inhibition, and working memory. *The Quarterly Journal of Experimental Psychology*, *59*(4), 745-759.

FLIPPING YOUR CLASSROOM: A METHODOLOGY FOR SUCCESSFUL FLIPPED CLASSROOMS

Pedro Isaias
Institute for Teaching and Learning Innovation (ITaLI), The University of Queensland, Brisbane, Australia

ABSTRACT

As higher education reinvents itself to respond to the needs of a new generation of learners and novel workplace demands, it pivots towards student-centred pedagogical approaches and focuses on the promotion of active and lifelong learning. The flipped classroom model emerges in this context to address the limitations of the traditional classroom. When successfully implemented, it can provide students with the opportunity to learn at their own pace and to develop self-learning competences that are useful both academically and professionally. This paper proposes a methodology for the effective deployment of the flipped classroom that aims to assist educators in their efforts to flip their classrooms. The methodology comprises five core aspects: pre-class content delivery, pre-class assessment, in-class content review, classroom active learning and in-class assessment.

KEYWORDS

Flipped Classroom, Blended Learning, Higher Education

1. INTRODUCTION

The incorporation of active learning activities within a classroom is often hindered by time constraints. Classes have a limited time period and teachers are faced with the intricate mission of delivering lectures and presenting active learning tasks. Flipped classrooms are being used as a method to increase the level of active learning during the classes (Kim et al., 2014). The flipped classroom refers to a pedagogical model that consists in delivering content via online lectures that the students can review at their own pace, before coming to the class, that assists them to be prepared to engage with the content during in-class learning activities (Mortensen and Nicholson, 2015). Despite the fact that the flipped classroom can be designed in learning settings that do not resort to the support of technology, they are primarily established in blended learning settings (Thai et al., 2017).

The flipped classroom is a student-centred learning approach that promotes students' independence and the development of active learning activities (McLaughlin et al., 2014). The core objective of adopting the flipped classroom method is to offer students the possibility to access the course content at their convenience, before they attend the class. This allows them to be prepared to actively engage with the materials in class, maximising deeper learning (Moraros et al., 2015). The evolution of technology facilitates the process of recording the video lectures to deliver content to the students prior to the class (Zappe et al., 2009), but they are not in themselves the centre of this methodology. It is rather the way in which they are incorporated into a different approach (Tucker, 2012). Adopting a flipped classroom approach provides the opportunity to break with the conventional structure of lectures that are based on the transmission of information by the teacher and the passive reception of this information by the students (Hutchings and Quinney, 2015).

The need to develop a methodology to guide the process of flipping a classroom derives from the fact that there is a variety of activities that can be associated with pre- and in-class activities, which can cause educators to be confused as to what type of activities actually work. Also, by learning from previous experiences it is possible to identify the aspects that are more effective to successfully flip a classroom. This paper begins by examining the flipped classroom model and then proposes a methodology for its successful implementation.

2. THE FLIPPED CLASSROOM APPROACH

Current evaluations of the flipped approach present differing opinions, but generally speaking the assessment they make is positive (Bishop and Verleger, 2013). Among the multiple existing definitions of the flipped classroom, Abeysekera and Dawson (2015) provide a summary of what it entails and define it as "a set of pedagogical approaches that: (1) move most information-transmission teaching out of class; (2) use class time for learning activities that are active and social and; (3) require students to complete pre- and/or post-class activities to fully benefit from in-class work." (p. 3). There is a wide variation between what different studies report having used as the pre-class content delivery assignments, although the majority seems to use a combination of asynchronous online video and quizzes or closed-ended problems. This variation exists equally in the type of activities that the teachers design for the in-class engagement with the material. Most studies seem to have a preference for using interactive learning tasks based on group work (Bishop and Verleger, 2013).

The flipped model popularity is associated with the multiple benefits it represents. It contributes to the empowerment of learners by endowing them with more control over their learning in the pre-class work that they can complete at a time they choose, in the classroom through their active participation and in the improvement of their lifelong learning aptitude (O'Flaherty and Phillips, 2015). The control that the students have over how they engage with the video lecture, what segments they review or are more interesting to them, is also an enabler of personalised learning (Danker, 2015, Moffett and Mill, 2014). The flipped classroom can enhance student-student and student-teacher interaction (Phillips and Trainor, 2014), foment student engagement and participation in the classroom and it can improve their learning outcomes (Thai et al., 2017). Previous research has showed that flipped classrooms are a valuable strategy to promote active learning also within the context of large classes (Danker, 2015). The fact that students have the possibility to prepare for the class in advance, makes them more available to expand on the material and interact more deeply with it (Kurtz et al., 2014). Time becomes less of a constraint, since the students can learn the material at their own pace, using as much time as they need (Bergmann and Sams, 2014). Moreover, since the students complete the assignments, which were previously allocated as homework, inside the classroom they can benefit from the direct help of their teachers and their peers (Danker, 2015). Traditionally, the teacher is present at the time of the delivery of content, but not when the students have to apply what they have learned during the completion of the homework assignments (Moffett and Mill, 2014).

The adoption of the flipped classroom implies changes to the role of the teachers. There are changes also at the level of the student's role. The students can assume an active and collaborative stance towards learning and engage more richly with the content of the class (Hutchings and Quinney, 2015). During the classroom the teachers predominantly assume the role of a mentor, guiding both individual and group work and prior to the class they are required to deliver learning content by using their technology competences (Dennen and Spector, 2016).

The implementation of the flipped classroom model requires educators to maximise its benefits, but also to understand the challenges it poses. Despite some claims that the effort of flipping the classroom is more substantial the first time the course is flipped (Moffett and Mill, 2014) and that it solely involves the reformatting of existing content (Bergmann and Sams, 2014) the time effort that it requires from educators is often cited as one of its most relevant challenges (Findlay-Thompson and Mombourquette, 2014, Ferreri and O'Connor, 2013, Mason et al., 2013). The pre-classroom preparation that is demanded of the students can similarly constitute a difficulty. In order for the flipped approach to be effective, the students have to learn to be self-learners (Findlay-Thompson and Mombourquette, 2014) and to review the materials before attending the classroom (McLaughlin et al., 2014). For those teachers who decide to deliver the content via online videos, the production of the lecture might prove challenging, as they have to convey the content with clarity and succinctness (Tucker, 2012). Another difficulty that may arise from delivering content online is the fact that not all the students have access to an internet connection. In these cases the accomplishment of the pre-class work might become compromised (Danker, 2015).

3. METHODOLOGY FOR FLIPPING CLASSROOMS

A flipped classroom can be organised in a variety of manners. The only constant among the different cases of flipped classrooms is the delivery of content prior to the classroom and the use of the classroom time to engage in active learning activities. The methods for delivering the content and the organisation of the in-class activities vary greatly, but it is important to establish a coherent link between the activities that are performed in the classroom and those that are completed outside, so that they can be mutually supportive. Also offering clear instructions and a guiding structure is key to ensure that the students always know the learning objectives (Kim et al., 2014).

In their study about a flipped psychology course, Isaias et al. (2017a) describe how these two components of the process can be successfully executed. In the case of the course in question, the content was delivered via online videos and the classroom activities were conducted in workshops and tutorials, where the learners had the opportunity to debate and interact with the content and work on their assignments.

To successfully deploy the flipped classroom method, teachers need to offer students with the possibility to have exposure to the content before the class, by providing learning materials (Kim et al., 2014). Likewise, it is essential to provide the flipped classroom with meaning and structure to assist the students in this transition from a passive attitude to the adoption of an active role (Moffett and Mill, 2014). In order to effectively flip a classroom, it is important that the students understand the objective of this approach, how it works and that they know and welcome their new responsibilities. Also, the teachers must accept this shift from conventional teaching practices and may require training on how to implement this technique, which cannot be reduced to a mere inversion of tasks with the support of video (Findlay-Thompson and Mombourquette, 2014).

The methodology that this paper proposes comprises five core aspects: pre-class content delivery, pre-class assessment, in-class content review, classroom active learning, in-class assessment. Each of these elements of the methodology is supported by core guidelines (Figure 1).

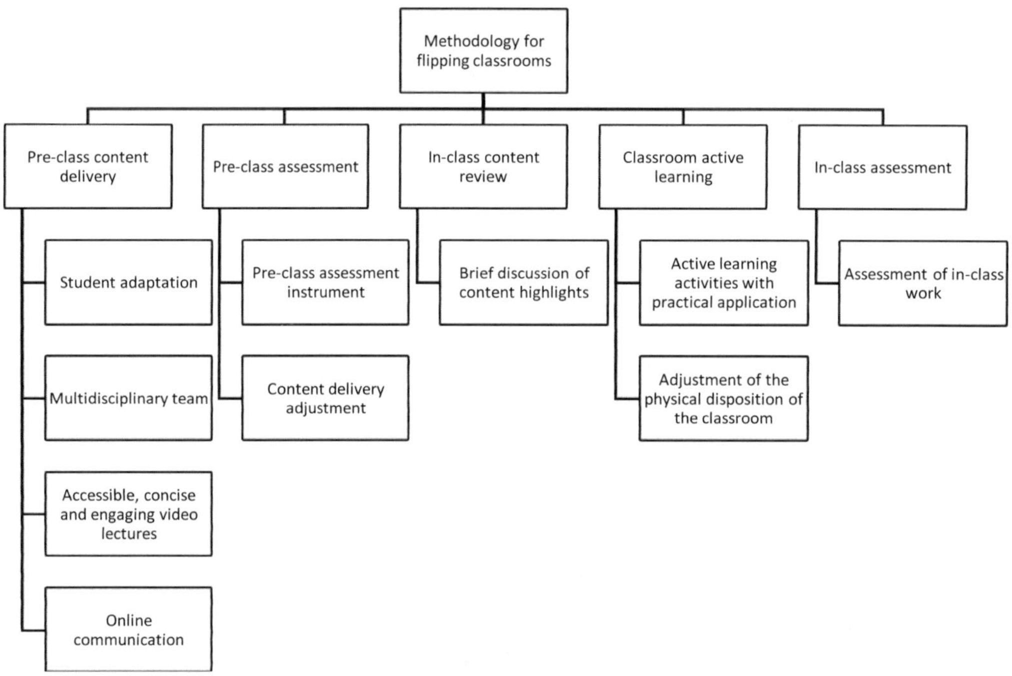

Figure 1. Methodology for flipping the classroom

3.1 Pre-class Content Delivery

When developing the pre-class activities, it is important to account for the students' workload and to design them to be engaging and brief. In previous studies, some students considered that the review of the online lectures required a significant time commitment (Isaias et al., 2017a). Teachers should ensure that the workload of the students is merely distributed between pre- and in-class and not increased (Loveys et al., 2016). In order to achieve an effortless transition to the flipped model, the teachers should limit the number of initial content topics, which will increase the amount of time that the learners have available to adjust to this new pedagogical approach. Also, the students should be encouraged to develop different learning strategies and to face the online preparation as an integral learning package (Isaias et al., 2018).

Before starting the flipped course, there is a need to assemble a multidisciplinary team that can bring different expertise to the process. The content must be delivered in a different format and that conversion requires knowledge at the level of the content, learning design and technology. Academics will need the assistance of other professionals to accomplish a successful flipped classroom. Also, the teaching team should have enough members to create and supervise the novel activities that are required in this approach (Isaias et al., 2018). Interdisciplinary teams are important to gather different types of experts that can account for all the aspects of designing a flipped classroom (Loveys et al., 2016).

There are three main aspects that video lectures should consider: access, conciseness and student engagement. In terms of access, it is crucial that the lectures are accessible to the students (Isaias et al., 2018). The development of technology has caused access to be facilitated. At the same time, learning management systems such as Blackboard, provide secure platforms for uploading the video lectures (Zappe et al., 2009). It is equally important that the lectures are accessible for the students to review at their convenience. Educators should equally resort to technology that is familiar and that the students can easily access, to decrease technological barriers (Kim et al., 2014). The employment of simple technology assists the pedagogical reliability of the flipped model (Loveys et al., 2016).

Conciseness, refers to the video lecture length, a subject where there are several recommendations deriving from previous research. The general advise to educators is to create brief videos (Bergmann and Sams, 2014). Zappe et al. (2009) concluded that the students would be more reticent to reviewing one hour video lectures and established that the ideal size should be kept maximum to 20-30 minutes. Kurtz et al. (2014), on the other hand, used videos that lasted a maximum of 10 minutes. In the context of MOOCs, for example, Guo et al. (2014) recommend dividing the lessons into videos with no more than 6 minutes. Isaias et al. (2018) underlined the importance of conciseness and created online lectures that lasted on average 3 minutes.

Student engagement, concerns the need to regard the creation of videos as an opportunity to deliver a lecture that transcends the options that are available in a classroom. Hence the videos should not be restricted to a delivery method where the teachers record themselves talking about the content. It is crucial to employ several resources, namely demonstrations and interviews, and take advantage of the technology that is available in terms of video production and animation. Moreover, the online lectures should include transcripts and use text in the video to highlight the most relevant content and help the students in following the lecture (Isaias et al., 2018). A valuable strategy to maintain students' interest about and engagement with the course content is to incorporate multimedia into the online lectures (Zappe et al., 2009). Teachers do not have to limit the presentation of the lecture to the use of video, they can create podcasts and use web-based whiteboards (Moffett and Mill, 2014). High quality content is also important. The teachers need to ensure that the content in the lecture is up-to-date, safe in terms of copyright and that it has been reformatted to fit this model. The video should also have a professional look (Isaias et al., 2018). The innovation afforded by the flipped classroom should not compromise the accuracy of content standards (Bergmann and Sams, 2014).

The teachers should determine if their subject can benefit from a flipped classroom format, since not all subjects are easily reformatted into this method (Isaias et al., 2018). The usefulness of videos for learning isn't universal, not all subjects benefit from the visualisation of videos, so it is important to develop other methods that can assist students to obtain a deeper understanding of content (Bergmann and Sams, 2014).

Since the flipped approach extends the classroom to online environments, it is valuable to guarantee that social interaction in these settings is assisted by social technology such as forums and social polling (Isaias et al., 2017a). Teachers should focus on promoting the creation of a learning community, by facilitating collaboration among the students (Kim et al., 2014). Furthermore, the creation of an online forum provides the teachers with an important communication channel that allows them to provide timely responses to the students questions before they attend the class (Moraros et al., 2015). Resorting to forums can equally be valuable in terms of information search and for assignment resources (Miranda et al., 2013). The use of social technology transcends the classroom and enables the students to contact with their colleagues and with other students worldwide and provides them with access to various opinions. When using forums, it is important to ensure that group discussions are facilitated and that there are features available, such as the possibility to add tags, to create more communication and to limit the occurrence of single posts. The interaction between students and teachers must also be assured (Isaias et al., 2018).

3.2 Pre-class Assessment

To ensure the students' preparation, teachers can resort to the use of online quizzes that the students should complete before attending the classroom. Compliance with the pre-class activities is vital as the better the students are prepared, the more they will be capable of learning (Herreid and Schiller, 2013) and the more they will benefit from the classroom activities. The activities for outside of the classroom can also include brief illustrative problems that the students are asked to complete after watching the videos (Zappe et al., 2009). Providing an incentive for the preparatory work, such as grading students' online comments on the videos is essential. It is fundamental to develop instruments to evaluate the students understanding of the material, like creating quizzes (Kim et al., 2014). The online quizzes represent a key element of assessment. Some students prefer them over a summative final exam and argue that they cause them less stress and help them to remain on track (Isaias et al., 2017a, Isaias et al., 2018).

With concern to content delivery adjustment, the online quizzes are equally useful to assist the teachers to use their results to determine the aspects that were less clear to the students and adapt the in-class activities according to those difficulties (Zappe et al., 2009, Phillips and Trainor, 2014).

3.3 In-class Content Review

Given that the videos are to be viewed prior to the classroom for student preparation, they shouldn't be replayed during the class (Phillips and Trainor, 2014). The in-class activities should be preceded by the teachers' report on the students' answers to the online questions and address any salient aspects of the online content. In the flipped classroom format, the teacher has the responsibility to examine the pre-class activities and ensure that any misunderstandings are cleared (Loveys et al., 2016).

The fact that the teacher is not present to personally transmit the concepts, might cause students to misunderstand the resources. They may equally feel overloaded with the study of the contents and may lack the confidence for self-study, which can hinder their learning progression (Kurtz et al., 2014). Hence, although the students watch the videos prior to coming to the classroom, it is beneficial to include a short review of the content of the video lectures before beginning the in-class activities (Isaias et al., 2018). This review should simply underline the most significant aspects of the content, rather than go through all the information of the video lecture. This reminds the students of the key aspects, enabling them to complete the classroom activities more proficiently and allows them to ask questions (Zappe et al., 2009). Moreover, in scenarios where the in-class activities will be assessed the absence of this discussion of content might prove detrimental to the students' learning. The students can become overly concentrated on and pressured by their assessment and miss the opportunity to really debate the content (Isaias et al., 2018).

3.4 Classroom Active Learning

The activities in the classroom should establish a connection between the online content and real-life scenarios (Loveys et al., 2016). The inclusion of practical situations for the application of the knowledge is essential to consolidate the content that the students' have reviewed. Also, the use of several active learning methods in flipped classrooms seems to be more beneficial for the students (DeLozier and Rhodes, 2017).

The classroom activities can be structured as tutorials. This format should be used to present the highlights of the video lectures, to develop engaging activities and to engage the students in interesting discussions of the content (Isaias et al., 2018). Loveys et al. (2016) described how they resorted to the creation of a tutorial to provide the students with the competences that they required to write a laboratory report. The students were asked to complete the pre-class activity and then attend the tutorial. In the tutorial they were presented with a brief lecture about writing reports and they were asked to review their pre-class assignment in pairs. In the case of the tutorial sessions conducted by Moraros et al. (2015), although they were in a classroom (a tutorial room), they were characterised as being post-class, since the students attended them after the classroom activities. In a study by Butt (2014), tutorials were also used to supplement the lectures. They lasted one hour and they were offered once a week in a computer lab to guarantee computer access to the students. During the tutorials the students were required to complete exercise.

The in-class activities can also assume a workshop format to engage in authentic activities with real life scenarios (Loveys et al., 2016). A central elements of using workshops is to assist the students to apply knowledge to practical and real world situations so that they can debate and reinforce the information that they've learned (Isaias et al., 2018). In Moffett and Mill (2014) study of a flipped classroom course, the in-class activities were organised in workshops, where an initial overview and discussion of content was followed by active learning tasks that were monitored by an audience response system. In Isaias et al. (2017a) study the authors used both tutorials and workshops for in-class activities. The tutorials were mainly used for assisting the students to complete their laboratory report and the workshops were created for the development of activities about the three main content areas developed of the course.

Active learning activities demand an adjustment of the physical space of the classroom. The traditional lecture theatres limit the possibilities of engaging in discussions due to the fact that the students are facing the front, so educators must choose rooms that are already arranged to foster discussion among the students or that can be set up that way (Isaias et al., 2018). Group work requires flexible spaces for learning (Hutchings and Quinney, 2015) and large lecture amphitheatres have fixed seating and hinder collaboration. Despite the fact that classrooms for active learning have a reduced student capacity, in comparison to larger lecture halls, they result in a more proficient use of space, since they improve the students' perception of the learning settings (Baepler et al., 2014). Houston and Lin (2012) describe how a room was rearranged to accommodate a conference table that enhanced the students engagement with the material and increased the discussion among students. The different set up of the room had a deep positive impact on interaction.

3.5 In-class Assessment

The workshops can also be used for preparing the learners for their assessment (Loveys et al., 2016). When organising the classroom structure, it is advisable to allocate enough time for assignment completion to enable students to apply the material they've reviewed in advance (Kim et al., 2014). For teachers who opt to use group activities, assessing the group discussions precludes the students from assuming a passive stance and it enhances their participation. Also, teachers should provide students with feedback on their assignments' drafts and ensure that enough support is available to assist their completion (Isaias et al., 2018). Is advisable to provide immediate and adaptive feedback on both individual and group work, to improve the work and for engagement (Kim et al., 2014). Moraros et al. (2015) required the students to collaborate in groups around a relevant topic and present their work to the class. This work was then assessed with a grade by the teacher. A strategy that can be employed to provide students with feedback on their workshop responses is to create a video after the completion of the assessment of the students to offer them examples of what the teachers expected of their answers. The video would elucidate the students on the feedback that they received and at the same time it would serve as a content debriefing (Isaias et al., 2018). The in-class assessment can equally be supported by the use of clickers to capture the students' answers (Ferreri and O'Connor, 2013, Zappe et al., 2009). The use of electronic assessment offers numerous advantages and it is widely employed by teachers, namely due to marking automation (Isaias et al., 2017b), which is a time saving feature.

4. CASE STUDY FOR THE PROPOSED METHODOLOGY

The work of Isaias et al. (2018) constitutes an example of the implementation of the methodology that is proposed. The authors described the process of flipping a psychology course in an Australian university (PSYC1030). Traditionally, the course was composed of a conventional lecture (2 hours) and one tutorial (1 hour) per week in a total of 12 weeks. In the flipped format, the content was delivered via a small private online course (SPOC) and the classroom time was divided into workshops and tutorials. This flipped approach was subject to a comprehensive evaluation that was provided by the students, the tutors and the course development team, through surveys and semi-structured interviews. Both the process that was followed and the evaluations support this methodology, as is portrayed in table 1.

Table 1. Case study's application of the methodology

Methodology elements	Guidelines	Evaluation and Procedures
Pre-class content delivery	Student adaptation to model	– Need to reduce the number of initial topics – New learning strategies for students are required
	Multidisciplinary team	– Lead course academic – Course academics – Media team – Technical team – Learning designer – Faculty project officer – Team of beta-testers
	Accessible, concise and engaging video lectures	– Accessible online – Average of 3 minutes – High quality and current content – Inclusion of transcripts
	Ensure online communication	– Forum – Social polling
Pre-class assessment	Create a pre-class assessment instrument	– Online quizzes
	Use the results of the assessment to adjust content delivery	– Need to identify areas of difficulty
In-class content review	Discuss the highlights of the pre-class content briefly	– Content discussion required
Classroom active learning	Develop active learning activities with practical application of the content	– The tutorials assisted the students with their laboratory report – The workshops included group work and the application of knowledge to practical scenarios
	Adjust the physical disposition of the classroom to suit active learning	– Tutorial rooms
In-class assessment	Assess the work that the students do in the classroom	– Individual and group assessment

In terms of pre-class content delivery one of the aspects that emerged from the evaluation of the course creators was the need for the students to adapt to the model. According to their assessment, it is important to assist the students in their transition to the flipped approach by restricting the number of initial topics that are to be covered in the content. Additionally, the students should be instructed to adjust their learning strategies to meet the demands of this new model. With regards to the composition of the team, it was multidisciplinary and it included a lead course academic, who produced the slides and some of the video resources; course academics, who perfected the scripts for the videos and designed interactive activities; a media team, responsible for the recording and edition of the videos; a technical team, in charge of developing tools for formative assessment; a learning designer, who developed the videos and the activities for formative assessment to build the SPOC; a faculty project officer, responsible for building the summative quizzes; and a team of beta-testers who revised the SPOC. The video lectures were made available online so that the students could easily access them. The team ensured that they consisted of current and high quality content, supported by transcripts. Demonstrations and interviews were equally included to convey the content in an engaging manner. Finally, the online communication between the teacher and the students and among the students themselves, was assured by the use of forums and social polling. The use of these communication tools was seen as positive by the course creators' evaluation, who claimed that the type of engagement that they foster is not possible to achieve in the traditional classroom.

With concern to the pre-class assessment, when flipping PSYC1030, the team developed online quizzes that the students were asked to complete. One quiz was done before they watched the video lectures, which was formative and after they viewed the videos they would complete another quiz, which was summative. Both the tutors and the students provided a positive evaluation of the use of quizzes. For the tutors they were one of the most effective aspects of the model and they endowed the students with a significant understanding of the main course concepts. The students claimed that the quizzes were a valuable tool to assist them to manage the course content. Furthermore, the evaluation of the course creators made it clear that it is fundamental to detect the areas that the students found more difficult and adapt the delivery of that content accordingly. Their viewpoints highlight the use of the results of the quizzes, as it is proposed in the methodology, as a valuable strategy to identify the content that needs further explanation.

According to the appraisal of the course creators it is necessary to allocate more time in the workshops for the discussion of the content. Some students also found this to be true in the tutorials. Hence, to address this shortcoming of the flipped PSYC1030, and reiterating the guidelines of the methodology, there is the need to include a brief discussion of content in the classroom.

In the flipped PSYC1030 the classroom time was divided into workshops and tutorials. According to the course creators' evaluation one of the key aspects of the experience was the use of the workshops for the application of the content. The workshops also enabled more time for discussion with the teacher and the inclusion of group work demanded the active participation of the students. The tutors' appraisal highlighted the importance of the workshops for promoting discussion, problem solving and critical thinking and the fact that they increased student participation. In terms of the tutorials, some students claimed that they were valuable for explaining the laboratory report and for providing assistance with their assignment completion. In the flipped PSYC1030, the physical space for the classroom activities was important to enable student discussion. The course creators underlined the fact that lecture theatres do not foment discussion. The teaching team used tutorial rooms and rooms that could be rearranged to fit the workshop format.

Finally, with regards to in-class assessment, as per the methodology, in the flipped PSYC1030 course, the students were assessed on the outcomes of their group work. They were asked to apply their newly acquired knowledge to the resolution of a practical problem that they had to address as a group and their collective answer was assessed. Individually, they were assessed on their laboratory report.

5. DISCUSSION

The process of flipping a classroom can be associated with the misconception that it requires merely an inversion of the events that occur in-class and outside the classroom. Flipping a course requires preparation and an understanding of the effort it demands. As more educators are implementing this pedagogical strategy there is a growing awareness of the time commitment it implies and of the different moving parts that together create a successful flipped classroom.

The methodology that is proposed in this paper presents a flexible structure that can assist teachers in their efforts of flipping classrooms. While it is composed of five key elements that are essential for the success of the flipped classroom it provides sufficient latitude to be adapted to several types of subjects, teaching styles and learning goals. This methodology is not to be taken as an attempt to provide a cookie-cutter approach, but as a guiding frame for those who wish to flip their courses.

Firstly, a pre-condition of the flipped classroom is the delivery of content prior to the classroom. The students must have access to pre-class content in order to prepare for the classroom activities. The content needs to be redesign to fit online delivery and independent learning and it must engage the students. It is valuable to resort to social technology to support this online portion of the flipped classroom to ensure that the students have appropriate communication channels to interact with the teachers and their peers. Secondly, the online delivery of content should be accompanied by one of more methods of assessment. The assessment is advised both to guarantee that the students complete their pre-class preparation and to provide the teachers with a depiction of the areas where the students had more difficulties. The creation of quizzes has been amply cited in existing studies as a valuable option for this type of assessment needs (Kim et al., 2014, Zappe et al., 2009, Phillips and Trainor, 2014, Isaias et al., 2017a).

Thirdly, the in-class activities should be preceded by a brief review of the content of the online lectures. The review has the objective of reminding the students of the highlights of the content and to respond to any difficulties that may arise with parts of that content. The teacher should equally use this time to provide the students with feedback to their pre-class assessment. Fourthly, the classroom can be structured as workshops and tutorials to promote a more active discussion of the content, to enable group work and to create active learning activities based on real scenarios. These formats are more conducive to active learning and peer discussion than the large lectures conducted in traditional amphitheatres. The activities can assume a variety of forms, but their underlying principle should be the practical application of the content and the promotion of active learning. Finally, to ensure the success of the flipped classroom model, educators are advised to create assessment methods for the in-class activities, to potentiate the students' participation. Both individual and group work can be assessed namely by resorting to electronic assessment.

6. CONCLUSION

The promise of a student-centred, active learning offered by the flipped classroom is driving educators to adopt this approach in their courses. The increasing popularity of this pedagogical method and its potential to improve the learning experience of students requires teachers to reflect about new teaching practices and to redesign their classes.

This paper intended to contribute with a methodology to guide teachers through the process of flipping their courses. Flipped classrooms can be designed in a variety of forms and they can be supported by multiple activities. Nonetheless, it is important to establish a guiding structure to ensure that the redesign of the courses into the flipped format actually results in an enhancement of active and deep learning and represents an improvement of the traditional classroom. Specifically, it is key to the flipped classroom format that the students have access to engaging content prior to the classroom; that they are asked to complete some form of assessment to ensure that preparation; that the content is briefly reviewed in the classroom to address any difficulties; that the in-class activities are comprised of active learning exercises based on real-life scenarios; and that these activities are assessed by the teacher to encourage student participation.

The rising importance of this format for education demands new and improved design and evaluation efforts that can attest its effectiveness. An important limitation of this paper concerns the use of findings from data collection methods that are based on the respondents' self-evaluation. While self-evaluation is valuable to gain insight into the different stakeholders' standpoint, it fails to provide an objective and quantifiable account of the experience. Future research ventures should focus on improving and providing a more empirical support for the methodology that is presented in this paper, namely by collecting the opinion of experts in this subject and resorting to more objective measurements pertaining to the specific learning outcomes.

REFERENCES

Abeysekera, L. & Dawson, P. 2015. Motivation and cognitive load in the flipped classroom: definition, rationale and a call for research. *Higher Education Research & Development,* Vol. 34, No. 1 pp. 1-14.

Baepler, P., Walker, J. D. & Driessen, M. 2014. It's not about seat time: Blending, flipping, and efficiency in active learning classrooms. *Computers & Education,* Vol. 78, No. Supplement C pp. 227-236.

Bergmann, J. & Sams, A. 2014. Flipping for mastery. *Educational Leadership,* Vol. 71, No. 4 pp. 24-29.

Bishop, J. L. & Verleger, M. A. The flipped classroom: A survey of the research. ASEE National Conference Proceedings, Atlanta, GA, 2013. 1-18.

Butt, A. 2014. Student views on the use of a flipped classroom approach: Evidence from Australia. *Business Education & Accreditation,* Vol. 6, No. 1 pp. 33-43.

Danker, B. 2015. Using flipped classroom approach to explore deep learning in large classrooms. *IAFOR Journal of Education,* Vol. 3, No. 1 pp. 171-186.

DeLozier, S. J. & Rhodes, M. G. 2017. Flipped classrooms: a review of key ideas and recommendations for practice. *Educational Psychology Review,* Vol. 29, No. 1 pp. 141-151.

Dennen, V. P. & Spector, J. M. 2016. The Flipped K-12 Classroom: Implications for Teacher Preparation, Professional Development, and Educational Leadership. *In:* Avgerinou, M. D. & Gialamas, S. P. (eds.) *Revolutionizing K-12 Blended Learning through the i²Flex Classroom Model.* Hershey, PA, USA: IGI Global.

Ferreri, S. P. & O'Connor, S. K. 2013. Redesign of a large lecture course into a small-group learning course. *American journal of pharmaceutical education,* Vol. 77, No. 1 pp. 1-9.

Findlay-Thompson, S. & Mombourquette, P. 2014. Evaluation of a flipped classroom in an undergraduate business course. *Business Education & Accreditation* Vol. 6, No. 1 pp. 63-71.

Guo, P. J., Kim, J. & Rubin, R. 2014. How video production affects student engagement: An empirical study of MOOC videos. *Proceedings of the first ACM conference on Learning@ scale conference.* ACM.

Houston, M. & Lin, L. Humanizing the classroom by flipping the homework versus lecture equation. Society for information technology & teacher education international conference, 2012. Association for the Advancement of Computing in Education (AACE), 1177-1182.

Hutchings, M. & Quinney, A. 2015. The Flipped Classroom, Disruptive Pedagogies, Enabling Technologies and Wicked Problems: Responding to" The Bomb in the Basement". *Electronic Journal of E-Learning,* Vol. 13, No. 2 pp. 106-119.

Isaias, P., McKimmie, B., Bakharia, A. & Zornig, J. 2018. Flipping the Classroom Effectively: Evaluation Results from a Course at The University of Queensland. *In:* Bastiaens, T., Van Braak, J., Brown, M., Cantoni, L., Castro, M., Christensen, R., Davidson-Shivers, G. V., Depryck, K., Ebner, M., Fominykh, M., Fulford, C., Hatzipanagos, S., Knezek, G., Kreijns, K., Marks, G., Sointu, E., Korsgaard Sorensen, E., Viteli, J., Voogt, J., Weber, P., Weippl, E. & Zawacki-Richter, O. (eds.) *Proceedings of EdMedia: World Conference on Educational Media and Technology.* Amsterdam, Netherlands: Association for the Advancement of Computing in Education (AACE).

Isaias, P., McKimmie, B., Bakharia, A., Zornig, J. & Morris, A. 2017a. How to flip a classroom and improve student learning and engagement: the case of PSYC1030. *In:* Sampson, D. G., Spector, J. M., Ifenthaler, D. & Isaías, P. (eds.) *Proceedings of the IADIS International Conference Cognition and Exploratory Learning in Digital Age.* Lisbon, Portugal: IADIS Press.

Isaias, P., Miranda, P. & Pífano, S. 2017b. Framework for the analysis and comparison of e-assessment systems. *In:* Partridge, H., Davis, K. & Thomas, J. (eds.) *Me, Us, IT! Proceedings ASCILITE2017: 34th International Conference on Innovation, Practice and Research in the Use of Educational Technologies in Tertiary Education.*

Kim, M. K., Kim, S. M., Khera, O. & Getman, J. 2014. The experience of three flipped classrooms in an urban university: an exploration of design principles. *The Internet and Higher Education,* Vol. 22, No. pp. 37-50.

Kurtz, G., Tsimerman, A. & Steiner-Lavi, O. 2014. The Flipped-Classroom Approach: The Answer to Future Learning? *European Journal of Open, Distance and E-Learning,* Vol. 17, No. 2 pp. 172-182.

Loveys, B., Riggs, K., McGrice, H., Snelling, C., Winning, T. & Kemp, A. The Rise of the Flip: Successfully engaging students in pre-class activities through the use of technology and a flipped classroom design template. 2016. ASCILITE.

Mason, G. S., Shuman, T. R. & Cook, K. E. 2013. Comparing the effectiveness of an inverted classroom to a traditional classroom in an upper-division engineering course. *IEEE Transactions on Education,* Vol. 56, No. 4 pp. 430-435.

McLaughlin, J. E., Roth, M. T., Glatt, D. M., Gharkholonarehe, N., Davidson, C. A., Griffin, L. M., Esserman, D. A. & Mumper, R. J. 2014. The flipped classroom: a course redesign to foster learning and engagement in a health professions school. *Academic Medicine,* Vol. 89, No. 2 pp. 236-243.

Miranda, P., Isaias, P., Costa, C. & Pifano, S. 2013. WEB 2.0 technologies supporting students and scholars in higher education. *In:* A.A., O. & P., Z. (eds.) *Online Communities and Social Computing. OCSC 2013. Lecture Notes in Computer Science, vol 8029.* . Berlin, Heidelberg: Springer.

Moffett, J. & Mill, A. C. 2014. Evaluation of the flipped classroom approach in a veterinary professional skills course. *Advances in medical education and practice,* Vol. 5, No. pp. 415-425.

Moraros, J., Islam, A., Yu, S., Banow, R. & Schindelka, B. 2015. Flipping for success: evaluating the effectiveness of a novel teaching approach in a graduate level setting. *BMC medical education,* Vol. 15, No. 1 pp. 27.

Mortensen, C. J. & Nicholson, A. M. 2015. The flipped classroom stimulates greater learning and is a modern 21st century approach to teaching today's undergraduates. *Journal of Animal Science,* Vol. 93, No. 7 pp. 3722-3731.

O'Flaherty, J. & Phillips, C. 2015. The use of flipped classrooms in higher education: A scoping review. *The Internet and Higher Education,* Vol. 25, No. pp. 85-95.

Phillips, C. R. & Trainor, J. E. 2014. Millennial students and the flipped classroom. *Journal of Business and Educational Leadership,* Vol. 5, No. 1 pp. 102-112.

Thai, T. N., De Wever, B. & Valcke, M. 2017. The impact of a flipped classroom design on learning performance in higher education: Looking for the best "blend" of lectures and guiding questions with feedback. *Computers & Education,* Vol. 107, No. pp. 113-126.

Tucker, B. 2012. The flipped classroom. *Education next,* Vol. 12, No. 1 pp. 82-83.

Zappe, S., Leicht, R., Messner, J., Litzinger, T. & Lee, H. W. 2009. Flipping" the classroom to explore active learning in a large undergraduate course. *Proceedings of the 2009 American Society for Engineering Education Annual Conference and Exhibition.* Washington, DC, USA: American Society for Engineering Education.

CLUSTERING AND ANALYSIS OF USER MOTIONS TO ENHANCE HUMAN LEARNING: A FIRST STUDY CASE WITH THE BOTTLE FLIP CHALLENGE

Quentin Couland, Ludovic Hamon and Sébastien George
Laboratoire d'Informatique de l'Université du Mans, LIUM - EA 4023, Le Mans Université, Avenue Olivier Messiaen, 72085 Le Mans, Cedex 9, France

ABSTRACT

More and more domains such as industry, sport, medicine, Human Computer Interaction (HCI) and education analyze user motions to observe human behavior, follow and predict its action, intention and emotion, to interact with computer systems and enhance user experience in Virtual (VR) and Augmented Reality (AR). In the context of human learning of movements, existing software applications and methods rarely use 3D captured motions for pedagogical feedback. This comes from several issues related to the highly complex and dimensional nature of these data, and by the need to correlate this information with the observation needs of the teacher. Such issues could be solved by the use of machine learning techniques, which could provide efficient and complementary feedback in addition to the expert advice, from motion data. The context of the presented work is the improvement of the human learning process of a motion, based on clustering techniques. The main goal is to give advice according to the analysis of clusters representing user profiles during a learning situation. To achieve this purpose, a first step is to work on the separation of the motions into different categories according to a set of well-chosen features. In this way, allowing a better and more accurate analysis of the motion characteristics is expected. An experimentation was conducted with the Bottle Flip Challenge. Human motions were first captured and filtered, in order to compensate for hardware related errors. Descriptors related to speed and acceleration are then computed, and used in two different automatic approaches. The first one tries to separate the motions, using the computed descriptors, and the second one, compares the obtained separation with the ground truth. The results show that, while the obtained partitioning is not relevant to the degree of success of the task, the data are separable using the descriptors.

KEYWORDS

Human Motion, Human Learning, Machine Learning, Clustering

1. INTRODUCTION

Motion capture is increasingly used in multiple domains such as video-game, animation movies, Virtual Reality (VR), sport, medicine, industry and education. Thanks to breakthroughs made in electronics, Human-Computer Interface (HCI) and data processing, it is reasonable to assume that capturing, editing and sharing human gestures will be soon generalized. This assumption has a strong impact on education and on every domain implying human movements. Indeed, different kinds of information can be extracted from human motion analysis. One can easily generate low-level descriptors such as kinematic and dynamic data (Nunes & Moreira, 2016)(Larboulette & Gibet, 2015). Gestures may have a meaning in verbal (Huang, *et al.*, 2015) or non-verbal communication (Chang, *et al.*, 2013). In addition, high-level data linked to human emotion (Kobayashi, 2007), intention (Yu & Lee, 2015) and action (Kapsouras & Nikolaidis, 2014) can be reified and built. Monitoring learner activities can imply the generation of a large amount of motion data that cannot be manually analyzed (Gu & Sosnovsky, 2014). Automatic methods, such as machine learning techniques, can ease such a task. This set of techniques can process high-dimensional data for classification purposes, features extraction, regression problems, etc. (Ng, 2016). In an educational context, these algorithms are used for learning analytics for instance, to study learner actions (Lokaiczyk, *et al.*, 2007) and/or behavior (Markowska-Kaczmar, *et al.*, 2010). Supervised learning can be used in order to classify motions. However, this kind of algorithms implies (i) that a large database of specific motions exists, (ii) that the different classes are known in advance. Furthermore, these works are rarely focused on motions that requires a learning effort from the user. There is a lack of work regarding the automatic extraction of relevant information in pedagogical situations from learner motions. This can be explained by several technical and scientific issues. Some of these issues could be overcome by the use of clustering algorithm, in order to avoid the constraints specific to supervised learning (database size, labeling), and by using morphology-invariant descriptors relevant to the given context. The goal of this work is to use kinematic descriptors along with clustering techniques in order to have a relevant data separation.

The remainder of the paper is structured as follows: section two presents a review of related work, our new approach are shown in section 3, the experimentation and its related protocol, results and discussion are detailed in section 4. Finally, perspectives and future work ends this study.

2. RELATED WORK

Human learning motion can use captured motion, in order to assist the student in his learning task. In this context, the motion is mainly represented as a sequential evolution of human postures through time. Usually, a fixed time-step separates each posture (called "frame"). One way to represent a posture is to build a set of joints, hierarchically structured thanks to a graph, each node describing a joint. This set of joints is organized according to a skeleton model, *i.e.* a tree data structure, in which the root represents the low body part of the torso (i.e. the hip bone) and the nodes represent the body joints. Each node contains the position and the orientation, related to its parent node. It is possible to extract kinematic and dynamic descriptors from this structure such as the speed of the joints, the acceleration, the displacement through time (Nunes & Moreira, 2016) (Larboulette & Gibet, 2015). Zhu and Hu worked on the learning of specific motions for reeducation (Zhou & Hu, 2008). The skeleton model was not systematically considered, because different kinds of sensors were used to gather motion data, depending on the observed movement ; thus, it wasn't systematically possible to construct a skeleton from these data. The data were used in order to analyze the patient's gait. No automatic analyses of the recorded movements were made, the observations and deductions of information were always made by a human expert. For Japanese archery learning, Yoshinaga and Soga developed a system based on a Kinect sensor to capture learner skeletons and its variations through time (Yoshinaga & Soga, 2015). Expert movements were also recorded and learners could compare their motions with the expert ones. The analysis was empirically made by humans.

Works using supervised and unsupervised algorithms to analyze facial expressions, gestures and actions exist. Among them, some were based on 3D captured data. Patrona *et al.* presented a framework for action recognition and evaluation based on extreme learning machine (Patrona, *et al.*, 2018). Using fuzzy-logic, a semantic feedback (depending on the activity context) is given to the learner, such as information about the velocity at specific frames, in order to improve the motion realized. This feedback requires a reference motion and a large corpus of existing motions, as the goal here is to classify the motion into predefined categories in different datasets (CVD exercise, MSRC-12 and MSR-Action3D). Hachaj and Marek used a set of expert rules relating to the learner displacements, *e.g.* the distance covered by the learning in a time step, in order to classify motions (Hachaj & Marek R., 2015). Although these approaches are efficient, the motion does not require a cognitive effort in terms of human learning. Furthermore, the goal is not to evaluate the success degree of the motion and the descriptors cannot be used to give pedagogical feedback. Lui *et al.* worked on video databases from which two sets of descriptors were extracted (Lui, *et al.*, 2011). These descriptors are, on the one hand, localized space-time features that are used with a Bag Of Features approach, and a manifold product on the other hand. The results showed a good data partitioning, especially with the manifold product set of descriptors. The performed motions are trivial in terms of cognitive effort, such as walking, jogging, running, and the descriptors cannot be used to give feedback to the learner. Due to the nature of the motions, the degree of success of the task is not evaluated.

With a sufficient amount of data for the training phase, supervised machine learning algorithms are efficient when the searched and estimated hypothesis is well designed for the problem complexity. However, these kinds of algorithms need a large amount of labeled data related to the given context. The data labeling is usually a costly task in terms of time and resources. Furthermore, some pre-processing steps can change the nature of the data (e.g. PCA), and some decision/separation frontier cannot be easily interpreted by humans (e.g. SVN, Neural Networks). Consequently, analyzing and giving feedback to the learner can be a hard task or impossible to perform. Unsupervised learning approaches, by nature, do not need labeling data to group them into different clusters. It seems that there's a lack of works using unsupervised machine learning algorithms to automatically extract useful pedagogical information from 3D motion data. This could allow to automatically detect the most distinguishing features of a set of motions, group them into learner profiles according to the observation needs of the teachers (i.e. high level descriptors) and help the expert in giving a better feedback to the learner. The presented work is based on the two following hypothesis: (i) for one identified task, it is possible to group motions in separable clusters, with each cluster made of motions with common features, and that (ii) it is possible to automatically group gestures according to the degree of success of the motion-based task. This approach, as well as an experiment are detailed in the next sections.

3. A CLUSTERING APPROACH FOR MOTION ANALYSIS

A motion is not usually described by a perfect example. Instead, in most of the cases, a targeted gesture is defined by one or several experts. Establishing the relevant features allowing to tell if the motion is successful or not depends on the context, the expectations of the experts, which can vary from one to another (i.e. given a learning situation, the set of discriminant features is not the same for every expert). Using supervised learning algorithms implies that a database containing non-trivial and labeled motions in terms of cognitive effort exists. The degree of success of the task of each sample must be stored within the labels. In practice, most of the databases focus on trivial motions, such as sitting, running, walking, etc. The chosen approach relies on the automatic analysis of motions through clustering techniques, in order to avoid most of the drawbacks of the supervised approach. The global context can be seen in Figure 1. From a motion corpus, a first pre-processing step applies several filters, in order to clean the data if needed (frames loss or corrupted, framerate variation, etc.). The next step extracts descriptors from the cleaned motions and the extraction of a wide range of descriptors is possible (Larboulette & Gibet, 2015). One should be careful about them, as some descriptors are morphology-invariant (*e.g.* the ones related to the joints distance), and some are not (*e.g.* the rotation of joints). From here, according to the observation needs of the teacher, the data are analyzed through their descriptors. These descriptors are then used in a clustering process, using the k-means algorithm, from which several metrics are computed to assess its quality. The use of an IT environment and especially a 3D virtual environment allows observing the motion and offering interactions that are hard, or not possible to perform in real environment, e.g. replay motion from several viewpoints, slow down, speed up, pause, etc. From these observations, the expert can then give feedback to the learner, while refining his observation needs.

This paper focuses on the clustering part of Figure 1., implying that clean data are available. An example of such data can be seen in Figure 2c. The goal is to find a set of descriptors, algorithms and metrics, such as (i) the motion corpus can be separated in different groups and (ii) the obtained separation can give an indication of the degree of success of the motion. Such separation would allow analyzing the properties of the clusters, giving information about what the characteristics of each motion type are, and thus giving a more accurate feedback about the needed advice to give for the improvement of the learner motion. The next section presents the experimentation conducted, in order to validate the presented hypotheses.

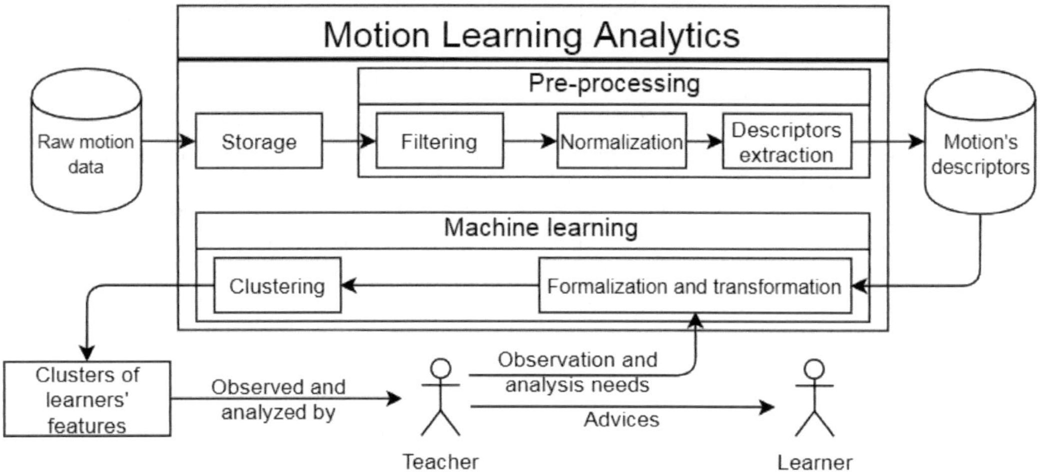

Figure 1. The main principles of a system for assisting the human motion analysis

4. EXPERIMENTATION ON CLUSTERING WITH KINEMATIC DESCRIPTORS

This section is dedicated to an experimentation for the validation of the two previous hypotheses. As a reminder, these assumptions are: (i) it is possible to separate the data into well-defined clusters, and (ii) it is possible to obtain a separation corresponding to the degree of success of the motion. The next paragraphs focus on the protocol used to test the hypotheses, present and discuss the results.

4.1 Protocol

For this experimentation, a database made of short motions requiring some dexterity was created. The Bottle Flip Challenge was the chosen task. The goal is to throw a bottle, such as it completely rotates once on the horizontal axis, and then lands correctly on a table. The distance from the person performing the gesture to the table was empirically set to 70cm (27.5 inches), indicated by a mark on the floor. A MOCAP suit named Perception Neuron and based on Inertial Measurement Units (IMU) was used to capture the motions (https://neuronmocap.com/). It allows capturing 72 joints (some of which are interpolated) at the rate of 60 frames per second. The skeleton of the subject was measured according to the measuring guide, in order to have data skeletons made in accordance with the user morphology. Due to the nature of the sensors, the experimental protocol ensures that (i) no device generating electromagnetic perturbation was close to the user, and (ii) all metallic accessories were removed (including rings, bracelets, watches, belt with metallic buckle, etc.). During the experiment, the MOCAP suit had to be regularly recalibrated, due to the inherent drift of the sensors. Each subject had to perform the motion a hundred times and for every throw, the success (or not) of the task was recorded.

Figure 1.a shows the artifacts of the suit sensors, on the hand's data. Such data are not usable, as the original signal is distorted by the noise. In order to compensate these errors, a Savitsky-Golay filter was applied on each motion (Figure 1.b). Then, the throwing part of the motion was automatically segmented to extract the motion part of interest. (Figure 1.c). From those cleaned data, descriptors were computed. Since the subjects have different body types, morphology-invariants descriptors were chosen: speed and acceleration (vector norm and direction, components along each axis in both cases). The descriptors were computed from three moments of each cleaned motion: beginning of the throw, maximum value of the speed norm for the dominant hand (corresponding to the release of the bottle), and end of the throw. The chosen clustering algorithm is the k-means, as it can gives an insight of the data possible separations, is faster to run than other clustering algorithms (execution time scales linearly with data size), and has easily explainable results. The k values ranged from 2 to 10 for this experimentation.

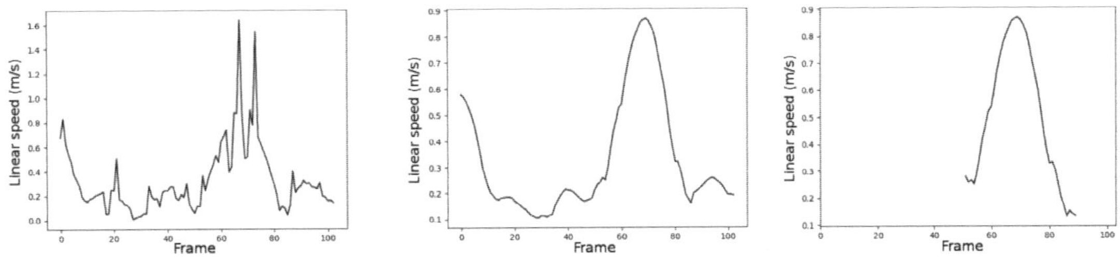

Figure 2. (a): speed of the captured motion through time of the right-hand of a user (b): initial speed filtered (c): extracted throwing part (Couland, et al., 2018)

In order to analyze the clustering results, a few metrics suited to our approaches were chosen.

The first approach was based on the hypothesis that there are various types of motions that can be gathered in separable clusters. In this context, the computed metric is the Average Silhouette Score (*ASS*) (Rousseeuw, 1987). The Silhouette Score (SS) is a metric which compute if a sample belongs well to the cluster it has been assigned (compared to other clusters). The Average Silhouette Score (ASS) is the mean of every sample SS . It gives an indication about the clusters homogeneity: the highest this value is, the better the clusters are separated. This value ranges from -1 to 1, with 1 meaning that every sample is close to the others in the same clusters (the clusters are well separated), and 0 indicating that the clusters are overlapping. This last case, a possible explanation is that the number of clusters is either too low or too high. An ASS between 0 and 0.25 means that no structure is found in the data, a value between 0.25 and 0.5 indicates that a weak structure is found (potentially artificial), an ASS above 0.5 suggests that a reasonable structure is found, while an ASS value above 0.7 means that a strong structure is found (Struyf, et al., 1997). In this context, the metric allows verifying the separation of the clusters, thus giving an indication about the degree of separation with the computed descriptors.

The second approach was based on the hypothesis that it is possible to obtain clusters corresponding to the degree of success of the motion. In our case, our degrees of success are either a successful, or failed throw. A metric such as the accuracy of the clustering seems to not be a relevant indicator. For example, if the k-means algorithm is considered, this metric, based on the computation of a Euclidian distance, is relative to the measured data, the required accuracy of the measuring system and the learning situation. This accuracy is often ascertained by an advanced expert both in the application domain and in computer sciences. In order to verify the difference between the ground truth and the obtained labeling (*i.e.* failed/success motion), the precision, the recall, the F1-score and the Adjusted Rand Index (*ARI*) were chosen. These metrics were only computed for *k=2*, as the ground truth is defined for *k=2* (successful/failed). As a reminder, the F1-score is a combination of two metrics (recall and precision) representing the labeling accuracy. This value ranges from 0 to 1, with 1 indicating a perfect matching. The ARI is a measure of the similarity between two data partitioning. This index's maximum value is 1, corresponding to a perfect matching between the two labeled clusters and their labeled data. 0 corresponds to a random cluster assignment, and negative values are obtained if the clustering is orthogonal, to an extent.

4.2 Results

The recorded data consisted in 1300 motions, performed by 13 different subjects. 11 subjects were right-handed, and 2 were left-handed. For the clustering, different sets of joints have been considered: hand (H), forearm (FA), arm (A), these body parts being the most solicited during the movement. The computed descriptors were: Speed Norm (SN), Speed value in x, y and z (Sxyz), Speed directions in x, y, and z (SDxyz), and Speed Norm and directions in x, y and z (SNDxyz). The precision (*P*), recall (*R*), F1-score (*F1*) and Adjusted Rand Index (*ARI*) are given for *k=2*, as it corresponds to the ground truth. The Average Silhouette Score (*ASS*) results are also given for *k=2*, as it is the k value that yields the best value in most of the case (the *ASS* values show non-significant variations for other k values when k=2 doesn't yield the best *ASS* values). The clustering was performed on: (i) the mixed data (left and right-handed together) (ii) left-handed data only and (iii) right-handed data only. Table 1. shows the results obtained on this experimentation. F1-score, *ASS* and *ARI* values slightly decreased when joints were added to the dominant hand, meaning that the dominant hand was the most important joint for this case. The highest *ASS* scores were obtained for speed values along the three axis, in the right-handed (0.73) and mixed data (0.54). Left-handed best *ASS* values are for the speed norm values (0.41), yet they are lower than the right-handed and mixed data *ASS* values for the same data (0.42 and 0.48). The *ARI* stayed close to 0, regardless of the joints and descriptors combination (ranging between 0.05 and 0).

Table 1. Clustering metrics for various joints combinations

Joints	H					H, FA					H, FA, A				
Metric	ASS	P	R	F1	ARI	ASS	P	R	F1	ARI	ASS	P	R	F1	ARI
	Left and Right-Handed														
SN	0.48	0.25	0.33	0.29	0.04	0.44	0.25	0.33	0.29	0.04	0.43	0.25	0.33	0.29	0.04
Sxyz	**0.54**	0.18	0.67	0.30	0.05	**0.52**	0.27	0.32	0.29	0.05	**0.51**	0.18	0.68	0.29	0.05
Sdxyz	0.24	0.21	0.53	0.30	0.00	0.27	0.25	0.25	0.25	0.04	0.22	0.18	0.72	0.27	0.04
SNDxyz	0.21	0.18	0.47	0.30	0.00	0.27	0.25	0.26	0.26	0.04	0.22	0.26	0.28	0.27	0.04
	Left Handed														
SN	**0.41**	0.39	0.39	0.39	0.02	**0.42**	0.38	0.39	0.39	0.01	**0.41**	0.31	0.61	0.39	0.01
Sxyz	0.35	0.32	0.57	0.39	0.00	0.34	0.32	0.57	0.39	0.00	0.33	0.35	0.43	0.39	0.00
Sdxyz	0.31	0.34	0.48	0.40	0.00	0.27	0.34	0.54	0.39	0.00	0.23	0.34	0.48	0.40	0.00
SNDxyz	0.27	0.34	0.49	0.40	0.00	0.25	0.33	0.48	0.39	0.00	0.22	0.34	0.52	0.41	0.00
	Right Handed														
SN	0.42	0.18	0.29	0.22	0.00	0.36	0.17	0.28	0.21	0.00	0.34	0.17	0.28	0.21	0.00
Sxyz	**0.73**	0.19	0.12	0.15	0.01	**0.71**	0.19	0.12	0.15	0.01	**0.71**	0.19	0.12	0.15	0.01
Sdxyz	0.28	0.15	0.45	0.28	0.00	0.20	0.16	0.49	0.27	0.00	0.26	0.19	0.13	0.15	0.01
SNDxyz	0.26	0.16	0.45	0.28	0.00	0.19	0.19	0.52	0.27	0.00	0.26	0.17	0.87	0.15	0.01

4.3 Discussion

The combination of the speed vectors in each axis is a good separation criterion, as suggested by results shown in section 4.2. The best ASS values were obtained for the descriptors extracted from the dominant hand, suggesting that other body parts only add noise. This can be partially explained by the fact that every joint motion is related to the other, and that the hand movement is the one with the widest range of values (in terms of speed).

While the *ASS* stayed at an acceptable value ($ASS \approx 0.5$) for the mixed data, better results were obtained when right-handed and left-handed people are separated ($ASS \approx 0.75$). The acquisition problems of the suite can explain this phenomenon (and are discussed below in this section). In terms of relative distance, the most discriminant features were the maximum speed value, in both Z (forward) and Y (upward) directions (regarding to the subject), as seen in Table 2.

Table 2. Relative distance of the clusters centroids, for the right hand, with the speed directions in x, y, and z, for k=2

	Beginning	Maximum	End
X (Side)	0.0398	0.5071	0.0110
Y (Upward)	0.0415	1.7497	0.0998
Z (Forward)	0.0847	2.0477	0.0536

The clusters were indeed separable, but the ARI stayed close to 0 for every case ($\max(ARI) \approx 0.05$), indicating a random cluster assignment. That means that the obtained clusters cannot be related to the outcome of the throw. The current descriptors (speed, acceleration and direction) with the proposed separation model are uncorrelated from the degree of success of the task. One can argue that, the considered task itself does not present a significant variation from one throw to another, in terms of speed and acceleration. Furthermore, the computed descriptors all relies on speed or acceleration, and that can possibly limit the variability of the results. Other higher level descriptors exist (Larboulette & Gibet, 2015), and could be used to analyze the motions. For example, the jerk (rate of change of the acceleration during the motion) can give an indication on how smooth the motion is, and the curvature, which is a measure of how fast a curve is changing through time, can give more accurate data about the wrist rotation. The geometric descriptors, such as the rotation of joints through time, and the center of mass displacement are also interesting values to consider.

In this experimentation, several problems arose. First, the distance between the subject and the table was not constant, as some people took a small step back before throwing. The table was also slippery, and the bottle slid on the table, thus the distance between the subject and the impact point of the bottle cannot be measured. Despite the fact that this measure can be an interesting feature to analyze.

The use of a MOCAP suit limits the experiment to its sensors accuracy and their constraints for a good use, opposed to, for example, an infrared camera system. Having accurate data for the wrist could have been interesting, as its movement is a crucial part of the motion. Furthermore, frame by frame data analysis showed that the data flow was not constant, and that the mandatory software used to gather the data used some undocumented method to counterbalance the data loss, that creates the artifacts seen in Figure 1.a. While the pre-processing steps took care of these problems, nothing can ensure that, the used method did not alter the initial data. Furthermore, the left side of the suit (from the shoulder to the hand) outputted noisy data. When the clustering was performed, mixing left-handed and right-handed data yielded worse results than keeping only the right-handed subjects, due to noisy nature of the left-handed data (Figure 3). This noise was visible on the captured data, and it is due to the fact that the suit has difficulties to handle a capture of the full body.

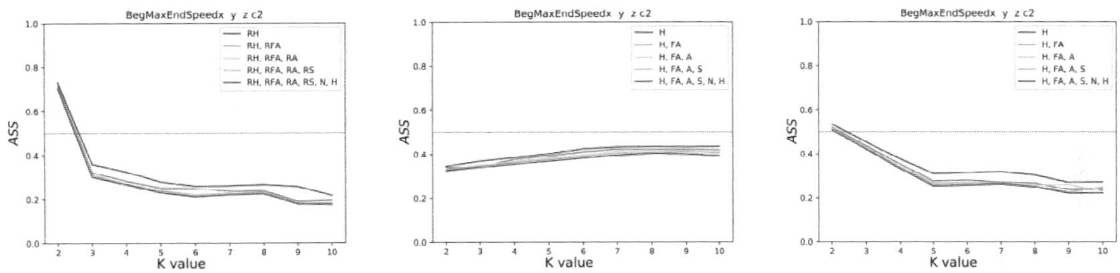

Figure 3. *ASS* score for various joints combinations and k ranging from 2 to 10 of (a) the right-handed subjects (b) the left-handed subjects (c) left and right-handed subjects together

As the motion variability of the chosen task can be discussed, another experiment was conducted to verify if the computed descriptors, combined with the k-means algorithm, can separate the motions according to the ground truth. In this experiment, a subject must throw a ball in one of two bins, placed in a line front on him (one placed 2m (6,56 ft) from them, another one placed 3.5m (11,48 ft) from them). The subject has to perform 100 throws, without any constraints about the throwing motion. For each throw, (i) the degree of success of the throw, (ii) the bin aimed at, and (iii) the type of throw (*i.e.* basket type launch, bowling type launch), were recorded . Having multiple labels for each motion allow for a wider range of tests, and allows to work on the degree of success, as well as the descriptors' ability to discriminate in various cases. Early results have shown that while the *ASS* and *ARS* values stay the same as the first experimentation for the successful/failed labeling, the clustering gives a good *ARS* for the throwing type, with the norm, and "norm + directions" descriptors. Further work is needed in order to validate these results on a larger scale.

5. CONCLUSION AND PERSPECTIVES

A new approach regarding the analysis of 3D motions was presented in this paper. The goal is to give a method to analyze the motion, through explainable descriptors extracted from it, leading to personalized feedback given to the learner in order to improve his motion. After acquiring and processing the motion data, some descriptors based on speed, acceleration and direction were extracted from it. These descriptors were then used in a clustering process, in order to find different explainable types of motions. This approach relied on two hypotheses: (i) it is possible to separate the motions into explainable clusters (ii) it is possible to obtain partitions corresponding to the degree of success of the task. While the second objective did not reach the expectations, the results of the first objective showed that the separation of clusters is indeed possible, validating the hypothesis, and the used descriptors (with the proposed method) in terms of discriminant features. The computation of more descriptors is planned, as the current ones may be limited, regardless of the application context. As the data are time series, the use of Dynamic Time Warping (DTW), computing a distance between motions (Morel, 2017), would provide another similarity measure between them, giving inter and intra-clusters information about the motions. Future work will also focus on performing recursive clustering on obtained clusters, in order to find if the motions, in each cluster, are separable according to the degree of success of the task or other features. The ongoing second experimentation will allow testing the new considered descriptors, as well as generalizing the context in which each descriptor is the best suited.

REFERENCES

Chang, C.-Y., Chang, C.-W., Zheng, J.-Y. & Chung, P.-C., 2013. Physiological emotion analysis using support vector regression. *Neurocomputing,* Issue 122, pp. 79-87.

Couland, Q., Hamon, L. & George, S., 2018. Enhancing Human Learning of Motions: An Approach Through Clustering. *European Conference on Technology Enhanced Learning.*

Gu, Y. & Sosnovsky, S., 2014. Recognition of Student Intentions in a Virtual Reality Training Environment. *Proceedings of the Companion Publication of the 19th International Conference on Intelligent User Interfaces*, pp. 69-72.

Hachaj, T. & Marek R., O., 2015. Full Body Movements Recognition - Unsupervised Learning Approach with Heuristic R-GDL Method. *Digital Signal Processing,* Volume 46, pp. 239-252.

Huang, J., Zhou, W., Li, H. & Li, W., 2015. Sign Language Recognition using 3D convolutional neural networks. *Multimedia and Expo (ICME), 2015 IEEE International Conference on,* pp. 1-6.

Kapsouras, I. & Nikolaidis, N., 2014. Action recognition on motion capture data using a dynemes and forward differences representation. *Journal of Visual Communication and Image Representation,* 25(6), pp. 1432-1445.

Kobayashi, Y., 2007. The EMOSIGN - analyzing the emotion signature in human motion. *Systems, Man and Cybernetics, 2007. ISIC. IEEE International Conference on,* pp. 1171-1176.

Larboulette, C. & Gibet, S., 2015. A Review of Computable Expressive Descriptors of Human Motion. *Proceedings of the 2Nd International Workshop on Movement and Computing,* pp. 21--28.

Lokaiczyk, R., Faatz, A., Beckhaus, A. & Goertz, M., 2007. Enhancing Just-in-Time E-Learning Through Machine Learning on Desktop Context Sensors. *Modeling and Using Context: 6th International and Interdisciplinary Conference, CONTEXT 2007, Roskilde, Denmark, August 20-24, 2007. Proceedings,* pp. 330-341.

Lui, Y. M., O'Hara, S. & Draper, B. A., 2011. Unsupervised Learning of Humain Expressions, Gestures, and Actions. *Face and Gesture 2011,* pp. 1-8.

Markowska-Kaczmar, U., Kwasnicka, H. & Paradowski, M., 2010. Computational Intelligence for Technology Enhanced Learning. *Intelligent Techniques in Personalization of Learning in e-Learning Systems,* pp. 1-23.

Morel, M., 2017. *Multidimensional time-series averaging: application to automatic and generic evaluation of sport gestures,* s.l.: s.n.

Ng, A., 2016. *CS229 - Machine Learning course, Lecture N 19: Stanford Engineering Everywhere, Stanford University.* [Online] Available at: https://see.stanford.edu/Course/CS229.

Nunes, J. F. & Moreira, P. M., 2016. *Handbook of Research on Computational Simulation and Modeling in Engineering.* s.l.:s.n.

Patrona, F., Chatzitofis, A., Zarpalas, D. & Daras, P., 2018. Motion analysis: Action detection, recognition and evaluation based on motion capture data. *Pattern Recognition,* Volume 76, pp. 612-622.

Rousseeuw, P. J., 1987. Silhouettes: A graphical aid to the interpretation and validation of cluster analysis. *Journal of Computational and Applied Mathematics,* Volume 20, pp. 53-65.

Sanchez-Mendosa, D., Masip, D. & Laepdriza, A., 2015. Emotion Recognition from Mid-level Features. *pattern Recognition Lett.,* 4(12), pp. 87-94.

Struyf, A., Hubert, M. & Rousseeuw, P., 1997. Clustering in an Object-Oriented Environment. *Journal of Statistical Software, Articles,* 1(4), pp. 1--30.

Yoshinaga, T. & Soga, M., 2015. Development of a Motion Learning Support System Arranging and Showing Several Coaches' Motion Data. *Procedia Computer Science,* Volume 60, pp. 1497-1505.

Yu, Z. & Lee, M., 2015. Human motion based intent recognition using a deep dynamic neural model. *Emerging Spatial Competences: From Machine Perception to Sensorimotor Intelligence*, Septembre, pp. 134-149.

Zhou, H. & Hu, H., 2008. Human motion tracking for rehabilitation - A survey. *Biomedical Signal Processing and Control,* pp. 1-18.

ANALYSING UNIVERSITY STUDENT ACADEMIC PERFORMANCE AT THE UNIT LEVEL

Eric Parkin, Simon Huband, David Gibson and Dirk Ifenthaler
Curtin Learning and Teaching, Curtin University, Perth, Western Australia

ABSTRACT

This paper describes the creation of a dataset to enable the analysis of student academic performance at the unit level at a large Australian University. The dataset was designed to enable academic leaders to explore research questions concerning student performance and pass rates in units. Four example research questions are presented here and explored, to demonstrate the value of the exploratory dataset, along with an overview of the methodology and tools used to synthesise the data. The data handling methodology and reflections on tools and processes may be useful for other analysts.

KEYWORDS

Data Integration, Exploratory Analysis, Hypothesis Testing, Analytics Tools and Methods, Pass Rates

1. INTRODUCTION

Universities are increasingly interested in improving their capability to make data informed decisions around Learning and Teaching. Curtin University has employed a Learning and Teaching analytics team to help enable this capability. Much the team's work involves combining and transforming institutional data to create datasets for the University's academic leaders to explore for insights, and to use to answer hypotheses about learning and teaching. The datasets are also used by the analytics team to conduct more complicated analyses at the request of academic leaders. This paper describes the creation of a dataset with information on student academic performance in units (known elsewhere as subjects). A sample analysis of four research questions follows, to demonstrate how the dataset can be used to answer hypotheses about learning and teaching.

The need for this dataset was prompted by requests from academic leaders for data on student academic performance, with statistics at the unit level. Faculties used existing data to identify units with low pass rates, but the data did not provide the detail required to explore some of their specific questions. Existing data addressed high-level reporting and strategic decision-making needs, rather than learning and teaching needs. One of the main differences in this tool, compared to other learning analytics tools used by the university, is that it enables analysis at the unit level. Other learning analytics tools used by the university have focused primarily either on students, such as by using machine learning to predict student attrition (Kevin EK Chai, 2015), or on courses (known elsewhere as degrees), by using clustering to find categories of students that attrition in courses is low, (David Gibson, 2015).

The issue of student attrition is related closely linked to academic performance in units. One study at another Australian institution found that "first year academic performance is a much stronger predictor of attrition than any demographic factors or educational background" (Andrew Harvey, 2014), and determined that "attrition is an institutional problem, but the causes often lie at the lower levels of course and subject" (Andrew Harvey, 2014). According to a recent report (Higher Education Standards Panel, 2017) it is apparent that student attrition and the factors driving it have been of concern since the Commonwealth claimed a role in higher education funding. Substantial resources have been committed over many years to exploring ways to reduce it. The consistently reported drivers of attrition, which are documented in the report, are summarised in Table 1.

Table 1. Drivers of attrition

Driver	Examples
The learning environment	Dramatic changes in learning culture from school to higher education New modes of learning (off-site, online, part-time)
The teaching ability of lecturers	Adequacy of level of training in teaching
Lack of student engagement	Helpful and unhelpful patterns of student/student and student/teacher interaction
High student staff ratios	Availability of lecturers and tutors to students
Lack of student support information and services	
Personal factors	Financial, social, emotional, health or other life events.

The adjusted attrition rate (the rate at which students do not complete their course, and do not return to study it at any Australian University) in Australia has changed little over the period from 2005 to 2014. The attrition rate fell from 15.04 per cent in 2005, down to a low of 12.48 per cent in 2009, before rising over the remainder of the period to 15.18 per cent by 2014 (Higher Education Standards Panel, 2017).

The panel report and the other historical studies of attrition do not seem to focus on why students choose either to course switch or leave, even though the rate difference between normal attrition and adjusted attrition (course or institutional switchers) is significant. For example, the three-year running national average from 2012 to 2014 is 6%.

The success rate measures units of study passed by commencing students and is understandably highly correlated with the adjusted attrition rate and adjusted retention rate, as poor academic performance is a major factor in a student's decision to discontinue studies. The success rate in 2015 was 83.72 % and has dropped from its peak in 2004 of 86.85 % (Higher Education Standards Panel, 2017).

This report also found that student characteristics alone appear to only explain a relatively small part of the overall variation in student attrition, with an adjusted R^2 of 22.55 for a full model consisting of institution, full-time or part-time, attendance mode, age group, basis of admission, field of education, socio-economic status, indigenous, non-English speaking background, and gender (Higher Education Standards Panel, 2017). The field of education, which may be the closest indicator related to units of study, had an adjusted R^2 of only 1.49, well below the leading indicator, institution, which had 18.83. This indicates that exploring unit of study success rates may need to be part of a wider array of inquiries and interventions that will impact institutional culture to have an impact on schools, faculty areas, and the larger university.

The paper is structured as follows: **Section 2** introduces the research questions used as a sample analysis, **Section 3** describes the methodology of creating the dataset and conducting the analysis, **Section 4** presents the results of the analysis, **Section 5** discusses plans for future improvements and **Section 6** concludes with a reflection on the methodology and results.

2. RESEARCH QUESTIONS

Curtin University is a large, multi-campus Western Australian University, with over 35,000 from diverse backgrounds studying undergraduate and postgraduate , including over 10,000 international students as of 2017, see Curtin's 'Office of Strategy and Planning' website for more detail (Curtin University Office of Strategy and Planning, 2017).

To demonstrate the capabilities of the dataset, the following research questions were formulated, based on typical questions the analytics team are asked by the University's academic leaders:

> **RQ1a:** Is there a difference in pass rates between international students and domestic students who studied a first-year communications unit in 2017?
> **RQ1b:** If there is a difference in pass rates, is this difference consistent with other first-year units?
> **RQ2:** Were students who attempted, but did not pass a first-year communications unit in 2017, less likely to have completed their attempt, compared to students who studied other first-year units?

RQ3: Were international students who entered via a particular 'enabling pathway' less likely to pass a first-year communications unit in 2017 than international students who entered via other pathways?
RQ4a: Is there a difference in pass rates between students on their first attempt and students on their second or subsequent attempt at a first-year communications unit in 2017?
RQ4b: If there is a difference in pass rates, is this difference consistent with other first-year units?

The 'communications units' refer to six communications-skills focused units from the University's four main Faculties (**Business and Law**, **Health Sciences**, **Humanities**, and **Science and Engineering**). At least one of these six units is compulsory for most undergraduate students.

To eliminate potential confounding factors, only student enrolments which met the criteria in Table 2 were included. To use as a control group in the analyses, a set of **'control units'** were selected, which included all enrolments that met all criteria in Table 2, excluding enrolments in communications units. Further detail about the units is shown in the results section.

Table 2. Student enrolment inclusion criteria

Category	Criteria
Year	2017 enrolments only
Campus	Enrolments at the University' main campus only
Attendance Mode	Face-to-face enrolments only (online students are excluded)
Year Level	First-year units only
Unit Level	Undergraduate units only (enabling and postgraduate units are excluded)
Result Type	Exclude units graded only as pass or fail (not marked out of 100)
Coursework or Thesis	Coursework type units only. Thesis-type units are excluded.
For Degree Enrolment	Students studying 'not for degree', e.g. doing a single unit, are excluded

3. METHODOLOGY

This section summarises the methodology used to create the dataset. The primary purpose of the dataset was to enable academic leaders to investigate unit outcomes, enabling investigation of the research questions was a secondary goal. The aim for the workflow was to rapidly develop a rapid prototype that could be quickly and easily modified and updated with new data and was easy for staff to engage with and can be summarised in the following steps:

1. **Explore Data**: find data sources and gain understanding of the data
2. **Extract Data**: extract data from the source systems
3. **Combine Data**: merge data to into a single table and derive new columns
4. **Finalise Data**: add calculated columns and aggregate data
5. **Share Data**: prepare data for dissemination and share it with academic leaders
6. **Analyse Data**: use the data to answer the research questions

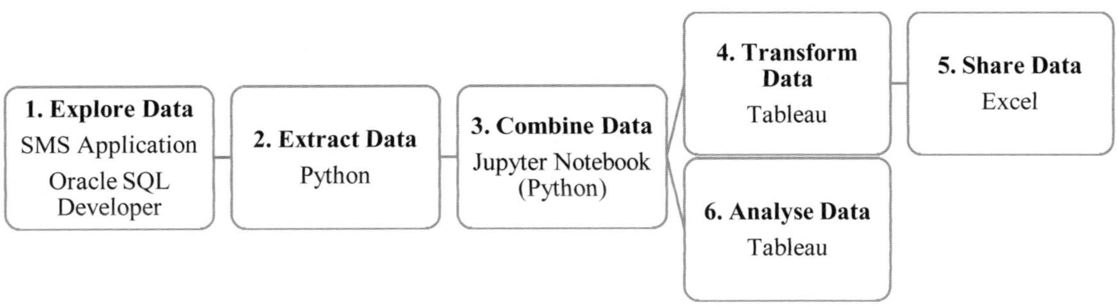

Figure 1. Data workflow

1. Explore Data

Gain an understanding data available, its structure, accuracy, and reliability, by exploring the Student Management System (SMS) application, and consulting with domain experts. Find the required tables and columns by referring to the database documentation and exploring the database using a database IDE (Oracle SQLDeveloper) in this case. The Result of this step will be a list of tables and columns, their sources, and notes/diagrams about the data, and how the tables relate to each other, i.e. primary and foreign keys.

2. Extract Data

Extract the data with Python script using the 'Pandas' 'read_sql' module to connect to the database (with login credentials), extract the tables, and save them as CSV files on a local (encrypted) storage device.

3. Combine Data

Combine the data into a single table with one row per enrolment. A Jupyter Notebook, using the 'Pandas' and 'NumPy' libraries, was the tool of choice for this step. Within in the notebook, import the CSV files, then sequentially transform and merge the tables into a single data frame. Use 'groupby' commands to derive new columns which require constructing from multiple rows (e.g. derive number of attempts by counting the number of rows with an enrolment in the same unit for the same student). Validate the data by running test commands to check for issues such as duplicates and inconsistencies between rows. Perform a 'sanity test' of the data by checking whether the data is sensible. Complete a final manual 'spot check' of the data by validating a selection of rows with the SMS Application. Correct any issues, re-execute the code, and repeat. Lastly, rename columns save as a CSV file on a local (encrypted) storage device.

Steps 1 to 3 will differ significantly for different institutions, but the combined table produced by step should be similar to the structure described in Table 3. Producing a dataset with these fields can be considered the goals of steps 1 to 3.

Table 3. Combined data structure

Group	Columns
Enrolment: (unique combination to define an enrolment in a unit)	Student ID, Unit Code (unique unit identifier), Year, Study Period (Semester/Term)
Course Details (determined by the course (degree) the student is studying	Course (degree) code and title, Undergraduate or Postgraduate course, 'Not for Degree' course flag, Basis for Admission (determines entry pathway)
Unit Details (determined by the unit code)	Unit title, Unit owning Faculty and School, Year Level, Postgraduate or Undergraduate unit, Campus, Internal or Fully Online
Enrolment Details (details about a student's enrolment in a unit)	Attempt Number, Enrolment Status (Pass/Fail/Withdraw), Grade and Mark
Student Details (unique per student)	International or Domestic Student flag

4. Transform Data

Transform the combined data into the final dataset, by connecting to the combined CSV file from a Tableau workbook and the set data types for each column. Create calculated columns to flag rows as 1 or 0, based on existing columns (e.g. 'domestic student pass', or 'zero mark'). Create a table and add rows for unit, campus, faculty, year, and semester. Set the granularity of the dataset by adding or removing rows (e.g. remove semester for a more aggregated dataset or add 'attendance mode' to create separate rows for online and face-to-face enrolments). Add filters to remove student enrolments which should not be included, e.g. 'not for degree' students. Validate the calculated columns by creating tables which flag inconsistencies, e.g. count rows which are flagged as both 'passed' and 'zero mark' (should be none).

This step could be done within other spreadsheet tools, or within the Jupyter Notebook (although this may be more time-consuming). One of the transformed datasets, focusing on students with multiple attemtps is shown in Table 4. Different columns can be used to focus on different information (e.g. international or domestic student statistics), but the 'Unit and course information' and 'Basic Enrolment Statistics' can remain.

Table 4. Transformed data structure, with data for multiple attempts

Group	Columns
Unit and Course Details	Unit Code, Unit Title, Faculty and School, Campus, Postgraduate or Undergraduate Unit, Year and Study Period
Basic Enrolment Statistics	Total Enrolments, Passes, Pass %, Fails, Fail %, Withdrawals, Withdraw %
First Attempt Statistics	No. on 1st Attempt, 1st attempt pass %, 1st attempt fail %, 1st attempt withdrawal %, 1st attempt avg. mark
Second Attempt Statistics	No. on 2nd Attempt, 2nd attempt pass %, 2nd attempt fail %, 2nd attempt withdrawal %, 1st attempt avg. mark
Third+ Attempt Statistics	No. on 3rd+ Attempt, 3rd+ attempt pass %, 3rd+ attempt fail %, 3rd+ attempt withdrawal %, 3rd+ attempt avg. mark

5. Share Data

Create a shareable from of the transformed datasets by copying data from Tableau text tables into separate tabs of a 'master' Excel workbook. Add a description tab with instructions, explanations of the data, and known issues. Create a separate workbook for each area by deleting data for other areas. Email the Excel workbooks to authorised personnel, for distribution more widely in their areas.

6. Analyse Data

The combined dataset produced in step 3 was used to conduct the analysis for this paper (with some of the transformed columns from step 4), the data was filtered to the scope in Table 2, and structured to create the aggregated tables shown in the results section, instead of to produce the more aggregated, unit level data.

4. RESULTS

This section presents the results of analysing the research questions presented in section 2. The findings presented here cannot be generalised to apply in all contexts, and can vary significantly when looking at individual units, and when looking at different types of units. These results are a sample only and are not intended to provide definitive answers to questions that are known to be inherently complex.

For context in the analyses to follow, overall enrolment and completion statistics for the communications units and control group units are shown in Table 5.

Table 5. Overall completion statistics for the communications units, and control group units

	Control Units	Communications Units	Difference
Number of Units	248	6	-
Enrolments	52565 **(100.0%)**	7726 **(100.0%)**	-
Passes	41433 **(78.8%)**	6467 **(83.7%)**	**+4.9%**
Fails	8280 **(15.8%)**	863 **(11.2%)**	**-4.6%**
Withdrawals	2842 **(5.4%)**	396 **(5.1%)**	**-0.3%**

RQ1a: Is there a difference in pass rates between international students and domestic students who studied a first-year communications unit in 2017?
RQ1b: If there is a difference in pass rates, is this difference consistent with other first-year units?

The completion statistics for international students and domestic students in the communications units and control units are shown in Table 6.

RQ1a Answer: The results show that the pass rates in the communications units is lower for international students compared to domestic students **(-3.8%)**. This lower pass rate for international students is accounted for, mainly by the higher fail rate **(+7.5pp)**, which is partly offset by the lower withdrawal rate.

Table 6. Completion statistics for international students

	Measure	Domestic Students	International Students	Difference
Communication Units	**Enrolments**	6508 **(100.0%)**	1218 **(100.0%)**	**-**
	Passes	5487 **(84.3%)**	980 **(80.5%)**	**-3.8pp**
	Fails	650 **(10.0%)**	213 **(17.5%)**	**+7.5pp**
	Withdrawals	371 **(5.7%)**	25 **(2.1%)**	**-3.6pp**
Control Units	**Enrolments**	47706 **(100.0%)**	4859 **(100.0%)**	**-**
	Passes	37725 **(79.1%)**	3718 **(76.5%)**	**-2.6pp**
	Fails	7221 **(15.1%)**	1086 **(21.8%)**	**+6.7pp**
	Withdrawals	2760 **(5.8%)**	82 **(1.7%)**	**-4.1pp**

RQ1b Answer: The results show that the pass rates are lower for international students more in the control units, however, the difference is more pronounced in the communications units **(-3.8pp** compared to **-2.6pp)**.

RQ2: Were students who attempted, but did not pass a first-year communications unit in 2017, less likely to have completed their attempt, compared to students who studied other first-year units?

'Non-completions' can be classified into four categories:

1. **'Fail (complete & low mark)'** – fail based on the student's mark (out of 100) being too low.
2. **'Fail (incomplete & non-zero mark)'** – student achieved a non-zero mark and failed on the basis of not meeting all pass criteria (e.g. student did not submit all compulsory assessments).
3. **'Fail (incomplete & zero mark)'** – student achieved a zero mark and failed on the basis of not meeting all pass criteria (these students likely have not participated in the unit, despite being enrolled).
4. **'Withdrawal'** – students decided to drop out of the unit after the cut-off date for fees (census date).

A breakdown of the non-completion statistics, as a proportion of all non-passing students, for the control units and communications units is shown in Table 7.

Table 7. Non-completion statistics

Measure	Control Units	Communications Units	Difference
All non-passes (withdrawals + fails)	11155 **(100.0%)**	1259 **(100.0%)**	**-**
Fails (complete & low mark)	5006 **(44.9%)**	344 **(27.3%)**	**-17.6pp**
Fails (incomplete & non-zero mark)	2156 **(22.6%)**	420 **(33.4%)**	**+10.8pp**
Fails (incomplete & zero mark)	786 **(7.0%)**	99 **(7.9%)**	**+0.9pp**
Withdrawals	2847 **(25.5%)**	396 **(31.4%)**	**+5.9pp**

RQ2 Answer: The results show that students who attempted but did not pass a communications unit were significantly less likely to have completed their attempt **(-17.6pp)**, than students who studied other units. The difference is accounted for by the higher rates of 'fails with incomplete attempts & non-zero mark' **(+10.8pp)**, 'fails with zero mark' **(+0.9pp)**, and withdrawals **(+5.9pp)**.

RQ3: Were international students who entered via a particular 'enabling pathway' less likely to pass a first-year communications unit in 2017 than international students who entered via other pathways?

The **'Enabling pathway'** looked at in this analysis, offers entry programs for students who do not meet the University's undergraduate entry requirements and is predominantly used by international students. The enrolment and completion statistics for these students are shown in Table 8.

Table 8. International student communications unit completion statistics by entry pathway

Measure	Other Entry Pathways	Enabling Pathway	Difference
Enrolments	1027 **(100.0%)**	191 **(100.0%)**	-
Passes	827 **(80.5%)**	153 **(80.1%)**	**-0.4pp**
Fails	181 **(17.6%)**	32 **(16.8%)**	**-0.8pp**
Withdraw	19 **(1.9%)**	6 **(3.1%)**	**+1.2pp**

RQ3 Answer: Of students who studied the communication units, the results show there is little difference in completion rates between international students who entered the university via the enabling pathway, and international students who entered via other pathways. Specifically, there is only a **-0.4pp** difference in pass rates, a **-0.8pp** difference in failure rate, and a **+1.2pp** difference in withdrawal rates.

RQ4a: Is there a difference in pass rates between students on their first attempt and students on their second or subsequent attempt at a first-year communications unit in 2017?
RQ4b: If there is a difference in pass rates, is this difference consistent with other first-year units?

The completion statistics for students on their first attempt, and students on their second or subsequent attempt, for both the communications units and control units are shown in Table 9.

RQ4a Answer: Students on their second or subsequent attempt at a communications unit, had a much lower pass rate than students on their first attempt **(-31.5pp)**. This is accounted for by the higher fail rate **(+22.3pp)** and higher withdrawal rate **(+9.2pp)**.

Table 9. Completion rates by first attempt and by second or subsequent attempts

	Measure	1st Attempt	2nd or Subsequent Attempt	Difference
Communications Units	**Enrolments**	7291 **(100.0%)**	435 **(100.0%)**	-
	Passes	6232 **(85.5%)**	235 **(54.0%)**	**-31.5pp**
	Fails	723 **(9.9%)**	140 **(32.2%)**	**+22.3pp**
	Withdrawals	336 **(4.6%)**	60 **(13.8%)**	**+9.2pp**
Control Units	**Enrolments**	48959 **(100.0%)**	3606 **(100.0%)**	-
	Passes	39428 **(80.5%)**	2015 **(55.9%)**	**-24.6pp**
	Fails	7114 **(14.5%)**	1166 **(32.3%)**	**+17.8pp**
	Withdrawals	2417 **(4.9%)**	425 **(11.8%)**	**+6.0pp**

RQ4b Answer: The lower pass for students on their second or subsequent attempt at a communications unit, is consistent with the control units, however, the difference is more pronounced in the communications units **(-31.5pp** compared to **-24.6pp)**.

5. FUTURE WORK

The Analytics team has plans to improve the pass rates dataset, including fixing issues, and making enhancements. These include: adding a row for student who have been left in an 'Enrolled' state, correcting for cases of duplicate enrolments present in some older source data, and combining unit codes with their replacements – allowing units that have been replaced to be analysed across multiple years. Additional columns are planned based on requests from academic leaders, including adding Tertiary Entrance Rank, and columns to flag the number of units failed in the same semester, and whether the student was ever granted a deferred assessment in a unit. Longer term goals for the analytics team are to make the dataset accessible via dashboards, and to combine the pass rates data set with the team's student retention dataset.

The analysis of the research questions could be improved by exploring the statistical significance of the results, and where there are highly significant results, investigating the data more deeply to find causal factors (e.g. attempt to find why the communications units have a greater prevalence of non-completion).

6. DISCUSSION/CONCLUSIONS

The methodology used to create the pass rates dataset, was effective in its goal of enabling the rapid creation of a prototype dataset. It required minimal computing infrastructure, and was capable of being used to investigate hypotheses about student academic performance in units. Due to the success of the project, the methodology and tools described, will likely be used by the analytics team in future projects, and is suggested for consideration by other institutions undertaking similar projects.

The issues and complexities encountered during the project, highlighted not only the importance of rigorous testing, but also of the importance of engaging with staff and of having a deep understanding of the data and how it is used within the organisation. Without such engagement and understanding, it is likely the datasets produced would have been flawed, and from previous experience, could have caused users to 'distrust' the accuracy of the data, and hence, refrain from using it. Being open about known issues in the data, and encouraging staff to report new issues, helped to improve trust.

The choice of sharing data with pre-calculated columns, in a 'flat' table structure, rather than as Pivot tables, helped lower the barrier for staff to engage with the data, and broadened its audience. The analytics team has received positive feedback on the usefulness of the data, had several requests for updated data and for improvements/additions to the dataset, evidencing the usefulness and accessibility of the data.

One major limitation of the dataset is that in its current form the data is 'static'. When academic leaders wish to view the data at a different level of aggregation, or with different filters, a new dataset would need to be created. Making the data available via dashboards could help solve this problem.

At present, no consideration has been given to release the data to external researchers for the purpose of open science. This will be considered in the future, however, ethical considerations complicate this task. Considerable care and effort would be required to cluster and anonymise the data, and was not a priority for this project.

ACKNOWLEDGEMENT

This paper was partly funded by the UNESCO Chair of Data Science in Higher Education Learning and Teaching position (Curtin University, 2018).

REFERENCES

Andrew Harvey, M. L., 2014. Beyond demographics: Predicting student attrition with the Bachelor of Arts degree. *The international Journal of the First Year in Hiher Education,* 5(1), pp. 19-29.

Curtin University Office of Strategy and Planning, 2017. *Curtin University Student Statistics 2013-2017.* [Online] Available at: https://planning.curtin.edu.au/stats/students2013-2017.cfm [Accessed 8 October 2018].

Curtin University, 2018. *UNESCO Chair of Data Science in Higher Education Learning and Teaching.* [Online] Available at: https://research.curtin.edu.au/projects-expertise/institutes-centres/unesco/ [Accessed 8 October 2018].

David Gibson, S. d. F., 2015. Exploratory Analytics in Learning Analytics. *Technology, Knowledge and Learning,* 21(1), pp. 5-19.

Higher Education Standards Panel, 2017. *Improving retention, completion and success in higher education.* [Online] Available at: https://docs.education.gov.au/system/files/doc/other/final_discussion_paper.pdf [Accessed 8 October 2018].

Kevin EK Chai, F. G., 2015. *Predicting the risk of attrition for undergraduate students with time based modelling.* s.l., 12th International Conference on Cognition and Exploratory Learning in Digital Age.

Note: This research received ethics approval by Curtin University's research integrity office, code: HRE2018-0519.

DIGITAL ETHNICITY

Nan B. Adams
Southeastern Louisiana University, United States

ABSTRACT

Digital Ethnicity is a concept based on Longstreet's (1978) model of the Aspects of Ethnicity. Digital Ethnicity was developed to describe the impact human interaction with digital communication technologies is having on cultural development. The ultimate goal for the development of Digital Ethnicity as a concept is to describe those aspects of digital ethnicity to achieve profiles of various digital ethnicities. These digital ethnic profiles are intended to guide thinking and provide insight into the social and educational needs of rapidly changing societal groupings by providing guidance for educational leaders, teachers and teacher education programs to prepare candidates who will be able to address the biological, social and cognitive changes brought about by pervasive use of digital communication technologies.

KEYWORDS

Learning Theory, Social Aspects of Technological Change, Digital Communication, Ethnicity

1. INTRODUCTION

Digital communication technologies pervade every facet of our lives. The influence of these technologies is changing human actions and beliefs; the construction of our social reality is in flux. A majority of the world's population 'text' rather than 'talk'; couples fall in love online and meet after the fact; gender identity is becoming a choice made not by biology but by a screen name or the physical appearance of an avatar. Social groups are formed in virtual space that provides new kinds of common identity to previously disparate individuals. Virtual schools prepare learners worldwide, while having no physical campus for teachers and learners to congregate. Palfrey and Gasser (2008) discuss the development of 'digital natives' whose "culture is global in scope and nature. Whether physically based in Rio de Janeiro, Shanghai, Boston, Oslo, or Cape Town, Digital Natives form part of global culture of their peers. They are connected to each other in terms of how they relate to information, how they relate to new technologies, and how they relate to one another" (p. 13). This first generation of Digital Natives are now in their late-30s and, as society dictates, becoming the new leadership for our nation and our world. Donald Trump was elected president of the United States. Although Trump is not a Digital Native, the reality of this outcome rests on manipulation of electronic media to influence beliefs and ultimately the outcome of an election – and it worked. A new 'Digital Ethnicity' has emerged, and it is critical to our collective futures to understand the implications.

2. BODY OF PAPER

Marc Prensky (2001a, 2001b) writes of Digital Natives and Digital Immigrants and how children are being socialized in vastly different ways than their parents. He states that "it is now clear that as a result of this ubiquitous [digital] environment and the sheer volume of their interaction with it, today's students think and process information fundamentally differently than their predecessors" (2001a, para 4). When discussing the implications for cultural loss due to the changes that are occurring to children immersed in interaction with digital technologies, Prensky (2001b) cites one key area of loss as the skill of reflection. He defines reflection as the ability to generalize and create mental models from our experiences and suggests that the implication for this loss is to develop educational strategies for developing reflection and critical thinking to counteract this seemingly media-induced loss in children.

Prensky (2009) continued his narrative writing of Digital Wisdom and calls for concerted efforts to realize the impact on child development both intellectually and socially and calls for teaching 'digital wisdom'. He states that "the digitally wise distinguish between digital wisdom and mere digital cleverness". He concludes that "It is through interaction of the human mind and digital technology that the digitally wise person is coming to be. I believe it is the time for the emerging digitally wise among us to embrace digital enhancement and to encourage others to do so." These aspects of child development are critical issues for teacher educators as they prepare teachers to address student learning styles and needs.

Schools have always been the institutions that prepare current and future society; they are where organized, formal learning is intended to take place. But is the intention of schools as the center of learning a reality? As virtual experiences increasingly replace traditional face to face activities, it is critical to study those aspects of society and the resultant ethnicities that are guided by this new communication style. Prensky's most current writings call for educational programs and practices that respond to the fact that today's adults grew up in the pre-Internet 20th century and do not yet fully understand their children are fast becoming "humans with enhanced brains, all networked together" (2017).

Koutropoulos (2011) in his critique of the monolithic assumptions of Prensky's Digital Natives, contends that from a social perspective and in contrast to writings about that portrayed digital natives as compliant, they are actually masters of their own destiny. Johnson (2006), a digital native herself teaching other digital natives, indicates that digital natives are complacent, actively seek authority figures and are unable to cast a critical gaze on their lives. This provides some argument for the role of teacher and learner in this digital age. Kouropoulos (2011) goes on to suggest that no organized research has been done to identify the real changes to education that should be developed in response to pervasive societal use of digital technology, and complains that we are not talking about pedagogy, and what is really good for the learners, but taking suppositions based on speculation rather than research to drive practice. Exploring the aspect of social value patterns included in this model to describe changes in our rapidly increasing digital society intends to provide insight into the demonstrated needs of learners that may be addressed by informed teaching practices.

Small and Vorgan (2008) discuss the effects of extensive interaction with digital technologies and observe that "as the brain evolves and shifts its focus toward new technological skills it drifts away from fundamental social skills, such as reading facial expressions during conversation or grasping the emotional context of a subtle gesture" (p.2). They talk of an increasing "brain gap" (p.3) resulting separate cultures. Small and Vorgan go on to discuss changes in communication preference style that often affects issues of privacy, how people meet socially, and often how they form loving attachments. Frank and Castek (2017) argue that learners must "develop the problem solving skills necessary for discerning accurate and reliable information, interacting with public services, communicating with friends, engaging in political activities, gaining employment, and participating in ongoing education (para 2)."

As digital technologies increasingly occupy the lives of young children, influencing their understanding of the world that surrounds them and influencing their development of communication and language skills, it is critical that deliberate analysis of the changes take place. Their engagement with these digital tools is shaping the preferences young children develop for their construction of reality and guides their interaction with their surroundings. The implications for the increased use of digital communication technologies on current and future educational practice are profound, and must be deliberately studied and addressed by education professionals to guide effective educational practice.

Longstreet's (1978) construction of the concept of ethnicity, originally developed to describe patterns, or aspects, that represent areas of social behavior that may exist among members of a social group, appears to provide an appropriate and useful framework for investigating the impact digital communication tools are having on cultures and societies. Her definition of ethnicity focuses on cultural development during the earliest stages of human development, prior to the onset of children's abstract thinking. This focus captures much of the timeframe given schools and teachers to accomplish the task of shaping formal and informal learning activities for students.

In a previous study (2010), the Digital Ethnicity concept utilized Longstreet's ethnicity model (1978) and was tested in terms of the digital environment. The Digital Ethnicity Scale investigated the different aspects of ethnicity using a digital lens. Four aspects of digital ethnicity were identified and correlated directly with the five originally identified aspects of ethnicity Longstreet proposed in 1978. The aspects of 1) Intellectual Mode 2) Orientation Mode and 3) Social Value Patterns were distinct. Verbal Communication and NonVerbal Communication aspects from the original model were combined to form the 4th aspect of Digital Ethnicity named Communication Mode. The ultimate goal for the development of the Digital Ethnicity Scale was to describe those aspects of digital ethnicity and collect these descriptions along with demographic data to achieve profiles of various digital ethnicities. These digital ethnic profiles may provide insight into the social and educational needs of rapidly changing societal groupings with hopes of providing guidance for future educational practice.

2.1 Why Ethnicity? Understanding the varying Definitions for the term 'Ethnicity'

For most, the word 'ethnicity' conjures both abstract and concrete meanings, which are often contextual. In the concrete uses of government and institutions, ethnicity usually denotes race. In the more abstract, it often means a group of humans who are identified through shared characteristics that may be real or assumed. This ambiguity seems to track the lack of agreement among scholars that has ebbed and flowed along with interest in the endeavor of building a consensus for meaning. Isajiw (1974) analyzed 65 sociological and anthropological studies and found that only 13 had definitions for the term ethnicity, with the remaining 52 having no explicit definition at all. With no real resolution in sight, the term has been defined as needed by institutions and individuals to gather data or describe groups of people.

Two major viewpoints guide the issue: 1) objectivists, who regard ethnic groups as cultural and social entities with distinct boundaries that are characterized by lack of interaction and relative isolation, and 2) subjectivists, who describe ethnic groups as culturally constructed categorizations that guide social behavior and interaction and define these groups by subjective self-categorizations (Jones, 1997). This begs the question of whether ethnic groups are based on shared, objective cultural practices that exist independently or the more subjective notion that ethnic groups are constructed by the processes of perception and derived social organization of their members.

2.1.1 Longstreet's Construction of Meaning for the Concept of Ethnicity

Longstreet (1978), unlike other scholars, provides the only constructed model for describing identified aspects of ethnicity. This model provides the socio-biological definition of ethnicity as being "that portion of cultural development that occurs before the individual is in complete command of his or her abstract intellectual powers and that is formed primarily through the individual's early contacts with family, neighbors, friends, teachers, and others as well as with his or her immediate environment of the home and neighborhood" (p.19). This construction of the concept of ethnicity, originally developed to describe patterns that may exist among members of a social group, provides an appropriate and useful framework for investigating the impact digital communication tools are having on educational practices of cultures and societies.

Our children are interacting with computers very young, even as early as 2 or 3 years of age, which puts them into the age when they are powerful learners of languages of all kinds – including the operational languages of computing. Longstreet's aspects of ethnicity are helpful in describing children growing up engaged and often surrounded by digital environments that encompass their early childhood. They are engaged in interactive video and computer games and other forms of digital communication at a time when biological development and ethnic understandings are most influenced, and yet these young children are not yet in command of their full abstract and intellectual powers and there is a lack of conceptual awareness of what is happening to them. The ultimate goal for the development of the Digital Ethnicity Scale is to describe those aspects of ethnicity using a digital lens and collect these descriptions along with demographic data to develop profiles of various digital ethnicities. These digital ethnicity profiles are intended to provide guidance for effective educational practices to serve the needs of a rapidly changing digital world.

2.1.2 Aspects of Ethnicity – The Underlying Theory and Working Model

Longstreet developed a functional model for the 5 aspects that may be used to describe her concept of ethnicity. These aspects are (a) social value patterns, (b) intellectual mode, (c) orientation mode, (d) verbal communication, and (e) nonverbal communication. A brief description of each follows:

1. Verbal communication may be described as the structure a person uses when communicating orally. The rules or patterns for this oral communication are learned by children prior to the development of their abstract intellectual abilities. The ability to learn language seems to be a universal capacity of humankind (Longstreet, 1978, p. 42).
2. Nonverbal Communication may be described as a system of facial expression, body movements and spatial arrangements that communicate meaning to others (Longstreet, 1978, p. 59).
3. Orientation Mode refers to patterns of behavior used, regardless of the presence of others, as ways of orienting oneself to the differing contexts of one's usual environment. It may be described as the way one communicates with themselves (Longstreet, 1978, p. 74). The orientation mode may be the most complex of the described modes. This mode is influenced by the social environment but ultimately becomes the ways one becomes comfortable in their own environment when no communication takes place.
4. Social Value Patterns are based on the sets of persistent behaviors that a group expects from its members and upon which it places certain values and upholds with certain beliefs (Longstreet, 1978, p. 89).
5. Intellectual Modes are described by Longstreet as the most emotionally charged aspect of ethnicity. This mode is not intended to deal with human innate intelligence, but rather reflect the way we externalize our thoughts, how we approach a problem, what gets our full attention, what details we are most likely to recall. Intellectual modes link intellectual performance to past experiences (Longstreet, 1978, pp. 106-107).

When seeking a model to describe human development through social interaction, and especially social interaction in digital communication environments, the notion of identity often emerges. The authors wish to acknowledge that identity focuses on the individual's definition of self (Erikson,1968), whereas ethnicity describes an individual's place or believed inclusion within a cultural group. This inquiry focuses on the individuals as they relate to a group.

2.2 Digital Ethnicity as a Specialized Form of Ethnicity

When constructing a scale to describe those aspects of ethnicity that may be influenced by early and pervasive interaction with digital communication technologies, consideration of which aspects to investigate was a challenging task. Longstreet predicted a variety of contextual ethnicities that may be distinct ethnicities. These distinct and specialized ethnicities were described as being grounded in one or more of the identified 5 Aspects of Ethnicity. For example, Scholastic ethnicity may be a distinct form of ethnicity grounded in intellectual mode but still related to and having impact upon the other modes identified within this construction of ethnicity. National ethnicity may be a distinct form of social value patterns and communication modes. Gender ethnicity may be a distinct form of orientation mode. In this vein, the current research has sought to describe Digital Ethnicity as a distinct form of the combined Communication Mode, which is a combination of verbal and non-verbal communication mode.

2.3 The Digital Ethnicity Scale

Over a period of 2 years, the Digital Ethnicity Scale (DES) was developed and refined to test the construct of Digital Ethnicity using Longstreet's Aspects of Ethnicity Model. The final version of the Digital Ethnicity Scale contained 12 items designed to measure the three aspects of Intellectual Mode, Orientation Mode, and Social Value Pattern. Consistent with the previous revision, the scale was analyzed using exploratory factor analysis. The final analysis was conducted by specifying a 3-factor solution with a Varimax rotation. Because of previous refinements to the items, the suppression level for the factor loadings was increased to .50.

The results of the 3-factor solution from the factor analysis are presented in Table 1. The results indicate that the items loaded as predicted with all items loading above the .50 criterion. The first factor contained the four items related to Orientation Mode and accounted to 17.87% of the variance. Factor 2 contained the Social Value Pattern items and accounted to 15.82% of the variance. The final factor contained the four items related to Intellectual Mode and accounted for 15.57% of variance. Finally, the reliability estimates ranged from .570 to .648.

Table 1. Factor Loadings for Revised 15 Item Digital Ethnicity Scale

Item	Factor 1	Factor 2	Factor 3
I respond to emails immediately	.694		
I would rather send email than talk on the phone	.675		
I leave my computer on all of the time just in case I need to get online	.652		
I am usually on the internet at the same time every day	.600		
Posting pictures, even misleading ones, on the web doesn't hurt anyone		.775	
It is okay if I pretend to be someone else online		.736	
It is okay to talk about my private life online with people I do not know		.590	
It is okay to download or copy music for free		.571	
Using a computer makes me smarter			.701
Because of the internet I am able to solve problems myself that I would not be able to do otherwise			.693
Computers make us question what we know			.656
The internet helps me make good decisions			.584
Proportion of variance explained	17.87	15.82	15.57
Reliability	.634	.570	.648
Identified Aspect of Ethnicity	Orientation Mode	Social Value Pattern	Intellectual Mode

2.3.1 Semantic Differentials to Measure Communication Mode

The initial analyses of the semantic pairs identified a 3-factor structure consistent with the findings of Osgood, Suci, and Tannenbaum (1957). For the final phase of the development, 13 semantic pairs were retained and biased/fair was replaced because it did not load on any factor during initial analyses. Additionally, two pairs were added to the set for a total of 16 semantic pairs. The structure of the 16-item set was examined using a factor analysis with an eigenvalue greater than 1 extraction criterion, Varimax rotation, and .50 display criterion for factor loadings. The results of the analysis are presented in Table 2.

Table 2. Factor Loadings for 16 Semantic Pair Set

Pair	Factor 1	Factor 2	Factor 3	Factor 4
hard-easy	-.833			
easy to understand-confusing	.795			
fluent-awkward	.776			
comfortable-anxious	.743			
chaotic-ordered	-.613			
wholly engaging-insufficient	.515			
trustworthy-bogus		.777		
ethical-corrupt		.702		
personal-impersonal		.566		
part of a community-isolated		.522		
informative-entertaining			.682	
public-privacy			.608	
influential-inconsequential			.558	
interesting-boring			.534	
choice-need				.762
text intensive-highly graphic				
Proportion of variance explained	22.28	15.79	10.81	8.20
Semantic Space Dimension	Evaluation	Potency	Activity	

The results of the factor analysis of the 16 pairs indicated a 4-factor solution that accounted for 57.08% of the variance. The first three factors corresponded to the dimensions of Evaluation, Potency, and Activity, respectively, and accounted for 48.88% of the variance. The fourth factor only contained one pair, choice/need, and represented an additional unique dimension. Osgood et al. (1957) acknowledged that semantic spaces would likely have more than the three dominant dimensions. Therefore, the structure of this set of semantic pairs is consistent with the common structure proposed by Osgood et al. Additionally, the failure of the text intensive/highly graphic pair to load on any of the factors suggests that is also represents a unique dimension. However, the variance accounted for by the dimension is not large enough to be extracted as a factor in the solution.

2.4 Discussion of Results

As digital communication technologies increasingly replace face-to-face communication and interactions, the experiences that construct human perceptions of reality are altered. Marshall McLuhan (1964) observed that "Everybody experiences far more than he understands. Yet it is experience, rather than understanding, that influences behavior" (p. 277). The Digital Ethnicity Scale seeks to describe those aspects of ethnicity that are influenced by immersive experience with digital communication tools.

When constructing a scale to describe those aspects of ethnicity that may be influenced by early and pervasive interaction with digital communication technologies, consideration of which aspects to investigate was challenging. We were unable to obtain consistent separate sets of data for the aspects of verbal and non-verbal communication. It appears that the digital media, not television but all other digital communication environments, has impacted the verbal forms of communication in ways that cannot be tested separately from nonverbal communication and in ways that do not exist in other environments. This fusion may well be a major characteristic of digital ethnicity, but not one that can as yet be characterized by the instrument we have developed. However, digital influences on those ethnic aspects of Social Value Patterns, Orientation Mode and Intellectual Mode provided distinct descriptions of digital ethnic behavior that appear to be useful for the development of an instrument focused on construction of digital ethnic profiles.

Just because this research did not find a description of the changes occurring to communication modes does not mean that these changes are not occurring. McLuhan's 1967 conception that the *Medium is the Message* provides insight into this media-induced change and is probably more relevant now than when it was originally discussed. Even more relevant may be pursuing the impact of the digital environment on the construction of meaning and even of reality.

3. CONCLUSION

3.1 Further Exploration and Expansion of the Theoretical Basis of This Research

There exists a large amount of interaction between the world around us and the digital environment – our students are currently experiencing multiple environments that the individual is negotiating. For example, students write on a computer, stop and talk, and they may well send copies of the writing back and forth digitally and then discuss the work verbally. The investigation of this negotiation of a variety of learning environments is not studied with this current inquiry. This should be part of further study, but may be informed by the development of digital ethnic profiles. The ability to understand and accommodate changing orientation and intellectual modes along with an understanding of changing social value patterns that result from interaction with digital media will inform educators and other social scientists as we work to understand this emerging digital society.

3.2 Recommendations for Future Research

Through exploratory analyses, the current research has identified the foundations of a scale that reflects Longstreet's aspects of ethnicity applied to the interaction with digital environments. However, the following recommendations should direct future research concerning the development and validation of the DES.

First, the analyses conducted in the present research were based on the total sample, which was skewed with respect to gender (72.3% females) and race (69.7% white), and did not examine the factor structure for subgroups. Future research should examine the scale properties for subgroups based on demographic characteristics such as gender, race, and age through techniques such as confirmatory factor analysis. Because the current research included only respondents who were 18 years old or older, future research should also attempt to sample and examine the scale properties for individuals who are under 18 years. This is particularly relevant based on Longstreet's assumption that ethnicity is developed prior to the onset of abstract thinking in children and the volume of technology to which today's children are exposed.

Second, the current research has provided a foundational set of items related to each of Longstreet's aspects of ethnicity. Although the reliability estimates for the final set of items was acceptable for exploratory analyses, future research should continue to refine and potentially add items to increase the reliabilities of the subscales. Enhancing the reliabilities will also impact usability of the scale for research and practice.

Third, the current research focused on the development of an initial item set related to Longstreet's aspects of ethnicity. However, in order for the scale to have practical applications, procedures to calculating and reporting results must be determined. This is based on the assumption that different profiles will exist based on selected demographic data.

Fourth, future research should undertake the reconceptualization of Communication Modes (as a possible combination of Longstreet's original Verbal and Non-Verbal modes) in terms of the digital environments.

Fifth, because this inquiry has combined all of the different digital environments into one (computers, video games, intelligent phones, webcams, etc.), an investigation into the different types of digital environments should be undertaken.

Finally, it is commonly understood that interaction with digital technologies is changing the structures of society and varying aspects of human nature. Digital environments for work and play will only increase, therefore, the theoretical constructs describing digital ethnicity should be pursued further. McLuhan's work of the 60s and 70s and Hall's undertakings may provide further avenues for investigation.

REFERENCES

Adams, N., DeVaney, T., & Longstreet, W., Investigating aspects of an emerging digital ethnicity: Development of the Digital Ethnicity Scale (DES). *Computers in Human Behavior*, 26 (2010) 1822-1830.

Erikson, E. (1968). *Identity: Youth and crisis*. New York, NY: W. W. Norton.

Isajiw, W. (1974). Definitions of ethnicity. *Ethnicity 1*, 111-24.

Johnson, K. (2006). The millennial teacher: Metaphors for a new generation. *Pedagogy, 6*(1), 7-24. Retrieved from http://muse.jhu.edu/journals/pedagogy/v006/6.1johnson.html

Jones, S. (1997). *The archeology of ethnicity*. London: Routledge.

Koutropoulos, A. (2011). Digital natives: Ten years after. *Journal of Online Learning and Teaching, 7*(4). Retrieved from http://jolt.merlot.org/vol7no4/koutropoulos_1211.htm

Longstreet, W. S. (1978). *Aspects of ethnicity*. New York, NY: Teachers College Press.

McLuhan, M. (1964). *Understanding media: The extensions of man*. New York, NY: McGraw-Hill.

McLuhan, M. (1967). *The medium is the message*. New York, NY: Bantam Book.

Osgood, C., Suci, G., & Tannenbaum, P. (1957). *The measurement of meaning*. Urbana, IL: University of Illinois Press.

Palfrey, J., & Gasser, U. (2008). *Born digital: Understanding the first generation of digital natives*. New York, NY: Basic Books

Prensky, M. (2001a). Digital natives, digital immigrants. *On the Horizon, 9*(5), 1-6. Retrieved from www.marcprensky.com

Prensky, M. (2001b). Digital natives, digital immigrants, part 2: Do they really think differently? *On the Horizon, 9*(6): 1-6. Retrieved from www.marcprensky.com

Prensky, M. H. (2009). Sapiens digital: From digital immigrants and digital natives to digital wisdom. *Innovate Journal of Online Education, 5*(3), 1-9. Retrieved from www.innovateonline.info

Prensky, M. (2017). *Education to better their world*. New York, NY: Teachers College Press.

Small, G., & Vorgan, G. (2008). *iBrain: Surviving the technological alteration of the modern mind.* New York, NY: Harper Collins.

SUITABLE JUDGEMENT ASSISTANCE OF VISUALIZATION METHOD FOR SENSOR LOG OVERLAPPING ON DAILY VIDEO

Takuya Ishioka[1], Naka Gotoda[2], Christian Alo[3], Takayuki Kunieda[2], Rihito Yaegashi[2] and Toshihiro Hayashi[2]
[1]Kagawa University, 2217-20 Hayashi-cho, Takamatsu, Kagawa, 761-0396 Japan
[2]Kagawa University, 1-1 Saiwai-cho, Takamatsu, Kagawa, 760-8521 Japan
[3]University of Applied Sciences, Bonn-Rhein-Sieg, Grantham-Alle 20, 53757 Sankt Augustin, Germany

ABSTRACT

Obtaining tacit knowledge in sports skill learning is difficult. Although, coaches can give their learners easy to understand instructions to obtain the tacit knowledge. The coaches monitor, analyse and interpret learners' physical movement based on the coaches' experiences, then they give the instruction. In self-training without coaches, it is difficult for learners to analyse own growing status and interpret their achievement goal. We developed an Automatically Superimposed-video Creating System (ASCS) in order to support analysis and interpret the learners' status and achievement level of the skill. Our system has several independent modules to create each instruction, and the learners can choose one module. We assume two achievement models to select suitable modules. Achievement models show a growing process of learners' skills in time series. We conducted a survey to find out the models. We found combined growth patterns which consisted of two assumed models. It suggests a possibility of the two assumed models. In addition, the survey suggested the relationship between modules and models.

KEYWORDS

Individual Training, Achievement Model, Tacit Knowledge, Status Prediction, Module Candidates

1. INTRODUCTION

It is important to obtain tacit knowledge of physical movement in sports technical skills learning (Schmidt and Wrisberg, 2004). However, obtaining tacit knowledge is one of the most difficult factors. Coaches monitor, analyse and interpret learners' achievement status of the goal skills through observing their movement. The coaches instruct them based on the status to transfer the coaches' tacit knowledge to them, giving the learners easy to understand instructions by face-to-face. Recently, the learners of sports techniques watch video learning materials created by experienced players, on web services such as YouTube, and they equip wearable sensors to monitor their own physical movement. These environments are constantly evolving and enable daily self-training without coaches. However, It is difficult for the learners to predict own achievement status through analysing the monitored data, and interpret the result of the analysis. Thus, they could not figure out how they should change their movement. For example, if the learner is not aware of their current achievement level, they cannot correctly evaluate own training to improve own skills, then they cannot figure out what action is suitable for them. Therefore, we believe it is useful for the self-training to introduce a system which observes the learner's achievement and presents suitable kind of instruction. The system creates instructions based on the analysis of the leaner's achievement level and the interpretation of the achievement status. Then it can support learners instead of human coaches.

The videos which are superimposed instruction can use for the easy to understand instruction. The superimposed-video can communicate instruction synchronous with video, and it is intensely. We propose an Automatically Superimposed-video Creating System (ASCS) to support the individual physical training. ASCS can superimpose the differences between trials of experienced players and learners in videos to give suitable teaching for the learners. ASCS generates superimposing information dependent on the learner's characteristics and preferences. ASCS-Engine interprets the learner's achievement status. The status consists of the learner's progress, and the progress shows a pattern of the learner's achievement. We assumed that the pattern consists of two models. If the difference between the learner's current achievement and the achievement goal is significant, the learners probably take a big change in their movement. If the difference is small, they take small steps, and it perturbates around the goal. The ASCS-Modules can interpret the models and display proper viewable instruction and superimpose on a target learning-material video. When watching those videos, the change of the learner's progress might be different depending on preferences and characteristics of the learner. ASCS-Engine predicts the learner's characteristics by comparing their achievement status and the models. Each ASCS-Module might have specific characteristics whose attach the module. There is a much different candidate of teaching method. However, we assumed two species of modules. One species modules create an instruction to show the learner's current achievement level, and other modules create an instruction to show the change of direction in their training. The preference has the relationship between characteristics and the suitable species of modules. The preference also has different selective candidate modules as ASCS-Modules.

We tackled to find out the relationship between characteristics and preferences. We developed three ASCS-Modules include typical methods (numeric displaying and sentence instruction displaying method), and a proposed method compared with advanced methods which use onomatopoeias and those font shape. The onomatopoeia can express the scale of change and change of direction of physical movement briefly.

In this study, we set the forehand stroke in tennis as the learning topic and surveyed the learner's achievement pattern. The survey found different achievement patterns in each learning which use different modules. We observed the possibility of the models through the patterns. Also, we observed the suggestion of the relationship between the characteristic and the preference.

2. RELATED WORKS REGARDING TO E-LEARNING ON SPORTS

2.1 An Approach to Display Information for Trainings

Matsuura et. al. applied a superimposed approach for the skipping-rope (Matsuura et al., 2010). In this study, the system creates graphs which reflects the learner's position of the head. The graphs are superimposed in videos which are taken while the user's training. The users watch a wave which appears on the graph in the video. The wave shows the consistency of a frequency and an amplitude. The learners master the skipping-rope by observing the wave and adjusting their movements. The system in the study displays the monitoring results, however, it does not give instructions based on the relationship between the characteristics and the references. We tried to give the learners appropriate instruction based on the relationship, predicting achievement status.

2.2 The Attachment of Visual Aspect with Onomatopoeia for Instruction

Jimenez et al. defined the onomatopoeia as "Generic term for an "echoic word" or "imitation word"" (Jimenez et al., 2014). They showed that it was possible to maintain the learner's motivation, using the onomatopoeia. In comparison to the general vocabulary, they mentioned that the onomatopoeia can express the reality more effectively. For example, the onomatopoeia can express a bold movement with short and easy word. Also it can express minute movement.

The research topic of Fujino et al. focused on the usage of onomatopoeias as a vocal instruction approach in Japanese sports (Fujino and Yamada, 2006). They defined "The Sports Onomatopoeia", and they researched to find out the learning effects of the onomatopoeias in addition to organising the onomatopoeias used in sports. In the research, the onomatopoeia was used as a tool to communicate movement by voice.

If we express onomatopoeia with letters, the onomatopoeia might gain both feature, voice and visual. The feature of visual is that when put it on a picture, it can improve the reality of the picture as a moment in the video. For example, the onomatopoeia is used in comics to express visual scene and movements through instinct. Expressing like that is difficult for the non-onomatopoeia words. Mixing the voice and vision of onomatopoeias, promote the effect of onomatopoeia in the instruction. The shape of fonts and arrangement of letters with onomatopoeia are used to make the way to movements more clearly, adjusting the nuance of the onomatopoeia. We tackled to set the onomatopoeia which instructs sports skill by voice into the learning video. To add the onomatopoeia instruction into the learning video, we combined letter of onomatopoeia and suitable shape of the letter appropriately. Moreover, we proposed a new teaching method using combined the letter and shape. The vital point to employee onomatopoeias into the method is to connect the instruction information with onomatopoeias appropriately to present the instruction impressively to the learners. We focused on the learner's characteristics at the time which the remarkable event is happened (e.g. The racket shoot the ball in tennis) because every moments are factor which configure a motion.

2.3 The ASCS: Focusing Judgement Assistance for Choosing Modules

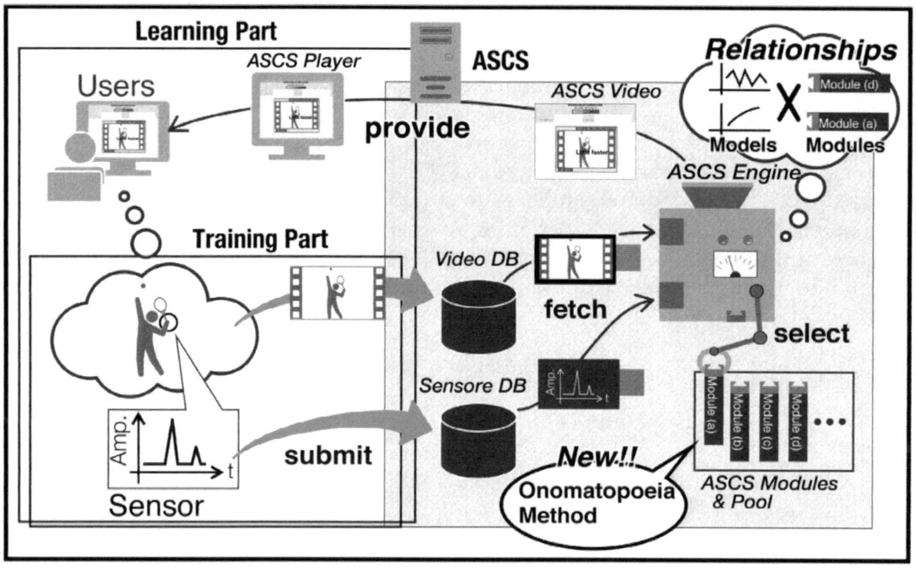

Figure 1. An Overview of Automatically Superimposed-video Creating System (ASCS)

Figure 1 shows the overview of the structure of Automatically Superimposed-video Creating System (ASCS) which we proposed in this research project. The system has a coach's trial video and sensor data to assistant the judgement of the learner. In the sports learning, the learner has several achievement statuses such as improving, decreasing and stable status. Regarding to the stable status, concretely speaking, there is two kind of stable status. We defined high level stable status as the status which keeps high achievement level and low level stable status as the status which keeps low achievement level. One of most worrying status is low level stable status because if the learner is not aware this status, the learner might not improve the learner's skill in the feature.

The ASCS predicts the learner's achievement status and supports to make the learners notice the status using characteristics. Also, ASCS can select the instruction species which are suitable for the leaner's achievement status, and provide suitable candidates of ASCS Modules for the learners. It enables the learners to choice a prefer instruction method from appropriate candidates at the current achievement. The ASCS Module is implemented based on the specific instruction method, and ASCS chooses the module based on the learner's characteristics. ASCS Modules refers to the coach's video and movement which is obtained by sensor log, and create instruction and superimposed-video. Generally, if the coach aware the gap between the achievement goal and the learner's achievement level, the coach communicate the change of direction for the learner's movement (e.g. swing the racket faster or swinging the racket slower) to the learner. Besides, if the coach observes that the learner's achievement is close to the goal, the coach communicates the current status of the learner's movement (e.g. your swing is a little bit faster) to the learner to adjust the learner's movement. Based on this discussion, in order to complement without coaches, the target of the system is to observe the learner's achievement level and predict the learner's status and provide appropriate instruction like the coach. If the learner uses ASCS, ASCS monitors the achievement levels and predicts the status. The learner gets appropriate instruction based on own status. Superimposed-videos is applied to the instruction in ASCS. The video contains the instruction which is created based on the learner's status and communicates differences between the learner's achievement level and coach's achievement level. The learners can gain the change of direction and the achievement level from the superimposed-video. The learner tries to improve movement at the next learning. In this study, the vital point is the relationship between the characteristics and the preferences. The characteristic is needed to determine the learner's status as a coach, and the characteristic needs models of achievement status. The preference is needed to feature the instruction method. the preference considers the distance between the leaner's achievement and the achievement goal and give instructions. Thus we survey the learner's achievement models and the preference of the modules. We tackled to find out the fundamental achievement model to design ASCS-Engine and ASCS-Modules.

The ASCS is designed based on a hypothesis that providing annotated videos to the learners and interactive changing of the instruction depending on the learner's status promotes and maintains the learner's motivations by the preferences. Thus we propose the ASCS-Video and functions of ASCS. We confirm the hypothesis throw a pre-study, and we design ASCS-Modules.

3. THE ASCS-MODULES TO PROVIDE JUDGEMENT METHOD

3.1 The Pre-Study: the Base of the Achievement Models Assumption

In this study, we assumed that the video which is extended by the instructional annotation for the learners promotes and maintains learner's motivations. The reason is that if the learner takes an instruction based on both, the characteristic and preference, the training might be more effective, and the motivation for the learning will maintain. We have conducted a pre-study to verify the hypothesis. Four tennis learners participated in this study. The participants divided into two groups. Both groups were given the same learning videos of forehand stroke. Only one group was given feedback which shows differences between the experienced player's movements and learner's movements. The learning targets of this pre-study were swing speed and spinning amount of ball on the forehand swing. These learning targets are fundamental techniques which are developed through iterative training. We monitored the participants' achievements process and conducted a questionnaire survey. Figure 2 and 3 show the growth process of swing speed. The line types shows the achievement models which configure the achievement process. The Figure 2 shows that both participants maintain the high level stable status in compare with Figure 3. Therefore, the instructional annotated video affects the physical training. Moreover, to maintain the high level stable status of the learner, would maintain the learner's motivation consequently.

From the graphs, we observed the two models: the exponentially growing model and the perturbational aspect model. The result of the survey shows that the solid line in figure 2 and 3 mainly consists of the exponentially growing model. Also, the broken line in the figures consists mostly of perturbational aspect model. The perturbating part in the figures is shown at trial 2 to 10 on figure 2 and trial 4 to 10 on figure 3. In this study, we defined the perturbation as a wavering state around a constant achievement level. The perturbation status is related to the stable status of the achievement status.

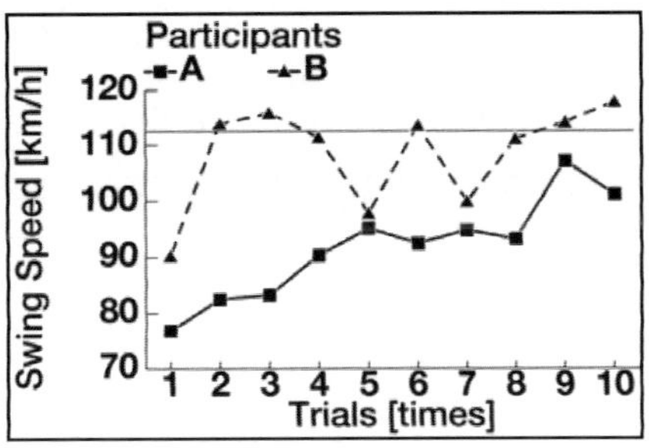

Figure 2. The result of swing learning with feedback

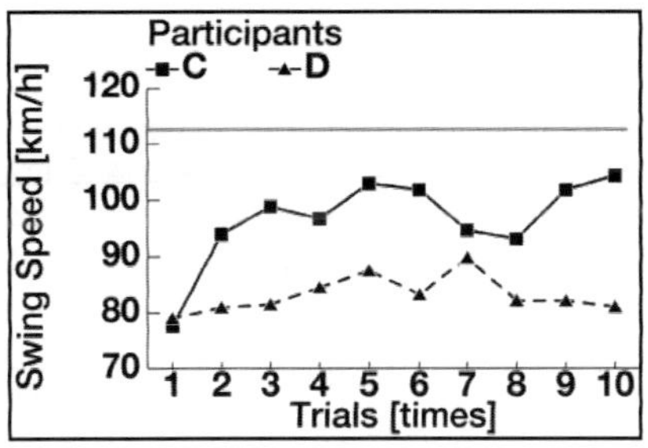

Figure 3. The result of swing learning, only watching videos

From the observation, we assumed two models which configure the achievement models: "Perturbation model" and "Exponential model". Also, we assumed that monitoring the model in the patterns, ASCS can predict the status the achievement status. The purpose of this study was to confirm that the achievement process pattern consists of two models, also, to find out the relationship between the characteristics and the preference.

We develop ASCS-Modules which were implemented based on four requirements which are needed to create instruction, for the experiment.

3.2 Module Definitions

This section describes the requirements for the ASCS-Modules. We defined these following four requirements;

a.) The modules accept two inputs of monitoring data.
b.) The modules should compare and interpret these monitoring data.
c.) The modules generate feedback instruction based on the comparison.
d.) The modules are able to superimpose the information in the videos.

Modules fetch in two sensor data: The coach's data and the learner's data. The system uses the coach's data as the achievement goal. The ASCS-Modules receive the current characteristic of learner's which the system determines from the achievement process. The modules create instruction information using the reference and the characteristic. The system monitors the learner's achievement process and determines current achievement status by predicting the current achievement model and comparing the achievement and the achievement goal to check the amount of difference.

The modules have preferences. The preference has the property of the instruction method. The property has two specifies. One specifies method's instruction communicates the leaner's achievement status to adjust the leaner's movement, and other species to communicate the change of direction to let leaner's movement change. We developed three different kind of ASCS-Modules includes two advanced methods and one proposed method whose have the preference. This study surveyed to confirm the possibility of the achievement models and find out the relationship between the characteristics and the preferences observing the learner's achievement progress using the developed ASCS-Modules.

3.3 The Implementation of ASCS-Modules

We developed three different kinds of ASCS-Modules. This section describes a used sensor for the examination in addition to three ASCS-Modules, Module (a), Module (b) and Module (c), which presents the instruction in different ways. We adopted Smart Tennis Sensor, produced by Sony Corporation, to monitor technical levels of learners. The sensor is attached to the butt cap of tennis rackets, it detects ball speeds, ball spinning levels when the racket hits the ball. The unit of the speed is km/h, and the level is shown by 21 gradations from -10 to 10. This study use the speeds and levels to develop instructions.

The modules were implemented with one proposed and two advanced annotation methods. The module (a) and (b) were implemented with showing differences from coaches by numeric instruction and sentence instruction method respectively, and the module (c) employed the proposed method which uses onomatopoeias and its font shapes. The feature of the proposed method is able to present the gaps in a visual and instinctive way. Figure 4 shows ASCS-Player and the superimposed video which is created by module (a). The learners use ASCS-Player not only to play ASCS-video (superimposed learning video) but also to play learning material videos and to upload the own sensor monitoring data to generate ASCS-Videos which is detected and monitored by Smart Tennis Sensor while training. Module (a) creates numeric instructing ASCS-Videos like shown on Figure 4. The instruction is showing the difference between coaches' target values and the learner's ball speed and ball spinning level. The instruction of speed is indicated on left hand side in km/h, and the difference of spinning level is indicated on right hand side in ASCS-Player. Figure 5 shows an instance of ASCS-videos created by module (b). The module (b) expresses the difference of sensor values between coaches and learners with sentence. The module expresses the difference of speed using "faster" or "slower" with 5 gradating words. The difference of spinning level is expressed by using "more spin" or "less spin" with 4 gradating words. When the learner's speed ball and spinning level are close to the coach's one, the module indicates "Hold it." In the ASCS-video, two sentences are superimposed in the video.

These sentences display to what extend speeds and spinning levels have to change. Figure 6 shows an instance of ASCS-video created by module (c). Module (c) is implemented with proposed method which uses onomatopoeias and its font shape. We proposed this method to present the difference between coaches and learners in a visual and instinctive approach. Module (c) adopted echoic words "Syuuu" as an onomatopoeia to express swing speeds of tennis racket, and the font shape and arrangement express pitch of instruction and positive or negative of modifying directions. The shape of the font is connected to the difference of the sensor values. For example, the fonts' shape change like shown on Figure 7, the thickness of the font expresses the perception of speed. the font's shape shifts to the right direction on the figure when the learner's speed is slower than the experienced player's speed, and it shifts to left direction on the figure when the learner's speed is faster than the experienced player's speed. Figure 8 and 9 shows relationship between the sensor values differences of the spinning levels and the letter arrangement. The curvier the letter arrangement the more spinning speed is needed. When the learner's spinning level is stronger than the experienced player's one, the font shape is generated like shown on Figure 8. On the other hand, when the learner's spinning level is weaker than the experienced player's one, the font shape is generated like shown on Figure 9.

Figure 4. ASCS-Player and ASCS-video with module(a)

Figure 5. ASCS-video with module(b)

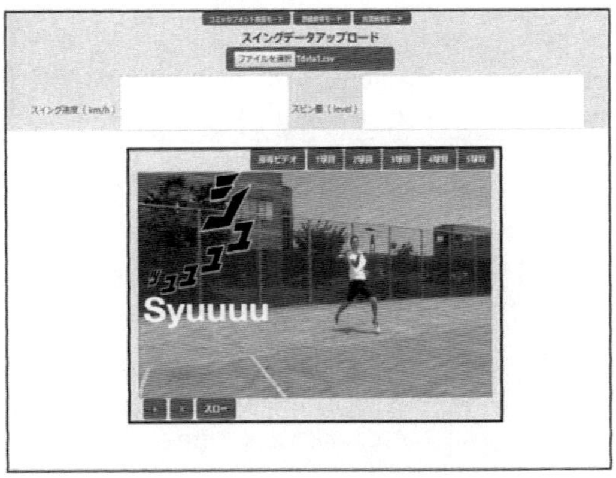

Figure 6. ASCS-video with module(c)

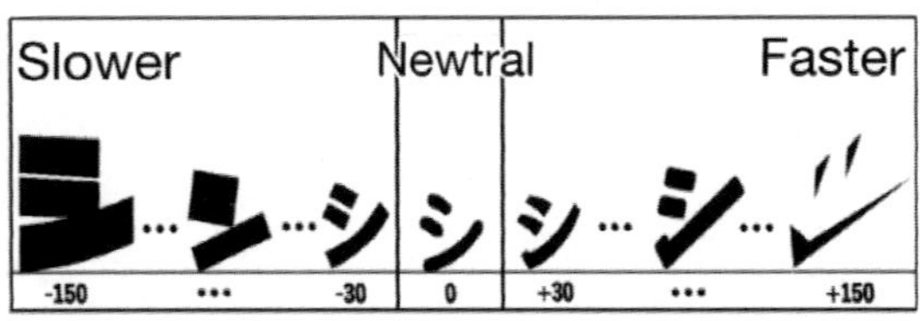

Figure 7. The Shifting of Fonts on Speed

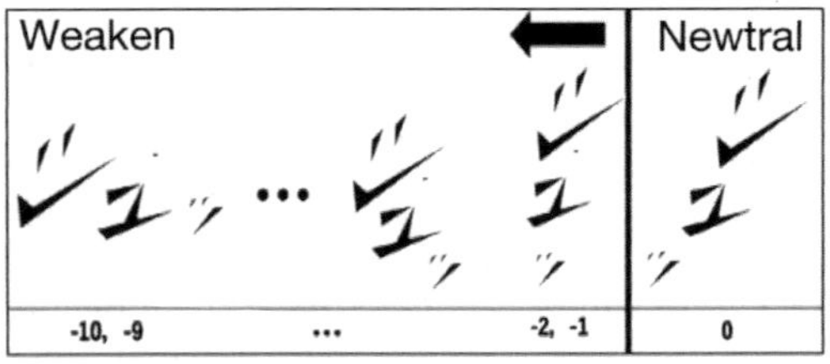

Figure 8. The Shifting of Fonts on Weaken Spinning Levels

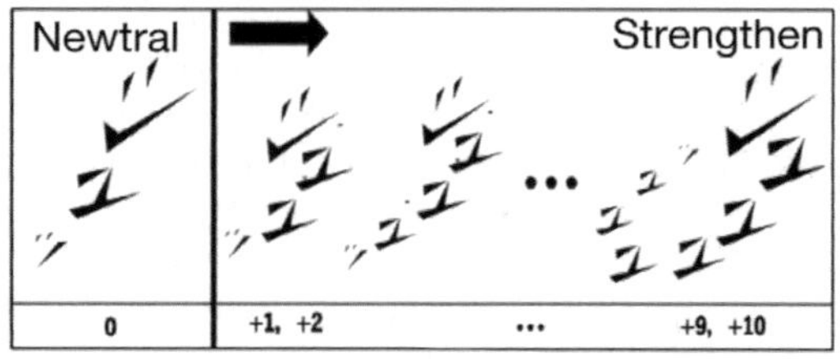

Figure 9. The Shifting of Fonts on Strengthen Spinning Levels

When the module (c) generates the instruction information, shapes and arrangements are combined, and the instruction is shown on Figure 6. In this study, we conducted a survey to find out the relationship between the characteristics and the preferences. The preference of module (a) is to show the achievement status. The preferences of the others are to show the change of direction. We tackled to figure out that either the achievement process pattern consists of the models which consist characteristics and how to affect the modules on the particular achievement status.

4. EXPERIMENT

4.1 Subject

Six male tennis players participated in this study (age: 21.83±0.69 years). We referred to National Tennis Rating Program (United States Tennis Association, 2005) to determine experience levels of the participants. Every participant‘s level was 4. We treated them as middle level tennis players.

4.2 Protocol

The participants were divided into 3 groups; Group A, Group B and Group C which were assigned to Module (a), Module (b) and Module (c) respectively. In this experiment, the participants' learning target was the balls speed of 112 km/h and the spinning level of +8. The procedure of this experimental training is 1) Warming-up (exercise and light tennis training), 2) Taking instruction of the experiment (how to use ASCS, and specifications of the sensor), 3) Watching learning video twice, 4) Training forehand-stroke (three times trial per a loop). 5)Taking ASCS-video instruction.

The participants repeat procedure 4) and 5) 10 times, the speed and spinning level is monitored every time.

4.3 Result

Figure 10 to 12 show the result of the experiment and the grey horizontal lines on each graph show the achievement goal of the learning in this study. Figure 10 to 12 show that every module has the positive effect on the learning. However, only participant E who module (c) was assigned, shows growth and the other learners did not show massive growth on the learning.

Regarding the achievement model, every result shows both models. Also, the growth patterns are different between the assigned modules.

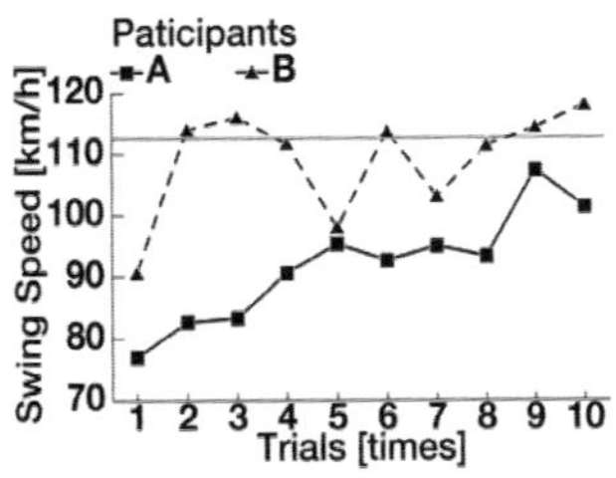

Figure 10. Swing-Module(a)

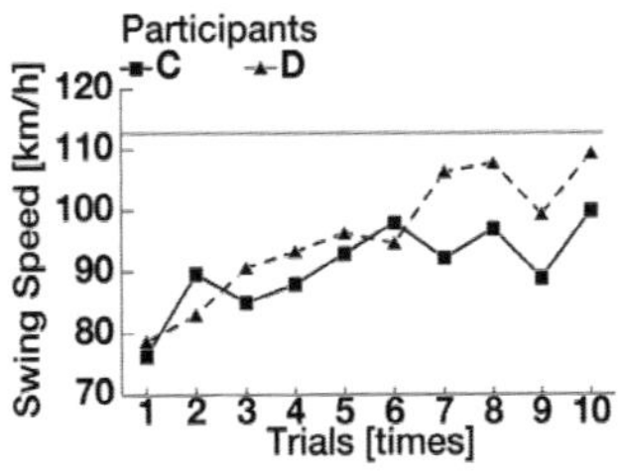

Figure 11. Swing-Module(b)

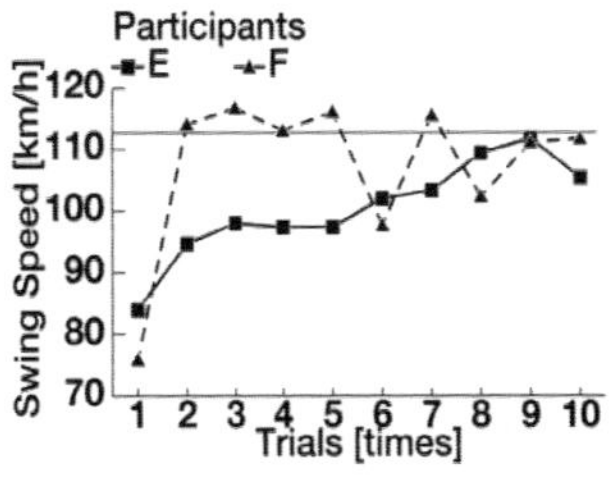

Figure 12. Swing-Module(c)

5. DISCUSSION

The result suggested that the achievement process consists of the assumption models: "Exponential model" and "Perturbation model".

The achievement process of the participant B, C and F considered to include the perturbation models noticeably from Figure 10 to 12. The process of participant D perturbated under the achievement goal. Thus it suggested that the stable achievement level status appears away from the goal. We confirmed the achievement progress which consists of "Exponential model" from all of result. The survey shows that the exponential model appears when the learner's achievement is improving, and the perturbation model appears when the learner's achievement status is stable status.

Regarding the modules, module (a) and module (c) brought huge change for the movement of participants B and F in Figure 10 and 12, and the participants reached to the achievement goal. The difference between the goal and first achievement is big on both participants, and at first trial, the modules brought a big change for the learners. However, the participants B did not take a big change. Thus, the participants A seems to gain the change of direction from the indicated instruction. Although the module indicates the learner's achievement status directly, it might be useful when the achievement status is stable status, and the level is close to the goal.

Regarding module (c), both participants almost reached to the goal. Moreover, on spinning learning, the participant grew. Therefore the module (c) might be useful for the improving achievement status. On the learning of swing, the participants who use module (b) did not reach to the goal. Although the participants D was continuously improving. Therefore, the module (b) might be useful for the improving state.

The survey showed that the module(b) and (c) might be useful when the learner's status is improving. The module (a) might be useful when the learner's status is stable status.. Moreover, module(c) has a possibility that it is useful for the stable state. The two models "exponential model" and "perturbation model" appeared on the learner's achievement process. The process suggested that "exponential model" appears when the status is improving, and "perturbation model" appears when the status is stable status. Also, we confirmed that the stable status has "high level stable status" and "low level stable status".

6. CONCLUSION

In this paper, we assumed that the relationship between the characteristics and the preferences. The characteristics predict the learner's achievement status based on the achievement models. "Perturbation model", "Exponential model". The preference is important to choose the ASCS-modules which provide instruction. The ASCS uses characteristics to select the different candidates of the ASCS-modules. We assumed the preferences of the modules and developed three ASCS-modules include one proposed method.

We surveyed to confirm the models and the relationship. The survey showed the models through the achievement pattern. The models suggested that the learner's achievement status: improving status, stable status. Also, the survey shows the possibility of the relationship.

In future work, we are going to conduct a study to confirm the suggestions by a bigger number of participants.

ACKNOWLEDGEMENT

This work was supported by JSPS KAKENHI Grant Numbers JP16K16321, JP18H03344, JP16H03089 and this research is also jointed work with Ricoh Co., Ltd.

REFERENCES

Schmidt, R. A. and Wrisberg, C. A., 2004. *Motor Learning and Performance.* Human Kinetics Publishers, Champaign USA.

Matsuura, K., et al, 2010. Learning and Competing Rope-Skipping Skills on a Community Site, *Proceedings of ED-MEDIA2010*, Tronto, Canada, pp.3204-3209.

Jimenez, F. et al, 2014. Effect Of Robot Utterances Using Onomatopoeia On Collaborative Learning. *Journal of Artificial Intelligence and Soft Computing Research*, Vol. 4, No. 2, pp 125-131.

Fujino, Y. and Yamada, T., 2006. Development of a "Japanese Sports Onomatopoeias" Computerized Dictionary for Understanding of Subtle Movement, *Proceedings of ED-MEDIA 2006--World Conference on Educational Multimedia, Hypermedia & Telecommunications*, Orlando, FL USA , pp. 1034-1041.

UNITED STATES TENNIS ASSOCIATION, 2005. NATIONAL TENNIS RATING PROGRAM https://assets.usta.com/assets/639/15/National%20tennis%20Rating%20Program.pdf > (2018-08-26)

LANGUAGE AND ELECTRONIC MEDIUM SKILLS DEVELOPMENT THROUGH AUTONOMOUS AND IDEOLOGICAL PRACTICES

Odette Bourjaili Radi
Dr. (PhD), La Trobe University, Victoria, Australia

ABSTRACT

The purpose of this paper is to report on how the concepts of autonomy and ideology are perceived by scholars, educators and researchers. The project is a preliminarily study to investigate the connections between the language and computer literacies, that would lead to further influences the implications on the development of traditional language learning. The study will be covering 180 secondary students in two private schools (one is only girls, referred to as G school and the other is co-educational, referred to as BG school). This paper will mainly focus on comparing the students' performance and use of the electronic medium at school and at home. The G school students do not bring nor use any of the electronic medium at school, except when the library computers are booked by their teachers for research. They handwrite their notes and assignments in their workbooks. Their education is focused on mastering the autonomous dimensions of a given literacy, the ideological dimensions can present much more compelling and in depth challenges. The literature reviews differentiate between language literacy and computer literacy acquisitions, the two literacies require different skills from each other. Even though, the BG students are using their electronic devices at school as well as in their domestic environment for homework. They are using the devices more than seven to nine hours a day. They access their textbooks as eBooks on their devices and they compose their notes and school work electronically. However, the G students are also practising on their personal computers and are familiar in operating the software and hardware as much as the BG students who spend a substantial amount of time each day on their electronic devices.

KEYWORDS

Language and Computer Literacies, Autonomous, Ideology and Electronic Devices

1. INTRODUCTION

The content of this paper will focus on the models of autonomous and ideological concepts, introduced by Brian Street, on both language and computer practices and how school age students in two private school develop their literacy skills in the two domains of 'language' and 'computers'. Some of the concepts raised by the literature apply to both language and computer literacy issues. Hence, this paper is intended to review the literature for I have recently started the research and intended to apply it in four areas: first, the definitional and conceptual issues of literacy; second, language literacy; third, computer literacy, which applies to the acquisition and development of computer skills, particularly those associated with electronic medium; fourth, the evolution of computer literacy to include new literacies, as new technological components emerge and interlock in computer usage to encompass Information and Communication Technology (ICT) literacy and its applications. The schools will be referred to by a code (BG is referred to the co-educational school–boys and girls) which is located in the north suburb of Melbourne and G is referred to girls' school which is located in the north-west suburb of Melbourne, Australia. In the courses of the curriculum, the G school students do not carry electronic devices for school use and are still using the printed textbooks and handwrite their school notes, comparing to BG school students who are reprimanded for not having their electronic medium devices on hand for using the eBooks which may also be associated with social media.

1.1 Definitional and Conceptual Issues of Literacy

Literacy definitions have expanded from an original focus on just reading and writing to include additional types relating to many aspects of contemporary society. Issues relating to literacy definitions have reflected many dimensions and explanations from different perspectives and disciplinary areas. Theorists such as Street (1984) have distinguished between an autonomous model and an ideological model of literacy. In the autonomous model, literacy is defined as a set of value-free skills, like decoding the printed words into sounds (decontextualising text) (Street 1995: 18-19). Viewed from this perspective - the acquisition of reading and writing skills is simply a cognitive process. There is no mention of how literacy enables people to function socially, culturally and politically. A corollary of the autonomous model of literacy is the presumption that learning to read and write, in and of itself will improve the social and economic conditions of people (Street 1995: 151-152). In critiquing the concept of autonomous literacy by scholars, Street brought into full light the awareness that literacy is not simply a set of context-neutral skills or competencies in mastering graphemes, phonemes or written and spoken texts. In developing a more inclusive alternative perspective, his focus turned to cultural dimensions of literacy involving attitudes, values, practices and conventions. He included that

> *The autonomous model of literacy works from the assumptions that literacy in itself – autonomously - will have effects on other social and cognitive practices. It assumed that the acquisition of literacy will in itself lead* [to] *higher cognitive skills, improved economic performance, greater quality, ... This model ... disguises the cultural and ideological assumptions and presents literacy's values as neutral and universal. ... The alternative ideological model of literacy offers a more culturally sensitive view of literacy practices as they vary from one context to another (Street 2005: 417-418).*

Street (1993) identified many issues relating to the models and notions of literacy. In relation to the ideological model of literacy, he argued that it

> *recognises a multiplicity of literacies; that the meaning and uses of literacy practices are related to specific cultural contexts; and these practices are always associated with relations of power and ideology. They are not simply neutral technologies. ... Literacy practices are constitutive of identity and of personhood – whichever forms of reading and writing we learn and use have associated with them certain social identities, expectations about behavior and role models. ..., 'what it is to be a person', to be moral and to be human in specific cultural contexts is frequently signified by the kind of literacy practices within which a person is engaged (1993: 139-140).*

Both models of literacy have been interpreted in different ways by different scholars. For example, Blake and Blake's (2005: 172) interpretation of the autonomous model is "the prevailing Western view of literacy, a single thought". In extending a modified view of literacy into the social domain, Bélisle (2006) included three complementary approaches to literacy that stand out in educational analysis:

> *an autonomous model of literacy is based on the assumption that reading and writing are simply technical skills; a socio-cultural model, based on the recognition of all literacies as socially and ideologically embedded; and a strong claim model based on anthropological statements of the revolutionary power of instrumented thinking processes (p. 52).*

After the 1990 International Literacy Year, Bélisle (2006) added that literacy had come to be seen in a broader way as knowledge acquisition: "to be literate is not only to identify and satisfy information needs through mastery of print", but involves the capacity and the inclination constantly to "continue constructing one's own knowledge, as learning is a lifelong learning endeavour, never fully attained" (p. 54). In line with Bélisle (2006), Kimber and Wyatt-Smith (2008: 330) reported that the strategy adopted an inspirational tone, "urging teachers to embrace and capture the potential of new technologies in classroom practice". They stated that pedagogies integrating ICT can enhance learning. "ICT provide tools and environments that support interactive conceptual learning, focused on constructing and creating knowledge. It exhorts teachers to empower students to purposefully select activities, applications and modes of communication and to engage students in simulations, modelling and creative activities". Kimber and Wyatt-Smith's (2008) work echoed Bélisle (2006: 64) who also reported that pedagogy is influential communication, providing children with the information and the tools to successfully integrate into society as concerned, autonomous and fulfilled actors.

Consequently, the autonomous model has been criticised many times over the years as a result of questioning its strategies, applications and goal directions particularly in response to the rapid development of technology and its wide use, by all ages, in contemporary society. According to Barton (2007: 118-119), the autonomous view suggests that "there is a 'great divide' between literate and non-literate, both at the individual level and at the cultural level, and that there are cognitive consequences associated with literacy itself". Subsequently, Reder and Deliva (2005) in agreement with Barton (2007) elaborated on the 'great divide' views of the consequences of literacy, which have posited fundamental and far-reaching cognitive differences as a consequence of being (or not being) literate, not only between societies and individuals, but also between local and global contexts. In his later writing, Street (2003) pursued the distinction between literacy events and literacy practices to further clarify the notions of literacy. He applied these notions to what was challenged in the "New Literacy Studies" (NLS) (Mandinach and Cline 2000).

Heath (2007: 204 – 206) was not satisfied with Street's explanations of the concepts of 'literacy and social practices' and looked at it from a contemporary perspective of how young people convey and receive information in the NLS/multimodality of 'literacy practices'. Heath stated that multimodal literacies involve all media forms that combine visual literacy, information literacy, digital literacy and conventions. The initial formulation of Street's theory of literacy was broadly applied without taking into account the extensive use of the electronic medium, its rapid changes moving away from traditional literacy and its impact on contemporary society and the young. It was only in his later writings that Street engaged more extensively with issues associated with digital/computer literacy.

1.2 Defining Language and Computer Literacies

Hence, Street's (1984) autonomous and ideological models of literacy that were subsequently replaced by the notions of literacy events and practices, partially apply to computer literacy. Many technological dimensions have been considered in moving to the current term of ICT and digital literacy (Markauskaite 2006). Markauskaite utilised Street's (1984) models by relating the different purposes of ICT literacy to different teaching and learning practices. She pointed out that

> *[i]n this model, ICT is an integral part of all literacy practices. ...* [She includes the notion of ICT literacy in a specific context with dimensions which are intended to provide benefits in the first instance]*; in an autonomous model 'benefits to individual'* [and in the second instance of the] *ideological model 'benefits to society' (Markauskaite 2006: 10 – 16).*

Understandings of computer literacy include literacy events with many dimensions underpinning literacy practices at the global level such as information literacy, visual literacy, technology literacy and digital literacy (Cohen and Cowen 2008, and Barton 2007). The term digital literacy developed to include media literacy and the ability to interpret information. Digital literacy encompasses computer hardware, software (particularly those used most frequently by businesses), the internet, cell phones, PDAs, iPods, iPads and other digital devices. McLean (2010: 14) stated that "..., social networking sites such as MySpace, Instagram, Twitter, Facebook and others offer their members opportunities to engage in multimodal consumption and production of a range of texts, including photos, videos, text comments, symbols and images". Young people using these skills to interact with society are called digital citizens (Lankshear and Knobel 2006: 12 – 24). Digital literacy also has different meanings, according to Leahy and Dolan (2010: 210 –221) which includes terms such as "computer literacy" (the technical knowledge of computer professionals); "Information literacy" includes the ability to verify, interpret and validate the information; "Cyber literacy" includes competence with using the internet, digital communication and the Web. Digital literacy is used to refer to the use of electronic equipment by all members of society, for personal and social interactions and for educational and business needs. It is underpinned by basic skills in ICT: the use of computers to retrieve, access, store, produce, present and exchange information, and to communicate and participate in collaborative networks via the Internet (McLean 2010: 13 - 22). Despite the need to become computer literate, Blake and Blake (2005: 172) reported that the use of ICT also requires language literacy skills, "[r]eading and writing are [also] used [in order] to transmit information, to interpret, to respond to the expression of human thought." Language literacy acquisitions are fundamentally essential for the exchange of information required in our society.

2. LANGUAGE LITERACY

More generally, in current usage, the term language literacy implies an interaction "between social demands/practices and autonomous individual competence, ranging from individual skills, abilities and knowledge, to social practices and functional competencies to ideological values and political goals" (Winch et al 2006: xxxii – xxxvi). Malatesha and Aaron (2010: 310) stated that "letter knowledge requires the ability not only to be aware of the phonemes of the language but also to relate these sounds to the letters of the alphabet". They added that increasing awareness of phonemes can also increase children's knowledge about reading and writing in a particular language. From an ideological perspective, language literacy is a broad term used to indicate not only the importance and the ability of individuals to read and write in a designated language, but also their ability to interpret the world as presented to them in the texts (Blake and Blake 2002: 10). Hence, writing is clearly a form of communication, which also connotes the activity of forming letters and words, and sentences which can signify meaning to a prospective reader.

2.1 Students' Writing

Handwriting has been largely forgotten in the literacy and ICT debates, but Ljungdahl (2010: 357) stressed that handwriting develops skills needed for good readers and writers. Increasingly, writing is done on the keyboard, enhancing legibility, but only in contexts where keyboards or alternative digital technologies are available. In other contexts, which are still frequent in both classrooms and high stakes environments such as examinations, the acquisition of handwriting skills free the student to focus on the quality of ideas and clarity of expression, including accurate spelling. In addition, good (consistent) handwriting visually reinforces the memory of word patterns and can help in speaking, spelling, and writing more effectively. This applies to the students at G school and was confirmed by their teachers. They read widely and saw a relationship between this and their effective writing skills. Carroll et al (1995: 5) asserted that the value is in the handwritten language when practised independently; the handwriting reinforces the acquisition of literacy skills. In line with Carroll et al (1995), De Craene and Cuthell's (2006: 1–5) study revealed that children, who handwrote their work and engaged more in reading printed texts, showed development in their motor and cognitive skills at a young age. In line with the literature, the G students who practised their handwriting skills were able to express their ideas and wrote lengthy essays. This strategy was consistent with strategies adopted by their teachers who expect their students to handwrite their drafts as many times as they needed until they reached the curriculum expectations. Their reasons were that students were provided with the opportunity to reflect on issues (such as spelling and grammatical errors, expressions and the like) that they might improve on by redrafting their pieces of writing. In support to the teachers consisting practices, Feder and Majnemer (2007: 312) asserted that "[f]ailure to attain handwriting competency during the school age years has, far-reaching negative effects on both academic success and self-esteem". Despite the widespread use of computers, they added, that "legible handwriting remains an important life skill that deserves greater attention from parents and educators" Ljungdahl (2010: 363 – 367). The data in Table 1 compares in percentage the settings of the two schools and their policies for using/not using electronic devices.

Table 1. BG students compulsory use of electronic devices and G students do not use any electronic devices at school

Students	No electronic devices at school %	Electronic devices %	Research projects using electronic devices at school %	Passing rate at Year 12 %
G school	80		20	70
Electronic devices used at home	20			
BG school				30
Laptop		45	80	
iPads		44		
Mobile Phones		11		
Total	100	100	100	100

Table 1 demonstrates 80% of students in G school do not own any electronic devices for school use, while 20% use their domestic personal computer (PC) to produce their school work. The question was asked of year 12 students how do they feel about being unable to use any electronic devices at school. Their responses were: "This helps us to improve our handwriting to be faster at composing the required writing which will earn us a high mark at the end of year exams. Handwriting the essays in the exam are easily readable and clear to the examiners". This makes a substantial difference in the passing rate of 70% of G students compared to 30% of BG students at the end of year exams. The G students' responses echoed in De Souza and Towndrow (2010: 26), who stressed the importance of handwriting for students who still use pen and paper format in their exams. While 100% of students at BG school were directed to solely use their electronic devices to perform all their school works. They stressed that at times, "we could not read our own handwriting". It is a hindrance to us at the end of year exams. Nevertheless, Ljungdahl (2010) stressed that handwriting develops skills needed for good readers and writers by stating that "[g]ood handwriting visually reinforces the memory of word patterns and can help in speaking, spelling, and writing more effectively" (p. 357).

The definitions of literacy are of increasing breadth and reflect a growing emphasis on context. The relevance of this study particularly relates to the text composition. This applies to G school where the students are contented to handwrite their school work and its outcomes. The social situations have changed and brought with them changes to the definition of language literacy with the additional emergence of new technologies in educational, domestic and workplace environments. For the purpose of this study, the main focus will be to compare the relationship between language literacy and computer literacy, which involves the use of computer peripherals and software applications and their tools.

3. COMPUTER LITERACY

Computer literacy definitions vary depending not only on the different levels of users from regular users to power users (software developers, programmers and network infrastructure experts), but also on how literacy is perceived and applied by educational and industrial/workplace theorists. Computer literacy involves not only the understanding of what is possible with (and what influences the use of) computers, but also the physical use of combined equipment (peripherals) and software applications (Williams 2002: 8). At a less specialised level and from the autonomous view, this applies to BG students; computer literacy involves the knowledge of how to turn on a computer, start and stop software applications as well as save, retrieve and print documents. In relation to software, Cohen and Cowen (2008: 546) defined computer literacy as "the ability to effectively use [autonomously] computer tools, such as word processors, spreadsheets, databases, presentation and [integration of] graphic software". From a possibly wider perspective, Moursund's (2003: 9) definition of computer literacy, that also reflects an autonomous model, is "a functional level of knowledge and skills in using computers and computer-based multimedia as an aid to communication with oneself and others for the purposes of learning, knowing and for using one's knowledge". Ideologically, the term computer literacy is commonly used to characterise a degree of knowledge and awareness about computers and their role in society. Computer literacy, according to Cartelli (2010, 1-6), applies to an understanding of computer characteristics, capabilities, and applications, as well as an ability to implement this knowledge in the skilful, productive use of computer applications suitable to individual roles in society. From an ideological view, computer literacy has evolved into a broad term that incorporates the use of the internet and other digital devices.

3.1 The Internet

The internet is an integral part of computer literacy. It is a "powerful tool and endless source of information, which is easy to find and easy to produce" (Knierzinger and Turcsanyi-Szabo 2001: 926). Computer literacy has evolved into a broad term that encompasses a range of related literacies, including digital, network, ICT, electronic devices in different fields of communication, including the internet (Cesarini 2002: 1–4). More recently, computer literacy has expanded to multidimensional related literacies known as ICT. The ideological dimensions of computer literacy or ICT revolve around online communication (globally), the internet and wireless electronic devices to facilitate access to digital resources.

The internet has become more and more important in young people's lives at school and at home. Ma et al (2008: 197) stated that "the Internet is affecting all subjects in K-12". Ma et al's study included those described by Tapscott's (1998) term the 'Net-generations' who are fluent with digital technology, including all sorts of digital and electronic devices.

4. RESEARCH METHODOLOGY

The nature of the present study has two methods associated with an ethnographic quantitative approach: (1) the implications of the increase in the use of ICT, and (2) the students' perceptions of and identified use of ICT both at home and at school (Burns 1997: 9-10). This methodology will be used to analyse the shift from reading the printed text and handwriting to engaging with electronic medium devices. Seeking students' opinions will be a source of descriptive data that will assist in arriving at a judgment of how computers are enhancing or hindering the development of language literacy skills compare to those who are not using the electronic devices. This is a preliminary start of observation and pre-surveying/discussing with students the main variables of electronic devices usage at home and at school. All students at BG school have to carry their devices to the classrooms in all subjects and also take them home to do their homework. There is a substantial difference between the two private schools. All BG students are obliged to use their devices according to their school policy. While the students at G school, are not allowed to bring to school any electronic devices. There is one pc in each classroom for the teachers to project any work into the electronic white board and the students copy the notes or summaries of the work into their exercise books.

4.1 Results

I have observed 90 students at the GB school and 90 students at G school all students are at secondary level. The BG school students use their devices between 7 to 9 hour a day between school and homework. While the G students only carry their textbooks and do not have any electronic devices to use. Figure 1 displays the percentage of middle school students at BG (Years 6 to 9) who use more than one device, while G school students do not use electronic devices at school but both BG and G students use them at their domestic environment.

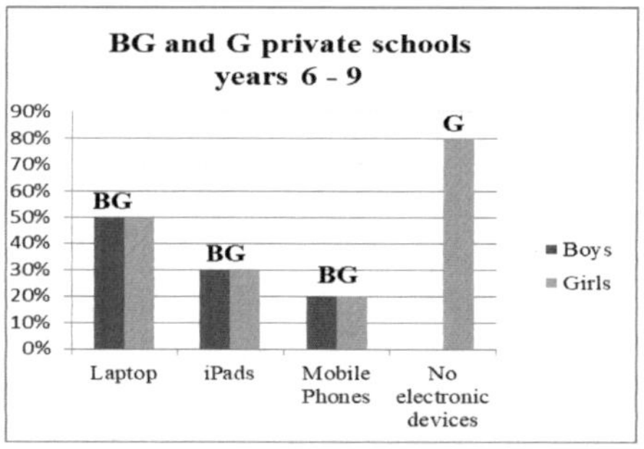

Figure 1. Middle school (Years 6 to 9) students' use/not use of electronic devices

Figure 1 demonstrates 50% of boys and 50% of girls at BG school are using their laptops to access information and use them for communication purposes. While 30% of boys and 30% of girls use their iPads and 20% use their mobiles phones. Their activities include homework and leisure time. Hence, 80% of students at G school do not use any electronic devices at all at school, but they still experience self-efficacy in operating their PC away from school. They are as familiar with the electronic devices as much as the BG students are. Regardless, they are also the Net-Generation (Rohatgi et al, 2016, 103-116), every day, students come into contact with computer technologies and learn about them in less formal ways outside the school. "IT skills are acquired through family, through friends, self-tuition, and through many other sources" (Milić, and Škorić 2010, 63). Hence, Hatlevik et al (2018, 107-119) stated that "... ICT self-efficacy is positively related to computer and information literacy when controlled for other student characteristics and background contextual variables". Furthermore, students' ICT self-efficacy at both schools plays important roles in understanding students' computer use and accessessing information literacy. However, the senior students at BG school are compelled to use more specific devices, depending on the demand of their subjects.

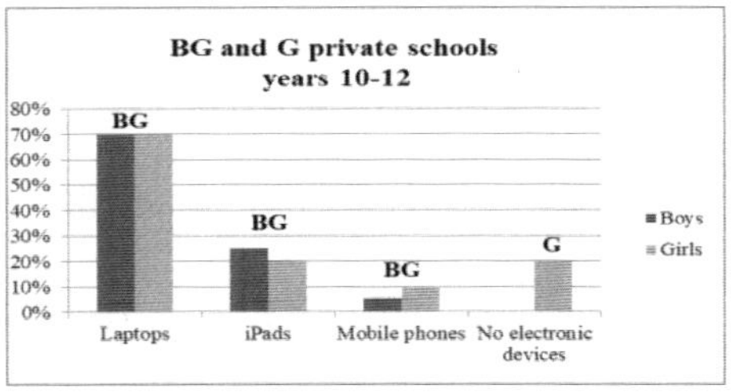

Figure 2. Senior (Years 10-12) students' use/not use of electronic devices

Figure 2 illustrates 70% of boys and 70% of girls are using laptops, while 25% of boys and 20% of girls are using iPads at the BG school. The mobile phones are less used, 5% of boys and 10% of girls may use their mobile phones to access and manipulate the required data. The experience Year 12 students who practiced the use of the electronic devices such as iPads with the inclusion of Bluetooth keyboard are able to save their work on Google drive. The question was asked how do they access their documents and why using the Google drive rather the iCloud drive. Their responses were that the iCloud provides only five gigabytes of free capacity to save their data and when the capacity exceeds the required amount, they have to pay money, where Google drive is not restricted to any data capacity and also free. The G students do not use electronic devices, 20% of them commented that the storage they used for their data is only in their exercise books. Further comments, it is safer, "we do not worry about computer viruses and the deletion of our work".

The use of ICT in different settings such as the home or school environment for different purposes such as recreation or working on school-related tasks may provide opportunities for students to gain mastery experience. As such, mastery experiences are considered "to be crucial antecedents of students' self-efficacy, which in turn determine their achievement" ideologically (Rohatgi et al, 2016, 103-116).

4.2 ICT Literacy

ICT literacy is a broad term that includes multiple communication devices, various services and applications associated with it. ICT literacy is increasingly regarded as a broad set of generalisable and transferable knowledge, skills and understandings that relate to communication tools used to access, manage, integrate, evaluate and create information in order to function in a knowledgeable society (Martin 2006: 8 – 9; Ainley 2010: 2). ICT literacy covers the new and emergent technological devices combined, introducing new literacies (internet, iPads and others) as they become available. Harris (2005: 34) stated that ICTs are "social information spaces". They are designed as much for the reciprocal "sharing of information" as they are for "seeking and disseminating information". He elaborates that "sharing" involves exchanging information amongst users and "seeking" implies going to sources outside one's immediate social system. Out-of-school and in-school digital literacies are used by youth interactively and purposefully, in ways that are increasingly "hypertextual", connected and communicative (Bussert-Webb and Diaz, 2012: 5). These changes have made computer literacy skills more available to include interactions and communications through social events and practices. The changes become more apparent in Street's notions. Literacy events and practices apply to the acquisition of computer literacy skills. The literacy events happen when the Net-Generation (Rohatgi et al, 2016, 103-116) acquired the new literacy and put it into practice. On the other hand, autonomously, the digital natives apply their own language which they have invented by engaging in the use of the electronic devices as they emerge. The digital culture that the young people identify with has shifted emphasis from the traditional written language to re-form a language that the Net-Generation created (Mountifield (2006: 172–173). They are digitally embodied in multimodal forms of literacy and are associated in the constructions of identity and community (Nævdal 2007: 1113). They will continue to apply their experience to further practice with more emergent technology.

5. CONCLUSION

Today, young people face a challenging situation. Whilst, they have the opportunity to benefit from powerful digital technologies which open up new learning opportunities, they also need to deal with handling and making sense of such devices in a complex and non-stable world. For example, the BG school students are constantly using their digital devices for seven to nine hours a day, increasing their accessibility and power to shape action and perception through the development of learners' understanding and application of creativity, computational thinking, media literacy and digital citizenship. However, the literature suggests that being competent in literacy implies that one knows which practices, attitudes and values are appropriate in a given situation. This applies to the G school students who are autonomously mastering the language literacy without the destruction of the digital devices, and the ideological dimensions can present much more compelling and in depth challenges. The prominent messages stemming from the literature and the comparison of the two schools are that young children should be developing an enriched vocabulary as an indicator of oral language proficiency which is essential for comprehension of both oral and written language. Though, technological changes have happened so rapidly that changes to literacy are shaped not only by technology, but by our ability to adapt and acquire the new literacies that emerge with its applications (Leu et al 2004; Florian 2004). Hence, the implications on young people's engagement in digital culture, from an autonomous and ideological view, have a focus on digital texts as social and textual entities.

Computer literacy and its relationship to language literacy development among school age children need further and continuous study. Technology is still advancing rapidly and further changes to the education system infrastructure and domestic environments are likely. It is, therefore, necessary to have a closer look at the ways in which individual student made use of the computers and their associated literacy tools. In future studies, a collaborative work between teachers and researchers will be necessary to progress the formulation of multimodal 'New Literacies' and 'digital literacies' and intermodal pedagogic 'spellings' and 'grammars' will be needed to accommodate the New Literacies Studies in classroom contexts. Further studies will assist in facilitating productive participation along these lines among the researchers and teachers in ICT, English and literacy education.

REFERENCES

Ainley, J. (2010). What can Australian students do with Computers. *Research Developments. ACER*. Camberwell Vol. 23, No 23, pp 1–4.

Barton D. 2007. *Literacy: An Introduction to the Ecology of Written Language.* Second Edition. Blackwell Publishing. Oxford.

Bélisle, C. 2006. Literacy and the digital knowledge revolution.: In Martin A. and Madigan, D. (Eds.). *Digital Literacies for Learning.* Facet Publishing. London, pp 51 – 67.

Blake, B. et al, 2005. *Literacy Primer.* Peter Lang. New York.

Burns, R. B. 1997. *Introduction to Research Methods. Third edition.* Longman, South Melbourne.

Bussert-Webb, K. M., and, Diaz, M. E. 2012. New Literacy Opportunities and Practices of Latino/a Children of Poverty In and Out of School. *Language and Literacy Journal.* Vol 14, No 1, pp 1–25.

Cartelli, A. 2010. Theory and Practice in digital competence Assessment International. *Journal of Digital Literacy and Digital Competence,* Vol 1, No 3, pp 1-17

Carroll, A. et al, 1995. Information Revolution. *National Geographic.* Vol 188, No 4, p 5.

Cesarini, P. 2004. Computers, Technology, and Literacies. *The Journal of Literacy and Technology*. Vol 4. No 1, pp 1-16.

Chen, X., and, Lee, V. G., 2010. Promoting Comprehension in Middle School and High School: Tapping into Out-of-school literacies of our Adolescents. In Kathy Ganske and Douglas Fisher (Eds.). *Comprehension Across the Curriculum Perspectives and Practices K – 12.* The Guilford Press. New York. Pages 119– 145.

Cohen, V. L., and Cowen, J. E., 2008. *Literacy for Children in an Information Age: Teaching, Reading, Writing and Thinking*. Thomson Wadsworth. Belmont.

De Craene, M., and Cuthell, J., 2006. 'Clickerati Generation Update: The Digital Divide Starts Early'. *The Educational Technology: ICT in Education,* pp 1–5.

De Souza, D. E., and Towndrow, P. A., 2010. The Generative Use of ICT in the Language Arts: Strategies in Learning Task Design and Implementation. In Caroline M. L. Ho, et al (Eds.). *Transforming Literacies and Language: Multimodality and Literacy in the New Media Age.* Continuum. London, pp 23–48.

Feder, K. P., and Majnemer, A., 2007. Handwriting Development, Competency, and Intervention. *Devlopmental Medicine and Child Neurology Journal.* Vol 49. No 4, pp 312–317.

Florian, L., 2004. Uses Of Technology That Support Pupils With Special Educational Needs. In Florian L., Hegarty, J. (Eds.). *ICT and Special Educational Needs: A Tool for Inclusion.* Open University Press. Buckingham, pp 7–20

Harris, F. J., 2005. I Found it on the Internet: Coming of Age Online. *American Library Association*. Chicago.

Hatlevik, E., et al, 2018. *Students' ICT self-efficacy and computer and information literacy: Determinants and relationship.* Computers & Education. Vol 118, pp 107-119

Heath, S. B., 2007. Afterword. In Ellis, V., Fox, C., and Street, B. (Eds.). *Rethinking English in Schools: Towards a New and Constructive Stage.* Continuum International Publishing Group, London, pp 199–206.

Kimber, K., and Wyatt-Smith, C., 2008. Assessing Digital Literacies: Can Assessment Ever Be the Same?: In Unsworth, L. (Ed.). *New Literacies and the English Curriculum: Multimodal Perspectives.* Continuum, London, pp 328–352

Knierzinger, A., and, Turcsanyi-Szabo, M., 2001. Internet, Education and Culture: Should We Care?. In D. Watson and J. Andersen (Eds.). *Networking the Learner. Seventh IFIP World Conference on Computers in Education (WCCE).* Kluwer Academic Publishers. Norwell, pp 925 – 932

Lankshear, C., Knobel, M., 2006. 'Digital Literacy and Digital Literacies: Policy, Pedagogy, and Research Considerations for Education'. ***Digital Kompetanse Journal.*** Volume 1. Number 1. Pages 12 – 24.

Leahy, D., and Dolan, D., 2010. Digital Literacy: A Vital Competence for 2010?. In N. Reynolds, and M. Turcsányi-Szabó (Eds.). *Key Competencies in the Knowledge Society. International Federation for Information Processing (IFIP) TC 3 International Conference*, KCKS 2010, Held as Part of WCC 2010, Brisbane, Australia, September 20-23, 2010. Proceedings. Vol 324, pp 210-221.

Leu, D. J, Jr., et al, 2004. Toward a Theory of New Literacies Emerging From the Internet and Other Communication Technologies. In R. B. Ruddell, and N. J. Unrau (Eds.). *Theoretical Models and Processes of Reading.* Fifth Edition. International Reading Association. Newark, pp 1570–1613.

Ljungdahl, L., 2010. Handwriting. In G. Winch, R. Ross Johnston, P. March, L. Ljungdahl and M. Holliday (Eds.). *Literacy: Reading, Writing and Children's Literature.* Fourth Edition. Oxford University Press. South Melbourne, pp 357–369.

Ma, H. J., et al, 2008. Digital Cheating and Plagiarism in Schools. *Theory into Practice.* Vol 47, No 3, pp 197–203

Malatesha, J. R., and Aaron P. G., 2010. Assessment of Reading Problems among English Language Learners Based on the Component Model. In A. Yücesan Durgunoglu (Ed.). *Language and Literacy Development in Bilingual Settings.* Guilford Press. New York, pp 304–331.

Mandinach, E. B., and Cline, H. F., 2000. It Won't Happen Soon: Practical Curricular, and Methodological Problems in Implementing Technology-based Constructivist Approaches in Classrooms. In S. P. Lajoie (Ed.). *Computers as Cognitive Tools: No more Walls.* Lawrence Erlbaum Associates. New Jersey, pp 377 –389.

Markauskaite, L., 2006. Towards an Integrated Analytical Framework of Information and Communications Technology Literacy: From Intended to Implemented and Achieved Dimensions. *IRinformationresearch.* Vol 11, No3, pp 1–23.

Martin, A., 2006. Literacies for the Digital Age: Preview of Part 1. In A. Martin and D. Madigan (Eds.). *Digital literacies for learning.* Facet Publishing, pp 3–25.

McLean, C. A., 2010. A Space Called Home: An Immigrant Adolescent's Digital Literacy Practices. *Journal of Adolescent &Adult Literacy,* Vol 54, No 1, pp 13–22.

Milić, M. and Škorić, I., 2010. The Impact of Formal Education on Computer Literacy. *iJET*, Vol 5, No 2, pp 60-63.

Mountifield, H., 2006. The Information Commons: a Student-Centred Environment for IT and Information Literacy Development. In Martin A., Madigan, D. (Eds.). *Digital Literacies for Learning.* Facet Publishing. London, pp 172 – 181.

Moursund, D., et al, 1995. *Effective Practice: Computer Technology in Education. International Society for Technology in Education.* Eugene, Oregon.

Nævdal, F., 2007. Home-PC Usage and Achievement in English. *Computers and Education.* Vol 49, No 4, pp 1112–1121.

Reder, S. and Davila, E., 2005. Context and Literacy Pratices. *Annual Review of Applied Linguistics.* Vol 25, pp 170–187.

Rohatgi, A., et al, 2016. The role of ICT self-efficacy for students' ICT use and their achievement in a computer and information literacy test. *Computers & Education.* Vol 102, pp 103-116.

Street, B., 1984. *Literacy in Theory and Practice.* Cambridge University Press. Cambridge

Street, B., 1993. Introduction: The New Literacy Studies: In Street, B. (Ed.) *Cross-Cultural Approaches to Literacy.* Cambridge University. Cambridge, pp 1–22.

Street, B., 1995. *Social Literacies: Critical Approaches to Literacy in Development, Ethnography, and Education.* Longman, London.

Street, B., 2003. What's "New" in New Literacy Studies? Critical Approaches to Literacy and Practice. *Current Issues in Comparative Education.* Vol 5, No 2, pp 77–91.

Street, B., 2005. Recent Applications of New Literacy Studies in Educational Contexts. *Research in the Teaching of English,* Vol 39, No 4, pp 417–423.

Tapscott, D., 1998. *Growing Up With Digital: The Rise of the Net Generation.* McGraw-Hill. New York.

Winch, G., et al, 2006. Introduction: To Literacy in the Modern World. In G. Winch, R. R. Johnston, P. March, L. Ljungdahl and M. Holliday (Eds.), *Literacy: Reading, Writing and Children's Literature,* Third Edition. Oxford University Press, South Melbourne. Pages. xxxi – xl.

Young, C. A., et al, 2008. Framing Research on Technology and Student Learning in English Education During an Era of Changing Literacy Practices. In B. L. Schrum, and A. D. Thompson (Eds.). *Framing Research on Technology and Student Learning in the Content Areas: Implications for Educators.* Information Publishing. Charlotte, North Carolina, pp 67–84.

A MODEL FOR ENRICHING AUTOMATIC ASSESSMENT RESOURCES WITH FREE-TEXT ANNOTATIONS

Luigi Di Caro[1], Sergio Rabellino[1], Michele Fioravera[2] and Marina Marchisio[2]
[1]*Department of Computer Science, University of Turin, Turin (TO), Italy*
[2]*Department of Mathematics, University of Turin, Turin (TO), Italy*

ABSTRACT

This paper discusses a model for structuring resources for automatic assessment in scientific education by means of textual descriptions. This study aims to support instructors in extending teaching strategies and expanding formative assessment in virtual communities of practice. The strategy to achieve these goals involves the implementation of a system for adaptively providing the students with instructional activities based on Natural Language analysis and ontological knowledge bases. The model is presented, and the feasibility of its use is discussed taking into account the results collected from the experimentation with instructors.

KEYWORDS

Automatic Assessment, Descriptors, Learning Objectives, Mathematics Education, Natural Language, Communities

1. INTRODUCTION

The development of e-learning courses typically involves some basic steps, such as choosing the hosting environment, creating learning resources, and storing the resources in the courses. Resources description and metadata can help their management through repositories; however, learners could experience difficulties in choosing among similar resources: even if it is easy to find data, it could be a challenge to retrieve an e-learning material that satisfies their needs – especially for those who do not have the complete awareness of what is needed to know in advance. The role of instructors/editors of an online course is still crucial to help students. At the same time, even e-instructors are not able to provide learners with uniform help.

The present research is aimed at scientific disciplines, especially Mathematics, and considers resources for automatic assessment (Barana, et al, 2015). It investigates the possibility to implement a system that automatically groups resources by means of the elements indicating their intended competencies. Through this system, instructors will no longer exclusively design learning paths but they will also be able to focus on the specification of the single nodes of possible paths. The research is aimed at

- supporting instructors in extending teaching strategies by the retrieval of shared resources;
- fostering learners' formative assessment by automatic recommendation.

This study is conducted by proposing and experimenting a model for the description of the scope of a resource (as well as of prerequisites and expected results) with instructors participating to a virtual learning community. The model provides for Natural Language descriptions: those will be the information exploited by an automatic recommender system integrated to the learning management system hosting the community. The model features are presented, and the results collected from the experimentation of its use by the instructors are discussed.

2. STATE OF THE ART

The next subchapters present the two main aims that guide the system and model development, namely resources retrieval and formative assessment, and the context in which they are applied – the Communities – for enhancing competence-based education.

2.1 Resources Retrieval

A lot of work has already been done in order to facilitate the storage and retrieval of shared e-learning resources. Several examples of online repositories exist, such as Merlot (http://merlot.org), CeLeBraTe (http://celebrate.eun.org), Wisc-Online (http://wisc-online.com). In the field of competency-based education, European Projects have been activated to help instructors share learning objects in an open perspective (Ravotto, 2011). In the Italian context, operational strategies have been proposed (Trinchero, 2017) for

- defining observable indicators for the skills being trained;
- building learning paths;
- designing a teaching that is based on national guidelines goals but insists on a plurality of cognitive processes, educational activities and assessment, tests and certification of competence;
- defining the levels of competence to be included in the final certification forms.

To overcome the problems that can occur in e-learning systems where the learning path is determined solely by human experts, strategies based on Natural Language have been developed and experimented (Vincent et al., 2014). Ontologies-enhanced approaches showed how external domain knowledge can help organize a corpus of digital materials and construct comprehensive knowledge representations to facilitate online learning (Huang et al., 2015).

2.2 Formative Assessment

There is no universally shared definition of "competence" (Winterton et al., 2006). In this paper, competence means the ability to cope with a task, or a set of tasks, managing to activate and orchestrate internal, cognitive, affective and resources, and to use the external resources available in a coherent and fruitful way.

Formative assessment is the way learners use information from judgments about their work to improve their competence. Since the nineties, the concern about formative assessment has grown to cover one of the major issues in the educational research. Paul Black and Dylan Wiliam conceptualized formative assessment through the following five key strategies (Black & Wiliam, 2009; Wiliam & Thompson, 2007):

1. clarifying and sharing learning intentions and criteria for success;
2. engineering classroom discussions and learning tasks that elicit evidence of student understanding;
3. providing feedback that moves learners forward;
4. activating students as instructional resources;
5. activating students as the owners of their own learning.

Matching similarities among digital materials is crucial for building mapped data sets of entities and relationships across entities, which are useful for the enhancing of automatic formative assessment strategies. The possibility to perform such an operation with ontology-based methods has been discussed in (Di Caro et al., 2018a; Barana et al., 2018a; Di Caro et al., 2018b).

2.3 Community

The use of automatic assessment systems has been proven effective in Mathematics education (Barana & Marchisio, 2016) and formative assessment (Barana et al., 2018b) especially in the context of Communities (Ellerani & Parricchi, 2010; Demartini et al., 2013). A Community is a system where

- instructors (discipline experts) manage one or more courses dedicated to a group of learners;
- tutors (discipline and ICT experts) help instructors with the testing of innovative methodologies for teaching, the creation of digital materials, peer collaboration, the sharing of resources and best practices, the use of advanced tools integrated to the LMS that hosts the online courses;
- instructors and tutors agree upon a framework of competences expected to be achieved by the learners at the end of the learning process.

A national-wide example of Community is the "Problem Posing & Solving". PP&S started as a project promoted by the Italian Ministry of Education, to ensure a growth in the information technology culture in teaching and learning in secondary school and building a "Problem posing & solving" culture (Brancaccio et al., 2014; Brancaccio et al., 2015). The project aims at developing an integrated training area that interconnects logic, Mathematics and Information Technology. The PP&S Community has adopted the following suite of technologies: an Advanced Computing Environment, an Automatic Assessment System and a web conference system integrated to the Virtual Learning Environment which hosts the Community.

The community of instructors who joined the SMART project is an example of Community in a European context (Brancaccio et al., 2016). It shares with PP&S the suite of tools and the methodology chosen for fostering Problem Posing and Problem Solving in different European countries. The Project offers a guided training, an accessible repository of free materials, and an open community to share practices.

3. THE MODEL

The features of an assignment reflect the educational strategy chosen by the instructor. Whatever the features, clarifying, sharing, and understanding learning intentions and criteria for success are fundamental requirements to activate learners' reasoning on their own objectives achievement and to stimulate the learner to undertake appropriate learning paths (Trinchero, 2014). It is proposed to associate digital materials to Natural Language descriptions which explicate the learning intentions and success criteria they were designed for. The model provides for the P-R-O triad of descriptors: Performance, Requirements, Objectives. The P-R-O triad elements are defined as follows, and meant to be included as metadata about the material:

- Performance (P): specific and essential description of what a student will be able to do as proof of having achieved the objective, which can be measured objectively.
- Requirements (R): declaration of objectives - considered as already achieved by the students - necessary and sufficient to provide the performance.
- Objectives (O): general description of the knowledge (to be acquired or recalled) and / or of the intellectual skills and abilities (to be developed) that students are required to demonstrate in order to be considered competent.

The three descriptors must be expressed in a student-centered perspective. Performance statement should explicate what the student will be able to do (that can be observed directly), the conditions under which the student will perform the task, the criteria for evaluating the student's performance, and optionally a degree of mastery needed. Requirements is the explicit declaration of previous knowledge and skills necessary and sufficient to achieve the Objectives of the material. Objectives, unlike Performance, is independent from the type of response of the material (since distinct types of questions can be exploited for testing an identical instructional objective). This statement should not simply describe a list of topics, that being too abstract and narrow, and not being restricted to lower-level cognitive skills.

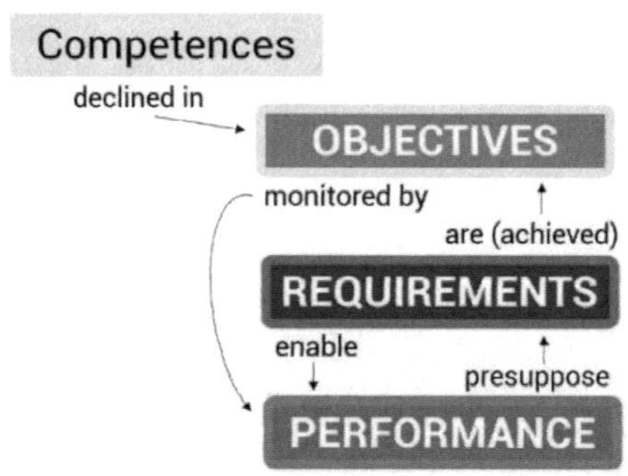

Figure 1. Relation between competences and the P-R-O descriptors

Figure 1 shows the P-R-O model relation with competences: competences can be declined in Objectives. The former can be monitored by a Performance, which is enabled by (presuppose) Requirements – which are intended as achieved Objectives.

Materials descriptors can express which the kind of performance required in terms of cognitive processes that need to be activated and the types of knowledge on which these processes operate. To this aim, the adoption of a taxonomic model is proposed. This is considered as the main reference affecting both instructors and learners: during the design phase, it is important to "space" in the definition of learning tasks; moreover, automatically subsuming cognitive processes and knowledge types implicit in a material is the key to adaptively advising students with variegated resources.

To detail the descriptors structure more deeply, this research considers Anderson & Krathwohl's taxonomy (Anderson et al., 2001). The authors proposed a classification of cognitive processes and knowledge types: 11 types of knowledge organized into 4 categories (Facts, Concepts, Procedures, Metacognition), and 19 basic processes organized into 6 categories (Remember, Understand, Apply, Analyze, Evaluate, Create) ordered by ascending cognitive complexity. Considering the authors' taxonomy, a material can be linked to a set of concepts couples referring to a two-dimensional matrix: the first dimension of the matrix represents the types of knowledge while the second dimension represents the cognitive processes involved. The connection between a material and a matrix element is established by identifying cognitive processes and knowledge type from its descriptors.

The use of Natural Language allows to overcome the limits implicit in the exclusive use of tagging, namely the inability to express complex data. The risk of the use of tagging is to achieve a semantic granularity that is either too synthetic or too high. In the domain of Natural Language it is possible to use a syntax from which to extract conceptual coherence: this allows to achieve both a greater freedom of expression by the designers and a minor effort for those who search for materials.

Inferring Anderson & Krathwohl taxonomy dimensions involves dealing with domain-specific verbs. The semantic disambiguation of a verb in terms of cognitive processes depends on the (disciplinary) element on which it is applied. The use of an ontological version of the taxonomy is proposed to be integrated with the OntoMath^{PRO} ontology, a bilingual ontology of mathematical knowledge, geared to be the hub for math knowledge in the Web of Data (Nevzorova et al., 2014). The developers share the sources with the Semantic Web community. This research proposes the further development and translation of OntoMath^{PRO} also in the Italian panorama.

4. EXPERIMENTATION

To validate and refine the model, quantitative and qualitative analyses on activities made by Community instructors is proposed. The main objective is to experiment the use of the model to equip the digital teaching materials with descriptors linked to the skills expected at the end of the educational path.

The experimentation requires a total estimated commitment of 6 hours within 4 weeks for each participant, and it develops through several activities within four main phases of inquiry:

- **Initial questionnaire**: inquiry about the methodology that instructors adopt to create materials.
- **Agreement activity**: evaluation of the consistency of the choice of descriptors with respect to the proposed model of sample questions. The activity follows a virtual meeting for the presentation of P-R-O descriptors model.
- **Workshop**: assessment of the descriptors – associated with questions – written by colleagues. The workshop follows the 'question design and submission' activity: each instructor autonomously elaborates 1 question starting from the specification of the descriptors. This activity is preceded by a 45-minute virtual meeting in which an example of design and implementation of a question (starting from the specification of the descriptors) is shown.
- **Final questionnaire**: inquiry about the activity carried out in the experimentation.

Questionnaires questions are open-answers or selections in Likert scale from 1 ("not at all") to 5 ("very").

5. RESULTS

Each of the next subchapters shows the results of the single phases of the experimentation. The subjects involved are secondary school teachers chosen among those who joined the PP&S project. To date, the Project involves 1,229 teachers (from all over Italy) of Mathematics, Computer Science, Physics, and other scientific disciplines, and 16,400 students. For this experiment, we chose a reduced set of (23) teachers, particularly active and proactive, dedicated to innovation and willing to experiment with new methodologies.

The experimentation did not provide for indemnity of any kind, it only issued a training certification by the University of Turin for each teacher involved.

5.1 Initial Questionnaire

The participants are not used to sharing content frequently: half of them shares less than 25% of the questions used with their students. At the same time, as Figure 2 shows, more than 50% of their questions are autonomously created. The other part of instructors' repository appears – on average – to be composed of questions taken from the Community (and possibly modified according to their needs).

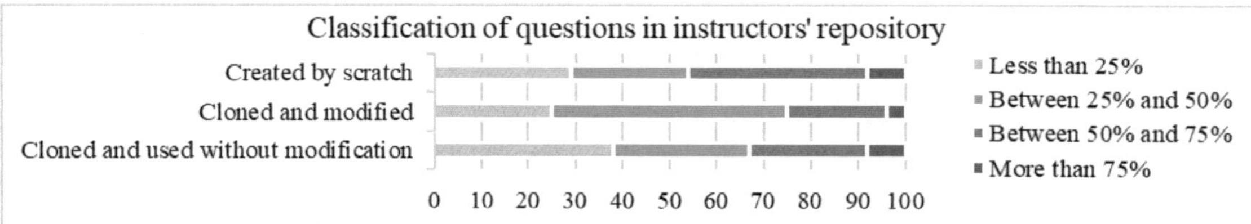

Figure 2. Percentage of questions created by scratch, cloned and modified, cloned and used without modification according to instructors' responses

The instructors' tendency to share a little percentage of their materials is accompanied by their low perception of the easiness of the search for questions in the Community: about 72% of them rates this aspect "enough" easy or less. They motivated their choices with open answers: among the features which contrast the easiness of the search engine they indicated the "heterogeneity of the quality of the questions", the frequent "poor specification of the topic of the questions", and the perceived "lack of immediacy in the research system". Some answers, like the latter, highly relate to the Automatic Assessment System features, while others – such as the former – deal with Community best practice: specifying topics and estimating the quality of shared materials should follow a common methodology in order to make it easy to retrieve. Topics can be part of the learning objectives description, which 80% of them specifies – mostly verbally – before submitting an assignment to students. Even among those who indicated that they do not specify learning objectives, the times of reflection about learning objectives during planning and realization of a question are rated "enough" or more. This tendency is similar when taking into account the time dedicated to reflecting about the way in which the question allows to measure the achievement of the objectives, and the requirements needed to answer the question. The rates slightly decrease when considering the phase of the use of questions with the students, in line with the presence of 20% of instructors who indicated that they do not specify learning objectives.

5.2 Agreement Activity

The survey on agreement of choice between different descriptors of proposed questions is proposed to assess instructors' understanding of the P-R-O model. The instructors are shown 4 questions, each of which has 4 different versions of each descriptor. For each of the 3 descriptors, each teacher is asked to "choose the sentence that appeals as the most appropriate for a given descriptor or suggest a different one"; the teacher can select one of the 4 choices or write his original proposal in the text area.

All instructors made the same choices, which matched an expert's opinion about which should be the most correct answers except for one case. This shows that the identification of distractors is an operation on which high degree of agreement can be achieved.

5.3 Workshop

Analyzing peer assessment rates and open answers enables to understand the following features:

- instructors' comprehension of the descriptors: Performance was the only one which someone misunderstood: it does not relate with the 'actual' solving path taken by the student. Instead, it describes what the student is required to do to communicate to the teacher the correct answer (supposing that he already found it); for an example, see the review of teacher 2 to the Performance of the author A in Table 1;

- instructors' writing methods: the majority of them wrote essential statements (composed by one or two phrases), while others widely expressed descriptors using also lists of phrases;

The activity highlighted the understanding of the intent of the authors of the questions: several reviewers appreciated peers' work and proposed modifications to questions to completely align them with the descriptors.

Figure 3 shows an example of workshop submission, while Table 1 shows the related descriptors proposed by the author (A) and by the reviewers (1, 2, 3).

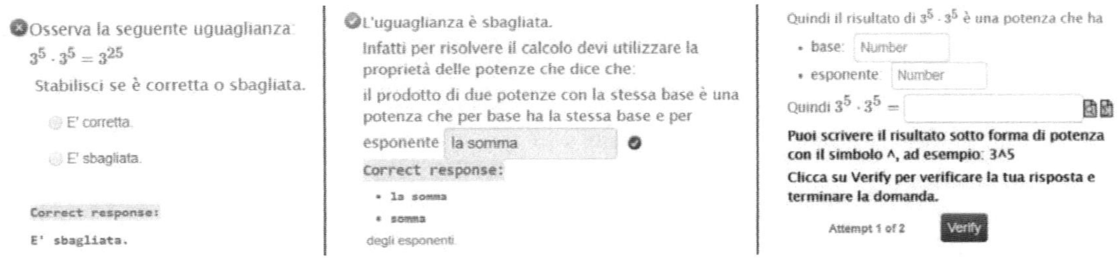

Figure 3. Question (composed of three parts) submitted by an instructor.

Table 1. Descriptors proposed by the author of the question (A) and by the reviewers (1, 2, 3)

	Performance	Requirements	Objectives
A	Assigned an already resolved expression (power product with the same base), verify the correct application of the corresponding property based on the explicit result.	Remembering the properties of the powers. Working with expressions that contain powers.	Analysing expressions with properties of powers, identifying: the use or not of the properties of the powers; the correct application of the property.
1	Indicate any correctness, by clicking on one of the two alternative options presented; write the operation that must be carried out among the exponents; identify and write the base and the exponent of the produced power; write the resulting power.	Knowing the concept of power at full exponent, identifying the base and the exponent; remembering the property of the product of similar powers; calculating the sum between positive integers.	Knowing and knowing how to apply theorem about the product of similar powers.
2	Given an equality of whether it is correct or not, enunciate a property of the powers, recognize the base and the exponent of a power, and apply a property of the powers.	Knowing the properties of the powers, knowing the meaning of the symbol =.	Recognizing the correctness or of the application of a property of the powers.
3	In my opinion the O-P-R descriptors are well explained, I would just have used the verb 'select' instead of 'verify' in the performance.		

5.4 Final Questionnaire

Instructors appreciated several aspects of the activity: 'Clarity of explanations', 'Adequacy of the topics covered', 'Completeness of the topics covered', 'Course progress modality' were rated more than 4.5 out of 5 on average (with standard deviation of less than 0.75). They showed high appreciation of the use of P-R-O triad in the activity: similar rates were obtained for the following aspects:

- Designing learning units through the specification of the P-R-O descriptor triad;
- Having the three-part P-R-O descriptors associated with learning units of other teachers available;
- Reasoning together with peers about learning units on the basis of the P-R-O modeling principles.

Overall, instructors believe that this model will be useful. The use of the P-R-O descriptors may be useful to reflect systematically on teaching, to elaborate material for students, to activate discussions within the Community, to share material in the Community, and to search for material. Those aspects were rated 4.16 or more on average (with standard deviation less than 0.93).

The descriptors were used by instructors during the phases of planning, realization and use of a question, as highlighted by the high average rates of Table 2.

Table 2. Average rates of descriptors appreciation considering three phases

	Design	Realization	Use
The use of the descriptor Performance helps reflect on how the question allows to measure the achievement of the intended goals	4.30 (0.80)	4.22 (0.91)	4.17 (0.77)
The use of the descriptor Requirements helps reflect on the requirements necessary to answer the question	4.63 (0.58)	4.33 (0.67)	3.70 (1.09)
The use of the descriptor Objectives helps reflect on the learning objectives	4.44 (0.75)	4.31 (0.74)	3.85 (0.86)

Open answers confirm both the appreciation of the overall activity and the expectation that the systematic adoption of the P-R-O model would be helpful to the Community. A selection of answers to the question "Indicate how you plan to use what was proposed during experimentation in your teaching" follow.

- **Helpfulness for the new instructors joining the community**: "Having just entered the PPS community, I have not yet mastered the use of the Automatic Assessment System, so I am not yet able to prepare ex novo questions; I would like to start using the questions in the archive and therefore I think it would be very useful if all the questions were accompanied by the proposed descriptors".
- **Alignment to everyday teaching practice**: "During the experimentation I realized that before formulating a test, I always reflected on objectives, performance and requirements, but I never explicitly wrote them. Now I will begin to do it, because I think it is essential to draw a learning path. I also think it is important to communicate it to the students so that they too have clear that each trial has its own purpose and is part of a larger project".
- **Positive effects of cooperation between peers**: "The questions proposed by our colleagues have been a useful tool, because they allow us to understand not only what are the objectives that guide us to create a test, but also how important it is to be clear and precise in the delivery we propose".

All the participants would like to participate to a second experimentation to further discuss and learn about the proposed model. Among the suggestions left through open answers, they indicated useful hints for future experimentations:

- having a list of counterexamples, that are incorrect associations of descriptors to materials;
- repeating, strengthening and supporting the activity with a supervising tutor;
- systematizing descriptors cross-review, to make them as objective and recognizable as possible;
- using a standardized vocabulary, so that terms are not subject to individual interpretations.

6. CONCLUSION

Associating descriptors to materials should increase the educational validity of the whole instructors' work, from the design phase to the sharing and finding of different resources. It could especially favour the selection of materials by instructors who join Communities for the first time, as they might not be familiar with the tools. Furthermore, clarifying learning intentions is crucial for interpreting students' results.

The main outcome of the experimentation is the creation of the first collection of shared resources associated with descriptors validated by experts: the elaborated materials and the guidelines to their preparation are made available to all the instructors in order to be used in their own didactics. Furthermore, workshop submissions will be reviewed in order to create a gold standard of resources described and counter examples with comments for the teachers who want to continue using this model. Reviewing instructors' work is also strategic for a careful development of the ontologies and the planning of the system's implementation. A web-based software will be integrated into Learning Management Systems hosting targeted Communities for the experimentation of the proposed model, so that experimentation involving students will enable to further investigate material authoring and automatic dispatching.

ACKNOWLEDGEMENT

We sincerely thank the teachers involved in the experimentation and the Scientific Committee of PP&S Project.

REFERENCES

Barana, A. et al, 2015. Automated Assessment in Mathematics. *Proceedings of 2015 IEEE 39th Annual International Computers, Software & Applications Conference*. Taichung, Taiwan, pp. 670-671.

Ravotto, P., 2011. Competence-based learning in Europe & the sloop2desc MODEL. *In Preparing the teachers for a competence-based education system*, pp.13-16.

Trinchero, R., 2017. *Costruire e certificare competenze nel secondo ciclo*. Rizzoli Education, Milano, Italy.

Vincent, T. et al, 2014. A new framework of concept clustering and learning path optimization to develop the next-generation e-learning systems. *In Journal of Computers in Education*, pp. 335-352.

Huang, C. et al, 2015. Constructing Learning Maps for Lecture Videos by Exploring Wikipedia Knowledge, *Proceedings (Part I) of 16th Pacific-Rim Conference on Multimedia*, Gwangju, South Korea, pp. 559-569.

Winterton, J. et al, 2006. *Typology of knowledge, skills and competences : clarification of the concept and prototype*. Office for Official Publications of the European Communities, Luxembourg.

Black, P. and Wiliam, D., 2009. Developing theory of formative assessment. *In Educational Assessment, Evaluation and Accountability*, Vol. 21, No. 1, pp. 5-31.

Wiliam, D. and Thompson, M., 2007. Integrating assessment with instruction: What will it take to make it work?. *In The future of assessment: Shaping teaching and learning*, pp. 53-82.

Di Caro, L. et al, 2018a. Alignment of content, prerequisites and educational objectives: towards automated mapping of digital learning resources. *Proceedings of The 14th International Scientific Conference eLearning and Software for Education*. Bucharest, Romania, pp. 335-342.

Barana, A. et al, 2018a. Developing Competence Assessment Systems in e-Learning Communities. *Proceedings of EDEN 2018 ANNUAL Conference*. Genova, Italy, pp. 879-888.

Di Caro L. et al, 2018b. Towards adaptive systems for automatic formative assessment in virtual learning communities. *Proceedings of 2018 42nd IEEE International Conference on Computer Software & Applications*. Tokyo, Japan, pp. 1000-1005.

Barana, A. and Marchisio, M., 2016. Ten good reasons to adopt an automated formative assessment model for learning and teaching Mathematics and scientific disciplines. *In PROCEDIA: SOCIAL & BEHAVIORAL SCIENCES*, Vol. 228, pp. 608-613.

Barana, A. et al, 2018b. Sharing system of learning resources for adaptive strategies of scholastic remedial intervention. *Proceedings of 4rd International Conference on Higher Education Advances (HEAd'18)*. Valencia, Spain, pp. 1465-1473.

Ellerani, F. and Parricchi, M., 2010. *Ambienti per lo sviluppo professionale degli insegnanti. Web 2.0, gruppo, comunità di apprendimento*. Francoangeli, Milano, Italy.

Demartini, C. et al, 2013. PP&S100 - una comunità di comunità di collaborative learning attraverso le nuove tecnologie. *Proceedings of DIDAMATICA 2013, Tecnologie e Metodi per la Didattica del Futuro*. Pisa, Italy, pp. 989-998.

Brancaccio, A. et al, 2014. Il progetto PP&S informatica a scuola. *In MONDO* DIGITALE, Vol. 13, No. 51, pp. 565-574.

Brancaccio, A. et al, 2015. Problem Posing and Solving: Strategic Italian Key Action to Enhance Teaching and Learning of Mathematics and Informatics in High School. *Proceedings of 2015 IEEE 39th Annual International Computers, Software & Applications Conference*. Taichung, Taiwan, pp. 73-88.

Brancaccio, A. et al, 2016. L'efficacia dell'apprendimento in rete degli immigrati digitali. L'esperienza SMART per le discipline scientifiche. *In MONDO DIGITALE*, Vol. 15, No. 64, pp. 803-821.

Trinchero, R., 2014. *Valutare l'apprendimento nell'e-learning*. Erickson, Trento, Italy.

Anderson, L.W. et al, 2001. *A taxonomy for learning, teaching, and assessing. A revision of Bloom's taxonomy of educational objectives*. Addison Wesley Longman, New York.

Nevzorova, O. et al, 2014. OntoMathPRO ontology: A linked data hub for mathematics. *Proceedings of KESW: International Conference on Knowledge Engineering and the Semantic Web*. Kazan, Russia, pp. 105-119.

SHARED COOPERATIVE ACTIVITIES IN PARENT-CHILD DYADS IN AN EDUCATIONAL ROBOTICS WORKSHOP

Katarzyna Potęga vel Żabik[1] and Łukasz Tanaś[1,2]
[1]*Copernicus Science Centre, Wybrzeże Kościuszkowskie 20 str., 00-390 Warsaw, Poland*
[2]*Department of Psychology, University of Social Sciences and Humanities, Warsaw, Poland*

ABSTRACT

Learning robotics can be performed individually or as a collaborative problem-solving activity. Effective pedagogy is based on the latter. In this paper, we offer a work-in-progress report of an observational analysis of parent-child dyads engaged in an educational robotics workshop in a Science Center. We chose this context because learning technological fluency is largely sustained by family-based interactions. We aim to observe what is the relationship between the occurrence of joint engagement in parent-child dyads and their effectiveness in beta-testing of an interactive robot. We use the concept of a shared cooperative activity (Bratman, 1992) as a framework for this analysis and argue for the importance of conducting such analyses in an ecologically valid learning environment.

KEYWORDS

Joint Attention, Shared Cooperative Activity, Collaborative Learning, Joint Engagement, Parent-Child Relationship, Educational Robotics Program

1. INTRODUCTION

The cornerstone of pedagogy is the ability of a teacher and a student to establish common ground in communication to provide personalized leadership for the trainee. This is manifested when learning takes the form of a shared cooperative activity (Bohn & Köymen, 2018) and it is what differentiates pedagogy from mere skill acquisition, as skill acquisition is a broader term, applicable to the learning process of most animals, whereas pedagogy is arguably a human-specific based on shared intentionality (Tomasello & Carpenter, 2007; McClung *et al.*, 2017). We offer a work-in-progress report of a study which aims to show the role of shared cooperative activities in an educational robotics program.

Despite the continually growing offer of educational robotics courses, most of them are addressed only to children and less frequently to parents or families. Parents consider robots as a useful educational instrument, but they rarely see themselves as active participants in robotics-related activities. Instead, they would delegate the teaching role to experts or receive a relatively autonomous self-guiding tool for their children (Feng *et al.*, 2011; Lin *et al.*, 2012). It is hypothesized that it might be challenging for parents with less technological fluency to engage in educational robotics activity with a child when they have to acknowledge their novice status (Bers *et al.*, 2004; Barron *et al.*, 2009). In consequence parental anxiety might limit the frequency of family educational interventions, and not only lessen the exposition to new technology, but also limit the opportunity to embed learning experience within a family system. There is ample body of evidence which shows that parental support during educational activities, and the quality of it, influences children's motivation, behavior and knowledge acquisition (Lee & Nie, 2015; Tenenbaum & Hohenstein, 2016; Sha *et al.*, 2016; Sadka *et al.*, 2018). Hence, it is worthwhile to focus on the methods which could boost parental confidence in using educational technology in a context that often disrupts traditional roles in a family. Shifting parent role from "know-it-all" to "novice" is often unfamiliar situation both for parents and children. The common assumption is that, in task-related context, parent automatically adopts supportive role (Grebelsky-Lichtman, 2014), but it was found that, *e.g.*, the complexity of the task can influence parent behavior. The more complicated the activity, the less cooperation-inducing parental communication becomes (Grebelsky-Lichtman, 2014). On the other hand, there is a modest data on dyadic cooperation in context of family courses in robotics (Bers & Urrea, 2000; Beals & Bers, 2006; Cuellar *et al.*, 2013, 2014; Roque *et al.*,

2016) or other family-focused, non-formal educational interventions (Sadka & Zukerman, 2017; Sadka *et al.*, 2018). Therefore, we decide to investigate dyad dynamics throughout the robotics workshop using bi-directional perspective.

Parent-child interaction is a constantly changing bidirectional dynamic process, in which participants are influencing each other on different levels (behavioral, emotional as well as motivational). Therefore many experts now argue that it might be more beneficial to analyze the dyad as a whole.

The concept of a shared cooperative activity (SCA) was popularized by a philosopher Michael Bratman (1992) and has subsequently been successfully operationalized and applied in various fields of psychology, including neuroscience (Newman-Norlund *et al.*, 2007). SCA happens when people decide to form a pair or a team to achieve some goal, which would be unlikely to be completed individually, and they assist and monitor their performance in the process SCAs are defined by three features: mutual responsiveness, commitment to the joint activity, and commitment to mutual support. Mutual responsiveness is based mainly on joint attention. In the simplest case, it involves a pair of agents, who are engaged in such activity which requires them to pay attention to each other's actions and respond accordingly. Mere joint attention is neutral with regards to the goals of the agents. People can have mutual, neutral (*e.g.*, "I do not care what you do") or opposing goals (*e.g.*, as in combat), but they are interdependent in a situation. Adding joint activity commitment introduces the element of a shared goal. Agents can have different reasons and motivations for this goal, but they communicate about a particular goal and make it theirs. An important quality of such a goal is that it is achieved only when all participants receive their rewards. Only then the collaborative action stops (Hamann *et al.*, 2012). Finally, the commitment to mutual support points to the fact that agents will play different roles in the activity, are prepared to monitor their role performance, as well as offer assistance when needed. As mentioned previously, this is a typical situation in pedagogy the digital age makes the value of SCAs even more apparent. There are similar to SCA concepts, which are wildly used in family studies, *e.g.*, mutuality, which Funamoto and Rinaldi (2014) defined as "concept in the parent-child literature that describes how harmonious, reciprocal, cooperative, and responsive this interaction can be" [pp.4]. Lack of shared goal component, which is an essential factor in family-based educational activities, makes the SCA most suitable for this study.

In this project, we aim to apply the concept of SCA's to the context of an educational robotics program. Our primary research questions are: how do parent-child SCA's change the quality of interaction in the context of robotics? Why do parent-child SCAs break down or are not established at all? Is it mainly due to the problems in mutuality? Inability or unwillingness to agree on the joint goal or perhaps difficulties in coordination of different roles and provision of mutual support? Additionally, we want to create a less domain-dependent measure of SCA's in parent-child collaborative problem solving, which could be used in other educational contexts.

2. EDUCATIONAL ROBOTICS WORKSHOP

2.1 Setting and Participants

Study took place during workshops which were organized in Copernicus Science Center (Warsaw, Poland) during a five-month period from January to May 2018 and additional workshops are planned in August 2018. Final sample of participants should reach at least 60 parent-child dyads. Participants are recruited on a volunteer basis through an internet advertisement. So far 56 children (24 girls), aged 9-14 (girls, $M = 10.83$, $SD = 1.46$; boys, $M = 10.84$, $SD = 1.35$) participated with their parents (29 mothers; mothers $M = 46.34$ years; SD = 4.15; fathers $M = 44.30$ years, $SD = 5.37$). All families live in the metropolitan area and all parents except one have a university degree. Their self-assessed socioeconomic status was relatively high ($M = 6.05$ $SD = 1.41$ using 10-point SSS MacArthur Scale; Adler & Stewart, 2007), but this is typical for individual visitors in the science center. Participants were gifted with free tickets to the science center. Parents gave written informed consent and children gave verbal consent for participation in the study.

2.2 Robot

Photon (Photon Entertainment LTD, https://photonrobot.pl/en/) is a commercially available educational toy designed with the intent to teach introductory computer programming concepts. Features of the robot include sensors for light, touch, sound, ground contrast and obstacle detection; measurement of traveled distance and angle of rotation; outputs, apart from motor functions, include changing colors of various body elements and playing sounds. Robot can be controlled via a set of applications with different types of interface, suited to changing levels of user's proficiency and age, starting from graphical programming by drawing to creating sequences similar to actual coding. Robot is advertised as a toy for children 5-years and older.

2.3 Workshop Scenario

Scenario design was influenced by social constructivism (Karagiorgi & Symeou, 2005) and Authentic Learning frameworks (Herrington and Parker, 2013) which are regarded as a well-suited methods for educational robotics (Mubin *et al.*, 2013; Chetty, 2017). Workshop design lets the participants gain knowledge in social, collaborative and interactive manner. Steps were taken to provide an authentic context and to make the task meaningful. The goal of the activity was to test various features of the robot and was a real beta-testing experience.

Workshops included a maximum of 16 participants and lasted 45 min. Each workshop was divided into 3 parts: introduction, testing and summary. Each parent-child dyad received the Photon robot along with a Samsung SM-T580 tablet with a control application based on a graphical interface. During the *introductory* part participants were familiarized with work requirements of a typical product beta-tester and given a 10 min instruction on how to use the robot and make a simple code in order to test different robot's features (See: Figure 1).

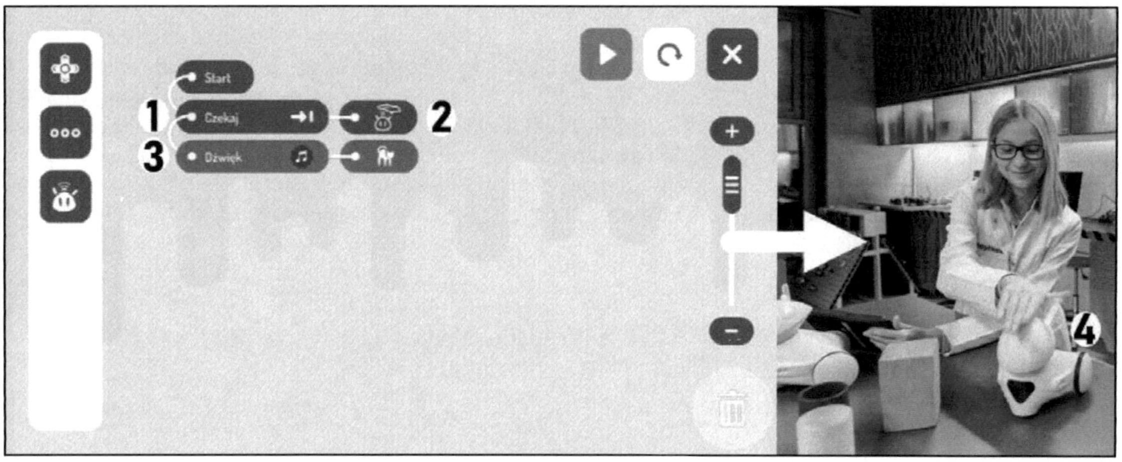

Figure 1. Graphical application interface (left) and Photon robot with the haptic sensor being tested (right). Participants received training in the use of the "wait until" function (1); variety of sensor inputs (2); and a sound output (3)

The *testing* phase was initiated with the statement: "Now test how this robot works. Is it possible to, somehow, make its sensors or motor malfunction? Under which conditions?". Participant dyads were asked to focus on different aspects of the robot and given different additional testing materials (See: Table 1). Testing phase lasted for 20 minutes and was videotaped for further coding. From this point on the workshop animators were passive and engaged only if needed. They only occasionally hinted or asked follow up questions, *i.e.*, "Perhaps check what is the lowest or highest sound which can be registered with the robot's sensor?".

Table 1. Description of the 5 beta-testing conditions and a list of the materials for the workstations

Beta-testing variants (no. of workstations):	*Additional beta-testing materials given to participants*
Touch & Sound detection (2)	Gloves (woolen, hardware and rubber), balloons, foil (copper and aluminum), magnets, radio that generates noise, Vernier sensors, music instruments.
Light detection (2)	Black carton box, flashlight with white, IR and UV light, white LED lamp, blue and red diodes, RGB ball, LED strip, laser, colored filter foils.
Contrast detection (1)	white and black sheet, orange-green mat, chessboard, various tapes - shiny, insulating, silver, whiteboard markers
Distance detection and motor & measurement of rotation angles (2)	Synthetic grass, carpet and blankets, acoustic sponge, foam pads, bubble wrap, twine, ruler, compass, professional protractor.
Obstacle detection (1)	Geometric figures from Plexiglas (various), model of a crystal structure, a sheet of golden, rigid foil, ruler, mirrors, 3D prints (various), bottle, tiles of plywood, Plexiglas, polypropylene and Teflon.

The *summary* part lasted 10 minutes and consisted of participants filling out their tester report and engaging in a group discussion on how the robot could improve. Finally, participants were asked to fill an evaluation questionnaire and a sociodemographic survey.

2.4 Data Coding and Preliminary Data Analysis

Video excerpts from the testing phase (20 min) of the workshop are currently being coded using the BORIS software (Friard & Gamba, 2016) for the occurrence of SCAs in the parent-child dyads and this will be matched with the assessment of beta-testing effectiveness of each dyad. Effectiveness is defined as the quantity and range of beta-testing actions that the parent-child team performed (*e.g.*, the number and variety of additional materials used, testing both high and low sensory/motor thresholds, originality of solutions, number of bug-fixing conclusions). Taking into account the limited time given to each pair for beta-testing and the semi-open-ended nature of the task we expect that their effectiveness will be positively correlated with the stability of their SCAs.

We operationalize the occurrence of SCAs by coding: a) frequency and total time of joint engagement (both agents attentive to each other or to the same object: hardware, software or additional materials); b) frequency and total time of bids for joint engagement on the part of both the parent and the child (due to limits on the quality of recorded audio, this will be mostly based on non-verbal attempts to initiate mutual attention); c) total time of work with division of labor (agents performing on task activity in different roles, *e.g.*, one controlling hardware and the other one software); d) frequency and total time of mutual support (occurrence of a disruption of ongoing activity by one agent in order to assist the other agent in their role).

Analysis of the workshop evaluation questionnaires enables us to offer some preliminary descriptive data on the general agreement between parents and children with regards to their perception of the workshop. We expect that the agreement in perception should reflect better SCAs of the dyad (See: Table 2).

Table 2. Preliminary descriptive data from the workshop evaluation questionnaire: level of agreement in perception of the situation between parents and children

Who spent more time interacting with the robot: parent/child/both?							
Child	Lack of agreement	Agreement	n	Parent	Lack of agreement	Agreement	n
Girls	11 (46%)	13 (54%)	24	Mothers	16 (55%)	13 (45%)	29
Boys	19 (59%)	13 (41%)	32	Fathers	14 (52%)	13 (48%)	27
Both	30 (54%)	26 (46)	56	Both	30 (54%)	26 (46%)	56
How difficult was this task for the child?							
	Lack of agreement	Agreement	n		Lack of agreement	Agreement	n
Girls	8 (33%)	16 (67%)	24	Mothers	18 (62%)	11 (38%)	29
Boys	23 (72%)	9 (28%)	32	Fathers	13 (48%)	14 (52%)	27
Both	31 (55%)	25 (45%)	56	Both	31 (55%)	25 (45%)	56

How did you and the other person enjoy the workshop? Columns describe the level of match in perception									
	None	One	Both	n		None	One	Both	n
Girls	5 (21%)	13 (54%)	6 (25%)	24	Mothers	5 (17%)	9 (31%)	15 (52%)	29
Boys	6 (19%)	7 (22%)	19 (59%)	32	Fathers	6 (22%)	11 (41%)	10 (37%)	27
Both	11 (20%)	20 (36%)	25 (45%)	56	Both	11 (20%)	20 (36%)	25 (45%)	56

Note. % values in a row. Difficulty (1 - definitely too difficult, 5 - definitely too easy). Time with the robot (mostly me, mostly the other person, equal). General enjoyment (5-point visual analogue scale). Agreement means that in particular dyad parent and child marked the same response. In case of "Enjoyment": same response for both child and parent (both); same response for child or parent (one); different ratings for both (none).

3. CONCLUSION

Study offers a framework for the analysis of shared cooperative activities in an educational robotics program which could be applied in a variety of informal and formal educational settings. Among the advantages of current proposal are: a) high ecological validity, as the study involves behavioral observation during an actual learning situation; b) time series data which can show patterns of SCA interactions for those dyads which are most successful at beta-testing; c) promise for development of a less task dependent measure of join engagement in the context of dyads (parent-child; teacher-student; student-student) as well as larger groups. Limitations include: a) exploratory character of the study, which lacks experimental manipulation which would enable us to understand the mechanisms responsible for the willingness or ability of both the parent and the child to create SCAs; b) commitment to a common goal was partially forced as it was presented to the dyads by the explainer; c) participants in the current study were self-selected and their characteristic (*e.g.* high SES) limits generalizability.

We hope that this framework will shed light on the determinants of parent-child mutuality and effectiveness in learning situations. Especially in situations which involve learning of/with new technologies, such as robotics or programming. High level technological fluency is largely sustained by family-based learning and parents do play a significant supporting role in creativity within the realm of new media (Barron *et al.*, 2009).

ACKNOWLEDGMENT

This research was supported by the National Centre for Research and Development (project funding agreement: 210/17/PK). We would like to thank Dagmara Kiraga and Joanna Śliwa and all members of the robotic laboratory who were instrumental to this project. Anna Gańko for made this research possible. We are appreciative of families who agreed to participate in this research. We are also grateful to prof. Maartje Rajimakers for preparing coding scheme and invaluable advices, dr Ilona Iłowiecka-Tańska and dr Maksymilian Bielecki for thoughtful comments.

REFERENCES

Adler, N. and Stewart, J., 2007. The MacArthur scale of subjective social status. *MacArthur Research Network on SES & Health.* Retrieved from http://www. macses. ucsf. edu/Research/Psychosocial/subjective. Php.

Barron, B., Martin, C.K., Takeuchi, L. and Fithian, R., 2009. Parents as learning partners in the development of technological fluency.

Beals, L. and Bers, M., 2006. Robotic technologies: when parents put their learning ahead of their child's. *Journal of Interactive Learning Research*, *17*(4), pp.341-366.

Bers, M.U. and Urrea, C., 2000. Con-science: Parents and children exploring robotics and values. A. Druin.

Bers, M.U., New, R.S. and Boudreau, L., 2004. Teaching and learning when no one is expert: Children and parents explore technology. *Early Childhood Research & Practice*, *6*(2), p.n2.

Bohn, M. and Köymen, B., 2018. Common Ground and Development. *Child development perspectives*, *12*(2), pp.104–108.

Bratman, M.E., 1992. Shared Cooperative Activity. *The Philosophical review*, *101*(2), pp.327–341.

Chetty, J., 2017. Combatting the war against machines: an innovative hands-on approach to coding. *Robotics in STEM Education* (pp. 59-83). Springer, Cham.

Cuellar, F., Penaloza, C. and Kato, G., 2013, August. Robotics education initiative for parent-children interaction. In *RO-MAN*, 2013 IEEE (pp. 364-365). IEEE.

Cuellar, F., Penaloza, C., Garret, P., Olivo, D., Mejia, M., Valdez, N. and Mija, A., 2014, October. Robotics education initiative for analyzing learning and child-parent interaction. In *Frontiers in Education Conference* (FIE), 2014 IEEE (pp. 1-6). IEEE.

Feng, H.C., Lin, C.H. and Liu, E.Z.F., 2011. Parents' perceptions of educational programmable bricks for kids. *British Journal of Educational Technology*, *42*(2), pp.E30-E33.

Friard, O. and Gamba, M., 2016. BORIS: a free, versatile open-source event-logging software for video/audio coding and live observations. *Methods Ecol Evol*, 7: 1325–1330.

Grebelsky-Lichtman, T., 2014. Parental patterns of cooperation in parent–child interactions: The relationship between nonverbal and verbal communication. *Human Communication Research*, *40*(1), pp.1-29.

Hamann, K., Warneken, F. and Tomasello, M., 2012. Children's developing commitments to joint goals. *Child development*, *83*(1), pp.137–145.

Herrington, J. and Parker, J., 2013. Emerging technologies as cognitive tools for authentic learning. *British Journal of Educational Technology*, *44*(4), pp.607-615.

Karagiorgi, Y. and Symeou, L., 2005. Translating constructivism into instructional design: Potential and limitations. *Journal of Educational Technology & Society*, *8*(1).

Lee, A.N. and Nie, Y., 2015. The 'Why'and 'How'of Engaging Parents in Their Children's Science Learning in Informal Contexts: Theoretical Perspectives and Applications. In *Science Education in East Asia* (pp. 93-121). Springer, Cham.

Lin, C.H., Liu, E.Z.F. and Huang, Y.Y., 2012. Exploring parents' perceptions towards educational robots: Gender and socio-economic differences. *British Journal of Educational Technology*, *43*(1).

McClung, J.S., Placì, S., Bangerter, A., Clément, F. and Bshary, R., 2017. The language of cooperation: shared intentionality drives variation in helping as a function of group membership. *Proc. R. Soc. B*, *284*(1863), p.20171682.

Mubin, O., Stevens, C.J., Shahid, S., Al Mahmud, A. and Dong, J.J., 2013. A review of the applicability of robots in education. *Journal of Technology in Education and Learning*, *1*(209-0015), p.13.

Newman-Norlund, R.D., Noordzij, M.L., Meulenbroek, R.G. and Bekkering, H., 2007. Exploring the brain basis of joint action: co-ordination of actions, goals and intentions. *Social Neuroscience*, *2*(1), pp.48-65.

Roque, R., Lin, K. and Liuzzi, R., 2016. "I'm Not Just a Mom": Parents Developing Multiple Roles in Creative Computing. Singapore: *International Society of the Learning Sciences*.

Sadka, O. and Zuckerman, O., 2017, June. From Parents to Mentors: Parent-Child Interaction in Co-Making Activities. In *Proceedings of the 2017 Conference on Interaction Design and Children* (pp. 609-615). ACM.

Sadka, O., Erel, H., Grishko, A. and Zuckerman, O., 2018, June. Tangible interaction in parent-child collaboration: encouraging awareness and reflection. In *Proceedings of the 17th ACM Conference on Interaction Design and Children* (pp. 157-169). ACM.

Sha, L., Schunn, C., Bathgate, M. and Ben- Eliyahu, A., 2016. Families support their children's success in science learning by influencing interest and self- efficacy. *Journal of Research in Science Teaching*, *53*(3), pp.450-472.

Tenenbaum, H.R. and Hohenstein, J.M., 2016. Parent–child talk about the origins of living things. *Journal of experimental child psychology*, *150*, pp.314-329.

Tomasello, M. and Carpenter, M., 2007. Shared intentionality. *Developmental science*, *10*(1), pp.121–125.

EFFECTS OF CONTENT AND LANGUAGE INTEGRATED LEARNING CLASS DESIGN BASED ON THE FIRST PRINCIPLE OF INSTRUCTION THEORY: A CASE STUDY

Hao Hao[1], Hitoshi Susono[2] and Masanori Yamada[1]
[1]*Kyushu University, Japan*
[2]*Mie University, Japan*

ABSTRACT

Content and Language Integrated Learning (CLIL) has emerged as a popular approach to language education in Europe and America in recent years. The main features of CLIL are learning foreign languages while gaining professional knowledge, enhancing student thinking, and improving the understanding of culture. However, CLIL has certain limitations, which a more effective course design may address. This paper aims to use the First Principle of Instruction (FPI) theory, one of the Instructional Design (ID) theories, to design CLIL in order to improve the course. This paper has selected the Japanese CLIL course in China as an example. The target learners are 16 students of the Japanese major at the university. The subject of the course is Intercultural Education. The results indicated that the FPI-based pre- and post- questionnaires revealed significant difference, as compared to those of the Japanese proficiency test. The analyses of the proficiency test, FPI, and CLIL indicated that there is a high correlation between the test and FPI whereas there is a moderate correlation between the test and CLIL and between FPI and CLIL.

KEYWORDS

CLIL, FPI, Foreign Language Learning

1. INTRODUCTION

Content and Language Integrated Learning (CLIL), which gained momentum in the 1990s, has spread in Europe in recent years, with significant advances in a relatively short period of time (Coyle, 2015). CLIL is a dual-focused educational approach wherein a student learns content while simultaneously learning a foreign language gain a certain level of mastery over both (Maljers et al., 2010). Through CLIL, students can enhance the sense of citizenship, increase awareness of the value of transferable skills and knowledge, and improve confidence and the ability to use language; CLIL may significantly increase the learner's thinking ability and offer an opportunity to the youngsters to be bilingual (Sabet et al., 2012). However, studies have also highlighted the shortcomings of CLIL, which more effective, integration of language and content, not only based on teaching experience may address. (e.g., Cenoz et al., 2014). Although CLIL-based courses are likely to be effective, a professional class design method can further improve its effectiveness (Meyer, 2010).

Using Instructional Design (ID) to create a model for CLIL is likely to solve some of the existing problems and expand CLIL's potential. This research focuses on the design and application of the First Principle of Instruction (FPI)-based CLIL program, which is a collection of fundamental principles of ID proposed by Merrill (2002). Statistical analysis, through testing and questionnaires, will be used to evaluate and improve the course design.

2. LITERATURE REVIEW

2.1 CLIL

CLIL is defined as a dual-focused educational approach wherein a foreign language is used to learn and teach content and language (Coyle et al. 2010). CLIL primarily has two features, a Conceptual Framework (4Cs), and five dimensions, displayed in Table 1. In 2005, the European Union (EU) formally recognized CLIL as a cross--curriculum class format (European Commission, 2005). Extensive research has proven that CLIL has improved the learning motivation, and professional performance, and language skills of the students. CLIL and non-CLIL students have different attitudes towards their mother tongue and second language, which may cause differences in their learning motivation (Sylvén, 2015). In a CLIL lesson, the use of foreign language learning strategies as well as geography-related content was facilitated and improved, at the same time, reading skills, lexicon, satisfaction and collaboration were enhanced (Dourda et al., 2014).

An effective integration and balance of content and language in a CLIL course will greatly influence learning. For example, if students are unable to comprehend what the teacher says, they cannot effectively grasp the content. Although CLIL has made significant progress in the last 20 years, it is also necessary to identify methods to continuously innovate CLIL (Dooly et al., 2015). In the current research, CLIL characteristics are employed to improve the quality and design of a class. (Meyer, 2010). So far, there seems to be no unified and effective way to design CLIL courses. In Thailand, researchers used design manuals to help teachers complete CLIL courses, as practice (Kewara, 2017). In this study, we expect to use ID to design CLIL courses, so as to stimulate more potential of CLIL and provide a possible way to design CLIL.

Table 1. The 2 Features (2F), 4Cs, and 5 Dimensions (5D) of CLIL (Coyle et al., 2010)

2 Features	2F-1.Integrating language and content and 2F-2.Flexibility to society and culture
4Cs	4C-1.Contents,4C- 2.Communication, 4C-3.Cognition, and 4C-4.Culture
5 Dimensions	5D-1.Progression in knowledge, 5D-2.Skills and understanding of content, 5D-3.Engagement in higher order cognitive processing, 5D-4.Interaction in the communicative context, and 5D-5.Development of appropriate communication skills, and acquisition of a deepening intercultural awareness

2.2 FPI

In 2002, Merrill advocated the First Principles of Instruction (FPI), which was based on existing ID theories and models. According to FPI, learning is promoted when: (a) learners are engaged in solving real-world problems, (b) existing knowledge becomes the foundation for new knowledge, (c) new knowledge is necessary to demonstrate to the learner, (d) new knowledge is applied by the learner and (e) new knowledge is incorporated into the learner's world (Merrill, 2002).

FPI was intended to identify universal principles of instruction that are common to various ID theories (Cropper et al., 2009). These include: (1) Star Legacy by the Vanderbilt Learning Technology Center, a software shell for instruction (Schwartz et al., 1999); (2) 4-Mat model used by teachers in K-12 education, which is divided into McCarthy (1996); (3) Instructional Episodes describing an instructional episode consisting of three major phases: (a) activation, (b) instructional, and (c) feedback, for supporting instruction rather than a theory (Andre, 1997); (4) Multiple Approaches to Understanding emphasizing the understanding of content rather than problem solving (Gardener, 1999); (5) Collaborative Problem Solving, which is just an extensive list of guidelines, organized under nine process activities: (a) Build readiness, (b) Form and normal groups, (c) Determine a preliminary definition, (d) Define and assign roles, (e) Engage in an iterative collaborative problem solving process, (f) Finalize the solution or project, (g) Synthesize and reflect, (h) Assess products and processes, and (i) Provide closure (Nelson, 1999). (6) Constructivist Learning Environments, which emphasizes problem solving and includes four phases; (a) Attention, (b) Demonstration, (c) Application, and (d) Integration (Jonassen, 1999); and (7) Learning by Doing, which is clearly problem- centered with a very strong emphasis on the application (Schank et al., 1999).

FPI uses cognitive strategy directly and indirectly through intrinsic goal orientation (Lee et al., 2016). In another study, the experimental group using FPI indicated a significant difference between pre- and post-tests at the remembering level and was more confident in solving future problems (Gardner, 2011). FPI is also used to design learning software, which provides a teaching framework for software design (DeWittet al., 2013). Other study has shown that students in biology courses designed with FPI as a framework have better remember level in final exams than students in traditional courses. (Gardner et al., 2017).It can be seen from the preliminary study that FPI has strong universality, using an FPI-based CLIL class is likely to improve the composition of the CLIL and address the issues in the current CLIL research.

3. METHOD

3.1 Course Design

Table 2. The relationship between the content of each class and the elements of FPI and CLIL

FPI Strategy level		Content of Lesson 1	Elements of CLIL (Table1)
Level 0 1-a	Information	Explain the definition of the Johari window and self-disclosure. Teach in Japanese.	4C-1, 5D-1, 2F-1
Level 1	Demonstration	Teacher to introduce herself first.	
1-a,1-b, 2-1-c	A. Consistent	Present the topic of the day. There are four learning activities from low to high throughout the lesson.	4C-2
3-b	B. Guidance	The teacher first introduces herself and provides real-life examples consistent with the subject. She then introduces the social and personal etiquettes that are followed by the Japanese society.	2F-2
3-c	C. Multimedia	Use PowerPoint and pictures to present information. The course materials were uploaded to the Moodle, and the students submitted their comments online at the end of the day.	4C-4
Level 2 4-a	Application	Students introduce themselves. Discuss self-disclosure and analyze their own type.	5D-2, 5D-5
1-a 2-b	A. Consistent	Students use the principles of the Johari window and self-disclosure given to reintroduce themselves.	5D-2
4-b	B. Feedback	Students were given feedback on discussion.	
4-b	C. Coaching	The students were given hints about problems they were unable to understand during the discussion.	
Level 3 4-c	Task-Centered	Give three different levels of self-introduction.	5D-3
2-a 2-b	A. Activation	Utilize the learned knowledge to evaluate the teacher's self-introduction.	4C-3
2-c	B. Structure	In addition to standing up and introducing themselves, there were other challenging activities. First, introducing themselves to the person next to them. Following which students stood in two columns and introduced themselves to the person opposite them.	
5-b	C. Integration	Rethink how to appropriately introduce themselves in diverse scenarios. Reflect on their self-disclosure and compatibility with others in the future.	4C-3
5-a 5-c	D. Peer-Collaboratio and Peer-Critique	Discuss in groups, exchange views, and then speak to the class.	4C-2, 4C-3, 5D-4

*The code "1-a" in the level column indicates the number of stages in the five stages of FPI. The five stages of FPI are as follows: 1.Task-Centered-a. Show task, b. Task level, and c. Problem progression; 2. Activation-a. Previous experience, b. New experience, and c. Structure; 3. Demonstration-a. Demonstration consistency, b. Learner guidance, and c. Relevant media; 4.Application—a. Practice consistency, b. Diminishing coaching, c. Varied problems; and 5. Integration-a. Watch me, b. Reflection, c. Creation

We first determined the content and learning objectives of the course depending on the elements of CLIL. Subsequently, we used FPI to design the content. The goals of this course are as follows, 1. Identify-personal communication styles, 2. Understand multicultural and 3. Improve language and communication skills.

The course covers the following along with cognitive exercise: 1. What is myself?, 2. Image and stereotype, 3. Meeting people, 4. Difference in values, and 5. Moving toward a multi-cultural symbiosis. In addition, the course content, taught only in Japan, covered Japanese etiquettes. We designed the FPI-based checklist to facilitate the design of and control the content, displayed in Table 2. The practice used Moodle at the end of every day to check and comment on the contents. In recent years, research is being conducted on the application of multimedia (as an essential FPI element) and information and communications technologies (ICT) in a class. In this study, we used the open-source solutions, Modular Object-Oriented Dynamic Learning Environment (Moodle), which is widely considered to be user-friendly in higher education (Paulsen, 2003).

3.2 Subjects

The participants were 16 junior Japanese language learners at the University in Republic of China. Among them, ten learners study at the N1 level of the Japanese-Language Proficiency Test (JLPT), five learners at the N2 level of JLPT, and one learner is without a determined level. The learners learned about intercultural education in five days for a total of 15 hours. The course, which was taught in Japanese, commenced with a pre-test and pre-questionnaire and ended with the post-test and post-questionnaire. The test comprised N1 and N2 of the JLPT, while the questionnaire was FPI based (see Appendix 1).

3.3 Data Collection and Analysis

The course lasted for 15 hours over five days. We conducted the pre- and pre-tests and FPI-based pre- and post-questionnaire in this course. Leaners were required to answer the pre-questionnaire before taking this class, and post-one at the end of this course. The post-questionnaire comprised questions about FPI and CLIL. The test included N1 and N2 of the JLPT, including six reading and two listening questions. Each N1 question was scored at two points, while N2 was scored at one point, totaling twelve points. The FPI-based questionnaire included 21 questions. Application contained five questions, while the remaining Task-Centered, Activation, Demonstration, and Integration comprised four questions. CLIL based questionnaire included seven questions, three questions for Content, one for Communication, one for Cognition, and two for Culture, and one about the Moodle. At the end of the course, a questionnaire was conducted on CLIL with one question about the Moodle. The qualitative analysis data was conducted using IBM SPSS Statistics 24.0.

4. RESULTS

Consequently, descriptive statistics and Wilcoxon signed - rank sum test analysis on the test data determined the distribution between the pre- and post-tests, pre- and post-questionnaires. Analysis of the FPI-based questionnaire, revealed that the post-questionnaire (Mean 89.38, Median 90.00, Standard Deviation (SD) 8.53, N=16) average was higher than that of the pre-questionnaire (Mean 74.94, Median 74.50, SD 6.65, N=16). Additionally, a significant difference ($p=0.001$) was noted in the distribution of the questionnaire. Similarly, the post-test average score was higher than that of the pre-test, although the results did not reveal any significant difference (See Table3).

Table 3. The descriptive statistics of test (N=16)

	Mean	Median	SD
Pre-test	8.56	8.00	2.10
Post-test	9.00	9.50	3.12

Subsequently, we used Spearman's rank correlation coefficient method to detect the correlation between each element of FPI and CLIL and the test scores. We added the scores of the problems under each of the FPI and CLIL elements, and the correlation analysis was carried out with the difference of test scores. Correlations among variables are presented in Table 4. A strong correlation was noticed between test scores and FPI, ρ=.97**, $p < .01$; test scores and Activation, ρ=.72**, $p < .01$; test scores and Demonstration, ρ=.57*, $p < .05$; and test scores and Application, ρ=.67**, $p < .01$. A strong correlation was observed between test scores and CLIL, ρ=.69**, $p < .01$; test scores and Contents, ρ=.68**, $p < .01$; and test scores and Culture, ρ=.57*, $p < .05$. A correlation also existed between the FPI and CLIL, ρ=.62**, $p < .01$; FPI and Contents, ρ=.60*, $p < .05$; and FPI and Culture, ρ=.56*, $p < .05$. Activation and CLIL were correlated, ρ=.55*, $p < .05$; Activation and Culture, ρ=.51*, $p < .05$; and Demonstration and Contents, ρ=.50*, $p < .05$. Moodle and Task-Center displayed no correlation with any variables.

Table 4. Correlations among FPI, CLIL and test scores

	Test scores	All of FPI	Task-Centered	Activation	Demonstrati-on	Application	Integration	Moodle
Test scores		.97**	.19	.72**	.57*	.67**	.27	
All of CLIL	.69**	.62**	.14	.55*	.30	.44	-.04	.12
Contents	.68**	.60*	.09	.48	.50*	.46	.04	.14
Communication	.12	.12	-.14	.07	-.17	.31	-.02	-.16
Cognition	.31	.31	-.32	.31	.45	.28	-.27	.36
Culture	.57*	.56*	.27	.51*	.28	.24	.04	.28
Moodle	-.20	-.24	-.04	.00	.09	-.18	-.23	

* $p < .05$. ** $p < .01$.

5. DISCUSSION

Data analysis of FPI-based questionnaire revealed that the average of post-questionnaire was not only higher than the pre-questionnaire but also significantly different. Further, a strong correlation was observed between FPI and CLIL. Thus, in addition to CLIL, FPI can be used as a tool for improving courses and the learning model of flipped classroom; the study indicates that the FPI provides teachers with a way to re-examine the existing teaching models (Hoffman,2014).

In terms of language learning, although the average score of the post-test is higher than that of pre-test, there is no significant difference after statistical analysis. This could be because the test was based on JLPT, and it is difficult to improve a learner's language ability in a short time. However, Dourda et al. (2014) have indicated that in the geographical CLIL class of primary school, the students' geographical performance and the vocabulary and reading ability of foreign languages improved significantly.

Although the pre- and post-test scores did not indicate a significant performance, the test scores were strongly correlated with the FPI and CLIL. In the correlation analysis of the various elements of FPI, a strong correlation was observed between the test scores and Activation, Demonstration, and Application, respectively. Without these three elements, the test scores between the Integration presented no correlation. In the construction strategy of FPI, Integration is at a high strategic level, and it is challenging and relatively difficult to integrate these elements into the curriculum (Merrill, 2013). Test scores and Integration indicated no correlation. In the analysis of the elements of CLIL, test scores and Content and Culture revealed a strong correlation, while Cognition and Communication displayed no correlation. We speculate that such a conclusion could be a result of FPI-based curriculum design without emphasizing the elements of CLIL. However, as the course content involves cultural exchange, there is a correlation between the test scores and Content and Culture.

6. CONCLUSIONS AND FUTURE STUDIES

In this study, we designed FPI-based CLIL courses. Moreover, there was a significant difference in the questionnaire about FPI. Although the test scores were not significant, there was a strong correlation between FPI and CLIL. FPI-based CLIL courses are likely to address the problems raised by previous studies.

There are a few limitations to this study. Since there is no accurate measurement of FPI scale, the questionnaire used in this practice was designed by referring to the questionnaire of other ID theories; hence, it is necessary to improve the reliability of the questionnaire. In the descriptive statistics, the SD value of test scores is large, indicating that there is an obviously personal difference between students. In future research, it is necessary to study the reasons for the differences between students. In addition, this study considered the JLPT, and did not involve teaching content. In upcoming studies, teaching content should be added to the test. In terms of correlation, we can interview the students and use qualitative analysis to discuss the cause of the correlations. Although Moodle was used in practice, it was limited to uploading learning materials and submitting homework. Timely feedback was not given after submission. Other functions of the Moodle collaboration tools should be used in future studies. Collaboration tools such as teleconference seem to be effective on language proficiency (e.g., Yamada and Kitamura, 2011; Goda et al, 2014). There are only 16 samples in this study, and the analysis results are not widely applicable. In the following study, the number of samples will be continuously increased to enhance the credibility of the data.

ACKNOWLEDGEMENT

This research was partially supported by JSPS Grant-in-aid for Scientific Research(S) (B) JP16H03080, and the Qdai-jump Research (QR) Program of Kyushu University.

REFERENCES

Cenoz, J. & F. Genesee, et al., 2014. Critical Analysis of CLIL: Taking Stock and Looking Forward. *Applied Linguistics,* Vol.35, No.3,pp 243-262.

Coyle, D., Hood, P., & Marsh, D., 2010. *CLIL: Content and language integrated learning.* Cambridge University Press, England, Cambridge.

Dooly, M., & Masats, D., 2015. A critical appraisal of foreign language research in content and language integrated learning, young language learners, and technology-enhanced language learning published in Spain (2003–2012). *Language Teaching*, Vol.48, No.3,pp 343-372.

DeWitt, D., Siraj, S., Alias, N., & Leng, C. H., 2013. Retrospective Evaluation of a Collaborative Learning Science Module: The Users' Perspective. *Malaysian Online Journal of Educational Technology*, Vol. 1, No. 2,pp 33-43.

Dourda, K., Bratitsis, T., Griva, E., & Papadopoulou, P., 2014. Content and language integrated learning through an online game in primary school: a case study. *Electronic Journal of e-Learning*, Vol.12, No. 3,pp 243-258.

European Commission, 2005, *Education and Culture at a glance*, European Commission, Brussels.

Gardner, J., 2011. Testing the efficacy of Merrill's First Principles of Instruction in improving student performance in introductory biology courses. *Unpublished doctoral dissertation*. Utah State University, Logan, Utah.

Gardner, J., & Belland, B. R., 2017. Problem-Centered Supplemental Instruction in Biology: Influence on Content Recall, Content Understanding, and Problem Solving Ability. *Journal of Science Education and Technology*, Vol.26, No.4, pp 383-393

Goda, Y., Yamada, M., Matsukawa, H., Hata, K., & Yasunami, S., 2014. Conversation with a chatbot before an online EFL group discussion and the effects on critical thinking, The Journal of Information and Systems in Education, Vol.13, No.1, pp. 1-7, 10.12937/ejsise.13.1

Kewara, P., 2017. Phrasebook: a Way out for CLIL Teachers in Thailand. *Latin American Journal of Content and Language Integrated Learning*, Vol.10, No.1,pp 49-73.

Hoffman, E. S., 2014. Beyond the flipped classroom: Redesigning a research methods course for e3 instruction. *Contemporary Issues in Education Research (Online)*, Vol.7, No.1,pp51-62

Paulsen, M., 2003. Experiences with Learning Management Systems in 113 European Institutions. *Educational Technology & Society*, Vol.6, No.4,pp 134-148.

Lee, S. & T. A. Koszalka, 2016. Course-level implementation of First Principles, goal orientations, and cognitive engagement: a multilevel mediation model. *Asia Pacific Education Review,* Vol.17, No.2,pp 365-375.

Maljers, A., Marsh, D., Wolff, D., Genesee, F., Frigols-Martín, M., & Mehisto, P., 2010. *Diverse Contexts-Converging Goals: CLIL in Europe*, Peter Lang, Frankfurt.

Merrill, M. D., 2002. First principles of instruction. *Educational Technology Research and Development,* Vol.50, No.3, pp 43-59

Merrill, M. D., 2012. *First Principles of Instruction*, John Wiley & Sons, NJ

Meyer, O., 2010. Introducing the CLIL-pyramid: key strategies and principles for quality CLIL planning and teaching. *Basic Issues in EFL-Teaching and Learning*, Winter, Heidelberg.

Sabet, M. K. & N. Sadeh, 2012. CLIL European-Led Projects and Their Implications for Iranian EFL Context. *English Language Teaching,* Vol.5, No.9,pp 88-94

Sylvén, L. K., 2015. CLIL and non-CLIL students' beliefs about language. *Studies in Second Language Learning and Teaching,* Vol.5 No.2,pp 251-272.

Yamada, M., & Kitamura, S., 2011. The role of social presence in interactive learning with social software. In B. White, I. King, & P. Tsang (Eds.), Social Media Tools and Platforms in Learning Environments: Present and Future (pp.325-335). Heidelberg, Germany: Springer.

Appendix 1. The questions of FPI questionnaire

Task-Centered

1. Where you given a specific task in this class?
2. Are you interested in this lesson?
3. Did the teacher tell you about the role of the task in this course?
4. Did you feel that the composition of this course changed from simple to complicated?

Activation

1. Were you able to recall your past experience in this course?
2. Did you relate the past experience to the new knowledge?
3. Did you use the past experience in this class?
4. Through this lesson, did you structure the past experience and new knowledge?

Demonstration

1. Did the teacher give examples during the class?
2. Was the example given by the teacher consistent with the learning content?
3. Did the teacher give a proper explanation when giving examples?
4. Was there a proper use of multimedia in the course?

Application

1. Was the new knowledge applied in class?
2. Were group activities aligned with the learning objectives of the course?
3. Did the teacher give appropriate guidance and feedback?
4. Did you feel that as your abilities improve, your teacher's guidance diminishes?
5. Did you feel that the topic of group activities has gradually changed from a single problem to a complex one?

Integration

1. Do you think what you learn in this class can be applied to your life?
2. Is the knowledge you have learned visible to others?
3. Did you do any reflection in class?
4. Have you ever thought about how to apply what you have learned in a creative way?

Appendix 2. The questions of CLIL questionnaire

1. Do you think the learning objectives of this course are clear?
2. Do you understand the content of the course?
3. Have you built your own knowledge system through this course?
4. Does this course deepen your understanding of the Japanese culture?
5. Do you think the Japanese culture introduced in the course is closely related to the learning theme?
6. The teacher taught in Japanese. Do you think it is necessary to add Chinese language to assist?
7. Do you think the Moodle aids your learning?

PROPOSING AND EVALUATING A MODEL OF CO-CONSTRUCTION OF THE LEARNING SCENARIO BY THE LEARNER

Guy Merlin Mbatchou[1,2], François Bouchet[1], Thibault Carron[1] and Philippe Pernelle[3]
[1]*Sorbonne Université, CNRS, Laboratoire d'Informatique de Paris 6, LIP6, F-75005 Paris, France*
[2]*Université Assane Seck de Ziguinchor, Ziguinchor, Sénégal*
[3]*Université Claude Bernard Lyon 1, France*

ABSTRACT

To improve the learning process, the evolution of learner's characteristics (cognitive, affective, prior knowledge, workflow, organization, ...) must be taken into account during the personalization or adaptation. This requires generating several scenarios (a description of activities, their order and links in the learning sequence as well as the expected outcome for the learner) adapted to the identified profiles. We propose a model which aims at improving learners' learning processes by giving them control over two key aspects: (1) the steps of the learning scenario to be followed: after each learning goal is completed, the learner chooses the next one among the possible ones (in terms of their current knowledge) while respecting pedagogical constraints (time and quality of the solutions produced according to satisfaction thresholds); (2) the assessment mode: the learner chooses a mode corresponding to their own goals in terms of mastery, while respecting the minimum thresholds set by the teacher. We assess our approach with learners in terms of (a) adequacy of the model with learners' expectations, (b) usability of the system and (c) learning experience satisfaction, through self-report questionnaires and an analysis of the data collected over 11 learners who used an implementation of our system on the LMS (Learning Management System) in the context of a real course on Economy. The results reveal an a priori acceptance of our model, a diversity of the scenarios constructed, and the use of 2 (out of 3) assessment modes to progress. We use these results to analyze current limits of the system and propose redesign ideas to minimize them.

KEYWORDS

Learner-directed Learning, Learning Challenge, Personalized Learning Scenario, Personalized Learning Goals, Co-construction of Learning Scenario, Learning Path

1. INTRODUCTION

The teacher creates a knowledge-based course with well-defined learning goals. The course is then organized in a scenario which guides teaching and learning. This standard scenario, as envisioned by the teacher, can be inappropriate or at least suboptimal for some learners, because the learning also depends on their personal characteristics (*e.g.* pace of work, cognitive styles, emotional factors, prior knowledge). To improve the learning process, it is therefore ideal for each learner to have their own personalized scenario. Moreover, while learning, some characteristics of the learner may change (*e.g.* more motivation to learn about a topic than another, less time because of personal issues), making the scenario, as defined initially, less and less appropriate. It would be difficult for the teacher, particularly in an online context, to detect the change in the learners' characteristics to propose a new adapted scenario. However, this detection is achievable by computer-based methods based on the exploitation of learning traces, learner modeling (Greer and McCalla, 2013) and intelligent tutoring systems (Ma et al., 2014). However, these methods usually require an important quantity of traces (hard for courses with few students enrolled) and when new profiles are detected the system may need reengineering or a refinement of some parameters. Thus, there can be issues relative to the real-time detection of changes in learner profiles to assign them an appropriate scenario. More fundamentally, various works on metacognition and self-regulation show that involving the learner, for instance by making them choose their learning goals, can lead to deeper learning and increased motivation (Harley et al., 2018), compared to a linear more passive way predefined by the teacher. This approach forces the learners to re-evaluate their decision if they realize they have chosen an activity for which they do not master yet all the required skills.

Following these observations, this paper focuses on the co-construction of the learning scenario by the learners, as they learn, to make the learning process or acquisition of knowledge more efficient. We use the term "co-construction" because although the next learning goal depends on the learner, the range of their choice is constrained by the teacher, to prevent them from making illogical choices (*e.g.* trying to acquire a competence before its prerequisite). In this context, our research questions are: (RQ1) Can we set up a model allowing each learner to co-construct his or her scenario during the learning process? (RQ2) Is such a model understandable and acceptable to learners? (RQ3) How do learners use the possibilities of co-construction made available to them? Our contribution is to provide learners with conceptual and technological tools to build their learning scenario in a learning context imposed by the teacher and supported by technology.

The remainder of this paper is organized as follows. In section 2, we present a brief overview of related works on personalization and adaptation of learning. Section 3 presents our model of co-construction of the learning scenario. Section 4 presents our implementation of the model in the LMS. Section 5 presents results of an evaluation of our approach in terms of acceptability of the model by learners, but also an evaluation of the system usability through an analysis of data collected in a preliminary experiment conducted in real situation with a class of students. We conclude on opportunities for some system redesign ideas.

2. RELATED WORK

The description of a learning scenario can be formalized with the Educational Modeling Language (EML) (Koper and Manderveld, 2004) which offers the modeling of reusable, interoperable, rich and customizable learning units. Through personalization and reuse, it is possible to design several scenarios, but the EML language does not provide ways to switch from one scenario to another during the learning. This is because the scenario design is generally based on the intentions of teachers (Emin et al., 2010) (teacher-centered pedagogy) and on pedagogical goals (Dalziel, 2008) (content-centered pedagogy). Some works have tried to be closer to a learner-centered pedagogy, for instance by taking into account teachers' intentions, activities to do by learners and learner interactions (Mariais et al., 2010).

To design a pedagogical scenario, (Esnault and Daele, 2003) defined 17 dimensions of question, taking into account learners' individual differences. However, to take this personalization into account, the scenario designer must know the learners' profiles in advance. Even if new scenarios can be designed by reuse and adaptation of existing ones (Riad et al., 2012), profiles can evolve during the learning process and no personalized path corresponds to the new profile. (Marne and Labat, 2014) proposed a scenario based on activities with several input and output states. The links between activities based on prerequisite relationships among them makes it possible to have several learning paths. However, their model, defined in a context of serious games, does not give the learner the possibility to choose the scenario to follow.

The Competence-based Knowledge Space Theory (CbKST) offers a model for structuring competences-based learning for personalization (Heller et al., 2006). From the relationship of prerequisite among competences, the model constructs several recommended learning paths (Kopeinik et al., 2012). Each path is composed of knowledge states (set of competences acquired in a particular field). From a knowledge state, the learner progresses in their learning by choosing a competence to acquire that will bring them into a new higher knowledge state. The learning is complete when the learner is in the terminal knowledge state (state with all acquired competences). Although the CbKST offers several learning paths, it does not consider learning constraints (temporal and qualitative related to satisfaction threshold of activities) in choices of paths, nor multi-goal activities (*e.g.* case studies), nor the conditions to change paths (*e.g.* a change can take place after a certain number of failures or the incapability to reach a fixed goal or a temporal constraint non-respected).

3. CO-CONSTRUCTION MODEL OF SCENARIO DURING LEARNING

3.1 Core Concepts of the Model

Knowledge acquisition is rarely linear: there are many ways to do it, depending on the learning goal. But to build a scenario, the course design model must allow it. Our model relies on five concepts (*cf.* Figure 1):

1. **Decomposition of knowledge by learning goal to be achieved.** Time constraints are associated with each goal. Satisfaction thresholds are added to constrain learners' efforts.
2. **Encapsulation of knowledge in learning resources for learning goals.** This encapsulation guarantees modularity in a course since a resource is reusable in another course without modification.
3. **Assessment of acquired knowledge.** We define activities to assess the learning. To prevent assessment from depending on only one activity, we define for each activity a percentage of participation in knowledge validation. An activity can also contribute to the validation of several knowledge.
4. **Prerequisites between knowledge.** There can be many ways to learn a course, but there are nevertheless order constraints, taken into account in our model by a prerequisites graph between the goals.
5. **Grouping learning goals into learning units.** To be close to the teachers' practice, the goals are grouped into learning units (generally parts, chapters, titles, ...).

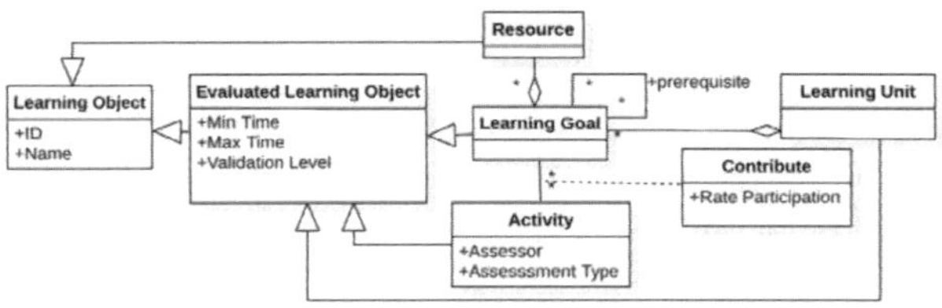

Figure 1. Class diagram of learning objects for course design

Our model constructs several learning scenarios by articulating the learning objects. In a previous work, we have also assessed our model acceptability (https://goo.gl/forms/ne1Uua4UeYPW3EeO2) from the teacher's point of view (Mbatchou et al., 2018), showing their willingness to use it. An experiment with 16 teachers from 8 specialties also allowed us to (1) detect and correct the inconsistencies in their educational productions; (2) find that certain goals of their course are not related to others; (3) find that there is little prerequisite relationship between goals; (4) to note the multiplicity of scenarios in their course.

3.2 Scenario Building

The model is meant to provide learners with an environment allowing them to learn the way they want while respecting the rules and constraints of learning. We assume that we do not have a priori learner profiles, as learners' profiles are dynamic and we do not want to regularly ask learners to self-report their motivation, time, etc. Learners need to build their scenario as they learn. The model is based on knowledge states to enable each learner to situate themselves in their learning and to progress. A knowledge state is a state that describes acquired and validated knowledge by a learner; it is composed by achieved learning goals. The knowledge states are produced and associated according to the Knowledge Spaces Theory to obtain different learning paths. The learning process is to guide the learner from initial state to final state. The learning constraints defined by the teacher when designing learning objects is an implicit guidance contributing to co-construction. Learning is supervised by a human tutor as a learning facilitator (role not detailed in this paper).

During the learning process, the system determines the learner's knowledge state and offers them a set of goals to achieve. Then for the chosen goal, the system proposes a set of resources and activities that will allow them to reach it. After an assessment that the knowledge is acquired, the system determines their new knowledge state. If they are unable to perform a given activity (resp. progress in a chosen scenario), the learner can abandon it and choose another activity (resp. scenario) offered by the system in the same scenario (resp. according to the learning goals).

The model integrates knowledge assessment modes to progress in learning. The choice of the mode depends on the challenge that the learner sets for themselves at any moment. Since the learner is situated in learning by their knowledge state, suppose a state with P goals $\{G_1, G_2, \ldots, G_P\}$. Each G_i has a set of learning activities $\{A^i_1, A^i_2, \ldots, A^i_{Ni}\}$ for validating the acquired knowledge. Each activity A^i_j has a percentage of participation P^i_j to achieve the goal G_i. When a learner chooses to perform the activity A^i_j we keep the obtained value V^i_j to compute the score obtained for this goal. The validation of each goal (G_i) is constrained by a threshold (S_i). To validate his state with P goals, the learner has the following modes:

Assessment mode by flexible compensation. The state is validated if $\sum_{i=1}^{P}\sum_{j=1}^{Ni} P^i_j V^i_j \geq \sum_{i=1}^{P} S_i$. So, learner can progress with few efforts made on certain goals because he can obtain them by compensation.

Assessment mode by restrictive compensation. With the previous mode, a learner can validate a state even with one goal with a very low level of satisfaction. To avoid this case, in compensation mode, the learner must make minimum efforts for each goal. The state is validated if $\prod_{i=1}^{P}\sum_{j=1}^{Ni} P^i_j V^i_j \geq \prod_{i=1}^{P} S_i$.

Strict assessment mode. This mode allows challengers learners to master all goals of a state before progressing. The state is validated if $\forall\, i, 1 \leq i \leq P, \sum_{j=1}^{Ni} P^i_j V^i_j \geq S_i$. The quality of the built scenario is better if the strict mode is used throughout the learning.

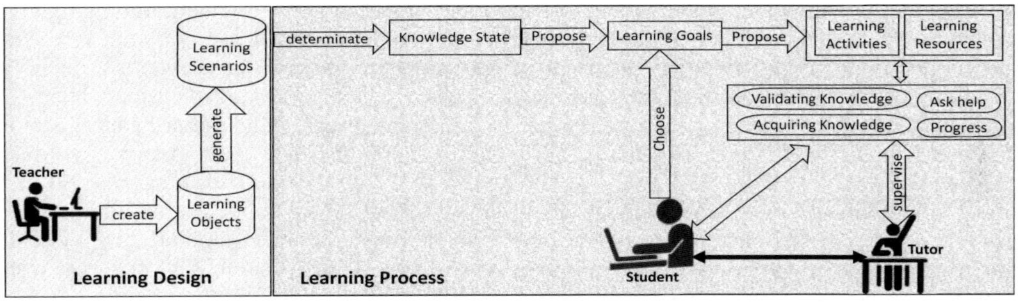

Figure 2. Learning process

4. SYSTEM OVERVIEW

We chose to implement our model as a plugin in MOODLE (Modular-Object Oriented Dynamic Learning Environment), which is the LMS used in our test university (the model being platform-independent). The plugin is named EGbKST (Educational Goal based Knowledge Space Theory) and has a dynamic interface for learning (*cf.* Figure 3) and a visualization interface of its results that is visible only at the request of the learner (not presented here). Learning is organized in dynamic blocks (Communication, Statistics, Resource, Goal and Activities) whose content and visibility depends on each learner and their knowledge state.

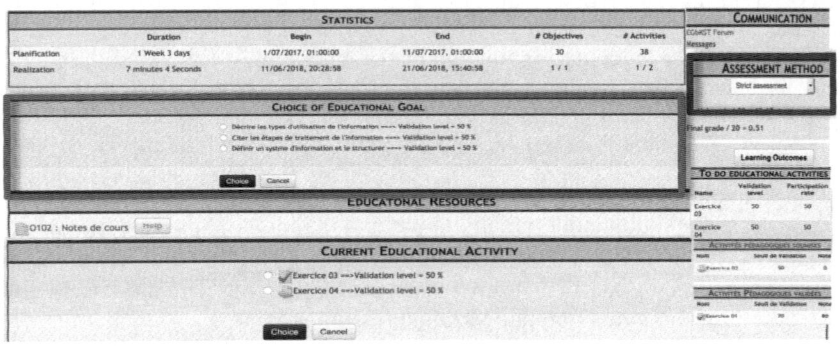

Figure 3. Learning interface

The learner initially chooses a goal to achieve (block in green). As soon as it is reached, the system offers them a new set of goals they can achieve and so on. The learning ends when the learner has achieved all the goals. The goals and the order in which they are chosen represent the scenario built by learner. The system allows to change current goal to choose another one if necessary. To progress in learning, the learner has a list of assessment modes (block in red) to choose from to express their desired degree of challenge. The efforts made and the chosen mode allow it to progress at a higher knowledge state.

So, we answered positively to our first research question, proposing a model that allows learners to co-construct their learning scenario.

5. ASSESSING CO-CONSTRUCTION OF SCENARIO BY LEARNERS

5.1 Methodology

The experiment was realized in 3 phases in a public university in sub-Saharan Africa, with nearly 3500 students enrolled in 21 academic sections and 120 teachers in 15 specialties (from bachelor to doctorate).

Phase 1: Assessing the acceptability of the model by the learners. To answer our second research question, we submitted a survey to students (https://goo.gl/forms/EgiVdEgE1z8mfFQr1). The survey questions are in affirmative form with responses on a 4-point Likert scale extending from "strongly disagree" to "strongly agree". The survey collected student opinion on the following aspects: (1) Current educational model: the question is to find if they find that (a) the courses have clearly defined and identifiable educational goals, (b) for the defined goals, do they have learning resources and activities to evaluate them? (c) can the learning be done in a different order than the teacher's? (2) Interests for a goal-based educational model: the question is to know if they think that a such model would facilitate their learning and success. The questionnaire was sent to all 3500 students, but we received only 85 responses (Consulted at 11-24-2017). This can be explained by the fact very few students are trained to take online courses (around 250 students have access to online training platform). Participants come from 14 academic sections and 3 teaching cycles. Their age varying between under 18 years to over 45 (M = 21.60, SD = 6.46). 80% of survey responses are from learners who have been trained in the use of online learning platform.

In view of the response rate, these results should be taken with caution, because it probably over represents certain categories of students (*e.g.* motivated, technophiles). To counter this potential bias, we also asked those questions to the 11 students who tested the system (*cf.* below).

Phase 2: Assessing the usability of the system. We tested the usability of our system during a real-life experiment on the "General Political Economy 1" teaching unit taught in the 1st year of the Legal Sciences academic section for 2 ECTS credits. Students ($N = 11$) are professionals in continuing training whose age vary between 24 to over 50 ($M = 36.22$, $SD = 6.38$). To carry out this experimentation, the teacher agreed to adapt his course according to our model (29 learning goals, 33 learning resources, 31 learning activities and a teacher-recommended scenario). Learning takes place over 2 weeks. The resources are a mix of files, hyperlinks and videos. The activities are of the production type and quiz (true/false, yes/no, matching, single choice and multiple choice). The experience is organized in 2 stages. Stage 1 took place in a 2-hour classroom session during which we explained to learners and tutors how the new teaching model worked. Stage 2 consisted to learn online under supervision of tutor.

Phase 3: Assessing the learning satisfaction of the learners. At the end of the course, learners filled a survey (http://foad.uasz.gouv.sn/mod/questionnaire/view.php?id=5274) evaluating their satisfaction with the new learning model. The survey questions are in statements with a 4-point Likert scale (from "strongly disagree" to "strongly agree"), focusing on the perceived impact of the model on ease of learning and contribution to success.

Assessment of the model acceptability (phase 1) is done with the Google Forms tool, with data saved in a CSV (Comma-Separated Values) file. During learning (phase 2), learner interactions with the system are recorded in a plain text log file in which each line contains a quintuplet (date, action, object, score, learner), corresponding to the action done by a learner on a learning object. The data (CSV file) of the learning satisfaction (phase 3) are collected from the Moodle platform of training.

To validate our third research question, we considered 2 indicators: diversity of scenarios and of assessment modes. **The diversity of scenarios** allows to determine if co-constructed scenarios are different. For each learner, we extract successive learning goals followed in chronological order. For those who have not completed their learning, we compare their learning sequence with the corresponding sequence in the reference teacher-recommended scenario (*e.g.* the first 5 steps for a learner who dropped out after 5 steps).

The diversity of scenarios is represented by the number of different scenarios and the distance between alternative scenarios (distance based on the Levenshtein distance - when computing distances between scenarios, we only consider sequences of identical length). **The diversity of assessment modes** allows to determine the willingness of each learner to progress according to the mode chosen at each learning stage. This indicator is broken down into 2 sub-indicators: the percentage of time that each assessment mode is used to progress, and for each mode, the number of learners who used it and the number of times used.

5.2 Results and Discussion

5.2.1 Acceptability of the Model by the Learners

The acceptance of the model is assessed in the general framework with all 85 respondents. We present below the results and then contrast them with the results obtained with the 11 students involved in the experiment.

Current educational model. The survey shows that the courses are organized mainly in chapters (81.2%) and often in parts (32.9%). 27% of participants estimate that certain learning goals do not have learning resources clearly associated to them. 3.5% of participants believe that in some courses, goals are not announced. Results are more concerning for exercises, for which 50.7% learners estimate that educational goals are not assessed. This finding justifies our approach to associate resources and exercises with each goal to better structure and facilitate learning. 70.6% of participants' estimate that the course could be better learned with a different scenario than the one imposed by the teacher. We conclude that current educational model contains weaknesses identified by learners and their wish reinforces our approach of co-construction.

Interests of pedagogical model based on goals. 81.2% of learners estimate that learning would be easier if it is organized and presented by goals and not by chapter. 91.8% of them believe they would obtain better results if they were assessed by goal. The results obtained from the 11 students of our experiment are similar to those obtained on the larger sample. The only difference is the availability (online) of resources and activities for the goals. This difference is justified by the fact that online course procedure requires the availability of resources and activities for each learning sequence.

We thus can respond positively to our RQ2: our approach seems in agreement with learners' expectations.

5.2.2 Scenarios Diversity

To visualize different scenarios followed by the learners, we represented each stage of the scenario of each learner with a different color (with gray corresponding to identical steps in teacher-recommended scenario – *cf.* Figure 4). We can see that the learners have built 4 of 11 possible scenarios (called call A, B, C and D), where scenario A is built by 72.7% of learners (*cf.* Figure 5) and corresponds to the one recommended by the teacher. We think this high preference rate is related to a system bias, because the proposed goals for the choice appeared numbered. Therefore, it seems normal that learners chose the natural order (increasing) of goals when they did not have strong preferences. The distance between the scenarios shows that scenario C (resp. D) is the most distant (resp. close) to the recommended one (*cf.* Figure 6). These results show that when giving choice to the learners to build their own scenario, they can build a variety of logical scenarios while respecting to pedagogical constraints. It should be noted that possible variability of the scenarios was limited by the fact that the teacher had chosen to impose the order of chapters. For example, it was not possible to move to a goal in chapter 2 as long as all the learning goals of the first chapter were not validated.

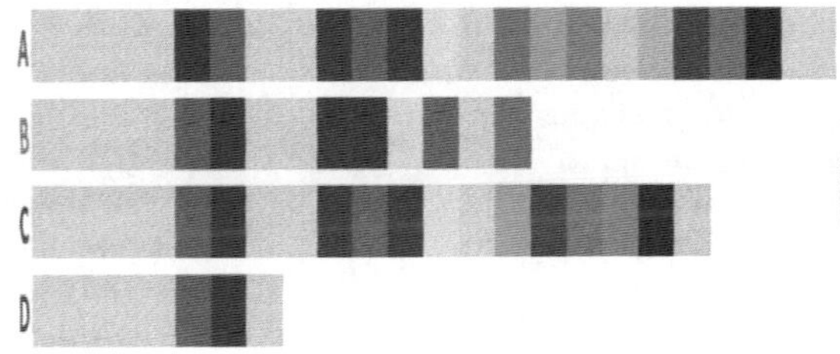

Figure 4. Visualization of 4 scenarios built by learners

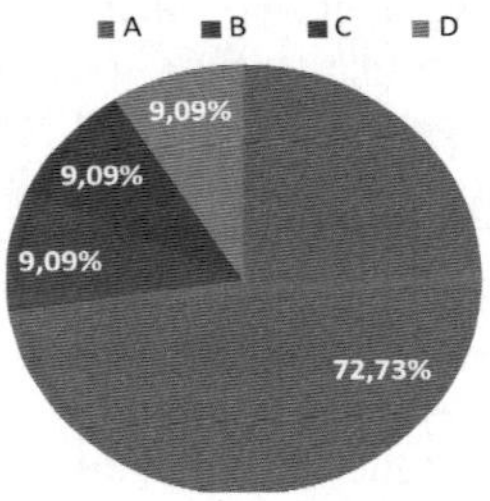

Figure 5. Representation of learners by scenario

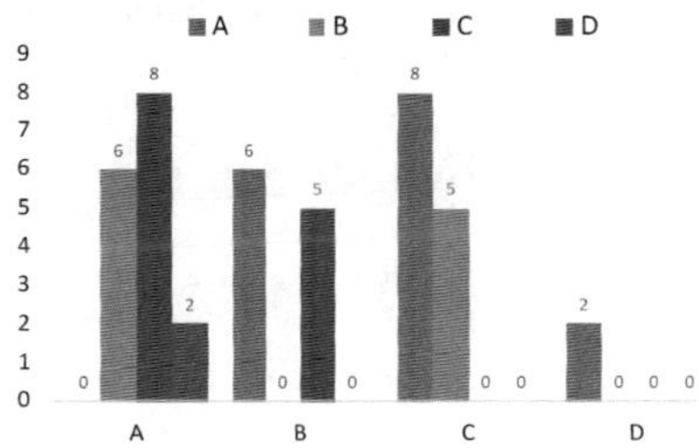

Figure 6. Levenshtein distance between different scenarios

5.2.3 Assessment Modes Diversity

Although the strict mode is the most difficult, we found that all learners used it more than 75% of the time (*cf.* Figure 8). This mode is selected by default at the beginning of learning, which can justify that all learners are assessed in this mode at least once. Nonetheless, the number of times used shows the desire to remain in this mode. This point of view is reinforced by a manual trace analysis which reveals that certain learners (*e.g.* L05 and L09 in Figure 7) return to certain activities to improve their score to stay in this mode. Except for 4 learners (*cf.* Figure 7), we find that they are challengers (learners who like to validate all activities without compensation). We think that once the learners have changed the assessment mode, they want to progress quickly and therefore preferred the flexible mode over the restrictive one. We also find that all learners who changed their mode stopped some time after and did not view all the educational content. This could mean that changing to flexible mode indicates future dropout, and that could be brought to the teacher's attention.

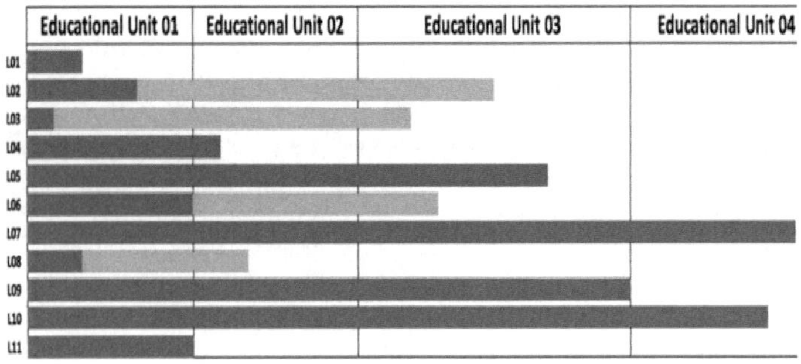

Figure 7. Scenario representation of each learner by assessment mode (Strict mode in green; Flexible mode in orange)

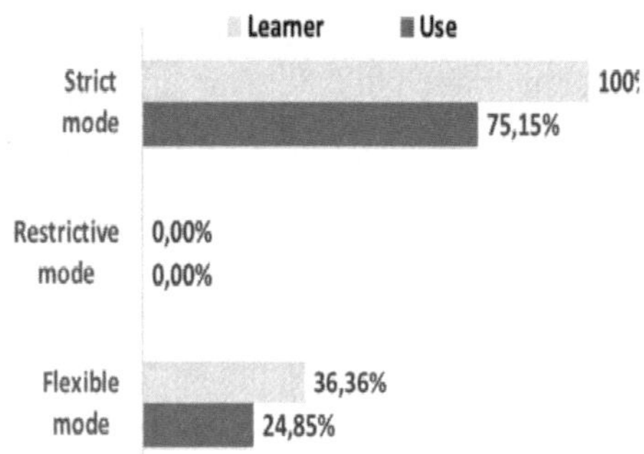

Figure 8. Representation of learners and progress number by assessment mode

5.2.4 The Learning Satisfaction of the Learners

54.5% (6 of 11) of learners answered to the post-study survey (4 of them reached the third learning unit). 50% estimate that their learning was facilitated by the initial goal announcement. 66.7% thought the course presentation by goal (*vs.* by chapter) facilitated their learning, confirming the value of our approach which propose to structure a course by goal to facilitate its accessibility. 50% said they liked choosing their learning path because they are central actors of their learning, confirming our observation that the diversity of scenarios is well appreciated and used. However only learner L07 explicitly declared thinking his success was related to our approach. Conversely, learner L02 said: "*This software causes a lot of problem because my progress was very slow. The internet connection caused me great prejudice. (...) I propose to let us continue with the old method.*". The main reason is that our approach requires frequent connection to assess their learning to unlock the next learning content, which can be an issue in the sub-Saharan African context.

5.3 Analysis for Reengineering

This experiment revealed system weaknesses to correct to avoid bias in the analysis of learners' behaviors.

Bias when constructing a scenario. To correct it, we will hide goal numbers and instead present for each goal metadata such as duration, validation threshold, description, the number of resources and activities. This change should allow for a greater diversity of scenarios and more meaningful choices.

Decision between challenge and progression. We realized that some learners stay on strict assessment mode while they are not progressing. We propose to find a mode that allows them to progress and recommend it. This decision is made because we think some learners forgot they could change their mode.

Choice of assessment mode. To avoid a default mode, we will explicitly ask learner to choose their assessment mode at the beginning of the learning.

Risk of school dropout. Whenever the learner changes their assessment mode to a less challenging mode, we will notify the teacher and ask the learner, the reasons of change to better understand their motivations.

6. CONCLUSION

Giving learners the opportunity to build their scenario while learning, making them a main actor of its co-construction, is not really considered in recent research in TEL. Our model shows that it is possible, and that the built scenarios respect educational constraints defined by the teacher. Experiments led with teachers and learners show their satisfaction and the ability of the model to improve both the learning and teaching processes. The diversity of scenarios built by learners revealed that some learners seem to prefer a different approach than the teacher's default one. Moreover, the model offers learners to modify their assessment mode at any time. Their desire to be challenged (strict mode used more than 75% of the time) is a sign that our model offers a motivating framework to better acquire competences. This is confirmed by the fact some learners returned on previous activities to improve their score to remain in a strict assessment mode. We observed that some learners prefer the challenging mode, even if it slowed down their progress. To avoid drop-out, we plan to identify this indicator moment and recommend using a less challenging mode.

Among the limits of this work, the context of our experimentation (few online learners in sub-Saharan Africa) does not allow us to fully validate our approach – integration to a MOOC could help reaching a more reliable conclusion. Moreover, our model is only applicable for learning by competences or educational goals. A first analysis of learning traces allowed us to define reengineering axes, which will give us more accurate learning tools and highlight the existing ones.

In future work, we will integrate into the model the analysis of the chosen scenario and present it to the learner. When they face difficulties while diverging from the reference scenario, we may redirect them towards the reference scenario. Moreover, traces analysis over several courses could help in identifying patterns and thus learner profiles and learning indicators that will help us to guide or redirect future learners.

REFERENCES

Dalziel, J., 2008. Using LAMS Version 2 for a game-based Learning Design. *J. Interact. Media Educ.* 2008.

Emin, V., Pernin, J.-P., Aguirre, J.L., 2010. ScenEdit: An Intention-Oriented Authoring Environnment to Design Learning Scenarios. *In: Wolpers, M., Kirschner, P.A., Scheffel, M., Lindstaedt, S., Dimitrova, V. (Eds.), Sustaining TEL: From Innovation to Learning and Practice, LNCS*. Springer, Berlin, Heidelberg, pp. 626–631.

Esnault, L. and Daele, A., 2003. Higher Education and ICT: Questions to Design Successful Pedagogical scenarios to Improve the Learning Process. Presented at the *E-Learn: World Conf. on E-Learning in Corporate, Government, Healthcare, and Higher Education, (AACE)*, pp. 944–951.

Greer, J.E. and McCalla, G.I., 2013. Student Modelling: The Key to Individualized Knowledge-Based Instruction. *Springer Science & Business Media*.

Harley, J.M., Taub, M., Azevedo, R., Bouchet, F., 2018. "Let's Set Up Some Subgoals": Understanding Human-Pedagogical Agent Collaborations and Their Implications for Learning and Prompt and Feedback Compliance. *IEEE Trans. Learn. Technol.* 11, 54–66.

Heller, J., Steiner, C., Hockemeyer, C., Albert, D., 2006. Competence-Based Knowledge Structures for Personalised Learning. *Int. J. E-Learn.* 5, 75–88.

Kopeinik, S., Nussbaumer, A., Bedek, M., Alber, D., 2012. Using CbKST for Learning Path Recommendation in Game-based Learning. In: *Proceedings of the 20th International Conf. on Computers in Education.* Singapore, pp. 26–30.

Koper, R., Manderveld, J., 2004. Educational modelling language: modelling reusable, interoperable, rich and personalised units of learning. *Br. J. Educ. Technol.* 35, 537–551.

Ma, W., Adesope, O.O., Nesbit, J.C., Liu, Q., 2014. Intelligent tutoring systems and learning outcomes: A meta-analysis. *J. Educ. Psychol.* 106, 901–918.

Mariais, C., Michau, F., Pernin, J.-P., 2010. The use of Game Principles in the Design of Learning Role-Playing Game Scenarios. In: *Proc. of the 4th European Conf. on Games Based Learning. Academic Publishing Ltd*, pp. 462–469.

Marne, B. and Labat, J.M., 2014. Model and authoring tool to help teachers adapt serious games to their educational contexts. *Int. J. Learn. Technol.* 9, 161–180.

Mbatchou, G.M., Bouchet, F., Carron, T., 2018. Multi-scenario modelling of learning. In: *Proc. of the 8th Conf. on Research in Computer Science and Its Applications.* Ziguinchor, Sénégal, *C. M. F. Kebe et al. (Eds.): InterSol 2018, LNICST* 249, pp. 1–13, https://doi.org/10.1007/978-3-319-98878-8_19.

Riad, B., Mourad, H., Nourredine, G., Hamid, S., 2012. The scenarization: a new task for teachers. *Procedia - Soc. Behav. Sci., World Conference on Learning, Teaching & Administration* - 2011 31, 732–737.

GAMESONOMY VS SCRATCH: TWO DIFFERENT WAYS TO INTRODUCE PROGRAMMING

Cristina Rebollo Santamaría, Carlos Marín Lora, Inmaculada Remolar Quintana and Miguel Chover Sellés
Institute of New Imaging Technologies, Universitat Jaume I, 12071 – Castellón, Spain

ABSTRACT

The first obstacles to overcome when a student has to face the task of programming for the first time are the abstraction level, the comprehension of a language with unfamiliar concepts for him/her and the specific syntax for each programming language. This work presents the qualitative results obtained in a study focused on the gain of skills for learning programming languages. The experiment has been carried out in a classroom with 50 university students from the second year of the Degree in Video Game Design and Development. Students have worked with Scratch programming language on their first year, a tool created to facilitate programming learning, and with Gamesonomy, a game engine created to ease video game development without programming knowledge. The main purpose of this work is focused on the question: which one of these two tools is more appealing, easy to understand and to use, as well as which one of them is more efficient for a further initiation on the traditional programming. To test them, the students have fulfilled an evaluation test for each tool. After the analysis of the results, it is concluded that Gamesonomy seems to be more efficient to develop logical thinking and to have a better transition to conventional programming languages.

KEYWORDS

Game Engine, Visual Programming, Logical Thinking

1. INTRODUCTION AND LITERATURE REVIEW

The ability to code computer programs is an important part in today's society. One of the main problems to face a student on his/her first year computer science, comes from the abstraction and the inherent complexity of a programming language with unknown concepts such as variables, loops, matrices, functions and rest of specific syntax for each different programming language.

In order to comprehend any programming language, it is essential to develop a logical thinking. In 2006 (Wing, J., 2006), the computational thinking concept was defined as "problem solving, system design and understating of human behavior, by using the fundamental concepts of computer science". According to Grover and Pea (Grover, S., Pea, R., 2013) programming is not only a fundamental ability of computer science and a key tool to develop cognitive tasks involved in computational thinking, but also a way to improve students' thinking skills.

We could consider two different programming ways: conventional programming (Van Roy P. et al., 2003), (Jackson M., 1980) and visual programming (Chang, S.K., 1990), (Good, J., 2011). The first one is based on writing code, and the second one is based on a friendly visual environment easy to use (Repenning, A., 2017). Some examples of these are Java, C, C++, C# and Python for the conventional ones and Scratch and App Inventor for the visual ones. More recently, the game engines (Gregory, J., 2014) came out as another kind of tools with visual environments who can contribute to learn to programming without coding. Some examples of these engines are GameSalad and Gamesonomy.

As the usage of a visual environment for programming facilitates the understanding of conventional programming concepts, the research of this study is focused on evaluating the effectiveness of the educational method of teaching with a visual programming language or a game engine as first step before learning conventional programming. For this study, Scratch (ScratchTool), (Resnick, M. et al, 2009) has been selected as visual programming language and Gamesonomy (GamesonomyTool), as game engine. The reasons for selecting them were, for one hand, Scratch was conceived to ease programming learning and nowadays it is one of the most extended visual programming languages due to its ease of use, and for the other hand, the ease of use and comprehension of Gamesonomy which was created to facilitate game development for non-programmers. This game engine deals with the learning process from a ludic point of view, in order to avoid the initial non-acceptance usually present on many conventional programing environments. It worth to be highlighted, that both tools help to reach a better understanding of computational concepts and ease the logic programing thinking.

However, which one is seen as more useful by the students? With the purpose to answer this question, an experiment has been carried out with 50 second year university students from the Degree in Video Game Design and Development. The students have been working with Scratch and with the Gamesonomy's Game Logic Editor on their first year. The subjects where these kinds of software have been used are semester subjects, they are not programming subjects, and students have no previous programming knowledge. For this purpose, the evaluation has been conducted by an acceptance test (Davis, F.D., 1989), (Davis, F.D., Venkatesh, V., 2004) with the same method used by Zarraonandia et al, (Zarraonandia T. et al., 2017).

The work presented on this paper is organized as it follows. On chapter 2 both tools will be described and compared, after that on chapter 3 a simple example will be performed to compare them, later on chapter 4 the methodology of the test and the results of the study on the students will be presented and discussed. Finally, on chapter 5 the conclusions and the future work will be presented.

2. DESCRIPTION OF THE TOOLS

The two analyzed tools, Scratch and the Gamesonomy's Game Logic editor, have several features in common: both are visual programming environments, are perceived as easy to use, have multiplatform support, improve the computational thinking, teach programming fundamentals and let to check the actions that the user is programming. Furthermore, the student learns mathematic concepts with them such as: space coordinates, variables, algorithms, randomness, etc. Besides that, the main differences between these tools came from the Gamesonomy architecture, in which there are no loop structures because the system is evaluating all the events in a continuous loop. Also, it has no dependency on complex data structure and has no need of logic expressions. Next, a presentation of both tools is detailed, emphasizing their features and functionality.

2.1 Scratch

Scratch is a programming language designed to ease the introduction to programming (ScratchTool). The system is made up on a visual programming environment where the user can learn about the coding syntax in an intuitive way. It uses a drag and drop technique with graphical blocks in order to create programs ready to make animations, interactive storytelling, games, interfaces and presentations.

Scratch objects or sprites are configured using scripts, having only their position and size as properties. Its functionality is based in the usage of a set of actions or behaviors to specify the performance of some graphical content or even some peripheral device. These actions and behaviors have a graphical puzzle shape, making the programing task very similar to fit the puzzle pieces together. This philosophy eliminates one of the main obstacles for the students when facing the coding for first time: the uncomfortable and unfamiliar aspect of the programing environments. The actions and behaviors are grouped into different categories of scripts, which in turn offer a drop-down list with all the different options that allow you to configure the specific script action or behavior to be performed. For each one of the blocks categories there is a color to ease its recognition. These categories of actions and behaviors offered by Scratch are defined below:

- Motion: To translate and rotate an object on the screen.
- Looks: To change the object visual aspect: image, size, etc.
- Sound: To play or stop audio sequences.
- Pen: To draw specific color, shadow or line thickness.
- Data: To create new variables and links it to the program.
- Events: Handlers to trigger specific events.
- Control: Conditionals such as if, else, and so on ... and loops such as forever, start and stop.

- Sensing: To manage peripheral sensors and their inputs.
- Operators: Mathematical, logics, random and position getters.
- More blocks: Own blocks and external controllers.

2.2 Gamesonomy

Gamesonomy is a game engine devised to facilitate the videogames creation and design (GamesonomyTool). It uses a very intuitive interface where no coding is required. In the same way as Scratch, it entails a visual programing environment aimed to teach coding in an intuitive mode. It is also used the drag and drop technique for the buttons representing actions and conditions, these buttons are arranged on a graphical decision tree where a specific behavior is defined.

Gamesonomy works under the concept of Actor. Every object present on scene is an Actor; it carries a set of properties and a list of rules. These rules are built from the combination of the actions and conditions in order to perform a specific behavior. Each one of these actions and conditions are represented by a button on the Game Logic Editor to ease its recognition. The rules are graphically represented by a flow chart created from the arrangement of the actions and conditions in it. To arrange an action or a condition, the user has to drag the button from the lateral menu to the flow chart, and then place it in the desired place. This way, it makes that the student is programing while is playing, making him/her to forget he/she is actually writing code. The actions on the Game Logic Editor define the behavior of the Actors. On Figure 1, the set of available actions is presented and they will be described in the following lines:

- Edit: To change every parameter by a specific value or expression. It works in the same way for game, scene or object properties.
- Animate: Animation setter and controller. It executes animations by adding and arranging sprites and setting the frames per second rate.
- Destroy: To delete the object from the scene when is triggered.
- Spawn: An automatic object copy generator.
- Play sound: To activate a sound in the game.
- Move: To translate the object a certain quantity of units on screen. It has a related action called Move To: To travel towards a specific position or object.
- Rotate: To rotate the object a certain number of degrees. There is also a Rotate to action.
- Push: To apply forces on the object. Also it has a related action called Push To and another one working with the same concept to apply angular forces called Torque.

Figure 1. Actions used for the game logic

Conditions are the event triggers. They define the actions to perform on a decision making determined by an occurrence. It has been defined just six as it is shown in yellow also at Figure 2.

- Check: To check if a boolean property is met.
- Compare: To compare two data values from some game, scene or object features.
- Collision: To check if two objects are colliding. It relies on the object's colliding shape.
- Timer: To perform actions after a determined amount of seconds.
- Touch: To manage user interaction with mouse or touch events through tactile devices.
- Keyboard: To check which key has been pressed on the keyboard.

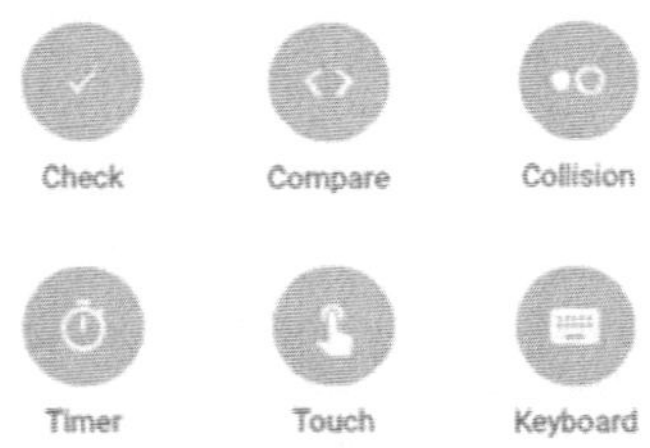

Figure 2. Conditions used for the game logic

Also, both conditions and actions are ready to work with numerical expressions and with mathematical functions: sin, cos, tan, asin, acos, atan, sqrt, random, and so on ... and the data types supported by this system are numbers and booleans.

3. PROGRAMMING EXAMPLE COMPARING BOTH TOOLS

Some code has been developed in order to understand the philosophy and the functionality of both tools. It has been tested with a mouse-following behavior: editable velocity conditions the time it takes an object to move from its original position to the point where the user has clicked the mouse. First of all, the pseudocode that solves the example that has been later programmed in Scratch and Gamesonomy is presented. This pseudocode is included only for the intended of performing a better understanding of the code. This section compares the way both programming environments face this example, but both tools allow the development of complete videogames.

3.1 Pseudocode

Figure 3 illustrates the necessary pseudocode to perform the example behavior. Let Player be the object to move across the screen and Mouse be the object that indicates the point in the screen where the object has to move to. Both have the position (x,y) property and the Player also has the dimension (size) and velocity properties by default.

```
OnClick {
    var x = Mouse.x - Player.x;
    var y = Mouse.y - Player.y;
    var distance = sqrt(x*x + y*y);
    if(distance < Player.size) {
          var directionVector= { x: x / distance, y: y / distance };
          Player.x += Player.velocity * directionVector.x;
          Player.y += Player.velocity * directionVector.y;
      }
}
```

Figure 3. Pseudocode of the action performed as example.

Each time the environment registers a click event on the screen, the spatial coordinates are stored on Mouse.x and Mouse.y. Then, the unitary direction vector from the Player position to the Mouse position is determined by calculating the distance between these two points. If the required movement is greater than the dimensions of the Player, this action is performed. Then, the direction vector is obtained for each component and finally the movement is performed taking into account the Player velocity previously set.

3.2 Programming Language Scratch

The previous example code has been implemented with the programming language Scratch. For this purpose, it has been arranged a set of blocks to compose an instruction puzzle as it is shown in Figure 4.

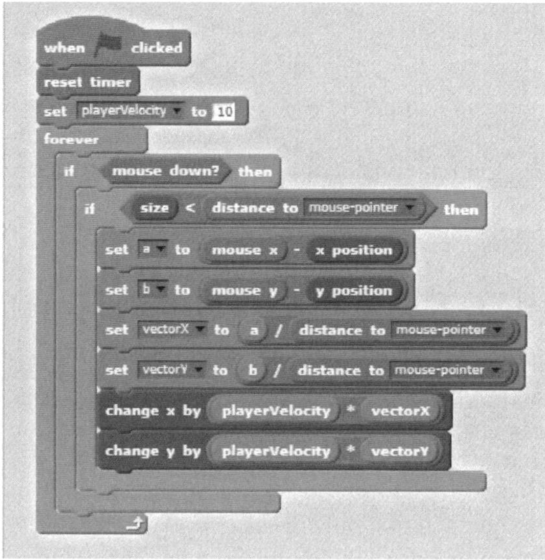

Figure 4. Action programmed with the Scratch Editor

It is known scratch sprites are configured using scripts, having only their position and size as properties. Each time the code is executed, the program enters on a continuous loop. This loop is controlled by two nested conditional statements 'if', which are met when the mouse has been clicked and the distance between the object and the mouse is greater than the object size. If that is an affirmative case, the direction vector is computed and the object position coordinates are updated in accordance with the object predetermined velocity and the director vector.

3.3 Gamesonomy's Game Logic Editor

Continuing with the same example, it is time to test it with the Gamesonomy Game Logic Editor and its flow chart. First, an object or actor is defined that will be the player of the example being programmed. The rule assigned to control the object movement is presented at Figure 5. Besides that, it should be noted that each time an action or condition is added to the Game Logic Editor, a new configuration window is opened to configure the properties of the action or condition.

The action or script assigned to the Player object follows a flowchart structure. Then, the condition under control of the mouse click, called TouchDown, has to be dragged to the graph, positioning it as root of the flowchart. Next, if the condition is met, the action MoveTo has to be dragged to the right branch, that enumerates the developed actions in the case of the root conditions meets. Each action has its own parameters to configure it. On the configuration window for this action, the value for the position of the click coordinates has to be set. They have been stored by the system in variables that Gamesonomy uses by default: game.touchx and game.touchy. Moreover, the velocity of the displacement is set by the programmer.

Only with this short configuration, the game engine updates the position of the object Player by adding the computed displacement on the proper direction.

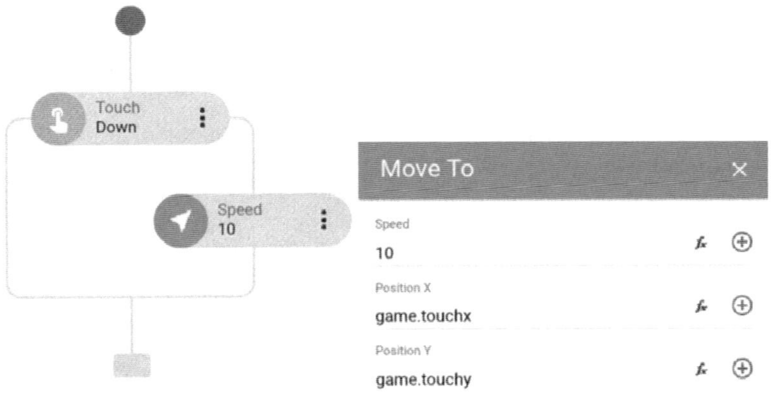

Figure 5. Action programmed with Gamesonomy's Game Logic Editor, and the Move To action configuration window

4. USER EXPERIENCE

Since the intention of this work is to know the real efficacy of Scratch and Gamesonomy after these tools have been used by the students, the direct feedback from them is essential to validate the concept. In order to generate a deeper and nuanced understanding there has been conducted a set of questionnaires (Gilchrist, V.J., 1992). For that purpose, an evaluation has been carried out in second year students of the Degree in Video Game Design and Development. The students had been working with these tools for one semester of the first year, and then with a conventional programming language on their second year. This situation will allow determining which one of these two tools is more suitable in order to learn and overcoming a conventional programming subject. The evaluation is based on acceptance test (Davis, F.D., 1989) with the same method used by Zarraonandia et al. (Zarraonandia, T. et al., 2017). This kind of user is ideal for this research: students who in their apprenticeship have to face to conventional programming languages, starting with no background skills (Hanks, K. et al, 2008).

4.1 Objectives and Hypotheses

The models and the learning strategy that use the tools evaluated in this paper are focused on the student, with the purpose to improve the computational thinking and their logical, abstraction and resolution skills. On an educational context, these practices let the students to comprehend how does it works in the real world and empowering them with essential skills to resolve complex problems (Johnson, L.A. et al., 2014).

The aim of the study is evaluate the learning efficacy and the motivational appealing of a visual programming language and a game engine to ease the further apprenticeship on a conventional programming language and to improve their logical thinking. In other words, this work assess the extent to this tools provide students a starting point to start learning programing.

In previous sections, the methodology of programming in visual environments has been explained, specifically through the use of Scratch and Gamesonomy. There is a conviction that this type of programming environments offers clear advantages for the understanding of programming concepts and facilitates the initiation of conventional programming. Based on this situation, with the intention of assessing which of the two tools is more effective, the results of the questionnaires filled in by the students will be analyzed. To this end, a series of objectives and hypotheses were proposed, shown in Table 1.

Table 1. Objectives and hypotheses

Objectives	Hypotheses
O1 - Identify the most effective visual programming tool to develop the student's logical thinking	H1 - Gamesonomy is more effective to develop the logical thinking
	H2 - Scratch is more effective to develop the logical thinking
O2 - Identify the most effective visual programming tool to facilitate the learning of a conventional programming language	H3 - Gamesonomy is more effective to facilitate learning of a conventional programming language.
	H4 - Scratch is more effective to facilitate learning of a conventional programming language
O3 - Identify the most effective tool for acquisition of computational, mathematical and logical concepts	H5 - Gamesonomy is more effective for acquisition of computational, mathematical and logical concepts.
	H6 - Scratch is more effective for acquisition of computational, mathematical and logical concepts

4.2 Protocol

To carry out this study, a sample of 50 students in the second year of the Degree in Video Game Design and Development is used. All students in the sample had used the Scratch visual programming language and Gamesonomy's Game Logic Editor for a semester in their first course. At the end of the second course, and after having taken a conventional programming subject, students were asked to evaluate different aspects of the two tools they had worked in the first semester, in order to collect their opinions.

For this purpose, they have to evaluate the proposed questions on a scale of one to five, with the value 1 corresponding to the lowest level of acceptance of the question, and the value 5 corresponding to the highest level of acceptance. These questions concern the comfort with usability and understanding of the method by specifically addressing to a measure of Perceived Ease-of-Use (PEOU) and Perceived Usefulness (PUSE) (Davis, F.D., 1989) (Davis, F.D., Venkatesh, V., 2004), as it is also attempted to understand the scope in learning of specific programming concepts. The tests were assessed with the average and the standard deviation. It is important to know the statistical significance of the results obtained in the comparison made between Gamesonomy and Scratch. For this purpose, the tests were evaluated with a signed rank based on a two-tailed test with 5% significance Wilcoxon Signed-Rank (Lazar J. et al., 2010).

4.3 Results

To gather information about PUSE and PEOU, this research is based on the questions at Table 2. This test collects information about the learning curve and satisfaction of use related to each of the tools investigated. The survey evaluates questions related to the achievement of concepts related to programming learning.

Table 2. Items and results for the PEOU and PUSE analysis

	Scratch		Gamesonomy	
Questions	Average	SD	Average	SD
PEOU				
Q1 It's easy to learn	3.76	0.73	4.72	0.62
Q2 It is quick to learn	3.67	0.80	3.93	0.78
Q3 It is intuitive	3.62	0.78	4.10	0.64
Q4 It facilitates understanding of conventional programming	4.28	0.73	4.50	0.77
Q5 It improves computational thinking	4.21	0.81	4.52	0.78
Q6 I will continue to program with this tool even though I know how to do it in a conventional programming language	4.12	0.76	4.33	0.46
Q7 I would recommend it to beginners	4.53	0.65	4.70	0.75
PUSE				
Q8 It represents the concept of visual programming	4.80	0.48	4.92	0.63
Q9 It facilitates the understanding of the loop concept	4.31	0.59	4.10	0,59
Q10 It facilitates the understanding of the concept of logic expression	4.21	0.77	4.32	0.63
Q11 It facilitates the learning of mathematical and logical concepts	4.47	0,57	4.71	0.77

Once the students learned and worked at Scratch and Gamesonomy, they realized that their capacity for abstraction and logical thinking had reached the level to learn a conventional programming language more effectively than if they had initially had to face this task without them. This is reflected in a general way in the PEOU test, with the Q4 and Q5 questions of both tools rated with an average of more than 4 out of 5. As for the comparison of these issues among the tools under study, it is worth noting that Gamesonomy is slightly favored, surpassing by 0.22 in the Q4 question and by 0.31 in the Q5 question. As for the measure of perceived ease of use, students clearly preferred Gamesonomy as it is reflected in questions Q1, Q2 and Q3. This would confirm hypotheses H1 and H3.

The results obtained in questions Q6 and Q7, which reflect the general satisfaction of the students with the two tools, should be highlighted. This satisfaction in both cases is above 4 out of 5. Question Q6 demonstrates that both Scratch and Gamesonomy are not considered as simple programming initiation tools, as students confirm their intention to continue using them even after they have learned conventional programming languages. Q7 question demonstrates this satisfaction as they see them as highly recommended for beginners in the world of programming. In both cases, Gamesonomy is slightly above in their assessments.

Looking at the results obtained for Perceived Usefulness (PUSE), the data shows that, except in the Q9 question, Gamesonomy is once again above in the rest of the aspects consulted. The lower acceptance of Gamesonomy in Q9 may be due to the fact that Gamesonomy is a game engine, and there are no loop structures because the system is evaluating all the events in a continuous loop. This means that the student never has to program loops and is therefore unaware that they are programming them and, it would be confirmed hypothesis H6. Q10 and Q11 questions confirmed that Gamesonomy is a better tool for the acquisition of computational, mathematical and logical concepts. This validates the hypothesis H5. Finally, as can be sawn in Q8 question, both Scratch and Gamesonomy have been assessed with values very close to 5, considering them as tools strongly representative of what is known as programming in visual environments, although Gamesonomy is slightly surpassing Scratch.

Concerning the statistical significance of the comparison test between Gamesonomy and Scratch, the Wilcoxon Signed-Rank results establish the test statistic value at 19, minor than the critical value of 73 established for the number of entries. Therefore, it is demonstrated that there is sufficient evidence to suggest that there is a substantial difference between them.

In summary, the results after the analysis of the data reflected in the PEOU test showed that students prefer Gamesonomy as the most effective tool to be used as a basis for computer thought configuration, and as a preliminary step for learning conventional programming languages. Questions related to the PUSE test confirmed that students consider both tools highly representative of visual programming. In addition, Gamesonomy would surpass Scratch as the best tool for acquiring computational, mathematical and logical concepts, while scratch would surpass Gamesonomy as the preferred tool for understanding the loop concept.

5. CONCLUSIONS AND FUTURE WORK

The presented work analyzes the effectiveness of the educational method of teaching programming using a visual programming language or a game engine, in order to facilitate the understanding of conventional programming. In particular, it is used Scratch as visual programming language and Gamesonomy, as game engine. The main aim of this study focused on answer the next question: which one of these two tools is more efficient, appealing, easy to understand and to use for a better transition to the traditional programming? To this end, students have worked with Scratch and Gamesonomy before facing a conventional programming language.

After training and later reflection of the students on the influence of these tools on the understanding of a conventional programming language, the students filled out a test with questions regarding the proposed question. The results of this test have concluded that although both tools are effective and highly representative of visual programming, students prefer Gamesonomy as more effective tool to be used as a basis for computer thought configuration, and as a preliminary step for learning conventional programming languages. The work also confirmed that students have efficiently acquired computational, mathematical and logical concepts with Gamesonomy, but for the understanding of the loop concept they have chosen Scratch.

As future work, we propose to expand this study by adding other tools, and augment the concepts to be studied, such as the use and understanding of complex data structures. It would also be interesting to carry out this study in primary and secondary school students, in order to discover whether this type of learning of programming increases technological vocations among young people.

ACKNOWLEDGEMENT

This work was supported by the Spanish Ministry of Science and Technology (Project TIN2016 - 75866 - C3 - 1 - R).

REFERENCES

Chang, S.K, 1990. *Principles of Visual Programming Systems*. Englewood Cliffs, NJ: Prentice Hall.

Davis, F. D., 1989. *Perceived usefulness, perceived ease of use, and user acceptance of information technology*, MIS Q. 13 (3).

Davis F.D., Venkatesh V., 2004. *Toward preprototype user acceptance testing of new information systems: implications for software project management*. IEEE Transactions on Engineering Management pp 31-46.

GamesonomyTool: URL http://www.gamesonomy.com [Online; Last accessed: 2018-05-19] (May 2018)

Gilchrist, V.J., 1992. *Key informant interviews*. In B. F. Crabtree & W. L. Miller (Eds.), Research methods for primary care, (3), pp 70-89. Thousand Oaks, CA, US: Sage Publications, Inc.

Good, J., 2011. *Learners at the wheel: novice programming environments come of age*. International Journal of People-Oriented Programming, 1(1), pp 1-24.

Gregory J., 2014. *Game Engine Architecture*. Second Edition, 2nd Edition, A. K. Peters, Ltd., Natick, MA, USA.

Grover, S., Pea, R., 2013. *Computational thinking in K–12: A review of the state of the field. Educational Researcher*. 42(1), pp 38-43. http://dx.doi.org/10.3102/0013189X12463051

Hanks, K. et at., 2008. *Sustainable millennials: Attitudes towards sustainability and the material effects of interactive technologies*. Proceedings Conference on Human Factors in Computing Systems. http://dx.doi.org/10.1145/1357054.1357111

Jackson M., 1980. *The Design and Use of Conventional Programming Languages; in Human Interaction with Computers*, pp 321-347; isbn:0126528500; H T Smith & T R Green eds; Academic Press.

Johnson, L.A. et al, 2014. *NMC Horizon Report: K-12* edition. Austin, Texas: The New Media Consortium. Retrieved from http://www.nmc.org/pdf/2014-nmc-horizon-report-he-EN.pdf.

Lazar J. et al., 2010. *Research Methods in Human-Computer Interaction,* Wiley Publishing.

Repenning, A., 2017. *Moving Beyond Syntax: Lessons from 20 Years of Blocks Programing in AgentSheets*. Journal of Visual Languages and Sentient Systems, 68-91. http://dx.doi.org/10.18293/VLSS2017-010

Resnick, M. et al., 2009. *Scratch: Programming for All*. Communications of the ACM, 52(1), 60-67.

ScratchTool: Research on scratch. URL https://scratch.mit.edu/info/research [Online; Last accessed: 2018-05-18] (May 2018)

Van Roy, P. et al., 2003. *The Role of Language Paradigms in Teaching Programming*. SIGCSE Bull. 35(1), 269-270. ISSN: 0097-8418. ACM, New York, USA. http://dx.doi.org/10.1145/792548.611908.

Wing, J., 2006. *Computational thinking*. Communications of the ACM, 49(3), 33-35. http://dx.doi.org/10.1145/1118178.1118215.

Zarraonandia T. et al., 2017. *Using combinatorial creativity to support end-user design of digital games*. Multimedia Tools and Applications 76(6).

ATTRIBUTES OF ENGAGEMENT IN CHALLENGE-BASED DIGITAL LEARNING ENVIRONMENTS

Dirk Ifenthaler[1], David Gibson[1] and Longwei Zheng[2]
[1]*Curtin University, Bentley, WA, Australia*
[2]*East China Normal University, Shanghai, China*

ABSTRACT

This study is part of a research programme investigating the dynamics and impacts of learning engagement in a challenge-based digital learning environment. Learning engagement is a multidimensional concept which includes an individual's ability to behaviourally, cognitively, emotionally, and motivationally engage in an on-going learning process. Challenge-based learning gives significant freedom to the learner to decide what and when to engage and interact with digital learning materials. In light of previous empirical findings, we expect that learning engagement is positively related to learning performance in a challenge-based digital learning environment. This study was based on data from the Curtin Challenge platform, including transaction data of 13,655 students. Findings indicate that attributes of learning engagement in challenge-based digital learning environments are, as expected, positively related to learning performance. Implications point toward the need for personalised and adaptive learning environments to be developed in order to cater for the individual needs of learners in challenge-based digital learning environments.

KEYWORDS

Learning Engagement, Data Analytics, Time On Task, Challenge-Based Learning

1. INTRODUCTION

Learners differ in their reasons for engaging in learning tasks and these inter-individual differences require personalised support while learning (Schunk & Zimmerman, 1994). In addition, research also reports intra-individual differences in engagement, i.e., during a learning dependent-progression engagement changes over time and requires adaptive support to cater for the learners' needs (Ifenthaler & Seel, 2005).

Learning engagement is generally regarded as the time and effort an individual invests on a specific learning activity (Kuh, 2009). Several studies focussing on learning engagement support the assumption that higher engagement of a learner corresponds with higher learning outcomes (Carini, 2012). However, most of these studies have been conducted in face-to-face learning environments. Accordingly, a confirmation of these findings in digital learning environments is still lacking.

This study seeks to close this gap by investigating the dynamics of learning engagement in a challenge-based digital learning environment using a data analytics approach. The context of the presented study is set in the *Curtin Challenge* which is a mobile ready interactive learning delivery platform that illustrates several features of game-inspired challenge-based learning while adding a layer of big data collection to enable research into teaching and learning. A learner interacts with Curtin Challenge content by pointing, clicking, sliding items, vocalizing, taking pictures and drawing as well as watching, listening, reading and writing as in typical digital learning environments.

2. LEARNING ENGAGEMENT

Learning engagement is a multidimensional concept and understood as the individual's ability to behaviourally, cognitively, emotionally, and motivationally interact with learning artefacts in an on-going learning process (Wolters & Taylor, 2012). A generally accepted assumption is that the more students engage with a subject matter or phenomenon in question, the more they tend to learn (Carini, Kuh, & Klein, 2006).

This assumption is consistent with the theory of self-regulated learning (Zimmerman, 2002) and concepts of engagement (Fredricks & McColskey, 2012). Accordingly, learning engagement is positively linked to desirable learning outcomes or learning performance (Klein, Kuh, Chun, Hamilton, & Shavelson, 2005).

While learning performance is linked closely with behaviours (Bandura, 1993), several assumptions are associated to the relationship between the performance of an individual and learning engagement. For example, Chen (2017) investigated the relationship between learning engagement and learning performance of students of ten schools based in Taiwan. Findings of the multilevel analysis indicate a significant positive relationship between learning engagement and learning performance. Recent findings also document that serious games drive learning engagement (Peng, Cao, & Timalsena, 2017). Similar implications focussing on learning engagement and learning performance have been reported in other contexts (Flowerday & Shell, 2015; Lin et al., 2016; Pourbarkhordari, Zhou, & Pourkarimi, 2016).

An impressive number of research studies have been conducted in the field of cognitive load with links to task characteristics and learning engagement (Kirschner, Kester, & Corbalan, 2011; van Merriënboer & Sweller, 2005). This line of research assumes an active role of the learner in learning processes, i.e., learners select tasks relevant to them (Corbalan, Kester, & van Merriënboer, 2011) and are actively engaged while interacting with the learning environment (Schwamborn, Thillmann, Opfermann, & Leutner, 2011).

In addition, research on reading utilises reading time measurements in order to identify learning engagement and linking those to learning performance (Graesser, Millis, & Zwaan, 1997). The general assumption is that the intensity of mental effort aimed at achieving a greater understanding, i.e., time spent on reading task, is critical during learning. Findings indicate that increased reading times as a sign of greater learning engagement are positively related to learning performance measured as comprehension scores (Miller, 2015; Miller et al., 2014).

3. CHALLENGE-BASED LEARNING ENVIRONMENT

The Curtin Challenge digital learning platform (http://challenge.curtin.edu.au) supports individual and team-based learning via gamified, challenge-based, open-ended, inquiry-based learning experiences that integrate automated feedback and rubric-driven assessment capabilities.

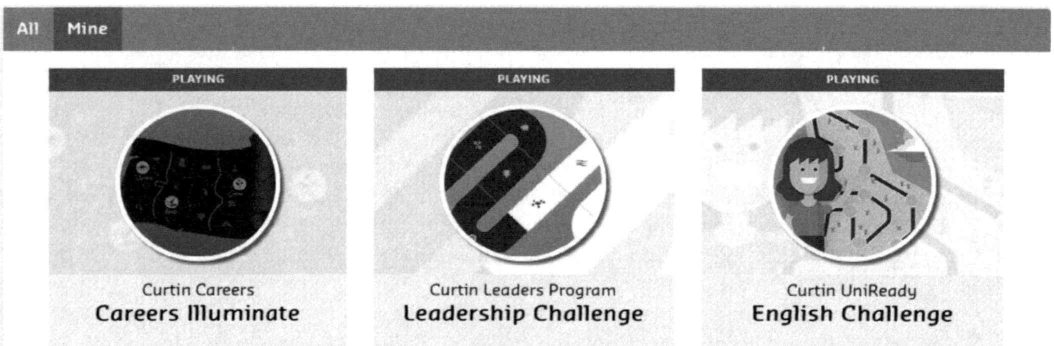

Figure 1. Three challenges currently available

A challenge is regarded as a collection of information and corresponding tasks linked to specific learning outcomes. Currently, there are three *Challenges* offered by Curtin University: *Careers Illuminate*, *Leadership Challenge*, and *English Challenge* (see Figure 1). This study includes analysis from the Career and Leadership Challenges which both require approximately up to one hour of learning time. Career Challenge includes 14 modules while Leadership Challenge includes eleven modules (see Figure 2 for individual modules).

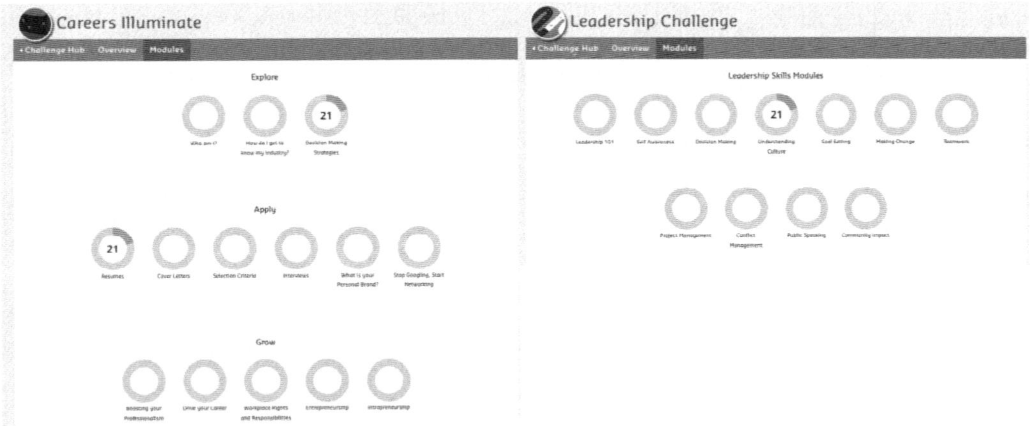

Figure 2. Modules overview for Career and Leadership Challenges

The design features of each module contain up to five activities including one to three different learner interactions or tasks. For example, the module *Who am I* in the Career Challenge is a collection of five activities containing learning interactions, such as choosing from among options, writing a short response to a prompt, spinning a wheel to create random prompts, creating, organising, and listing ideas, or matching items. Each page can contain one or several such interactions, and the learner does not have to submit the page in order for the data to be captured. Data is constantly being captured, which creates information about the timing, sequence, and completeness as well as the content of the interactions (i.e., navigation event and sequences). The data record is thus highly granular, providing an opportunity to examine the dynamics of the activity as well as the contents of the artefacts created by the learner for every click on every activity or module page.

4. HYPOTHESES OF THE PRESENT STUDY

In light of previous empirical findings on learning engagement (Chen, 2017; Flowerday & Shell, 2015; Kirschner et al., 2011; Miller, 2015; Miller et al., 2014), we expect that learning engagement is positively related to learning performance in a challenge-based digital learning environment. Attributes of learning engagement in the challenge-based digital learning environment are conceptualised through several actions: (a) launching a specific activity (task), (b) spending active time on the task, (c) entering a written response, and (d) finishing a task. The learning performance measured in this study is computed by the number of correct answers in a subset of tasks designed with embedded feedback to the student. The hypotheses of this study focus on the attributes of learning engagement and its relation to learning performance in both Career and Leadership Challenge. We assume that launching specific activities (tasks) is related to the learning performance in challenge-based digital learning environments (Hypothesis 1). Further, we assume that spending active time on tasks is related to the learning performance (Hypotheses 2). Also, we expect that the length of written responses is related to the learning performance (Hypothesis 3). The final assumption focusses on the relationship between finishing tasks and learning performance (Hypothesis 4).

5. METHOD

5.1 Data Source

The data set of the Career Challenge consists of 52,675,225 rows of raw data containing information of $N_C = 8{,}951$ students (3,571 male; 5,380 female) with an average age of $M = 25.72$ years ($SD = 6.64$). The Leadership Challenge includes data from $N_L = 4{,}704$ students (1,825 male; 2,879 female) with an average age of $M = 23.96$ years ($SD = 5.47$) with information stored in 19,517,647 rows of raw data. In a period of 24 months (January 2016 – January 2018), students spent a total of 10,239 hours interacting with the Career Challenge and 14,546 hours interacting with the Leadership Challenge.

5.2 Data Analytics Strategy

Raw data from the Career and Leadership Challenge were cleaned and transformed into a transaction data set in which each row represents an event of one user. The dependent variable *learning_performance* (LP) was computed as the number of correct answers in an activity. The variables reflecting attributes of learning engagement were computed as follows: *launching_task* (LT) as the number of activities started by a student; *time_on_task* (TT) as the duration in seconds spent in an activity; *written_response* (WR) as the number of words submitted by a student; *finishing_task* (FT) as the number of activities finished by a student.

6. RESULTS

In order to test the above presented four hypotheses, regression analyses were computed to determine whether attributes of learning engagement (i.e., launching task, time on task, written response, finishing task) were significant predictors of learning performance in challenge-based digital learning environments. The analyses were computed separately for the Career and Leadership Challenge.

6.1 Career Challenge

Table 1 shows zero-order correlations of attributes of learning engagement and learning performance for the Career Challenge. All correlations were significant at $p < .001$. High positive correlations were found between launching task (LT; $M = 6.73$; $SD = 8.95$) and learning outcome (LP; $M = 8.38$; $SD = 13.19$), time on task (TT; $M = 4118.09$; $SD = 6623.88$), as well as written response (WR; $M = 166.92$; $SD = 284.62$). Moderate positive correlations were found for written response and learning outcome as well as time on task. Low positive correlations were found for the remaining variable combinations.

Table 1. Zero-order correlations, means and standard deviations of attributes of learning engagement and learning performance for the Career Challenge

	Zero-Order *r*				
	LT	TT	WR	FT	LP
LT	-				
TT	.771***	-			
WR	.724***	.685***	-		
FT	.355***	.290***	.331***	-	
LP	.839***	.628***	.660***	.340***	-
M	6.73	4118.09	166.92	1.24	8.38
SD	8.95	6623.88	284.62	4.40	13.19

Note. *** $p < .001$; LP = learning outcome; LT = launching task; TT = time on task; WR = written response; FT = finishing task; $N_C = 8{,}951$

The linear regression analysis for the Career Challenge is presented in Table 2, yielding a ΔR^2 of .713 ($F(4, 8950) = 5568.79$, $p < .001$). Clearly, the number of activities started by a student (LT; $\beta = .80$, $p < .001$) positively predicted the learning performance. In addition, the number of activities finished by a student (FT; $\beta = .04$, $p < .001$) and the number of words submitted by a student (WR; $\beta = .13$, $p < .001$) positively predicted the learning performance. In contrast, the duration students spent on a task (TT; $\beta = -.09$, $p < .001$) was negatively correlated with the learning performance.

Table 2. Regression analyses predicting learning performance by attributes of learning engagement for the Career Challenge

	R^2	ΔR^2	*B*	*SE B*	β
LP	.713	.713			
LT			1.177	.015	.80***
TT			.001	.001	-.09***
FT			.115	.018	.04***
WR			.006	.001	.13***

Note. *** $p < .001$; LP = learning performance;
LT = launching task; TT = time on task;
FT = finishing task; WR = written response; $N_C = 8{,}951$

In sum, the four hypotheses are accepted for the Career Challenge, confirming significant relationships between attributes of learning engagement and learning performance.

6.2 Leadership Challenge

Table 3 shows zero-order correlations of attributes of learning engagement and learning performance for the Leadership Challenge.

Table 3. Zero-order correlations, means and standard deviations of attributes of learning engagement and learning performance for the Leadership Challenge

	Zero-Order *r*				
	LT	TT	WR	FT	LP
LT	-				
TT	.698***	-			
WR	.759***	.789***	-		
FT	1.00***	.697***	.759***	-	
LP	.901***	.667***	.711***	.921***	-
M	26.74	11132.30	661.78	26.52	10.76
SD	22.97	14535.29	782.97	23.05	11.96

Note. *** $p < .001$; LP = learning outcome; LT = launching task;
TT = time on task; WR = written response; FT = finishing task; $N_L = 4{,}704$

The linear regression analysis for the Leadership Challenge is presented in Table 4, yielding a ΔR^2 of .850 ($F(4, 4703) = 6652.32$, $p < .001$).

The number of activities started by a student (LT; $\beta = 1.50$, $p < .001$) positively predicted the learning performance. In addition, the duration students spent on a task (TT; $\beta = .05$, $p < .001$) positively predicted the learning performance. In contrast, the number of activities finished by a student (FT; $\beta = -.61$, $p < .05$) was negatively correlated with the learning performance.

In sum, the hypotheses 1, 2 and 4 are accepted for the Leadership Challenge, confirming significant relationships between attributes of learning engagement and learning performance.

Table 4. Regression analyses predicting learning performance by attributes of learning engagement for the Leadership Challenge

	R^2	ΔR^2	*B*	*SE B*	β
LP	.850	.850			
LT			.782	.127	1.50***
TT			.038	.000	.05***
FT			-.318	.129	-.61*
WR			.001	.000	.00

Note. * $p < .05$; *** $p < .001$; LP = learning performance; LT = launching task;
TT = time on task; FT = finishing task; WR = written response; $N_L = 4{,}704$

7. DISCUSSION

The times of direct comparisons of technology-mediated and face-to-face learning environments are over (Alavi & Leidner, 2001), hence, research needs to identify key factors influencing learning processes and learning outcomes. This study aimed to investigate the dynamics of engagement in challenge-based digital learning environments and its relationship to learning performance. Hypotheses were developed based on previous research from face-to-face learning environments. Our analyses focussed on data from the Challenge platform including transaction data from 13,655 students.

The analytic results showed that learning engagement in challenge-based online learning environments is significantly related to learning performance. These findings support previous studies conducted in face-to-face situations (Chen, 2017; Lin et al., 2016; Pourbarkhordari et al., 2016). Significant attributes predicting the learning performance of the student appeared to be the number of activities started and the number of activities finished by a student. This is a reflection of active engagement with the learning environment (Kirschner et al., 2011). At the same time, better learners seem to spend less time on a specific task in the Career Challenge. This may be interpreted as a reflection of existing prior knowledge or a progression towards an advanced learner (Ifenthaler & Seel, 2005). Another significant indicator predicting learning performance in the Career Challenge was the number of words submitted in open text activities. On a surface level, these findings are also related to studies conducted in writing research and clearly reflect the impact of the variation in learning engagement (Graesser et al., 1997; Miller et al., 2014).

This study and its findings are limited in several aspects that must be addressed. First, due to limited access of student data, for example, course load, past academic performance, or personal characteristics, linking additional data to the reported engagement and performance measures has not yet occurred. Combining such additional data, we expect will provide a more detailed insight into the multidimensional concepts to be investigated in a future study. Second, both challenges did not include an overall performance measure which has been validated against an outside criterion. Accordingly, a revision of the learning and assessment design should include additional or revised measures which follow accepted criteria or competence indicators. However, without the externally validated benchmarks, there is sufficient available data which can be used to improve the existing learning design through algorithms focussing on design features and navigation sequences of learners (Agrawal, Golshan, & Papalexakis, 2016; Ifenthaler, Gibson, & Dobozy, 2018; Lockyer, Heathcote, & Dawson, 2013). Third, as we included the analysis of open text answers in our analysis model, this approach is limited by the overall potential of the simple approach natural language processing (NLP). Further development of our analysis in future studies will include a focus on deeper levels of syntactic complexity, lexical sophistication, and quality of writing as well as a deep semantic analysis compared to expert solutions (Crossley, 2013; Ifenthaler, 2014).

8. IMPLICATIONS AND FUTURE RESEARCH

Analyses of the learning performance transcript, even when automated and multileveled, is a mixture of *conditional and inferential interpretation* that can utilize several frames of reference while adding layers of interpreted evidence, insights concerning the complexity and additional dimensionality to our understanding of the performance and our ability to re-present the performance in the light of our understandings (Gibson & Ifenthaler, 2018).

The Curtin Challenge platform is being developed to support both individual and team-based learning in primarily open-ended ill-structured problem solving and project-based learning contexts (Eseryel, Law, Ifenthaler, Ge, & Miller, 2014). The platform can also support self-guided learning, automated feedback, branching story lines, self-organizing teams, and distributed processes of mentoring, learning support and assessment (Gibson, 2018; Gibson & Ifenthaler, 2018).

The data traces captured by the Curtin Challenge platform are highly detailed, with many events per learning activity, which brings the potential for measuring indicators of physical, emotional and cognitive states of the learner. The data innovation of the Curtin Challenge platform is the ability to capture event-based records of higher frequency with the potential to analyse higher dimensional aspects of learning engagement, which we believe may be in turn useful for analysis of the embedded learning design's effectiveness and impact on the physical, emotional and cognitive layers of learning caused or influenced by digital engagements. The data from the challenge-based learning platform forms a high-resolution analytics base on which researchers can conduct studies into learning design and into how to achieve better outcomes in scalable digital learning experiences (Gibson, 2018; Gibson & Jackl, 2015).

Future research will focus on the analysis of several large extant data sets from the Curtin Challenge platform. Currently, the possibility of adaptive algorithms based on learning engagement and learning performance are being investigated. Such algorithms will enable meaningful micro analysis of individual performance as well as personalised and adaptive feedback to the learner whenever it is needed.

ACKNOWLEDGEMENT

This work is part of the UNESCO Chair of Data Science in Higher Education Learning and Teaching (http://www.curtin.edu.au/UNESCO) which focusses on advancing global knowledge, practice and policy in applying data science to transform higher education learning and teaching that improves personalization, access and effectiveness of education for all.

REFERENCES

Agrawal, R., Golshan, B., & Papalexakis, E. (2016). Toward data-driven design of educational courses: A feasibility study. *Journal of Educational Data Mining, 8*(1), 1–21.

Alavi, A., & Leidner, D. E. (2001). Research commentary: technology-mediated learning — a call for greater depth and breadth of research. *Information Systems Research, 12*(1), 1–10.

Bandura, A. (1993). Perceived self-efficacy in cognitive development and functioning. *Educational Psychologist, 28*(2), 117–148. doi:10.1207/s15326985ep2802_3

Carini, R. M. (2012). Engagement in learning. In N. M. Seel (Ed.), *Encyclopedia of the sciences of learning* (pp. 1153–1156). Boston, MA: Springer.

Carini, R. M., Kuh, G. D., & Klein, S. P. (2006). Student engagement and student learning: testing the linkages. *Research in Higher Education, 47*(1), 1–32. doi:10.1007/s11162-005-8150-9

Chen, I.-S. (2017). Computer self-efficacy, learning performance, and the mediating role of learning engagement. *Computers in Human Behavior, 72*, 362–370. doi:10.1016/j.chb.2017.02.059

Corbalan, G., Kester, L., & van Merriënboer, J. J. G. (2011). Learner-controlled selection of tasks with different surface and structural features: Effects on transfer and efficiency. *Computers in Human Behavior, 27*, 76–81. doi:10.1016/j.chb.2010.05.026

Crossley, S. A. (2013). Advancing research in second language writing through computational tools and machine learning techniques. *Language Teaching, 46*(2), 256–271.

Eseryel, D., Law, V., Ifenthaler, D., Ge, X., & Miller, R. B. (2014). An investigation of the interrelationships between motivation, engagement, and complex problem solving in game-based learning. *Journal of Educational Technology & Society, 17*(1), 42–53.

Flowerday, T., & Shell, D. F. (2015). Disentangling the effects of interest and choice on learning, engagement, and attitude. *Learning and Individual Differences, 40*, 134–140. doi:10.1016/j.lindif.2015.05.003

Fredricks, J. A., & McColskey, W. (2012). The measurement of student engagement: A comparative analysis of various methods and student self-report instruments. In S. I. Christenson, A. L. Reschly, & W. C. (Eds.), *Handbook of research on student engagement* (pp. 763–781). New York, NY: Springer.

Gibson, D. C. (2018). Unobtrusive observation of team learning attributes in digital learning. *Frontiers in Psychology, 9*(834), 1–5. doi:10.3389/fpsyg.2018.00834

Gibson, D. C., & Ifenthaler, D. (2018). Analysing performance in authentic digital scenarios. In T.-W. Chang, R. Huang, & Kinshuk (Eds.), *Authentic learning through advances in technologies* (pp. 17–27). New York, NY: Springer.

Gibson, D. C., & Jackl, P. (2015). Theoretical considerations for game-based e-learning analytics. In T. Reiners & L. Wood (Eds.), *Gamification in education and business* (pp. 403–416). New York, NY: Springer.

Graesser, A. C., Millis, K. K., & Zwaan, R. A. (1997). Discourse comprehension. *Annual Review of Psychology, 48*, 163–189. doi:10.1146/annurev.psych.48.1.163

Ifenthaler, D. (2014). AKOVIA: Automated Knowledge Visualization and Assessment. *Technology, Knowledge and Learning, 19*(1-2), 241-248. doi:10.1007/s10758-014-9224-6

Ifenthaler, D., Gibson, D. C., & Dobozy, E. (2018). Informing learning design through analytics: Applying network graph analysis. *Australasian Journal of Educational Technology, 34*(2), 117–132. doi:10.14742/ajet.3767

Ifenthaler, D., & Seel, N. M. (2005). The measurement of change: Learning-dependent progression of mental models. *Technology, Instruction, Cognition and Learning, 2*(4), 317–336.

Kirschner, F., Kester, L., & Corbalan, G. (2011). Cognitive load theory and multimedia learning, task characteristics and learning engagement: The Current State of the Art. *Computers in Human Behavior, 27*(1), 1–4. doi:https://doi.org/10.1016/j.chb.2010.05.003

Klein, S. P., Kuh, G. D., Chun, M., Hamilton, L., & Shavelson, R. (2005). An approach to measuring cognitive outcomes across higher education institutions. *Research in Higher Education, 46*(3), 251–276. doi:doi.org/10.1007/s11162-004-1640-3

Kuh, G. D. (2009). What student affairs professionals need to know about student engagement. *Journal of College Student Development, 50*(6), 683–706. doi:10.1353/csd.0.0099

Lin, W., Wang, L., Bamberger, P. A., Zhang, Q., Wang, H., Guo, W., . . . Zhang, T. (2016). Leading future orientations for current effectiveness: The role of engagement and supervisor coaching in linking future work self salience to job performance. *Journal of Vocational Behavior, 92*, 145–156. doi:10.1016/j.jvb.2015.12.002

Lockyer, L., Heathcote, E., & Dawson, S. (2013). Informing pedagogical action: Aligning learning analytics with learning design. *American Behavioral Scientist, 57*(10), 1439–1459. doi:10.1177/0002764213479367

Miller, B. W. (2015). Using reading times and eye-movements to measure cognitive engagement. *Educational Psychologist, 50*(1), 31–42. doi:10.1080/00461520.2015.1004068

Miller, B. W., Anderson, R. C., Morris, J., Lin, T. J., Jadallah, M., Sun, J., & D., T. (2014). The effects of reading to prepare for argumentative discussion on cognitive engagement and conceptual growth. *Learning and Instruction, 33*, 67–80. doi:10.1016/j.learninstruc.2014.04.003

Peng, C., Cao, L., & Timalsena, S. (2017). Gamification of Apollo lunar exploration missions for learning engagement. *Entertainment Computing, 19*, 53–64. doi:10.1016/j.entcom.2016.12.001

Pourbarkhordari, A., Zhou, E. H. I., & Pourkarimi, J. (2016). How individual-focused transformational leadership enhances its influence on job performance through employee work engagement. *International Journal of Business and Management, 11*(2), 249–261. doi:10.5539/ijbm.v11n2p249

Schunk, D. H., & Zimmerman, B. J. (1994). *Self-regulation of learning and performance: Issues and educational applications*. Hillsdale, NJ: Erlbaum.

Schwamborn, A., Thillmann, H., Opfermann, M., & Leutner, D. (2011). Cognitive load and instructionally supported learning with provided and learner-generated visualizations. *Computers in Human Behavior, 27*, 89–93. doi:10.1016/j.chb.2010.05.028

van Merriënboer, J. J. G., & Sweller, J. (2005). Cognitive load theory and complex learning: Recent developments and future directions. *Educational Psychology Review, 17*(2), 147-177.

Wolters, C. A., & Taylor, D. J. (2012). A self-regulated learning perspective on student engagement. In S. Christenson, A. Reschly, & C. Wylie (Eds.), *Handbook of research on student engagement* (pp. 635–651). Boston, MA: Springer.

Zimmerman, B. J. (2002). Becoming a self-regulated learner: An overview. *Theory into Practice, 41*(2), 64–70.

RELATIONSHIP BETWEEN GOAL ORIENTATION, CONCEPTION OF LEARNING AND LEARNING BEHAVIOR

Mai Yokoyama and Kazuhisa Miwa
Nagoya University, Japan

ABSTRACT

This study examined the causal relationship of goal orientation and conception of learning on learning behavior; previously, these concepts were examined separately in preceding studies. A sample of 185 fourth-grade university students participated in the study. A covariance structure analysis revealed that the causal effect regarding goal orientation to learning behavior through conception of learning, in which the mediational role of conception of learning was confirmed. Learning goals had a positive effect on autonomous learning conception and had a negative effect on forced learning conception. While performance-avoidance goals had a negative effect on autonomous learning conception, it had a positive effect on forced learning conception. In addition, autonomous learning conception had a positive effect and forced learning conception had a negative effect on learning behavior.

KEYWORDS

Goal Orientation, Conception of Learning, Learning Behavior

1. INTRODUCTION

Goal orientation and conception of learning are decisive factors that regulate learning behavior such as motivation for learning and/or learning approach.

1.1 Goal Orientation

According to goal achievement theory (Dweck 1986), which explains the differences in learning behavior based on a student's goals when executing tasks, a student's goals may be classified into two categories: learning goals and performance goals. The purpose of the former is to acquire new knowledge and skills through challenging activities while that of the latter is to seek positive and avoid negative evaluations. Students who are oriented toward learning goals tend to select challenging tasks and persevere even when they encounter failure, regardless of whether or not they are confident in their abilities. Performance goal-oriented students behave similarly to students with learning goal orientation provided they are confident in their abilities; however, if they lack confidence in their abilities, they are less likely to persevere until they have completed the tasks. Elliot and Dweck's (1988) findings support the latter statement. According to Ames and Archer (1987, 1988), learning goals have a positive effect on both academic achievement and endogenous motivation. Furthermore, emphasis has been placed on the superiority of learning goals.

Elliot and Harackiewicz (1996) divided a performance goal into a performance-approach goal in which a student tries to outperform others and a performance-avoidance goal, which is the desire to avoid performing more poorly than others do. Elliot and colleagues found that performance-approach goals result in positive effects on endogenous motivation and academic performance whereas performance-avoidance goals have negative effects on them, thus, demonstrating the importance of distinguishing between approach and avoidance utilities (e.g., Elliot & Church, 1997; Rawsthorne & Elliot, 1999).

Previous research has shown that learning behaviors are associated with a student's goal orientation (Bandura, 2012) in which learning goals and performance-approach goals have positive influences whereas performance-avoidance goals have negative effects on learning behavior (Liem et al., 2008).

1.2 Conception of Learning

Research on students' conceptions of learning can be traced to the late 1970s and early 1980s, primarily in Europe (e.g., Säljö, 1979; Van Rossum & Schenk, 1984). Marton et al. (1993) found qualitatively different conceptions of learning among students of the British Open University in which learning was recognized as an increase in knowledge, memorizing and reproducing, applying, understanding, seeing something in a different way or as and changing as a person.

Previous studies have revealed that there are differences in learning behavior, which are dependent on how people conceptualize learning. Van Rossum and Schenk (1984) conducted an empirical study on learning behavior in relation to reading materials. Students who perceived learning as memorizing adopted superficial learning behavior in which they only read a summary whereas students who perceived learning as the abstraction of meaning or an interpretative process aimed at the understanding of reality adopted deep learning behavior in which they read the sentences while processing the relationship between the paragraphs. Dart et al. (2000) suggested that students who had qualitative conceptions such as personal fulfillment and experiential conceptions like a process not bound by time were more likely to utilize deep approaches to learning in contrast to students who had quantitative conceptions such as an increase of knowledge who were more likely to rely on superficial approaches.

Takayama(2000), who constructed a scale of conception of learning of Japanese students consisting of nine categories that included lifelong learning, and compulsion/duty, found that subjective exploration, growth/improvement and learning/repetition(effort) have positive influences on deep learning behavior including checking one's own understanding or making associations of uncommon knowledge. On the contrary, obligation/compulsion has negative influences on it (Takayama, 2002).

As noted previously, goal orientation and conception of learning have been viewed as regulating factors that affect learning behavior. Goal orientation involves a student's belief about their goals and what they have learned. Conception of learning is a student's belief on how to view the process of learning. Both concepts are thought to be personal characteristics formed through experiences and are closely related. There are two possibilities: (1) goal orientation may be a predictor of conception of learning that affects learning behavior; or (2) conception of learning may be a predictor of goal orientation that affects learning behavior. In this study, the relationship between goal orientation and conception of learning, and its effects on learning behavior were examined.

Coal orientation and conception of learning form the basis of students' learning behavior. To clarify these relationships is extremely important in considering the problems of education and learning at the place of educational practice.

1.3 Purpose

The first aim of this study was to examine three models of goal orientation and conception of learning on learning behavior (Fig. 1) and to compare their validities by using covariance structure analysis.

Model 1: Conception of learning mediation model

Model 2: Goal orientation mediation model

Model 3: Independent model

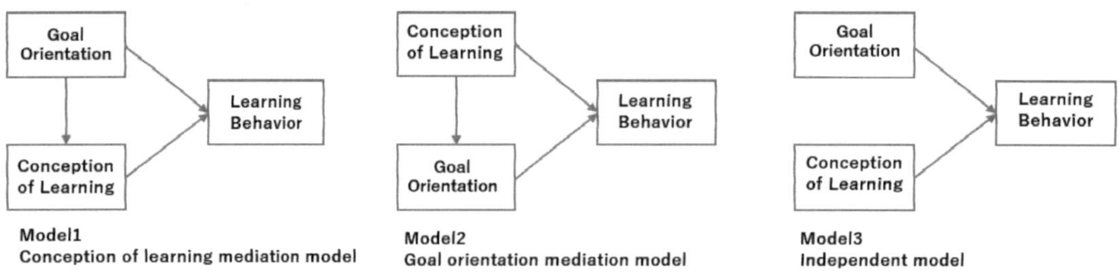

Figure 1. Three Models of Goal Orientation and Conception of Learning on Learning Behavior

The second aim of this study was to focus on the subordinate structures of goal orientation, conception of learning and learning behavior, and to clarify the causal relationship among the three.

Previous studies on goal orientation and conception of learning have mainly dealt with test scores of specific subjects and short-term learning behavior observed over a series of a few minutes. However, it is important to conduct research on learning tasks that are completed over a long-term process and that are based on a student's proactive attitude. Consequently, in the current study, graduation thesis research, as the learning task, that was conducted in a university was investigated.

2. METHOD

Subjects

The participants included 185 fourth-grade university students from the School of Integrated Arts and Sciences of a Japanese public university.

Procedures

The study was conducted in February 2018. The participants answered questionnaires during the presentation session of their graduation thesis.

Measures

The participants were asked to indicate their agreement or disagreement for each item in the questionnaires on 5-point likert scale, ranging from do not agree at all to completely agree.

Goal Orientation

The questionnaire comprised 18 items, which was modified from Mitsunami (2010) translated from the Achievement Goal Scale developed by Elliot and Church (1997).

Conception of Learning

The questionnaire comprised 24 items. The items were partially modified from Takayama's (2002) scales. **Learning Behavior**

The questionnaire consisted of 8 items. The items were partially modified from Mitsunami's (2010) scales. The items were modified to measure student's motivational beliefs and learning outcomes in the context of undertaking graduation work.

3. RESULTS AND DISCUSSION

The first objective of the study, Purpose 1, was to examine three causal models of goal orientation and conception of learning in relation to learning behavior. First, the variables of goal orientation, conception of learning, and learning behavior were clarified by performing factor analysis (3.1.). Subsequently, covariance structure analysis was conducted by using the variables clarified by the factor analysis. Furthermore, the suitability of the three models was compared (3.2.).

The second objective, Purpose 2, was to clarify the relationship between the subscales of goal orientation, conception of learning and learning behavior based on the results of the covariance structure analysis (3.3.).

3.1 Structure of the Scales

3.1.1 Goal Orientation Scale

Factor analysis (principal factor with promax rotation) of goal orientation was performed. We found three factors with eigenvalues were 1 or more. The analysis was conducted again; items that were loaded at .40 or less as well as items that were loaded at .40 or more on two or more factors were excluded. The details of each item and the results of the analysis are presented in Table 1. The following three factors emerged: Performance-Avoidance Goal, Learning Goal and Performance-Approach Goal. An average value of the items was regarded as the respective value of each factor.

Table 1. Goal Orientation Items and Factor Loadings

Factors and Items	I	II	III	h^2
Factor I . Performance Avoidance Goal(α=.87)				
I worry about the possibility of getting a bad grade.	**.83**	-.11	-.09	.61
I often think to myself, "What if I do badly?".	**.76**	-.07	.01	.56
My fear of performing poorly is often what motivates me.	**.74**	-.24	.14	.63
It is important for me to understand the content as thoroughly as possible.	**.67**	.33	-.12	.56
I just want to avoid doing poorly.	**.65**	-.06	.06	.44
My goal is to get better grades than most of the students.	**.60**	.07	.23	.58
I desire to completely master the material presented in classes.	**.50**	.15	.14	.40
Factor II . Learning Goal(α=.75)				
I hope to have gained a broader and deeper knowledge when I am done with classes.	.07	**.80**	-.03	.65
I prefer course material that really challenges me so I can learn new things.	-.22	**.64**	.22	.49
I want to learn as much as possible from class.	.27	**.67**	-.17	.50
I prefer course material that arouses my curiosity, even if it is difficult to learn.	-.26	**.56**	.10	.35
Factor III. Performance Approach Goal(α=.76)				
I am striving to demonstrate my ability in relation to others.	.07	-.09	**.76**	.58
I am motivated by the thought of outperforming my peers.	.03	.16	**.61**	.47
It is important to me to do better than the other students.	.10	.07	**.58**	.43
Contribution rate (%)	31.5	14.0	6.3	
Accumulated contribution rate (%)	31.5	45.5	51.8	

3.1.2 Conception of Learning Scale

Factor analysis (principal factor with promax rotation) of goal orientation was conducted. Four factors with eigenvalues were 1 or more were found. The analysis was conducted again; items that were loaded at .40 or less as well as items that were loaded at.40 or more on two or more factors were excluded. In Table 2 the details of each item and the results of analysis are presented. The following four factors emerged: Autonomous Development Duty and Memorizing, Growing Mind and Effort. An average value of the items was regarded as the respective value of each factor.

Table 2. Conception of Learning Items and Factor Loadings

Factors and Items	I	II	III	IV	h^2
Factor I . Autonomous Development(α =.90)					
Learning is something we continue to do as long as we live.	**.91**	.11	.03	-.13	.70
Learning is something that will continue after becoming a member of a society.	**.82**	-.10	.01	-.06	.72
Learning is something that will continue throughout life.	**.81**	-.02	-.02	-.04	.63
Learning is trying to know what you are deeply interested in.	**.76**	-.05	-.07	.04	.60
Learning is actively exploring your interests.	**.69**	-.08	-.01	.07	.57
Learning involves learning what you truly want to do voluntarily.	**.53**	-.15	-.02	.11	.42
Factor II . Duty and Memorizing(α=.84)					
Learning is being forced by parents or teachers.	.04	**.76**	-.10	-.03	.56
Learning is accurately memorizing the contents of materials.	-.10	**.75**	.16	-.11	.65
Learning is being forced to do things that you do not want to do.	-.10	**.73**	-.16	.02	.64
Learning is memorizing the textbook contents at a desk.	-.02	**.68**	.22	-.01	.53
Learning is being forced to do things that you do not want to do.	.03	**.68**	-.22	.06	.50
Learning is memorizing answers accurately for examinations.	.03	**.49**	.06	.14	.28
Factor III. Growing Mind(α =.74)					
Learning involves human beings' forming a spiritual core.	.09	-.02	**.71**	-.03	.57
Learning means living a life like a human being.	.04	.09	**.70**	.03	.54
Learning is not accumulating knowledge, but forming a person's attitude.	-.11	-.10	**.65**	.01	.37
Factor IV. Effort(α=.76)					
Learning is what you acquire with effort.	-.07	-.08	.08	**.91**	.80
It takes much time and effort to learn.	.10	.13	-.08	**.68**	.54
Contribution rate (%)	30.3	15.5	6.6	3.4	
Accumulated contribution rate (%)	30.3	45.8	52.5	55.9	

3.1.3 Learning Behavior Scale

Factor analysis (principal factor with promax rotation) of learning behavior was performed. It was determined that the first eigenvalue was sufficiently larger than the second eigenvalue and subsequently, that one factor solution was desirable. The analysis was conducted again; items were loaded at .40 or less were excluded. In Table 3, the details of each item and the results of analysis are shown. An average value of the 6 items was regarded as the learning behavior variable.

Table 3. Learning Behavior Items and Factor Loadings

A Factor and Items	I	h^2
Factor Ⅰ. Learning Behavior(α=.81)		
I tried to improve the quality of my graduation thesis as much as possible.	**.82**	.68
Even though it was difficult, I worked on it without giving up.	**.71**	.50
I studied what I did not know, or I asked my teacher and my friends about it.	**.69**	.47
I set goals and plans.	**.60**	.37
I often tried to read and understand the contents.	**.59**	.35
I was prepared to be able to respond to any questions in the presentation.	**.49**	.24
Contribution rate (%)	43.5	

3.2 Structural Equation Modeling

Using structural equation modeling (path analysis), we assessed how well the three models fit the data.

In Model 1, goal orientation affects learning behavior directly or through the conception of learning. First, it was hypothesized that the three variables of goal orientation would predict the relation of the four variables of conception of learning. Second, it was hypothesized that the three variables of goal orientation and four variables of conception of learning would predict the learning behavior variable based on the research results of Liem et al.(2008) and Takayama(2002). Subsequently, covariances were added between the variables of goal orientation and error variables of learning conception based on the correlation coefficient analysis results. The paths which were not significant, that is, less than the 10% level, were deleted and the analysis was conducted again.

In Model 2, conception of learning affects learning behavior directly or through goal orientation. The same procedure carried out for Model 1 was conducted.

In Model 3, goal orientation and conception of learning regulate learning behavior independently. It was hypothesized that the three variables of goal orientation and four variables of conception of learning would be related to learning behavior based on the research results of Liem et al.(2008) and Takayama(2002). Based on the results of the correlation analysis, covariances were added between the variables of goal orientation and learning conception. The paths, which were not significant, that is, less than the 10% level were deleted and the analysis was conducted again.

In Table 4, the results of evaluating the models are shown. The model fit was evaluated by the following indices: the goodness of fit index (GFI), the adjusted goodness of fit index (AGFI), the comparative fit index (CFI), and the root mean square error of approximation (RMSEA). Values above .95 for GFI, AGFI and CFI, and below .07 for RMSEA were regarded as a sufficient fit (Hooper at all, 2008). The result revealed that Model 1 accommodates the data very well. This result showed that students' conceptions of learning partially mediated the relationship between learning orientation and learning behavior

Table 4. Results of evaluating the models

Model	GFI	AGFI	CFI	RMSEA
1	.988	.956	1.00	.000
2	.941	.847	.915	.109
3	.984	.918	.963	.089

3.3 Path Analysis for Causality

We examined the effects of goal orientation and conception of learning on learning behavior with Model 1, which was the most suitable of the three models. The covariance structure analysis result of Model 1 is depicted in Figure 2. The numerical values of the unidirectional arrows are the standardized path coefficients and the numerical value of the bidirectional arrows are the correlation coefficients.

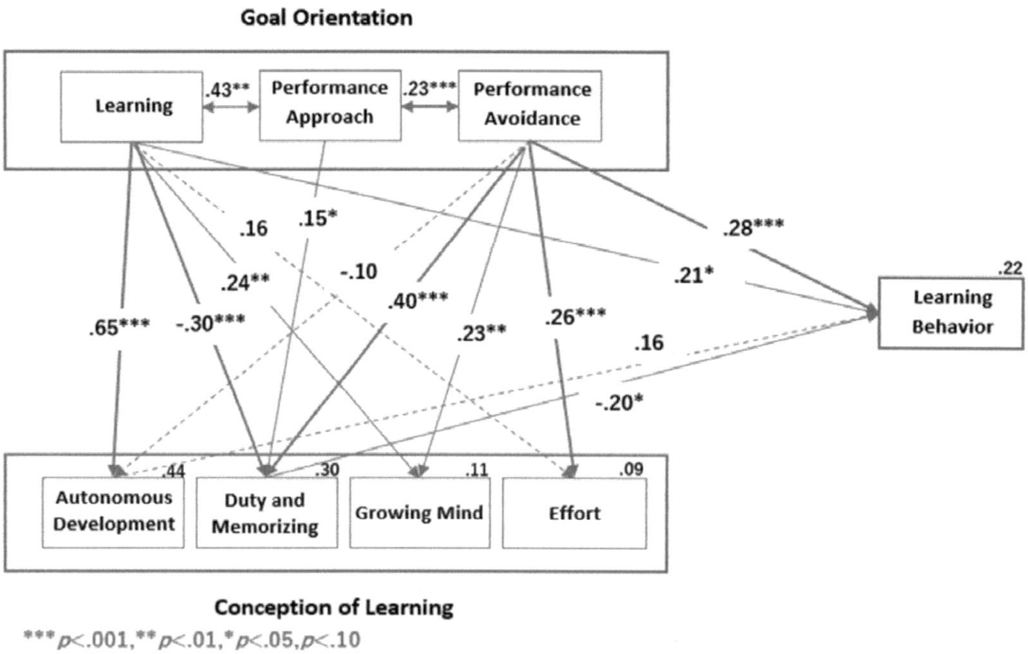

Figure 2. The Covariance Structure Result of Model 1

Learning Goal(β=.21) and Performance-Avoidance Goal(β=.28) had direct positive effects on Learning Behavior. In many previous studies (e.g. Liem et al., 2008), performance-avoidance goals have been considered to have a negative effect on learning behavior; however, a positive effect was confirmed in this study. The learning behavior component in the graduation thesis study determines whether or not students will be able to graduate. This constraint may result in students' attitudes such as "I do not want to get bad grades," thus, resulting in a positive effect and promoting positive learning behavior.

Learning Goal had a positive effect (β=. 65) on Autonomous Development, and a negative effect (β=-.30) on Duty and Memorizing. On the contrary, Performance-Avoidance Goal had a negative effect (β=.-.10) on Autonomous Development and a positive effect (β=. 40) on Duty and Memorizing. Consequently, while goal-oriented students tended to regard learning as autonomous, but not mandatory activities, performance-avoidance goal-oriented students were more likely to regard learning as mandatory, but not autonomous activities.

In addition, Autonomous Development had a positive effect (β=. 16) on Learning Behavior while Duty and Memorizing had a negative effect (β=. -.20) on Learning Behavior. Our findings provide support to Takayam's(2002) study. It indicates that if students regard learning as autonomous, their active learning behaviors may be promoted whereas if they regard learning as mandatory, their active learning behaviors may be suppressed.

In summary, both learning and performance-avoidance goals have direct positive effects on learning behavior; however, although the former has an indirect positive effect, the latter has an indirect negative effect on learning behavior through Autonomous Development and Duty and Memorizing, respectively.

4. CONCLUSION AND LIMITATION

In this study, we examined the causal relationship of goal orientation and conception of learning on learning behavior; previously, these concepts were examined separately in preceding studies. The results of the covariance structure analysis revealed that the causal effect in the model regarding goal orientation to learning behavior through conception of learning, in which the mediational role of conception of learning was confirmed.

Learning goals had a positive effect on autonomous learning conception and had a negative effect on forced learning conception. While performance-avoidance goals had a negative effect on autonomous learning conception, it had a positive effect on forced learning conception. In addition, autonomous learning conception had a positive effect and forced learning conception had a negative effect on learning behavior. The relation of paths connecting goal orientation and learning behavior through the conception of learning reveals that the learning goal has a positive effect, but the performance-avoidance goal has a negative effect on the learning behavior indirectly through Autonomous Development and Duty and Memorizing, respectively.

In this study, we examined graduation thesis research that was conducted in a university as a learning task. Depending on the nature of learning tasks to be examined, it is a possible that a different result may be reached. Furthermore, it is recommended that other learning tasks be examined. In addition, although self-evaluation by students was treated as a measure of learning behavior, in order to guarantee objectivity, it is recommended that adding a more objective viewpoint such as evaluation by teachers be included.

REFERENCES

Ames, C., & Archer, J. ,1987. Mothers'beliefs about the role of ability and effort in school learning. *Journal of Educational Psychology,* Vol.79, pp.409-414.

Ames, C., & Archer, J. ,1988. Achievement goals in the classroom: Students'learning strategies and motivation process. *Journal of Educational Psychology*, Vol.80, pp.260-267.

Antonio Valle, Ramón G. Cabanach, José C. Núnez, Julio González- Pienda, Susana Rodríguez, Isabel Piñeiro, 2003. Multiple goals, motivation and academic learning. *British Journal of Educational Psychology*, Vol.73, pp.71-87.

Arief Darmanegara Liem, Shun Lau, Youyan Nie, 2008. The role of self-efficacy, task value, and achievement goals in predicting learning strategies, task disengagement, peer relationship, and achievement outcome . *Contemporary Educational Psychology*, Vol.33, pp.486-512.

Bandura,A., 2012. On the Functional Properties of Perceived Self-Efficacy Revisited. *Journal of Management*, Vol.38, No.1,pp.9-44.

Dart, Barry C., Burnett, Paul C., Purdie, Nola M., Boulton-Lewis, Gillian M., Campbell, Jenny, & Smith, David ,2000. Students' conceptions of learning, the classroom environment and approaches to learning. *The Journal of Educational Research*, Vol.93, No.4, pp. 262-270.

Dweck, C. S. , 1986. Motivational processes affecting learning. *American Psychologist*, Vol.41, pp.1040-1048.

Elliot, A. J. ,1999. Approach and avoidance motivation and achievement goals. *Educational Psychologist*, Vol.34, pp.169-189.

Elliot, A. J., & Church, M. A.,1997. A hierarchical model of approach and avoidance achievement motivation. *Journal of Personality and Social Psychology*, Vol.72, pp.218-232.

Elliot, A. J., & Harackiewicz, J. M., 1996. Approach and avoidance achievement goals and intrinsic motivation: A mediational analysis. *Journal of Personality and Social Psychology*, Vol.70, pp.461-475.

Elliott, E. S., & Dweck, C. S. ,1988. Goals: An approach to motivation and achievement. *Journal of Personality and Social Psychology*, Vol.54, No.1, pp.5-12.

Hooper, D, Coughlan, J and Mullen, M ,2008. Structural Equation Modelling: Guidelines for Determining Model Fit. *ElectronicJournal of Business Research Methods*, Vol.6, No.1, pp.53-60.

Marton, F., Dall'Alba, G., & Beaty, E. ,1993. Conceptions of learning. *International Journal of Educational Research*, Vol.19, pp.277-300.

Mitsunami, M. ,2010. Influence of Achievement Motive and Goal Orientation on Learning Behavior : Different in Cognitive Strategies. *Japanese Journal of Educational Psychology*, Vol.58, pp.348-360.

Rawsthorne, L. J., & Elliot, A, J. ,1999. Achievement goals and intrinsicmotivation: A meta-analytic review. *Personality and Social Psychology Review*, Vol.3, pp.326–344.

Säljö, R. ,1979. Learning in the learner's perspective. I. Some common sense conceptions, In *Reports from the stitute of Education*, No.76, Gothenburg, Sweden: University of Gteborg.

Takayama, S. ,2000. Characteristics and Structure of Studen Conception of Learning. *Memoirs of the Faculty of Education. Literature and Social science*, Vol. 34, pp.1-10.

Takayama, S. , 2002. The Relationship between Learning Conception, it's Determinants and Learning Strategies. Memoirs of the Faculty of Education. *Literature and Social science*, Vol.37, pp.19-26.

Van Rossum, E. J., & Schenk, S. M. ,1984. The relationship between learning conception, study strategy and learning outcome. *British Journal of Educational Psychology*, Vol.54, pp.73-83.

STUDY ON THE FACTORS CONTRIBUTING TO THE MOTIVATION OF MATHEMATICAL STUDIES AT THE UNIVERSITY

Anna Vintere
Latvia University of Life Sciences and Technologies, Liela Sreet 2, Jelgava, Latvia, LV-3001

ABSTRACT

The mathematics studies at university develop the cognitive abilities of the person, influence studies of special subjects as well as contribute to the development of professional competence. Nevertheless, several studies have been carried out to show that the quality of mathematical studies is decreasing and students' preparation and knowledge deteriorates. The article describes factors influencing the development of mathematics education, seeing motivation as a key element of successful teaching and learning. The article includes theoretical analysis of topical issues like the definitions of learning motivation, its influencing factors, which contribute to the development of mathematical thinking and competence, etc. Based on the analysis and evaluation of the scientific literature as well as taking into consideration the author's reflection, experience and observations, in the study the authors found out the factors influencing mathematics learning at the university, which include internal motives (attitude), rational thinking (potential values of mathematics and advantages in the labor market) and external factors (teaching of mathematics at the university). The findings illustrated by the results of the survey of the students from Latvia University of Life sciences and Technologies (LLU) and Riga Technical University (RTU) on the mathematics learning and teaching. The study proves that the higher the students' achievements in mathematics, the more positive attitude towards mathematics and mathematics studies at the university.

KEYWORDS

External Factors, Cognitive Abilities, Internal Motives, Mathematics Learning, Motivation, Rational Thinking

1. INTRODUCTION

Mathematics always has been an important factor for the person's intelligence and personality forming and development, as well as a key to understanding the world around us, a base for scientific and technological progress. In accordance with Servais (1957) mathematics develops intellectual qualities such as logical thinking - ability to reason deductively, ability to abstract, generalize, classify, ability to think, analyse, and criticize. He pointed out that mathematics plays an important role both in the development of intellect and in the development of personality. Mathematical knowledge is a fundamental basis for the person's cognitive development (Kangro, 2006). According to Evans (2000), mathematical knowledge is not only a fundamental basis for the person's scientific development, but it also relates to the area of specific emotional experience, which is characterized by clearness of mind, unexpected fantastic discovery and full comprehension. Mathematics is also viewed as a dynamic process in which a person creates and implements his mathematics according to his abilities and needs (Dunn et al, 2000).

The mathematics studies at university develop the cognitive abilities of a person, influence studies of special subjects as well as contribute to the development of professional competence ensuring highly qualified specialists for the knowledge-based, skill and technology-intensive industries. Practical contribution of mathematics as a tool to the idea of sustainable development of society, for example, is reflected in the Textbooks for pedagogues, curriculum leaders and ministries of education by UNESCO, highlighting the role of mathematics in providing decision-making tools and developing understanding of the complex system related to sustainability (Textbooks for sustainable..., 2017).

Taking into account the above-mentioned aspects, in the study process of mathematics, due attention should be paid to the development of intellectual potential of students, building and developing the qualities of mathematical thinking. In spite of the above mentioned, several studies have shown that the quality of the mathematics studies is decreasing and the level of students' preparation and knowledge is getting worse. There are several factors that influence the development of mathematics education.

First of all, a decreasing mathematical knowledge is observable among first year university students in recent years. The lack of mathematics prerequisite skills at tertiary level has been recognised as an issue since the late 1970s and is known as the 'mathematics problem' (Rylands & Coady, 2009). It's also a problem in Latvia.

Secondly, as mentioned above, mathematics is one of the essential knowledge necessary to live and work. Unfortunately, the research, made by the author, shows that more than one fifth of Latvian students (22.7%) rate their knowledge in mathematics as insufficient, while 36.8% of respondents - as satisfactory. Only 11.5% of students who have completed higher mathematics courses are confident in their math skills (Vintere, 2018).

Thirdly, it is well known that in recent years several universities have reduced the time allocated to mathematics studies, but the content has remained unchanged or even increased. Therefore, the situation is that teaching of mathematics consists mainly of transmitting of main concepts to students, mostly focusing on task-solving techniques. Traditional teaching involves the passive transmission of abstract, symbolic and existing mathematical structures to students, thus forcing them to adopt thinking structures developed by others which do not motivate students to get better results. In turn, students are interested in explaining in detail how the particular mathematical calculation techniques are applied in real life context.

Many authors agree that there is a variety of factors and circumstances that have an impact on the teaching and learning, university life etc. (Kahu, 2013). Several studies show that motivation is a key element of successful teaching and learning. According to the Gould (2010), there are several reasons for low learning motivation of pupils and students, for example, the underestimation of the importance of mathematics education by the society in general, the crammed curriculum in schools and higher educational establishments, redundant content of appraisal and training materials, inability of training programs to meet the needs of students etc. (Gould, 2010).

For reasons above, the aim of this article, based on the literature review, to find out the factors contributing to the motivation of mathematical studies at the university. To illustrate the student's motivation to master mathematics based on the factors developed and to reflect students' views on teaching and teaching of mathematics, data from the survey carried out at two of the largest universities: University of Latvia's Life Sciences and Technology (LLU) and Riga Technical University (RTU) were used.

2. MATERIALS AND METHODS

The problem has been approached by analysing and evaluating the scientific literature for the development of the methodological basis of this study. The article includes theoretical analysis of topical issues like the definitions of learning motivation, its influencing factors, which contributes to the development of mathematical thinking and competence, etc.

There are several approaches to motivation in scientific literature. One of the approaches defines motivation as a "need" that forces a person to do or not do something by looking at motivation as interconnectedness of beliefs, perceptions, values and interests. Seeing the need as the main motivation for learning, it is essential to identify the needs that encourage students to learn (Broussard & Garrison, 2004). In this context the main task of the study process is to develop competencies for the implementation of professional activities.

Another approach describes motivation as a psychologically and physiologically regulative process of dynamic, psychic human activity that determines its persistence, organization, activity and progress (Šteinberga, 2013).

In Latvia, motivation is also defined as a set of certain motives that promote human behavior in a particular direction. Motivating is the incention to choose one of the alternatives to achieve personal goals" (Praude & Beļcikovs, 2001). The motivation is also the internal psychic forces of the person, which encourage this person to work (Renge, 2004).

Learning motivation engages students in the learning process and creates a lasting interest in it. With the increasing personal motivation, the productivity of the problem solution also increases - the content and structural properties of the intellectual activity are subordinated to the actions of the person (Kongro, 2010). The learning motivation is characterized by the education system, the organization of the educational process, the subjective qualities of the students - age, gender, intellectual development, abilities, a claim stick, self-evaluation, etc., teachers' system of the attitudes towards the student.

Learning motivation depends on different motivational factors: professional, cognitive, personal prestige, pragmatic (getting a diploma), with the first two being dominant among students with higher success (Ильин, 2002). According to Ilyin (Ильин), the main factors in creating positive learning motivation are: (1) identification of the goals of the current and further studies; (2) the theoretical and practical significance of the knowledge to be acquired; (3) the emotional form of the presentation of learning material; (4) demonstration of perspective directions in the development of scientific concepts; (5) emphasizing the professional orientation of the teaching activity, (6) integrating the problem tasks into the structure of the learning activity, (7) securing the psychological climate based on curiosity and cognitive interest in the academic group. On the basis of the acquired motivation, students develop a definite attitude towards different study subjects, including mathematics (Ильин, 2002).

Several scientific studies have shown that emotions and motivation play an important role in the mathematics study process, considering them as factors characterizing the personal intellectual activities and development of mathematical thinking. Evans (2000), studying the relationship between emotions and mathematical thinking, recognized that the fear of mathematics is rather difficult to separate from other emotions that arise in the process of learning mathematics: confidence, diffedence, pleasure, dislike, anger, boredom (Evans, 2000). In turn, Wedege recommends solving emotion-related problems in mathematics through a contextual approach (Wedege, 1999).

Attitude is also considered to be an important factor in the development of mathematical thinking, with attitude being understood as an integrated personality trait, formed in a unit of life experience, knowledge acquisition, experience, and manifesting itself in values, goals, ideals, and norms (Kangro, 2010). Swedish researchers' findings show that in so-called school mathematics an encounter occurs between the subject of mathematics and people's attitudes, experiences, feelings and thoughts, which sometimes creates special problems in education. Many people associate mathematics with feelings of failure, anxiety, humiliation, suspicion and disassociation. The experience of school mathematics thus becomes a life-inhibiting stigma even creates learning blockades. A person who feels anxiety and suffers learning blockages when faced with this subject is therefore likely to conclude that the subject is meaningless; it neither improves understanding of the environment nor adds to practical knowledge (Gustafsson & Ouwitz, 2004).

The results of the survey of students from two major technical universities in Latvia: Latvia University of Life sciences and Technologies (LLU) and Riga Technical University (RTU) are used to illustrate students' motivation to learn mathematics and to reflect students' views on the current mathematical study process. The survey was carried out during May, 2017 - March, 2018. The survey questionnaire includes several diagnostic blocks, but this paper analyzes the answers to questions that describe the motivation to learn mathematics. Statements describing the motivation of mathematical learning, were grouped according to Muchinsky, who distinguishes three groups of the motivation: internal motives, rational thinking and external factors (Muchincky, 2000). The factors influencing mathematics learning at the university are summarized in Table 1.

Table 1. The factors influencing mathematics learning at the university

Groups of the motivation	Characteristics	Statements
Internal motives	Mathematics learning experience, attitude	a) Mathematics have always been my favourite subject b) Mathematics, which I studied, could have been more complicated c) I do not like mathematics d) I did not understand most mathematical concepts that I studied
Rational thinking	The potential values of mathematics	a) Mathematics was an interesting and meaningful subject b) Knowledge in mathematics helped me to understand other subjects c) The knowledge and abilities of mathematics, mathematical thinking helps me to achieve more in my life d) Mathematics develops thinking, helps to make a decision in a particular situation, find new ideas.
	Advantages in the labour market	a) The need for mathematical knowledge in the contemporary labour market b) Studying mathematics develops logical thinking, accuracy and concreteness of future specialists c) A person who understands mathematics will easily deal with tasks that require thinking d) Employers highly value people who have a good understanding of mathematics
External factors	Teaching of math at the university	a) Mathematics was taught formally and jadedly b) Most students do not understand math and try to learn the laws by heart c) Linking the course of mathematics with real-life situations d) Usage of mathematics in a particular specialty

3. FINDINGS

According to the survey results, the external factors, characterising by the teaching of mathematics at the university, are the most important factors that determine the motivation of mathematics learning. As the time allocated to mathematics studies in universities in Latvia has been reduced, with the same content remaining, teachers only explain the main concepts, focusing on task-solving techniques during the lectures. In turn, students are interested in a detailed explanation of how precisely the particular mathematical calculation methods are applied in practice. Survey results show that there is the need to link mathematics studies with the calculations that are actually used in a particular specialty.

According to the students' answers, mathematics at universities should be taught in solving real-life problems with the help of mathematics and the lecturers should explain examples of real life where the particular teaching substance is used. According to students' opinion, it could make it easier to perceive and understand the mathematical concepts. Students also draw attention to the need to demonstrate the connection of higher mathematics with other study subjects and its application in them. Study results show that teaching mathematics have to be concerned with the environment and the chosen future profession, with practical examples in life / profession, thus creating interest in students as well as motivating them to succeed in mathematics and competence development (Vintere, 2018).

Students recognized internal motives (mathematics learning experience) in the second place. The study demonstrates the coherence of students' mathematical competence with self-esteem learning experience and attitude. The higher the student values his knowledge in mathematics, the higher the self-assessment of mathematical competence (Vintere, 2017). Respondents evaluated their knowledge of mathematics by excellent, good, satisfactory and in-sufficient. The results of students' mathematical competence self-assessment, which see their mathematical knowledge as excellent, are shown in the figure 1.

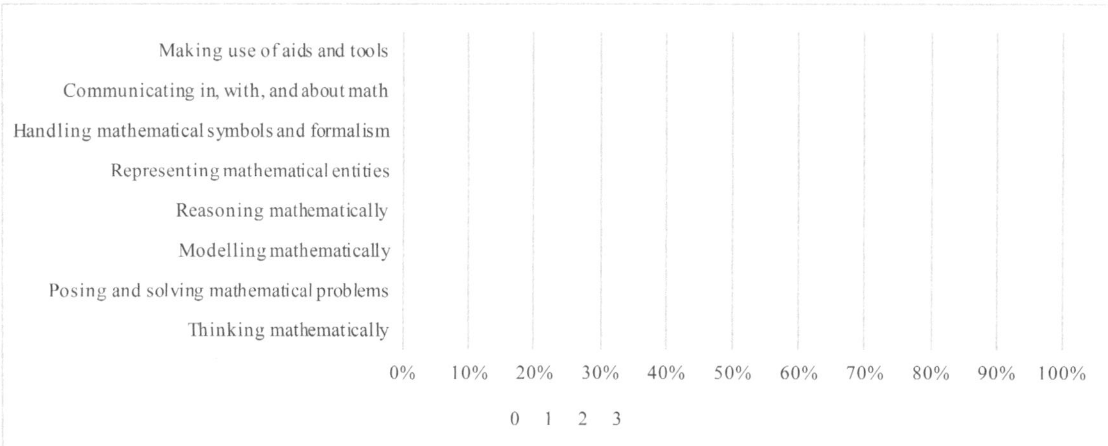

Figure 1. Self-assessment of mathematical competence of students with excelent mathematical knowledge (N=261)

The concept "mathematical competence" is based on Danish KOM (Competencies and the Learning of Mathematics) project. The respondents were asked to assess their mathematical competence on a 4-stage Likert scale, by writing in the questionnaire numbers from 0 to 3, where 0 – "I have not mastered this skill", but 3 – "I can apply mathematical knowledge in different situations of life, etc."

More than two thirds of students claim that their mathematical knowledge can be applied in different life situations and they can formulate a mathematical problem, as well as solve it. 78% of students, who rate their knowledge in mathematics as excellent, have obtained competence of "thinking mathematically" which include abstraction and generalisation of results; understanding of the certainty mathematical considerations. Almost 69% of these students can identify and specify mathematical problems; solve mathematical problems, have personal capabilities to decide if the question is considered as a problem.

The results of students' mathematical competence self-assessment that see their mathematical knowledge as in-sufficient are shown in the figure 2. Only 7% of these students can apply mathematical knowledge in different life situations. The worst skill gained is an ability of reasoning mathematically (Niss, 2003): ability to understand and assess already existing math argumentation and the notion of proof and to recognise the central ideas in proofs; knowledge/ ability to distinguish between different kinds of math statements; construction of chains of logical arguments and hence of transforming heuristic reasoning into own proofs (reasoning logically).

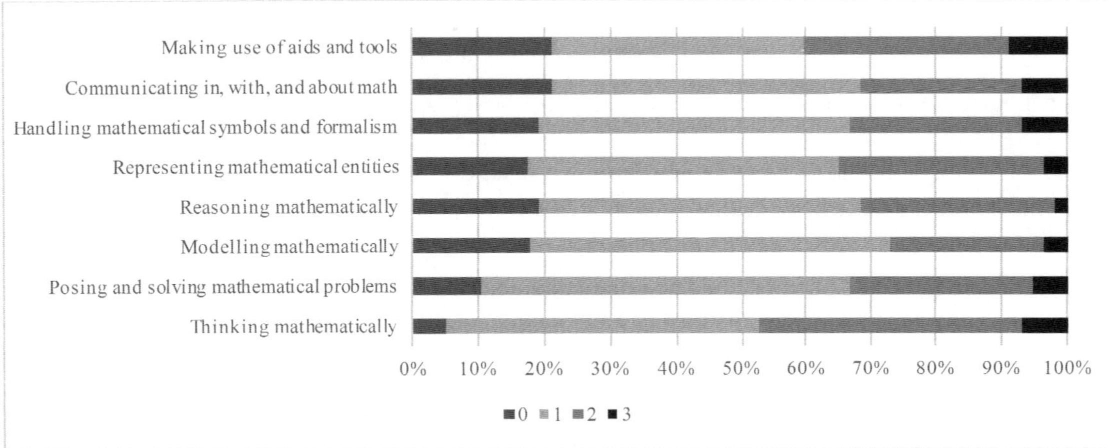

Figure 2. Self-assessment of students' mathematical competence with insufficient mathematical knowledge (N=461)

Rational thinking is, according to students, only a third factor. Evaluating students' attitude towards the potential values of mathematics, it should be noted that for 76.9% of students, who rate their knowledge in mathematics as exalted, mathematics helped to understand other subjects. They mathematical competences which are characterized by abilities to ask and answer questions in and with mathematics are very high.

According to a study by Havighurst (1972) on the relation between different life cycles and educational needs, at the age of 18-30, education is usually linked to career prospects and employment prospects. Mathematics is an area that needs to be as knowledgeable as possible so that an individual can successfully pursue his or her career. However, in this study, only 54.7% perceive the need for mathematical knowledge in today's labour market conditions, while 18.2% of respondents deny the connection between mathematical knowledge and employment, which undeniably reduces student motivation for achieving good results. An average 56% of respondents agree or even strongly agree with the statement "Mathematical thinking helps solving life and professional problems", 44% of them have the opposite opinion. 68% of total respondents agree with the statement "People who understand mathematics will easily deal with tasks that require thinking". Only 33% of students from computer sciences and information technologies specialties recognize the role of mathematical thinking in solving various problems.

4. CONCLUSION

Motivation is a key element of successful mathematics teaching and learning - a positive attitude to maths motivates learning more and making progress and achieving their goals.

The study shows that the first factor influencing mathematics learning at the university is internal motives (mathematics learning experience, attitude), second - rational thinking (potential values of mathematics and advantages in the labour market) and third - external factors (teaching of mathematics at the university).

Based on the students' views on the teaching mathematics at the university, the learning result could be more correlated not only with the repetition of a rule, algorithm solving examples, but it should be correlated with a deeper understanding of mathematics; the methods of teaching/learning of mathematics have to conform to the student's expectations, the process of learning should be more involving, interesting.

In order to influence motivation of the mathematics learning at the university it is important to develop positive attitudes of students towards the relevance of mathematics in professional activities and to enhance learning motivation on this basis.

Practical impact - the methodology and factors that influence the teaching of mathematics at a university described in the study can be used to promote and evaluate the motivation for learning other subjects.

Self-assessment method used in the empirical study. Therefore, the results are based on respondents' opinion.

It was a case study, and it only reflects the views of students who participated in it. The results were used only to illustrate findings. They do not provide generalization.

ACKNOWLEDGEMENT

The author expresses gratitude to Dr.oec. Evija Kopeika, researcher of the Riga Technical University for cooperation and support in conducting the students' survey.

REFERENCES

Broussard, S., & Garrison, M. (2004). The relationship between classroom motivation and academic achievement in elementary school - agreed children. *Family and Counsumer Sciences Research journal*, 106-120.

Evans, J. (2000). *Adults' Mathematical Thinking and emotions*. London: Routledge Falmer.

Dunn, R. & Griggs, Shirley A. (2000). Practical approaches to using learning styles in higher education: the how-to steps. In: *Practical approaches to using learning styles in highe education*. (Dunn R., Griggs, Shirley A.) Westport: Greenwood Publishing Group, Inc., 2000. Pp. 19 – 32.

Gould, M. (2010). GIScience grand challenges: How can research and technology in this field address big - picture problems? *ArcUser*, 13(4), 64–65. Available: http://www.esri.com/news/arcuser/1010/files/geochallenges.pdf

Guay, F., Chanal, J., Ratelle, C., Marshy, H., Larose, S., & Boivin, M. (2010). Intrinsic, identified, and controlled types of motivation for school subjects in young elementary school children. *British Journal of Educational Psychology*, 711-735.

Gustafsson, L., Ouwitz, L. (2004) *Adults and Mathematics – a vital subject*. ISSN 1650 -335X, NCM, 2004.

Havighurst, R.J. (1972). *Developmental tasks and education*. (3rd.ed) New York: McKay.

Ильин Е.П. (2002) Мотивация и мотивы. СПб: Питер. (In Russian)

Kahu, E.R. (2013). Framing student engagement in higher education. *Studies in Higher Education*, 38 (5): 758-73.

Kangro, I. (2006). Matemātikas studiju organizācijas problēmas. No: Red. Prof. A. Kangro Izglītības vadība. Rīga: Latvijas Universitātes Akadēmiskais apgāds. 697. s.j. (In Latvian)

Kangro, I. (2010) Studentu matemātiskās domāšanas attīstība profesionālās kompetences veidošanās procesā. *Promocijas darbs Doktora zinātniskā grāda iegūšanai pedagoģijā Augstskolas pedagoģijas apakšnozarē*, Rīga, 2010, 323.lp. (In Latvian)

Muchincky, P. M. (2000). *Psicologia Aplicada Al Trabajo*. Madrid: S.A. Ediciones Paraninfo.

Niss M., Mathematical competencies and the learning of mathematics: *The Danish KOM project. Mediterranean Conference on Mathematics Education, Athens, Greece: Hellenic Mathematical Society and Cyprus Mathematical Society*, 2003, pp. 115-124.

Praude, V., & Beļčikovs, J. (2001). Menedžments: teorija un prakse.Rīga: Vaidelote (Preses nams). (In Latvian)

Reņģe, V. Kad vēl nav par vēlu sākt mācīties? *Psiholoģijas pasaule*, (2004,gada 8) lpp. 2-5. (In Latvian)

Rylands, L. & Coady, C. (2009). Performance of students with weak mathematics in first-year mathematics and science. *International Journal of Mathematical Education in Science and Technology*, 40(6), 741–753.

Serve, V. 1957. Teaching mathematics in secondary schools. *Mathematical Education*, Vol.1, pp. 22-32. (in Russian)

Šteinberga, A. (2013). Pedagoģiskā psiholoģija.Rīga: RaKa. (In Latvian)

Textbooks for Sustainable Development. A Guide to Embedding. (2017). UNESCO MGIEP, 186 p. Available: http://unesdoc.unesco.org/images/0025/002599/259932e.pdf

Vintere A. (2017) Mathematical competences and competence-based mathematics learning for sustainable development. *Proceedings of the 8th international scientific conference "Rural Development 2017: Bioeconomy Challenges"*, Kaunas, Lithuania, 23-24 November, 2017 / Aleksandras Stulginskis University, Ministry of Agriculture of the Republic of Lithuania. - Kaunas, 2017,1386-1390 pp.

Vintere A. (2018) Study on engineering students experience in mathematics learning in context of sustainable development. *17th International scientific conference "Engineering for rural development": proceedings*, Jelgava, Latvia, May 23 - 25, 2018 Latvia University of Life Sciences and Technologies. Faculty of Engineering. Latvian Academy of Agricultural and Forestry Sciences. - Jelgava, 2018. - Vol. 17, 1186-1191pp.

Wedege, T. (1999). To know or not to know - mathematics, that is a question of context. *Educational Studies in Mathematics Education*, 39, 205-227.

BR-MAP: CONCEPT MAP SYSTEM USING E-BOOK LOGS

Masanori Yamada[1], Atsushi Shimada[2], Misato Oi[3], Yuta Taniguchi[2] and Shin'ichi Konomi[1]
[1]*Learning Analytics Center, Kyushu University*
[2]*Faculty of Information Science and Electrical Engineering, Kyushu University*
[3]*Innovation Center for Educational Resource, Kyushu University*
744, Motooka, Nishiku, Fukuoka, 8190395, Japan

ABSTRACT

This preliminary study developed the concept map tool "BR-Map" using learning logs on eBook viewer, and investigated the relationships between self-regulated learning (SRL) awareness, learning behaviors (usage of BR-Map, and one-minute paper and report submission), and learning performance. Psychometric data and learning logs were collected in the lecture course, and their relationships were analyzed using Spearman's correlation analysis. The results indicated that awareness of intrinsic value, use of cognitive learning strategies, and self-regulation had significant correlations with the usage of BR-Map. The awareness of cognitive learning strategies had significant correlation with standard deviation of one-minute paper submission hours. With regard to relationships between the BR-Map usage and learning behaviors, the relationships between the usage of BR-Map and one-minute paper submissions, which was a regularly weekly assigned task, were found.

KEYWORDS

Cognitive Learning Tool, Learning Analytics, Self-Regulated Learning

1. INTRODUCTION

1.1 Cognitive Learning

Cognitive learning research has been conducted for a long time in the field of educational technology research. Not only input but also consideration of, and interaction with, learning materials deepen information processing in both the mind and brain, and promote learning outcomes. Cognitive learning tools play an important role in enhancing learning outcomes, according to many previous researches (e.g., Leopold and Leutner, 2012). Concept maps are an effective cognitive learning tool for the enhancement of learning outcomes. Previous research (e.g., Clariana, et al, 2013; Yamada, 2010) indicated that a concept map makes learners aware of learning objects and the presence of peers. Concept maps promote cognitive learning performance and strategies (Fiorella and Mayer, 2013, 2017).

Perry and Winne (2006) evaluated the effects of the integrated cognitive learning tool, "gStudy," which was developed based on a self-regulated learning (SRL) model that centered on meta-cognitive skills. Learners become aware of academic strengths and weaknesses through metacognition. gStudy records learner's learning behaviors, promotes the cognitive learning process, and gives learners feedback. The concept map seems to be effective not only in improving learning performance but also the enhancement of metacognition. As further research, tracing and visualizing the learning process including the SRL process from input to consideration of concept maps and other learning support systems is desirable for creating an effective learning environment.

1.2 SRL and Learning Analytics

Self-regulated learning (SRL) is one of the important viewpoints for understanding learning behaviors. SRL is the active learning process used to regulate and monitor learning cognition, motivation, and behavior, and to set personal learning goals, including social aspects (Wolters, Pintrich, & Karabenick, 2003; Schunk and

Zimmerman, 2008). SRL also relates to metacognition (Schunk, 2008) and information processing (Winne and Hadwin, 1998). SRL seems to be a useful concept for understanding learners' learning features. The effects of SRL seem to be different for high- and low-performers. Schunk and Zimmerman (1998) further compared the learning behaviors of novice and expert SRL learners. Their results indicated that skillful learners controlled their learning process—such as making their learning plan, monitoring and reflection with their metacognition—and then they felt high self-efficacy, and had high internal motivation and learning performance.

Advances in Information and Communication Technology (ICT) can be of benefit to both learners and teachers to enhance SRL awareness and skills. When using ICT, learners can control when, what, and how they learn, without restrictions of time, learning space, and printed materials (Cunningham and Billingsley, 2003). Greene and Azevedo (2009) suggested 13 indicators of SRL in the context of computer-based learning such as help-seeking, expectation of adequacy of information, time and effort spent in planning. Recent research trends are focusing on the relationships between learning performance and SRL. Winne and his research colleague (2006) developed "gStudy" with a log analyzer, which constituted an early research about SRL in terms of learning analytics. Learning analytics is defined as "to clarify education and learning environment improvement using various data such as logs about learners and learning environment, with information processing methods" (e.g., Ifenthalar, 2015; Ogata et al, 2015). Goda et al (2013) suggested that SRL factors are useful to predict learning performance, and their successive study (2015) suggested that high-level SR learners can control and manage their learning plan in the context of their everyday lives, using a blended learning environment with ICT. Azevedo et al. (2017) suggested a framework for visualizing SRL awareness using multimodal data in e-learning settings. Yamada et al. (2017) suggested that the use of cognitive learning strategies—such as annotation as well as appropriate reading time for learning materials—play an important role in enhancing SRL awareness. Using ICT, learning behaviors that contribute to enhancing SRL awareness can be analyzed to support learning from the perspective of cognitive learning in the flow from input to consideration. This study aims to develop a concept map, "BR-Map," using learning logs stored on an ebook viewer that plays an important role in input, and investigate as a preliminary research the relationship between the usage of the concept map and SRL.

2. METHODS

2.1 Subjects and Course

Forty-four university students participated in this research. The course consisted of eight classes (one per week). The main learning object was to understand educational theories, principles, and history. There were two criteria for the grade: submitting a one-minute paper after every class, and a report. Students had to submit the one-minute paper within a day for a normal grade, but the teacher would accept it one day late (in such cases, the score would be reduced by half). The one-minute paper had to contain an abstract of the class and a discussion. The teacher explained the report themes three weeks before the submission deadlines. Students were required to submit the one-minute papers and reports on LMS.

2.2 BR-Map

BR-Map is a concept map tool using logs stored on an ebook viewer, "BookRoll," (Ogata et al, 2017) displayed in Figure 1. This is a simple and normal concept map tool with an interface as displayed in Figure 2, but BR-Map uses the logs on the ebook viewer. The usage flow of BR-Map is as follows: 1) The learner reads an ebook on BookRoll, 2) Learners highlight part(s) or attach memos on the ebook, 3) Learners open BR-Map, 4) BR-Map reads the logs of highlight(s) and memo(s) from the BookRoll database, 5) BR-Map lists all logs of highlight(s) and memos and displays them as objects on the left pane, 6) Learners click the object on the left pane, and drag-and-drop it on the right pane—the "concept map area," 7) Learners make a concept map by connecting objects using an "arrow". BR-Map allows learners to make many concept maps, using the "tab" function, and to save concept maps as a .png file. BR-Map was developed as a Moodle plug-in. The teacher adds one BR-Map plugin on a section in their course. BR-Map reads all the highlights and memo logs of all ebooks in the course.

BR-Map consists of two parts, the frontend and the server end. The frontend was developed using HTML/CSS and JavaScript using libraries including jsPlumb (for arrow presentation), html2canvas (for concept map presentation), canvg-browser (convert concept map to picture format (png)), EventBus (for event management), download.js (for download function), and jQuery. The server side consists of two servers—a web server using nginx 1.12 and a database server MySQL 5.7. Moodle 2.8.5 and PHP 5.6 were installed on the web server.

2.3 Data Collection

Students were asked to answer the motivational strategies for learning questionnaire (MSLQ) (Pintrich and DeGroot, 1990). The MSLQ, which consists of five factors (self-efficacy (SE), internal value (IV), cognitive strategies (CS), self-regulation (SR), and test anxiety (TA); 44 items in all, rated on a seven-point Likert scale), was used for the subjective evaluation of learners' SRL skills (see appendix). Students were asked to complete the MSLQ in the third class and again in the last class. The second method of data collection was the concept maps. The number of objects and links on the concept map of each learner were counted. The third method was the log of submission times of the one-minute papers and report. The submission time increased the earlier a student submitted the assignment. For example, if a student submitted the one-minute paper one hour before the deadline, the submission time was 1; if a student submitted the regular report 100 hours before deadline, submission time was 100. The final method was to measure report quality. A teacher evaluated the report quality as a score in the range of 0 to 40.

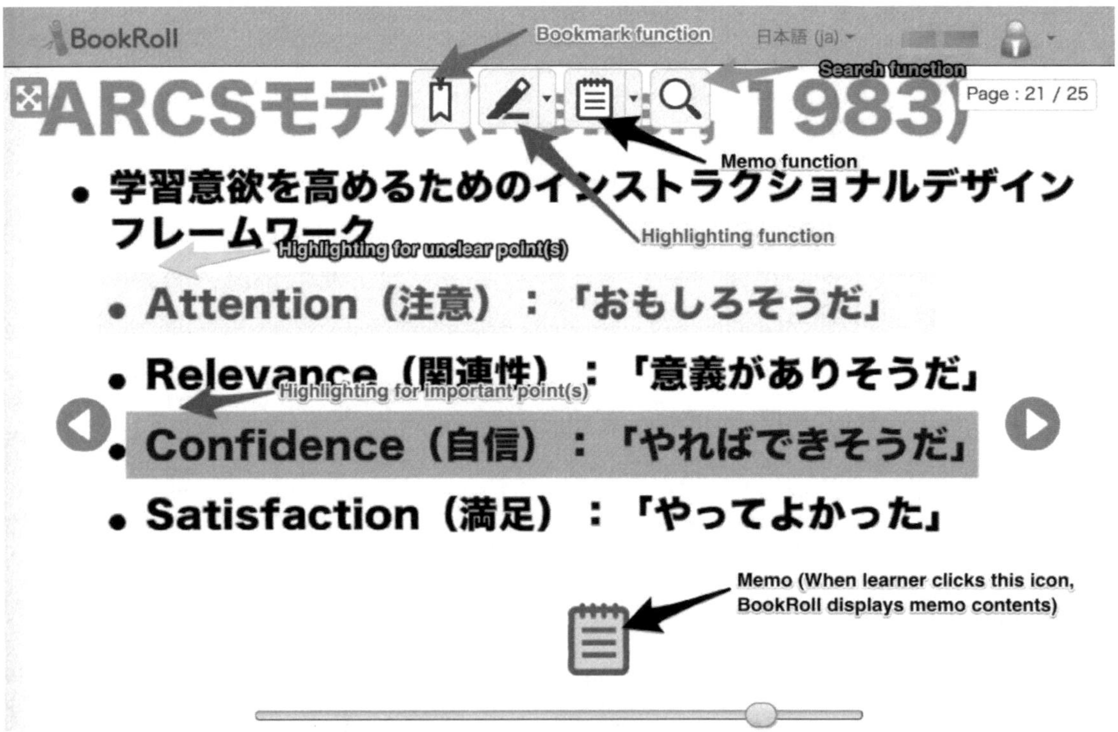

Figure 1. Interface of "BookRoll" (Ogata et al, 2017)

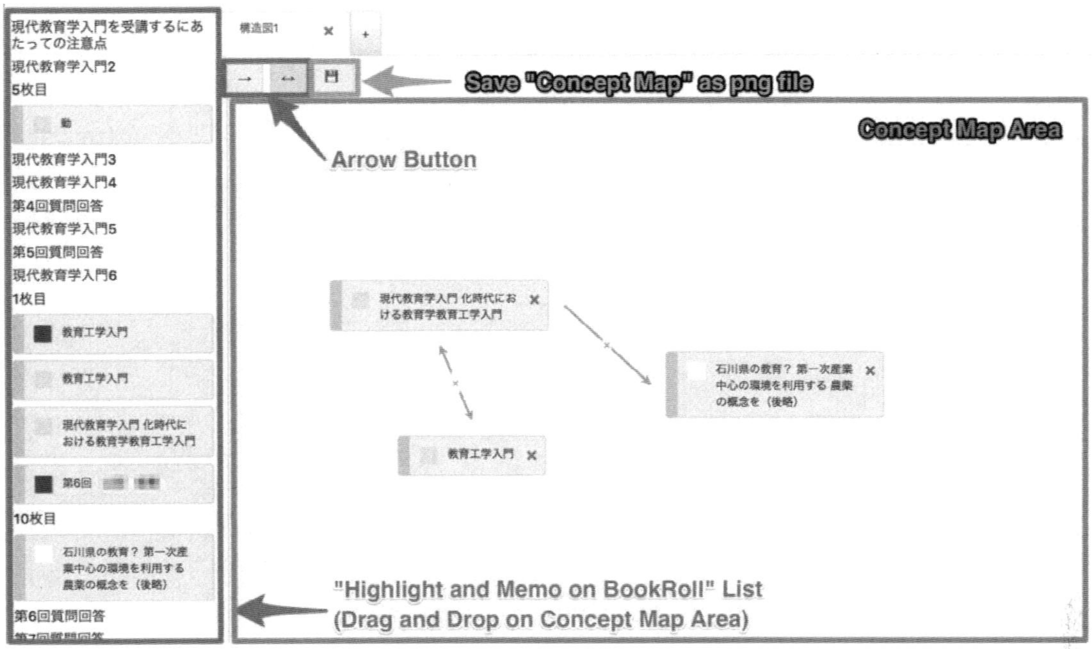

Figure 2. Interface of "BR-Map"

3. RESULTS

Of the 44 first-year students, 24 answered the questionnaire in class. We conducted Spearman's correlation analysis to investigate the relationship between SRL, submission time of the one-minute paper and report, standard deviation of the one-minute paper's submission times and the report score. In sections 3.1 and 3.2 below, we provide the descriptive data, and the results of the correlation analysis are given in section 3.3.

3.1 Descriptive data and Wilcoxon Signed-Rank Test for SRL

Table 1 shows the average, standard deviation, and median results of the Wilcoxon signed-rank test for each SRL factor. The score for each factor was calculated from the sum of each item in each factor. Table 2 displays the descriptive data of the concept map, submission time, and report quality. These results show that MSLQ factors except self-efficacy significantly declined between pre- and post-questionnaires. However, SDs of internal value, cognitive strategy use, and test anxiety declined very much—that is, factors of MSLQ declined overall, but lower-level learner scores improved and individual differences became small.

3.2 Descriptive data for Learning Behaviors

Tables 2 and 3 show learning behaviors and learning performance. In BR-Map usage, learners tended to create nodes more, though learners used link functions to some extent. With regard to submission of the one-minute paper and report, almost all of the learners kept the deadline. Learners tended to submit the one-minute paper between noon and evening. The SD of the one-minute paper submission hours indicated learning habits. For example, if the SD is 0, it indicates that a learner submits the one-minute paper at the same hour every week. In this study, eight out of 24 learners had an SD of submission hour less than 1. One-third of the learners had a stable learning habit. Interestingly, in five of the eight learners, the average of submission hours for the one-minute paper was less than 10 hours in five lectures. This means that these learners submitted their one-minute paper around the end of the day (from 22:00 to 23:59).

3.3 Correlation Analysis

The Wilcoxon signed-ranked test results revealed that awareness of SRL declined significantly overall. However, what kinds of learning behaviors and SRL awareness were affected by the use of BR-Map? Is awareness of SRL, learning behaviors, and learning performance related to the use of BR-Map? To investigate the relationships between psychological perspectives, learning behaviors, learning performance, and BR-Map usage, Spearman's correlation analysis was conducted. The differences between post- and pre-rating data for SRL were calculated. Table 4 shows the results.

Table 1. Average sum scores and Wilcoxon signed-ranked test results for each factor in MSLQ

Item	Average score (SD)		Median		*Z*	sig
	Pre	Post	Pre	Post		
Self-efficacy (min: 9, max: 63)	31.79 (7.45)	32.29(7.90)	32.00	33.00	-0.20	p = 0.84
Internal value (min: 9, max: 63)	46.71 (11.23)	42.08 (4.93)	49.00	42.00	2.82	p = 0.00
Cognitive strategy use (min: 13, max 91)	62.50 (12.51)	57.50 (5.99)	61.50	58.00	2.50	p = 0.01
Self-regulation (min: 9, max: 63)	37.08 (3.45)	33.13 (4.01)	37.50	34.00	3.09	p = 0.00
Test anxiety (min: 4, max 20)	16.29 (5.55)	14.00 (1.69)	16.00	14.00	1.83	p = 0.06

Table 2. Average sum score of nodes and links in BR-Map

Item	Average score (SD)	Median
Node	8.67 (6.79)	9.00
Link	3.88 (3.85)	2.50

Table 3. Average, SD, and median of learning behaviors and learning performance

Item	Average	SD	Median
Submission time for one-minute paper in the deadline (Min 0 – Max: 5)	4.92	0.28	5.00
Delayed submission time for one-minute paper	0.16	0.38	0.00
Sum of submission time (hour) for one-minute paper	26.38	17.51	24.00
Submission time (hour) of S.D. for one-minute paper	2.70	1.89	2.88
Submission time (hour) for report	20.08	31.18	11.50
Report score (Min 0 – Max 40)	32.71	4.97	33.00

Table 4. Spearman's correlation analysis results between MSLQ, node and link in BR-Map, learning behaviors, and learning performance

	Node	Link	One-minute paper submission	One-minute paper delayed submission	One-minute paper submission hours	S.D of One-minute paper submission hours	Report submission hours	Report score
SE	0.20	0.11	-0.04	0.06	0.26	-0.01	0.24	0.01
IV	0.30	**0.49***	0.18	-0.07	0.22	0.31	-0.10	-0.04
CS	0.34	**0.44***	0.18	-0.07	0.26	**0.36†**	0.03	0.04
SR	**0.43***	**0.47***	0.11	-0.19	0.24	0.12	-0.13	0.11
TA	0.09	0.10	0.18	-0.11	0.00	0.06	-0.05	0.02
Node	-	**0.76*****	**0.42***	**-0.54****	**0.53****	0.19	**0.42***	0.22
Link	**0.76*****	-	**0.36†**	**-0.42***	**0.41***	0.15	0.15	0.15
Report score	0.22	0.15	**0.40†**	**-0.45***	-0.20	-0.10	0.08	-

***: p < 0.001, **: p < 0.01, *: p < 0.05, †: p < 0.1

The results indicated that self-regulation and the number of links were correlated with the number of nodes, and internal value, cognitive strategies use, and self-regulation were correlated with the number of links. With regard to the relationships between learning behaviors, learning performance, and BR-Map use, the number of nodes was correlated with one-minute paper submissions, one-minute paper submission hours, and report submission hours positively, and with one-minute paper delayed submissions negatively. The number of links on BR-Map was correlated with one-minute paper submission and one-minute paper submission hours positively, and with one-minute paper delayed submissions negatively. However, the usage of BR-Map did not have any significant direct relationships with the report score.

4. CONCLUSION AND FUTURE RESEARCH

This study aimed to develop and conduct a formative evaluation of BR-Map from the perspective of self-regulated learning. It is hypothesized that BR-Map supports SRL skills—in particular, cognitive learning strategies use—directly, and it usage seems to be affected by the learning habit of reading learning materials regularly. The results of this study support the hypothesis to some extent. The usage of BR-Map was significantly correlated with the awareness of self-regulation and the use of cognitive learning strategies in MSLQ, and the submission times and hours of the one-minute paper. However, the usage of BR-Map was not significantly correlated with learning performance directly. According to many previous studies, supporting SRL leads to learning performance (e.g., Wolters et al, 2003; Yamada et al, 2016). There are two possible reasons; one is that learners could not effectively use the concept map on BR-Map for report writing. BR-Map allows learners to understand learning contents in a cross-class manner, but it did not focus on the report theme that the learners wrote. Second, BR-Map seems to enhance the understanding of learning materials, but it did not help learners in developing their ideas on the report theme. The class required learners to select a report theme and write abstracts of the theme and their idea. When learners did not include their idea in their report, it could lead to lower scores.

As future research, there are four points that need to be taken up. First, to improve BR-Map functions. Several learners asked to modify BR-Map, for example, adding memos on BR-Map and displaying the thumbnails of learning materials (slides) on the left pane. These functions seem to improve usability and affect awareness of learning objectives. Second, analysis of the relationships with ebook viewer logs—such as page flipping, highlighting, and memos—is required because these behaviors were considered to have direct effects on comprehension and self-regulated learning (Yamada, et al, 2017), as mentioned in section 1. Third, to analyze learning behaviors and learning performance with more data in order to investigate the effects of BR-Map. And finally, to develop a dashboard to collect and visualize the learning process using BR-Map, which would be essential for enhancing the effects of learning analytics on learning support. BR-Map is a cognitive medium that connects input and consideration. Learning logs stored on BR-Map seem to be useful to understand the learner's learning process. A dashboard to collect and visualize learning logs on BR-Map can be effective in understanding the status of the learner's learning process, which promotes effective learning support.

ACKNOWLEDGEMENT

This research was partially supported by Grant-in-aid for Scientific Research JP16H03080, JP17K18659, and JP18K18657 and the Qdai-jump Research (QR) Program of Kyushu University.

REFERENCES

Azevedo ,R., Millar, G.C., Taub, M., Mudrick, N.V., Bradbury, A.E., & Price, M.J. (2017). Using Data Visualizations to Foster Emotion Regulation during Self-Regulated Learning with Advanced Learning Technologies: A Conceptual Framework, Proceedings of Learning Analytics and Knowledge 2017, 444- 448.

Clariana, R.N., Engelmann, T., and Yu, W. (2013). Using Centrality of Concept Maps as a Measure of Problem Space States in Computer-Supported Collaborative Problem Solving", Educational Technology Research and Development, 61(3), pp. 423–442.

Cunningham, C. A. & Billingsley, M. (2003). Curriculum Webs: A Practical Guide to Weaving the Web into Teaching and Learning. Boston, MA: Pearson Educational, Inc.

Fiorella, L., and Mayer, R. E. (2013). The relative benefits of learning by teaching and teaching expectancy. Contemporary Educational Psychology, 38(4), 281–288. doi: 10.1016/j.cedpsych.2013.06.001.

Fiorella, L., and Mayer, R.E. (2017). Spontaneous spatial strategy use in learning from scientific text, Contemporary Educational Psychology, 49, 66-79. doi: 10.1016/j.cedpsych.2017.01.002

Goda, Y., Yamada. M., Matsuda, T., Kato, H. & Miyagawa, H. (2013). Effects of Help Seeking Target Types on Completion Rate and Satisfaction in E-Learning, Proceedings of INTED 2013, pp. 1399-1403

Goda, Y., Yamada, M., Kato, H., Matsuda, T., Saito, Y. & Miyamaga, H. (2015). Procrastination and other learning behavioral types in e-learning and their relationship with learning outcomes, Learning and Individual Differences, Vol.37, pp.72-80.

Greene, J.A., and Azevedo, R. (2009). A macro-level analysis of SRL processes and their relations to the acquitision of a sophisticated mental model of a complex system, Contemporary Educational Psychology, 34(1), 18-29. doi: 10.1016/j/cedpsych.2008.05.006

Ifenthaler, D. (2015). Learning Analytics. In J. M. Spector (Ed.), The SAGE Encyclopedia of Educational Technology (pp. 447-451). Thousand Oaks, CA: Sage.

Leopold, C., and Leutner, D. (2012). Science text comprehension: Drawing, main idea selection, and summarizing as learning strategies, Learning and Instruction, 22 (2012), pp. 16-26. doi: 10.1016/j.learninstruc.2011.05.005

Ogata, H., Yin C., Oi, M., Okubo, F., Shimada, A., Kojima, K. and Yamada, M.(2015). e-Book-based Learning Analytics in University Education, Ogata, H et al (Eds.). Proceedings of the 23th International Conference on Computers in Education, pp.401-406.

Ogata, H., Oi,M., Mohri, K., Okubo, F., Shimada, A., Yamada, M., Wang, J., and Hirokawa, S. (2017). Learning Analytics for E-book-Based Educational Big Data in Higher Education, H.Yasuura, C.-M.Kyung, Y.Liu, Y.-L.Lin. (Eds.) Smart Sensor at the IoT Frontier, Springer, 327-350

Pintrich, P. R. (1999) The role of motivation in promoting and sustaining self-regulated learning. International Journal of Educational Research, Vol.31, No.6, pp.459-470.

Perry, N. E., and Winne, P. H. (2006). Learning from Learning Kits: gStudy Traces of Students' Self-Regulated Engagements with Computerized Content, Educational Psychological Review, 18, 211-228. doi: 10.1007/s10648-006-9014-3

Schunk, D. H., and Zimmerman, B. J. (1998) Self-Regulated Learning: From Teaching to Self-Reflective Practice. New York, NY: The Guilford Press.

Schunk, D. H. (2008). Metacognition, self-regulation, and self-regulated learning: Research recommendations. Educational Psychology Review, 20(4), 463-467.

Winne, P., & Hadwin, A. F. (1998). Studying as self-regulated learning. In D.J. Hacker, J.Duntosky & A.C. Graesser (Eds.) Metacognition in educational theory and practice, pp.277-304, Mahwah NJ: Erlbaum.

Winne, P.H., Nesbit, J.C., Kumar, V., Hadwin, A.F., Lajoie, S. P., Azevedo, R., and Perry, N. E. (2006). Supporting Self-regulated Learning with gStudy Software: The Learning Kit Project, Technology, Instruction, Cognition and Learning, 3(1), 105-113

Wolters, C. A., Pintrich, P. R. & Karabenick, S. A. (2003) Assessing Academic Self-Regulated Learning. Paper prepared for the Conference on Indicators of Positive Development: Definitions, Measures, and Prospective Validity. Sponsored by ChildTrends, National Institutes of Health.

Yamada, M. (2010). Development and Evaluation of CSCL Based on Social Presence, Proceedings of World Conf. E-Learning in Corporate, Government, Healthcare, and Higher Education, J. Sanchez and K. Zhang (Eds.), Assoc. for the Advancement of Computing in Education, pp. 2304–2309. www.editlib.org/p/35889.

Yamada, M., Goda, Y., Matsuda, T., Saito, Y., Kato, H., and Miyagawa, H. (2016). How does self-regulated learning relate to active procrastination and other learning behaviors?, Journal of Computing in Higher Education, 28(3), pp.326-343.

Yamada, M., Shimada, A., Okubo,F., Oi, M., Kojima, K., & Ogata, H. (2017). Learning analytics of the relationships among self-regulated learning, learning behaviors, and learning performance, Research and Practice in Technology Enhanced Learning,12, 13.doi: 10.1186/

GAMIFIED MICRO-LEARNING FOR INCREASED MOTIVATION: AN EXPLORATORY STUDY

Till Halbach and Ivar Solheim
Norwegian Computing Center, Oslo, Norway

ABSTRACT

This work investigates in how far gamification and micro-learning, implemented by the novel technologies H5P and xAPI, are suitable to increase the motivation and learning performance of pupils with cognitive and behavioral challenges. The context for the field trials is the Norwegian SOL framework (short for Systematic Observation of Reading) in 6th and 7th grade. The results show that, albeit there are technical deficiencies, the technology is well suited for crafting engaging learning experiences. The prototype developed in the course of the project is capable of assessing task fidelity and pupil performance. With the proper statistical analysis, it can be a valuable ingredient for useful teacher assets such as monitoring tools.

KEYWORDS

On Demand, Just in Time, Micro-Learning, Mobile App, Gamification, H5P, xAPI

1. INTRODUCTION

Recent numbers show that, in Norway, two out of three young pupils drop out of higher secondary school (Lillejord et al. 2015). The costs of a single dropout are estimated to be around EUR 90,000 (Falch et al. 2009), accumulating to huge sums for society. The goal of the PLA Project – Personalized Learning Arena (Norsk Regnesentral 2018) – was to address this problem and to investigate how the high number of dropouts can be reduced by developing digital educational tools targeting vulnerable groups, i.e., pupils with reading difficulties, including dyslexia, and those lacking motivation for attending school.

The project was organized between 2015 and 2018 according to the user-driven research-based innovation program of the Research Council Norway. As such, the participating SME Conexus, one of the largest EdTech companies in Norway, played a central role as technology provider, and with responsibility for implementation and integration. The research institute Norwegian Computing Center, along with the interest organization Dyslexia Norway and Gjesdal municipality, were in control of research-related aspects, methodology, and content strategy, as well as user trials and evaluation.

The main case in the PLA Project was the "learn to read" framework called SOL (translated to Systematic Observation of Reading), which is specific to Norway and currently implemented in a number of schools with a total reach of approximately 130,000 pupils in about 30% of all Norwegian municipalities (Gjesdal kommune 2011). SOL consists of 10 steps which cover a pupil's anticipated reading progress, from pre-alphabetical reading over phonological and orthographical reading to, finally, an adult's literary reading ability. SOL is quite an extensive framework, and thus we decided to focus on two topics on Level 6 as explained below. The basic idea is to provide tools and tasks that the pupils find challenging, to be used for additional training and exercise on reading topics.

This work contributes to the field of exploratory learning technologies in multiple ways: Firstly, it introduces the research project to a wider audience and explains the approach chosen, including the technologies mYouTime, H5P, and xAPI. The content strategy and production of content is briefly discussed afterwards. Then, the assessment of the solution is explained in detail, with experiment description, results, and discussion, before the conclusion is drawn at the end.

2. CHOICE OF TECHNOLOGY

Our technology provider Conexus offered the application mYouTime combined with H5P (explained below) as the main platform for content management and distribution (Conexus as 2018b), both linked to their Engage platform for tracking and analysis (Conexus as 2018a).

mYouTime and Engage were considerably improved throughout the project as a result of extended requirements and preliminary testing. In particular, mYouTime had to be integrated in Engage for performance monitoring.

2.1 mYouTime & Engage

mYouTime is quite a generic application and hence suitable for a wide range of domains, but originally it targets micro-learning and just-in-time content delivery. The application exists as a web application and as apps for iOS and Android operating systems, i.e., for smartphones and tablet computers. This aspect alone contributes to an increased motivation with the target group due to, at the time of writing, the fascination these devices and apps have on children at that age, their "coolness" and "x-factor".

A user with content generation privileges can author plain texts and rich media, including hyperlinks and H5P, or record video, audio, stills, and combinations thereof. The majority of users, though, will only "consume" the content made by others. The app is based on learning units, or lectures, which in turn compound of slides of the aforementioned content types. Newly sent lectures arrive first in a user's inbox and trigger a smartphone notification, before they can be addressed and finally archived.

A lecture may theoretically consist of an arbitrary number of slides (with an upper limit of 20). The time needed to finish a single lecture depends, in addition to the slide count, on factors like the duration of contained timed media, such as video and audio, the amount of text, the content's difficulty, and similar, and is of course influenced further by human factors such as reading pace, ability for rational thinking, and others. It is hence neither feasible nor desirable to quantify the optimal number of slides. However, keeping lectures short and the slide count low is of uttermost importance in order to exploit all advantages of the "micro" in micro-learning and for the pupils to stay motivated.

mYouTime is linked to another application in Conexus portfolio, Engage (previously Vokal). Engage is a tool for teachers. Its purpose is, among others, to track and show the performance and progress of pupils, and to enable comparisons across individuals and groups, such as classes, teachers, and schools. Engage is only available as a web application.

2.2 H5P & xAPI

H5P is a free and open-source JavaScript-based framework for implementing interactive content for the Web (H5P Consortium 2018). The name stands for HTML 5 Package, referring to the combination of HTML, CSS, and JavaScript in a single container for deployment in a suitable content management system. H5P supports different types of interactivity and content, such as questionnaires, quizzes, interactive videos, audio recordings, and more. At the time of writing, 39 different types are known. We employed a subset of these in this work. It should also be mentioned that the available content types offer plenty of gamification elements to boost motivation: interactivity (dragging, choosing, buttons, etc.), user control (previous and next buttons, play/stop, etc.), feedback (instant flagging of wrong answers, display of achieved vs. maximum point score, progress bar, etc.), continuous playing ("try again" button, etc.), loss avoidance (motivating messages even for low point scores), exploration possibilities (possible to terminate a lecture at any time without disadvantage), competition (for tasks with time constraints), and other. The effect of all these elements cannot be underestimated, as seen in the results.

In the H5P type "Mark the words", the pupils had to mark particular words in a text, in our case those that included a particular sound when read aloud. In "Memory Game", six (our choice) pairs of identical words had to be found. "Drag the words' was an exercise where 4-9 (our choice) given words had to be dragged to appropriate placeholders in the text. "Multiple-choice quiz" consisted of a series of questions, where the pupils partly had to mark the correct word among all available options, and partly where the correct answer (a word) had to be dragged upon an illustrating image. Finally, "Interactive video" was used like an audio book, where a voice read a piece of text out loud. In between the playback was paused several times, and upon each pause a multiple-choice quiz with one to three questions was shown.

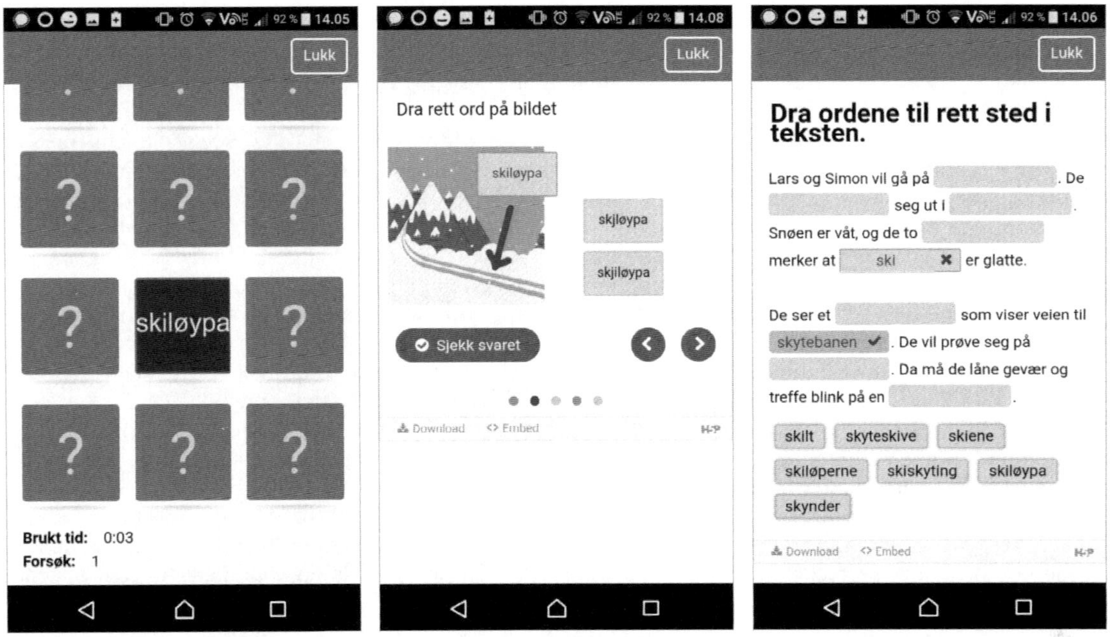

Figure 1. Illustration of H5P content types " memory game " (left), “quiz with drag the image” (middle), and “drag the words” with immediate feedback (right)

To sum up, an H5P content type is capable of supporting a single or multiple tasks and, in the prototype, the majority of lecture slides consisted of H5P content types. A lecture could thus be said to consist of a series of H5P types.

H5P generates xAPI data (ADL 2018), which are basically variable-value messages in JSON format. xAPI messages carry information about pupil activity, such as task completion, duration needed, points achieved, and similar. These messages are usually stored in databases dubbed Learning Record Store (LRS) for tracking and analysis purposes, a strategy we have followed in this work as well.

3. EVALUATION

The app, mYouTime and H5P combined with backend Engage, was evaluated at a school in Gjesdal municipality in Western Norway during 10 days in March 2018. It turned out that it was difficult to recruit pupils from the target group for this research project, but eventually we had six pupils with reading challenges, all of them in 6th and 7th grade. They had various complex cognitive and behavioral challenges. Four of them were male, two female. The evaluation was approved in advance by the Norwegian Center for Research Data. In addition, we had asked the pupils’ parents for their consent.

The entire evaluation was carried out in a browser in Google Chromebook, i.e., utilizing mYouTime’s web interface. The pupil had to go to mYouTime’s website, which basically starts the app, and then to login with the national login solution Feide, which requires entering of the social security number and a password. After the pupils had received a demonstration of the app, they were given a schedule with five to seven lectures for every day of the evaluation, corresponding to an estimated entire duration of 15-20 minutes. Most of the tasks were new, but some were also repetitions. Tasks could also be repeated if all other (scheduled) tasks were solved before the stipulated duration. Additionally, the pupils were encouraged to try the app at home, too.

All data reported from mYouTime and H5P were gathered and analyzed in the aforementioned Engage tool. As an additional measure, the data were stored in a suitable LRS.

3.1 Content Production

In total 26 lectures were crafted for the evaluation, each consisting of two to five tasks, or three to five slides. A task was implemented by means of H5P as mentioned above; see the screen dumps in Figure 1 for how some of the H5P content looked like. The lectures covered two topics on Level Six of the aforementioned reading learning program SOL concerning automating word recognition. The choice of topics, selection of words, and tasks was carried out by the reading experts who also have central responsibility for the maintenance and development of SOL.

Topic 1 was about the spelling and pronunciation of the [ʃ] sound, which can be written as sj, skj, and sk in Norwegian. The topic was presented as 10 lectures with similar structure but different texts and words. Each lecture was based on a short simple text with roughly 50 words on the average, four to nine of which included the sound of concern. Text and words were repeated throughout up to five different tasks, each implemented as an H5P type. The following H5P types were utilized for Topic 1: “Mark the words”, “Memory Game”, “Drag the words”, “Interactive Video”, and “Multiple-choice quiz”.

Topic 2 covered the spelling of the 400 most popular Norwegian words and was implemented as 16 different lectures with similar structure but varying words. One lecture was compound of three slides. On the first slide, the pupils had to read and memorize 25 words. Both next slides showed the same set of words but with (five) hidden misspellings, respectively, where the task was to find them.

The basic idea behind all these tasks is repetition of a limited set of words over a given time span to train the pupils’ automatic recognition of words, and to vary the way this is done to maintain engagement and avoid boredom.

4. RESULTS & DISCUSSION

During the evaluation, it became clear quickly that Engage was not working as expected due to technical difficulties with regard to the integration of mYouTime and H5P data in Engage. It was, however, possible to extract the data from the LRS and analyze them manually.

In total 5216 xAPI messages were generated and stored in the LRS during the trial. Most H5P content came with the correct descriptor, other were just given a very generic "other" value, which basically could mean anything. Not surprisingly, this complicated the interpretation of LRS data significantly. The basic problem here was the lack of a unique identifier that allowed to associate an LRS entry with a particular piece of content. This identifier lack also made it impossible to reliably associate LRS data with a particular task in case of multiple identical content types in the same lecture, say two "mark the words".

Another problem was that the "interactive video" type contained other H5P types; in this case a "multiple choice" type. However, as detailed above, also native "multiple choice" type content had been crafted, and sadly it was hence not possible to differentiate both in the LRS. In addition, the multiple-choice content type erroneously did not track a pupil’s duration correctly, which rendered this content type useless.

Concerning xAPI values, only the statement types “answered” and “completed” were found in the LRS, meaning that a pupil’s progress could only be tracked for completed tasks, as there were no “has started”-type messages. Finally, the xAPI’s timestamp field could not be used to pinpoint events exactly in time as it turned out that the messages had been buffered and sent in bundles to the LRS in order to save network capacity. As a result, for instance, bundled “answered” messages had timestamps with only millisecond differences, which of course could not have been generated in real life. The order of generation, though, was maintained by the system, which allowed to track a pupil’s progress over time.

The most important fields of xAPI messages stored in the LRS were those carrying values for duration, score, and score range. Together with a field for the topic and a field for the pupil/student/user, this could be exploited to derive detailed statistics as explained in the following.

Simply counting the LRS entries with a particular topic, optionally normalized by the number of tasks and number of pupils, gives the popularity of lectures, see Figure 2, left side. Such information can be used to optimize task giving and to rule out particular unpopular tasks. Related to this is the comparison of task fidelity for a particular topic to the task fidelity for all similar topics, i.e., topics of the same nature but with different content/values, computed over all pupils. This is shown on the right side of Figure 2. The plot shows the task fidelity in terms of duration and score for the task “SOL6.3-1” (“mark misspelled words”) compared to the entire series "SOL6.3" with tasks of the same type but different values/words. The scatter plot also shows the smoothed trend (regression line) and confidence interval (gray). It can be seen that the durations achieved in "SOL6.3-1" lay much more scattered than those for the series. This corresponds with the lectures' statistical values as shown in Table 1, where the average duration accomplished in "SOL6.3-1" is roughly 76% higher than that of "SOL6.3". At the same time, the average relative score of "SOL6.3-1" is 22% lower than that of "SOL6.3". It can be concluded that with this lecture, the pupils both needed more time to succeed, and they achieved lower rates, which places this particular task among the more difficult tasks in the entire series. That is, the amount and possibly choice of words should be reconsidered.

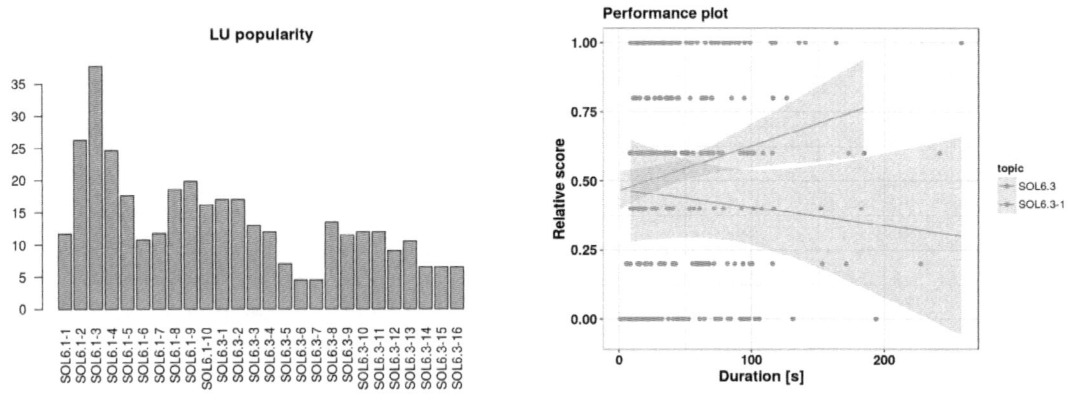

Figure 2. Lecture fidelity in terms of task finalization count (left), and score-duration comparison including regression curve and confidence interval (right)

Table 1. Comparison of score and duration of all pupils for the specific task SOL6.3-1 against all tasks SOL6.3 of the same type (but different values)

Lecture	Score	Duration [s]
SOL6.3-1	0,42	79
SOL6.3	0,54	45

The LRS data also give answers to aspects regarding specific task characteristics. For instance, we included numerous variants of the H5P task "Drag the words", where a set of words had to be put into appropriate placeholders in the text. It was possible to configure the task to give instant feedback in terms of a green background and a check mark as soon as a word had been dropped over a placeholder, but we were not sure if this was the right decision. Maybe this meant too much help and too little independent work? The data's verdict, however, is clear: With instant feedback enabled, the maximum score was unachieved in 12% of all trials, happening to 5 out of 6 pupils. The numbers were computed by filtering LRS data for the case that score and maximum score were unequal, and then simply counting the occurrences and names of pupils. The fact that 80% of all pupils did not achieve maximum score despite instant help advocates for that this feature does not help too much.

The main objective with xAPI messages, though, is to track and evaluate individuals. We propose to measure a pupil's performance as the product of score and duration. Given a particular topic and task, the performance of one specific pupil can be compared to peers, the entire class, or any other group of interest. As an example, "Girl2" is compared to the other participants in the evaluation for the task "Mark the words" for the topic "SOL6.3-2". The score here is normalized to the maximum score possible. Each point in the scatter plot in Figure 3 represents a pupil's termination of a task. As can be seen, the majority of trials by "Girl2" are in the lower part of the plot (and below the smoothing line), meaning her scores are below average, and all her registered durations are moderate to high (none are low). This corresponds to the mean scores as given in Table 2, but when it comes to the mean duration, it turns out that "Girl2" uses approximately as much time as the others.

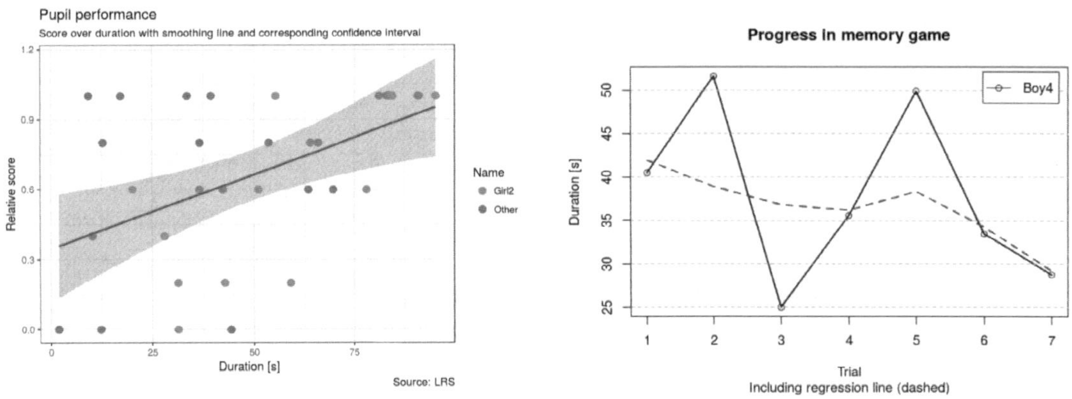

Figure 3. Pupil performance in terms of score-duration points including regression curve and (gray) confidence interval for the lecture "SOL6.3-2" (left), and with progression in duration over time for the task "Memory game" (right)

So in total, "Girl2" has likely more severe reading challenges than the others, but the trend can be said to be weak only. It is apparent, though, that it does not suffice simply to calculate and compare the average of some values for accurate tracking, as the scatter plot clearly illustrates.

Table 2. Comparison of average score and average duration of a particular groups for the lecture "SOL6.3-2"

Group	**Score**	**Duration [s]**
Girl2	0,53	52
Other	0,73	49

The memory game is quite useful for tracking a pupil's progress in duration, as all reported scores were equal to one, meaning all cards were correctly paired in the long run. I.e., duration was the only parameter that changed over several trials. This is depicted on the right hand in Figure 3 for the task "Memory game" in the lecture "SOL6.1-10" for "Boy4". As seen, the boy had seven trials, and his performance was quite flunky. However, when we smoothen the points by means of a locally-weighted polynomial regression, we can witness a 25% performance improvement, i.e., more than 10 s reduction in duration over this few number of trials. This shows not only the appropriateness of the task, but also the boy's ability (and willingness) to learn.

To conclude, the data generated by H5P as stored in the LRS can nicely be used to derive statistics in order to improve tasks by looking for high durations and low scores, but tracking progress is limited to completed tasks only. With a sufficient number of data points reported by H5P, it is possible derive meaningful trends in pupil performance as well. It is stressed that, even though the number of trial participants was low, the volume and variety of tasks elegantly allowed to arrive at meaningful results, rendering the solution and its inherent technology fit for the purpose as anticipated.

4.1 Supplemental Interviews with Pupils and Teachers

So far, we have shown how task quality and pupil performance could be sufficiently achieved and controlled. However, the main objective for the solution was to improve the pupils' motivation and eventually reduce the number of dropouts. This is a very ambitious goal and was not possible to measure given the scale of the trial and the limited time frame. Still, we were able to derive some trends by combining the above statistical analysis with an additional source of data in a qualitative approach. More precisely, pupils and teachers were interviewed after the trial about their experience, challenges, and perceived learning benefits. The interviews confirm and elaborate on the findings so far as follows.

The pupils clearly found the H5P tasks both motivating and useful for learning. Some of them were in the risk zone for dropping out of school, but experienced the trial as positive and engaging due to the strong gamification elements. This neatly confirms other research, for instance (Peirce 2013; Nolan & McBride 2014), which states that educational games can be highly useful in a learning context. In particular relevant and motivating feedback is crucial. E.g., the memory game provides the score and congratulates when answers are correct. Also the time used on specific tasks is made visible for the pupils once the task is finalized – a motivating factor in itself. It becomes important for the pupils to solve these tasks as quickly as possible in competitive time comparisons. A corollary from this is that even pupils with motivation challenges can keep their attention over a longer period of time because they become motivated to solve more tasks to show both the teacher and for themselves that they can do this both fast and in a correct manner. The statistics showing a 25% improvement over time can be explained by the factors mentioned here.

What the above numbers do not show: It was further crucial that the teachers were able to provide personalized assistance during the trial. Although Engage suffered from various technical difficulties, teachers could follow the pupils' progress by looking at the log, and thus the teachers had a sufficient overview of the pupils' progress at any time. It is clear that thereby also teachers benefit from the developed solution. Notable events could be caught and followed up quickly, for example when a pupil for various reasons did not do a particular task she was told to do. Such technological enablers are particularly important for the given target group with pupils often struggling with lack of motivation and sense of failure at school.

The trial also provided valuable results for the design of digital learning materials in the optimal way. Pupils with reading difficulties and dyslexia will usually try to avoid reading longer texts and sections, if they can avoid it. Some of the tasks we crafted were more verbose than others, and several pupils actually skipped reading crucial parts of it, e.g., where to draw the words. For "draw the words" tasks, we expected the main text (including dropzones) to be read first in order to be able to quickly understand where words should be placed correctly. To our surprise, however, most pupils used a more time-consuming "trial and error" strategy where they would try random words and see if they fit. This will usually take much longer time. Nevertheless, this should *not* lead to the conclusion that texts of a certain length should always be avoided; pupils need to practice this, too, but the trial shows that this challenge should be addressed when designing interactive tasks for reading training.

Concluding, the trial provides several leads for the appropriate design of learning tasks for this target group.

5. CONCLUSION

This paper explores the possibilities that lay in gamification and micro-learning, in this solution instantiated by novel technologies like H5P and xAPI, to increase the motivation and learning performance of pupils with cognitive and behavioral challenges. We describe the technologies involved and the setup of the field trials in detail, including content production, and the results and the opportunities and limitations given by this solution are discussed afterwards.

H5P is very powerful and promising, but it also is quite novel still, and as such some of its aspects are simply not mature enough for a production-level system. This applies in particular to partly insufficient and partly inconsistent messaging, as well as to some missing or erroneous values. Another drawback is that learning units are currently not tracked in real time, so reports on progress are inherently somewhat delayed. Apart from that, H5P-generated xAPI messages can with advantage be stored in an LRS and statistically analyzed. We have succeeded with deriving detailed statistics to assess task fidelity, and to identify particularly difficult or unpopular tasks. The paper also describes how a pupil's performance in terms of score and duration can be compared with other individuals and groups.

Interviews with both pupils and teachers have confirmed that the gamification elements provided by H5P have a positive effect on the learning performance of pupils with cognitive and behavioral challenges, and they are capable of increasing the pupil's motivation considerably. As a consequence, the high number of dropouts of school could be reduced, even though a tight project schedule and budget have not allowed to validate this claim. The trials have also shown that close monitoring of the pupils' learning progression is vital, and that teachers need to have the right analysis tools to be able to quickly follow up deviations from the learning schedule.

All in all, with a little improvement H5P is well suited for engaging learning experiences for the given target group as a minimum, and potentially also for other pupils.

ACKNOWLEDGEMENT

The authors thank the Research Council Norway for BIA funding, the participating municipalities and all pupils for their contributions, and the anonymous reviewers for helpful comments for the improvement of this work.

REFERENCES

Conexus as, 2018a. Conexus - For a smarter learning planet. Available at: http://www.conexus.net/ [Accessed May 25, 2018].

Conexus as, 2018b. mYouTime. Available at: http://myoutime.com/ [Accessed May 25, 2018].

Falch, T., Johannesen, A.B. & Strøm, B., 2009. Kostnader av frafall i videregående opplæring. *Senter for Økonomisk Forskning.*

Gjesdal kommune, 2011. SOL - Systematisk Observasjon av Lesing. Available at: http://www.sol-lesing.no/ [Accessed November 16, 2015].

H5P Consortium, 2018. H5P – Create and Share Rich HTML5 Content and Applications.

Lillejord, S. et al., 2015. Frafall i videregående opplæring: En systematisk kunnskapsoversikt. *Oslo, Norway: Kunnskapssenter for utdanning.*

Nolan, J. & McBride, M., 2014. Beyond gamification: reconceptualizing game-based learning in early childhood environments. *Information, Communication & Society*, 17(5), pp.594–608.

Norsk Regnesentral, 2018. PLA — Personlig (mobil) læringsarena | Norsk Regnesentral. Available at: https://www.nr.no/nb/projects/pla-—-personlig-mobil-læringsarena [Accessed May 25, 2018].

Peirce, N., 2013. Digital game-based learning for early childhood. *A state of the art report. Dublin, Ireland: Learnovate Centre.*

The Advanced Distributed Learning Initiative (ADL). n.d. "Experience xAPI." Accessed July 26, 2018. https://www.adlnet.gov/research/performance-tracking-analysis/experience-api/.

CODING AND COMPUTATIONAL THINKING WITH ARDUINO

Veronica Rossano, Teresa Roselli and Gaetano Quercia
Department of Computer Science – University of Bari
Via Orabona, 4, Bari - Italy

ABSTRACT

The Computational Thinking recently has been recognised as one of the basic knowledge to be developed since childhood. Coding and computers are not just programming, but tools that help students to develop problem solving skills and more deep understand of the way things work. For these reasons, great attention has been focused on this topic both from a pedagogical and technological point of view. In this paper, a first approach to Computational Thinking using ARDUINO is presented. To this end, some learning activities have been designed to introduce middle school students, without any experience in coding, to the process of building the algorithm from simple exercises to more complex tasks. The pilot test involved 25 subjects, many of them do not like to study mathematics, science and technology, but the results were promising. The approach was appreciated by the students and the results of the questionnaires confirmed the learning effectiveness too.

KEYWORDS

Computational Thinking, Coding, Problem Solving, Arduino

1. COMPUTATIONAL THINKING

The importance of Computational Thinking (CT) was underlined since the 1980s when Seymour Papert stated that for children developing procedural thinking was necessary to develop basic skills about problem solving and deep learning. Papert defined LOGO (Papert, 1980, 1991) programming language that allows children to use a turtle to manipulate the computer and build simple programs. The current challenge of educational technology field is to make aware children that computers, and technologies in general, can be smart only if they are programmed by humans. One of the most dangerous and widespread misconceptions among young people is "technology is smart since the circuits are smart". Moreover, as Jeannette Wing (2006 - p. 33) stated, computational thinking is "a universally applicable attitude and skill set everyone, not just computer scientists, would be eager to learn and use". Several empirical evidences confirm that coding is effective in improving problem solving skills, divergent ways of thinking, creativity, communication and group work (Choi et al., 2013, Vaca-Cárdenas, et al., 2015, Siegle, 2017, Lye, 2014).

Following this trend, Google has activated the Exploring Computational Thinking (ECT) program (https://edu.google.com/resources/programs/exploring-computational-thinking/#!home) where a collection of lesson plans, videos, and other resources on computational thinking (CT) are published. To prove that CT is effective in any school subjects, the website offers didactic resources that can be used in different subjects, for example Algebra, Music, US-Story and so on.

The aim of the research is to verify if the use of physical technology, such as Arduino board, can be effective in teaching coding and develop computational thinking skills, in general. To this aim, a learning path has been designed and developed. The activities have been organised in order to introduce junior high school students, with no experience in coding, to the process of building the algorithm from simple exercises to more complex task. In addition, to make more engaging the activities some wooden models have been realised to allow students to see the effects of the programming on physical objects.

The paper is organised as follows: the next section describes the technological solutions available for learning coding and CT; section 3 describes the learning activities defined for the learning path; section 4 describes the pilot study to measure both the student's appreciation of the technological approach to education and the student's knowledge gain. Finally, some conclusions and future works are described.

2. TECHNOLOGICAL SOLUTIONS

It is clear that children are attracted by technology. The electronic devices have now entered in their everyday life: video games, computers, smartphones. Until a few years ago, these tools were used exclusively by adults, but today with the generation of "digital natives" it is common to see smartphones in children's hands.

Different technological solutions have been implemented in order to support the acquisition of computational thinking skills. Bee Bot®, as an example, is a floor robot that pupils, starting from 3 years old, can program using directional commands (e.g. forwards, backwards, left and right turns) to follow a path. For the same learning purpose there are also unplugged solutions. The Montessori play set, named Cubetto (https://www.primotoys.com/fr/), for example, is based on a tangible approach, children will be able to learn programming without the support of screens or the need to master basic bed-writing skills. Other solutions, combine technology with phisical objects, such as Coding blocks from Osmo (https://www.playosmo.com/en/) that is a tangible play platform to learn coding with physical blocks that interact with iPad and iPhone. There are also solutions based on software approach, the most known is the Hour of Code (https://code.org/) where different games based on Scratch are supplied. Scratch (Maloney, 2010) is a visual programming language that can be easly used by children to build media-rich projects, such as stories, games and animation. It is based on Papert's Logo project and currently is one of the most used language to introduce the programming at different ages (Vaca-Cárdenas et al., 2015).

To improve motivation and engagement in programming skills acquisition, in the latest years also robotic education is spreading. The idea is to create artifacts that can be programmed to do some tasks. The idea is to allow students to work with real hardware that will be able to do real physical work when programmed. The LEGO® Mindstorms are an example, they allow to develop programmable robots based on Lego building blocks. This approach has been successfully applied in different contexts (Haak et al. 2018, De Vries et al. 2018, Umbleja et al., 2017). Another device commonly used in teaching and learning contexts is Arduino (Plaza et al., 2018), an open source hardware and software for building digital devices and interactive objects that can sense and control objects in physical and digital world. Arduino board uses a variety of microprocessors and micontrollers that can be programmed using a language similar to C. The microcontrollers, unlike microprocessors which integrate only the processing unit (CPU), include permanent and volatile memories and I/O ports. This makes Arduino an autonomous system: the program, saved in the permanent memory, instructs the microprocessor which uses volatile memory to store data useful during the execution of the program. Moreover, there are different sensors which allow Arduino to measure light, temperature, degree of flex, pressure, proximity, acceleration, carbon monoxide, radioactivity, humidity, barometric pressure. Thus, the Arduino board can be used in order to solve real complex problems with physical objects, allowing students to program artifacts that can be touched with hands. The learning process is, in this way, more engaging and motivating.

3. DESIGN OF LEARNING ACTIVITIES

Until now, there are a lot of teaching experiences using coding to introduce the concept of problem solving and computational thinking from the early years of school (Lye & Koh, 2014). In this context, the research aims at defining a path for the acquisition of the basic concepts of programming with the use of Arduino and Scratch4Arduino. The learning path is addressed to 12-14 years old students and aims at improving motivation and engagement in technology subjects. The lessons were designed to introduce: the algorithm definition, the logical connective, the if-then-else and the while statements. The lesson involved the following tools: the Arduino Uno logic board, the IDE Scratch for Arduino and some wooden models built for this specific purpose.

Activity #1. Led controlled by switch

Learning objective: introduction to the electonic components of Arduino. No coding activity is required to handle this task. The Arduino board has been used as a power source. The circuit built in this way allows the LED to light up when the switch is pressed.

Activity #2. Blinking led

Learning objective: introduction to the algorithm concept. The idea is to write a simple program that is able to make the led bliking when the user makes an action, for example the user uses the spacebar.

Activity #3. Blinking led more than once

Learning objective: introduction to the while statement. Starting from the algorithm defined in the previous activity, the students were asked to build a program that repeats the instructions more than once.

Activity #4. Turn on and turn off the led

Learning objective: introduction to the if-then-else statement. Starting from the program in Activity #2 the idea is that the led should be turned on if the user pushes a specific button and turned off otherwise.

Activity #5. AND operator

Learning objective: this activity was designed in order to introduce the AND logical operator. Starting from the program in Activity #4 the idea is that the led should be turned on if the user pushes two specific buttons and turned off otherwise.

Activity #6. OR operator

Learning objective: introduction to the OR logical operator. Starting from the program in Activity #4 the idea is that the led should be turned on if the user pushes one of two specific button and turned off otherwise.

Activity #6. The Traffic Light

Learning objective: this activity allows the student to apply the knowledge acquired with the previous activities in real task. The idea is to build a program to tackle two traffic lights controlling a crossroads. In order to make simpler the problem solving process, a wooden model was used to see its effects on phisical objects (figure 1).

Figure 1. The wooden traffic light model

Activity #7 Rail crossing

Learning objective: this activity allows the student to apply the knowledge acquired with the previous activities in a more complex task. In order to make more engaging the activity a real world problem was proposed. The aim is to build a program to control both the traffic lights and the rail crossing (Figure 2). The user presses a button to close the bar, while the red lights start flashing. When the train has passed, the user presses another button to open the bar. The red lights shall continue to blink until the bar is completely open.

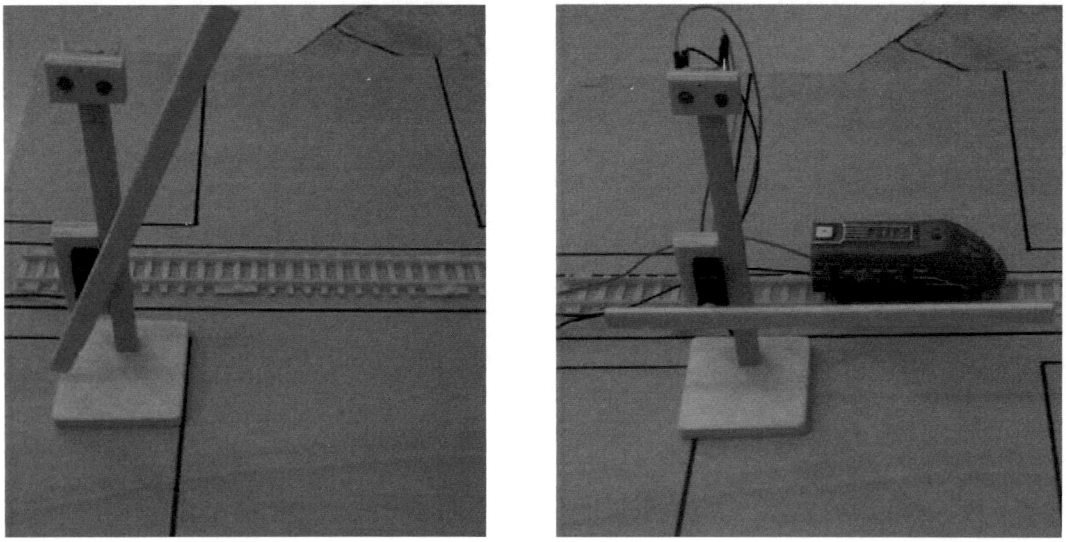

Figure 2 The wooden rail cross activity model

4. THE PILOT STUDY

4.1 The Resources

The pilot study was carried out in the laboratory of the school. It is composed of 20 Pentium 4 equipped with Windows XP Professional. The "Scratch 4 Arduino" tutorial was installed on these machines. Two wooden models used in Activity#6 or Activity#7 were built before the experiment.

4.2 The Participants

The participants were 25 students (11 girls and 14 boys) of the middle school in Terlizzi, a town near Bari, attending the 3rd class. All participants were 13 years old. Together with the teacher, we chose not to inform the participants about the activity in advance, in order to study their reaction and interest. None of the students had ever worked with Arduino and Scratch.

4.3 The Experimental Design

The within-subject design has been applied for the evaluation of effectiveness. The experiment was organized in five sessions distributed in two weeks: three meetings in the first week, two meetings in the next one.

Before the activity was presented, a pre-test was administered to collect information concerning previews knowldege about CT and coding. The pre-test was divided into two sections: the demographic section and the knowledge assessment section. The first section made up of twelve questions, was useful to understand how and how long the students use the PC, how much they are attracted by the technology (smartphone, game platforms, etc.), if they know the programmer's work and whether they have ever tried to program anything. The second section consists of six questions to assess previous knowledge about computational thinking. Specifically, in the first question the knowledge about the algorithm definition is investigated; two questions measure the ability to build an algorithm, to make easy the concept some algorithms related to daily activities were proposed (e.g. brushing teeth, making a phone call with the smartphone); two questions measure the knowledge of logical connectives AND and OR (in this case we use a colored figure on which to assess the truth value of some statements); the last question verifies the knowledge about flow-chart.

After the pre-test, the planned activities were carried out. In the first week Activities #1, #2, #3 and #4 were completed and in the second week Activities #5 and #6 were completed. Activity #7 was only presented to the class, but no actions were required from the students side.

The post-test was aimed at assessing the improvements of student's knowledge and the appreciation of the teaching approach. All the knowledge assessed in the pre-test were measured also in the post-test.

4.4 The Results

The pre-test reveals that 24 out 25 students got a pc at home. The students were asked to self-assess their level of e-skills, the average ratings was 7/10. Moreover, students usually spend 1.5 hours a day to study and/or play with PCs. Many of them do not like subjects such as Mathematics, Science and Technology, indeed the teacher confirms that their average grade was 5.5/10. As regards the computational thinking, only one student knows the binary system, no one knows the programmer's work, only 3 students have tried to program something; the students are interested in using technology (mean value 7.44/10).

For what concerning the algorithm skills, all students have many difficulties. Some of them have been able to build the algorithm only guided by the tutor and/or the teacher. The knowledge about the logic connectives was very low (mean 4.2), the grade obtained in the pre-test are reported in figure 3. In addition, data reveal that almost the whole sample has well-consolidated knowledge of flow charts and their proper use.

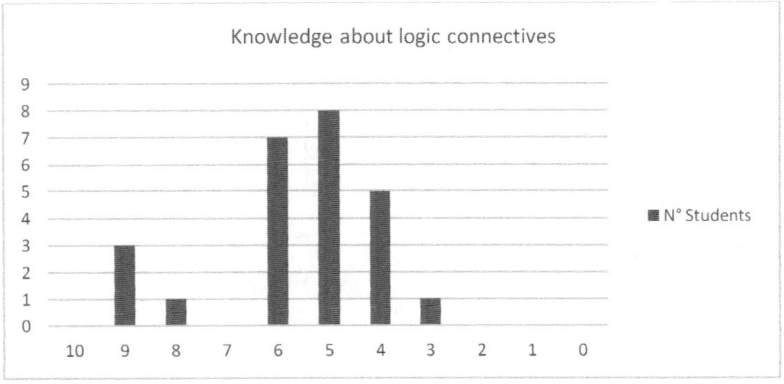

Figure 3. Previous knowlege about logic connectives AND and OR

4.4.1 Appreciation of the Teaching Approach

The 19 out of 25 students appreciate using Arduino 1, most of the sample (21 out of 25) considered enjoyable to assemble the circuit, and almost all the sample (23 out of 25) considered the whole project engaging. An unexpected result was that many students reported difficulties using Scratch (Figure 4), indeed 21 out of 25 students stated that they had no difficulties in carrying out the proposed activities thanks to the methodological approach adopted.

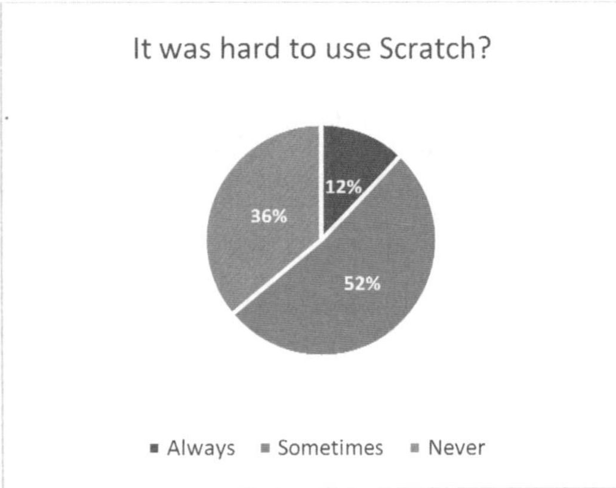

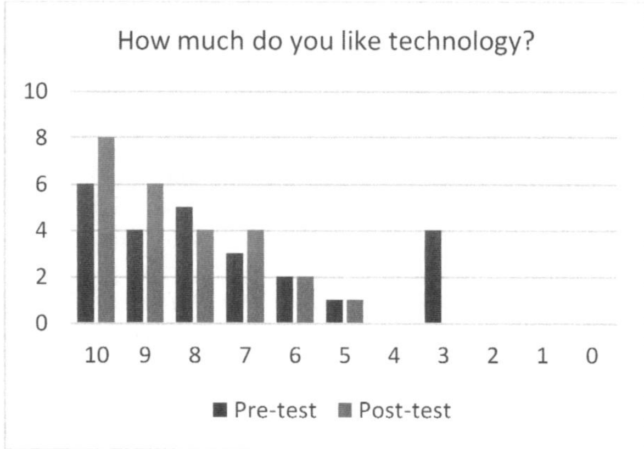

Figure 4. Students judge not simple using Scratch

Figure 5. The improvement of student's interest in technology

An interesting result was related to the question, already posed in the pre-test, "How much are you attracted by technology and innovation?". As Figure 5 shows the distribution of the grades has changed, higher values than the pre-test were obtained, this could mean that thanks to this experience they see another application of technology and perhaps they perceive a higher utility of it.

4.4.2 Student's Knowledge Gain

All students stated that they learned from this new experience. This perception was confirmed by the student's higher marks obtained in the post-test (Figure 6).

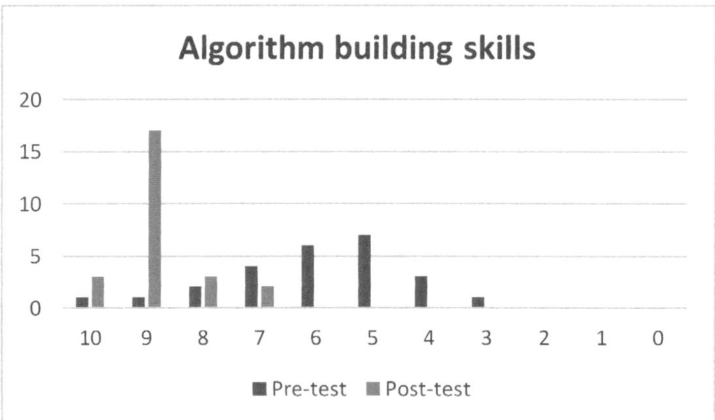

Figure 6. The improvement of ability to build an algorithm

All pupils achieved excellent evaluations of their ability to use logical AND and OR connectives (average grades 9.36 out of 10).

5. CONCLUSION

The importance of Computational Thinking in all levels of education has been largely recognised in the latest years. Problem solving abilities are necessary to tackle all daylife activities since childhood. The spread of learning initiatives is a confirmation that fostering CT skills is basic for all students. In this view, the research aims at introducing computational thinking and coding using Arduino board. In particular, a learning path was defined to let the students acquire knowledge and abilities about the algorithm, the logical connective, the if-then-else and the while statements. The pilot study conducted in a junior high school confirms that the learning activities were engaging and motivating for the students and teacher. All students actively participated in all the proposed tasks, the teacher was surprised by some of them who usually show less interest in all kinds of proposed activities.

In the future, an experimentation with a larger sample should be conducted. Moreover, it would be interesting to record the difference among male and female performances, that in this case it has not been annotated. A more exhaustive learning pathway should be designed to ensure that all basic programming knowledge is acquired.

ACKNOWLEDGEMENT

We would like to thank the junior high school “Gesmundo – Moro – Fiore” in Terlizzi (Ba), in particular the principal Maria Chiapparino, the teacher Silvana Chiapparino, and finally all students involved in the study.

REFERENCES

Choi, B., Jung, J. & Baek, Y. (2013). In what way can technology enhance student learning?: A preliminary study of Technology Supported learning in Mathematics. In R. McBride & M. Searson (Eds.), *Proceedings of SITE 2013--Society for Information Technology & Teacher Education International Conference*. New Orleans, Louisiana, United States: Association for the Advancement of Computing in Education (AACE), pp. 3-9.

De Vries, C., et al., 2018. Using LEGO Kits to Teach Higher Level Problem Solving Skills in System Dynamics: A Case Study. *Advances in Engineering Education*, 2018, Vol. 6, N.3.

Maloney, J., et al., 2010. The scratch programming language and environment. *ACM Transactions on Computing Education* (TOCE), Vol. 10, N. 4, 16.

Marques, A., Guimarães, C., Salgado, A., (2019). Scratch 3 – Beginners programming course in 3rd year of primary school. *Lecture Notes in Electrical Engineering*, 505, pp. 1160-1166.

Haak, V., et al., 2018, Conception of a Lego Mindstorms EV3 simulation for teaching C in computer science courses. *In: Global Engineering Education Conference (EDUCON)*. IEEE, pp. 478-483.

Lye, S. Y., & Koh, J. H. L. (2014). Review on teaching and learning of computational thinking through programming: What is next for K-12?. *Computers in Human Behavior*, 41, 51-61.

Papert, S. 1980. *Mindstorms: Children, computers, and powerful ideas*. Basic Books, New York.

Papert, S., 1991. Situating constructionism. In *I. Harel & S. Papert (Eds.), Constructionism*. Norwood, NJ: Ablex, 1–11.

Plaza, P., et al., 2018. Traffic lights through multiple robotic educational tools. *In: Global Engineering Education Conference (EDUCON)*, IEEE, 2018, pp. 2015-2020.

Siegle, D. (2017). Technology: Encouraging creativity and problem solving through coding. *Gifted Child Today*, 40(2), 117-123.

Vaca-Cárdenas, L. A., Bertacchini, F., Tavernise, A., Gabriele, L., Valenti, A., Olmedo, D. E., ... & Bilotta, E. (2015). Coding with Scratch: The design of an educational setting for Elementary pre-service teachers. *In Interactive Collaborative Learning (ICL)*. IEEE, pp. 1171-1177.

Umbleja, K., 2017. Learning to Program with Lego Mindstorms–Difference Between K-12 Students and Adults. In: *International Conference on Interactive Collaborative Learning*. Springer, Cham, p. 447-458.

Wing, J. 2006. Computational thinking. *Communications of the ACM*, Vol. 49, N. 3, pp. 33–36

PROBLEM-BASED LEARNING AND COMPUTER-BASED SCAFFOLDS IN DISTANCE EDUCATION

Mahnaz Moallem[1] and Elizabeth Igoe[2]
[1]*Ph.D. Towson University*
Towson University, College of Education, Dept. of Educational Technology and Literacy
8000 York Rd. Towson, MD 21252-0001
[2]*M.S.*

ABSTRACT

What effects does PBL have on student learning outcomes, knowledge acquisition, and higher order thinking skills? This question continues to influence the adoption and implementation of problem-based learning (PBL) since its' inception. The answer to this overarching question is still lacking. This chapter responds to this question by first analyzing and synthesizing the literature regarding the factors that influence the effectiveness of PBL to identify questions that designers and researchers should ask about results of learning. It then explores important characteristics of PBL compared with its' analogous pedagogies and approaches of project-based learning, case-based reasoning, inquiry-based learning, learning design and/or design thinking in an effort to understand how features of each approach influence the effectiveness of learning outcomes. Further, the chapter examines how PBL approaches and pedagogies define learning outcomes and how various learning outcomes are measured. Finally, the chapter offers a synthesis of research on the effectiveness of PBL and recommendations for the future researchers and designers.

KEYWORDS

Problem-Based Learning, Effectiveness of PBL, PBL and Student Learning Outcomes, PBL Analogous Pedagogies, Comparison of PBL with its Analogous Pedagogies

1. INTRODUCTION

Problem-based learning (PBL) is an instructional approach rooted in constructivist and experiential learning theories. Research and theory on learning suggest that by having students learn through the experience of solving problems, they can learn both content and thinking strategies (Hmelo-Silver, 2004; Savery, 2006). In PBL, student learning centers around a complex problem that does not have a single correct answer or solution. Students learn content, strategies, and self-directed learning skills through collaboratively engaging in problem-solving, reflecting on their own experiences, and engaging in self-directed inquiry (Hmelo-Silver, Duncan, & Chinn, 2007). It has been maintained in the literature that PBL positively influences learning outcomes along with learners' higher order thinking skills such as creative thinking, problem-solving, logical thinking and decision making (Şendağ & Odabaşı, 2009). With the advent of reform movements in education, such as 21st Century Learning Skills, PBL is increasingly being advocated for and adopted by institutions of higher education.

However, while the utilization of PBL has expanded, disputes exist regarding the amount of scaffolding and guidance provided to students during implementation. Scaffolding is a temporary guidance provided to assist learners with the learning process. Kirschner, Sweller and Clark (2006) argue that PBL represents a minimally guided instructional practice. In contrast, Hmelo-Silver, Duncan and Chinn (2007) argue that PBL is not a minimally guided instructional approach, but "rather provides extensive scaffolding and guidance to facilitate student learning" (p. 99).

This dispute is relevant in higher education as the rate of online education programs continue to rise. PBL has traditionally been conducted in face-to-face settings using cooperative learning groups. Less is known regarding the successful implementation and facilitation of PBL online. Online education has emerged as a popular alternative to face-to-face classroom instruction. Most online courses are delivered asynchronously, allowing instruction and communication between students and instructors to occur independent of time and location. However, the traditional implementation of PBL poses significant challenges to asynchronous online instructors in terms of scaffolding both individuals and groups.

The purposes of this study were to (1) design, develop and pilot test five self-directed, computer-based modules to support scaffolding in an online graduate level course utilizing Problem/Project-Based Learning (PBL), (2) collect data to assess the effectiveness of computer-supported scaffolding (hard scaffold) provided in the modules to assist students in problem identification, application of conceptual and domain-specific knowledge and skills of argumentation, and (3) use the results of the data to identify recommendations for future researchers and designers.

2. REVIEW OF THE LITERATURE

PBL is one of a family of constructivist, experiential learning approaches, which situate learning in a meaningful task (Hmelo-Silver, 2004), such as project-based learning (PrBL) and inquiry learning (IL) (Savery, 2006). Despite some differences among these approaches, the focus of each is a question, issue, case or problem that learners attempt to solve or resolve (Jonassen, 1999). In addition, problem-based approaches share the same assumptions about active, constructive and authentic learning experiences (Jonassen, 1999). Due to the similar characteristics, problem-based approaches such as PBL (Problem-based Learning), PjBL (Project-based Learning) and IL (Inquiry-based Learning) are often used in combination and play complementary roles in practice.

2.1 Process of Implementing PBL

PBL, as its name implies, situates learning in the context of a problem. The PBL learning cycle, also known as the PBL tutorial process, typically starts with the presentation of a problem rather than a lecture or reading assignment intended to impart discipline-specific knowledge to the student (Savery, 2009). The problem is ill-structured in nature and refers to an academically or professionally relevant issue (Yew & Schmidt, 2012) that students learn more about through the process of investigation and production of viable solutions. Students work in small collaborative groups to identify relevant facts from the provided problem scenario. As a group, students analyze the problem, generate possible explanations, as well as identify key issues and concepts they need to learn more about in order to solve the problem (Hmelo-Silver, 2004; Savery, 2009; Yew & Schmidt, 2012). After this period of teamwork, students disperse for a phase of self-directed study. Students independently research and investigate selected learning issues identified by the group. "They then regroup to share what they have learned, reconsider their hypotheses, and/or generate new ideas in light of their new learning" (Hmelo-Silver, 2004, p. 242). A tutor/facilitator is present during the group discussions to help facilitate the learning processes and the development of metacognitive skills (Savery, 2009; Yew & Schmidt, 2012).

PBL tutors/facilitators do not directly transmit/teach the content knowledge to students. Instead they support the students' learning process by observing the students, pushing them to think deeply by asking probing questions and encouraging students to articulate their thinking, modeling problem-solving strategies, and promoting collaboration among group members (Hmelo-Silver et al., 2007; Sockalingam, Rotgans, & Schmidt, 2011). It is noted in the literature that the role of the tutor or facilitator is critical to the successful implementation of PBL (Hmelo-Silver, 2004; Savery 2009). The tutor provides the initial guidance and supports with process skills, such as metacognitive modeling for individuals and groups, during collaborative group work (Savery, 2009). The tutor is responsible for both moving the students through the various stages of PBL and for monitoring the group process to assure that all students are actively involved (Barrows, 1988; Hmelo-Silver, 2004).

2.1.1 Role and Types of Scaffolding or Guidance in PBL

Scaffolding can be defined as support provided by a teacher, facilitator, tutor, peer, or a computer- or paper-based tool that allows students to meaningfully participate in and gain skill at a task that they would be unable to complete unaided (Belland, 2014). This concept of scaffolding has been connected to Vygotsky's zone of proximal development (ZPD), defined as the "distance between the child's actual developmental level as determined by independent problem solving and the higher level of potential development as determined through problem solving under adult guidance and in collaboration with more capable peers" (Belland, 2014; Reiser, 2004; Vygotsky, 1978, p. 86). Enabling the learner to bridge this gap between the actual and the potential depends on the resources or the kinds of support provided (Puntambekar & Hübscher, 2005).

The original notion of scaffolding assumed that a single more knowledgeable person, such as a parent or a teacher, would help an individual learner, providing him or her with exactly the help he/she needed to move forward (Puntambekar & Hübscher, 2005). Strategies for scaffolding include (a) enlisting student interest, (b) controlling frustration, (c) providing feedback, (d) indicating important task/problem elements to consider, (e) modeling expert processes, and (f) questioning (Belland, 2014; Wood et al., 1976).

However, the reality of modern classrooms and the emergence of computer technologies has broadened the definition of scaffolding, expanding the potential sources of scaffolding and how scaffolds are delivered to students. Thus, scaffolds can be defined as tools, strategies or guides that support students in gaining higher levels of understanding that would otherwise be beyond their reach (Brush & Saye, 2002; Hannafin, Land, & Oliver, 1999; Simons & Ertmer, 2005). Scaffolds may assume multiple forms depending on the learning environment, the content, the instructor, and the learners (Simons & Ertmer, 2005). Brush and Saye (2002) conceptualize two categories of scaffolds: *soft* and *hard scaffolds* (Brush & Saye, 2002; Saye & Brush, 2002). *Soft scaffolds* are dynamic situational aid provided by a teacher or peer. Soft scaffolding requires teachers to continuously diagnose the understandings of learners and provide timely support based on student responses (Brush & Saye, 2002; Saye & Brush, 2002). This type of support is generally provided "just in time," where the teacher monitors the progress students are making while engaged in a learning activity and intervenes when support or guidance are needed. In contrast, *hard scaffolds* are static supports that can be anticipated and planned in advance based on typical student difficulties with a task (Brush & Saye, 2002; Saye & Brush, 2002). Such scaffolds can take the form of printed materials, such as worksheets, scripted cooperation and structured journals (Hmelo-Silver, 2004; Schmidt et al., 2011), or embedded within multimedia and hypermedia software to provide students with support while they are using the software (Brush & Saye, 2002).

3. COMPUTER-MEDIATED SCAFFOLDING: A DESIGN FRAMEWORK

Incombered by the review of the PBL literature, a conceptual framework was constructed to guide the design and development of problem-based, self-directed, computer-based modules to support scaffolding in an online graduate level course. As shown in Figure 1, the framework was designed to propose how the core characteristics of PBL can be used to create computer-based hard scaffolds to facilitate problem-based learning in the absence of an instructor or facilitator.

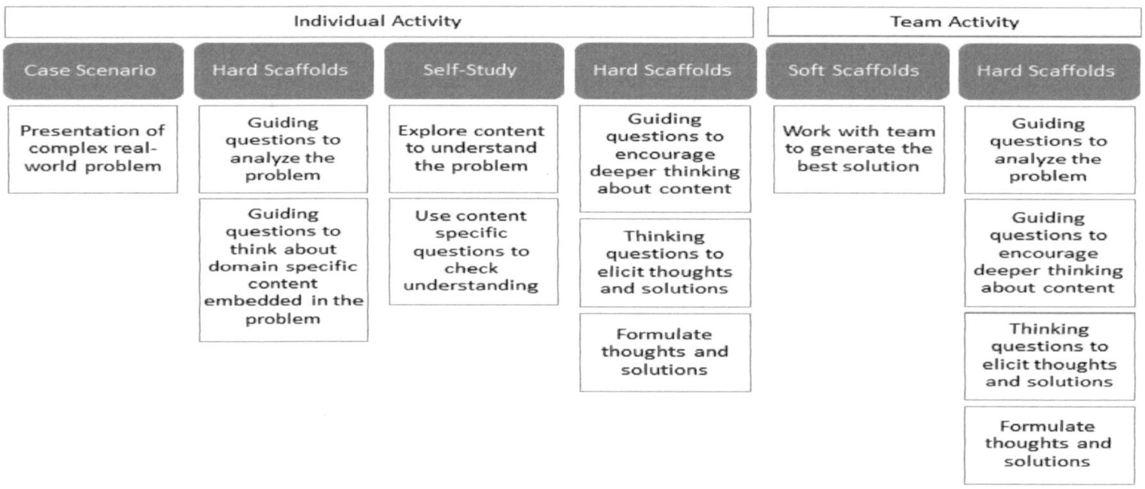

Figure 1. Design framework for online PBL modules

3.1 Top Hat: An Interactive Content Development Tool

A web-based PBL environment was specifically designed and developed for the purposes of this study. Top Hat was selected and used to develop the instructional materials. Top Hat is a commercially available, web-based teaching platform which offers two products marketed towards engaging higher education students in and outside of class: "*Lecture*," a classroom response system which allows for interactive slide presentations, and "*InteractiveText*," interactive learning materials to help students study. The latter product was used to develop the PBL modules for this study.

Interactive text, is a modern conceptualization of traditional textbooks. One of the unique elements of *InteractiveText* is the ability to embed questions within content. There is also a feature to allow students to respond with a drawing or graphical representation. Additionally, students can view each other's responses and engage in dialogue within the threaded discussion. These questioning functions allow an instructor to assess students' understanding in real-time or in advance of a class session. An instructor could use the data from assigned *InteractiveText* to identify issues and direct instruction towards areas where students are struggling.

3.2 Incorporating Scaffolds in Top Hat Modules

Using the Top Hat environment and the proposed framework, three online modules were developed. Each module focused on a targeted content embedded in an ill-defined problem statement. The students were to carefully read and analyze the problem statement to identify underlying concepts and issues, study them individually and then meet with their collaborative group to discuss and come up with the best solution. Thus, each module began with a real-world, ill-defined problem, which was used as the context for the instruction. In order to replace the human tutor who would normally guide learners' discussion when reviewing and analyzing the problem statement, a series of hard scaffolds in form of consecutive questioning were provided to assist students in problem identification and analysis while exploring and applying conceptual and domain-specific knowledge. Furthermore, the successive questioning as a hard scaffold was aimed to encourage deeper thinking, elaboration, and argumentation. The following explains two types of hard scaffolds that were used to assist the learners.

Analytical questions. Following the presentation of the problem, a series of "thinking questions" were provided to assist the learner in analyzing the problem. This line of questioning was designed to act as cognitive and metacognitive scaffolds by modeling the types of questions students should be asking of themselves. The thinking questions were related to both the domain-specific thinking, as well as self-regulation skills.

Domain-specific guiding prompts and questions. In addition to analytical questions, students were guided to review related readings and other multimedia materials to explore domain-specific knowledge. The resources provide real-world examples and explanations of theoretical concepts, model expert behavior/thinking, or demonstrate a concept in action.

4. THE METHODOLOGY

As indicated earlier, the Top Hat modules were designed to support and be incorporated into the activities of an existing online course. "Organization and Management of Instructional Technology" is an elective course offered to students in an instructional technology graduate program. Participants enrolled in this course are primarily graduate students seeking a master's degree or a certificate in instructional technology. The study was piloted during the fall semester 2016 and was conducted again in the spring semester of 2018. During fall 2016, the course met regularly once a week for three hours via WebEx while during spring 2018 no weekly virtual meeting was scheduled and the course was delivered asynchronously. In fall 2016, participants were both on campus (1) and at a distance (4) logging in for the class through the WebEx teleconferencing system. The researchers were present in the classroom during class sessions to observe live discussions and take notes.

The following questions guided the data collection process:

- To what extent do the Top Hat modules impact students' content knowledge acquisition and thinking skills?
- To what extent do the hard scaffolds in the Top Hat modules affect students' thinking and argumentation skills?
- What were students' perceptions of the Top Hat modules?

A design-based approach was used to systematically study the process of implementing and evaluating the learning materials. According to this iterative approach, the intervention could simultaneously be designed, developed, implemented and studied (Wang & Hannafin, 2005). During implementation, formative evaluation data was collected to systematically analyze the effectiveness of the modules and identify changes before implementing it again in spring 2018. This paper reports the results of 2016 pilot study. Both qualitative and quantitative data were collected and analyzed during fall 2016 to inform decisions. Data was collected from multiple sources including pre-posttests, student written responses to open-ended questions, student perception surveys and classroom observations.

Participants. A group of 5 students (3 female, 2 male) volunteered to participate in the evaluating the Top Hat intervention in fall 2016. None of the volunteers had previously participated in or completed the course. Additionally, three of five participants were completely new or novice to the process PBL.

5. RESULTS

Pre-posttest results for three modules were analyzed. Tests contained both close-ended questions (i.e., multiple choice and True/False) questions and open-ended questions which required short written responses. Close-ended questions were scored for correctness, while open-ended responses were scored using the rubric described above. In general, participants achieved an increase in their overall score from the pretest to the posttest. The average score among participants demonstrated growth in content knowledge and achievement for all three modules (Table 1).

Table 1. Summary of average pre-posttest growth

Test	Points Possible		Average Pretest Score		Average Posttest Score		Average Growth	
Module 2	22	100%	13	59%	16.5	75%	3.5	16.5%
Module 3	23	100%	14.6	63%	18.3	80%	3.7	16%
Module 4	19	100%	11.5	62%	13.75	72%	2	11%

While the results demonstrate that participants' scores improved from pre to posttest, each module pre-posttest included items which resulted in an average decline or minimal gain in scores among participants (Table 2).

Table 2. Summary of items with negative or minimal gain

Test	Item	Points Possible	Average Pretest Score		Average Posttest Score		Average Growth	
			#	%	#	%	#	%
Module 2	3	4	2.5	63%	2.75	69%	0.25	6%
	6	4	2.5	63%	2.25	56%	-0.25	-6%
Module 3	1	5	4.6	92%	4.2	84%	-0.40	-8%
Module 4	2	3	1.25	42%	2	67%	0.75	25%
	4	5	3	60%	3.25	65%	0.25	5%

Item 6 in the Module 2 experienced a 6% decline in average scores. The majority of participants' scores did not change between pre and post, while one participant's score declined. Additionally, Item 3 showed little gain (6%) compared to the other items. Each of these items asks participants to explain a concept and provide an example to support their answer. The lower scores reflect a difficulty providing reasoning and argumentation for more complex concepts within written responses. It is worth noting that Item 4 required participants to use the context of their course project in their response. While the item did achieve a small gain (5%), it is telling that the module did not appear to improve their performance when applying the content to their project.

To assess the effects of hard scaffold on students' thinking and argumentation skills, written responses to open-ended assessment items within the Top Hat modules were scored and analyzed (see Table 3). The online activities for Modules 3 and 4 consisted of two parts; an individual activity followed by a team activity. The two parts were scored separately.

Table 3. Summary of Top Hat scores

Top Hat Module	**Points Possible**	**Average Score**	
		#	%
Module 2	47	28.1	65%
Module 3: Individual Activity	5	3.25	65%
Module 3: Team Activity	21	12.25	58%
Module 4: Individual Activity	8	4.67	58%
Module 4: Team Activity	15	7	47%

The average scores for open-ended responses were low (Table 4). However, it should be noted that among the five participants scores often varied widely per item. Scores appear to have been impacted by the weight placed on the level of argumentation and justification. Many open-ended questions consisted of both Level 1 and Level 2 components described in the scoring rubric (worth 4 points or more). The mediocre average scores reflect a general difficulty with the skills of argumentation and justification which made up the bulk of the possible points.

Participants generally lacked detailed reasoning or justification to support and explain their thinking. This could be because students are not used to defending their thoughts in writing, lack skills and knowledge regarding argumentation and reasoning, or that they felt rushed when completing the activity so they didn't take time to fully expand on their thoughts for each question. The low scores could also point to a lack in conceptual content knowledge or prior experiences which could have affected their ability to provide thoughtful and well-constructed arguments. Additionally, the low scores could indicate that the metacognitive and cognitive scaffolds did not support or provide enough guidance for students to fully achieve the learning task.

The results for team activities mirror the findings for individual activities. Scores were affected by the team's level of argumentation within responses. Both teams tended to provide superficial answers with very limited reasoning or justification within their responses. However, it should be noted that the question prompts in team activities focused on the application of domain-specific knowledge and the presentation of team generated solutions. The question prompts did not necessarily specifically request reasoning in writing, but practice in the domain would expect justification for solutions. Teams were observed discussing their answers and reasoning, but this collaboration was not reflected in the written responses. This could be due to the fact that one team member was acting as the scribe for the team and did not include all the conversation or thinking that led up to the compilation of the response. Or, it could be due to the format of the question prompts and embedded scaffolds. It is evident that the scaffolds did not provide enough guidance to teams to elicit the expected components of the written response.

The implementation of the Module 4: Team Activity consisted of the three participants enrolled in the course. As such, the team activity was designed to allow the team to use the context of the course project during the team activity. The opportunity to work within the context of their project did not appear to improve open-ended responses. However, the team was observed skipping past questioning scaffolds and moving straight from question prompt to question prompt. It can be assumed that the embedded questioning scaffolds did not attract attention within the modules or were perceived to be extraneous. The format of the question prompts directed much more attention as they required action from participants.

A survey was conducted to evaluate student perception of the Top Hat modules. The survey consisted of 23 items and each item was accompanied by a 5-point Likert scale, with 1 denoting the most disagreeable and 5 denoting the most agreeable. The survey questions were categorized under the dimensions of PBL approach, scaffolds, learning evaluation, and the web-based platform (Top Hat). The results of students' perceptions of Top Hat materials are shown in Tables 4-7.

Results indicate that participants generally agreed that the PBL approach was helpful and effective for interacting with and learning the content, as shown in Table 4. However, questions regarding skills associated with PBL, items 4-10, such as collaboration and communication demonstrate a slightly wider range of responses, as illustrated by the standard deviation calculations. This is important to note because these skills are typically scaffolded by a facilitator in PBL during collaborative group sessions. During the Top Hat intervention, early group discussion on problem analysis was not facilitated by the instructor/tutor. The results demonstrate that the hard scaffolds were not sufficient to take the place of the presence of a facilitator, as scaffolds offered by an instructor or a trained tutor are provided on spot and in response to learners' thoughts (soft scaffold). Thus, it is likely that a human facilitator could better model thinking processes and promote skills of communication, collaboration and critical thinking, especially with students that are new or novice to the PBL approach. However, with such a small sample size it is difficult to generalize.

Table 4. Student perceptions of PBL approach

No	Statement	N	Mean	Std
1	The Top Hat modules helped me identify what I needed to learn more about.	5	3.8	0.84
2	The cases presented in the Top Hat modules were relevant.	5	4.4	0.89
3	I used prior knowledge and experiences to help me analyze the cases.	5	4.6	0.55
4	I had a chance to collaborate with other students.	5	4	1.73
5	Interacting with other students improved my learning.	5	4.2	1.10
6	I experienced quality interactions with the other students in terms of learning.	5	3.8	1.79
7	Learning by interacting with other students enhanced my confidence	5	3.8	1.79
8	The interactions with the other students enhanced my communication skills.	5	3.8	1.79
9	The interactions with the other students enhanced my collaboration skills.	5	3.8	1.79
10	Working with group members helped me make connections between ideas.	5	3.4	1.67

Students' perception of the Top Hat scaffolding questions indicate that participants perceived the recommended resources embedded in the Top Hat modules to be helpful and effective for interacting with and learning the content.

Table 5. Students' Perception of Top Hat Scaffolds

No	Statement	N	Mean	Std
1	The questions in Top Hat helped me identify critical issues in the cases.	5	3.4	1.67
2	The questions in the modules prompted me to think more deeply.	5	3.2	1.48
3	It was easier to learn with the guidance of questions incorporated in the Top Hat materials.	5	3.2	1.48
4	The videos, articles and other resources included in the Top Hat modules helped me make sense of the content.	5	4.4	0.89
5	The Top Hat materials provided guidance to the construction of new knowledge.	5	3.8	0.84

Table 6 shows how the participants evaluated the learning processes that they experienced. The results reveal that participants perceived the Top Hat product to be a helpful learning tool and the intervention to be effective.

Table 6. Students' evaluation of learning

No	Statement	N	Mean	Std
1	Top Hat materials helped in my learning of the content.	5	3.4	1.14
2	The Top Hat modules improved my understanding of the content.	5	3.8	1.10
3	I have gained new knowledge as a result of completing the Top Hat modules.	5	3.8	1.10
4	I feel better prepared to apply the content to my project after completing the Top Hat modules.	5	3.8	1.10
5	This type of activity is suitable for how I learn.	5	3.6	1.14

Table 7. Students' perceptions of Top Hat

No	Statement	N	Mean	Std
1	The Top Hat platform was easy to use.	5	4.4	0.89
2	I enjoyed the Top Hat modules.	5	3.8	1.10
3	I would use Top Hat again if given the opportunity.	5	4.4	0.89

6. DISCUSSION

In general, the results of the 2016 study are encouraging for the use of hard scaffolds to promote problem-solving in an online environment, where the presence of a tutor is less feasible compared to a synchronous (virtual) or face-to-face learning environment. It appeared that hard scaffolds provided an opportunity for students to question their knowledge and thinking, and encourage them to dig deeper into the content. Also, the Top Hat modules and the embedded hard scaffolds are perhaps more important for asynchronous online PBL courses where regulating one's learning process is more critical. Furthermore, while participants' reasoning skills did not seem to improve as a result of embedded hard scaffolds, their domain-specific knowledge seemed to show improvement, which indicates that participants gained conceptual knowledge. Additionally, participants seemed to find the learning materials engaging and helpful in learning the content and appeared to enjoy interacting with the course content through the Top Hat PBL modules. However, it is evident that the design and implementation of online modules could be used to modify the design of hard scaffolds embedded in the online PBL modules in spring of 2018.

REFERENCES

Barrows, H.S. (1988). *The tutorial process*. Springfield, IL: Southern Illinois University School of Medicine.

Belland, B.R. (2014). Scaffolding: Definition, current debates, and future directions. In J.M. Spector et al. (Eds.), *Handbook of research on educational communications and technology* (pp. 505-518). New York, NY: Springer Science+Business Media.

Brush, T. A., & Saye, J. W. (2002). A summary of research exploring hard and soft scaffolding for teachers and students using multimedia supported the learning environment. *The Journal of Interactive Online Learning*, *1*(2), 1-12.

Hannafin, M., Land, S., & Oliver, K. (1999). Open learning environments: Foundations, methods, and models. In C. Reigeluth (Ed.), *Instructional design theories and models* (Vol. II). Mahway, NJ: Erlbaum,

Hmelo-Silver, C. E. (2004). Problem-based learning: What and how do students learn? *Educational Psychology Review*, *16*(3), 235-266.

Hmelo-Silver, C. E., Duncan, R. G., & Chinn, C. A. (2007). Scaffolding and achievement in problem-based and inquiry learning: A response to Kirschner, Sweller, and Clark (2006). *Educational Psychologist*, *42*(2), 99-107.

Jonassen, D. H. (1999). Designing constructivist learning environments. In C. M. Reigeluth (Ed.), *Instructional design theories and models: A new paradigm of instructional theory* (Volume II, pp. 215-239). New York, NY: Routledge.

Kirschner, P. A., Sweller, J., & Clark, R. E. (2006). Why minimal guidance during instruction does not work: An analysis of the failure of constructivist, discovery, problem-based, experiential, and inquiry-based teaching. *Educational Psychologist*, *41*(2), 75-86.

Puntambekar, S., & Hübscher, R. (2005). Tools for scaffolding students in a complex learning environment: What have we gained and what have we missed?. *Educational Psychologist*, *40*(1), 1-12.

Reiser, B. J. (2004). Scaffolding complex learning: The mechanisms of structuring and problematizing student work. *Journal of the Learning Sciences*, *13*(3), 273-304.

Savery, J. R. (2006). Overview of problem-based learning: Definitions and distinctions. *Interdisciplinary Journal of Problem-based Learning*, *1*(1), 9-20.

Saye, J. W. & Brush, T. (2002). Scaffolding critical reasoning about history and social issues in multimedia-supported learning environments. *Educational Technology Research and Development*, *50*(3), 77-96.

Schmidt, H. G., Rotgans, J. I. & Yew, E. (2011). The process of problem-based learning: What works and why. *Medical Education*. 45. 792-806.

Şendağ, S., & Odabaşı, H. F. (2009). Effects of an online problem-based learning course on content knowledge acquisition and critical thinking skills. *Computers & Education*, *53*(1), 132-141.

Simons, K. D., & Ertmer, P. A. (2005). Scaffolding disciplined inquiry in problem-based environments. *International Journal of Learning*, *12*(6), 297-305.

Sockalingam, N., Rotgans, J., & Schmidt, H. (2011). Student and tutor perceptions on attributes of effective problems in problem-based learning. *Higher Education, 62*(1), 1-16.

Vygotsky, L.S. (1978). Mind in society: *The development of higher psychological processes.* Cambridge, MA: Harvard University Press.

Wang, F., & Hannafin, M. J. (2005). Design-based research and technology-enhanced learning environments. *Educational technology research and development*, *53*(4), 5-23.

Wood, D., Bruner, J. S., & Ross, G. (1976). The role of tutoring in problem-solving. *Journal of child psychology and psychiatry*, *17*(2), 89-100.

Yew, E. H. J., Schmidt, H.G. (2012). What students learn in problem-based learning: a process analysis. *Instructional Science*, *40*(2), 371-395.

PROBLEM-BASED LEARNING IN THE DIGITAL AGE

Ditte Kolbaek
Aalborg University, A.C. Meyers Vaenge 15, DK-2450 Copenhagen SV, Denmark

ABSTRACT

Problem-based and project-organized learning (PBL) was originally developed to facilitate collaboration between physically present students; however, due to digitalization, collaboration, dialogues, and other PBL activities should take place online as well. With a theoretical point of departure from Dewey and a methodological point of departure from netnography, this study focused on a blended learning module at Aalborg University, where teaching is based on PBL. A primary research question was investigated: "How can IT support collaborative learning among learner communities in a PBL Master's program at Aalborg University?" The ways teachers and groups of students could benefit from utilizing IT as a platform for learning were examined. Netnography was the chosen methodology, and the data consisted of the course materials, the reflections, and the dialogues available online. The study showed that including more students allows for more discussions and reflections than including fewer students given teachers describe the task thoroughly and support the online dialogue. In addition, online collaboration allows students to return to the dialogue and re-use it as a resource for their dissertations, teachers can benefit from the online reflections and discussions to improve the educational design of the course, and researchers can obtain rich data from online reflections and dialogues.

KEYWORDS

Problem-Based Learning, Online Learning, Collaborative Learning, Workplace Learning, Learner Communities, Netnography

1. INTRODUCTION

It is well-established that dialogue, reflection, and collaboration are important elements of student learning (Dewey, 1916; Hmelo-Silver, 2012; Kolmos, Fink, and Krogh, 2006; Lazonder and Harmsen, 2016), and many universities integrate these elements through PBL. The literature highlights several advantages of PBL, for example the ability to stimulate critical, reflective, and creative thinking (Blackburn, 2015). Moreover, it accentuates student centeredness (Abercrombie, Parkes, and McCarty, 2015), students' active participation (Tambouris et al., 2014), and authentic ways for students to collaborate and create knowledge. With its roots dating back to Dewey, (1910), Piaget (1974), and Lewin (1948), PBL has been practiced in Denmark since the 1970s (Kolmos et al., 2006). Thus, most of the literature on PBL focuses on the practice of learning in offline face-to-face settings. Researchers have only recently begun to examine the role of learning technologies in PBL and the use of PBL for virtual classrooms and online learning (Lajoie et al., 2014).

A literature review revealed that PBL faces new challenges in online settings. Some studies showed that project work is not as beneficial for online students as it is for students who meet regularly on campus because online students must motivate themselves and solve problems alone (Lauersen, 2006). Online learning is also criticized due to the social isolation of students and technical issues that can. In this study, learning activities in an online learning setting for a specific course were examined to answer the following question: "How can IT support collaborative learning among learner communities in a PBL Master's program at Aalborg University?"

This article focuses on Aalborg University, where the pedagogical foundation is PBL, which is referred to as the "Aalborg PBL model" (www.aau.dk). According to the Aalborg PBL model, the students find an issue that makes them wonder, and they formulate the speculation as a question. This is the starting point for learning. The curriculum of the course frames the problem definition and analysis, and the students work in supervised groups during the planning, management, and completion of the project that addresses the problem. Finally, the students defend the project report orally. Most often, this defence is evaluated by the teacher and an external examiner as a final grade for the course.

Technology can provide additional support mechanisms for real-time supervision that are not available when PBL is conducted in a face-to-face setting (Lajoie et al., 2014). In addition, Learning Management

Systems, such as Moodle, require new teaching practices (Ravitz and Blazevski, 2014). This paper discusses how PBL can utilize IT to enhance reflection, dialogue, and collaboration among students in the digital age, and an analysis of a learning design for PBL in an online setting is presented.

2. THEORETICAL FOUNDATION

This section presents the theoretical foundation, which includes Dewey's conclusions (1910) related to PBL, as well as a comparison between PBL in a face-to-face setting and in an online setting.

2.1 Dewey and PBL

According to Dewey (1910,), thinking begins with a dilemma or state of perplexity that demands a solution. The difficulty of the problem causes students to reflect, which involves considering the definition and the location of the problem and briefly developing potential solutions that require further inquiry and experimentation to accept or reject the premature solution (Dewey, 1910, p. 72). To think critically, students must be curious and should spend a sufficient amount of time inquiring about the nature of the problem and investigating the facts before they can "digest impressions and translate them into substantial ideas" (Dewey, 1910) for solutions. Inquiry initiates critical thinking, and this type of thinking occurs differently for different students (Dewey, 1910); hence, it may be beneficial for students to work in groups to reflect collaboratively, enhancing the inquiry process. The inquiry includes two movements: induction, or developing ideas, and deduction, or developing, applying, and testing ideas (Dewey, 1910). Inquiry includes data gathering, analysis, and synthesis, and these steps lead to the development of premature ideas that must be evaluated to become suggestions for solutions. The students' "own good (or bad) judgment is the guide" when they evaluate data to identify conflicts in the definition and location of the problem and to analyse facts (Dewey, 1910, p. 106). From problem identification to solution suggestions, the process includes different ways of thinking, beginning with the sense of difficulty caused by perplexity and continuing with reflection, which leads to the identification of the problems that require inquiry.

The outcome of educational thinking is twofold (Dewey, 1910). First, the student identifies the meaning of the problem and the location of the problem. Second, the student develops suggestions for solutions to the problem that initiated the thinking process. Although several learning theorists' findings inspired the PBL model (Kolmos et al., 2004), Dewey's findings were the foundation for the general views of learning, collaboration, and inquiry related to PBL.

Both in Dewey's writings (e.g., 1910, 1916) and in various framings of the models, phases, and steps of PBL (Tambouris et al., 2014), the teacher's role is not restricted to the supervision of students' collaborative thinking and project work. Learning involves more than individual reflection and creative processes. Dewey (1910) provided guidelines for teachers and suggested how teachers can best help students memorize and recite content, but he emphasized that the teacher's attention should be focused on instruction and supervision to support and enhance students' reflection and collaboration skills. In Dewey's writings, it is implicit that the teacher is in physical proximity with his or her students on a regular basis, as this was a common instruction practice at the time. He died in 1952, which was long before the invention of personal computers and the internet; however, while the issue of proximity is still a focus, proximity can be either physical or online.

2.2 PBL Activities Face-to-Face and Online

When PBL occurs in an on-campus setting, students usually prepare for class at home, whereas most interactions between the teacher and the students and between the students usually occur on campus. Hence, the activities of the students and the teacher are distributed to different times and spaces, and the teacher's access to the students' activities is thus limited by time and space. Activities "disconnected from the teacher" involve the students' preparation for class and group work, including problem formulation and writing project-reports. The activities within "physical proximity with the teacher" include lectures, in-class discussions, supervision, and the final exam. The teacher is usually only involved on campus, so the teacher only has access to students' reflections, collaboration, and progress when discussed during supervision sessions. The lack of physical proximity limits supervision, instruction, and learning activities for traditional PBL; hence, efforts should be made to improve proximity between students and teachers.

In online settings, PBL allows for participating in collaborative activities across time and space. Students do not need to find an available room for collaboration or supervision; they only have to agree on a time for the synchronous activities (Nortvig, 2015). In addition, they only require a common space online in which to contribute asynchronously to the dialogues at a time that is convenient for them. Thus, all student activities can occur within proximity of the teacher because the teacher is reachable online. The students can engage in lectures, dialogues, supervision, collaboration, and other activities from any location, as they do so online.

3. METHODOLOGICAL CONSIDERATIONS

This section explains the methodology and methods utilized to investigate the role of PBL in the digital age in a specific research setting.

3.1 Netnography

To analyse an online PBL learning design, netnography is appropriate because it is a methodology used for online field work in which IT represents the main resource for data collection (Kozinets, 2012, p. 102). Netnography allows researchers to investigate activities in online learning settings without physical presence, which means that researchers can be present in these settings at any time from any location and can investigate learning activities and course material years after the courses end.

Research on online data is intangible, and most data are text-based, although they may include sounds and pictures as well (Hughes, 2012). When the data lack sound and pictures, researchers cannot analyse body language cues, such as gestures, tone of voice, or clothing (Kozinets, 2015). The distance between the persons under study and the researcher often eliminates social cues, such as age, gender, and ethnicity, and the distance also reduces the researcher's impact on the participants because they cannot see or hear the researcher (Kozinets, 2015). In this study, the researcher investigated online learning activities, but she was not able to analyse body language cues. However, the researcher knew the students from teaching the course and from supervising the students online. The exploration of the course design took place two years after the course ended. In this way, research distance was developed.

3.2 Research Setting and Data Collection

The data were gathered from the Master in ICT and Learning program (MIL) at Aalborg University, specifically from a course entitled "Proactive Review: An Educational Design for Organizational Learning." The course was offered in 2013 and 2015 and was valued at five ECTS, with a student workload of 137½ hours. The requirements for attending MIL are a professional bachelor degree such as teacher or nurse, or alternatively ad BA in humanity or social science, or alternatively a MA, as well as relevant work experience for at least two years and good skills in IT and English language. In both years half of the students held a Master's Degree and the other half held a professional bachelor degree. The first lecture took place face-to-face, and the remainder of the course consisted of online activities only. The educational design of the course stayed the same over the two years except for the choice of tools for online collaboration being Google Group in 2013 and Moodle Forum in 2015. The difference in the choice of technology is a matter of availability. The students suggested Google Groups as the common IT platform, as Aalborg University did not provide a learning management system with collaboration tools in2013. This changed in 2015, and Moodle was an easy choice.

The data were collected from Moodle and included the teacher's lesson plans, lists of literature, slides from the initial face-to-face lecture, exercises, and students' written conversations and online reflections in 2015; the conversations and reflections in Google groups in 2013; and the slides from the videoconference in 2013 and 2015.

MIL students worked as professionals at private or public organizations and study part-time, and they were located all over Denmark and Norway. As they were geographically dispersed, it was important for them to study and collaborate online. Proactive review is an educational design for organisational learning consisting of seven open questions asked in a specific sequence. The proactive review course presented this educational design and enabled the students to try it out in roleplays, before they experimented with proactive reviews in their work places, which was followed by reflections. It should be noted that many elements of the course are not described in this article because the focus is the learning activities, and the online tools utilized are mentioned but not described in detail. The teacher prepared for the course by selecting relevant texts. For the in-class lecture she prepared oral presentations, in-class group work, and role-playing activities, and she prepared the online spaces for online presentations, reflections, inquiries, and analyses. Students prepared for the introduction by reading the texts. The flow of the proactive review course is shown in Table 1.

Table 1. Activities and technologies of the online PBL proactive review course

Time	**4 hours**	**6 weeks**	**3 weeks**	**2 hours**	**2 weeks**	**1 week**
	Week 1	**Week 2-7**	**Week 8-10**	**Week 10**	**Week 11-12**	**Week 13**
Teacher activities	Present theory Conduct experimentation with proactive reviews Supervise reflections on experimentation	Students experiment with proactive review at their workplaces	Supervise online reflections and inquiries of different theories of organizational learning	Supervise collaborative reflections on difficulties and relevant theories Supervise problem identification	Supervise collaborative analyses and idea-generation and reflection	Read reports Examine/ evaluate
Setting	Face-to-face	Field	Discussion forum (Moodle/ Google Group)	Video conference (Adobe Connect)	Moodle/ Google Groups	Folder file on Moodle
Student activities	Become curious about the topic Experiment with role play Form groups Groups decide location for experimenting with proactive review	Experiment Identify a difficulty in running a proactive review	Individual and collaborative reflection on the identified difficulties Inquire by including data collection for theories Formulate a problem based on the difficulty	Present the problem	Analyse the problem Develop ideas for solutions Reflect collaboratively and test the ideas	Write the report, including the location of the problem Suggest solutions

The proactive review course began with a face-to-face introduction in which students were introduced to theories related to organizational learning and proactive review as an educational design for organizational learning (Kolbaek, 2014). The teacher's aim was to stimulate students' curiosity about learning in the context of work, specifically the educational design for collaborative learning. During the introduction, the teacher briefly presented relevant theories and the format for the proactive review. She initiated experimentation with proactive reviews during role playing activities, and she supervised students' reflections on role play by asking them to provide specific feedback. The students formed small groups that served as learner communities to discuss the theories and to choose a specific theory as their focus. The role-playing activities enabled the students to experiment with proactive reviews at their workplaces. They chose a location to try out at least one proactive review, and then they prepared for their proactive review. The outcome of the introduction was a common understanding of a proactive review and a plan for subsequent work.

For the first six weeks after the introduction, the students were occupied with other courses required for the master program. During this period, the learner communities prepared and implemented at least one proactive review at the workplace. Then, they formulated a difficulty they experienced during their experiments. The teachers did not interfere in the group work or in the experimentation with proactive reviews. The learner communities chose the online space for collaboration on their own without interference from the teacher. The student outcomes of the experimentation period were acquiring experience with an educational design for organizational learning at the workplace and developing curiosity regarding a difficulty they faced.

For the following three weeks, some learner communities used Google Group, and others used private Facebook groups, FaceTime, Skype, emails, etc. Using the common Moodle forums (2015) or Google Group (2013), the teacher supervised the students' collaborative reflections and inquiries of different theories of organizational learning. The learner communities reflected on a specific difficulty and inquired about the issue through the lens of a theory they chose, which the group presented in an online discussion forum. This was followed by individual comments on at least two theories presented by other groups and by individual replies to at least two of the comments from fellow students. The outcome of the three weeks of reflection and inquiry was thus the identification of problems. By the end of the three weeks, the learner communities had formulated problems based on a difficulty they experienced, and each group presented their problems to fellow students and to the teacher during a two-hour video conference using Adobe Connect. In 2015, 17 students presented seven problems: "who is to participate," "do the participants need to have shared a task," "which contexts are suitable for proactive reviews," "which competences are required for supervising proactive reviews," "how to introduce proactive reviews in an organization," "how to ensure commitment to the agreements in a proactive review," and "how does the supervisor capture all the good ideas generated during a proactive review." In 2013, 12 students presented three themes for discussion: "power distance," "prerequisites for the participants," and "preparation for a proactive review."

Over the following two weeks, students analysed the problems by gathering examples (data) from fellow students' experiences that enabled them to generate ideas for solutions. Students then reflected collaboratively to test their ideas. The teacher supervised the online collaborative analysis, idea generation, and reflection and ensured that all students actively contributed. If the dialogues waned, the teacher commented or asked questions to initiate reactions. If the dialogues lost focus, the teacher led students back to the topic. During the 2015 course when a Moodle discussion forum dialogue wavered, the teacher intervened 14 times—an average of twice per dialogue (the dialogues included 93 contributions and an average of 4.6 contributions per student, and the students contributed equally). In 2013, the dialogue took place using Google Group, and the teacher intervened 21 times—an average of seven times per dialogue (the dialogues included 75 contributions and an average of 4.5 contributions per student, and the students contributed equally). The outcome of these two weeks of thinking and collaboration was the creation of tentative solutions to the problems identified. The online space had no effect on the activity of the groups or the need for teacher intervention.

The exam at the end of the course consisted of a group or individual student report, including the location of the problem based on the theories, suggestions for solutions, and reflections on the learning process during the course. Students uploaded their final reports in Moodle, and all the students passed the exam.

4. ANALYSIS

This analysis involves examining activities that support learning, such as curiosity, problem location, experimentation, identification of difficulties, reflection, problem identification, inquiry, analysis, and suggestions for solutions. In addition, the use of the different technologies utilized in the blended learning course is analysed (Dewey's 1910, 1916).

The students collaborated in a digital space, and when they wrote their reflections in the digital space, they made the reflections accessible to teachers, fellow students, and researchers. Inspired by Dewey (1910), this study explored how the teacher initiated curiosity and experimentation as well as how she stimulated the students' identification of a difficulty to initiate reflection, make inquiries, and perform analyses to develop suggestions for solutions to the problems identified. The teacher created curiosity about learning in the context of work by presenting theories and by enabling students to experiment with proactive reviews during role-playing activities. The students' curiosity, along with the teacher's requirements for the course, allowed the students to plan for further experimentation. The teacher emphasized that there must be a problem location, and the students chose a workplace as their specific problem location. For this course, the data showed that online collaboration did occur without a need for teacher supervision. Thus, the teacher did not support or interfere with the students' experimentation with proactive reviews, but she asked the students to discuss the difficulties they encountered during experimentation. The teacher provided the students with the confidence to share their difficulties, and these difficulties became the basis for reflection and inquiry.

The teacher supported reflection online in different ways. First, by asking students to choose a theory as their focus, the teacher motivated them to reflect on the theories they found most relevant or interesting. Second, by asking students to decide which workplace would be most suitable for experimenting with a proactive review, the teacher induced the students to discuss their individual workplaces and to reflect on the pros and cons of each before making their choice. Third, by asking the students to identify a problem to present during the video conference followed by an online dialogue, the teacher prompted the students to reflect on their experiences of implementing the proactive reviews. Fourth, by asking the students to reply to the questions raised in the online dialogue and by asking them to involve the theories in their replies, the teacher motivated the students to reflect on the theories in connection to the problems they or their fellow students experienced during their proactive reviews. All these questions were uploaded to Google Group the first year and to the Moodle front page the second year. Using this forum as a meeting point for the course, the teacher was able to reify and maintain the goals for the course. Thus, in the forum, she linked the face-to-face meeting (and the activities taking place there) with the independent off-campus experimental phase. Moreover, the Google Group/Moodle front page was used as a link between the problem identification during the video conference session and the following online asynchronous period as well as between the course material (theories) and the students' experiments and problem identification.

To identify a problem, the teacher asked the groups to move from difficulties in a specific case (namely, the proactive review they experienced) to the more general problems of a proactive review and to write and share their thoughts in the Google Group/Moodle Forum. In 2013, students identified three problems, which they formulated as headlines for their inquiries; in 2015, students identified seven problems, which the teacher asked to be formulated as questions. When the students formulated the problem, they were able to share their thoughts to a higher extent with less support from the teacher. When teaching using a video conference, it is recommended that the lesson be well-structured and planned so that all students feel engaged and are eager to participate and collaborate (Gill and Richardson, 2005). Online synchronous dialogue is important to supporting the trust that develops "when people have enough information about others to understand them and accurately predict their behaviour" (Thompson, 2015, p. 126; cited in Callister and Love, 2016, p. 247). During the course under investigation, the video conference session continued the online dialogue, and it also created a foundation for further collaboration. The video conference also allowed the teacher and the students to exchange body language and other nonverbal cues, such as smiles, nodding, and eye contact, which supported trust-building. Furthermore, body language cues could be used to indicate which group or individual student most needed help from the teacher.

The teacher initiated the students' inquiry process when they were asked to investigate their various workplaces to determine which would be suitable for implementing a proactive review. The teacher asked the students to inquire about and analyse the problems by gathering data from their experiments and by searching for more information based on relevant theories. The inquiries were shared online in discussion forums in Moodle or Google Group, where students took their point of departure of the entire experience from the experiment and added more details by including more data and relevant theories. Furthermore, the teacher supported inquiries by asking students to participate in the dialogues, which probed their insights regarding different problems and different workplaces as contexts for proactive reviews. The teacher supported inquiries in physical settings (the workplaces) as well as online settings (Google Group in 2013 and Moodle in 2015).

The teacher supported the students' collaboration skills by requiring the preparation and supervision of the proactive review, during which all students participated. The teacher also supported the students' collaboration skills by asking them to share their reflections and inquiries online and to read and comment on fellow students' thoughts. The teacher sustained student collaboration by asking the learner communities to identify problems that occurred during the proactive reviews and to contribute to the online dialogue with comments and questions. Because all students could read what the teacher wrote to a single group, online supervision enabled the supervision of the entire group at the same time. Moreover, the supervision of each group was more focused because the evolution of the students' arguments was easily followed in the forum.

The teacher continuously reinforced the creation of solutions to the problems identified by the students by leading the students through the process of educational thinking. This process began with experimenting and was followed by experiencing difficulties. This led to reflections on the experiment and the identification of the problems that occurred during the proactive review, which were investigated and analysed before tentative solutions were presented and discussed by fellow students. The teacher required suggestions for solutions in the final report, which included the location of the problem as well as the students' reflections regarding the learning processes. The reports served as important feedback for the teacher because they provided valuable insights into the students' learning processes and outcomes related to the course.

5. DISCUSSION AND CONCLUSION

In this study, the question "how can IT support collaborative learning among learner communities using PBL for a Master's program at Aalborg University" was explored. The IT utilized consisted of Google Group, Moodle, and video conferences from which the data were collected. Hence, this study could be classified as a netnographic study (Kozinets, 2012). Most of the data were text-based and lacked body language cues, such as gestures or tone of voice, but the researcher knew the gender, age, and ethnicity of the students because she had met them face-to-face during the introductory seminar. To establish and maintain trust and confidentiality (Hughes, 2012), the discussion forums of Google Group and Moodle were only accessible to the teacher and the students. When the teacher wanted to utilize the data for research, she asked the students for consent, which they willingly provided.

This study shows that the online students did not struggle to motivate themselves, although the students in 2013 needed more teacher support than the students in 2015. The teacher contributed 21 times to three different problem threads in 2013, whereas she contributed only 14 times to the seven problem threads in 2015. The reason could not be differences in student-competences, as approximately half of the students held a professional bachelor degree, and half of the students held a Masters' degree and several years of experience in IT as the basis to attend the MIL programme. So another reason for the reduced need for teacher support could be the number of students. It appears to have been easier for 17 students to maintain the pace online than it was for 12 students. Thus, the extended number of students may have led to livelier interactions online. The framing of the problem could also have contributed to this outcome. It appears that problems formulated as questions enable students to discuss the problems to a higher extent than if the problem is formulated as a headline. Technical problems do not seem to cause difficulties. When the teacher asked the students to find an online space for collaboration, they did so without assistance. The discussion forum can easily become silent and inactive without supervision because students may feel isolated. This study showed that inactivity and isolation can be resolved if the teacher requires a certain amount of activity, such as two comments and two replies to comments.

In contrast to so-called traditional teaching in face-to-face settings, this approach to teaching PBL online has several advantages: reflection as an activity is reified in the online space, and as such, the activity is not only a process but also an object that can be re-consulted and meta-reflected at a later time. The students can benefit from these written dialogues and reflections by returning to them when appropriate, such as when writing a thesis.

Moreover, due to the digital traces of activity, the teacher can easily track and take action with students who do not follow the course plan. Therefore, supervision can be targeted toward individual students, and collaboration in groups can be supported individually as well. The teacher can add to or change the program to enable as many students as possible to pass the exam. Because all students passed the exam, the teacher's support does not need to occur in a face-to-face or in a synchronous setting; a timely online presence seems to be more efficient for maintaining inquiry, dialogue, collaboration, and reflection. IT supported collaborative learning among learner communities using PBL for a Master's program at Aalborg University by creating proximity between students and the teacher, between students in the learner communities, and between the learner communities.

REFERENCES

Abercrombie, S, Parkes, J., and McCarty, T. 2015. Motivational influences of using peer evaluation in problem-based learning in medical education. *Interdisciplinary Journal of Problem-Based Learning.* 9(1), p. 8.

Blackburn, G. 2015. Innovative e-learning: technology shaping contemporary problem-based learning: a cross-case analysis. *Journal of University Teaching & Learning Practice.* 12(2), p. 5.

Callister, R. R., and Love, M. S. 2016. A comparison of learning outcomes in skills-based courses: online versus face-to-face formats. *Decision Sciences Journal of Innovative Education.* 14(2), pp. 243–256.

Dewey, J. 1910. *How we think.* New York: Heat.

Dewey, J. 1916. *Democracy and education: an introduction to the philosophy of education.* New York: The Macmillan Company.

Gill, D., Parker, C., and Richardson, J. 2005. Twelve tips for teaching using videoconferencing. *Medical Teacher.* 27(7), pp. 573–577.

Hmelo-Silver, C. E. 2012. International perspectives on problem-based learning: contexts, cultures, challenges, and adaptations. *Interdisciplinary Journal of Problem-Based Learning.* 6(1), p. 3.

Hughes, J. ed. 2012. *SAGE internet research methods.* London: SAGE Publications Ltd.

Kolbaek, D. 2014. *Learning from experience in the context of work: a seven-year study of proactive review as an educational design for learning from experience in a global, high-tech company classified as big business.* Aalborg: Aalborg Universitetsforlag.

Kolmos, A., Fink, F. K., and Krogh, L. eds. (2006) *The Aalborg PBL model: progress, diversity and challenges.* Aalborg: Aalborg Universitetsforlag.

Kozinets, R. V. 2012. Marketing netnography: prom/ot (ulgat) ing a new research method. *Methodological Innovations Online.* 7(1), pp. 37–45.

Kozinets, R. V. 2015. *Netnography: redefined.* London: SAGE.

von Krogh, G., Ichijo, K., and Nonaka, I. 2000. *Enabling knowledge creation: how to unlock the mystery of tacit knowledge and release the power of innovation.* Oxford: Oxford University Press.

Lauersen. E. 2006. Problem-based learning as a way of organizing learning and teaching at the university. In: Kolmos, A., Fink, F. K., and Krogh, L. eds. *The Aalborg PBL model: progress, diversity and challenges.* Aalborg: Aalborg Universitetsforlag

Lajoie, S. P., Hmelo-Silver, C. E., Wiseman, J. G., Chan, L. K., Lu, J., Khurana, C., and Kazemitabar, M. 2014. Using online digital tools and video to support international problem-based learning. *Interdisciplinary Journal of Problem-Based Learning.* 8(2), p. 6.

Lazonder, A. W., and Harmsen, R. 2016. Meta-analysis of inquiry-based learning effects of guidance. *Review of Educational Research.* 86(3), pp. 681–718.

Nortvig, A. M. 2015. *At sidde på skolebænken i egen sofa.* Aalborg: Aalborg University Press. English title (the author's translation): *To go to school while sitting on your own couch.*

Ravitz, J., and Blazevski, J. 2014. Assessing the role of online technologies in project-based learning. *Interdisciplinary Journal of Problem-Based Learning.* 8(1), p. 9.

Tambouris, E., Zotou, M., and Tarabanis, K. 2014. Towards designing cognitively-enriched project-oriented courses within a blended problem-based learning context. *Education and Information Technologies.* 19(1), pp. 61–86.

BUILDING COLLABORATIVE CREATIVITY THROUGH AN ITERATIVE APPROACH

Paula Hodgson, Kristof Corolla and Wai Yee Angel Ho
The Chinese University of Hong Kong, Shatin, N.T. Hong Kong

ABSTRACT

Instilling a creative mind is the foundation to prepare future architecture students. University educators can adopt an iterative approach in which students go through cycles of learning. This paper reports student experiences on a three-cycle team project in an architecture course that was part of a master program. This consisted of the group development of a single design proposal to build a large prototype on the roof in the School of Architecture building. Students had to self-select which solution to go forward with, starting with four teams of two in the first cycle, then two teams of four in the second cycle, and one final team of eight in the third cycle. Students needed to reflect on their individual experience and role within the team in a reflective cycle research model that was intended to enable independent and collaborative learning from a given action-based experience. Individual reports were analysed, and the students commonly showed learning through making mistakes and experienced collective efforts by all team members in the process of collaborative creativity.

KEYWORDS

Architectural Education, Creativity, Iterative Approach, Collaborative Learning

1. INTRODUCTION

Architectural educators create a learning environment that draws students' talents and imagination because these students will create landscapes for future generations. According to the charter of the United Nations Educational, Scientific and Cultural Organization (UNESCO) with the International Union of Architects (UIA) for architectural education, one of the core skills in architectural education is the 'ability to work in collaboration with other architects and members of interdisciplinary teams' (p.6). Educators play a significant role in marking student performance, and students experience negativity when a group of tutors provide different critiques as an educational experiment on design studio pedagogy (Ciravoğlu, 2014). A transformative pedagogy adopted in architectural education is studio pedagogy that aims to break down the social relationships of hierarchy between educator and learners and competition between learners (Dutton, 1987). Students as designers have opportunities to sharpen their critical thinking skills, build confidence in taking a stand and be able to communicate their points verbally, or present their work in written format with visual illustrations (Hadjiyanni, 2008). The studio setting allows students to take responsibility to make critiques between one another, and the teaching professor provides guidance on the creative thought processes. Students take active roles in problem analysis and solution justification to work on an authentic local design project with the participatory process (Kowaltowski *et al.*, 2007).

Creativity is one of the core competences that student architects need to acquire in the journey of becoming professional architects. Creativity is not a unitary process but requires conscious and unconscious information processing (Dietrich, 2007). A variety of strategies can be adopted, including critical analysis, imagery, habit breaking, relationship seeking and interpersonal interactions (Smith, 1998). 'Imagery alone cannot be sufficient to improve an idea, and good representational skills [that] are crucial in the developmental phases' of design (Hasirci and Demirkan, 2007: 269). Creativity through interpersonal strategy can enable team members to stimulate one another through building on peer ideas, where each member has veto power in the process of decision making.

Using computer software to generate solutions has been widely adopted in architecture and the construction industry, with 50 percent of the construction industry in North America have adopting building information modelling (BIM) for 3D model-based processing (Becerik-Gerber and Rice, 2010). An iterative approach in architectural design with modelling is deployed that may speed up preliminary safety analysis of automotive systems to allow rapid adoption in the development cycle in the real world (Rupanov *et al.*, 2014). This paper will explore the learning experiences of an advanced architectural design studio that adopts an iterative approach to providing students with rigorous expertise in the concepts, architectural design and design development of working with real-time structural performance simulation engines as a design tool. In addition, it will introduce students to methods for procedural design, digital modelling, digital fabrication, and robotic fabrication. They are expected to develop competence in using the technical tools in order to extend and advance the use of new tools and technologies into architectural design for contemporary practice.

2. STUDIO 'FORCE MATTER 2: CALIBRATION'

Studio 'Force Matter 2: Calibration' takes the high density of Hong Kong's built environment and the lack of available space for new construction as the challenging starting point to advocate lightweight additive architecture. Existing podium and tower structures are used as a substrate for the integration of additional public programs within high-performing structural additions. Weight constraints and limitations from proximity to build fabric become drivers for non-standard architectural design interventions. Students have to learn how to work with geometry, form, performance, materiality and materialization in the context of architectural design addition to a high-density built environment.

Setting up workflows that rely on feedback between material experimentation and notational design with digital design tools, students may experience the complexity of creating a one-tenth scale model to build a large-scale physical manifestation while exploring model making. Iterative design processes are set up that allow for interaction between the numerous factors that define a project. The main tools used in this setup are virtual real-time physics simulation engines, and students are expected to use them to do digital fabrication. They are required to produce a 3D digital design model and all usual architectural drawings to test programmatic requirements and response to site conditions. Apart from learning about principles of modelling (both computational and physical) at various scales to iteratively develop and transform a medium into large-scale intervention, they have to create a full-scale physical model in which a combination is sought between conventional structural systems and lightweight tectonics using bending-active structures to explore the non-standard spatial possibilities for large span areas with minimal live loads.

Each student submits a short critical reflective report on their individual experience with the project and role within the team, supported by evidence of that contribution (e.g. imagery, screenshots, drawings and pictures) to reflect on the action-based experience.

2.1 Creating a 1:10 Prototype in the First Cycle

Among the eight students, a team of two was formed with one student, who had taken the foundation elective course, taking a leading role paired with someone who took a supporting role. The lead teammate would be familiar with the digital tools that were used in the initial design prototype. This meant that it would be a good opportunity for the lead member to teach the supporting member as a form of peer learning in the first cycle.

Students were set to be familiarized with design and physical model construction systems for the development of structurally high-performing geometry setups. Each team used digital physics simulation engines that served as a test basis for the physical model making. Bamboo sticks were used to build a 1:10 scale model. By the end of the first cycle, the paired teams were required to make a PowerPoint presentation that included a time-lapse video of the model construction and to show the first one-tenth scale model. Afterwards, individual students cast their votes as to which two design concepts most involved architectural experimentation and innovation with structurally high-performing systems. Models of the top two votes were selected for the second cycle, a scale-up development. Members of the other two teams would join the selected teams to form two teams of four.

2.1.1 Starting with Errors

Even working with a prototype in the first cycle, students working in creative fields often make errors, and this was observed in their reflections:

> 'This is the first time we tested out Kangaroo with singularity, one of the fatal mistakes that we have made in the design is that we have inserted too many anchor points at the base to pull the desired shape and as a result the grid distorted more than 40mm. We underestimated the difficulties when we tried to bend the bamboo strips from the cover to form the column, strips went chaotic and hard to manage. So we failed to achieve our ideal double-column structure…we placed four anchor points in the skylight to hold up the skylight in position. As a result, the skylight was rectangular in shape instead of circular.' – student D
>
> 'I did struggle in doing simulation with Kangaroo. I failed several times because of the incorrect structural grid as well as the location and amount of anchor point setting. Though I have generated some successful simulations at last, I didn't really understand the failure part from every case I did.' – student O

2.1.2 Evidence of Teamwork

In the first cycle, teaming students with a foundation elective meant that they needed good teamwork, with one playing a leading role and the other a supporting role (with no prior experience in using software for model design and digital fabrication):

> 'I prepared the drawings and diagrams while my teammate combined the PowerPoint, and together we tried to figure out reasons that led to failure.' – student T
>
> 'With the help of my teammate, I could be able to understand the system and help to do some model design using Kangaroo.' – student F
>
> 'In phase 1, design experimentation was implemented as teamwork…. I learned a lot about grasshopper scripting from the discussions with my teammate. I did benefit a lot from the knowledge exchange between the peers throughout the entire phase. I put most of my effort and contribution in the assembly of the physical model while picking up the computation design method.' – student O

2.1.3 Solving Problems by Students

Students were expected to demonstrate architectural applications of recently developed digital design and fabrication tools. They would certainly encounter problems and needed to learn to solve problems by themselves.

> 'Professor has provided a grasshopper tool for generating diagonal grid, but this method must fix the singularity points by ourselves. – student N
>
> 'We did figure out a new way to generate a structural grid by using diamond grid component in Lunchbox plug-in software.'– student O

2.2 Creating a 1:5 Prototype in the Second Cycle

In the second cycle, the two teams of four students needed to develop and refine their designs into projects that incorporated all material and force behaviour, restrictions and opportunities in a symbiotic manner into a single well-resolved architectural production. The teams used bamboo sticks to create a 1:5 scale model in the second iteration, knowing that only the best model design would be selected for the rooftop construction. All students joined in voting for the best project.

2.2.1 New Team, New Roles

Forming new teams could invite more opportunities to try out new tasks. However, the collective wisdom would take time to function.

> 'I participated in both digital and physical model work in the first cycle. I took a role in preparing the material and model making in the second cycle. I made the wooden base bench for the 1 to 5 scale mock-up model…double checking in between the digital 3d model and physical model.' – student D
>
> 'Together as a team we marked and trimmed the bamboo lengths and tried to divide the whole fabrication into two parts (the column and the skylight). I was responsible for helping the skylight

part, but it was not smooth in the beginning as we went too fast and connected too many intersections. In the end, we were too confused and had to redo. It was a challenge later, even with a 1:5 model. We got difficulties merging the parts together because of the height and numbering problem.' – student T

'Although I know I would not be selected by the designer, I became more confident and wanted to make more contributions to the team. So I designed a series of simulations in the computer based on Lonhin's modeling file for more selections.' – student F

'I extrapolated the grid into 2D drawings for assembly and mainly assisted to build the scale model.' – student P

2.2.2 Lesson Learned

Using the same materials as in the first cycle, errors experienced in the first cycle could be avoided in the second, with new teammates' experience made the second cycle smoother than the previous one.

'I had ensured that the bamboo strips we used still contained enough moisture and bend well' [failed working out in the first cycle] – student D

'The failure in the first stage gave me a lot of lessons for the later process. I found a method to build the column rapidly.' – student F

'To prevent grid distortion [happened in cycle 1], we tried fewer anchor points with curve pull, and trimmed the ground part for grids that distorted the most and tried to tune the same rest length in the script. In Round 2, things went smoother as we had shared the lesson from failure with new teammates.' – student T

2.3 Creating a 1:1 Construction in the Third Cycle

All students worked together to implement the final design proposal. Construction detailing needed to be developed and tested through small-scale prototypes. Implementation strategies needed to be tried, coordinated, and realized. In the third cycle, students were set to construct a large-scale physical model to demonstrate the appropriate application of the selected tectonic systems, amplify its potential and incorporate its limitations. Instead of using bamboo sticks, new materials were used including PVC pipes with a different degrees of tensile strength to fit between joints, together with an estimate of how the whole structure might be created and mounted on a plywood base so that the full-scale construction could stand exposed to the weather on the rooftop of the School of Architecture. During the final review, the entire process and the end product were comprehensively presented. The team of eight was split into two sub-teams at the initial stage; one team was responsible for digital rhino modelling and documentation, and the second team took charge of material sourcing, design and testing. Nevertheless, the full-scale construction required more human resources and time to construct, and new materials and scale presented new challenges and unanticipated errors.

2.3.1 Role Shifting

After two rounds of competition, team members might have experienced different roles. However, the team process differed from the two cycles. Initially two sub-teams were formed to prepare for full-scale production.

'I was also responsible for searching for materials and ordering PVC pipes, screws, plywood board, zip ties and various tools fast in order to quickly test the trial design details...responsible for fixing the pipes with the base according to the anchor point markings...took role to do the documentation and drawings preparation...selecting the most representative photos and editing them through Photoshop.' – student D

'The third cycle brought me so many troubles during the computational process to come up with an ideal form for the bending-active shell structure for building on the roof, and I prepared the digital fabrication files, like the numbering and the length of the pipes, the wooden baseplate and the fixing point.' – student R

'I was in the sub-team for sourcing materials and testing initially. Later I was involved in digital documentation, including photo and video-taking and editing...kept track of all expenses.' – student P

2.3.2 More Errors

After two cycles of applying digital design and fabrication and making smaller-scale prototypes in the indoor environment, new challenges emerged because the materials used, ways of connection between materials and making anchors were all different.

> 'At the beginning, we suffered from the different rest length of each grid, and the shape of the model is out of control.' – student R

> 'Some material was bad quality or did not fit our use...the PVC pipes ordered were slightly thinner than the original ones, weaker in strength so more easily broken after we bent them and easier to collapse after exposure to sunlight.' – student D

> 'We ordered the rubber rings and iron nails from the internet for cheaper cost. However, the size of inner radius written in the description was a bit smaller than our original sample.' – student P

> 'Not all of us were present in the briefing for the tasks when we figured out ways to number the tubes. Sometimes, the tubes were marked wrongly, with confusing starting points adding to the construction time to cut the zip ties and shift the grids again.' – student T

> 'In the process of assembling the skylight part, we didn't check the connection carefully enough and found a lot of joints were connected incorrectly. Hence we spent extra time in redoing the skylight part.' – student O

> 'We made wrong calculations of the numbers for grid distance, wrong measurements of extensions at end points, wrong counts of the numbers of rubber rings, and loss of marking traces when moving the rubber rings to expected spots. All these issues showed up.' - student W

2.3.3 Testing and Fixing

In preparing for the full-scale construction with new materials and methods of connecting pipes and the plywood base, testing with software and the actual materials was needed beforehand.

> 'The pulling force was too much for the Kangaroo to keep the rest length remaining the same, and the whole model distorted. In order to solve this problem, we extended the flat grid to a larger one and reduced the number of pulling forces for it. It turned out to be a pretty good result.' – student R

> 'We tested the connection details for 1:1 construction, including the connection joints between pipe and wood base, pipe-to-pipe joints, a fixing method for the wood base to the ground on site.' – student O

> 'I offered a proposal that we can try to heat the pipe until it was soft and then quickly connect another pipe with it...It took several minutes to get some typical failures. Gradually I found the principle and tested the connection at three scales: the connection only, pipes of short length and pipes of full length. I was responsible to connecting pipes and repairing the broken pipe connections with heat. Then I tried to use the rainspout to fix the iron wire, and it succeeded.' – student F

> 'Before we built the scale model, we also built part of the column at full scale to test the pipes...After that, we did some mock-up and tested the feasibility of the connection details. Although the ground-fixing method seemed to work, the professor suggested a better solution. After more testing, we decided to adopt his solution.' – student P

> 'Quality of the pipes was not as good as our original sample. As we screwed at the overlapping part, the holes became the weak point and broke easily. Therefore, we bought PVC glue and solved the problem.... We did not prepare the edge profile pipe to the length measured with the intersection points in the digital model. We broke the bundle in half to form two arches for better and more stable support of the edge.' – student P

2.3.4 Unfolding Challenges

Although tests were conducted, mounting different materials required much more planning and coordination.

> 'The most difficult part was erecting the column at the beginning of construction. After forming the grid and then a loop, we had to hang the column down from one storey above and opened up the pipes like a flower. After we popped the structure up, it was difficult for us to work on the highest point of the edge.' – student P

> 'We ran out of screws and zip ties during the assembly process.' – student O

'The pop-up process was the most difficult stage as we did not expect that the form would turn out to be this floppy. Pipes we chose were heavy and yet not stiff enough to support themselves. We tried diagonal wires, cables and boundary outlines to stiffen the opening of the structure, but results were not satisfactory. Since the stiffness I applied in Kangaroo simulation was high, the pipe material system did not fit in as well as bamboo did in previous models. Pipes were more fragile than we had expected, and we were certainly not aware of how they might react when exposed to strong sunlight and sudden rains. I think lack of testing the new material is another reason that the structure ended up being floppy' – student W

3. DISCUSSION

The course aimed to engage students through critically investigating and evaluating theoretical concepts and drivers behind evolving architectural design while tackling novel situations and ill-defined problems. The three-cycle project presented different challenges, including software to generate geometric solutions, do experiments with materials, calculate the cost of production, build a full-scale model and take and edit video footage of the production process. The iteration process enabled students to work in teams and experience the principles of modelling (both computational and physical) at different scales to iteratively develop and transform a medium into large-scale intervention.

It was characteristic that mutually agreed roles were taken up by different teammates in the three cycles. These students readily took up leadership, support, design, sourcing, documentation and workmanship roles in different cycles. Higher student learning efficiency can be manifested because there are opportunities for students to discuss and share knowledge and experiences (Ruengtam, 2013). During the process, students were working hard to learn about the potential and strengths of themselves and their teammates for each specific role. Each member performed varied roles in different cycles while functioning effectively and efficiently to construct a full-size model. They needed to perform as a team rather than as smart individuals.

This trial-and-error method was the common strategy used in solving problems. Throughout the process, students made different kinds of mistake and varied attempts to look for solutions. They learned either by themselves, or from advice by peers, technical staff and the professor, as indicated in their reflections, and during the peer-group comments in each cycle of presentation. However, the third cycle seemed to present most challenges to the whole team, from sourcing materials and testing connections to the process of mounting and reinforcing the edge. They should have conducted more material testing, because the weight and flexibility of the pipes were so different from bamboo sticks. Eventually, they can train to think like architects constructing real-size projects through the reality-based studio as a chance to experience a kind of apprenticeship to their future professional life (Tokman and Yamacli, 2007).

4. CONCLUSION

Dynamic processes in studio are the cornerstone of architectural education. Instead of working independently or each team competes with one another, students are explored through teamwork as new ways to represent architectural concepts verbally, graphically and by means of physical models. This requires a high level of careful planning, implementation and modification to make every step accurate and complete to achieve final success in the team project collectively. The iteration process can surely be replicable in different disciplines as team projects. Students can be actively engaged when working in pairs and scaling up to four and eight as a team with a component of competition. However, the final project needs to be designed in such a way that every member can fairly contribute to different aspects. The collective learning experience aims to build a range of essential skills for being future architects, because their next task is to work on individual project. This study, based as it is on a master program with eight students, worked well with mature students who already knew each other well and could thus work collaboratively as a team. Further research can be made on professional competence and practices through the iteration process in a design studio.

ACKNOWLEDGEMENT

The project is funded by Teaching Development and Language Enhancement Grant for 2016–19 of the Chinese University of Hong Kong.

REFERENCES

Becerik-Gerber, B., and Rice, S. (2010). The perceived value of building information modeling in the US building industry. *Journal of Information Technology in Construction*, Vol. 15, No. 15, pp. 185–201.

Ciravoğlu, A., 2014. Notes on architectural education: an experimental approach to design studio. *Procedia – Social and Behavioral Sciences*, Vol. 152, pp. 7–12.

Dietrich, A., 2007. Who's afraid of a cognitive neuroscience of creativity? *Methods*, Vol. 42, No. 1, pp. 22–7.

Dutton, T., 1987. Design and studio pedagogy. *Journal of Architectural Education*, Vol. 4, No. 1, pp. 16–25.

Hadjiyanni, T., 2008. Beyond concepts – a studio pedagogy for preparing tomorrow's designers. *International Journal of Architectural Research*, Vol. 2, No. 2, pp. 41–56.

Hasirci, D., and Demirkan, H., 2007. Understanding the effects of cognition in creative decision-making: a creativity model for enhancing creativity in the design studio process. *Creativity Research Journal*, Vol. 19, No. 2–3, pp. 259–71.

Kowaltowski, D.C.C.K., Labaki, L.C., de Paiva, V., Bianchi, G. and Mösch, M.E., 2007. The creative design process supported by the restrictions imposed by bioclimatic and school architecture: a teaching experience. *Proceedings of 2nd PALENC Conference, and 28th AIVC Conference: Building low energy cooling and advanced ventilation technologies in the 21st century*. Crete, Greece, pp. 577–81.

Ruengtam, P., 2013. Modeling of cooperative/collaborative learning technique: a case study of interior architectural program. *Procedia – Social and Behavioral Sciences*, Vol. 105, pp. 360–9,

Rupanov, V., Buckl, C., Fiege, L., Armbruster, M., Knoll, A., and Spiegelberg, G., 2014. Employing early model-based safety evaluation to iteratively derive e/e architecture design. *Science of Computer Programming*, Vol. 90, pp. 161–79.

Smith, G.F., 1998. Idea-generation techniques: a formulary of active ingredients. *The Journal of Creative Behavior*, Vol. 32, No. 2, pp.107–34.

Tokman, L., and Yamacli, R., 2007. Reality-based design studio in architectural education. *Journal of Architectural and Planning Research*, Vol. 24, No. 3, pp. 245–69.

UNESCO/UIA, 2011. *Charter for Architectural Education* (revised edition 2011), Tokyo, Japan, pp. 1–6.

COMPARISON OF DEVELOPED IN "EFFICIENSEA2" PROJECT PLATFORM "BALTICWEB" WITH STANDARD ECDIS

Inese Barbare[1], Andrejs Zvaigzne[2] and Dmitrijs Goreļikovs[2]
[1]*Rigas Technical University, 1 Kalku Street, Riga, Latvia*
[2]*Latvian Maritime Academy, Flotes Street 12 K1, Riga, Latvia*

ABSTRACT

The paper examines the definition and concept of Electronic navigation (e-navigation), Electronic Chart Systems (ECS) and Electronic Chart and Display Information System (ECDIS). In paper are provided compare of positive and negative aspects for alternative e-navigation platform "BalticWeb", developed in "EfficienSea2" project with certified, internationally approved and accepted Electronic Chart Display and Information System (ECDIS) using on the STCW based criteria about electronic chart system. In addition, the paper represent new evaluation algorithms' testing methods created in Latvian Maritime Academy as part of "EfficienSea2" project. Paper is intended to familiarize wide range of specialists with positive and negative sides for last developed ECDIS, ECS and e-navigation systems and demonstrate subsequent possible ways of development for those systems. The discussion is about a good practice of exploratory testing and cooperation between higher education institutions and research institutions in developing, testing and implementing new digital devices that will be needed by the employer. As a result, the student got new knowledge and as the future worker has participated in the development of future work tools, expressing an opinion on their added value in practice.

KEYWORDS

ECDIS, e-Navigation, EfficienSea, BalticWeb, Exploratory Testing, IT Knowledge

1. INTRODUCTION

E - Navigation trends are developing fast enough today. This is due to the advancement of technology and the ability to provide faster data transmission, or the availability and quality of the internet on the ships. This direction improved with every moment. The e-navigation concept, as one of the basic ideas, is to create a linked system, with unified data access to users and, as soon as possible, to retrieve instant information in the system. Establishing such a unified system with a well-designed interface that enables the operator (navigational officer) to filter the information provided so that there are no inconsistencies due to the amount of excessive information that could potentially reduce the human factor impact on collisions, grounding etc. Within the framework of this research, the author had the opportunity to work with the European-supported project "EfficienSea2" e-navigation platform "BalticWeb" and the previously created platform "ArcticWeb".

During the research, it became clear, that these two platforms were not evaluated on a single scale, taking into account the functions and capabilities provided by the platforms. Therefore the authors decided to carry out a practical part study with a system analysis only for the platform "BalticWeb", but to give the respondents the opportunity get acquainted with the platform "ArticWeb" and its functions. Involving students of Latvian Maritime Academy in research process enables the development of collaborative learning methods and gives students the opportunity to express their views on future technology devices in their professional careers after completing their studies.

2. DEFINITIONS

Electronic Chart and Display Information System (ECDIS) is a computerized navigational system meeting the requirements of the International Maritime Organization that can be applied as an alternative to paper navigational charts. Obtaining information on-line, it continuously updates ship's position in respect of the coastline, conspicuous objects, navigational marks and invisible objects (IMO, 2012), (IECP, 2008). An ECDIS that does not comply or follow the relevant performance standards is classed as an Electronic Chart System (ECS).

Electronic Chart System (ECS) – This system is not certified as a 'type approved' ECDIS and does not meet or comply with IMO/SOLAS performance standards. The ECS may allow the use of Electronic Navigational Charts (ENC) and Raster Navigational Charts (RNC) with comparable functionality to a 'type approved' ECDIS, but should not be solely relied upon for navigation as the system is not tested nor certified.

E-navigation is defined as "the harmonized collection, integration, exchange, presentation and analysis of marine information on board and ashore by electronic means to enhance berth to berth navigation and related services for safety and security at sea and protection of the marine environment." (IMO, 2009).

The e-navigation not only as physical installation, nor merely as provision of a service but as a strategic framework for the development of current and future technological infrastructure on board and ashore. Thus, the term "e-navigation" currently includes systems and services, but the e-navigation user requirements have evolved and it is intended that the term also include an increased focus on more material elements. It should be noted that in the absence of e-navigation, systems and equipment diversity would continue to evolve provided with various degrees effectiveness. E-navigation development and elaboration is a way to optimize this development and to ensure attention to the further development of a holistic approach to safe navigation (IMO, 2009).

Exploratory testing - An approach to software testing that is concisely described as simultaneous learning, test design and test execution. Cem Kaner, who coined the term in 1984, defines exploratory testing as "a style of software testing that emphasizes the personal freedom and responsibility of the individual tester to continually optimize the quality of his/her work by treating test-related learning, test design, test execution, and test result interpretation as mutually supportive activities that run in parallel throughout the project" (Kaner, 1988).

2.1 "BalticWeb" Platform

The developed platform, called "BalticWeb" at this moment exist in Beta version (shown on Figure 1), was introduced in the project "EfficienSea2". It looks and works like conventional Electronic Charts Display and Information System (ECDIS), but not all ECDIS functions are implemented, as system is going to be a maritime map-centric portal. The site will aggregate relevant maritime data and information:

- Notices to Mariners and Navigational Warnings;
- Sea Traffic - Live Vessel position and information (AIS);
- No-Go area service. (The service is fully operational but the UI is being changed and improved);
- Satellite imagery service from NASA;
- Nautical Charts from Sjofartsverket and Geodatastyrelsen;
- Simulated Route planning, optimization and exchange service;
- OpenSeaMap.org overlay.
- It is advisable to keep all the given values.

For a closer look on the "BalticWeb" functionality, data and display please follow below link: https://balticweb.e-navigation.net/ (see Figure 1).

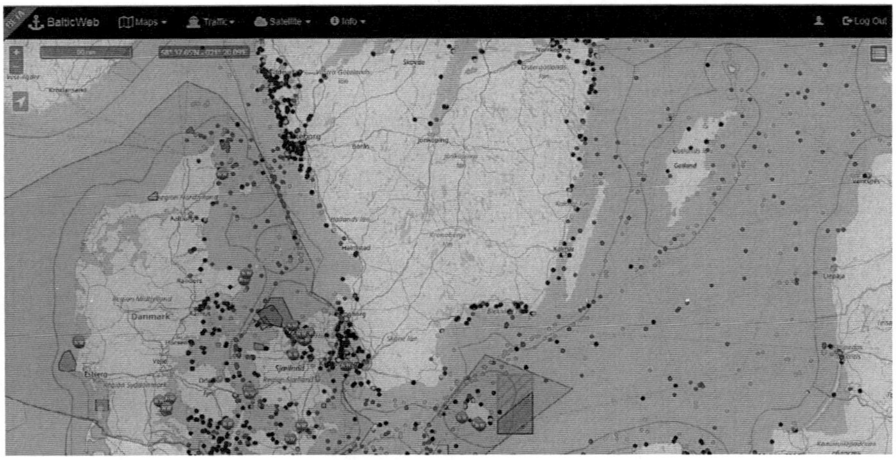

Figure 1. "BalticWeb"

2.2 Development of Testing Algorithm

Because of adopting at 2012 requirements for ECDIS mandatory use at certain types of vessels, IMO guidelines aimed at facilitating the transition from paper charts to Electronic Chart Systems was developed as for shipping companies, as well as for vessel's command. It is called "Transitioning from paper chart to ECDIS navigation. Usage of ECDIS as the primary means for navigation, in general, is different process, comparing with using paper charts. Important on-bridge work processes have changed especially route and route planning control. These processes need special attention." (IHO, 2010). The electronic chart system evaluation algorithm is based on the use of the STCW Convention, the 2010 Manila amendments, which describe requirements for seafarers in respect of ECDIS education use. The amendments cover full range of possible actions, which must be able to carry out ECDIS operator (IMO, 2010). Requirements for training of seafarers were revised for generating electronic chart system's evaluation criteria. Evaluation criteria summarize individual chapters in relation to their application. Rating scale is designed individually, so that it can be universally applied to all evaluation criteria and for calculating total mark. To test usefulness of the evaluation, algorithm was used to compare the "BalticWeb" e-navigation systems, ECDIS systems "Navi-Sailor 4000" and ECS systems "NaviFisher" and "iSailor".

The aim was to develop a universal evaluation algorithm, which may be used for evaluation of any electronic chart systems and examine this algorithm's effectiveness during testing of various Electronic Chart Systems. The testing being done on the basis of developed evaluation algorithm, it is compile structured set of tasks to be met by using an Electronic Chart Systems. In order to maximize objectivity and accuracy of results, in addition to officially approved by IMO and IHO ECDIS, were evaluated "Navi-Fisher" and "iSailor" systems. They were selected to examine the evaluation algorithm as for certified systems as well as for non-certified or partly certified systems, it is necessary to clarify the evaluation algorithm usefulness.

2.3 Background of Exploratory Testing

All exploratory testing based on knowledge, but some of this knowledge is gained during the testing. Other knowledge is already in the tester's possession. Other differences across exploratory testers are "styles" of exploration – 1) Subject matter experts who come up with scenarios that rely heavily on use of product and 2) Technique experts who know certain techniques and look for situations to use them in (Tinkham, Kaner, 2003). J. Lyndsay says that most commercial testers make use of unscripted techniques. Their unscripted approaches are most often undisciplined, and hidden from individuals outside the immediate team. He has also found that an individual tester typically makes use of a single style of unscripted testing, or focuses on a single type of target. This second characteristic can potentially be addressed with explicit exposure to a wider range of exploratory techniques (Lyndsay, 2006). G.M. Weinberg describes some abstract machines and makes observations, some based on stimulus. The observations are analysed, and a hypothesis reached and tested (Weinberg, 2001).

3. OBJECTIVE OF THE RESEARCH

The goal of the research was to compare the alternate e-navigation platform "BalticWeb" with a certified, internationally approved and accepted Electronic Chart Display and Information System (ECDIS) using an algorithm for the evaluation of the electric chart system developed on the basis of the STCW, developed in the Latvian Maritime Academy. For testing purposes was created two focus groups consisting of 12 persons. In groups were included students of Latvian Maritime academy as well as Captains with work experience more than ten years. For every person was issued the same scoring algorithm. During development procedure of algorithm was gathered data from 2010 Manila amendments for the STCW Convention: requirements of the training of seafarers working with Electronic Chart Systems. Data was processed to obtain full list of requirements for electronic chart functions and features. Requirements were used to draw up the criteria for the evaluation algorithm.

3.1 Research Description

The work was completed in 4 stages, which took place at the Latvian Maritime Academy in navigational stimulator laboratory premises. Respondents were given two copies of the assessment criteria, a task sheet and a questionnaire, on the e-navigation platform.

3.1.1 The 1st Stage - Analysis Of The Platform "BalticWeb"

During the first stage of the work, respondents were divided up into navigational stimulator booths and using laptops, 50 minutes were considered for all the functions offered in the "BalticWeb" platform and subsequently according to the evaluation criteria, evaluation of the offered functions and full analysis of the platform. The author did not introduce respondents to the alternative e-navigation platform interface, so that it would be possible to evaluate the complexity of the platform (see Figure 2).

Figure 2. Respondents are testing the "BalticWeb" platform

3.1.2 The 2nd Stage - Identical Evaluation Algorithm

In the second stage, respondents were assigned by navigational stimulator booths and were given the task of analyzing the available features and capabilities of the ECDIS Navi Sailor 4000 system using an identical evaluation algorithm that was used in the first part of the practical part. For this task, respondents were given 30 minutes.

3.1.3 The 3rd Stage - Analysis of the ECDIS Navi Sailor 4000 System

In the third stage, respondents were given the task of setting up a small passage plan with four waypoints on the ECDIS Navi Sailor 4000 system and using the "EfficienSea2" platform "BalticWeb" as an additional program. In response to this exercise, respondents assessed whether this platform could be an additional navigation tool that could be used together with the ECDIS system while navigating in the region. After completing this part, respondents looked at the features and capabilities offered by ArticWeb.

3.1.4 The 4th Stage - Analysis of the Platform "ArcticWeb"

As part of the fourth part of the work, was filling in a questionnaire on the operation of the "EfficienSea2" "BalticWeb" platform. For evaluation to be as objective as possible, whether the e-navigation platform to be tested meets the standard requirements, the evaluation criteria are divided into 13 chapters covering a specific function: (1) Risks of disinformation; (2) Detection of misrepresentation of information; (3) System performance and accuracy, access to primary information source; (4) Setting up and maintaining display; (5) Operational use of electronic charts; (6) Route Planning; (7) Route Monitoring; (8) Alarm indicators; (9) Manual correction of a ship's position and motion parameters; (10) Ship's electronic log; (11) Chart updating; (12) Operational use of electronic navigational systems where radar/ARPA is connected; (13) Operational use of electronic navigational systems where AIS is Connected.

There were 5 marks on the rating scale:

- Implemented (I) – Described task/option is implemented and is fully operational and independent from other options; (4 points)
- Defective (D) -Described task/option is implemented but is not available under certain circumstances; (3 points)
- Restricted (R) – Described task/option is implemented, but restricted in access or dependent on other functions; (2 points)
- Not Reliable (NR) – Described task/option is implemented, but is limited in functionality or is inaccurate; (1 points)
- Not Implemented (NI) – Described task/option is not implemented; (0 points).

Grades can be applicable to all criteria. In order to facilitate the progress of system's evaluation, each mark has been granted number of points and, after each criterion checking, for each function was calculated definitive number of points. The maximum points score for all marks is 508 points, which means 100% of the system compliance with the criteria. All criteria are equivalent; scoring algorithm does not provide preferences for concrete function. At the end of the evaluation is given to mark the entire system. Scoring algorithm is used to compose the tasks list and evaluate the electronic chart system after receiving results of testing. The objectives were drawn up so that the test should considering all criteria.

3.2 Results of the Study

The first "EfficienSea2" platform "BalticWeb" was evaluated according to the developed algorithm. As respondents worked for the first time with this platform, they were given 50 minutes. The compiled criteria were not translated into Latvian so that there would be no incompatibilities when translating professional terminology. Summing up the results, the "BalticWeb" platform got an average of 21.8%, against the 100% algorithm used for evaluation criteria. The responses provided by respondents were different, with percentage rates varying from 14.8% to 25.2%. The average percentage score of 21.8% is obtained by adding the final score of all 12 respondents and pulling out the average number (see Table 1).

Table 1. Comparison of "BalticWeb" with the evaluation algorithm. The result in percentage

Respondents	Percentage
1	14,8%
2	16,2%
3	22,8%
4	22,0%
5	21,1%
6	21,9 %
7	23%
8	24%
9	25%
10	25,1%
11	25,2%
12	21,0%

These final ratings were obtained by adding up all the results from each of the 13 chapters. On the chart number 2, the percentage of the average results from each respondent's answers is compiled by each chapter. Accordingly, it will be able to judge which department has received the most negative / most positive assessment (see Chart 1).

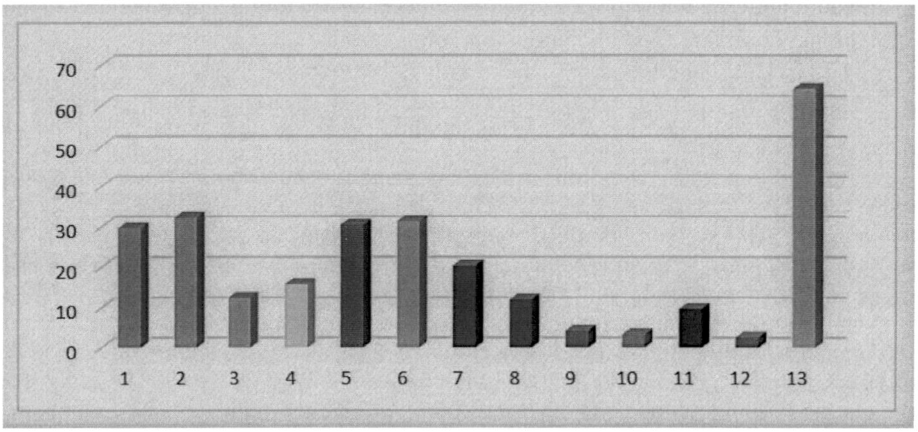

Chart 1. Average rating of "BalticWeb" Chapters

As can be seen from Chart 1, the lowest ratings in the "BalticWeb" platform have been received from Chapter 9 - Vessel position monitoring and correction, Chapter 10 - Vessel logbook and Chapter 12 - Operational use of electronic maps in total RLS / ARPA. Compares all 13 chapters in total, with the maximum possible score that could be obtained, it can be concluded that Chapter 13 - Operative use of electronic charts with attached AIS is the only one department that has received more than 50 percent.

In the second stage, the ECDIS Navi Sailor 4000 system was tested. The features and capabilities of this system are well known to respondents, since all of them are ECDIS certified users. Respondents were given the task of using an identical evaluation algorithm as it was used in examining the "BalticWeb" platform. As with this system, all respondents had worked, then 30 minutes were spent on doing this work. Summing up all the results, ECDIS "Navi-Sailor 4000" won 89.5% on average, against the 100% benchmark algorithm used.

The responses provided by respondents were different, with percentage variables ranging from 83.8% to 92.3% (see Table 2).

Table 2. Comparison of ECDIS with the evaluation algorithm. The result in percentage

Respondents	Percentage
1	86,8%
2	86,0%
3	83,8%
4	91,0%
5	90,9%
6	91,3%
7	92,3%
8	90,5%
9	89,9%
10	89,7%
11	89,6%
12	92,0%

As can be seen from results, all chapters are estimated relatively equally, with the lowest rating of 84.8%, which was received by Chapter 12 - Operational use of electronic maps in total RLS / ARPA (if added) and with the highest result for Chapter 9 - Control and correction of the position of the vessel. When evaluating all results, it is logical that the results of all chapters are about 90% because ECDIS "Navi Sailor 4000" is an IMO approved electronic chart display and information system.

In the third phase of the practical work, it was planned that respondents would be given the task of creating passage plan in Danish strait on the ECDIS system and using the "BalticWeb" platform in addition. Initially, each respondent set up the passage plan individually for the navigator bridge simulator. Later the installation of the "BalticWeb" platform on one of the monitors in the navigation simulator was created. In the third part of the practical work, it was possible to make passage using directly in parallel with the ECDIS system and the "BalticWeb" platform. When one of the respondents set up a passage plan, each respondent was given the opportunity to use the ECDIS system with the "BalticWeb" platform and create an identical passage as it was done with the ECDIS system only. Thus, the respondent was able to compare two types of workplaces.

In the fourth phase of practical work, respondents were provided with questionnaires for evaluating the "BalticWeb" platform. The results of the survey are summarized in diagrams. After completing the third part, respondents were given an opportunity to be acquainted with the features and capabilities of the "ArticWeb" platform. Such a subtle study was not conducted for the analysis of this program, since the possibilities and functions offered by the ECDIS Navi Sailor 4000 are not in the same ranking criteria table. Respondents acknowledged that the "ArcticWeb" platform had a well-developed and functional ice and meteorological report that would significantly help navigate the Arctic regions. Otherwise, the "ArcticWeb" platform cannot be a complement to the ECDIS system.

Summarizing the results of the evaluation algorithms performed by respondents, where the "BalticWeb" platform was compared with the ECDIS system, it is evident that this new platform needs many improvements. Compared to "ArcticWeb", based on the "BalticWeb" platform, the latter has far more advanced improvements. The options that are responsible for marking the "No-Go" region, where 66% of respondents rated this option as highly efficient, 17% needed improvements and 17% that this feature does not help, are of high quality. As the next option, portraying navigation alerts and notices to seamen, 34% of respondents said that this option worked great, but 66% rated that a well-functioning option, but where minor improvements were needed and an option with an identical score, where 66% of respondents rated it as good, requiring minor improvements, and 34% said that this option works great as the AIS function for obtaining information on other ships. From this, it can be estimated that the "BalticWeb" platform is a potential auxiliary program for the ECDIS system in the Baltic region, as 66% of the respondents assessed that this platform could be an additional program for the ECDIS system only after improvements.

According to diagrams „Navi-Sailor" system meets compiled criteria up to 90.3%, „Navi-Fisher" comply with 86.9%, „iSailor" comply with the to 48.9% and BalticWeb corresponds to 59.4%. „NaviSailor" and „Navi-Fisher" Electronic Chart Systems have been already certified for large vessels by IMO and IHO, thereafter gained more points during the examination. But the system "iSailor", used for yacht and small boats navigation scored significantly fewer testing points, when newly developed, and at this moment not officially certified, BalticWeb system. Whereas certified systems have shown better results, we can be conclude that evaluation algorithm shows the difference between Electronic Chart Systems with various level of functioning. So algorithm is useful and can be used to estimate the electronic chart system. Developed evaluation algorithm is not intended for resolving opportunity of certification for tested electronic chart system, it can be applied only for evaluating of examined systems' functional level.

4. CONCLUSION

The "BalticWeb" platform, after several improvements in the system, could be accepted as a future e-navigation program, which would complement the Electronic Chart Display and Information System for the Baltic Sea Region only. According to the results of the evaluation algorithm it is observed that the "BalticWeb" platform has potential as a supplement to the ECDIS system in the Baltic Sea. Potentially, the "BalticWeb" can become an additional program for the ECDIS system, due to the user interface that is easy to see and easy to use. There is no need to install specialized navigational technical equipment hardware, you need a computer or tablet computer with secure Internet access.

Involving students in the project as testers gives them an educational effect in mastering the course for ship navigators. The four-level testing with the final questionnaire is in line with the above-mentioned researcher scenarios for system testing. Collaboration during testing with experienced masters who practice different types of navigation maps extends the student's vision and provides insight into future work environments where it will be possible to work with different types of navigational charts.

ACKNOWLEDGEMENT

This project "EFFICIENSEA2 – efficient, safe and sustainable traffic at sea" has received funding from the European Union's Horizon 2020 research and innovation program under grant agreement No 636329.

REFERENCES

Kaner, C., 1988. "*Testing Computer Software*". TAB Books, Blue Ridge Summit, PA, USA.

Lyndsay, J., 2006. "*Four Exercises for Teaching Exploratory Testing*". Workroom Productions, London, U.K.

Tinkham, A., Kaner, C., 2003. "*Exploring Exploratory Testing*". The National Science Foundation, Florida, USA.

Weinberg, G.M., 2001. "*An Introduction to General Systems Thinking*". Dorset House, London, U.K.

International Maritime Organization, 2012. *International Convention for the Safety of Life at Sea (SOLAS)*. Consolidated Edition, London.

International Electro-technical Commission, 2008. *Publication 61174. Maritime navigation and radio communication equipment and systems - Electronic chart display and information system (ECDIS) - Operational and performance requirements, methods of testing and required test results*. London.

International Maritime Organization, 2009. *MSC 85/26: Strategy for the development and implementation of e-navigation*. London.

International Hydrographic Organization (January 2010). "*S-66 facts about electronic charts and carriage requirements*" Switzerland.

International Maritime Organization, 2010. *The Manila Amendments to the Seafarers' Training, Certification and Watchkeeping (STCW) Code*, STCW/CONF.2/34, (August 2010), Manila

Short Papers

DEVELOPING TRANSVERSAL COMPETENCES IN ENGINEERS

Juliana de Melo Bezerra, Cristiane Aparecida Martins, Lara Kühl Teles,
Neusa Maria Franco de Oliveira, Maria Margareth da Silva, Leila Ribeiro dos Santos
and Raquel Caratti Piani
Instituto Tecnológico de Aeronáutica – ITA, São José dos Campos – SP, Brazil

ABSTRACT

The development of transversal competences is essential for the success of engineers, who need to have the ability to adapt to the new and changing demands posed by modern society and scientific advances. It is a challenge for professors to teach and evaluate transversal competences, since such competences are related to attitudes and values. We present a program, held in an Engineering school, with the goal of motivating young people in STEM (Science, Technology, Engineering and Mathematics) areas. Results from the designed initiatives pointed to success in the development of transversal competences, including problem solving, communication, leadership, teamwork, self-management, creativity and innovation.

KEYWORDS

STEM, Education, Non-Cognitive, Competences, Engineering, Student

1. INTRODUCTION

Other than the well-known need for technical knowledge, it has become increasingly important for engineers to improve their social skills and attitudes for professional purposes. This is known as transversal competence. Engineers need to have the ability to adapt to the new and changing demands posed by modern society and scientific advances. Such competences can even improve the chances of employability by influencing the selection of one candidate over another in the labor market. Transversal competences contribute to a more flexible workforce capable of adapting more quickly to the constant changes that occur in an increasingly interconnected world (Rico et al, 2013; Linares et al, 2015).

There are different categories of transversal competences, for instance: cognitive, methodological, linguistic, individual, and interpersonal skills. Cognitive skills rely on the ability to understand and use thoughts and ideas. Methodological skills include time management, learning strategies, decision making, and problem solving. Linguistic skills encompass both oral and written communication. Individual skills are related to the ability to express feelings or perceptions of an issue. Interpersonal skills include the ability to work in a team, and express ethical or social commitments in a socially appropriate way (Rico et al, 2013). Yanaze and Lopes (2014), when studying the job market in the electrical and computer engineering area, identified the need for the following key transversal competences: communication, teamwork, leadership, problem-solving and analysis skills. Prinsley and Baranyai (2015), while investigating the importance of skills in marketplace, highlighted transversal competences such as critical thinking, problem solving, interpersonal skills, and time management.

Universities recognize the importance of the study program design and its relation to the professional profiles and the competences or skills needed, including transversal competences. Transversal competences are not directly related to the theoretical content of the curricula, but to attitudes, values and procedures. It characterizes a challenge for professors to teach and evaluate such competences (Rosa et al, 2013; Linares et al, 2015). In this paper, we focus on the following transversal competences: problem solving, communication, leadership, teamwork, self-management, creativity and innovation. We present a program held in an Engineering institute in partnership with a health-care company. The primary goal of the program was to foster STEM (Science, Technology, Engineering and Mathematics) education for young people as well as incentivizing our engineering students in STEM areas. Initiatives were then designed to maintain the goal of the program, while supporting the development of transversal competences of our students.

2. A PROGRAM TO SUPPORT TRANSVERSAL COMPETENCES DEVELOPMENT

In this section, we describe the initiatives performed during the program, over a period of 8 months, and the associated results related to the acquisition of transversal competences.

2.1 Program Initiatives and Transversal Competences

The team was composed of six professors, one professional communicator and 34 undergraduate students. Students had to participate in three social initiatives. One social initiative was the promotion of events with the objective of developing transversal skills of the program students. The other two social initiatives, lectures and workshops, aim to spark in children (in middle and high schools) an interest in STEM. Lectures (lasting one hour each) were conducted in schools, while workshops (with duration of three hours) were held in our institute. During 2017, the undergraduate students gave 40 lectures, to a total of 1,586 students aged between 10 and 19 years-old. The workshops were divided into: 'reused workshops' and 'new workshops'. During the first semester, the students selected six workshops already established in 2016 and submitted each one to 120 children. In the second semester, the students defined eight new workshops and applied at least one of them to 240 children. Three events were held just for students on topics such as financial education, professional behavior, and careers in STEM. A specific event regarding leadership, which was open to our community, was also promoted with the presence of speakers discussing the theme in a round table debate.

The way social initiatives were conceived and managed aided students to develop important transversal skills, including problem solving, communication, leadership, teamwork, self-management, creativity and innovation. In our program, students were in charge of all decision making, providing an interesting place to exercise problem solving. Problem solving includes the ability to gather and integrate information, identify alternatives, select the best solution, and evaluate the consequences (Salas et al, 2000). In lectures, students had to prepare or identify materials (presentations or videos), choose the school and schedule the lecture itself, along with evaluating the lecture. In workshops, students needed to develop a hands-on activity clearly stating STEM concepts and desired practices, select the public who would participate, organize the day on which to perform the workshop, and finally to evaluate it. In events, students had to select topics of interest with program participants, to identify and invite people to talk about such topics, to organize the day of the event itself, as well as evaluating it.

During our program, students worked in teams, characterizing the competence of teamwork, but also involving leadership and communication skills. Teamwork can be defined as the set of interrelated behaviors and actions that occur among team members while performing a task. Leadership is the ability to direct and coordinate activities of other team members, assign tasks and motivate team members. Communication considers the process by which information is clearly and accurately exchanged between two or more team members (Salas et al, 2000). Communication was essential for making the program initiatives feasible. Leadership was practiced in two dimensions by students: inside and outside the group. Leadership inside the group was naturally expected. Leadership outside the group includes the interactions needed to performed initiatives, for instance: to be a leader of a group of children during lectures or workshops, and to be the leader of the organization of an event given the interface with lecturers and the public.

Self-management is about knowing what to do at any given moment, including other critical skills such as initiative (being able to work without always being told what to do), organization (plan time and things to do), responsibility and accountability (Bernd, 2008).Since students had to organize themselves in order to provide results for the program by respecting goals and deadlines, and also to conciliate their participation in the program with their academic demands, an improvement in self-management was a likely outcome. We worked based on self-directed work teams and distributed decision making. Creativity is the ability to produce original ideas and items, as well as the combination of existing work and objects in different ways for new purposes. From the viewpoint of engineering education, it is very important to have innovative engineers, since they contribute creatively to design items, processes, and services to meet society demands (Kanematsu and Barry, 2015; Catarino, P. et al, 2016.). In our program, students could train their creativity and innovation, as students needed to be inventive to design lectures, workshops and events to motivate and involve the public.

2.2 Results

We invited students that conducted the program in 2017 to evaluate their participation regarding the developing of transversal competences when participating in the following initiatives: lectures, reused workshops, new workshops, and events. We had 23 respondents to the evaluation questionnaire. Firstly, students evaluated the degree of involvement in the performed activity using a 5-point scale ranging from 1 (poor) to 5 (excellent). The resultant median was 4 for all initiatives, meaning that students had a high degree of involvement in the program. Following that, students used a 6-point Likert scale (with the values: strongly agree, agree, slightly agree, slightly disagree, disagree, and strongly disagree) to assess the sentence "As result of the initiative participation, I developed or enhanced my competence" to each transversal competence: problem solving, communication, leadership, teamwork, self-management, creativity and innovation. Results are shown below. Figure 1a shows the degree of agreement regarding the development of transversal competences when working on the 'lectures' initiative. Figure 1b, Figure 1c and Figure 1d present results respectivelly regarding 'reused workshops', 'new workshops' and 'events'.

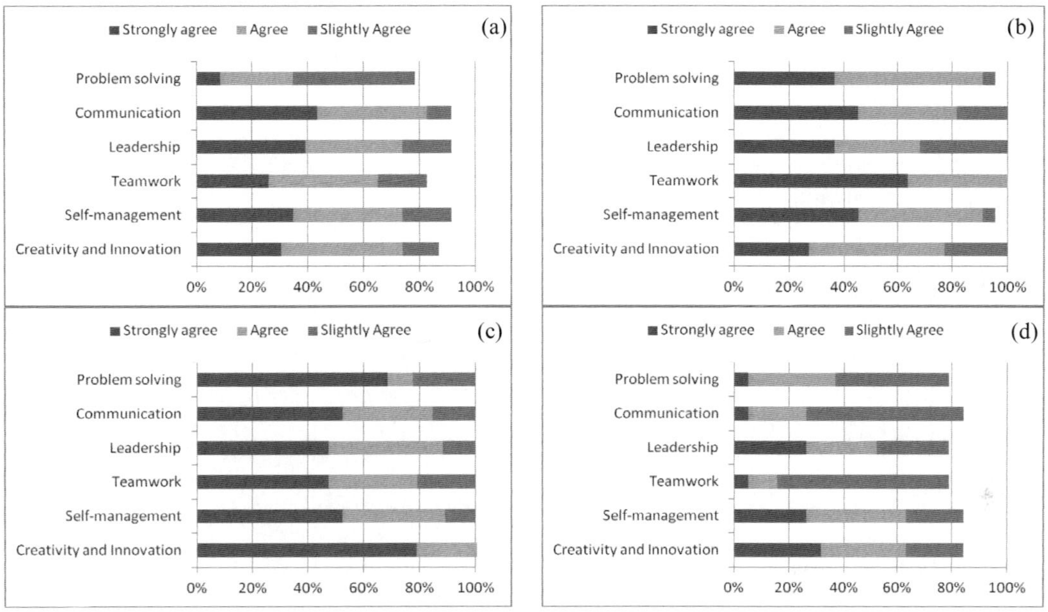

Figure 1. Transversal competences developed in (a) lectures, (b) reused workshop, (c) new workshops, and (d) events

According to the students' feedback, all initiatives contributed substantially to the development of transversal competences. Comparatively, workshops were more effective than lectures, which in turn were more effective than events. The low performance of 'events' was in part expected, since the students that organized this initiative could experience better outcomes, while students that only attended events only acquired knowledge and expertise from speakers. We believe that there is potential here to have other kinds of more formative events and not only informative ones, in order to work with students and advance their competences. 'Lectures' initiative had good results especially regarding communication, leadership, and self-management. With the continuation of the program, if students started to reuse materials, we may experience a reduction in items such as creativity and innovation, so it is important to continuously stimulate students to reinvent the way of giving lectures.

'Workshop' initiatives were the best way to foster transversal competence, as can be seen by the rate of 'strongly agree' answers. An interesting difference in results lies between 'reused workshops' and 'new workshops'. 'New workshops' were more effective to develop problem solving, and creativity and innovation, since students had to create different strategies and define an authentic hands-on activity. In the 'reused workshops', students had to learn about an existent workshop, so they practice competences but not to the same extent. Teamwork competence was well evaluated in 'reused workshops', not only because of the need to interact with other students who had created the workshop, but mainly due to the number of times they performed the workshop for children. Despite the potential preference of students for 'new workshops', the 'reused workshops' initiative is a strategy to keep promoting workshops for the community while new workshops are being created. In this way, the program can achieve better results in terms of number of children involved. The revision of workshops is also an important activity, in order to improve material related to workshops, aiming to minimize errors and doubts when other people reproduce them. It is also critical to maintain new workshops, due to the diversity that they bring to our portfolio.

3. CONCLUSION

The program presented is an example how to help students apply the technical knowledge and skills while also activating problem solving, communication, leadership, teamwork, self-management, creativity and innovation. We believe that such skills support students to make appropriate and effective choices toward achieving career goals related to STEM during and after university. In the coming versions of the program, we hope to stimulate the reinvention of current initiatives by including other types of activities, such as bringing workshops to public spaces. We also intend to propose new initiatives, such as mentoring programs for children, as well as the formation of a network of practitioners that share the program goal of fostering STEM education. We believe that these challenging actions are likely to support our students in developing their transversal competences. We argue that, based on the program outcomes stated in this paper, it is possible to reflect how engineering schools can stimulate the development of transversal competencies by proposing new programs, not only focusing on research, but also by including an extended mission of schools aligned to the needs and demands of society.

ACKNOWLEDGEMENT

A special thanks to Johnson&Johnson company for funding the program.

REFERENCES

Bernd, S., 2008. The importance of soft skills: Education beyond academic knowledge. *In Journal of Language and Communication.*

Catarino, P. et al, 2016. Take this Waltz on creativity: The engineering students' conceptions. Proceedings of International Conference of the Portuguese Society for Engineering Education (CISPEE).

Kanematsu, H. and Barry, D.M., 2015. Creativity and Its Importance for Education. *In STEM and ICT Education in Intelligent Environments*, Vol. 91, pp 3-7.

Linares, R.H. et al, 2015. Transversal Competences of University Students of Engineering. *In Croatian Journal of Education*, Vol.17, No. 2, pp 383-409.

Prinsley, R, and Baranyai, K., 2015. STEM skills in the workforce: What do employers want?. *Paper Series of the Australian Government*, No. 9.

Rico, M. et al, 2013. Everything Matters: Development of Cross-Curricular Competences in Engineering Through Web 2.0 Social Objects. *In Sampson, D. G. et al, Ubiquitous and Mobile Learning in the Digital Age*. Springer New York.

Rosa, J.L.S. et al, 2013. Evaluation of Transversal Competences of the Engineering Students and their Relation to the Enterprise Requirements. *In Enterprise Resource Planning Models for the Education Sector: Applications and Methodologies*. IGI Global.

Salas, E. et al, 2000. Teamwork: emerging principles. *In International Journal of Management Reviews*, Vol. 2, No. 4.

Yanaze, L.K.H. and Lopes, R.D., 2014. Transversal Competencies of Electrical and Computing Engineers considering market demand. *Proceedings of Frontiers in Education Conference (FIE)*, IEEE.

Start@unito: A SUPPORTING MODEL FOR HIGH SCHOOL STUDENTS ENROLLING TO UNIVERSITY

Barbara Bruschi, Valter Cantino, Roberto Cavallo Perin, Francesca Culasso, Barbara Giors, Marina Marchisio, Carla Marello, Matteo Milani, Lorenza Operti, Alberto Parola, Sergio Rabellino, Matteo Sacchet and Laura Scomparin
University of Turin, Italy

ABSTRACT

Students need help in transitioning from high school to university. It's important to facilitate their guidance in choosing the course of study and consequently their experience with the first exams, reducing the abandonment. The University of Turin, financially supported by the banking institution Compagnia di San Paolo, has invested in e-learning creating Start@unito: a Learning Management System that delivers twenty freely available, self-paced, online courses on different topics. The paper discusses the model adopted by Start@unito and the first results obtained.

KEYWORDS

e-Learning, Learning Management System, Open Online Courses, Self-Paced MOOC, Transition between the Secondary School and the University Education System, University Guidance

1. INTRODUCTION

Technology Enhanced Learning (TEL) has been widely and rapidly spreading since the beginning of the new millennium; universities are the right place in which best practices in teaching and learning should be adopted. E-learning provides many advantages (Ross, Morrison, & Lowther, 2010): there are a variety of solutions available; if built correctly, the system can accommodate everyone's needs; the contents are available anytime; there is a higher coverage; it is cheaper for students and more affordable; the impact on the environment is lighter; the main kind of users are millennials: they were born surrounded by technology. Of course, TEL is not effective by itself, but it needs a lot of knowledge and deep understanding of how these technologies can work to their full potential, and this should be the standard for teachers (Hicks, 2011). Technology should help students overcome difficult steps throughout their career and fill the gap between secondary and tertiary education. According to the annual report 2016 of the University of Turin (https://www.unito.it/sites/default/files/relazione_annuale_2016.pdf), around one third of the courses of study show a dropout rate higher than 20%. The main objectives of the recent experience at University of Turin, the "Start@unito" project, financed by Compagnia di San Paolo, are to improve the success rate on first year university exams and to help students with university guidance in the choice of their course of study. The project aims at using a Learning Management System (LMS) to create and provide Open Online Courses which can be accessed by everyone, but specifically targeted to the last year high school students, because a successful transition from secondary school to University is a crucial phase for both students and institutions (Barana, Bogino, Fioravera, Floris, Marchisio, Operti, & Rabellino, 2017; Barana, Bogino, Fioravera, Marchisio, & Rabellino, 2016; Barana, Bogino, Fioravera, Marchisio, & Rabellino, 2017). The project uses good practices developed both in local and European contexts (Brancaccio, Marchisio, Meneghini, & Pardini, 2015). Users can follow online self-paced open courses before their application at the University, and after submitting a final test they obtain a certificate of attendance. After the enrolment at the University of Turin, students can attempt the official exam and, if passed, add it to their career obtaining an immediate recognition of their efforts. This paper discusses the methodologies adopted and the results obtained.

2. THEORETICAL FRAMEWORK

Regarding online courses there are two main aspects to take into account: didactics and technology. From the didactical point of view there are six main theories: Behaviourist, Situated, Informal and lifelong, Collaborative, Learning and teaching support, Constructivist (Naismith, Lonsdale, Vavoula, & Sharples, 2004), the last one being the most suitable for online self-paced courses. In any case, the university didactics should optimize individual learning, involving the students in activities of collaborative exchange, comparison, negotiation, conception and planning of cognitive and/or real object (Ravinelli, & Serina, 2014). From the technological point of view, digital technologies can be a great advantage while dealing with learning, because of their enhanced interactivity (giving prompts and feedbacks, facilitating remote interaction among peers or with the instructor). With these features, digital environments have a positive impact on motivation and self-confidence, very important properties for lifelong learning (Barana, Conte, Fioravera, Marchisio, & Rabellino, 2018). Furthermore, automatic assessment provides the possibility of assigning grades and offering immediate feedback via computer. Real time information given to students and teachers by digital technologies promote the processes of formative assessment (Barana et al., 2018). Regarding the existing experiences in Italy, it is important to mention EduOpen (https://learn.eduopen.org/) and Federica (http://www.federica.unina.it/). With the project Start@unito, 20 online courses are available (and 34 more are under preparation): no other Italian university provides such an amount of full university courses. Around the world, there are many experiences of MOOC providers, like Coursera (https://www.coursera.org/) and edX (https://www.edx.org/). Openness is a key feature for the courses of the project Start@unito, declined as "contents available anytime to anyone". A disadvantage of this approach is the absence of tutoring, the learning process being completely self-paced. To reduce the downsides, during the design of the courses every solution that could accompany the student was considered, exploiting all the competencies developed by professors in the University of Turin.

3. ADDRESSED PROBLEM

After graduating, students have to choose their path, facing up to the transition between the secondary school and the university education system. Universities are used to organizing many guidance activities, useful to get to know all the details about competencies, outcomes, job opportunities. Despite this, when students start their career at university, they usually face other difficulties:

- **different approach to the subject**: during high school, teachers usually follow the main learning trend of the class and it is very difficult to adapt teaching to best, average and below average students, all together;
- **mandatory exams not easy to pass**: scientific courses of study have got Maths and Physics exams in their program, which students underrate, but which are actually the basis of future knowledge;
- **lecture rooms full of students**: having too many students in one room could be a real problem, both for professors and students, and for security issues too;
- **self-consciousness of their study**: university students have to become directly responsible for their own approach to learning and not everyone knows how to handle this;
- **change of course of study** after the enrollment: students do not get enough help during this transition;
- **admission tests** to access some of the bachelor courses: students who fail it, usually select another transitory course of study.

Online learning can be a partial answer to many of these problems. Worldwide universities provide free and open access to educational content via MOOCs (Grainger, 2013): this is not effective in improving students' guidance if open learning plans are not designed for this objective but mainly for advertising purpose (Barana et al., 2017; Barana et al., 2016; Barana, Bogino, Fioravera, Marchisio, & Rabellino, 2017).

4. THE MODEL

The project Start@unito starts from the experience gained through various activities, such as Orient@mente (Barana et al., 2017; Barana et al., 2016; Barana et al., 2017) that contains open online courses for realignment, recovery of gaps, and test preparation, developing a model for the design, implementation and availability of official university teachings through Open Online University Courses. In the following subsections we analyze the components of the model in greater detail.

The Open Online University Courses are developed to achieve the following objectives. The first one is **supporting students**. Following complete online university courses, students can see the different approach to teaching, getting an overview of what the university offers. Another important objective is the spreading of knowledge and education (University Third Mission). Expected consequences of these advantages are the reduction of the first year dropout rate and a largest number of passed exams. The second objective is **improving the outcomes of the evaluation criteria of first year university students**, increasing the number of ECTS that first year students obtain; by guiding students through their first exams, the positive outcomes are expected to raise. The third objective is **enhancing the use of e-learning in university teachings**. With more than 60 professors involved, who attended a training course, more people in university are now aware of the potential of online courses.

The actors involved in the model were divided into a procedure created for team working, the so-called Deming Cycle: Plan, Do, Check, Act.

Plan: the leading group of the project is the Scientific Committee, composed of professors of the university who have already gained experience about online learning. Chief of the Scientific Committee is the Vice-Rector. Another key member of the committee is the project manager, expert in digital education. They were supported by two Research Fellows Coordinators, who were experts and became more expert about e-learning and surroundings.

Do: a group of professors, experts in their own teaching topic, were engaged to create online courses, supported by coordinators and Junior Research Fellows, with a master degree or a PhD in the subject. With the guidance of professors of the Department of Philosophy and Educational Sciences, of the staff of the IT and E-learning bureau (DSIPE) and of an interdepartmental center, Cinedumedia (http://www.cinedumedia.it/), they learned about many areas of e-learning. Respecting teaching autonomy, professors and fellows attended a training cycle in which, in compliance with the aim of the project and with the tools available, they planned and rethought the contents in terms of learning objects. This training was very useful, because even the most experienced teachers are more accustomed to traditional or blended teaching: they had to rethink how to achieve the educational objectives. The University of Turin is trying to create a culture on digital education among all its professors. Training consisted of 10 lessons equally distributed between methodology (how to design an online course, how to obtain the best in communication and effectiveness) and practice (how to construct online resources, how to manage the adopted tools). Cinedumedia was also involved to help with video technologies and perform a presentation of every course.

Check: coordinators in collaboration with DSIPE staff were involved in validating the online contents, platform and communication management, online support and data analysis.

Act: platform managers and researchers provide adjustments according to feedbacks, methodologies and related topics. The main role in this phase was provided by the technical platform manager, experienced in handling and developing the virtual learning environment Moodle.

The tools to reinforce the early career of university students are provided by the LMS Moodle, a platform designed to provide educators, administrators and learners with a single robust, secure and pluggable system able to create custom learning environments (https://moodle.org/). The platform allows the integration of external tools, which allow a full learning and interactive experience, like web conferences tools or STEM oriented-tools. The use of an Advanced Computing Environment (ACE) is a great advantage, not only for scientific disciplines (Mathematics, Physics,...) but also for other topics involving a scientific approach. Our choice was to integrate Maple, which is a powerful ACE, very useful to analyze, explore, visualize, and solve mathematical problems. This environment can manage numeric and symbolic computations, geometric visualizations in two and three dimensions and interactive worksheets with embedded components. It is extensively used in several university activities like courses, exams and other projects. A useful component of this tool is MapleNet, the online worksheet player, which turns native worksheets into Moodle resources (Baldoni, Cordero, Coriasco, & Marchisio, 2011). The use of an Automatic Assessment System (AAS) helps universities in the testing and monitoring of students, who can find free and accessible tests validated by university experts. The native moodle assessment tools can be extended with the AAS Maple T.A. that is based on Maple engine, thus inheriting many benefits, such as numeric and symbolic computations, geometric visualizations in two and three dimensions, interactive components, algorithms and randomly generated variables. Maple T.A. integration allows assignments to be executed as Moodle resources, and students' results to be automatically updated in the gradebook (Barana, Marchisio, & Rabellino, 2015). The main multimedia content is video, and for this purpose the integrated tool chosen is Kaltura Video Platform, which provides live and on-demand video SaaS (Software as a Service) solutions to thousands of organizations around the world (https://corp.kaltura.com/). Besides the high quality of the player, the chance to integrate quizzes in video, provided by Kaltura, is a powerful learning method, which allows students to immediately check their comprehension.

The platform (http://start.unito.it/) hosts 20 online courses (number which is going to increase) divided into thematic areas, covering many basic topics about first-year university lectures. Every course is presented by a description of the main outcomes and a presentation video; some short details about the courses are also shown. All of them are first-year courses, also provided in presence. Every course can also cross different disciplines and, because of this, they are usually followed by students from different courses of study. Courses have a similar structure. They are divided into sections. The Moodle grid format is used to simplify students' navigation through sections. During the design of courses, previously experimented learning methodologies, such as immediate and interactive feedback (Barana et al., 2018) in tests with automatic evaluation or adaptive digital resources (Barana, Fioravera, Marchisio, & Rabellino, 2017) were adopted. The first contents that students can reach are an introduction to the course, the learning outcomes, how the exam works and other information on how to better attend the course. Then, all the other materials, regardless of the topic, are organized following the main structure of a classic learning object:

- **Entry test and Introduction**, in order to see if the student has the right prerequisites and to make him aware on what he is going to learn in the following steps.
- **Online contents**: short resources in which just one concept is introduced in a short way.
- **Summary**: map of all the concepts studied, with hyper references to the referred resource
- **Exit test** with immediate feedback and the possibility to check answers and get a grade
- **Deepening** (External resources): videos, journals, articles, blogs, scientific sites, official pages, data, which could be useful for the student to have a look at.

Other tools available are:

- **Glossary**: the main terms used in the online course are inserted here; students can check it whenever they want and all the concepts, everytime they appear in the course, are highlighted.
- **Progress bar**: every resource can be marked as viewed or completed. Completion progress is then highlighted in a panel showing a bar and the percentage of progress along the online course.
- **Gradebook**: in every moment, students can check their grades and their test details.

The model is characterized by the following properties.

- **Accessibility**: an high-legibility font designed for people with dyslexia is adopted (http://www.easyreading.it/en/); in addition, all resources consider many accessibility details like color contrast, short sentences, transcriptions of videos, etc.
- **Adaptability**: the structure and all tools chosen generate a versatile model.
- **Consistency**: this model is adopted by many projects within the University of Turin and students can easily become familiar with it throughout their career.
- **Control**: coordinators perform analysis and, if necessary, corrections; students are supported by immediate and interactive feedback.
- **Convenience**: the environment is useful and suitable for research on new technologies, thanks to the integration of multiple resources.
- **Free availability**: materials are distributed under Creative Commons license, they can be re-used in schools or in other learning contexts.
- **Efficiency**: first point of contact between learners and institutions.
- **High-quality**: the online contents are created by qualified personnel continuously improving their skills and collaboration among experts from distinct ranges of expertize.
- **Sustainability**: contained costs for students, they just pay for their device and its connection.
- **Usefulness**: students are more aware of their enrolment choices, positively affecting institutions and improving the quality of courses.

5. RESULTS AND DISCUSSION

The 20 online courses were opened on 1st March 2018, immediately after University Guidance Days. Access to platform is granted using Social Networks authentication API (Google and Facebook). In the summer the number of accesses increased. July and August is a good time frame for online learning: students just ended high school and they are evaluating which path may be the right one for their future. The actual amount of subscribed students is 4383. The number of subscriptions to courses can vary depending on several factors, like an attractive title, the advertisement, the presentations made in schools, the interest in the discipline. After completing the course, students are asked to fill an evaluation questionnaire. Analyzing the completion progress of students subscribed to courses, we notice that only a small percentage of students completed more than 40% of the course and attended it regularly. This is in line with the open characteristic of Start@unito courses: users can just have a look to a full university course and have an idea on how it works.

6. CONCLUSION

Start@unito is something that comes after a wide research experience of the University of Turin about digital online education. Looking at these first results, we can say that the starting point is very promising. Even after meetings with teachers and students in schools and during University Guidance Days, everybody was very interested in the great occasion that Start@unito project represents. High school teachers asked to be able to use some of the resources of online courses with their students, in order to deepen topics introduced during their lessons. This way of spreading tertiary education is a very useful service, especially for the most disadvantaged people, both economically or with learning and working issues. Working students can find and download all the materials, studying them during their free time; students with learning difficulties have available recovery activities that allow them to fill gaps; foreign, off-site or particularly gifted students can start to study before enrolling at the University and anticipate exams. Students who normally attend the course in presence can use the online course as a support for traditional lessons. People, unwilling to enrol at the University, but curious and interested in deepening some themes to broaden their knowledge and acquire some additional interpretative key can find materials prepared by experts and freely usable. High school teachers can find materials available at any time to enrich their lessons with insights and food for thought. That is why the University decided to extend the number of courses available amounting, for the academic year 2019-2020, to 34 new open online courses, including some missing disciplines, like pedagogy, chemistry and various foreign languages. Moreover, to promote the internationalization and the mobility of students, many of the new courses will be taught in English.

ACKNOWLEDGEMENT

The authors thank Compagnia di San Paolo for the support, Rector Prof. G. Ajani, Dr. M. Bruno, the staff of Board of Education and Student Services, Ing. A. Saccà, the staff of Portal Management, ICT services of the Computer Science Department, Cinedumedia, teachers, research fellows and personnel at Turin University.

REFERENCES

Baldoni, M., Cordero, A., Coriasco, S., & Marchisio, M. (2011). Moodle, Maple, MapleNet e MapleTA: dalla lezione alla valutazione. In M. Baldoni, C. Baroglio, S. Coriasco, M. Marchisio, & S. Rabellino (Eds.), *E-Learning con Moodle in Italia: una sfida tra presente, passato e futuro* (pp. 299-316). Torino, Italy: Seneca Edizioni.

Barana, A., Bogino, A., Fioravera, M., Floris, F., Marchisio, M., Operti, L., & Rabellino, S. (2017). *Self-paced approach in synergistic model for supporting and testing students: The transition from Secondary School to University*, Proceedings of 2017 IEEE 41st Annual Computer Software and Applications Conference (COMPSAC), 404-409.

Barana, A., Bogino, A., Fioravera, M., Marchisio, M., & Rabellino, S. (2016). *Digital Support for University Guidance and Improvement of Study Results*, Procedia - Social and Behavioral Sciences, 228, 547-552. D

Barana, A., Bogino, A., Fioravera, M., Marchisio, M., & Rabellino, S. (2017). *Open platform of self-paced MOOCs for the continual improvement of academic guidance and knowledge strengthening in tertiary education*, Journal of e-Learning and Knowledge Society, 13(3), 109-119. doi:10.20368/1971-8829/1383

Barana, A., Conte, A., Fioravera, M., Marchisio, M., & Rabellino, S. (2018). *A Model of Formative Automatic Assessment and Interactive Feedback for STEM,* Proceedings of 2018 IEEE 42nd Annual Computer Software and Applications Conference (COMPSAC), 1016-1025. doi:10.1109/compsac.2018.00178

Barana, A., Fioravera, M., Marchisio, M., & Rabellino, S. (2017). *Adaptive teaching supported by ICTs to reduce the school failure in the Project "Scuola dei Compiti"*, Proceedings of 2017 IEEE 41st Annual Computer Software and Applications Conference (COMPSAC), 432-437. doi:10.1109/COMPSAC.2017.44

Barana, A., Marchisio, M., & Rabellino, S. (2015). *Automated Assessment in Mathematics*, COMPSAC Symposium on Computer Education and Learning Technologies, Taichung, 670-671. doi:10.1109/COMPSAC.2015.105

Brancaccio, A., Marchisio, M., Meneghini, C., & Pardini, C. (2015). *Matematica e Scienze più SMART per l'Insegnamento e l'Apprendimento*, MONDO DIGITALE 14(58), 1-8.

In Cinedumedia - Università degli Studi di Torino. Retrieved from http://www.cinedumedia.it/

In Coursera | Online Courses & Credentials by Top Educators. Join for Free. Retrieved from https://www.coursera.org/

In EasyReading. Retrieved from http://www.easyreading.it/en/

In EDUOPEN LMS. Retrieved from https://learn.eduopen.org/

In edX | Online courses from the world's best universities. Retrieved from https://www.edx.org/

In Federica, l'e-Learning dell'Università di Napoli Federico II. Retrieved from http://www.federica.unina.it/

Grainger, B. (2013). *Introduction to MOOCs: avalanche, illusion or augmentation?*, Policy brief of Unesco institute for information technologies in education.

Hicks, S. (2011). *Technology in today's classroom: Are you a tech-savvy teacher?*, The Clearing House, 84(5), 188-191.

In Kaltura Video Platform - Powering Any Video Experience. Retrieved from https://corp.kaltura.com/

In Moodle - Open-source learning platform | Moodle.org. Retrieved from https://moodle.org/

Naismith, L., Lonsdale, P., Vavoula, G., & Sharples, M. (2004). *Mobile technologies and learning,* Futurelab Literature Review Series, Report No 11.

Ravanelli, F., & Serina, I. (2014). *Didactic and Pedagogical View of E-learning Activities Free University of Bozen-bolzano*, Procedia - Social and Behavioral Sciences, 116, 1774-1784. doi:10.1016/j.sbspro.2014.01.471.

In Relazione Annuale 2016, UniTo. Retrieved from https://www.unito.it/sites/default/files/relazione_annuale_2016.pdf

Ross, S., Morrison, G., & Lowther, D. (2010). *Educational technology research past and present: balancing rigor and relevance to impact learning*, Contemporary Educational Technology, 1(1), 17-35. doi:10.4236/jss.2014.22002

FOSTERING STEM EDUCATION CONSIDERING FEMALE PARTICIPATION GAP

Juliana de Melo Bezerra, Lara Kühl Teles, Cristiane Aparecida Martins, Neusa Maria Franco de Oliveira, Maria Margareth da Silva, Leila Ribeiro dos Santos and Raquel Caratti Piani
Instituto Tecnológico de Aeronáutica – ITA, São José dos Campos – SP, Brazil

ABSTRACT

Despite the technological development, the digital era, and the fact that Science, Technology, Engineering and Mathematics (STEM) permeates all the modern world, the number of students choosing to pursue a career in STEM areas is very small in comparison to other careers. In particular, considering the gender, the gap increases even more. In this work, we present an industry-university program designed to stimulate STEM education and fostering the female interest and development in these areas. Considering our female undergrad students, the proposal was to engage them in the process, as the main agents. Our students prepared and gave lectures in schools about STEM areas. Together with some faculty members, they also developed and applied workshops based on hands-on and minds-on learning activities to spark young girls' curiosity in STEM areas. In all activities, it was performed an evaluation of learning outcomes, as STEM skills and interest. The program showed to be effective producing very positive remarks.

KEYWORDS

STEM, Education, Gender, Program, Student

1. INTRODUCTION

Science, Technology, Engineering and Mathematics (STEM) permeate everything nowadays. Innovations that emerge from these fields underpin much economic development leading to the establishment of creative enterprises, rewarding careers, and leading nations (Kanematsu and Barry, 2015). STEM workforce is essential to countries increase innovative capacity, meet economic needs and reach global competitiveness (Beede et al, 2011). The modern definition of STEM education includes the notion of integration by emphasizing logical and conceptual connections across different STEM fields, meaning that STEM is the purposeful integration of the various disciplines as used in solving real-world problems (Xie et al, 2015). For example, an engineer needs a well-developed understanding of the various science disciplines, math, and technology to support and provide context for their engineering designs and applications (Breiner et al, 2012). Moreover, STEM education is multi-faceted and goes beyond by supporting the developing of curiosity, inquisitiveness, critical-thinking, innovation and problem-solving capacities (Bruton, 2017).

It is important to introduce young children to the topics of STEM and to motivate as well as encourage them to pursue STEM subjects in every grade. Acting on a young age can have a lasting impact on learners, as it can set the stage for their later engagement and success in these fields (Gonzalez and Kuenzi, 2012; Bruton, 2017). By acquiring STEM concepts, students can perform better and be better prepared for advanced education or jobs in STEM fields (Ryan et al, 2011). Despite robust progress toward equity, one critical issue related to STEM education is the gap gender. Women are vastly underrepresented in STEM jobs and among STEM degree holders (Beede et al, 2011; Xie et al, 2015). Cultural beliefs introduce in women, during different stages of development, a bias perception about their competence to STEM. Other aspect that reduces women interest in STEM is the presence of stereotypically masculine objects in these fields (Correll, S.J., 2001; Christie, et al, 2017). An indicated answer to this issue is to increase young women's exposure to successful women in STEM careers, aiming to strengthen female students' self-identification with STEM and enhance their motivation to pursue STEM careers (Stout et al., 2011).

Based in the importance and demands of STEM education, as well as the discrepancies in female participation in STEM areas, we identify three main needs. The first one is to provide opportunities to explore concepts and engage in children problem-solving, while developing their knowledge and skills. The second need is to enable children to make informed choices about careers in STEM and related areas. The third need is an effort to increase participation of females in STEM areas. In this paper, we present a program established by a partnership between industry and university, whose objective is to incentive young students in STEM and to contribute to the increase in female participation in STEM. We describe the program actions and the associated results.

2. STEM EDUCATION PROGRAM

The demand of the program was presented by a company, concerned to the female gap in their position jobs. The initiative was part of a broader effort to accelerate the development of women leaders and to support women at all stages of their life to improve global health and well-being and drive sustainable economic growth. The team that conducted the program in 2017 was composed by six professors, one communication professor, and 34 undergrad students of a renowned Engineering Institute. All participants were women. The Institute accepted the challenge to propose and manage the program, since it would to contribute not only to society, but also to the development of its own undergrad students.

2.1 Actions

The program had mainly two actions, named lecture and workshop. Regarding lecture, our undergrad students were in charge to produce or identify materials, including presentations and videos. The lecture was divided in three topics. The first topic introduced STEM concepts and presented famous women in STEM. The second topic in lecture presented the female gap in STEM, using data about the number of male and female professionals in distinct countries, and about the economic benefit for nations that reach a balance between male and female workforce. The third topic in lecture present focus on opportunities and careers in STEM, where we present information of our Engineering Institute, including courses, laboratories, student projects, interchange opportunities, and life in campus. Lectures took place in middle and high schools of our country for both boys and girls. To include boys in lectures was natural due to the mixed configuration of the classes in visited schools. Moreover, to have boys in lectures was essential to take the opportunity to stimulate them in STEM too, but mainly to present them the importance and need of women in STEM. The fact of having our undergrad students as lecturers was also a benefit of the program, since they have a language more adequate to reach the young public, and they were in fact STEM female representatives assuring the possibility of women take STEM careers.

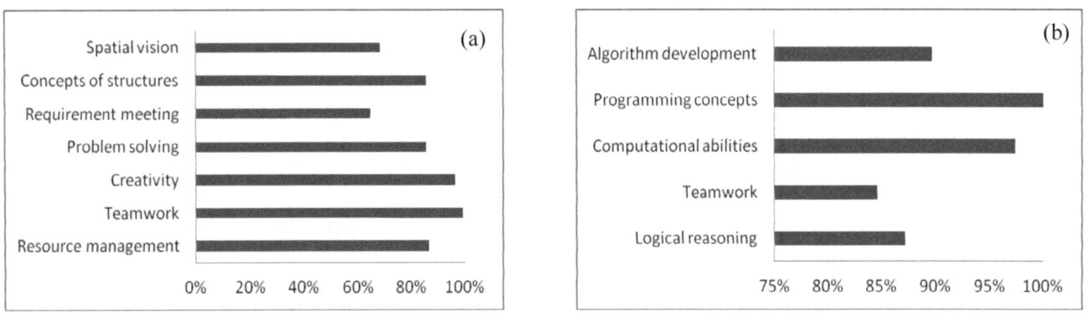

Figure 1. Percentage of students who declared to have acquired STEM skills in (a) "LEGO constructions" and (b) "Robotics with LEGO" workshops

Workshop was an initiative designed to spark girls' curiosity in STEM areas through hands-on and minds-on learning activities. Workshops were conducted inside our institute facilities, in a way to bring girls to campus and make them be part of it. The public was only girls, in a way to attack directly the gender gap by stimulating girls in STEM education. At the first semester, we applied workshops already developed in

2016, including “LEGO constructions”, “Binary bracelets and logic gates”, “Robotics with LEGO”, “Game Programming”, “3D Printer”, and “Circuits with Circuit Scriber”. Our students developed new workshops for the second semester, but now focusing on low-cost activities, in order to make feasible both our expansion and reproduction of activities in other schools later. The eight new workshops, conducted during the second semester of 2017, as follows: “Mathplayground – learning Plane Geometry through Geoboards”, “Civil Engineering – playing with structures”, “Optics – propagation and emission of light”, “Spectrometer – characterization of light”, “Water rocket”, “Plastic plate activities for Math class”, “Acid/Base Science Experiment”, and “Introduction to Electronic and Programming using Arduino Uno”.

2.2 Results

Regarding the achievements of program actions, we had 40 lectures in seven distinct cities of our country mainly in the region of our institute. Together lectures reached 1,586 students, being 951 girls and 635 boys, between 10 and 19 years-old. For workshops, we received a total of 360 girls of middle schools (from 10 to 15 years old). In the first semester of 2017, each one of the 120 girls performed the six workshops available, characterizing an immersive program in STEM. In the second semester of 2017, 240 girls experienced only one workshop, due to an objective of expanding our initiatives to a larger public and increase program visibility.

We conducted initial evaluations regarding the gains in STEM education associated to workshops in the first semester of 2017, in a way to know how productive and assertive the proposed workshop was in developing STEM abilities and skills. For instance, Figure 1a shows the evaluation of “LEGO constructions” workshop with 110 respondents; and Figure 1b presents the evaluation of “Robotics with LEGO” workshop with 39 respondents. The evaluation of each workshop was made independently, in a sense of being more aligned to workshop subjects and objectives. It was an interesting assessment, but we decided to improve it by standardizing the evaluation questionnaire both to lectures and workshops in order to be able to compare outcomes of all actions and to analyze the overall program achievement.

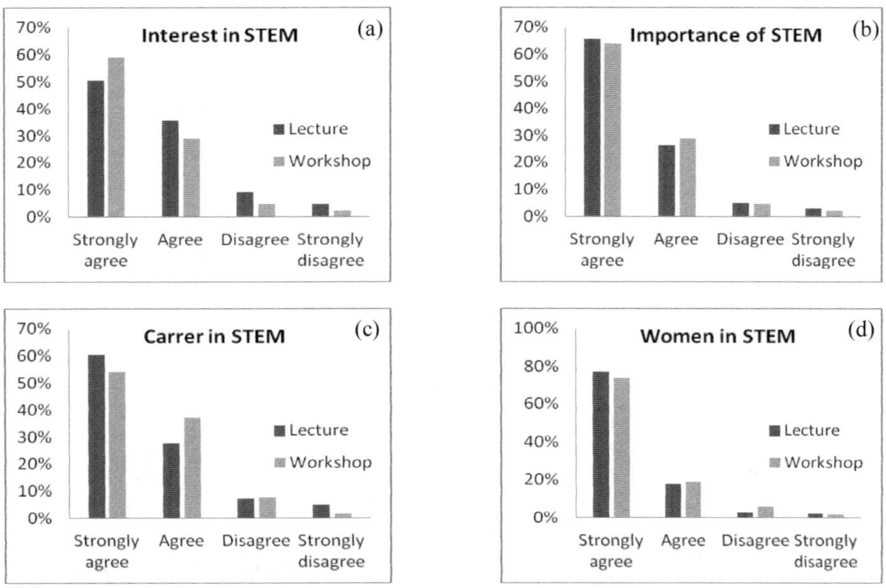

Figure 2. Evaluation of lectures and workshops considering: (a) perceived interest in STEM, (b) recognition of STEM importance, (c) knowledge of careers in STEM, and (d) understanding of women importance in STEM

Students that participated in lectures (during the year) and workshops (during the second semester of 2017) were invited to evaluate their experience after program actions considering the following perspectives: “The lecture/workshop contributed to increase my interest in STEM”, “After the lecture/workshop, I was able to understand the importance of STEM to society progress”, “After the lecture/workshop, I was able know career option in STEM", "After the lecture/workshop, I understood the importance of women in STEM". As respondents, we had 211 girls that participate of a workshop, and 157 students (98 girls and 59 boys) that attended a lecture. The results are depicted in Figure 2. According to Figure 2a, lectures and workshops sparked the interest in STEM, but workshops were a little more effective. Figure 2b shows that lectures and workshops had similarly effect on presenting STEM relevance to society progress. According to Figure 2c, workshops promote interesting experiences that make girls identify possibilities of careers in STEM, whereas lectures could also present such possibilities based on examples of STEM projects and courses. Figure 2d shows that students comprehended the importance of women in STEM with interesting marks. For instance, considering 'strongly agree' and 'agree' together, lectures contributed to 95.09% and workshops to 92.5%, numbers superior to the other investigated perspectives.

3. CONCLUSION

We presented a program designed to stimulate STEM education together to contributing to female involvement in STEM arena. The program actions, lectures, and workshops have a fundamental difference regarding the period that the student is submitted to STEM concepts. A lecture was mainly an exposition, even interactions and questions were stimulated, where students acquired information during approximately one hour. Each workshop was designed to last three hours in a group of at most 30 girls, so they could receive more attention by the workshop conductors and take more time working with STEM concepts. Although this difference, according to the results of program evaluation, both lectures and workshops succeed in stimulating STEM education. Moreover, program actions supported the dissemination of the importance of women in STEM careers and promoted the involvement with STEM to young girls. The program exemplifies actions that can be structured to spark STEM education and support female inclusion in STEM. We argue that the problem that motivated this paper is in fact a great challenge, which can only be overcome with a set of complementary initiatives around the work. The presented program can contribute to inspire the definition of new other programs, as well as the improvements of existing ones.

ACKNOWLEDGEMENT

A special thanks to Johnson&Johnson company for funding the program.

REFERENCES

Beede, D.N. et al, 2011. Women in STEM: A Gender Gap to Innovation. *U.S. Department of Commerce: Economics and Statistics Administration*, No. 04, pp 1-11.

Breiner, J.M. et al, 2012. What Is STEM? A Discussion About Conceptions of STEM in Education and Partnerships. *In School Science and Mathematics*, Vol. 112, No. 1, pp 3-11.

Bruton, R., 2017. STEM Education Policy Statement 2017-2026. Irish Department of Education and Skills.

Christie, M. et al, 2017. Understanding why women are under-represented in Science, Technology, Engineering and Mathematics (STEM) within Higher Education: a regional case study. *In Production*, Vol. 27, e20162205.

Correll, S.J., 2001. Gender and the Career Choice Process: The Role of Biased Self- Assessments. *In American Journal of Sociology*, Vol. 106, No. 6.

Gonzalez, H.B. and Kuenzi, J.J., 2012. Science, Technology, Engineering, and Mathematics (STEM) Education: A Primer. *Congressional Research Service (CRS)*, R42642.

Kanematsu, H. and Barry, D.M., 2015. The Importance of STEM for Modern Education. *STEM and ICT Education in Intelligent Environments*, pp 25-30.

Ryan, B. et al, 2011. Understanding STEM: Current Perceptions. *In Technology and Engineering Teacher*, Vol. 70.

Stout, J.G. et al., 2011. STEMing the Tide: Using Ingroup Experts to Inoculate Women's Self-Concept in Science, Technology, Engineering, and Mathematics (STEM). *In Journal of Personality and Social Psychology*, Vol. 100.

Xie, Y. et al, 2015. STEM Education. *In Annual Review of Sociology*, Vol. 41, pp 331-357.

COGNITIVE DESTRUCTIONS AS A CHALLENGE FOR LEARNING IN THE POST-LITERACY EPOCH

Marina Yurtaeva, Natalia Glukhanyuk, Tatiana Rasskazova and Anna Muzafarova
Ural Federal University named after the first president of Russia B.N.Yeltsin
Address 19, Mira Street, Ekaterinburg, 620002 Russia

ABSTRACT

The article is devoted to the issue of learning from the cognitive perspective. As life-long learning is an integral part of our modern life, the authors were attracted by the phenomenon when even young people demonstrate cognitive "resistance" to learning. This particular study is focused on cognitive destructions as challenges to learning and is based on the idea of non-linear nature of a cognitive style. Eighty subjects participated in the study with different types of psychological tests employed, including Stroop test, embedded figure test, tolerance of ambiguity, assumptive worlds, personality characteristics in decision making. The main findings are the following: cognitive degradations, which are based on different types of rigidity, which impedes not only the process of learning but also social behaviour of a person as well; the second finding is the intensity of tolerance of ambiguity in a subgroup with extreme analytical thinking is a destructive cognitive phenomenon, one of the manifestations of a negative mental attitude - the closure to the experience. The results prove that the subjects with extreme types of cognitive styles tend to demonstrate a "close" type of mind. This raises the discussion of different understanding of the rigidity phenomenon and gives fruit for thought and prospects of further research into the field of the role of cognitive resources in learning.

KEYWORDS

Cognitive Resources, Life-Long Learning, Rigidity/Flexibility of Cognitive Control, Field-Dependence/ Field-Independence, Cognitive Destructions

1. INTRODUCTION

Globalisation of life and education is an integral part of our life, where learning is a key factor. The modern world with its diversity of sources of information and variety of sources of learning is, in fact, the world of post-literacy (McLuhan et al., 2011), where ideally people are learning their whole life, as it is an essential survival skill. Even if people do realise that their life depends on learning, their learning abilities differ and their learning is not always as effective as teachers want it to be. In this article, we tried to explore the possible reasons for learning effectiveness/ineffectiveness from the psychological perspective, namely, the differences in cognitive styles.

The development of the theory of learning is impossible without a systematic study of the cognitive sphere of the individual, both from the standpoint of searching for reserves, and destruction, deformation. Traditionally, research is aimed at the strengths of cognition. Our research focuses on cognitive degradation, i.e. mental phenomena weakening the ability to learn and self-learning, the integration of a new mental experience, social adaptation. Accordingly, requiring the development of new approaches to learning, including learning through life. The basis of the work is the use of a cognitive-style approach to the study of a person's mental life, which makes it possible to identify specific intellectual-personal ways of processing information inextricably linked with the features of the organization of mental experience.

Using the results of our empirical study, we try to prove that high speed indicators of intelligence can mask the destructive phenomena of the cognitive sphere. The choice of classical methods of cognitive style is justified by their wider experimental possibilities, approximation to objective tests, an alternative to self-reports, which diagnose not cognitive styles, but personality traits. So the study was focused on two cognitive styles: field dependence / polarity dependence (analyticity / synthetism); rigid / flexible cognitive control (rigidity / flexibility).

Our research assumption of cognitive destruction is based on 1) the idea of extreme values of cognitive style, as predictors of psychological maladjustment; 2) the phenomenon of the quadripolar structure of the cognitive style and its nonlinear structure, in particular, the isolation of special style groups as a result of splitting the poles of the style continuum; 3) the different nature of cognitive rigidity. 3) the idea of involuntary intellectual control (Kholodnaya, 2002); 4) a fundamental provision on the cognitive-personal nature of the style; 5) the different nature of cognitive rigidity.

2. METHODS AND MATERIALS

At different stages of the study, students from Russian universities took part in it: the total number of participants is 80 students (M = 19.4, SD = 1.68). Research methods administered individually for each participant in the study are the following: "Embedded figures test" G.Witkin (1950); Stroop test (1935). In addition, methods used to measure indices of tolerance of ambiguity and personal characteristics in Russian: the scale of tolerance to the ambiguity of N.Y.Stanley Budner (1962) and D.L.McLain (1993), as well as the questionnaire "Personal factors in decision-making" by T.Kornilova (1994), assumptive worlds by R. Janoff-Bulman (1989). To analyse the obtained data we used SPSS cluster analysis.

2.1 Cognitive Style: "Field-Dependence/Field-Independence"

During the splitting of poles of the cognitive style of field-dependence / field-independence, 3 subgroups were singled out. Thus, the field-dependence (synthetic) is represented by one subgroup, which is explained by the age and educational status of the subjects. Let us turn to an analysis of the splitting of the field-dependence (analytic), in particular, to a comparison of its extreme and moderate values. It is definitely established that the extreme values of the analytic style are associated with high tolerance of ambiguity, i.e. openness to new experiences and knowledge. It can be concluded that an analytical approach is more preferable in cognition and learning.

According to the research of Kholodnaya, highly analytical people demonstrate a minimal effect of mobility and flexibility. It is noted that their intellectual behaviour is distinguished by a high speed of structuring the field combined with a weak integration of their behaviour with the field (Kholodnaya, 2002). Thus, this subgroup is least influenced by situational factors, but it is also true that their behaviour modulation dependence on the context is low. The question arises: what is the reason for the high degree of tolerance of ambiguity in this category of subjects, in comparison with other subgroups? Or does a person with high analytical abilities react with cognitive closure, whereas the result is a consequence of protective mechanisms?

In the course of the experiment, it was established that participants in the study, showing concern and ambiguity about their own abilities, often turned to the "role model". Therefore, the first explanation of the result is related to the role of stability-anxiety in regulating the volume of working memory needed to solve a cognitive problem (Grimley et al., 2008). Probably, the extreme values of analytical thinking contribute to reducing the effects of emotional stress on the processing of information, which causes the emergence of new pieces of experience.

The second explanation of the result is determined by the fact that this subgroup takes extreme positions in the behaviour-style continuum. It is known that the effect of extreme values of cognitive style is associated with a decrease in the indicators of mental adaptation (Kholodnaya, 2002). It is shown that individuals with extreme values of analytical thinking, more often than other behaviour-style groups prefer to use psychological protection in the form of repression. In this case, the intensity of tolerance of ambiguity in a subgroup with extreme analytical thinking can be interpreted as a destructive cognitive phenomenon, one of the manifestations of a negative mental attitude - the closure to the experience. Its destructive significance lies in the weakness of the integration processes, as a component of the development process. The challenge for learning is that the new experience, knowledge is not integrated with the personality, which is expressed in the appearance of prejudices, stereotypes, the inertness of thinking.

2.2 Cognitive Style: Rigidity / Flexibility of Cognitive Control

Splitting the field of a flexibility of cognitive control (flexibility) and the field of a rigidity of cognitive control (rigidity) resulted in differentiating two style subgroups in each field. Thus, in this study, we obtained 2 groups with extreme values of cognitive style. We base our work on the idea of the unity of style, therefore we believe that ignoring the interfering context as one of the features of a subgroup with extreme values of flexibility, as well as abstracting from a distracting field (background) subgroup with extreme values of analyticity, is a manifestation of cognitive destructions related with rigidity.

In the literature, the phenomenon of rigidity is described in terms of inertia, stiffness, which is not comparable with high-speed indicators observed in subgroups with high flexibility and analytical thinking. At the same time, one important aspect of rigidity should not be overlooked, which has been repeatedly discussed in theories of intellectual development, for example by H. Werner. The phenomenon of rigidity is based on the mechanism of isolation, described as the fragmentation of various sub-regions of experience. In other words, there is a lack of integrity of an individual, which is achieved through integration. E. Frenkel-Brunswick stressed that the phenomena of disintegration and chaos, as well as the concreteness, literality of perception of reality, in fact, are different aspects of the same phenomenon, which is based on a combination of extremity and primitiveness of cognitive responses of ambiguity (E. Frenkel-Brunswik, 1949).

Special attention should be paid to the fact that "the benevolence of the outside world" is expressed in a subgroup with extreme flexibility. The combination of high values for this indicator of assumptive worlds with low risk readiness can be seen as one of the manifestations of the work of the negation mechanism, the expression of which will be the desire to "hold on" to defensive illusions, reinterpret new events and impressions within the framework of established patterns and beliefs. Mental attitudes of such people are aimed at protecting themselves against information that threatens their cognitive patterns.

The analysis of the subgroup with extreme rigidity values showed the severity of dysfunctional cognitive schemes in relation to the self, such as low self-esteem, belief about the uncontrollability of events of one's own life. Rigid people are fixed on negative impressions which do not allow them to maintain positive basic patterns that are significant in terms of psychological security and openness to new experiences. The cognitive resource deficit does not allow them to restructure the situation, see it from different perspectives and change the mode of attitude towards it.

3. CONCLUSION

This article was inspired by the research of life-long learning in post-literacy epoch and aimed at investigating the reasons of ineffective learning from the perspective of cognitive styles. Eighty university students were selected for the study. We employed different traditional cognitive tests to find out individual styles in learning. Our study was based on the idea of quadripolar structure of learning style as opposed to a bipolar one. Our type of approach helped us to focus on destructive aspects of cognitive sphere of a personality such as dogmatism and rigidity. The results demonstrate that apart from positive features, such as intelligence, creativity, intellectual talent, cognitive styles, learning activity, tolerance of ambiguity, openness to new experiences, the need for cognition, we focused on problem areas in cognition. We paid special attention to dogmatism, rigidity, authoritarian style of communication and behaviour, intolerance of ambiguity, the need for closure as features that might negatively affect the process of learning. The analysis of the obtained data proved that extreme values in cognitive styles: field-dependence/field-independence and rigidity/ flexibility of cognitive control are the two styles that have negative impact on learning.

This study has allowed us to identify cognitive degradations, which are based on different types of rigidity. The most dangerous type is the first type of rigidity associated with disintegration, when high indicators of cognitive resources are aimed at maintaining a closed mind (compartmentalisation, isolation, denial) that is a strategic challenge not only for learning but also poses a serious strategic threat to other social systems, because it affects the problem of dogmatism and its cognitive basis. We can argue that individuals with high rates of cognitive processes are not "ordinary" the usual sense of the word. Since the ability for learning is not only a quantitative but also a qualitative characteristic, which implies the presence of a variety of ways of tackling the problem, solving it, creating the cognitive image in different ways.

Whereas individuals with high rates of cognitive processes tend to cope with problems too "straightforwardly" not seeing different ways of dealing with it.

There are a number of questions that arise from this study that make up the basis for further studying the indicated issue: 1) why those individuals who have a high cognitive resource demonstrate a closed position in cognition; 2) what happens to these people during the cognitive aging process; 3) how, with the help of training, we can correct destructions in cognition; 4) how to motivate these people for life-long learning. The answers to these questions require further research that can be carried out within the framework of an interdisciplinary approach, its methodology provides an opportunity for a comprehensive description of the closed mind attitudes and ways of correcting them, by involving approaches, research designs, methods and techniques from various sciences.

ACKNOWLEDGEMENT

The reported study was funded by RFBR according to the research project 17-29-09136.

REFERENCES

Ambrose, D. and Sternberg, R.J. eds., 2012. *How dogmatic beliefs harm creativity and higher-level thinking*. Routledge.

Bayer, S., Lev-Wiesel, R. and Amir, M., 2007. The relationship between basic assumptions, posttraumatic growth, and ambiguity tolerance in an Israeli sample of young adults: A mediation-moderation model. *Traumatology*, 13(1), p.4.

Frenkel-Brunswik, E., 1949. Intolerance of ambiguity as an emotional and perceptual personality variable. *Journal of personality*, 18(1), pp.108-143.

Friedland, N., Keinan, G. and Tytiun, T., 1999. The effect of psychological stress and tolerance of ambiguity on stereotypic attributions. *Anxiety, Stress & Coping*, 12(4), pp.397-410.

Furnham, A. and Marks, J., 2013. Tolerance of ambiguity: A review of the recent literature. *Psychology*, 4(09), p.717.

Grimley, M., Dahraei, H. and Riding, R.J., 2008. The relationship between anxiety- stability, working memory and cognitive style. *Educational studies*, 34(3), pp.213-223.

Janoff-Bulman, R., 1989. Assumptive worlds and the stress of traumatic events: Applications of the schema construct. *Social cognition*, 7(2), pp.113-136.

Kholodnaya M.A., 2002. *Cognitive styles: on the nature of individual mind.* – Per Se, Moscow. (In Russian) (Холодная М.А., 2002. Когнитивные стили: о природе индивидуального ума. –Per Se, Москва)

Kornilova T.V., 1994. The diagnosis of "personality factors" in decision making. *Voprosy Psykhologii*, (6), pp.99-109 (in Russian) (Корнилова, Т.В., 1994. Диагностика «личностных факторов» принятия решений. *Вопросы психологии*, (6), pp.99-109.)

Kruglanski, A.W., 2013. *The psychology of closed mindedness*. Psychology Press.

McLain, D.L., 1993. The MSTAT-I: A new measure of an individual's tolerance for ambiguity. *Educational and psychological measurement*, 53(1), pp.183-189.

McLuhan, M., Gordon, W.T., Lamberti, E. and Scheffel-Dunand, D., 2011. *The Gutenberg galaxy: The making of typographic man*. University of Toronto Press.

Stanley Budner, N.Y., 1962. Intolerance of ambiguity as a personality variable. *Journal of personality*, 30(1), pp.29-50.

Stroop, J.R., 1935. Studies of interference in serial verbal reactions. *Journal of experimental psychology*, 18(6), p.643.

Witkin, H.A., 1950. Individual differences in ease of perception of embedded figures. *Journal of personality*, 19(1), pp.1-15.

EXPLORING THE IMPACT OF A STEM INTEGRATION TEACHER PROFESSIONAL DEVELOPMENT PROGRAM ON EARLY CHILDHOOD TEACHER'S PEDAGOGICAL BELIEFS

Hengameh Kermani[1] and Jale Aldemir[1]
[1]*Ph.D.*
University of North Carolina Wilmington
University of North Carolina, Watson College of Education
601 South College Rd. Wilmington, NC 28403, USA

ABSTRACT

The purpose of this study was to investigate how STEM-focused professional development training influence early childhood teachers' knowledge, beliefs, and pedagogies. Four pre-K teachers participated in this study. The data collected was qualitative in nature. Interview data were transcribed, coded and emerging themes were identified. The findings showed that all four teachers were positively impacted by the STEM professional development, resources and the materials available to them to implement the STEM units/projects. Consequently, children were positively impacted because of their teacher's professional learning and high confidence about teaching STEM-related activities.

KEYWORDS

Early Childhood, Integrated STEM, Teacher's Belief, Professional Development

1. INTRODUCTION

A growing body of research indicates that experiences with science, Technology, Engineering, and Mathematics (STEM) is critical in preparing students to think critically, creatively, and solve problems. These are valuable skills students need to succeed in school, work and life (see Aronin and Floyd, 2013; Chesloff, 2013). This raising awareness of STEM education needs has led to a push for STEM education in middle grades and high schools giving limited attention to the teaching of the STEM in early childhood setting. Lately, a core of research specialists, curriculum developers, and early childhood advocates have called for STEM education in the early years since young children are perfectly adapted to learn STEM concepts (e.g., Alade et al., 2016). For example, Chesloff (2013) argued that STEM education should start in early childhood since "concepts at the heart of STEM—curiosity, creativity, collaboration, critical thinking—are in demand" (p. 27).

Although children show natural curiosity about their world and remarkable capacity for independent learning, they need adult assistance to support, guide and build on their interests to ensure adequate early STEM experiences (Early Childhood STEM Group, 2017). Unfortunately, research shows that many teachers, particularly early childhood teachers, not only lack confidence about teaching STEM subjects but are also ill-prepared in content and pedagogy to effectively engage young children in developmentally appropriate STEM learning (Bagiati & Evangelou, 2015; Nores & Barnett, 2014). Moreover, the implementation of a STEM curriculum is strongly dependent on teachers' attitudes and beliefs toward STEM (Roehrig et al. 2007). Studies (Wang et al., 2011; Park, Dimitrov, Patterson & Park, 2017) have indicated that Professional Development is needed in STEM education for K-12 teachers, especially pre-K teachers, as their beliefs and attitudes about STEM affect their students' perceptions and interest towards STEM subjects.

The purpose of this study was to explore the impact of a STEM integration teacher professional development program on early childhood teachers' pedagogical practices and beliefs about teaching STEM in pre-K settings.

2. EARLY CHILDHOOD TEACHER BELEIFS

There is limited research looking at early childhood teachers' pedagogical beliefs regarding STEM integrated curriculum. Kagan defines teachers' beliefs as "tacit, often unconsciously held assumptions about students, classrooms, and the academic material to be taught" (Kagan, 1992, p. 65). Different constructs such as teachers' early formal and informal education, school context, media, and culture could affect their pedagogical beliefs on how certain subject matters should be taught. Fang (1996) argues that "teachers' theoretical knowledge and beliefs" (p. 49), influence how they design and implement their curriculum and how they interact with their students. Chen et al. (2014) report that early childhood teachers' beliefs about what is more important in young children's education influence their decision as to what to prioritize in the classroom. The authors further argue that the misinterpretation of child-centered Developmentally Appropriate Practice (DAP) causes practitioners to think that content areas such as math/science are inappropriate to prioritize in early childhood education. This notion is an example of how teachers' beliefs often function as mechanisms to either confirm or refute new professional knowledge and skills that demand a change in their existing teaching practice (Nespor, 1987). Therefore, the view of early childhood teachers presented in this paper help us explore some of the pedagogical beliefs that they have about a newly recognized phenomenon, which is science, technology, engineering and math (STEM) integration in early childhood education curriculum following a series of professional development sessions

Therefore, the view of early childhood teachers presented in this paper help us deconstruct some of the pedagogical beliefs that they have about a newly recognized phenomenon in early childhood field, which is STEM integration in curriculum following a series of professional development sessions.

3. THE METHODOLOGY

Participants and setting. The data reported in this study are from two separate yet similar larger studies that investigated the effect of STEM education in early childhood settings. The two studies were conducted in 2013-13 and 2013-14 academic years respectively. Participants included two teachers (Brook and Megan) from a public Pre-K Center and two Pre-K teachers (Jenna and Tammy) from a Head Start program in a small town located in the South Eastern part of North Carolina. Pseudonyms were used to protect the participants' identity. All four teachers were female (three White and one Black) ranging in age from 29 to 40 years old. As B-K licensed lead teachers in their classroom, they were responsible for planning and implementing the curriculum as well as the assessment of their students. The teachers' experience at the Pre-K level ranged from three to ten years of teaching as lead teachers. All four teachers volunteered to take part in this study and were willing to share their project work and documentation as part of this research. The studies these teachers participated were reviewed and approved by our university' institutional review board (IRB).

Data collection. The data was collected through an interview protocol lasting for 90-120 minutes each. Observational notes of professional development sessions as well as researchers' field notes of participants' teaching practices were utilized to triangulate what emerged from the interview data.

Data analysis. The data collected for this study is qualitative in nature. Interview data were transcribed and coded into categories to explore the emerging themes regarding early childhood teachers' pedagogical practices and beliefs about teaching STEM integrated curriculum.

Professional Development. The lead teachers in each study received a series of professional development sessions that were designed to help teachers develop both content knowledge and pedagogical knowledge as it relates to STEM curriculum. Each teacher participated in three formal professional development sessions over the course of study (March – May). Professional development sessions were continuous (90 minutes each) and facilitated by the researchers and a former kindergarten teacher with expertise in science and engineering. The content of each professional development session targeted the STEM curriculum topics that were pre-selected by the teachers themselves: living and non-living, ocean animals, and the human body in the 1st study; weather and water, motion and the human body in the 2nd study. All the topics were explored via project-based learning activities. In each session, the participants discussed, brainstormed on teaching strategies and activities, investigated and practiced the process, as they would do in a classroom with a group of young children. Moreover, the two researchers served as a mentor and support engaging teachers in conversations about their practice and helping out with planning and implementing of units/projects when needed.

4. FINDINGS

Five themes emerged from the analysis of the interview data. Researchers' observational notes of teachers' classroom practices helped triangulate the themes. The following section explains each theme exemplified with quotations from the participants' interviews.

Impact on teacher learning/understanding of STEM curriculum. The professional development was designed to allow teachers to become familiar and comfortable with both content and pedagogy surrounding STEM curriculum. Teachers in both studies were provided with STEM related resources that they could utilize in their classrooms. Furthermore, the research team supported teachers' curriculum plans with materials that they desired and the research team found helpful. In their interview, all four teachers reported how their pedagogical practice was impacted by such professional development–they explained it helped them widened their knowledge and skills in STEM subjects. Jenna and Brook specifically noted how they came to realize that they had often stayed within the boundaries of the common practice employed in their programs in regards to curriculum planning. STEM professional development sessions encouraged them to try out different pedagogical practices such as intentional teaching or trying different modalities to search new information.

Increased confidence about teaching STEM. As part of the professional development, the participants were provided with hands-on learning experiences that focused on pedagogical and STEM content knowledge. As mentioned earlier, our goal was to provide the teachers with some of the same STEM integrated experiences that their students will have in the classroom. This increase in the pedagogical and STEM content knowledge helped boost teachers' level of confidence both in the planning and implementation of the STEM integrated curriculum. Furthermore, as teachers gained more comfort in handling the STEM related activities and materials, they showed more commitment to the STEM. That being said, it is important to note that although all four teachers implemented the STEM curriculum in their classroom, not all showed the same level of knowledge, comfort and pedagogical skills in STEM. This variance in teachers' knowledge, skills and comfort level seemed to have affected what was accomplished in those classes. Nonetheless, all teachers showed some level of confidence with STEM subjects that helped them with both planning and implementation. For example, in her interview, Tammy explained about how the STEM project helped her shift her focus from getting the right answers to using the right process when planning and implementing STEM integrated lessons.

Need for STEM related materials and resources including access to technology. Integrated STEM curriculum requires appropriate and stimulating materials/resources for teachers as well as children to investigate, problem-solve, design, and test and retest hypotheses. Schools that have little to no funds to afford appropriate materials and/or consumable supplies may hinder early childhood teachers from effectively engaging their students with STEM related activities. As part of this study, each classroom received a collection of STEM related materials and resources for children as well as teachers. All teachers revealed in their interview that the provision of STEM related materials and resources motivated both their learning and teaching practice.

Impacts on children's learning. A common theme found in teachers' interviews was the extent and quality of learning that occurred among children. Overwhelmingly, teachers explained that STEM curriculum offered their students numerous opportunities to be active, engaged, and take initiatives in their own learning. Based on the observational notes taken by the researchers, we saw a significant association between teachers' content and pedagogical knowledge and children's learning. The higher the teachers' competence in pedagogical and STEM content knowledge the greater the students' level of engagement and conversations surrounding the STEM units and activities. This observation/finding is well supported by previous work showing a direct association between the instructional approach of the teacher and student achievement, indicating that students are more likely to learn from teachers with higher levels of instructional competency (e.g., Brophy & Good, 1986; Polly et al., 2013).

Challenges with integrating a STEM integrated curriculum. In their interview, although all four teachers unequivocally marveled about the benefits of STEM project, they also explained of a number of challenges in implementing it. As part of the study, teachers were asked to complete reflective journals; collaborate with other teachers to plan if possible; facilitate children's technology use; and document children's learning. However, teachers explained in their interviews that it was hard to keep up with all these while at the same time addressing the goals/assessment required by state and their school curriculum/curricula. Teachers from Public Pre-K used a combination of curricula, Opening the World of Learning (OWL), Number Worlds and CIRCLE, whereas teachers from Head Start program used Creative Curriculum. The quotations in Table 1, row 6 highlight some of the challenges noted by these teachers.

5. DISCUSSION

The data collected from interviews of early childhood teachers from two similar studies revealed that all four teachers were positively impacted by the STEM integrated professional development, resources and the materials available to them to implement the STEM units. Consequently, children were positively impacted because of their teacher's professional learning and high confidence about teaching STEM-related activities. An early childhood teacher's beliefs in what and how young children should learn could critically impact children's acquisition of various emergent knowledge and skills in preschool years. Opportunities to improve teaching practice (e.g., teacher research), ongoing professional development support (e.g., integrating STEM), administrative policies that provide a democratic and liberated work environment for teachers, and most importantly teachers' positive self-efficacy to take on challenges would help early childhood teachers constantly reflect on their beliefs and make more conscious decisions regarding pedagogical issues. The conversations that we had with early childhood teachers in this study made us pay closer attention to the factors affecting teachers' pedagogical beliefs about integrating STEM in their classrooms.

REFERENCES

Aronin, S., & Floyd, K. (2013). Using an iPad in inclusive preschool classrooms to introduce STEM concepts. *Teaching Exceptional Children*, *45*(4), 34—39

Alade, F., Lauricella, A., Beaudoin-ryan, L., & Wartella, E. (2016). Measuring with Murray: Touchscreen technology and preschoolers' STEM learning. *Computers in Human Behavior*, 62, 433–441.

Bagiati, A., & Evangelou, D. (2015). Engineering curriculum in the preschool classroom: the teacher's experience. *European Early Childhood Education Research Journal*, *23*(1), 112-128.

Brophy, J. and Good, T. (1986) Teacher behaviour and student achievement'. In M. Wittrock (ed) *Handbook of research on teaching*. New York: Macmillan.

Chen, J., McCray, J., Adams, M., & Leow, C. (2013). (2013). A survey study of early childhood teachers' beliefs and confidence about teaching early math. *Early Childhood Education Journal, 42*, 367-377.

Early Childhood STEM Working Group (2017). *Early STEM matters: Providing high-quality STEM for all young learners*. UChicago STEM Education & Erikson Institute. Chicago, IL.

Fang, Z. (1996). A review of research on teacher beliefs and practices. *Educational Research*, *38*(1), 47-65.

Chesloff, J. D. (2013). STEM Education Must Start in Early Childhood. *Education Week*, *32* (23), 27.

Kagan, D. M. (1992). Implications of research on teacher belief. *Educational Psychologist, 27,* 65-90.

Nespor, J. (1987). The role of beliefs in the practice of teaching. *Journal of Curriculum Studies*, *19*(4), 317-328.

Nores, M., & Barnett, W. S. (2014). Access to high quality early care and education: Readiness and opportunity gaps in America. National Institute for Early Education and Center on Enhancing Early Learning Policy report.

Park, M., Dimitrov, L., Patterson, L., & Park. D. (2016). Early childhood teachers' beliefs about readiness for teaching science, technology, engineering, and mathematics. *Journal of Early Childhood Research*, *15* (3), 275-291.

Polly, D., McGee, J., Wang, C., Lambert, R., Pugalee, D., & Johnson, S. (2015). The Association between Teachers' Beliefs, Enacted Practices, and Student Learning in Mathematics. *The Mathematics Educator, 22*(2). Retrieved from http://tme.journals.libs.uga.edu/index.php/tme/article/view/253

Roehrig, G. H., Kruse, R. A., & Kern, A. L. (2007). Teacher and school characteristics and their influence on curriculum implementation. *Journal of Research in Science Teaching, 44*, 883-907.

Wang, H., Moore, T., Roehrig, G. H., & Park, M. S. (2011). STEM Integration: Teacher Perceptions and Practice. *Journal of Pre-College Engineering Education Research (J-PEER)*, *1*(2), 1–13.

COMPARATIVE STUDY OF TEACHING MATHEMATICS IN TWO UNIVERSITIES IN LATVIA

Evija Kopeika[1] and Anna Vintere[2]
[1]Riga Technical University, Daugavgrivas Street 2, Riga, Latvia
[2]Latvia University of Life Sciences and Technologies, Liela Sreet 2, Jelgava, Latvia, LV-3001

ABSTRACT

The role of mathematical education in everyday life, professional activities, attitude towards the role of mathematical knowledge in the labour market is widely discussed in the literature. To improve the studies of mathematics according to the trends in society development, it is necessary to find out the mathematics teaching philosophy as well as to reflect views of the students on the issues of mathematics learning experience and mathematics teaching at university. The structure of mathematical study process for energy and electronics specialties at the RTU and LLU and the survey results, which was carried out at the Latvia University of Life Sciences and Technologies (LLU) and at the Riga Technical University (RTU), are analysed in this article. The questionnaire includes three diagnostic blocks: the role of mathematics in everyday life; in professional work / in relation to the labour market, and mathematics for the general development of a person. The total sample of the research included 887 cases. The results showed that the RTU students were more confident about their mathematical knowledge. They were ready to apply the acquired knowledge of mathematics in a new context and situation, while students of the LLU had more developed ability to use the acquired knowledge and apply in specific situations. A self-assessment method was used in the study; the results were based on respondents' opinion. Since this was a case study and it only reflects the views of the students who participated in the survey, the results did not provide generalizations, however, the study was conducted to identify problems, to carry out a more in-depth study of them and to search for solutions.

KEYWORDS

Mathematics, Mathematics Study Process Organization, Self-Assessment, Teaching Mathematics

1. INTRODUCTION

Human capital has become the cornerstone of economic and social well-being in the 21st century. In contemporary knowledge-intensive economies and societies, individual and societal progress is increasingly driven by technological advances. Prosperity requires nations to retain their competitive edge by developing and sustaining a skilled workforce, maintaining a globally competitive research base, and improving the dissemination of knowledge for the benefit of society at large. In this context, higher education represents a critical factor in innovation and human capital development and plays a central role in the success and sustainability of the knowledge economy (Dill and Van Vught, 2010).

In order to find out how the mathematical teaching guidelines and philosophy affect the skills and abilities of students to apply them comprehensively, from the spring of 2017 till June 2018 the researchers conducted a study in the 2 largest Latvian universities – the Latvia University of Life Sciences and Technologies (LLU) and the Riga Technical University (RTU). The questionnaire included three diagnostic blocks: the role of mathematics in everyday life; in professional work / in relation to the labour market and mathematics for the general development of a person. The study used a self-assessment method, therefore, the results were based on respondents' opinion. The results did not provide generalizations, however, the study was conducted to identify common problems, to carry out an in-depth study of them and to search for solutions.

Respondents were required to evaluate the indicated statements by expressing approval or rejection of the four-step *Likert* scale: *I fully agree*, *I agree*, *I disagree*, and *I completely disagree*.

The survey involved 887 respondents, and since the questionnaires were filled in sufficient quality, leaving no blank response windows, all evaluations have been taken into account in the calculations. As the specialties of the two universities differed significantly, in order to make the results to be maximally usable and equally assessable, in the study that is reflected in this article, one student group was selected and analysed from both universities: young people who study energy and electronics specialties from the RTU, and students of the energy specialties at the LLU.

2. MATERIALS AND METHODS

In order to maximally integrate mathematical knowledge and skills of young specialists into both routine problem solving and in professional circumstances, it was necessary to evaluate the basic guidelines and goals of the existing mathematics programs. The study had two parts: 1) to compare and study the aims of mathematics teaching in RTU and LLU; 2) to evaluate the competences acquired in RTU and LLU.

Questionnaires were sent to all students of LLU and RTU (both on-site and out-of-school) to assess students' competence in mathematics, not only by using database records of student achievements in higher mathematics, additional sections in higher mathematics in energy and electronics specialties, but also to understand to what extent applicants use their acquired skills to prepare for the labour market. The activity of respondents depending on the university has been shown in Table 1.

Table 1. Distribution of respondents depending on the university

		Absolute values	Percentage
University	LLU	244	28%
	RTU	643	72%
Total		**887**	

According to Table 1 the number of students at both universities might not seem proportional, but the sample size in each institution was logical since in 2016 14,997 applicants studied in the RTU, and 4353 in the LLU (which were 29% of the RTU students) In turn, emerging electronics and energy specialists constituted 26% of all respondents.

The future labour market cannot exist without comprehensive knowledge and competences in mathematics.

In 2000 a number of higher education institutions across Europe took part in the project "Tuning Educational structures in Europe" in which several competences were set as learning outcomes – instrumental, interpersonal and systemic. In many ways mathematical knowledge is ingrained in these competences (cognitive, methodological, technological etc. abilities). In 2006 the European Commission declared to strengthen key competences for personal fulfilment, development, and employability. They also included mathematical competence: 1. ability to solve everyday problems, using thinking patterns (logical or spatial), depicting/portraying (formulas, constructs, graphs, diagrams etc.); 2. ability to identify structure and links, repeatability and systematicity. In 2016 in the World Economic Forum "The Future of Employment" three out of ten main targets were directly connected to mathematical knowledge – solving complex problems, critical thinking and creativity.

Mathematical knowledge in the study process is crucial since: 1. the problem-solving in mathematical situations and the demonstration of relationships improves logical thinking, the ability to solve complex problems; 2. while studying comprehensive and complex solutions to mathematical problems, students develop systematic competences and critical thinking; 3. while working in a group on more complex non-routine tasks students develop their creativity.

When evaluating the teaching methods, basic principles and objectives of mathematical teaching in the RTU and LLU, it should be noted that they differed significantly, although the programs were similar. Therefore, it is important to take into account how differences in attitudes affect the knowledge acquired during the course of studies and the ability to apply them.

The study objectives in the LLU: to acquire mathematical knowledge and practical skills necessary for the study of future special courses. The study objectives in the RTU: to acquire basic knowledge in mathematics necessary for the successful mastering of specialty subjects;

The study results in the LLU: to develop students' logical thinking and application skills in relation to specialty subjects and their basic objects in order to provide students with the ability to analyse solutions for the most complex tasks. The study results in the RTU: to develop students' logical thinking and application skills in relation to specialty subjects and their basic objects in order to provide students with the ability to analyse solutions for the most complex tasks.

Assessing approaches for achieving these objectives, students of the equivalent specialty studies in mathematics – energetics and electronics – were selected.

The questionnaire analysis showed that the volume of RTU lectures in higher mathematics (within the framework of ECTS 13.5) was 80 hours, whereas in the LLU it was 72 hours; practical lessons were 96 hours and 72 hours respectively, as well as 40 hours of laboratory work in the LLU, which demonstrates that the LLU teaching process of mathematics emphasized practical tasks, solving various general tasks both in mind and using computer programs. In turn, the RTU worked more on theoretical material, presenting theories in classes and discussing with the students not only the basic elements of mathematics, but also their physical and economic core functions, and when the guidelines were set out and part of them were proved, the attention was paid to the use of practical skills applications in specific situations. In order to find out which of these approaches was more effective, students' answers to several questions related to mathematical competences, as well as some test results were studied and analysed.

At the beginning of the studies (September 2017), for maximizing the further work efficiency and adapting the forms of training for the particular study course, all students were invited to complete the preliminary knowledge test consisting of several simple examples in which students could demonstrate their basic knowledge and skills in mathematics

According to the preliminary test the assessment of 46% of RTU and 37% of LLU students' knowledge was insufficient, for 29% of RTU and 27% of LLU students – mediocre, but good and excellent only for 24% and 32% of the students. This could be due to the fact that after the end of study period, the break was 3 months, for college and technical schools` graduates – even one and a half years.

In order to help young people to understand the study material taught at the university, young people are offered optional (for those RTU students who have passed the test unsuccessfully – compulsory) subject "Additional chapters in elementary mathematics", during which it is possible to repeat forgotten concepts.

LLU and RTU researchers, having conducted a student survey, in which students evaluate their knowledge themselves, discovered that students were sufficiently self-critical and understood that good skills in mathematics are necessary to become a high-end specialist in electronics or energy. The results of the tests and student self-assessment were equivalent. Despite the low evaluation of mathematical knowledge, 78% of students said they were ready and willing to devote more time to math, either working independently or consulting with instructors, or in groups, creating "maths fan clubs" which RTU Electronics and Mobile Communication specialty students have been organizing for several years.

A university should create such study environment that would interest students in active participation during the study process, in developing creative tasks at home, not being afraid to enter into disputes and discuss problems and obstacles with educators. When students feel more comfortable they develop their judgment, ability to detect problems, analyse and develop rational scenarios for solutions. It is important to create positivism rather than fear – a positive attitude towards learning and work motivates for better results, including in mathematics studies. In order to create or improve this environment, it is necessary to find out the attitude and assessment of the students. Students were asked: "Please express your opinion on teaching mathematics at a university" from several aspects.

The students` answers were not unambiguous and they thoughts were changing. For example, 56% of RTU and 77% of LLU students emphasized that mathematics classes at university are formal and boring, but in response to the next question, 75% of RTU and 76% of LLU students claimed that the same training had been interesting and meaningful. Such results indicate that individual responses were influenced by several factors that require more precise data analysis; for instance, one of the topics to be learned was more simple whereas another was harder (students remember last lesson the best), how many lectures respondents had listened to, whether they had only attended lectures or only practical classes, maybe they periodically went to both classes, if students had attended special consultations provided by instructors. Having summed up all these factors and discussed problems with students, one can conclude that students who had understood the mathematical connexions in high school and were also doing their best at the institution of higher education, did not experience difficulties in learning mathematics and being able to subsequently use it in the acquisition of professional study subjects. Whereas those students that had rather poor maths knowledge at the beginning of their studies at university (initial test results – 0-3), but were diligent at participating in all classes, consultations and different activities provided by educators, successfully overcame their difficulties when the objectives were clearly given. The electronics students of RTU who had insufficient maths assessment in the beginning of the studies, but attended 100% of lectures and consultations had a positive growth of average grade in mathematics during the study year.

When comparing the answers of the applicants from both universities, it was clear that the differences were not significant, and the RTU students' assessment of the study process and their acquired knowledge only slightly exceeded the results of the LLU. For example, 82% of RTU and 81% of LLU students admitted that the knowledge acquired in the higher education institution in mathematics helped them to understand other subjects.

3. CONCLUSION

The investigation of the multilateral learning process, both from the scope and quality of the inquiry, and from the attitude and skills of students and teachers, allowed the researchers to understand the opportunities for intellectual growth and cognitive development as well as their role in the learning process.

The study conducted the comparison of the results of the higher mathematics study process in 2 largest universities of Latvia – RTU and LLU, and the following conclusions were made:

- the results of the initial tests demonstrated that in the 2017/18 academic year the results of the energy students of the LLU were slightly higher than those of RTU electronics students;
- 45% of RTU electronics students fully acknowledged that the acquired knowledge in mathematics helped them to understand other subjects and solve various problem tasks and develop scenarios for their solution, while 37% of them agreed with the statement; in LLU the numbers accordingly were 51% and 30%;
- both universities had a mathematics support system for students – preparatory courses, course of elementary mathematics repetition, internet/ e-resources, additional consultations, etc.
- RTU students were confident about their mathematical knowledge. One of the reasons for this situation might be that the purpose of RTU mathematics courses is more specific, but in LLU it is more broad and includes seven mathematical competences;
- RTU students were ready to apply the acquired knowledge of mathematics in a new context and situation, while students of the LLU had more developed ability to use the acquired knowledge and apply in specific situations of life.

The **self-evaluation method** was mostly used in the research, thus the results were based on the opinion of the respondents, and therefore the results cannot be generalized, but they can be used to identify problems and to explore them further.

REFERENCES

Dill, D. and F. Van Vught (eds) (2010), National Innovation and the Academic Research Enterprise; Public Policy in Global Perspective, the Johns Hopkins University Press, Baltimore.

Uysal E. (2014). The Mathematics Education for the Engineering Students of 21st Century. *The Online Journal of Hew Horizons in Education,* 4(2), 65-72. Retrieved from http://www.tojned.net/?pid=showissue&issueid=96

www.aic.lv/ar/macibsp/4_2_LV%20likumdos_Bol.pdf

AN INVESTIGATION INTO PARENTS' CONCERNS ABOUT PROGRAMMING EDUCATION IN JAPANESE PRIMARY SCHOOLS

Yukiko Maruyama
Tokai University, Hiratsuka Kanagawa, Japan

ABSTRACT

To investigate the effects that experiences of programming have on parents' concerns about programming education in primary schools, a survey was carried out before and after a programming seminar for children and their parents. Participation in the programming seminar seemed to boost parents' expectations and decrease their anxieties about introducing programming education to primary schools. Findings also suggest that parents' attitudes and confidence in involvement in supplementary instruction at home improved. Since the survey is ongoing, the number of participants in this study was limited. It is necessary to carry out a statistical analysis with more participants.

KEYWORDS

Programming Education, Primary School, Parents' Concerns, Computing Thinking, Logical Thinking, Problem-Solving

1. INTRODUCTION

There have been widespread attempts to introduce computational thinking to primary/secondary or K-12 education (Barr 2011, Grover 2013). The term "computational thinking" was first used by Papert (1993), and popularized by Wing (2006). According to Wing, " 'Computational thinking' involves solving problems, designing systems, and understanding human behavior, by drawing on concepts that are fundamental to computer science." (p. 33). Additionally, she stated that computational thinking is a fundamental skill for everyone and that it should be added to every child's analytical ability. The article drew the attention of many education researchers and educators, and many researches related to computational thinking in K-12 have since been carried out. In the United Kingdom, a new subject, "computing," was introduced to primary and secondary schools. In the primary teachers' guide for the subject "computing," the importance of computational thinking is repeatedly stated.

As computational thinking increasingly draws attention, programming education is also receiving attention as one of the ways of teaching computational thinking. Lye and Koh (2014) state that "programming is more than just coding, for it exposes students to computational thinking which involves problem-solving using computer science concepts, and is useful in their daily lives" (p.51). In Japan, the central council for education in the Ministry of Education, Culture, Sports, Science, and Technology submitted a report that mentioned the introduction of programming education to primary schools. Another council report said that programming education in primary schools should not aim to merely teach students coding, but rather to foster students' programming thinking. Programming thinking is considered to be a similar concept to computational thinking and a part of computational thinking. However, the misconception that the aim of programming education is to learn coding has begun to spread among parents. The parents' role in primary education is very important, and their attitudes toward education have considerable influence on children's attitudes. Indeed, some researchers have investigated parent-child collaboration in learning programming (Lin and Liu 2012, Hart 2010). Parents' misconceptions and anxieties related to programming education could become obstacles to their involvement in children's learning. To smoothly and appropriately introduce computer education to primary schools, it is important to know parents' concerns about programming education. Moreover, it is necessary to encourage parents' involvement in programming education.

This study aims to establish a support system for parents to get them involved in programming education in primary schools. This paper provides the results of a preliminary investigation into the influence of participation in a programming seminar for children and parents on changes in parents' concerns about programming education in Japanese primary schools.

2. INVESTIGATION

The survey for this study was conducted in August 2018. Participation in the survey took place at programming seminars for children and their parents, which were organized by the author. Three kinds of programming seminars were held. One was for first and second grade primary school students and their parents, and wooden robots were used as teaching materials. Another one was for third to sixth grade students and their parents, and toy robots were used. The last one was for first to sixth grade students and their parents, and visual programming language was used. Participants were recruited via brochures distributed through seven local public primary schools in Kanagawa which is nearby Tokyo. Participants required to attend to seminars as a group of students and their parents or guardians. Sixty-three groups of students and parents took part in the seminars. Two of them include two students, and one group include both parents.

Participants in seminars were handed two questionnaires at the reception of programming seminars and were asked to fill them before and after the seminar respectively; this was voluntary. Fifty-four valid responses were obtained. Of the 54 participants in the survey, 40 were mothers, 13 were fathers, and one was a grandfather of primary school children. The average age of participants was 42.0. The ages of participants and school years of their children are shown in Tables 1 and 2, respectively.

Table 1. Ages of participants

Age	Frequency
-39	15
40-44	23
45-49	8
50-54	3
55-	1

four were non-responses

Table 2. School years of participants' children

School year	Frequency
1	7
2	7
3	7
4	15
5	10
6	9

Questionnaires included the following sections, 1) demographics of participants and their children (for pre-questionnaire), 2) participants' perceptions of programming, 3) attitudes toward programming education in primary schools, 4) expectations of introducing programming education to primary schools, 5) anxieties regarding the introduction of programming education, and 6) participants' experiences of computer usage (for pre-questionnaire). There were other questions that sought responses from children, but the results of these questions have not been included in this paper. Table 3 shows items in part 3, 4 and 5.

With regard to part 5, two researches related to English education in primary school(Morita 2011, Makino 2008) were referred for making the items. The reasons for referring is as follows.

1)There are few research related to programming education in primary school focusing on parents' concerns.

2)English education will be introduced into primary school as a subject in Japan from 2020. Compared with programming education, English education in primary school appears to get more attention from researchers. Therefor there are many insightful researches. It is apparent that useful suggestions for researches on programming education can be gained from those researches.

The aim of study by Morita (2011) was to establish the learning environment at home for English education. They stated that it is necessity to know parents' concerns regarding English education to establish the environment. Therefor they considered studiously items for questionnaire for investigating parents' concerns and decided to include items about parents' anxieties regarding English education.

Makino (2008) carried out a survey on parents' concerns on English education in primary school. The results of the survey showed that parents were anxious about contents and policies of education and teachers.

3. RESULTS

The survey is still ongoing and the number of responses at this stage is not enough for a statistical analysis. This paper provides a summary of the changes in parents' attitudes, expectations, and anxieties regarding programming education, and discusses their attitudes toward supplementary instruction at home before and after the seminars.

With regard to attitudes toward programming education in primary schools, participants were asked to choose a response from a five-point Likert scale ranging from 1- I completely agree to 5 - I completely disagree for six items in Table 3. Figure 1 shows changes in the average values of each item for all participants' responses before and after the seminars. A low value means positive attitudes for items 1, 2, 3, and 5, and negative attitudes for items 4 and 6. Although parents' attitudes changed and became positive, a tendency for participants to agree with the statement "Elementary school is too early to learn programming" was identified.

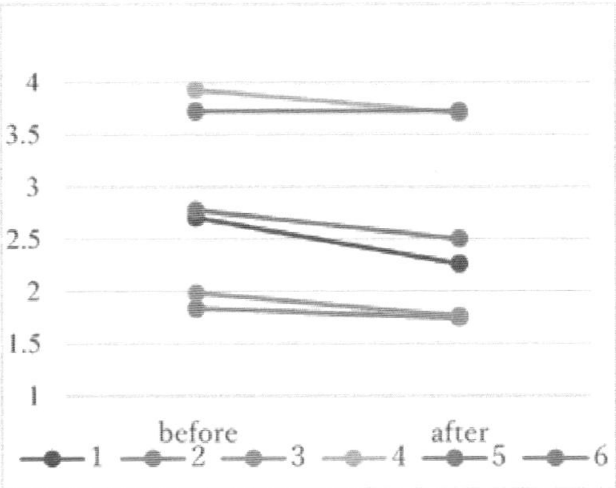

Figure 1. The mean value of responses to questions concerning parents' attitudes

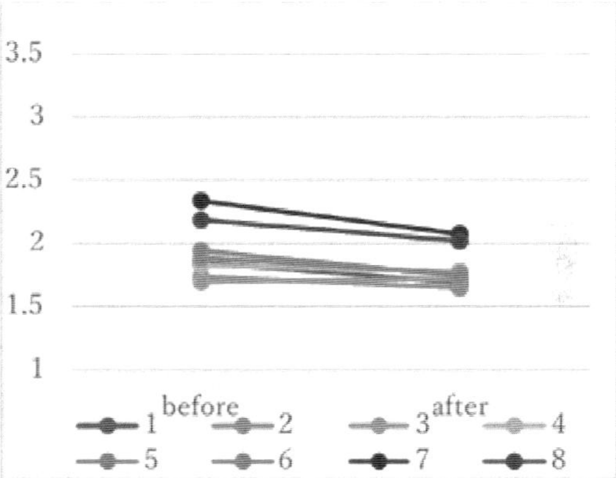

Figure 2. The mean value of responses to questions concerning parents' expectations (1-8)

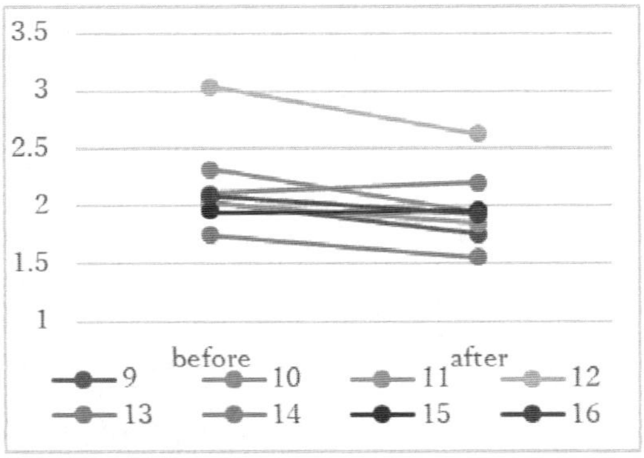

Figure 3. The mean value of responses to questions concerning parents' expectations (9-16)

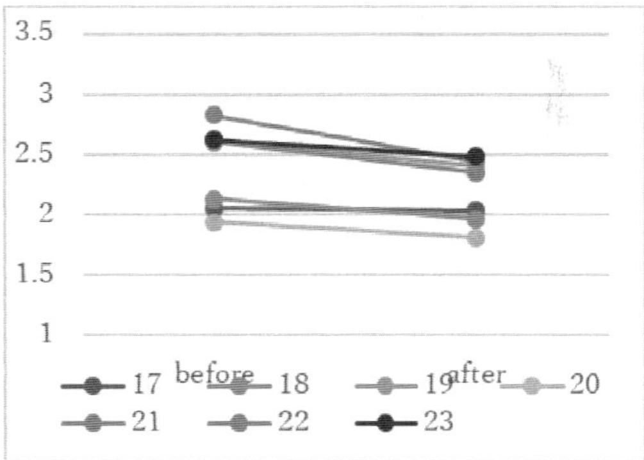

Figure 4. The mean value of responses to questions concerning parents' expectations (17-23)

With regard to expectations for introducing programming education, participants were asked to respond according to a five-point Likert scale ranging from 1 - I fully expect it, to 5 - I do not expect it at all, for 23 items in Table 3. Figures 2, 3, and 4 show changes in the average values of each item for all participants' responses before and after the seminars. A low value indicates high expectation. Overall, parents' expectations seemed to rise, especially for the statements, "Children will learn to be creative," "Children will learn how to express themselves," and "Children will be better able to communicate."

With regard to anxieties regarding the introduction of programming education, participants were asked to choose a response from a five-point Likert scale ranging from 1- I am very anxious to 5 - I am not anxious at all, for 10 items in Table 3. Figure 5 shows changes in the average values of each item for all participants' responses before and after the seminars. Only for the statement "There are not enough teachers to provide instruction" did parents' anxiety increase.

Overall, it seems that patents' attitudes toward programming education became positive, the expectations for introducing programming education increased, and anxieties decreased.

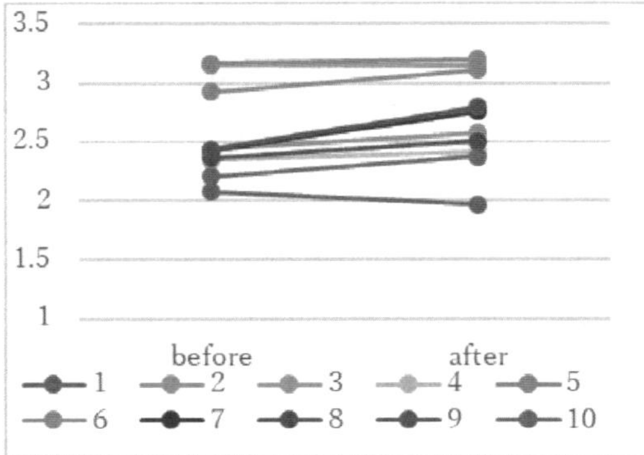

Figure 5. The mean value of responses to questions concerning parents' anxieties

With regard to attitudes toward supplementary lessons at home, participants were asked to answer three questions; 1.) Do you think supplementary instruction outside of school will be necessary for programming education? 2.) Do you think you will be involved in supplementary instruction for programming education at home? and 3.) If you will be involved in supplementary instruction at home, how much confidence do you have in your involvement? Figures 6 to 8 show the result. Before the seminars, more than half of the participants replied with "Do not think really so" or "Do not think so at all" to question 1. However, about 70% of the participants replied with "Very much think so" or "Think so somewhat" after the seminars. Concerning the necessity for supplementary instruction, participants' awareness seems to have increased. Concerning question 2, the number of participants who answered "Will not be very involved" decreased from 11% to 2%. On the contrary, the number of participants who answered "Will be actively involved to a certain extent" increased from 17% to 30%. Concerning question 3, the number of participants who answered "I'm not confident at all" decreased from 32% to 9%. On the contrary, the number of participants who answered, "I'm somewhat confident" increased from 23% to 35%. It seemed that the attitude and confidence in involvement in supplementary instruction at home also improved.

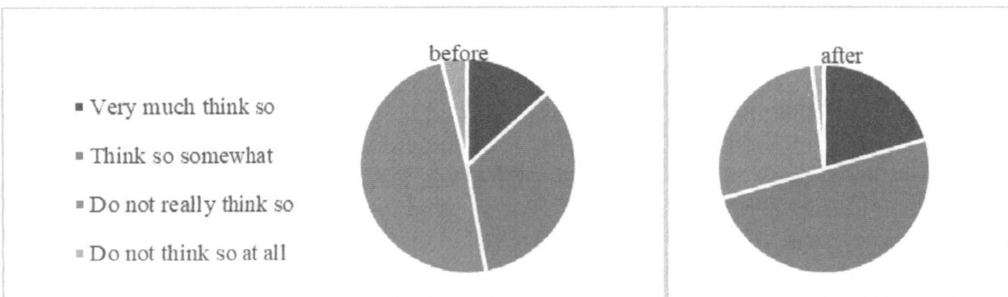

Figure 6. Views on necessity of supplementary instruction

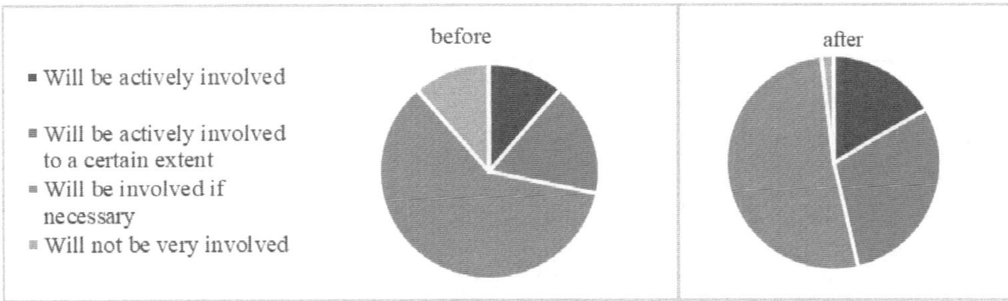

Figure 7. Involvement in supplementary instruction

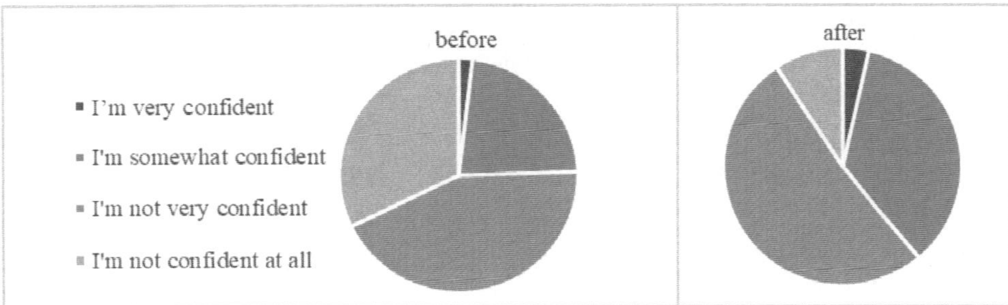

Figure 8. Confidence in involvement in supplementary instruction

4. CONCLUSION AND FUTURE WORK

It seemed that participation in programming seminar boosts parents' expectations and decreases anxieties about introducing programming education to primary schools. It also suggests that parents' attitudes and confidence in involvement in supplementary instruction at home improved. Since the survey is ongoing, the number of participants was limited. It is necessary to carry out statistical analysis with more participants. A brief acknowledgement section may be included here.

REFERENCES

Barr, V., and Stephenson, C., 2011. Bringing computational thinking to K-12: What is involved and what is the role of the computer science education community? *Acm Inroads*, Vol. 2, No. 1, pp. 48-54.

Grover, S., and Pea, R., 2013. Computational thinking in K–12: A review of the state of the field. *Educational Researcher*, Vol. 42, No. 1, pp. 38-43.

Hart, M. L., Making contact with the forgotten K-12 influence: Are you smarter than YOUR 5th grader? *Proceedings of the 41st ACM technical symposium on Computer science education*, Wisconsin, USA, pp. 254-258.

Lin, J. M.-C., and Liu, S.-F., 2012. An investigation into parent-child collaboration in learning computer programming. *Educational Technology & Society*, Vol.15, No.1, pp162–173.

Lye, S. Y., and Koh, J. H. L., 2014, Review on teaching and learning of computational thinking through programming: What is next for K-12? *Computers in Human Behavior*, Vol. 41, pp. 51-61.

Makino, M., 2008. Parental perception of English activities at elementary schools – focusing on expectation and involvement-, *Research Institute for Communication, Kansai University of International Studies, Studies on Communication*, 6, 61-73 (in Japanese).

Morita, A., 2011. Data analysis of parents' involvement in primary school English language education, *Waseda review of Education*, 25, 1, 163 – 172 (in Japanese).

Papert, S. 1993. *Mindstorms: Children, Computers, and Powerful Ideas*, 2nd ed, Basic Books, New York.

Wing, J.M. 2006. Computational Thinking, *Communications of the ACM*, Vol. 49, No. 3, pp. 33-35.

Table 3. Questions concerning parents' attitudes, expectations and anxieties about introducing programming education

Attitudes (How do you feel about programming being taught in school?)
(1) Everyone needs to know how to program.
(2) Programming should be taught from elementary school.
(3) Programming will be required in future societies, so it should be taught in elementary school.
(4) Elementary school is too early to learn programming.
(5) Programming should be part of the elementary school curriculum.
(6) Programming will affect students' other studies, so it should not be taught in elementary school.
Expectations (Do you expect the following outcomes as a result of introducing programming education?)
(1) Children will become skilled at using computers
(2) Children will like using computers
(3) Children will learn to think logically
(4) It will help with work in the future
(5) Children will learn how to use information and communications technology (ICT)
(6) Children will learn ICT skills
(7) It will foster personnel with advanced ICT skills
(8) Children will learn problem-solving skills
(9) Children will learn to be creative
(10) Children will learn how to express themselves
(11) Children will acquire problem-identification skills
(12) Children will be better able to communicate
(13) Children will be inclined to use computers
(14) Children will be able to use a computer to write compositions
(15) Children will be able to use a computer to draw pictures
(16) Children will understand how a computer works.
(17) Children will be able to write computer programs.
(18) Children will learn how to use the internet.
(19) Children will understand arithmetic and science.
(20) Children will think about the steps one must follow when performing a task.
(21) Children will be better able to study other subjects.
(22) Children will be better able to communicate their thoughts.
(23) Children will be better able to work with others.
Anxieties (Are you anxious about the following items concerning programming education in primary schools?)
(1) There are not enough teachers to provide instruction
(2) The aim of programming education is not clear
(3) Perhaps programming will adversely affect the study of other subjects
(4) The content taught differs depending on the school and teacher
(5) The burden on children will increase
(6) I wonder whether my child can keep up
(7) I wonder whether I can provide guidance at home?
(8) Perhaps there are inequalities in the degrees of comprehension
(9) Contents of programming education are not clear
(10) I wonder whether the teacher can take care of the whole class.

SELF-EVALUATION OF OPEN ANSWERS AS A BASIS FOR ADAPTIVE LEARNING SYSTEMS

Egon Werlen and Per Bergamin
Institute for Research in Open-, Distance- and eLearning (IFeL)
Swiss Distance University of Applied Sciences (FFHS), Switzerland

ABSTRACT

The continuous measurement of learning behavior or learning outcome by appropriate sensors is fundamental for the implementation of technology-based adaptive learning courses. An adaptive system needs such learning data to adapt the instruction to the needs of students. Depending on the learning objective, the sensors use information generated within tasks as basis for instructional adaptation, such as closed clear answers to learning tasks or more ambiguous open answers. In the second case, the use of self-evaluation concepts is one possibility. However, the automation and corresponding generation of learning data for adaptive systems is difficult because the answers are not clearly correct or incorrect. In a preliminary study we constructed a corresponding self-evaluation scaffold in the context of a Blended-Learning course in health psychology with 60 adult students. The goal of the study was to analyze if self-evaluation delivers valid data for sensors of an intended adaptive learning system, and what influences the accuracy of the self-evaluation. Therefore, we conducted an external evaluation of the students' answers. The correlation of the self-evaluation with the external evaluation was moderate ($r=.50$; $p < .001$), and there was a large overlap of 65.9% between self- and external evaluation. The difference between self-evaluation and external evaluation can partly be explained by the task and subtask used, the difficulty of the task and the quality of the answers. In this respect, these results provide us with initial insights into what must be taken into account when designing corresponding sensors with an open response format. The analyses have also encouraged the development of a technology-based adaptive course on the basis of corresponding sensors.

KEYWORDS

Self-Evaluation, Validity, Adaptive Learning, Sensors, Measurement

1. INTRODUCTION

Technology-based adaptive learning systems require a continuous flow of learning data in order to continuously and effectively adapt learning objects or instructions to the current needs of learners. For this purpose, sensors (measuring methods) must be found which, for example, provide the system with regular data on whether and how well a learner has solved certain tasks. In learning modules that aim at factual knowledge and its reproduction and in which clear answers can be determined, as is often the case in basic courses in natural sciences or vocabulary training in language courses, sensors usually deal with numbers or precisely defined terms. However, at all levels of education, especially university level or professional education, there are often no clear correct or incorrect answers to certain tasks. In such cases the solution can be the use of open answers. Such open answers cause additional challenges for the implementation of adaptive systems.

One way to measure the correctness of open answers is to compare the learners' self-evaluation with given standard answers. On this basis, we have developed a scaffold in the context of processing case vignettes in a module of health psychology, in which students compare their answers and evaluation of counselling procedures and activities with a standard answer and comment on it.

2. THEORETICAL BACKGROUND AND RESEARCH QUESTION

Modern adaptive learning systems are characterized by various adaptive instructional interventions in a dynamic technology-based learning environment. Learning content, navigation and learning support continually change during the learning process that are adapted to the individual requirements of the learners (Wauters, Desmet, & van den Noortgate, 2003).

Wauters et al. (2003) distinguishes three basic factors for adaptation: 1) personal characteristics (stable, situational), 2) content-specific characteristics, and 3) context-based characteristics. Information from all these factors may be used to adapt the learning process. They have to be measured and stored. For the development and implementation of our adaptive system on the basis of open questions and corresponding answers, we rely on a model of Zimmermann, Specht and Lorenz (2005). In this approach the measurements are described as Sensors. The data of the sensors are analyzed and categorized in the Analyzer. It determines the basis of the adaptation (e.g. person, content, context, ...). The Controller implements the adaptation mechanism and determines what threshold and in which way the learning process is adapted, i.e. it defines the object of adaptation (content, prompts, form, etc.). Based on the decision of the Controller, the Presenter displays the concrete objects of adaptation.

A first central component are the sensors, their measurement quality strongly influences both the way the system functions and the quality of the entire system. To measure the correctness of the students' open format answers we implemented the above-mentioned self-evaluation concept in form of a scaffold guiding comparison process for the students. The scaffold with the name OPeL (Online Prompting e-Learning) was realized in the standard Learning Management System of our university (Moodle; version 1.9 and 3.2) by using its different question types following a stepwise sequence: a) problem/situation (vignette) presentation b) question, c) student answer, d) standard answer presentation e) students' comparison of the solutions f) self-reflection about differences. For different vignettes, a combination of several of these sequences was possible. Such combinations were mainly arranged to evaluate whole episodes of entire behavioral changes. In the development of the entire adaptive system, steps d), e) and f) provide the learning data for the sensor.Bourke (2014) cites Boud's (1991) definition of self-evaluation as "the involvement of students in identifying standards and/or criteria to apply to their work and making judgements about the extent to which they met these criteria and standards". It's primarily the second part of this definition that fits to our work. The students judge their own answers in comparison to a sample answer using their own standards and criteria for the comparison. The students were not trained to identify their standards or criteria. Research shows rather mixed findings to such self-evaluation approaches. There are authors reporting good results of self-evaluation (Plant, Corden, Mourad, O'Brien, & van Schaik, 2013 for pediatric crisis resource management skills; Bachman, & Palmer, 1989 for communicative language ability), others found an inappropriate validity for self-assessment (e.g. Maderick, 2013 for digital competences). Ross (2006) reports that the validity of self-assessments (i.e. comparison with teacher assessment or tests) gives mixed results. He cites the meta-analysis of Steven Ross (1998) who found a mean correlation of r=.63 within a range of r=.15 to r=.80 (k=60).

The goal of the present investigation is whether the self-evaluation within the implemented scaffold delivers valid data for sensors of the intended adaptive learning system. Further, we want to know what influences the accuracy of the self-evaluation of the answers (under-, and overestimation).

3. METHODS AND HYPOTHESES

In the course Fundamentals of Health Psychology at our university the answers from fife case vignettes used in the years 2014 to 2017 were evaluated. The mean age of all course participants was 39 in a range of 24 to 52 (and one participant 74). 36 students never used any of the proposed tasks. Of the 60 students performing at least one of the tasks 87% were women. 285 processed case vignettes with a total of 791 evaluable answers and the associated self-evaluation were evaluated. In these analyses, we included only the first attempt, if a student executed the same case vignette several times. The self-evaluation was encouraged with the request to "Compare your answer with the sample answer". The students rated their agreement on a ten-point Likert-scale from "complete disagreement" to "complete agreement", with no other indications. Three questions on a nine-point Likert-scale included in the tasks were to measure the cognitive load (Brunken,

Plass, & Leutner, 2003) of the students while completing the tasks. The intrinsic load was measured asking for the difficulty of each subtask ("How high do you estimate the difficulty of the task you just completed?“; "extremely easy" to "extremely difficult"), the extraneous load was asked for with the influence of the learning environment ("How much did the learning environment (presentation, question type, etc.) help you to solve this task?“; "did not help at all" to „was very helpful"), and the germane load was asked for with the mental effort ("How high do you estimate your mental effort to solve the task you have just solved?“; „very little effort“ to „very large effort").

To evaluate the students' self-evaluation of their answers we conducted an external rating by the teacher of all students' answers with the same scale as the students did. Additionally, the quality of the answer (formulation, errors), the students' engagement (elaboration, effort to give correct answer) and the insight contained in the self-reflexion related to the differences between students' answer and sample answer (recognizes differences, understands differences). Further ratings by other collaborators are planned. Quality, engagement, and insight were measured on a three-point scale with the possibility to give half points.

In order to evaluate the self-assessment of students' answers, we conducted on the same scale an external rating of all students' answers by the teacher. In addition, the quality of the answer (formulation, mistakes), the students' engagement (elaboration, effort to give correct answer) and the insight into self-reflection with regard to the differences between the students' answer and the model answer (recognizes differences, understands differences) were checked. Quality, commitment and insight were each measured on a three-point scale with the possibility of awarding points. The following three hypotheses formed part of our explorative analysis: 1) There is a significant correlation between self-assessment and external assessment; 2) The percentage of under- and overestimation does not exceed 50% of students' answers; 3) The difference between self- and external assessment is predicted by the task, the cognitive burden of the task and the characteristics of the students' answers (quality, commitment). Statistical analyses were conducted with R (3.3.4; R-Core-Team, 2017). For the generalized linear mixed-model, we used the lme4 pack- age of Bates et al. (2014), the p-values were calculated by means of Satterthwaite's approximation with lmerTest (Kuznetsova et al., 2017), and the pseudo- R^2 of the fixed effects with MuMln by Nakagawa and Schielzeth (2013).

4. RESULTS

The mean value of all self-evaluations was 5.81 (SD = 3.12). The average value of all external evaluations was 6.34 (SD = 2.86). The correlation between self- and external evaluation was r = .50. The agreement of the self- and external evaluations with a difference of 0 to 2 points was 65.9%. The complete match was 18.2%. There were 15.4% underestimations (including 4.0% with 6 to 9 points lower self-evaluations; high underestimation) and 18.7% overestimations (including 3.2% with 6 to 9 points higher self-evaluations; high overestimation).

We conducted a regression analyses looking for variables that influence the difference between self- and external evaluation. The table 1 shows the results of the regression analysis predicting the difference between self- and external evaluation. The explained variance of the fixed effects is 18.9%. The model is significantly better than the intercept only model (chi^2=150.45, df=9, p<.001). This difference is influenced by the task, the subtask, the difficulty of the subtasks, and the quality of the students' answers. There were five tasks, one of them was applicated only the first year (task 5). The regression analysis predicted for the first, the third (both: case vignettes following the Transtheoretical Model) and the fourth task (Health Action Process Approach) a larger difference (positive values indicating an overestimation) compared to the second task (Health Action Process Approach). For the fifth task (Social Cognitive Theory) a smaller difference was predicted (negative values indicating an underestimation). Looking at the percentages of under- and overestimation confirmed this analysis: The second task (Health Action Process Approach) and the fifth task (Social Cognitive Theory) had with 20% and 32% the highest percentages of underestimation and the lowest overestimation (17% and 7%). The first and the third task (both: Transtheoretical Model) had the lowest underestimation (9% and 5%) and with 27% and 25% the highest overestimation. The fourth task (Health Action Process Approach) was in between (underestimating 11%; overestimation 17%).

Table 1. Full Model (fixed effects) of the prediction of the difference between self-evaluation and external evaluation by task, subtask, difficulty of the subtask and quality of the answer

Predictor	β	CI (95%)	P	
Intercept	2.59	2.10 ; 3.08	< .001	***
Task 1	1.09	0.79 ; 1.38	< .001	***
Task 3	1.21	0.93 ; 1.49	< .001	***
Task 4	0.77	0.48 ; 1.05	< .001	***
Task 5	-1.41	-1.75 ; -1.07	< .008	**
Subtask 2	0.47	0.25 ; 0.70	.036	*
Subtask 3	0.96	0.72 ; 1.19	< .001	***
Subtask 4	0.26	-0.27 ; 0.79	.625	
Difficulty of subtask (self)	-0.26	-0.31 ; -0.21	< .001	***
Quality of answer (external)	-0.88	-1.04 ; -0.73	< .001	***
Observations	703			
N_{VP}	60			

After an introducing text with the case vignette, all but the second task had three subtasks. Over all five tasks, the second and the third subtask had a significantly more positive difference between self- and external evaluation, indicating higher overestimations. The first subtask had the highest underestimation (19% vs. 11% and 12%), the third subtask hat the highest overestimation (26% vs. 17% and 16%). The fourth subtask (existing only on the second task) hat a low underestimation (7%) and a high overestimation 29%. That corresponds to less underestimation and more overestimation at the latter subtasks. The predicted values for each subtask are shown in figure 1.

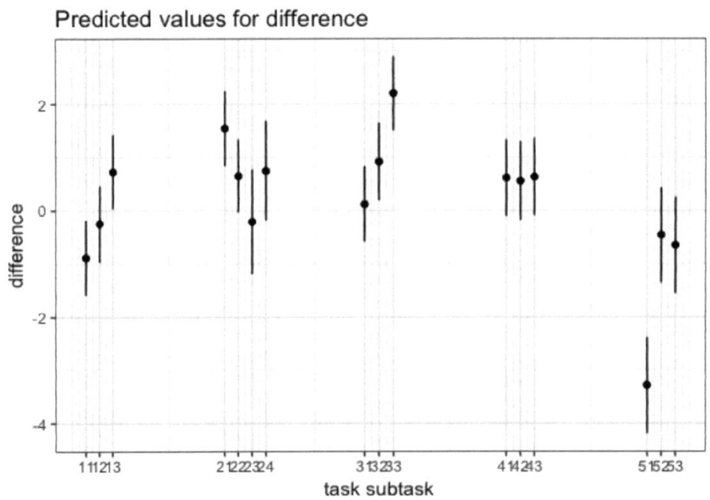

Figure 1. Predicted values for the difference between self-evaluation and external evaluation for all tasks and subtasks (task subtask: e.g. 11 = task 1, subtask 1)

The influence of the difficulty of the text and the quality of the responses was significantly predictive for the difference between self- and external evaluation of the answers. Concerning task difficulty, the easier a task as estimated by the students the higher the overestimation of the task. If the quality of the responses, rated by the teacher, was low, an overestimation was more probable.Other variables showed no influence on the differences between self- and external evaluation or showed high covariation and were therefore excluded.

5. DISCUSSION

In line with our first hypothesis, we found a correlation between self-assessment and external assessment of r=.50 (p<.001). This correlation falls in the range of correlations found in the meta-analysis by Ross (1998) with an average of r=.63 and a median of r=.49. With 65.9% most of the students estimated their answers with a difference of 0 to 2 points compared to the external evaluation confirming the second hypothesis. However, we have also found an underestimation of 15.4% and an overestimation of 18.7%. These values correspond to a formative self- and external assessment of foreign language courses (French, English) reported by Leonzini (2009). She found an underestimation of 13.3% and an overestimation of 20.2% in six classes within three years with a total of 110 students who were attending the degree course in Primary Education and in Social Services at the Faculty of Education of the University of Trieste. Poppi and Radighieri (2009) also report similar results from 20 students assessed in English reading comprehension. They found an underestimation of 15% and an overestimation of 25%.

It may also be noticed, however, that students with higher task difficulties increasingly underestimate the correctness of their answers. For example, Suzuki (2015) reports more misfits with difficult tasks (questions) compared to simpler tasks (but he gives no indication of the direction of the misfits). This contradicts somehow the findings of Leonzini (2015) that "students with a higher degree of competence were more inclined to under-estimation, while the less proficient students over-estimated themselves" (S. 123).

In this context, the main question to be resolved is how to deal with the 15% underestimates and 19% overestimates, especially the high underestimates (4%) and the high overestimates (3%). However, according to our hypothesis, the results of our regression analysis show that self-evaluation depends on the task (and sub-task), the difficulty of the task and the quality of the students' answers. This has an impact on the further development of adaptive learning environments with self-evaluation as sensors. In order to better explain the differences between self-assessments and external assessments of students' answers, we have to evaluate these differences with predefined criteria regarding possible causes for deviations in the next step. This should help to design tasks that reduce the proportion of under- and overestimates. In our first adaptive course with self-assessments as sensors we will divide case vignettes into several parts, stimulate different aspects and analyse the effects. The influence of the externally evaluated quality of the students' answers also points to differences in the motivation of the students. Therefore it is important to control the motivation of the students and to support them in their work.

Some restrictions of the study are still to be pointed out at present. The external evaluations were only made by the teacher of the course. This holds the danger of a bias. Future studies should include further raters. The framework (OPeL) from which the data were taken was not designed to test sensors for adaptive learning courses, but as a scaffold to promote meta-cognitive reflections when answering the tasks and checking the answers . In addition, the framework was implemented in two different Moodle versions (1.9, 3.2), which may have influenced several parameters (e.g. cognitive load, motivation).

6. CONCLUSION

The overlap of self-evaluation and external evaluation of the students' answers of our task with case vignettes is large but there remains a considerable amount of under- and overestimations. To get a good sensor for an adaptive learning system for open answers with a grey area of correctness we need to manage reasons for under- and overestimations. From our findings we got first insights to focus more on task-difficulty and motivation. Thus, to prevent under- and overestimations is to strive for a medium task difficulty and well-built tasks. Several studies mention the need of a training or guidance for the self-evaluation (e.g. Poppi et al., 2015). Bad quality of answers, i.e. students made little effort to formulate a well written answer, gives more overestimations. That may be due to poor motivation or uneasiness with self-evaluation. Therefore, an extended instruction e.g. by some advanced organizers on how to self-evaluate and introduce some relevant criteria might help to get more valid students self-explanations (e.g. Hsu, Lai, & Hsu, 2015; in the context of scaffolds for inquiry learning). Another way to get better matching of self- and external evaluation may be the use of a scale with fewer response options. Therefore, we transformed on a trial basis the data that were collected with a 10-point Likert-scale in a 4-point Likert-scale. The correlation of self- and external evaluation with this 4-level sensor remained nearly identical (r=.48; p<.001). Converted to a 4-point sensor, we estimate 14.5% of the answers with a larger deviation between self-evaluation and external evaluation (more than 1-point difference). That is 3.4% (n=24) of the answers with an overestimation and 11.1% (n=78) of the answers with an underestimation. Thus, we estimate a 10% higher accuracy.

All in all, we got the impression that it is possible to use the presented self-evaluation scaffold as a sensor in an adaptive system. The study encouraged us to implement the proposed sensors on an adaptive learning system using open answers as a source of adaptation.

ACKNOWLEDGEMENT

Many thanks to Dr. Stéphanie McGarrity of the Institute for Research in Open-, Distance- and eLearning (IFeL) of the FFHS for proof reading and her valuable comments.

REFERENCES

Bachman, L. F. and Palmer, A. S., 1989. The construct validation of self-ratings of communicative language ability. In *Language Testing*, Vol. 6, No. 1, pp. 14-29.

Bannert, M., 2009. Promoting self-regulated learning through prompts. In *Zeitschrift für Pädagogische Psychologie*, Vol. 23, No. 2, pp. 139-145.

Bates, D. et al., 2014. Fitting Linear Mixed-Effects Models using lme4. In *Journal of Statistical Software.* Vol 67, No. 1, pp. 1-48.

Boud, D., 1991. *Implementing student self assessment.* Green guide, no. 5. Higher Education and Development Society of Australasia Incorporated (HERDSA), Sidney.

Brunken, R. et al., 2003. Direct measurement of cognitive load in multimedia learning. In *Educational psychologist*, Vol. 38, No. 1, pp. 53-61.

Maderick, J. A., 2013. *Validity of subjective self-assessment of digital competence among undergraduate preservice teachers.* Dissertation, University of Nevada, Las Vegas. http://digitalscholarship.unlv.edu/cgi/viewcontent.cgi?article=2942&context=thesesdissertations

Friedrich, H.F. and Mandl, H., 1997. Analyse und Förderung selbstgesteuerten Lernens. In F.E. Weinert & H. Mandl (Eds.). *Enzyklopädie der Psychologie, DII/4, Psychologie der Erwachsenenbildung.* Hogrefe, Göttingen, pp. 237-293.

Hsu, Y. S. et al., 2015. A design model of distributed scaffolding for inquiry-based learning. *Research in Science Education*, Vol. 45, No. 2, pp. 241-273.

Kuznetsova, A. et al., 2017. lmerTest Package: Tests in Linear Mixed Effects Models. In *Journal of Statistical Software.* 82(13).

Leonzini, L., 2009. *Motivation and self-reflection: The ELP as a tool to raise learners' awareness and to enhance self-assessment.* In F. Gori, *Il Portfolio Europeo delle Lingue nell'Università italiana: studenti e autonomia.* EUT Edizioni Università di Trieste, pp. 109-125.

Nakagawa, S. and Schielzeth, H., 2013. A general and simple method for obtaining R^2 from Generalized Linear Mixed-effects Models. In *Methods in Ecology and Evolution,* Vol. 4, pp. 133-142.

Plant, J. L. et al., 2013. Understanding self-assessment as an informed process: residents' use of external information for self-assessment of performance in simulated resuscitations. In *Advances in Health Sciences Education*, Vol. 18, No. 2, pp. 181-192.

Poppi, F. and Radighieri, S., 2009. The role of ELP and self-assessment in effective language learning. In F. Gori, Il *Portfolio Europeo delle Lingue nell'Università italiana: studenti e autonomia.* EUT Edizioni Università di Trieste, pp. 83-89.

Ross, J. A., 2006. The reliability, validity, and utility of self-assessment. In *Practical Assessment Research & Evaluation*, Vol. 11, No. 10.

Ross, S., 1998. Self-assessment in second language testing: A meta-analysis and analysis of experiential factors. In *Language testing*, Vol. 15, No. 1, pp. 1-20.

Suzuki, Y., 2015. Self-assessment of Japanese as a second language: The role of experiences in the naturalistic acquisition. In *Language Testing*, Vol. 32, No. 1, pp. 63-81.

Wauters, K. et al., 2010. Adaptive item-based learning environments based on the item response theory: Possibilities and challenges. In *Journal of Computer Assisted Learning*, Vol. 26, No. 6, pp. 549-562.

Zimmermann, A. et al., 2005. Personalization and context management. In *User Modeling and User-Adapted Interaction*, Vol. 15, No. 3, pp. 275-302.

DIGITAL QUANTITATIVE ASSESSMENT OF QUESTION-ASKING-BASED EXPLORATION

Noam Tor and Goren Gordon
Curiosity Lab, Department of Industrial Engineering, Tel Aviv University, Tel Aviv, Israel, 6997801

ABSTRACT

Curiosity is one of the 21st century skills and is especially paramount in the digital age. However, curiosity is multifaceted and can be expressed in many ways. Furthermore, assessment of curiosity is often based on self-report or subjective observations. We present work in progress for the development of a digital quantitative assessment game for question-asking based exploration. The student selects her question-based exploration in a simulated alien world, wherein the game extracts several important quantitative measures which are derived from graph theory and compute different values of questions, e.g. novel information, exposed uncertainty and uniqueness. To evaluate the tool, we aim to conduct a large study with Youth University students who will play with the game and administer a curiosity-based questionnaire to their class guides, as an external validation.

KEYWORDS

Curiosity, Assessment, Question-Asking, Tablet Game, Children's Exploration, Graph Theory

1. INTRODUCTION

In the Information Age, where knowledge is just a click-away, curiosity becomes one of the most significant aspects of human learning. Research on curiosity has shown its great effect on learning processes. Curiosity drives the curious person to actively explore and seek new information - ask questions, test hypotheses etc. (Engel, 2011; Jirout and Klahr, 2012a). As a result of this active learning, the person's learning process and information acquirement will usually be much greater and more effective (Chi and Wylie, 2014; Fisher et al., 2013). This effect was also demonstrated in brain study researches, which showed that the more curious people are while learning new information, the better they will remember it (Gruber et al., 2014).

Curiosity, however, is multifaceted and can be expressed in many ways (Engel, 2015). It can lead to physical exploration of objects, to uncertainty seeking (Jirout and Klahr, 2012a) and to question asking (Jirout, 2011). The latter is usually associated with more developed curiosity expression, as it is one of the main venues for seeking epistemic knowledge, mainly in the educational system.

In order to better understand curiosity and how to promote it in the educational system, one must have a proper assessment tool. The most used tool for assessing one's curiosity is a self-reporting questionnaire (Kashdan et al., 2018, 2009). While there has been great advancement in these questionnaires and their validation, they still suffer from all the disadvantages of a self-report. Another common assessment method is subjective observation, e.g. observing students in the classroom and assessing their behavior (Engel, 2015).

In this work, we strive to create a more objective and quantitative assessment tool for curiosity, by leveraging digital technology and gamification. We have created a novel tablet game, in which students can explore a simulated alien world by selecting which question to ask about which object. They thus navigate a pre-defined "concept network". This novel game promotes exploration via visual question-asking, i.e. selecting icons of either "what"/"how"/"why" for each selected object, thus enabling us to administer to a wide age-range of students. Furthermore, by constructing a unique "concept network" to explore, we define novel measures of questions, namely, breadth which measures how many answers a question has; depth which measures how many new questions stem from a question's answers and; specificity which measures how many other questions have the same answer. We hypothesize that these quantitative measures can bring to light individual differences and that these are linked to expressions of curiosity.

The contribution of this paper is the presentation of a novel digital quantitative assessment tool for question-asking based curiosity exploration, that enables the extraction of several behavioral parameters related to exploration and learning.

2. RELATED WORKS

The strong relation between curiosity and effective learning has an important meaning for the educational system. Curiosity is usually expressed in behaviors (such as active information seeking, concentration, visible interest etc.) which are deeply related to improved academic performance (Schiefele et al., 1992). It has been shown that even though intelligence and effort play a great part in predicting scholarly success, curiosity is a no less important, strong, and distinct predictor for it (von Stumm et al., 2011). Furthermore, these mentioned visible behaviors that derive from curiosity, also lead to higher teacher ratings of attention, motivation, competence and persistence (Jirout and Klahr, 2012b), for the curious child is much more engaged in class. These results suggest that being curious in school can greatly and positively affect academic performance.

In recent years, several digital curiosity assessment tools have been developed for children. These tools, usually tablet applications, are intended to be more objective and behavioral-based than the current questionnaire type assessments. One application is the Fish Task app (Jirout and Klahr, 2012b), which aims to determine uncertainty seeking. This app is portrayed as a game in which children are in a submarine with two windows. They can open one window and see a fish through it. The two windows differ in the uncertainty of which fish will be outside. Thus, one window is presented with one fish next to it, indicating that with certainty that fish is outside the window. Another window can be presented with five fish next to it, indicating that one of those five fish is outside the window, but the child cannot know until he opens it. Thus, the child needs to select which window to open, i.e. which amount of uncertainty he seeks. The app is designed to explore many differences in uncertainty in a repetitive yet step-wise manner (Jirout and Klahr, 2012b).

A second application created for the task of curiosity assessment is the Free Exploration app (Gordon et al., 2015) in which children can move different characters on the tablet and receive information about them. Measures such as exploration time were used as a proxy of curiosity. These games represent a beginning of a solution for the current subjective measurement methods. However, one important expression of curiosity does not appear in these games, namely, question-asking (Engel, 2011; Harris, 2012).

In the world of game design, uncertainty and hidden information have a great role, for they are directly linked to the player's game experience (Costikyan, 2013). Uncertainty can trigger curiosity, challenge and engage the player to the game, but that is only if it comes in the right balance (To et al., 2018). Too little uncertainty might create a lack of interest. Too much uncertainty can invoke fear of failure and can be very irritative. We used this link between uncertainty and games to design a game in which we will be able to test players' tolerance for uncertainty and look for patterns in the methods they choose to gather information, via question asking, about the game's hidden model.

3. METHODS

Question World game. We created a tablet game we called *Questions World*. In *Questions World*, the player encounters different alien worlds which they can explore. Their interaction with the worlds is by selecting different objects within them, e.g. aliens, technology or indigenous plants, and selecting which question to ask: *How* does it work? *What* is it made of? *Why* is it here? Each object-question pair results in a verbal utterance of an answer, which is part of a different arch-story for each alien world, and the appearance of more objects which the child can interact with.

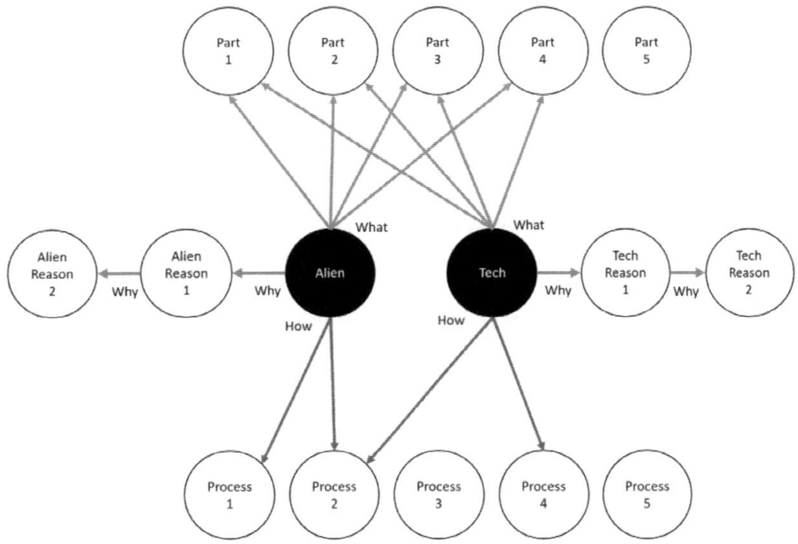

Figure 1. The "Concept Network". The nodes represent the game objects (the starting objects are signed as white over black), and the arrows represent the questions that can be asked about the object, that leads to the discovery of new items. For instance, asking "What is it made of?" about the Alien, will make Parts 1,2,3 and 4 appear on the screen (but the player cannot ask any questions about the parts). This graph is partial - it does not include all the items and questions that can be asked about each item

We have created a Directed Graph-based model that represents the questions-answers connections between the different objects in the world, which we called "the concept-network" (Figure 1). A graph G is an ordered pair *(V(G), E(G))* consisting of a nonempty set *V(G)* of nodes (or vertices), and a set *E(G)*, disjoint from *V(G)*, of edges (Bondy, 1976). A directed graph is a graph in which the vertices have a direction – a start node A, and an end node B. In our game, the nodes are represented by the world's objects, and the vertices are represented by the questions that can be asked about the object (that lead to new objects). Thus, the concept network is a directed graph (a question about an object "points" to the object that represents the answer, but this does not mean that it also points the other direction). This type of modeling lets us create different mathematical parameters for the subjects' questions-asking patterns.

The concept-network (i.e. the graph of objects and questions), is identical for all worlds, but the story differs. The network was constructed such that graph-parameters of each question type is different, with the assumption that these parameters reflect a basic curiosity-based behavior goal. The concept-network was built in a way that each question asked about a different object has its own values of parameters. For each object o and question q we have calculated the following parameters values: Breadth, $B_{o,q}$, the number of answers for the question; Specificity, $S_{o,q}$, the sum of the inverse of the number of questions that lead to the answer, for each answer; and Depth, $D_{o,q}$, the number of new questions that are potentially available from the given answer.

Let $A_{o,q}$ be the set of objects that are the answers to question q about object o and K_i be the set of object-question pairs that lead to object i. Then:

$$\mathrm{B}_{o,q} = | A_{o,q} |, \; D_{o,q} = \sum_{i \in A_{o,q}} \sum_{j \in \{why, what, how\}} D_{i,j}, \; S_{o,q} = \sum_{i \in A_{o,q}} \frac{1}{| K_i |}$$

These measures represent different possible *value* of a question, namely, breadth represents the amount of information that question can provide; depth represents possible new uncertainty an answer can provide and; specificity represents the uniqueness of a question with respect to other questions.

In total, the player visits 5 alien worlds: worlds 1, 2 and 5 are time-limited; world 3 is limited to only five questions; and world 4 is limited to one question type (what/how/why). This is designed so as to assess initial exploration (world 1); change in exploration patterns (comparison between worlds 1, 2 and 5); structured inte-subject comparison (world 3) and categorical force-choice comparison (world 4). We hypothesize that each game thus provides a rich set of exploration parameters that can then be correlated with external measures of curiosity.

4. CONCLUSION

In this contribution, we have presented a work in progress for the development of a novel digital curiosity assessment tool that emphasizes question-asking based exploration. In future work we aim to validate the tool via an extensive study using a wide range of students and external validations, such as teachers' and parents' questionnaires.

ACKNOWLEDGEMENT

The authors would like to thank Tel-Aviv Youth University for their support and Dvir Kleper for this insightful comments. The work is supported by the National Institute for Testing and Evaluation, Israel. G.G. is a Jacobs foundation fellow.

REFERENCES

Bondy, J.A., 1976. Graph Theory With Applications. Elsevier Science Ltd., Oxford, UK, UK.

Chi, M.T.H., Wylie, R., 2014. The ICAP Framework: Linking Cognitive Engagement to Active Learning Outcomes. Educ. Psychol. 49, 219–243.

Costikyan, G., 2013. Uncertainty in Games. MIT Press.

Engel, S., 2015. The Hungry Mind: The origins of curiosity in childhood. Harvard University Press.

Engel, S., 2011. Children's need to know: curiosity in schools. Harv. Educ. Rev. 81, 625–645.

Fisher, K.R., Hirsh- Pasek, K., Newcombe, N., Golinkoff, R.M., 2013. Taking Shape: Supporting Preschoolers' Acquisition of Geometric Knowledge Through Guided Play. Child Dev. 84, 1872–1878.

Gordon, G., Breazeal, C., Engel, S., 2015. Can Children Catch Curiosity from a Social Robot?, in: Proceedings of the Tenth Annual ACM/IEEE International Conference on Human-Robot Interaction. ACM, pp. 91–98.

Gruber, M.J., Gelman, B.D., Ranganath, C., 2014. States of Curiosity Modulate Hippocampus-Dependent Learning via the Dopaminergic Circuit. Neuron 84, 486–496. https://doi.org/10.1016/j.neuron.2014.08.060

Harris, P.L., 2012. Trusting what you're told: How children learn from others. Harvard University Press.

Jirout, J., Klahr, D., 2012a. Children's scientific curiosity: In search of an operational definition of an elusive concept. Dev. Rev. 32, 125–160.

Jirout, J., Klahr, D., 2012b. Children's scientific curiosity: In search of an operational definition of an elusive concept. Dev. Rev. 32, 125–160. https://doi.org/http://10.1016/j.dr.2012.04.002

Jirout, J.J., 2011. Curiosity and the development of question generation skills, in: 2011 AAAI Fall Symposium Series.

Kashdan, T.B., Gallagher, M.W., Silvia, P.J., Winterstein, B.P., Breen, W.E., Terhar, D., Steger, M.F., 2009. The curiosity and exploration inventory-II: Development, factor structure, and psychometrics. J. Res. Personal. 43, 987–998.

Kashdan, T.B., Stiksma, M.C., Disabato, D.D., McKnight, P.E., Bekier, J., Kaji, J., Lazarus, R., 2018. The five-dimensional curiosity scale: Capturing the bandwidth of curiosity and identifying four unique subgroups of curious people. J. Res. Personal. 73, 130–149.

Piotrowski, J.T., Litman, J.A., Valkenburg, P., 2014. Measuring Epistemic Curiosity in Young Children. Infant Child Dev. 23, 542–553.

Schiefele, U., Krapp, A., Winteler, A., 1992. Interest as a predictor of academic achievement: A meta-analysis of research.

To, A., Ali, S., Kaufman, G., Hammer, J., 2018. Integrating Curiosity and Uncertainty in Game Design, in: Gordon, G. (Ed.), The New Science of Curiosity. Nova, pp. 169–202.

von Stumm, S., Hell, B., Chamorro-Premuzic, T., 2011. The Hungry Mind: Intellectual Curiosity Is the Third Pillar of Academic Performance. Perspect. Psychol. Sci. 6, 574–588.

TRANSFER LEARNING OF COGNITIVE CONTROL USING MOBILE APPLICATIONS

Vincent Setiawan, Tricia Jing Yi Chor, Yee Qi Lai, Gan Wang, Wei Lok Yap and W. Quin Yow
Singapore University of Technology and Design, 8 Somapah Road, Singapore 487372, Singapore

ABSTRACT

This research aims to explore the transfer learning of cognitive control skills using mobile applications. We explored whether mobile application can serve as a viable platform in training interference control, specifically the color Stroop task. Mobile phone's advantage lies in its portability and its ability to reach many people. Forty undergraduates from the authors' university were involved in the experiment. We introduced the use of a mobile application to present training exercises as well as to record answers and reaction times. Half of the participants were given standard logical thinking questions whereas the other half was given different types of Stroop task as a form of training, followed by the color Stroop test as a test of transference. The results showed that mobile app training using different types of Stroop task significantly improved the performance on the color Stroop Task in reaction time. Future studies can explore transfer learning of other types of cognitive control as well as explore our findings for other age groups.

KEYWORDS

Cognitive Control, Mobile Applications, Transfer of Learning

1. INTRODUCTION

Executive control, also known as cognitive control, is a group of mental processes where you must go against your intuition to achieve a wanted outcome. Exerting cognitive control is difficult as it is easier to go with the flow rather than oppose it. To exert control, an individual need to recalibrate his or her intuition and train it for the correct action (Diamond, 2013). In general, there are several types of cognitive control, e.g., prepotent response inhibition, mental-set shifting, updating and monitoring, and cognitive flexibility (Friedman & Miyake, 2004; Miyake & Friedman, 2012). Stroop task is one instance where suppressing of automatic or dominant responses is required, namely, the prepotent response inhibition aspect of cognitive control.

In a typical Stroop experiment, a reaction-timed task is used to illustrate the nature of automatic processing versus conscious visual control (Stroop, 1935). Participants were shown colored words filled with a different ink color and asked to name the ink color as fast as possible instead of the word. Participants tended to be slower in naming when the ink color was different from the text than when they were the same. (also known as the Stroop effect) Research on the Stroop effect has been extended to other tasks such as picture-word (Rosinski et al., 1975) and directional tasks (Shor et al., 1972)

Our experiment aims to explore the transferability of cognitive control, in particular, inhibitory control, using mobile application. Transfer learning has been observed from a spatial compatibility task to a color Stroop Task where manual response using keyboard is required for both tasks (Marini et al., 2011). Besides near transfer, far transfer learning from a mental-set shifting task into an inhibitory control task, e.g., from task-switching training to Stroop task, has also been observed (Karbach & Kray, 2009). However, none of these experiments have been done in the context of mobile devices.

Limited research has explored training of cognitive control in the context of mobile devices. It was shown that auditory attention, visual search, and resistance to distractor interference could be improved through mobile-application based cognitive training or mobile-based games (Bless et al., 2014; Oei & Patterson, 2013). Neither of these literatures explored training of inhibitory control with mobile devices. Cognitive control and Stroop tasks are typically conducted in a closed-door setting where participants are shown prompts on the computer and answer verbally or press on keyboard to indicate their answer. Use of mobile devices for cognitive control tests are rare and have not been done before for Stroop tasks. Mobile devices have huge potential in the training of cognitive control because it provides avenue for individuals to improve their cognitive control whenever and wherever they are. Moreover, mobile devices are more affordable compared to personal computers while allowing for accurate record of responses and ease of data processing.

In our experiment, we focused on Stroop task as the main indicator of transfer learning between inhibitory control tasks, that is, whether training using one type of Stroop task would improve the performance on another. We introduced the use of a mobile application where training exercises were presented to the participants and response time (RT) and accuracy to the color Stroop test was recorded. We hope our experiments can pave the way for future researchers to consider the use of mobile devices for similar experiments to reach out to more participants as well as to improve the ecological validity of the experiments.

2. EXPERIMENT METHOD

2.1 Participants

Forty undergraduate students from the authors' university participated in this study (*M* = 22 years, *SD* = 1.42; 31 males; 20 in control condition). Half of the participants were randomly assigned to a control condition, where they were given standard logical thinking questions (control group), and the other half was given different types of Stroop task as a form of training (experimental group).

2.2 Materials

We created an Android application to present the training exercises in a user-friendly and portable way. All our experiments were done on Mi Note 2 and Samsung Galaxy Note 5. In the training phase, participants in the control condition were given 10 general logical thinking questions, while participants in the experimental condition were given 10 Stroop-like questions instead (see Figure 1 and 2).

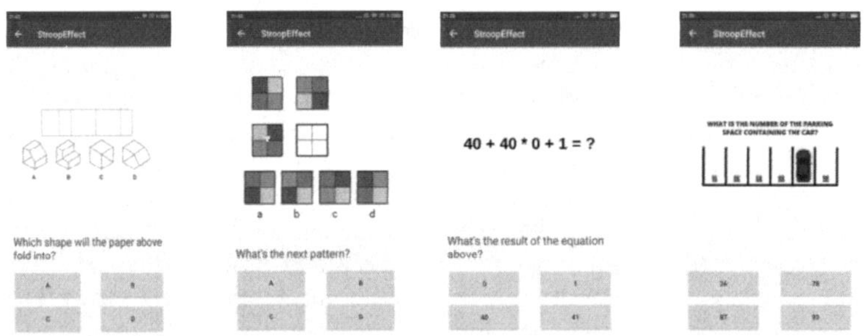

Figure 1. Examples of non-Stroop related control group question

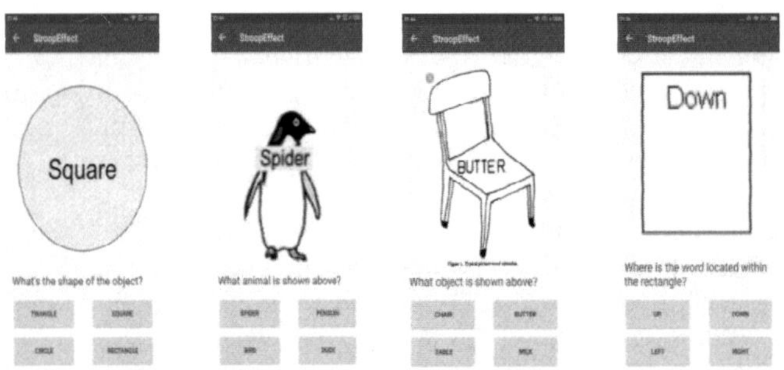

Figure 2. Examples of Stroop task training question

Figure 3. Examples of test question

In the test phase, all participants were given 10 color-word Stroop questions where the text was incongruent with the color it was printed in (see Figure 3). The button layout for the response key to color-word Stroop tasks were fixed to minimize the time taken for the participants to look for the correct button.

2.3 Procedure

Participants were recruited at different venues at the authors' university, such as cafeteria and library, and completed the study individually. Each participant was given a mobile device and told to answer a set of questions, untimed. After the first 10 questions were completed, the experimenter explained to the participants that the subsequent questions would be timed and instructed the participants to try to answer the questions correctly and as fast as they could. Participants were told to choose the option that corresponds to the color of the text, ignoring the text written. Participants were also asked to familiarize themselves with the buttons layout to minimize the contribution of the time taken to look for the correct options out of the total reaction time recorded. Participants' RT and the number of correct responses for the test questions were recorded and analyzed as the dependent variables of the study.

Upon completing all the questions, the mobile application presented a form to the participants that asked about gender, contact details, and color vision of the participant. All participants reported that they had normal color vision. The experimenter then explained the purpose of the experiment to the participants and concluded the experiment.

3. RESULTS

We hypothesized that the skills learned from a Stroop task presented on a mobile device is transferable to another. We first checked the normality of our RT data. Shapiro-Wilk test revealed that the p-value is 0.11, thus we concluded that the data comes from a normal distribution.

3.1 Response Times

We then computed the mean RT for each group. As shown in Figure 4, the average RT for the experimental group was approximately 120ms faster than that of the control group (M = 1225.53 vs. 1344.39 respectively).

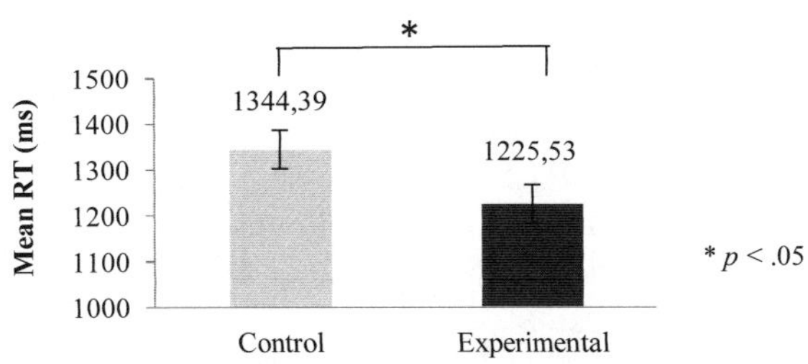

Figure 4. Mean RT of control vs. experimental group

One-way ANOVA test on RT showed a significant effect of transferability ($F(1,38) = 4.85$, $p = .034$). The experimental group was significantly faster in responding correctly to the Stroop task than the control group.

3.2 Accuracy

The average percentage of correct responses was found to be the same for both groups at 97%. Since the accuracy data was not normally distributed (p -value for Shapiro-Wilk test < .001), we ran a nonparametric test on the comparison of accuracy between the two groups. Mann-Whitney U-test for independent samples showed that $p = .93$. The response accuracy for the two groups did not differ significantly from each other.

4. CONCLUSION

In conclusion, we obtained evidence that mobile application can be used as a platform to train cognitive control in young adults. Results showed that participants in the experimental group at test were significantly faster than participants in the control group, demonstrating that training did improve performance. However, no significant difference in accuracy was found. This is likely because, given the (low) level of difficulty of the task, most participants were able to identify the correct answer albeit taking a slightly longer time. This is in congruence with past research on Stroop and Stroop-related tasks (Chen & Johnson,1991).

Our results serve as a motivation for greater integration of mobile application in the training of cognitive control for young adults. Mobile devices are light, portable, and are usually more intuitive than desktop computers or laptops. Given that cognitive control skills predict many life successes (Diamond, 2013; Imbrosciano & Berlach, 2005), it is important that adults can regularly train their cognitive control on the go while children can play with such mobile applications to develop their emerging cognitive control skills.

It is noteworthy that the environment in which different participants complete the test was not standardized as they were in different venues in the university. Some venues might be noisier (cafeteria) while others quieter (library). On the other hand, conducting the study in varied environments would give ecological validity to the effectiveness of the study. This would allow the mobile application to be effectively deployed in different settings that are natural and practical, such as at home and in the classroom.

As our sample population was predominantly undergraduate male, future studies should replicate the same research with equal number of male and female participants, and sampling a larger population other than those in the authors' university, such as children or older adults. Lastly, future studies should consider extending it to other components of executive control, such as mental-set shifting, both within-component transfer as well as between-component transfer, to explore whether this finding is specific to the color-word Stroop task, or it could be extended to other control tasks.

ACKNOWLEDGEMENT

We are grateful to the students who participated in this study. This work was partially supported by the SUTD-MIT IDC grant (IDG31700102) awarded to the last author. Correspondence concerning this paper should be addressed to Vincent Setiawan, Singapore University of Technology and Design, 8 Somapah Road, Singapore 487372. E-mail: vincent@mymail.sutd.edu.sg.

REFERENCES

Bless, J. J., Westerhausen, R., Kompus, K., Gudmundsen, M., Hugdahl, K. Self-supervised, mobile-application based cognitive training of auditory attention: A behavioral and fMRI evaluation. *Internet Interventions, 1*(3), 102-110.

Chen, J. Y., & Johnson, M. K. (1991). The Stroop congruency effect is more observable under a speed strategy than an accuracy strategy. *Perceptual and Motor Skills, 73(1), 67-76.*

Diamond, A. (2013). Executive Functions. *Annual Review of Psychology*, *64*, 135–168.

Friedman, N. P., Miyake, A. (2004). The relations among inhibition and interference control functions: a latent-variable analysis. *Journal of Experimental Psychology: General, 133*, 101–35.

Imbrosciano, A., & Berlach, R. G. (2005). The Stroop test and its relationship to academic performance and general behavior of young students. *Teacher Development, 9(1), 131-144.*

Karbach, J., & Kray, J. (2009). How useful is executive function training? Age differences in near and far transfer of task-switching training. *Developmental Science*, *12*, 978-990.

Marini, M., Iani, C., Nicoletti, R., Rubichi, S. (2011). Between-task transfer of learning from Spatial Compatibility to a color Stroop task. *Experimental Psychology, 58, 473-479.*

Miyake, A., & Friedman, N. P. (2012). The Nature and Organization of Individual Differences in Executive Functions: Four General Conclusions. *Current Directions in Psychological Science, 21*(1), 8–14.

Oei, C. A., Patterson, D. M. (2013). Enhancing Cognition with Video Games: A Multiple Game Training Study. *PLoS ONE, 8* (3).

Rosinski, R. R., Golinkoff, R. M., & Kukish, K. S. (1975). Automatic semantic processing in a picture-word interference task. *Child Development*, *46*, 247–253.

Shor, R. E., Hatch, R. E., Hudson, L. J., Landrigan, D. T., & Shaffer, H. J. (1972). Effect of practice on a Stroop-like spatial directions task. *Journal of Experimental Psychology*, *94*, 168–172.

Stroop, J. R. (1935). Studies of interference in serial verbal reactions. *Journal of Experimental Psychology*, *18*, 643–662.

APPLICATION OF SECOND LIFE IN PROMOTING COLLABORATIVE LEARNING

Amit Sharma* and Salman Nazir
Training and Assessment Research Group (TARG), Department of maritime operations, University of Southeastern Norway, Postboks 4, 3199, Borre, Norway

ABSTRACT

Increasingly, Massive Multiplayer Online Games (MMOG) and Virtual Worlds are being utilized for development of key competencies and 21st century skills in education. This paper is aimed at proposing a conceptual framework for the virtual world known as Second Life for potential application in Maritime Education & Training (MET). The need for developing collaboration as a competency for future seafarers and past applications of Second Life in supporting training and education is discussed. The expected outcomes from the proposed research activities will lead to establishment of a global MET community in Second Life that could facilitate communication and knowledge exchange across universities.

KEYWORDS

Collaborative Learning, Distributed Cognition, Second Life, Virtual Environment, Distance Education

1. INTRODUCTION

Research literature has indicated that Massive Multiplayer Online Games (MMOG) and virtual worlds can facilitate the development of 21st century skills such as problem solving, collaboration and critical thinking by their unique nature and opportunities they provide in term of reflective practices (Hartley et al. 2014). In this regard, King (2013) has also drawn attention towards the shortcomings of the existing educational frameworks and how MMOGs or virtual spaces can promote acquisition of skills related to Information and Communication Technologies (ICT), collaboration and leadership in the modern distributed workplaces. Second life is one of such popular virtual world where users can interact with the environment and each other via their own graphical representation or "Avatar" and offers unique opportunities in addressing the needs highlighted above. There are several other virtual worlds in addition to Second life which offer similar experience such as *OpenSim, There, Kaneva* etc. But relatively ease of access, richer immersive experience and the ability to create complex environment has enabled Second life to remain popular among the users of virtual worlds and researchers alike.

A key characteristic of modern sociotechnical systems such as maritime domain is the distributed nature of operations. As the systems have evolved over the years with increasing use of technology and automation of tasks, the result has been unchecked rise in number of information elements, associated functions and interfaces at the workplace. These changes had a distinctive effect on the nature of operations as they are now increasingly being executed by a specialized team of individuals with technological artefacts playing a fundamental role. In this regard, an example of the most elementary ship operation i.e. Navigation can be considered. Navigation which essentially involves safely guiding the ship from Port A to Port B is carried out by a group of individuals known as "bridge team" with the Captain being overall in charge. They are further supported by Pilot services and/or Vessel Traffic Services when in the vicinity of the port. At a more abstract level, the routing instructions and ship owners' standing orders are influential in making deciding the route of the ship. This example portrays the various levels of control involved in the navigation of a merchant ship and each of the level can be thought of as a Joint Cognitive System with technological artefacts seamlessly joining the levels and supporting the communication and flow of information. The cognition required to

* Corresponding author. Email: amit.sharma@usn.no

determine actions and execute decisions is essentially distributed amongst different levels. Figure 1 illustrates the above description.

With such distributed expertise in practice supporting critical operation of navigation onboard ships, it is imperative that non-technical skills such as collaboration and leadership are inculcated in education and training of seafarers. The regulatory bodies concerning Maritime Education and Training (MET) has recognized these trends and have incorporated the guidelines related to the development of non-technical skills of seafarers along with the regular technical skills, as can be seen in latest amendments proposed under Standards of Training, Certification and Watchkeeping regulations (STCW) 2010.

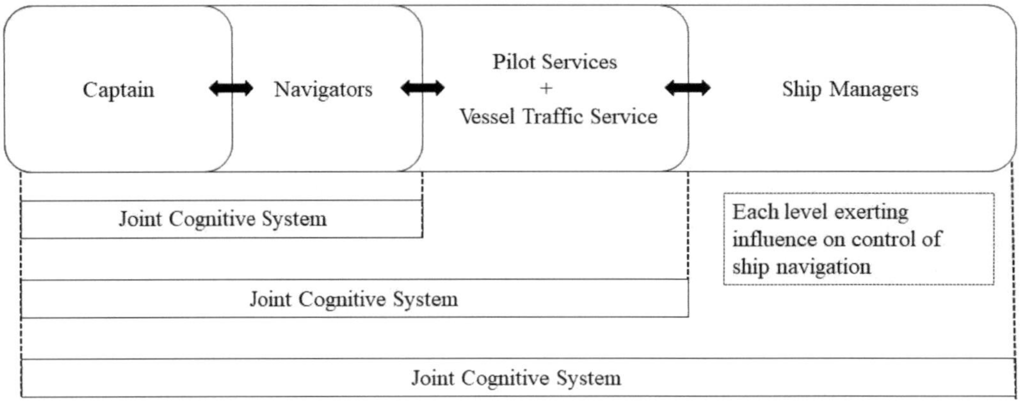

Figure 1. Various control level for ship navigation (Adapted from Hollnagel, 2002)

However, in the research literature related to MET, there is still insufficient application of pedagogical interventions applied with the aim of developing collaboration as competency for the modern seafarers. Collaborative learning can be defined as co-construction of knowledge and competence development where individuals with different but complementary expertise have the opportunity for creative thinking, introducing new ideas and taking creative actions (Goggins & Jahnke, 2013). Collaborative learning is argued to provide other benefits associated with it rather than pure cognitive gains such as social and motivational gains occurred during learning (Stribjos, 2011). Such approach is required in the future frameworks for maritime training where learning and knowledge creation will be framed as part of work integrated in the working processes. The need to address these challenges becomes vital with the current technological developments taking place in maritime domain. Increasing automation and development of autonomous vessels will in near future demand that the operators collaborate with a wide range of individuals with sophisticated ICTs at their disposal. It is therefore required by the researchers and practitioners in MET to utilize novel frameworks from the learning sciences to shift the learning paradigm from dominant behaviorist to constructivist approaches which actively promote co-construction, collaboration and dialogue between the trainee and its peers.

2. SECOND LIFE

Second life is an online open world virtual platform created by Linden Lab (http://lindenlab.com/) in 2003 and since then has increasingly being used for various purposes such as role-playing, arts, education, work simulation etc. It boasts of about 600,000 active users as of 2017 (Jamison, 2017). Second life's popularity has been attributed due to the platform offering relatively advanced technology in terms of day/night cycles, communication modes, weather system, character mobility and so on. It even has its own currency system with the currency called "Linden Dollars" which enables the platform to have its own economic system with transactions worth of millions of US dollars. Although for some advanced featured within Second life, it is required from users to buy them using Linden Dollars. However, it is also possible to experience the platform with basic features free of cost.

In relation to Second life and opportunities it offers for educational research, several studies have been conducted. In Mørch, Hartley, and Caruso (2015), the authors demonstrated how participants from a teacher preparation program were able to cultivate interpersonal problem-solving skills utilizing role playing in Second Life. Similarly, In Prasolova-Førland, Fominykh, Darisiro, and Mørch (2013), the authors utilized the platform of Second Life for training aspects of cultural awareness for military operators preparing for international deployments. Boulos et al. (2007) provides examples from health and medicine domain as to how Second Life is being used for dissemination of health-related information and by aged individuals as well by persons having physical disability for recreational purposes. Muir, Allen, Rayner, and Cleland (2013) in their study demonstrated how Second Life can be used by teachers for handling diverse student behaviors and engaging in reflective discussions in the classroom. These studies show how Second Life has been used by educators and practitioners involved in training for different purposes and facilities it offers in different contexts. Figure 2 below, provides some snapshots of how the platform appears for an ordinary user in various virtual locations within it.

Figure 2. Environment of Second life as appearing in certain locations recreated by the platform

3. APPLICATION OF SECOND LIFE FOR MET

The authors are currently involved in developing experiments and activities that would involve utilization of Second Life for the maritime trainees situated at department of maritime operations, University of Southeastern Norway (USN). At present, two potential application of Second Life for MET are proposed: (1) Organization of Student workshops with topics from syllabus involving maritime courses and (2) Development of a Global MET community aimed at replicating many of the existing functions of a maritime school in a virtual space and provide a platform for collaborative discussion between participants from different countries. Figure 3 below highlights the conceptual framework for the process.

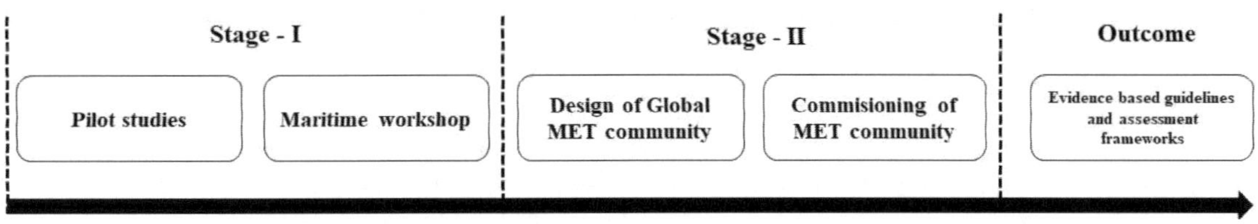

Figure 3. Conceptual framework for utilization of Second Life for MET

USN is a part of 4 university consortium involved in uplifting the maritime competence in Norway. There are 2 workshops organized by MARKOM2020 annually, selecting latest research challenges in maritime domain (www.targ.com\workshops). In this context, a virtual workshop can either substitute or may provide an additional arena for the actual workshops planned by the organizing practitioners. It is also observed that due to travel and financial investments usually required in such workshops it has limited student participation. As such a virtual workshop can offer inexpensive and engaging experience to students with considerable less investment of resources required from either the organizer or the students themselves. As normal ICT tools (Slide show or voice-based communication) along with communication modes can be adequately replicated in such settings the above objective can be utilized. Interaction analysis technique can be utilized to analyze the data from Stage – I which will help establish guidelines for creating a virtual space replicating a maritime school.

In the Stage - II of the project, an online space will be created/commissioned in Second Life with the functionalities offered by the platform which will be dedicated for creating a Global MET community with dedicated space for the participants of different countries/institutes to demonstrate their existing projects, organize exhibits and promote networking amongst them. Table 1 below, outlines the approach in each stage and respective outcomes.

Table 1. Planned activities and proposed research methods for realization of research objectives

Stage	Planned activities	Proposed research methods	Outcome
Stage - I	Pilot studies, Organization of in-house maritime workshop	Virtual ethnography, Interaction analysis	Framework for designing Global MET community
Stage – II	Initial surveys with instructors & experts, Creation of Virtual space	Semi-structured interviews. Design based research	Evidence based guidelines and assessment framework for collaborative learning in MET

The students and teachers participating in the virtual community will thus get an opportunity to explore different aspects of maritime operations with both local and international participants. Some of the possible implications of this research would be increased knowledge sharing across universities, enhanced cultural sensitivity and opportunity for reflective practice. Such development can also help bridge the knowledge gap by increased dissemination from relatively technical advanced countries to the developing countries and facilitate dialogue. The data gathered from this stage will be further analyzed for establishing guidelines for online courses and assessment framework which can be solely directed in cultivating collaboration as a competency for the maritime operators.

4. CONCLUSION

For catering to increasing need for development of crucial non-technical skills, the use of virtual platform called Second Life is proposed. The conceptual framework described is aimed to utilize the platform for proposing guidelines for developing frameworks which facilitate the acquisition of collaboration as a competency for future maritime trainees.

ACKNOWLEDGEMENT

This work is supported by the PhD research fellowship awarded to the first author by the department of maritime operations, University of Southeastern Norway. The authors would like to thank Anders Mørch, Professor at Department of Education, University of Oslo for his guidance.

REFERENCES

Boulos, M. N. K., Hetherington, L., & Wheeler, S. (2007). Second Life: an overview of the potential of 3-D virtual worlds in medical and health education. Health Information & Libraries Journal, 24(4), 233-245.

Goggins, S.P. & Jahnke, I (2013). CSCL@ Work: Computer-supported collaborative learning at the workplace—making learning visible in unexpected online placesacross established boundaries In S. P. Goggins, I. Jahnke, & V. Wulf (Eds.), Computer-Supported Collaborative Learning at the Workplace: CSCL@Work (pp. 1-20). Boston, MA: Springer US.

Hollnagel, E. (2002). Cognition as control: A pragmatic approach to the modelling of joint cognitive systems. In Hollnagel, E. & Woods, D. D. (2005). Joint cognitive systems: Foundations of cognitive systems engineering. (pp.1-25) Boca Raton, FL: Taylor & Francis

Jamison, L. (2017). The digital ruins of a forgotton future. Retrieved from https://www.theatlantic.com/magazine/archive/2017/12/second-life-leslie-jamison/544149/

Hartley, M.D., Ludlow, B.L., & Duff, M.C. (2015). Second Life: A 3D virtual immersive environment for teacher preparation course in a distance education program. Rural Special Education Quarterly, 34(3), 21-25

King, E. M. (2013). Massively Multiplayer Online Role-Playing Games: A Potential Model of CSCL@Work. In S. P. Goggins, I. Jahnke, & V. Wulf (Eds.), Computer-Supported Collaborative Learning at the Workplace: CSCL@Work (pp. 205-224). Boston, MA: Springer US.

Mørch, A. I., Hartley, M. D., & Caruso, V. (2015). Teaching interpersonal problem-solving skills using roleplay in a 3D virtual world for special education: A case study in Second Life. Paper presented at the 15th International Conference on Advanced Learning Technologies (ICALT), 2015 IEEE. Hualien, Taiwan, 464-468

Muir, T., Allen, J., Rayner, C., & Cleland, B. (2013). Preparing pre-service teachers for classroom practice in a virtual world: A pilot study using Second Life. Journal of Interactive Media in Education, 2013(1), 1-17

Prasolova-Førland, E., Fominykh, M., Darisiro, R., & Mørch, A. I. (2013). Training cultural awareness in military operations in a virtual Afghan village: A methodology for scenario development. Paper presented at 46th Hawaii International Conference on the System Sciences (HICSS), 2013 Hawaii, USA, 903-912

Strijbos, J.-W. (2011) Assessment of (computer-supported) collaborative learning. IEEE transactions on learning technologie, 4(1), 59-73.

THE NARRATIVE OF THE FACEBOOK SCANDAL FROM TWEETS: NARRATIVE ANALYSIS OF #DELETEFACEBOOK

Yasmine Khosrowshahi and Ananda Mitra
Wake Forest University, Winston-Salem, NC 27106, USA

ABSTRACT

This paper offers an analysis of the narrative emerging from nearly 11,000 tweets related to the scandal surrounding Cambridge Analytica and Facebook. The narrative analysis demonstrates that the users were annoyed with the way their information was used but were also unhappy with the fact that users need to be more mindful and attentive of the way in which they use Facebook. The methodology used a text analytic process to analyze the content of the tweets which serve as narrative bits or narbs.

KEYWORDS

Narb, Narrative Analysis, Tweet, Facebook, Cambridge Analytica

1. INTRODUCTION

The issue of privacy arose around Facebook when a scandal involving Cambridge Analytica was released in early March. It is estimated that nearly 87 million users were affected by the scandal. Forbes explains that the scandal actually started several years back when Facebook exposed the data from millions of users to an academics researcher (DeMars, 2018). That academics researcher, a Russian-American named Aleksandr Kogan, used a quiz app, similar to a personality quiz app Psychometrics Centre made, called "thisisyourdigitallife" (Meredith, 2018). The app was used to pull more data from users than they should have been allowed to. The Atlantic Media Company says that 270,000 people installed Kogan's app on their Facebook account. Just like any Facebook developer then, Kogan was able to access data about those users and their friends (Meyer, 2018). Kogan then sold all the data to Cambridge Analytica (CA) to then use as part of the 2016 US election for marketing and advertising for Trump. The information created targeted ads at users on Facebook. Christopher Wylie, a key player in the scandal, says, "We exploited Facebook to harvest millions of people's profiles and built models to exploit what we knew about them and target their inner demons. That was the basis the entire company was built on" (Staff, Al Jazeera, 2018). Since the news broke, many have put out the #DeleteFacebook hashtag to promote the end of using the social media platform (Rosenberg, 2018). The objective of this paper is to use the micro-blogging the hashtag in order to understand the stories circulating in the digital world around this scandal from early March. Here, we argue that the data collected explains how privacy in the digital world is extremely valuable to users and that once their trust has been broken, they use the digital world, ironically, the let their voices be heard.

2. NARRATIVE PARADIGM

The construct of looking at culture, communication and human behavior and beliefs through the lens of a narrative was suggested by the work of Walter Fisher who in turn based his work on earlier scholars who identified the importance of story-telling and narratives in the process of making meaning of everyday life as people operate within the cultural and social spaces that they occupy (see, e.g., Andrews, 1982; MacIntyre, 1981; Ricouer, 1977, 1983, 1984; White, 1984). Fisher suggested, people can operate as a narrative being where the act of creating and articulating a coherent and rational narrative becomes a part of being human. In doing this, the narrative paradigm offers a different way of analyzing and understanding communication, and the way in which people act.

There are many aspects of the narrative paradigm that merit examination in the early Twenty-first Century of Big Data, particularly when the analysis of large data sets seeks to provide an account of how persons come to believe and behave (see, e.g., Kosinski, et. al. 2013). The narrative paradigm suggests that it is possible to examine a story to seek internal coherence and fidelity of a story. In this case, the story related to gun violence is examined through the narbs that were produced around the hashtag: "deletefacebook."

3. NARRATIVE DATA AND ANALYSIS

In this case, the narbs were composed of nearly 11,000 tweets that were collected when the hashtag "deletefacebook" soon after the issue gained attention in 2018. The specific tweets were collected, and the content of the tweets were then analyzed to extract a narrative map which is a visual representation of specific narrative.

The outcome of the process is the creation of a narrative map composed of narrative categories, which are shown as circles or "nodes" on the map, that are connected with each other by the lines connecting the nodes. The volume of occurrence of each category in the corpus of narbs (visually represented by the diameter of each node of the map) and the strength of relationship between categories (visually represented by the thickness of the line connecting the nodes).

4. FINDINGS

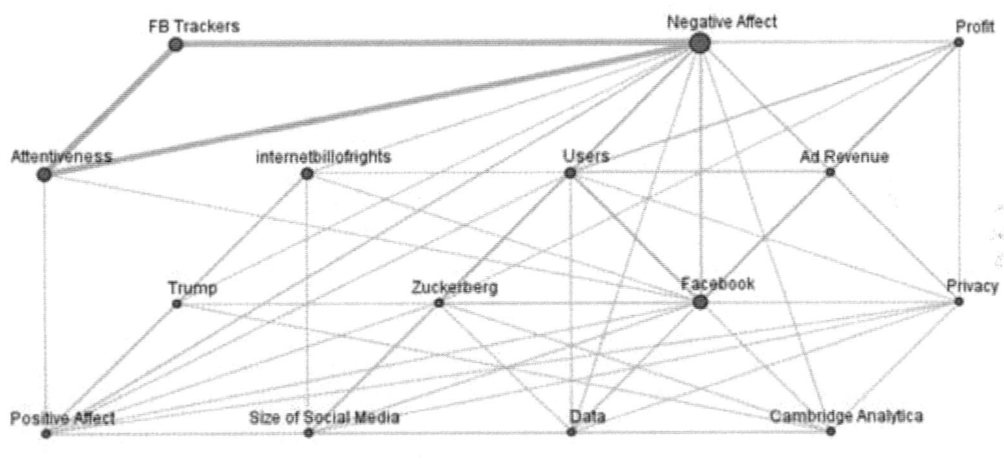

Figure 1. Narrative map of the categories extracted from the narbs

The interpretation of the narrative map (Figure 1) shows a strong negative affect with almost all of the narbs collected to create the map. It portrays a deep frustration towards the scandal related to Facebook. The strong negative affect connected with the idea of Facebook tells the story that the use of the social media platform is considered negatively. With a small connection to positive affect and an overall controversial topic since the scandal, Facebook continues to be the center of much concern regarding what is truly private in the digital world. The concern of being tracked on Facebook and how closely we pay attention to those trackers is demonstrated by the connection among FB trackers, attentiveness, and negative affect. When the scandal came to light it was clear that no one ever imagined that their privacy was being invaded as they used social media platforms. The thick lines indicate a strong relationship where FB trackers and attentiveness are negatively associated. It seems that the less attentive that users are, the more likely they are to fall victim to trackers such as the FB trackers. The Atlantic Media Company even explains how the app was created similar to a personality quiz app. Just by the trust users had in the previous app, they used it, not realizing, that it opened access to data about the users and their friends which was then saved in a private database instead of being deleted immediately (Meyer, 2018). When it got to the hands of Cambridge Analytica, they "used it to make 30 million 'psychographic' profiles about voters" (Meyer, 2018). The trust users had in the digital world allowed them to have low attentiveness to what they were actually doing, thereby voluntarily using the app without knowledge of what it was taking from them. The connection between negative affect and a number of other categories including Internet bill of rights, Trump, users, data, Facebook, Cambridge Analytica, Ad Revenue, and profit also demonstrates that scandal led to a chain of micro-blogging about all the different negative relationships.

The narrative codes also explain the relationship among categories that were spoken about with a negative affect directly linked to it on the map. The triangle for users, Facebook, and negative affect validates the point that users had a negative affect towards Facebook after the scandal broke out. The lines show a strong relationship between users and negative affect and user and Facebook but a weak relationship between Facebook and negative affect. This indicates that the focus is around the users more than Facebook. Many sources discuss what Facebook did to users, not stating a negative or positive affect but rather just an understanding of how it took users information. This fits the triangle and if there are sources written about this relationship then many of the tweets extracted must have done the same. It is also clear that the triangles that negative affect create are all connected with users as well. Therefore, Internet bill of rights, data, Ad Revenue, and profit all create triangles individually with user and negative affect to show that users are negatively affected by each of these categories.

Negative affect seems to be the category with the most relationships and interconnectedness on the map. The strongest of which is the triangle for FB trackers, attentiveness, and negative affect discussed above. What is also clear in the narrative is the fact that there is no connection between negative affect and Zuckerberg, which suggests that, in this narrative, there is no negative affect for Zuckerberg. While many categories had negative affects however, many categories had an equal amount of positive and negative affects. For instance, Trump had the same weak relationship with negative affect as with positive affect. This suggests that in this narrative Trump was not strongly affected by the scandal overall. Much of what Cambridge Analytica did was in favor of helping Trump win the election, which it did, thus creating that positive affect. However, with the reveal of the motives behind what CA did, a negative affect can also be linked to Trump. There were also many other categories such as users, Facebook, privacy, and attentiveness that had both positive and negative affects indicating that for many categories, there were split feelings and opinions.

In addition to the thickness of the lines indicating a stronger relationship, the size of the circle also indicates the number of narbs the category has. So for instance, negative affect has the largest circle on the map, meaning there are the most narbs for that category. Aside from negative affect, Facebook Tracker, attentiveness, and Facebook all have larger circles than the rest of the categories and these are the categories talked about most. Most of the categories on the map have the same size circle and same line thickness which means that they are equally all talked about in regard to the hashtag. It is clear that negative affect and its relationship with the categories, especially Facebook Tracker and attentiveness, are the most spoken about.

Another interesting triangle is the connection with users, Zuckerberg, and Facebook. Since the Facebook scandal, many users have blamed the founder of Facebook, Mark Zuckerberg, thus it would make sense that there would be a correlation among the three categories. In addition, since Zuckerberg went in front of congress, there was even more talk about him in relation to users and Facebook. It even seems as if the lines should be thicker from much discussion about the relationship among these three categories. Many articles and sources have surfaced regarding the situation in front of congress. Facebook even streamed it live however this narrative indicates that there was not a strong connection with Zuckerberg, Facebook, and users.

5. CONCLUSION AND DISCUSSION

The variety of connections suggest that people have many opinions in regard to the hashtag #DeleteFacebook. The narrative, created from the narbs, tells a story about the reaction prompted from the invasion of privacy. Many aspects such as the privacy of thought are presented in the digital space. A common way to do that on Facebook may be through status updates. Communicating on the social media platform allows an individual or a group to have a presence in the digital world. It creates a sense of agency; power. Privacy is meant to protect analog thoughts. This protection is needed because we believe there is a threat. Researchers have found that privacy is extremely important to Facebook users but not enough of them are aware enough about the level of privacy they have on the social media site (Netchitailova, 2012). This narrative reveal that privacy was negatively affected because users realized that nothing was safe for them given that Facebook took their personal information.

The Facebook scandal has affected millions of people who now have a better understanding that nothing is safe in the digital world. These findings can be further embellished in many ways. It is likely that this sample of narbs that were used to create this narrative could have come from a group with directly ties to Facebook. Facebook has around 2.19 billion monthly active users, many of which the scandal directly affected. This would explain the fact that this scandal grew to a point where congress was involved, and the narrative map created a large negative affect. The issue can be further explored in many different ways such as expanding on the hashtag used to collect the data.

In addition, the narrative created from the hashtag gives a largely one-sided account on the negative affects since the hashtag itself is negative. It would be interesting to look closer at the positive affects if there are any. Much of the cause of the scandal is related to political motives for the 2016 US election. In this story the issue has a strong correlation to the feelings of those with a strong opinion towards the breach in privacy. The narbs tell a personal narrative about how this scandal reveals the lack of privacy in the digital world and how that negatively affected others..

REFERENCES

Andrews, J. D. (1982). The structuralist study of narrative: its history, use and limits. In. P. Hernadi (Ed.). *The horizon of literature* (pp. 99-124). Lincoln, NE: The University of Nebraska Press.

Beres, D. (2018). It's Time to Protect Yourself - and Your Friends - from Facebook." *Mashable.*

DeMers, J. (2018). What Marketers Can Learn From The Facebook Scandal. *Forbes Magazine.*

Fisher, W. R. (1984). Narration as Human Communication Paradigm: The Case of Public Moral Argument, *Communication Monographs*, 51, 1–22.

Fisher, W. R. (1985a). The Narrative Paradigm: An Elaboration, *Communication Monographs*, 52, 347–367.

Fisher, W. R. (1985b). The Narrative Paradigm: In the Beginning, *Journal of Communication*, 35, 74–89.

Staff. (2018). Cambridge Analytica and Facebook: The Scandal so Far. *News | Al Jazeera.*

Kosinski, M., Stillwell D. J., & Graepel, T. (2013). Private traits and attributes are predictable from digital records of human behavior. *Proceedings of the National Academy of Sciences.*

M Pilgun, G Gradoselskaya (2015): — Political Communication on Facebook: Russian Casel. Revista Latina de Comunicación Social, 70, pp. 726 to 749.

MacIntyre, A. (1981). *After virtue: A study in moral theory (2nd ed).* Notre Dame, IN: The University of Notre Dame Press.

Meredith, S. (2018). Here's Everything You Need to Know about the Cambridge Analytica Scandal. *CNBC.*

Meyer, R. (2018). The Cambridge Analytica Scandal, in 3 Paragraphs. *The Atlantic.*

Mitra, A. (2010). Creating a Presence on Social Networks via Narbs. *Global Media Journal*, 9(16).

Mitra, A. (2011). Using narratives from social network to manage teacher-student interaction. In (Méndez-Vilas, Ed.), *Education in a technological world: communicating current and emerging research and technological efforts.* Formatex Research Center.

Mitra, A. (2014b). *Digital DNA: Managing Identity in Social Networking Sites.* New Delhi, India: Rupa Publications.

Mitra, A. (2018). *Needs Assessment: A Systematic Approach to Data Collection, 2nd Edition.* Sagamore Publishing: Urbana-Champaign, IL.

Netchitailova, E. (2012). Facebook as a Surveillance Tool: From the Perspective of the User. *Triple C.*

Ricouer, P. (1977). The model of the text: Meaningful action considered as text. In F. R. Dallmayr & T. A. McCarthy (Eds.), *Understanding and social inquiry* (pp. 316-334). Notre Dame, IN: The University of Notre Dame Press.

Ricouer, P. (1983). The narrative function. In J. B. Thompson (Ed.), *Paul Ricouer, hermeneutics and the human sciences: Essays on language, action, and interpretation* (pp. 274-296). Cambridge, UK: Cambridge University Press.

Ricouer, P. (1984). *Time and narrative* (Vol. 1, K. McLaughlin & D. Pellaur, Trans.). Chicago, IL: The University of Chicago Press.

Rosenberg, M. (2018). How Trump Consultants Exploited the Facebook Data of Millions. *The New York Times.*

COGNITIVE ENERGY FLOW MODEL CONCEPT FOR VIRTUAL STUDENT

Viktors Zagorskis, Atis Kapanieks, Aleksandrs Gorbunovs and Zane Kadakovska
Riga Technical University, TSC, Kronvalda 1, Riga, Latvia

ABSTRACT

Complex mathematical approaches exist in biological, social, and educational sciences, creating models to understand and explain cognition processes in human brain. Yet, the logged raw data is just an initial learners' behavior footprint in Virtual Learning Environments. Exploratory Data analysis would help to deepen the understanding of cognition processes in students' brain. The challenge is: the evaluation of usability of e-learning courses before the large-scale implementation. With this aim, we combine knowledge elements explored from logged learners behavior data and cognitive theories to formulate a computer model for Virtual Student's evolution. We assume that some of the brains energetic expenses in learning and memorization are due to energy-extraction skills from cognitive abilities, knowledge, information, etc. We also assume that the Virtual Student model can perform energy flow modeling by extracting energy from the environmental learning objects and losing the power in a tedious learning process. The research shows that on a Virtual Student's cognitive energy flow model based approach can potentially improve the model compliance with real student's behavior model and can be applied to predictive analytics classification problems in both inexpensive small and large-scale applications.

KEYWORDS

Cognitive Energy, E-leaning, Agent, Virtual Student

1. INTRODUCTION

A Since 1950th, intelligent agents used to use almost in all of the computer systems with the aim to get the system objects information, to rethink and provide local feedback or public actions. Usually, intelligent agents follow some road-map: (1) Perception, (2) Cognition, and (3) Actuation. These are functional properties of almost all the independent autonomous agents. Among the number of different agents categories, Learning Agents are more advanced because they have a similar to human ability to learn from experienced interaction with the host learning system.

The goal of this paper is to reflect the improved Learning Agent Model with additional specific properties: (1) emotional states, (2) ability to forget the learned facts, (3) need for rest, and (4) agent's energy flow. Concerning that, we propose the improved model based on the agent's energy flow assumption, that is the crucial point of interest. For instance: no energy - no action in learning process.

The new approach goal is to create the preliminary model that would further help to simplify real learners' classification problems using traditional predictive analytics methods in Virtual Learning Environments (VLEs) where (1) usage of Machine Learning Methods is not cost-efficient or (2) the environment has a new learning course and learners have not produced any data yet.

We expect that proposed Learning Agent namely Virtual Student (VS) cognitive energy flow model based approach improves agent model to be applicable for Predictive Analytics (PA) applied on real learners without non cost-efficient Machine Learning (ML) operations. This is the current research question.

The research organized as follows: Section 2 - the reflexion of related theories, methods, and approaches. In Section 3, that is the most important in the research we propose the concept of the Virtual Student's Cognitive Energy Flow Model. In Section 4 we provide a discussion of results and conclude the paper.

2. RELATED WORK

The full theory of intelligence is not yet in existence, although we assume that Master Theory of Cognitive Development should exist in the future [Domingos, 2015], and is applicable in a Human or Artificial World. Overall, Artificial Intelligence (AI) are held on a couple of key concepts: Sensing, Perception, Cognition, and Semantic [Sheth et al., 2015]. Assuming that Computer-Agent have Senses to receive various data from the digital learning environment host, the next conscious process in a computational sequence is the Perception: a cyclic process of interpreting data. Perception involves both interpretation and exploration with a strong reliance on background knowledge patterns of the domain of application [Gregory, 1997].

Cognition utilizes all the data received from a Perception act. Similarly like in a perception process, cognitive computing context is provided by existing knowledge base [Modha et al., 2011]. Finally, Semantics layer involves mapping observations from various stimuli on Computer-Agent input staying out of current research scope.

Of full value, cognitive process implementation serves goals to complete matching microarchitectures: (1) Senses (Intensity of Sensation), (2) Affection (Weber's Law - quantifying the perception of change in a given stimulus), (3) Attention (Rate, Duration, Degree, Inertia), (4) Perception (Temporal, Qualitative, Quantitative(Simple, Complex)), (5) Association (Law of Association), (6) Memory & Imagination (Cache Operative(a couple of seconds), Middle, Long Term Storage Network), and (7) Action (Emotions & Thoughts). Individual cognitive system requirements can cause simplification of the whole architecture or more detailed research and design of the specific item.

Levels of Cognitive Learning. We find an applicable reduced version of Bloom's taxonomy: (1) Memorization, (2) Understanding, and (3) Application.

Cognitive Cycles. Research results in psychology [Franklin and Graesser, 1997,Anderson et al., 2004] show that cognition in autonomous agents, whether artificial, animal or human, can be thought of as consisting of repeated perception-understanding-action cycles.

On Cognitive Cycles Timing. Results from studies in neurosciences determine the length of time taken by each of the phases of the cognitive cycle and are well known. Some results successfully adopted for specific architectures, for instance: LIDA (Learning Intelligent Distribution Agent) [Madl et al., 2011].

Mental Energy in Learning Process. Formulation of Mental Energy (a hard mental effort) in scientific magazines belong to Julian Huxley [Huxley, 1944]. It is a generally recognized truth that physical events can be looked at in two ways: from the mechanistic and from the energic standpoint [JUNG, 1969]. Time and Energy. The fundamental principle of causality and a proportional connection between

Intelligent Agents. Overall, exist more than one Intelligent Agents classification schemes proposed by Russell [Russell and Norvig, 2003] and Weiss [Weiss, 2013]. We follow Russel classification, where group agents divided into five classes based on their degree of perception and capability. Russell evolves five agent groups: (1) simple reflex agents,(2) model-based reflex agents, (3) goal-based agents, (4) utility-based agents, and (5) learning agents. Intelligent Agents can act either as a single instance or in groups: multi-agent systems. In the current paper, we discuss a single instance model.

3. DISCUSSION AND OUTCOMES

We specify some crucial principles we follow creating Agent's named Virtual Student's model: (1) Reliable Mental Energy Flow Model for Virtual Student is the primary interest of our research, (2) Virtual Student's Learning Process is a Mental Energy Flow expressed as a consuming of Internal Energy or growing from inherited Learning Objects, (3) Every single mental activity is a transition along the learning path rewarded with a specified but finite Energy Portion - Energy Token if the change has a direction to the comfortable emotional condition, (4) If the transition has a direction to the uncomfortable emotional condition, Virtual Student becomes fined by Energy Token Decreasing, (5) Virtual Student initially has enough Energy Tokens to overcome threshold level to join the Learning Course, or to start to explore specific Learning Object, and (6) Virtual Student runs based on the principle of causality and a proportional (linearity is not the obligation) relation between time and energy.

On research roadmap, firstly we draft the digital Ecosystem boundaries for Virtual Student's evolution. Then, we specify Virtual Student's properties. Finally, we propose the Virtual Student Learning Model implementation ready concept.

3.1 Virtual Student Ecosystem

Learning Energy Network. Here, we invent the isolated learning network with boundaries for Virtual Student operations when sensing, and declare rules for reasoning (perception, cognition) and acting. Learning network bounds energy consumption or production. We specify three top class energy-related objects for the ecosystem and their properties: (1) System Energy Depot - D, (2) Virtual Student's Energy Buffer - VS, and (3) Learning Object Energy Storage - LO.

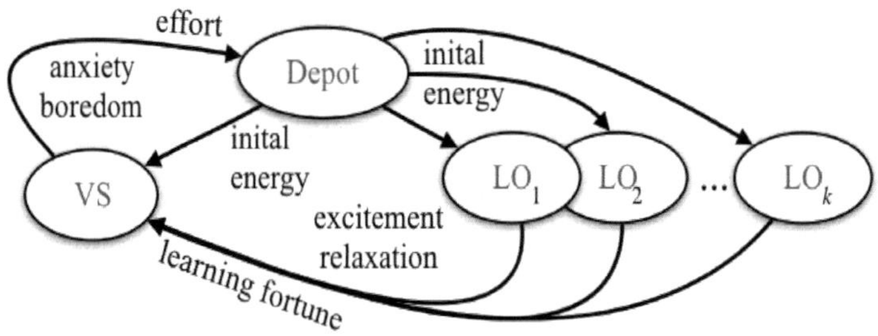

Figure 1. Energy Flow Model for Virtual Student's Ecosystem: System Energy Depot (Depot), Virtual Student's Energy Buffer (VS), and k Energy Storages for Learning Objects (LO1 . . . LOk)

3.2 Virtual Student Properties

We invent following groups of static and dynamic properties: (1) need the rest in daily workout process, (2) ability to forget the learned facts, (3) emotional states, and (3) cycling through motivational sequences. Newly invented and research specific properties we discuss in this paper.

Emotional States. With the Emotional States, we understand real learners' emotional conditions playing a specific role in the learning modeling confidence. We specify following emotional states: very pessimistic, skeptical, confident, and very confident. Considering correlation to Virtual Student's energy model, we elaborated the Emotional States factors.

Virtual Student's Motivational Sequences Model. To form Virtual Student emotionally motivated interactions with ecosystem layers and components required for cognitive learning process modeling, we adopt a commonly occurring Motivational Sequence model [Van der Molen, 1984)]. Virtual Student's attempts to catch and hold certain pleasant states like excitement or relaxation are alternating with unpleasant ones like flat, tiresome states. Four alternating model states (see Figure 2) represent cycling through comfort levels: excitement, anxiety, relaxation, boredom mapped to the timeline. We argue that a tendency to begin to learn at the emotional excitement phase correlates with the real learners' motivation keen to learn.

Alternating Emotional states represent stochastic emotional cycling process leading to Energy Fluctuation in the proposed Virtual Student Learning Model.

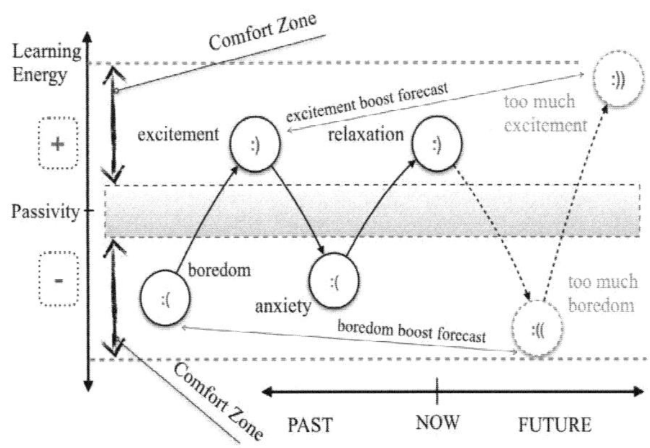

Figure 2. Energy Fluctuation model. Scenario: Suspicious Energy boosting in both directions leaving a Comfort Zone moving towards extreme threshold levels

3.3 Virtual Student Learning Model

From Franklin's results [Franklin and Graesser, 1997], we take into consideration the existence of universal cognitive cycling paradigm: cognition in autonomous agents is subject independent - whether artificial, animal or human. This is the crucial concept point to follow.

We find that Stringer's Action Spiral model [Nasrollahi, 2015,Stringer, 2013] stated existence of look-think-act cycles in cognitive learning correlate with similar results proposed by Anderson [Anderson et al., 2004]. By adding operation control logic we combine both motivational cycling and cognition cycles approaches in to one coherent system presenting Virtual Student Learning Model concept. Figure 3 depicts the Virtual Student Learning model in dynamics. Each transition on the scheme denoted as a colored circle object with a sequence number inside.

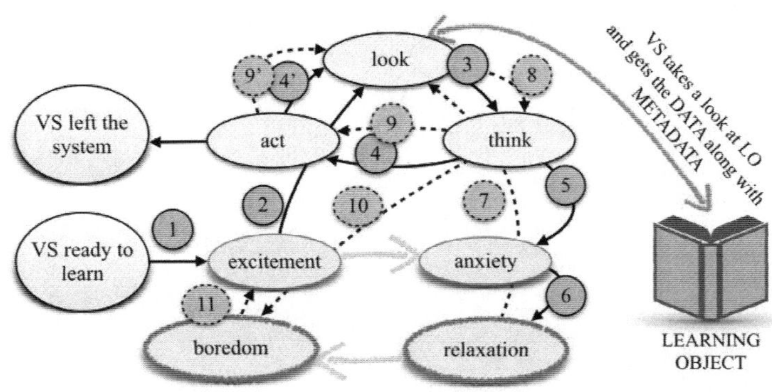

Figure 3. Interaction of Virtual Student Learning model States in a Spatial Design

The main algorithm controls the learning process interacting with every module with the aim to supervise ecosystem energy flow. On a condition of insufficient enough energy, what is the worst scenario, Virtual Student is dropped out of the course. In the case of acceptable quality of interaction with learning objects, the mission completed.

4. CONCLUSION AND FUTURE DIRECTIONS

Summarizing research results regarding energy aspects of the discussed model, **we conclude**: (1) proposed Ecosystem for Virtual Student evolution has clear operating conditions to simulate the learning process based on the energy balance principles, (2) Learning Energy redistribution flow among the system objects can be observed and controlled by the main system algorithm, (3) Ecosystem model's Energy Quantity is constant for every simulation run. For **future works** we consider to follow the crucial concept point: cognition for every autonomous agent is subject independent: (1) to study Virtual Student model computer implementation depending on model Verification results on the model validation stages, (2) to translate conceptual model to operational one and verify it by implementation ir real VLE. Further research by applying validation to the proposed model with an implementation in the Virtual Learning Environment might clarify the aspect of Virtual Student's potential.

ACKNOWLEDGEMENT

This research has been supported by a grant from the European Regional Development Fund (ERDF/ERAF) project Technology Enhanced Learning E-ecosystem with Stochastic Interdependences - TELECI, Project No.1.1.1.1/16/A/154

REFERENCES

[Anderson et al., 2004] Anderson, J. R., Bothell, D., Byrne, M. D., Douglass, S., Lebiere, C., and Qin, Y. (2004). An integrated theory of the mind. Psychological review, 111(4):1036.

[Domingos, 2015] Domingos, P. (2015). The Master Algorithm: How the Quest for the Ultimate Learning Machine Will Remake Our World. Basic Books.

Franklin and Graesser, 1997] Franklin, S. and Graesser, A. (1997). Is it an agent, or just a program?: A taxonomy for autonomous agents. In Proceedings of the Workshop on Intelligent Agents III, Agent Theories, Architectures, and Languages, ECAI '96, pages 21–35, London, UK, UK. Springer-Verlag.

[Gregory, 1997] Gregory, R. L. (1997). Knowledge in perception and illusion. Philosophical Transactions of the Royal Society of London B: Biological Sciences, 352(1358):1121–1127

[Huxley, 1944] Huxley, J. (1944). On living in a revolution, by Julian Huxley. Harper New York, [1st ed.] edition.

[JUNG, 1969] JUNG, C. G. (1969). Collected Works of C.G. Jung, Volume 8: Structure & Dynamics of the Psyche, pages 3–66. Princeton University Press.

[Madl et al., 2011] Madl, T., Baars, B., and Franklin, S. (2011). The timing of the cognitive cycle. 6:e14803.

[Modha et al., 2011] Modha, D. S., Ananthanarayanan, R., Esser, S. K., Ndirango, A., Sherbondy, A. J., and Singh, R. (2011). Cognitive computing. Commun. ACM, 54(8):62–71.

[Nasrollahi, 2015] Nasrollahi, M. A. (2015). A closer look at using stringer's action research model in improving students'.

[Russell and Norvig, 2003] Russell, S. J. and Norvig, P. (2003). Artificial Intelligence: A Modern Approach. Pearson Education, 2 edition.

[Sheth et al., 2015] Sheth, A. P., Anantharam, P., and Henson, C. A. (2015). Semantic, cognitive, and perceptual computing: Advances toward computing for human experience. CoRR, abs/1510.05963.

[Stringer, 2013] Stringer, E. (2013). Action Research. SAGE Publications.

[Weiss, 2013] Weiss, G. (2013). Multiagent Systems. The MIT Press.

STRENGTHEN ENTREPRENEURIAL CAPACITY IN ENTREPRENEURIAL COMPETITIONS

Su-Chang Chen[1], Hsi-Chi Hsiao[2], Jen-Chia Chang[3], Chun-Mei Chou[4] and Dyi-Cheng Chen[5]
[1]*Professor, Department of Marketing and Logistics Management, National Penghu University of Science and Technology*
[2]*Chair Professor, Department of Business Administration, Cheng Shiu University*
[3]*Professor, Graduate Institute of Technological and Vocational Education, National Taipei University of Technology*
[4]*Professor, National Yunlin University of Science and Technology*
[5]*Professor, Department of Industrial Education and Technology, National Changhua University of Education*
Taiwan

ABSTRACT

With high unemployment rates, many countries treat entrepreneurial education as one of the effective measures to solve the problem of social unemployment. In recent years, the government of Taiwan, industries, and schools hold various entrepreneurial competitions to cultivate students' entrepreneurship and realization of entrepreneurship. However, many entrepreneurial competitions are based on originality instead of entrepreneurship. Moreover, students encounter obstacles to carry out their ideas in entrepreneurial competitions. Thus, introducing experiential learning into entrepreneurial competitions and allowing students to develop their ideas of entrepreneurship through experience and stimulation of entrepreneurial competitions may reinforce students' entrepreneurial capacity and authentic entrepreneurship. This study mainly aims to introduce entrepreneurship orientation in experiential learning entrepreneurial competitions in order to cultivate participant students' entrepreneurship and enhance their entrepreneurial capacity and even achieve entrepreneurship. This is student-centered experience learning teaching model. This study treats the sixth College Students' Rural Residency Competition, as held by the Soil and Water Conservation Bureau, COA in Taiwan as an example. There are 126 students in the competition are investigated with questionnaire. According to results, experiential learning can strengthen students' partial entrepreneurial capacity.

KEYWORDS

Entrepreneurship, Entrepreneurial Capacity, Experiential Learning, Entrepreneurial Competition, College Students' Rural Residency Competition

1. INTRODUCTION

Entrepreneurship is popular in Taiwan. With high unemployment rates, many countries treat entrepreneurial education as one of the effective measures to solve the problem of social unemployment, as they provide effective learning courses to enhance graduates' entrepreneurial intention and skills (Chen & Lai, 2007;Chen and Cheng, 2012). In order to allow students to have entrepreneurial competence, entrepreneurial education should cultivate their entrepreneurship abilities and innovative concepts, as students actively learn, they can treat entrepreneurship as an option for their future career, meaning they can create a personal career through entrepreneurship, and according to their own professional skills and interests, to solve the social problem of students' difficulties in gaining employment (Chang et al. 2011).

Experiential learning means the participants voluntarily join in a series of activities, and obtain knowledge and insights from the experience, which they can apply to daily life and work. Kolb (1984) argued that knowledge is derived from experience, and learning is the process in which experience is transformed to construct knowledge. Experiential learning can be classified into four stages in an experiential learning cycle: experiential, reflecting, generalizing, and applying. That is to say, the Experiential Learning theory is a four-stage cycle in learning or problem solving. The first stage is specific experience; the second is observation and reflection; the third is abstract thinking; and the fourth is active validation (Kolb, Rubin,

& McIntyre, 1971). It is an instructional process to obtain knowledge from personal life experience (Dellaportas & Hassal, 2013; Kolb, 1984).

Entrepreneurial capacity is the key success factor of entrepreneurship. Thus, Chang (2003) argued that, before being entrepreneurs, individuals must have entrepreneurial capacity. Thus, "entrepreneurial capacity" is the potential competence possessed by entrepreneurs, including three elements: first, entrepreneurial drive: individuals develop the motive of entrepreneurial behavior; second, perceived venture feasibility: individuals' competence to recognize the execution of the objective behavior as entrepreneurship; third, propensity to act in entrepreneurship: individuals' continuous characteristics of entrepreneurial behavior, including internal and external control personalities and innovation and goal-oriented behavior. Liñán et al. (2011) argued that entrepreneurial capacity should include the competence to recognize opportunities, creativity, problem-solving competence, leadership, communication skill, R&D competence for new service or product, and the ability to control market situations.

In recent years, the government, industrial circles, and schools hold various kinds of entrepreneurial competitions, such as the TiC100 entrepreneurial competition, the Long Teng Smile Competition, the Innovative Entrepreneurship Project, the U-STAR College Graduates' entrepreneurship service project, and the WeWin entrepreneurial competition, in order to cultivate students' entrepreneurship and even the realization of entrepreneurship (Chen and Cheng, 2012; Hsiao et al., 2012). However, Chen and Cheng (2012) argued that, in many entrepreneurial competitions, students participated only to win prizes, instead of accomplishing entrepreneurship. They also encountered obstacles to realize their ideas in entrepreneurial competitions. Chen and Lai (2007) stated that entrepreneurial competitions in Taiwan were only based on originality, and not entrepreneurship. Thus, if Experiential Learning can be introduced into entrepreneurial competitions, and we allow students to develop their ideas of entrepreneurship through experience, the stimulation of such entrepreneurial competitions will reinforce students' entrepreneurial capacity, and even help them achieve real entrepreneurship. This is the motive of this study.

In short, this study aims to introduce entrepreneurship orientation in experiential learning entrepreneurial competitions to cultivate students' entrepreneurship, enhance their entrepreneurial capacity, and even achieve entrepreneurship.

2. RESEARCH METHOD

The College Students' Rural Residency Competition, as hosted by the Soil and Water Conservation Bureau, COA, aims to encourage young students to learn to interact with rural community residents and develop common consensus through their personal originality or specialty, participate in or assist with the public affairs of rural communities, and provide assistance in the process of community promotion of rural reconstruction, in order to approach rural villages, farmers, and agriculture. This competition guides more young people to create sustainable rural villages through new thoughts and skills. The College Students' Rural Residency Competition has been implemented since 2011, and in the last 5 years, it has recruited 300 teams of college students from 15 colleges.

In order to accomplish the research purpose, this study adopts questionnaire survey. It distributes questionnaires to 200 students of the sixth College Students' Rural Residency Competition in Taiwan, and retrieved 126 valid questionnaires, for a valid return rate of 63%.

The items of questionnaire are based on the scale of entrepreneurial capacity by Liñán et al. (2011), including the competence to recognize opportunities, creativity, problem-solving competence, leadership, communication skill, R&D competence of new services or products, and competence to control market situations. The measurement is based on a Likert 5-point scale. In the returned samples, the Cronbach's Alpha of the scale of entrepreneurial capacity is 0.894, which shows a certain degree of reliability.

This study measures the size and discrete situations of items of entrepreneurial capacity according to means and standard deviations, and analyses the differences of the entrepreneurial capacity of subjects with different personal background variables through variance analysis.

3. RESULTS AND DISCUSSION

There are 46 male subjects (36.5%) and 80 females (63.5%). There are 45 subjects of public normal universities (35.7%), 31 subjects of private normal universities (24.6%), 23 subjects of public universities of science and technology (18.3%), and 27 subjects of private universities of science and technology (21.4%). In addition, 36 subjects (28.6%) have taken courses related to entrepreneurial management, while 90 subjects (71.4%) have not; 49 subjects suggest that their parents practice entrepreneurship or commerce (38.9%), while 77 subjects (61.1%) do not; 56 subjects are the eldest in the family (44.4%), 45 subjects are second (35.7%), and 25 subjects are third or above (19.8%).

Table 1 shows subjects' scores in different items of entrepreneurial capacity. The mean of entrepreneurial capacity is 4.01, which denotes medium and high levels. It means that according to the subjects, participation in an experiential entrepreneurial competition can reinforce their entrepreneurial capacity. Among the items, the score for problem-solving competence is the highest, followed by communication competence, and then, competence to control rural market situations. This result is similar to the interview results, meaning it relies on future planning of entrepreneurship-oriented courses. Thus, students can learn before and during their residency, which might strengthen their competence in this aspect.

Table 1. Subjects' scores in different items of entrepreneurial capacity

Item	Mean	Standard deviation	Ranking
Communication competence	4.21	0.773	2
distinguishing competence	3.88	0.845	6
Creativity	4.11	0.772	3
Problem-solving competence	4.25	0.726	1
Leadership	3.94	0.756	4
R&D competence	3.90	0.828	5
Control competence	3.81	0.883	7
Entrepreneurial capacity	4.01	0.625	

According to Table 2, subjects who have taken entrepreneurship courses show higher entrepreneurial capacity than those who have not taken such courses, and the difference is significant. Hence, entrepreneurship courses can reinforce students' entrepreneurial capacity. Therefore, systematic planning of entrepreneurship oriented teaching materials, as well as instruction before and during students' residency, will significantly upgrade their entrepreneurial capacity.

Table 2. The t test of taking entrepreneurship courses or not

	Number	Mean	Standard deviation	t value	p value
Yes	36	4.27	0.466	3.002	0.003
No	90	3.91	0.652		

The remaining dimensions, such as gender, type of school, parents' practice of entrepreneurship, ranking in the family, and grades in the competition do not show significantly different entrepreneurial capacities.

4. CONCLUSION AND RECOMMENDATIONS

According to the results of the questionnaire survey, students who have taken courses of entrepreneurship show superior entrepreneurial capacity acquisition than those who have not taken such courses. Therefore, the systematic planning of entrepreneurship oriented teaching materials and instruction before and during students' residency will considerably enhance their entrepreneurial capacity.

Thus, this study suggests that, in the future, we can develop outlines for the teaching materials of experiential entrepreneurship and assignments to allow students' experience, knowledge, skills, and attitude, as obtained during their experiential residency, to effectively reinforce their entrepreneurship and entrepreneurial capacity.

In addition, teaching materials can be developed as videos, while assignments and instruction can be based on the teaching strategies of online platforms through the flipped learning concept.

ACKNOWLEDGEMENT

The authors would like to acknowledge the financial support of the National Science Council, Taiwan for the contract number of MOST 104-2516-S-346-001.

REFERENCES

Chang J. C., Chen S. C., Chen, C. P., and Chou C. M., 2011. Discussion on the necessity of implementing entrepreneurship education in advanced technical vocational education from the perspective of innovation and creative. *2011 Cross-Strait Applied Science (Technical and Vocational) Higher Education Academic Conference.* China: Shanghai.

Chang S. H. 2003. *The construction of entrepreneurial capacity mode and its application in entrepreneurship education (I).* Taiwan National Science Council Special Project Number: NSC91-2516-S212-002.

Chen S. C., and Cheng, L. L., 2012. The dilemmas and strategies for promoting entrepreneurship education in Taiwan. *Journal of Guangdong Polytechnic Normal University, 33*(1), 30-32.

Chen., Y. F., and Lai, M. C. ,2007. The Entrepreneurial Curricula in Taiwan. *Journal of entrepreneurshipResearch, 2*(3), 117-147.

Dellaportas, S., & Hassal, T. (2013) Experiential learning in accounting education: A prison visit *The British Accounting Review, 45*(1), 24-36.

Hsiao H. C., Chen S. C., Chou C. M., Chang J. C., and Jing L. L., 2012. Is entrepreneurial education available for graduate? *African Journal of Business Management, 6*(15), 5193-5200.

Kolb, D.A. (1984). *Experiential Learning: Experience as the Resource of Learning and Development.* Englewood Cliffs, NJ: Prentice Hall.

Kolb, D.A., Rubin, I.M., and McIntyre, J. (Eds., 1971). *Organizational Psychology: An Experiential Approach.* Englewood Cliffs, N.J.: Prentice Hall.

Liñán, F., Rodríguez-Cohard, J. C., and Rueda-Cantuche, J. M. (2011). Factors affecting entrepreneurial intention levels: a role for education. *International Entrepreneurship and Management Journal*, *7*(2), 195-218.

SCHOOL DIGITALIZATION FROM THE TEACHERS' PERSPECTIVE IN RUSSIA

Irina Dvoretskaya
Institute of Education, Higher School of Economics , Myasnitskaya, 20, Moscow, 101000, Russian Federation

ABSTRACT

In this study, we would like to show the analysis of latent factor structure of school digitalization from the teachers' perspective based on pilot SELFIE (Self-reflection tool for digitally capable schools) data. The survey of 685 teachers who took part in the pilot SELFIE study in Russia were subjected to an exploratory factor analysis. Five factors of technology-enhanced teaching emerged. Taking into consideration the lack of recent studies in internal drivers of digital transformation in Russia, this study contributes to the understanding of changes happening within a complex system such as the school system is. Further perspectives for digital transformation's aspects analysis based on SELFIE data are also proposed.

KEYWORDS

ICT in School Education, Digital Transformation of Schools, Innovative Teaching and Learning

1. INTRODUCTION

Nowadays the integration of ICT into education still seems very promising from the perspective of government, IT companies and digital evangelists. We know that innovative teaching enhanced by digital technology, contributes to the 21st century skills of students, so it become sufficient for modern school to employ the digital technologies potential. However, regarding the technology-supported educational reform there is a certain gap between declared digital-oriented goals of education policies and classroom practices that are slow to change(Cuban, Kirkpatrick and Peck, 2001; Vrasidas, 2015).

The national context of digital innovations in Russian schools during the last 10 years can be characterized by the following initiatives:

1. Federal Dedicated Program "Development of Informatization in Russia for the Period up to 2010" that includes some regional educational initiatives for educational services and software development.
2. In 2010, new educational standards were introduced considering 21st century skills as a necessary part of students' learning outcomes.
3. In 2010, «Education System Informatization» federal project sponsored by the World Bank was completed. The objective of this project was to support schools in the pedagogical use of ICT in teaching and learning.

The deficit of current national school informatization action programmes is supposed to be covered by priority project «Digital school»(Russian Federation, 2017), currently under development. At the same time the level of ICT usage and pedagogical change in Russian schools may be identified as low according to many experts. It means that for successful programmes' implementations the evidence-based aproaches on recent data should be offered.

The primary aim of this research is to explore the latent factor structure of digital transformation in Russian school through the perspective of school teachers. The main motivation for this study is the fact that very few past studies aimed to identify the factors affecting teachers' pedagogical use of technologies in Russian context. At best, only small-sampled studies were conducted dedicated to ICT competence as a main driver of changes.

Regarding large-sampled studies in which Russian schools took part during the last 10-15 years, it is possible to name SITES 2006 (Law et al., 2008) and Innovative Teaching and Learning Research(ITL) in 2011(Shear et al., 2011)). In the SITES 2006 the teacher-level factors of pedagogical use of ICT are highlighted, focusing on connectedness, traditional importance and life-long learning. This criteria may be sufficient for digital-age learning, according to more recent works. ITL proved that innovative practices dissemination should be supported with additional efforts and measures in Russia naming collaborative environment, professional development, a shift toward student centricity, and digital infrastructure among factors of teaching in the digital age.

In respect to the growing role of school teachers for knowledge economy, this paper addresses the question of drivers of pedagogical use of ICT in the Russian classrooms. In our analysis, we want to identify the latent factor structure that explains the nature of technology-enhanced teaching in Russia suggested by the pattern of responses. So the research question can be formulated as follows: which latent factors should be considered as influencing the pedagogical use of digital technologies among Russian school teachers'?

The knowledge of how teachers are changing their ICT related practices tailoring them to the dynamic context can serve as a tool for education strategy's elaboration.

2. METHODOLOGY

To carry out all analysis in this study we used R software with psych package.

2.1 Sample

In this study, the dataset of teachers' questionnaires (N=685) was drawn from the SELFIE tool dataset, in primary, lower secondary and secondary schools. SELFIE tool is developed by the European Commission Joint Research Centre. In 2017 it was piloted in more than 600 schools from 14 European countries. Based on DigCompOrg (Kampylis et al, 2015) framework, SELFIE tool helps to make visible the core of educational transformation in school to educators from the perspective of three main actors of the school system, namely school leaders, teachers and students. As a tool, it aims to support schools in reflecting their digital capability and practices. The main focus of the tool is learning, and not technology. The validity of the tool was confirmed(Munoz Castano et al., 2018).

Schools for the study were chosen from IITE and UNESCO Associated Schools Project Network (UNESCO ASP) within the scope of the SELFIE project pilot where Russia took part in October 2017.

2.2 Procedure

To obtain the study objective, the Exploratory Factor Analysis (EFA) was performed. The initial number of items was 60. The sample size (N=685) is adequate for the factor analysis as the case-to-variable ratio is 10:1.To ensure the degree of reliability of the SELFIE questionnaire, we calculated Cronbach's Alpha coefficient, which was found to be 0.96, indicating that the level of reliability of the Teachers' questionnaire of SELFIE is excellent.

To check the sampling adequacy for exploratory factor analysis, we also made the Káiser-Meyer-Olkin sampling adjustment test and the Barlett square test which ($p < 0.001$) showed that all variables from the dataset fit well.As KMO was 0.96 and in the Barlett a Chi-square= 27751.92, it indicated that we could continue to the EFA.

The sample was initially analyzed with maximum likelihood (ML) extraction methods and promax rotation. After the first step of EFA some items were omitted from further analysis as they have low factor loadings (<0.50). Items with missing values (optional questions) were also excluded from the analysis. In addition we eliminated items related to the SELFIE user experience. So the number of factors for EFA was 25.

With the reduced number of items we analyzed the sample with ML extraction method and promax rotation again. Here we used oblique rotation as factors were assumed to be correlated (Dean, 2009). Now it was possible to extract five factors that explained the 60.1% of variance.

3. RESULTS

In Table 1 the results of factor analysis are summarized. For interpretation of factors, we decided to discard the factor loadings of less than 0.50. Analysis of items on each factor emerged 5 areas of digital transformation in school from teachers' viewpoint. Each factor consists of varying quantity of items, grouped in five categories.

Table 1. Promax rotated factor structure: reduced dataset with 25 variables

	% of common variance	Name of the factor	№ of items
Factor 1	9,3%	Pedagogical Leadership	3 items
Factor 2	10,3%	Shift toward student centricity	4 items
Factor 3	15,9%	Digital infrastructure	7 items
Factor 4	15,5%	Digital-age learning environment	7 items
Factor 5	9,3%	Digital culture	4 items

Factor 1, «Pedagogical Leadership», comprised 3 items related to the contribution of teacher to the school digital strategy and to the regular review of the outcomes of using digital technologies in teaching and learning. This factor is aligned with DigCompOrg framework and «Leadership and governance practices» element (Kampylis et al, 2015).This factor claims the role of teachers' engagement to the holistic vision on digitalization, and how teachers understand the importance of open discussion and skilled communication digital technologies in school (Department of Education and Skills, 2015).

Factor 2, «Shift toward student centricity», contains 4 items capturing how teachers perceived digital technologies in teaching and learning, and how they evaluate its potential (Scherer et al., 2015). This factor proves the idea of the way how student-centered practices affect student learning outcomes (Shear et al., 2011).

Factor 3, «Digital infrastructure» contains 7 items, pointing out the digital infrastructure for learning. This factor is aligned with DigCompOrg framework and its «Infrastructure» element.

Factor 4, «Digital-age learning environment», contained 7 items related to the digital environment in school and described the way of using digital technology for teaching and learning. It reveals the changing role of pedagogical approaches with the focus on 21st century skills.

Factor 5, «Digital culture» comprised 4 items, capturing how teachers empower their students with digital skills by building digital culture (Scherer et al., 2015). This factor mainly referred to the developing of relevant skills for successful participation in modern social life (Kampylis et al, 2015) and knowledge economy.

4. CONCLUSION

The current study mainly aimed to explore latent factors that encompass digital transformation in school from teachers' perspective in Russia. This analysis is an initial step towards the explanation of the effective use of digital technologies in schools based on SELFIE data.

Our results suggest 5 factors of ICT incorporation in teaching and learning. Interestingly, that neither collaboration nor ICT competence factors were explored among them. So it is possible to say that teachers tend to focus on new pedagogical practices and innovative approaches rather than on general digital skills. At the same time, collaborative culture in schools is the subject for deeper analysis on SELFIE dataset. Limitations of this study include relience on self-report data, and participating schools have an access to the perfecting methods and teaching materials which UNESCO ASP provide them with, so it might influence teachers' responces.

The latent factor structure obtained shows the need to integrate corresponding measures for more effective use of digital technologies in the school education. It can be crucial for investment optimization on ICT for teaching and learning programmes, and for next school informatization action programmes.

As such, the results of the study could also inform key stakeholderss, e.g. policy makers, school leaders and principals, teacher educators on how to take measures to better support Russian teachers for pedagogical uses of ICT in their classrooms. Based on factor structure findings we can accentuate two parts of practical measures:

- teachers' professional development in schools should include additional possibilities, such as mentorship, development of the school as a learning community and different informal activities. It alignes with factors 1 and 5. The design of professional development model and its implementations is a subject for further studies.
- from organizational perspective, some new activities and policies should emerge in order to support student-shift centricity, as well as digital culture in teachers' community.

Further work will include more detailed interpretation of factors and confirmatory factor analysis in order to establish the construct validity. The next step could be the analysis of factors that may be used as predictors of innovative ICT use in Russian classrooms. To carry out this type of activity the regression analysis of technology enhanced teaching practices and contextual factors at the teacher's school must be planned. In addition to it, the analysis conducted on wider sample will help to elaborate factor structure depending on school characteristics.

REFERENCES

Cuban, L. et al, 2001. High Access and Low Use of Technologies in High School Classrooms: Explaining an Apparent Paradox. *American Educational Research Journal*. SAGE Publications, Vol. 38(4), pp. 813–834.

Dean, J. 2009. Choosing the Right Type of Rotation in PCA and EFA. *Shiken: JALT Testing & Evaluation SIG Newsletter*, Vol. 13, pp. 20–25.

Department of Education and Skills, 2015. *Digital Strategy for Schools Digital Strategy for Schools Enhancing Teaching, Learning and Assessment*. Department of Education and Skills, Dublin.

Kampylis, P. et al, 2015. *Promoting Effective Digital-Age Learning - A European Framework for Digitally-Competent Educational Organisations*.European Union.

Law, N. et al, 2008. *Pedagogy and ICT Use, CERC studies in comarative education*. IEA, Hong Kong.

Munoz Castano, J. et al., 2018. Within-school Differences in the Views on the Use of Digital Technologies in Europe : Evidence from the SSELFIE Tool. Theoretical framework : DigCompOrg The SELFIE tool Description of SELFIE ' s pilot phase and questionnaire s', *EDULEARN18 Conference Proceedings*. Palma de Mallorca, Spain.

Scherer, R. et al, 2015. Becoming more specific: Measuring and modeling teachers' perceived usefulness of ICT in the context of teaching and learning, *Computers & Education*. Vol. 88, pp. 202–214.

Shear, L., et al, 2011. *Innovative teaching and learning research: 2011 findings and implications*. SRI International, Menlo Park.

Vrasidas, C., 2015. The rhetoric of reform and teachers' use of ICT. *British Journal of Educational Technology*, Vol. 46(2), pp. 370–381.

Government of Russian Federation, 2017. On priority project «Digital School». Available at: http://government.ru/orders/selection/401/30822/ (Accessed: 9 June 2018).

DIGITAL LIFE, MATHEMATICAL SKILLS AND COGNITIVE PROCESSES

Maria Lidia Mascia[1], Simona Perrone[2], Dianora Bardi[2], Mirian Agus[1], Maria Pietronilla Penna[1] and Daniela Lucangeli[3]
[1]*Department of Pedagogy, Psychology, Philosophy, University of Cagliari, Italy*
[2]*Impara Digitale Association, Bergamo, Italy*
[3]*Department of Developmental Psychology and Socialisation, University of Padova, Italy*

ABSTRACT

A consistent part of the literature shows the significant role of digital experience in digital natives' cognitive processes. The main goal of the current study was to investigate the impact of digital learning on the improvement of mathematical skills and on some change in cognitive processes in 166 primary school children from schools located in different parts of Italy. Participants were divided in two group: one group experienced the study of math mainly through digital tools, the other spent more time on pencil-and-paper trainings. All our participants were assessed with a battery of tests measuring numerical and cognitive abilities. Our results suggest the positive effect of a different type of training for the empowerment of visuo-spatial and numerical abilities. Specifically, effects of a digital experience are particularly evident in some specific numerical areas, such us accuracy, speed, semantic and syntactic numerical knowledge. Also, participants with greater experience of digital trainings score higher on spatial orientation.

KEYWORDS

Digital Learning, Mathematics, Educational Technology, School, Cognitive Processes

1. INTRODUCTION

Cognitive flexibility, problem solving, speed of processing, spatial orientation and visuo-spatial abilities are abilities that have an impact on maths proficiency. Therefore, these are also crucial factors to succeed in nowadays'society (Moffitt, et al., 2011). In Italy, where this study has been carried on, OCSE data show that high-proficiency math students are the 9.9% of the students' population compared to the 12.6% of the European sample (PISA – OCSE, 2012). What these data tell us about? We think they show how much Italy falls behind other EU countries in terms of digital education in school contexts. Indeed, we rank 25 out of 28 in terms of connectivity and human capital (PNSD, Ministero dell'Istruzione e della Ricerca, 2015). However, ICT is a fact we cannot neglect nowadays; it becomes extremely important for Italy to regain positions in the digital world scenario and to strengthen research in the field of digital learning and education. It is within these boundaries that this study takes place. Our starting point in this work is the assumption that computer-based interventions can contribute to increase math skills (Agus, Mascia, Fastame, Melis, Pilloni and Penna, 2015; Mascia, Agus, Fastame & Addis, 2016). Indeed, ICT allows teachers to make up learning materials that are more familiar to children than the old-fashioned paper and pencil. A crucial example comes from the study of Zhang et al., where two-year old toddlers were able to use iPads with little direction from adults (Zhang, Trussel, Gallegos, Asam, 2015). Another plus of digital education is that digital devices offer personalized learning strategies (token economy, chunking, scaffolding) for children with special needs, and they guarantee an easy way to manage and analyze data coming from the interventions that are put into practice (Wayman, 2005; Papadakis, Kalogiannakis & Zaranis, 2016). Thus, because of the wide presence of digital tools in our life, and their potential implications on learning, we consider of extreme importance a further and deepen investigation of the phenomenon, focusing on the digital tools that allow the best user experience. For example, the opportunity to give immediate feedback to individual learners, especially if they have learning disabilities, seems to be the only way this population can improve their math performances. Also, the individual usage allows learners to work on math problems at their own pace, which can be particularly useful for struggling students who need more time to solve a problem (Baker, Gersten, & Lee, 2002; Hassler, B., Major, L., Hennessy, S.2015). Unfortunately, the actualization of these practices is barely feasible in Italy today, where the percentage of digital devices per student is one out of eight (PNSD, Miur, 2015).

2. METHOD

One of the main concerns about digital education is that it can impact negatively on cognitive variables that are crucial for the child's development and learning (Li & Ma, 2010; Livingstone, 2011; Highfield & Goodwin, 2013). However, studies comparing digital and analogical education do not display a similar outcome (Falloon, 2013; Berge & Muilenburg, 2013). Hence, persuaded that personalization of the educational could decrease anxiety while learning and could offer many advantages to school curricula, we conducted our research in primary school – where the basic and essential skills are tackled – and we tested our sample on two different cognitive measures: visuo-spatial abilities and spatial relations. Furthermore, numerical skills have been measured to analyze the learning outcomes of the intervention. The results fall within a wider research about the use of digital tools in learning founded by Acer for Education and led by CNIS and Impara Digitale.

3. PARTICIPANTS, MATERIALS AND PROCEDURE

One hundred and sixty six 8-year-old children took part into this research study. All of them have been recruited through previous contact with primary schools all over Italy. Therefore, the sample is equally distributed over the whole Nation. Participants were for the 47.9% female. Participation to the research was voluntary and no economic compensation has been offered to families or schools. Sampling was random and non-probabilistic. However, before the participation to the study, each family had to fill in a consent form where the nature of the research and data treatment was explained. Standardized tests have been administered to children to measure numeracy skills, visuo-spatial abilities, and fluid intelligence. Interviews to the teachers allowed us to divide the sample in "digitalized children", namely those who learned mathematics mainly through apps, softwares and digital tools, and "non-digitalized children", those who mainly had an analogical approach to the subject. The participants were divided into two experimental groups that followed two type of trainings, in computerised and pencil-and-paper formats, for 12 weekly sessions. In order to assess respectively abilities, at pre and post-test, our participants compiled a battery of standardised tests: to measure numeracy skills, we administered the ACMT 6-11 battery of tests (Cornoldi, Lucangeli, & Bellina, 2012), for visuo-spatial abilities we used Thurstone's PMA test (Thurstone & Thurstone, 1962) and for fluid intelligence Ravens' Coloured Progressive Matrices (cfr. Ed. It. Belacchi, Scalisi, Cannoni, et al., 2008; Brouwers, Van de Vijer & Van Hemert, 2009).

4. FINDINGS

The mean and standard deviations for AC-MT (Written calculation, Accuracy, Speed, Semantic and Syntactic numerical knowledge), PMA and CPM scales were examined. A Manova and a correlation analysis have been applied. Our results show that students with a greater experience in digitalized version of mathematical trainings have better results in some of the mentioned mathematical areas. The multivariate tests were significant for the covariates (Wilks' lambda [6, 159] = .897, p=.000). Then univariate tests indicated a significant effect of 'greater experience in digital trainings' in terms of Accuracy (F(1, 164) = 10.453, MSE = 455,949 p=.011, partial ηp2= .060), Speed (F(1, 164) = 13.626, MSE = 43926,343 p = .000, partial ηp2= .070), Semantic and Syntactic numerical knowledge (F(1, 164) = 11.433, MSE = 106,98 p = .001, partial ηp2= .065) and spatial orientation (F(1, 164) = 6.587, MSE = 113.339 p = .011, partial ηp2= .032).

The correlation study (Table 1) confirms the relationship between the cognitive variables analyzed in this study and mathematical abilities.

Table 1. Correlation analysis

			1	2	3	4	5	
Spatial orientation	r	1	1					
	Sig. (2-tailed)							
Written operations	r	2	,189*	1				
	Sig. (2-tailed)		,011					
Numerical Knowledge	r	3	,130	,377**	1			
	Sig. (2-tailed)		,090	,000				
Accuracy	r	4	-,203**	-,483**	-,552**	1		
	Sig. (2-tailed)		,007	,000	,000			
Speed	r	5	-,132	-,488**	-,486**	,720**	1	
	Sig. (2-tailed)		,084	,000	,000	,000		
Fluid intelligence	r	6	,403**	,200**	,378**	-,379**	-,289**	1
	Sig. (2-tailed)		,000	,008	,000	,000	,000	

5. CONCLUSION

We can now conclude that the use of digital tools in learning numerical and mathematical skills has had a positive impact on primary school children in their third year of study. First, the use of the digital version of mathematical trainings is more effective than the paper-and-pencil mathematical in some specific areas, in particular, in terms of interaction and in terms of spatial orientation.

Therefore, we can conclude that our findings are consistent with those by previous researches (Brouwers, Van de Vijer & Van Hemert, 2009; Burns, Kanive, De Grande, 2012; Zaranis, Kalogiannakis & Papadakis, 2013) and that the use of digital intervention supports the development of numerical knowledge in children (Pitchford, 2015), especially when it comes to improve some specific cognitive processes, such as the spatial orientation. In our sample, no differences were found in fluid intelligence. To conclude, we think that a tailored and personalized digital education has a crucial role in the effectiveness of learning.

REFERENCES

Agus, M., Mascia, M. L., Fastame, M. C., Melis, V., Pilloni, M. C., & Penna, M. P. (2015). The measurement of enhancement in mathematical abilities as a result of joint cognitive trainings in numerical and visual-spatial skills: A preliminary study. In *Journal of Physics: Conference Series* (Vol. 588, No. 1, p. 012041). IOP Publishing.

Belacchi, C., et al. (2008). *Manuale CPM*, Organizzazioni Speciali.

Bennet, S., Maton, K., Kervin, L. (2008). The "digital natives" debate: A critical review of the evidence. *British Journal of Education Technology*, 39(5), 775-786;

Berge, Z. L., & Muilenburg, L. (2013). Seamless learning: An international perspective on next-generation technology-enhanced learning. In *Handbook of mobile learning* (pp. 133-146). Routledge.

Brouwers, S., A., Van de Vijer, F., J., R., Van Hemert, D., A. (2009). Variation in Raven's Progressive Matrices scores across time and place, *Learning and Individual Differences*, 19(*3*), 330-338;

Burns, M., K., Kanive, R., De Grande, M. (2012). Effect of a computer-delivered math fact intervention as a supplemental intervention for math in third and fourth grades, *Remedial and Special Education*, 33(*3*), 184-191.

Cornoldi, C., Cornoldi, C., Lucangeli, D., & Bellina, M. (2012). *AC-MT 6-11. Test di valutazione delle abilità di calcolo e soluzione dei problemi*. Gruppo MT. Con CD-ROM. Edizioni Erickson.

Falloon, G. (2013). Young students using iPads: App design and content influences on their learning pathways, *Computers & Education*, 68, 505-521;

Highfield, K., Goodwin, K. (2013). Apps for mathematics learning: A review of "educational" apps from the iTunes app store, Mathematics Education: Yesterday, Today and Tomorrow. *Proceedings of the 36th annual conference of the Mathematics Education Research Group of Australasia,* 378-385;

Li, Q., Ma, X. (2010). A met-analysis of the effects of computer technology on school students' mathematics learning, *Educational Psychology Review*, 22(*3*), 215-243.

Livingstone, S. (2011). Critical reflections on the benefits of ICT in education, *Oxford Review of Education*, 38(*1*), 9-24.

Mascia, M. L., Agus, M., Fastame, M. C., & Addis, A. (2016). *Enhancement in Mathematical Abilities: A System Approach. In Towards a Post-Bertalanffy Systemics* (pp. 243-249). Springer, Cham.

Ministero della pubblica istruzione e della ricerca, (2015). Piano nazionale scuola digitale.

Moffit, T., E., Arseneault, L., Belsky, D., Dickson, N., Hancox, R., J., Harrington, H., L., Houts, R., Poulton, R., Roberts, B., W., Ross, S., Sears, M., R., Murray Thomson, W., Caspi, A. (2011). A gradient of childhood self-control predicts health, wealth, and public safety, *PNAS*, 108(*7*), 2693-2698.

OCSE-PISA, (2012). Rapporto nazionale a cura di Invalsi.

Papadakis, S., Kalogiannakis, M., & Zaranis, N. (2016). Comparing tablets and PCs in teaching mathematics: an attempt to improve mathematics competence in early childhood education, *Preschool and Primary Education*, 4(*2*), 241-253.

Pitchford, N., J. (2015). Development of early mathematical skills with a tablet intervention: A randomized control trial in Malawi, *Frontiers in Psychology*, 6(*485*), 1-12.

Thurstone, T. G., & Thurstone, L. L. (1962). *Primary mental abilities tests*. Science Research Associates.

Wayman, J., C. (2005). Involving teachers in data-driven decision-making: Using computer data systems to support teacher inquiry and reflection, *Journal of Education for Students Placed at Risk*, 10, 295-308;

Zaranis, N., Kalogiannakis, M., & Papadakis, S. (2013). Using mobile devices for teaching realistic mathematics in kindergarten education, *Creative Education*, 4(*7*), 1-10.

Zhang, M., Trussell, R., P., Gallegos, B., Asam, R., R. (2015). Using math apps for improving student learning: An exploratory study in an inclusive fourth grade classroom, *TechTrends,* 59(*2*), 32-39.

MIXED DIGITAL MESSAGES: THE ABILITY TO DETERMINE NEWS CREDIBILITY AMONG SWEDISH TEENAGERS

Thomas Nygren[1] and Mona Guath[2]
[1]*Department of Education, Uppsala University, Box 2136 , 750 02 Uppsala, Sweden*
phone: +46 73 6468649
[2]*Department of Psychology, Uppsala University, Box 1225, 751 42 Uppsala, Sweden*

ABSTRACT

In this study we investigate the abilities to determine credibility of digital news among 532 teenagers. Using an online test we assess to what extent teenagers are able to determine the credibility of different sources, evaluate credible and biased uses of evidence, and corroborate information. Many respondents fail to identify the credibility of false, biased and vetted news. We identify a digital divide between people with and without the ability to determine credibility. We also find that a large proportion of the respondents struggle to identify the source of information in Sweden's most read online newspaper. Respondents struggle to determine the bias of news reports regarding racism and weight loss, but are better at debunking manipulated images. Respondents who value the importance of credible news and who indicate that they have learned media literacy in school seem to hold a mind-set helping them to determine credibility better than other respondents. Our findings provide a basis for further research of how to better understand and support digital civic literacy in classrooms and society.

KEYWORDS

Credibility, Sourcing, Fact-Checking, False News, Bias, Media Information Literacy

1. INTRODUCTION

New media may connect people across cultural and ideological borders, but also foster mistrust. Digital news media is pivotal to stimulate conversations and active citizenry (e.g., Lee, Shah, & McLeod, 2013). However, digital media and modern journalism can also in many ways facilitate the spread of exaggerations, rumours and lies (e.g., Vosoughi, Roy, & Aral, 2018). Today mainstream and non-mainstream news are mixed in digital environments making it difficult to assess credibility (Fletcher & Park, 2017). This implies new requirements for both readers and society (e.g., McGrew et al, 2017, 2018). Scholars argue that teaching and learning what we label *digital civic literacy* is absolutely essential to informed and engaged citizenship (e.g. Kahne & Bowyer, 2017). We define *digital civic literacy* as the ability to navigate digital civic information in critical and constructive ways, and we acknowledge that simply having access to information is not enough. Digital civic literacy enable citizens to engage with political and social topics in critical and constructive ways, but it has proven to be quite a challenge to implement digital tools and digital literacy in education (Balanskat et al. 2013). Previous research highlights how prior beliefs, coherence of the message, and cognitive ability may affect people's ability to assess the credibility of information (Lewadowsky et al., 2012). It has also been noted how attitudes to news, scientific curiosity and socio-economic factors may influence how people navigate new information, facts and digital environments (e.g., Strömbäck, Djerf-Pierre, & Shehata, 2013; Kahan et al., 2017; Hatlevik et al., 2015). People use cues and heuristics to estimate credibility, which may be helpful, but they may still fail to separate false and biased news from authentic information regarding debated topics (e.g., Wineburg & McGrew, 2018).

The aim of the current study was to investigate youths' ability to assess the credibility of information on the Internet and how this relates to personal characteristics and beliefs, which in turn will enable us to suggest educational measures to support and scaffold young people's abilities to assess online information.

2. METHOD AND DESIGN

Researchers in education and psychology designed and piloted, in close collaboration with in-service teachers, online multiple choice tests in order to assess and compare youths (*N* = 532) age 15-19. The tests consisted of 22 questions whose contents and measured variables are presented in Table 1. The design of the tests was inspired by previous research on civic online reasoning (McGrew et al., 2017). In the present test, the participants were also asked for their self-rated ability to find news online, critical ability, the importance of credibility of news, how reliable information on the Internet is, and how much media literacy education they have had in school. All self-rated variables were on a 5 point scale, with the exception of media literacy, which was on a 10 point scale. Finally, demographic variables and media habits were measured (see Table 1 for a more detailed account).

Table 1. Overview of questions and measured constructs in the online test. The measured constructs refer to abilities that have been identified as important for the detecting of false news online. The questions are referred to in the text with the names in parentheses

Measured construct	Question
Detecting sponsored material (sourcing)	Screenshot from IT journal (Techworld) Screenshot from evening paper 1 (Aftonbladet) Screenshot from evening paper 2 (Expressen)
Comparing articles (corroboration)	Two articles about weight loss (weight loss) Two articles about the government's policy on racism (racism)
Scrutinising comments and images (evidence)	Edited photograph of a smoking girl (smoking) Article about the government's energy goals (energy goals) Article about the climate change (climate change) Reader's comment on incomes (income) Edited photograph on daisies in Fukushima (Fukushima)
Self-rated abilities	Media literacy education (media literacy) Reliability of information on the Internet (information reliability) Source criticism on the Internet (fact-checking ability) Finding information on the Internet (critical ability) Importance of news credibility (credibility importance)
Background variables	Gender Form (youths)/Age group (adults) Secondary school focus (youths) Political party sympathies (1 or more parties) News format (e.g., paper news, radio etc.) News source (e.g., local newspaper, evening paper etc.)

3. RESULTS

We first computed the total number of correct answers for all question items that could be classified as correct or incorrect, where the questions with embedded advertisements (see Table 1) was coded as correct if all answers were correct. The mean number of correct of maximum 8 for each for each form were: ninth form compulsory (M = 3.38, SD = 1.72), first form secondary (M = 3.42, SD = 1.74), second form secondary (M = 3.62, SD = 1.74), and third form secondary (M = 3.48, SD = 1.82). The items that the pupils found most difficult were Aftonbladet (12% correct), Expressen (21 % correct), Techworld (34% correct), racism (43%) and weight loss (53%).

This should be contrasted with the mean credibility ratings for the articles: climate change (M = 6.02, SD = 2.26), energy goals (M = 4.69, SD = 2.13), and income (M = 4.05, SD = 1.87). Hence, there were no clear differences between the articles, notably, the false news article (climate change) was rated as the most credible article. The self-rated abilities were: fact-checking ability (*M* = 3.99, *SD* = 0.743), credibility importance (*M* = 3.95, *SD* = 1.12), critical ability (*M* = 3.99, *SD* = 0.743), media literacy (*M* = 7.18, *SD* = 2.07), and information reliability (*M* = 2.87, *SD* = 0.755).

In order to relate performance to background variables and self-rated abilities we performed a number of regressions. Results showed that for Expressen, speaking Swedish at home and high ratings on media literacy were associated with an increased probability of correct answers, whereas a higher self-reported rating on fact-checking ability was associated with a decreased probability of number of correct items. For Aftonbladet, a higher rating on credibility importance was associated with an increased probability of number of correct items and for Techworld, speaking Swedish at home was associated with an increased probability of number of correct items.

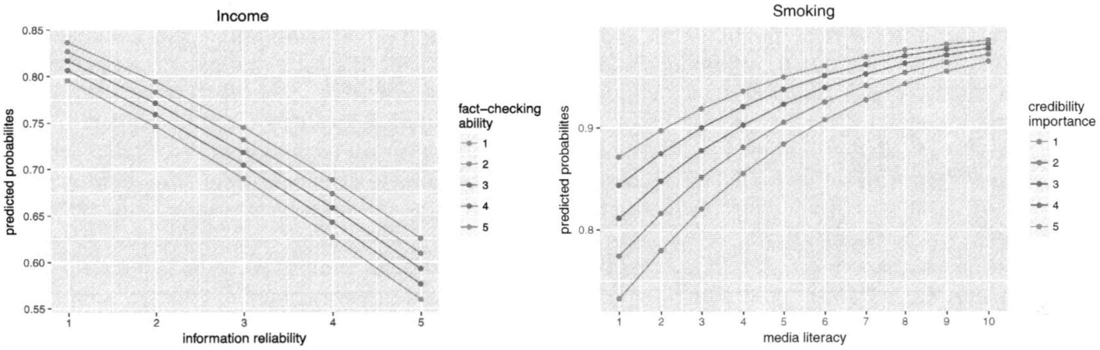

Figure 1. Panel 1 depicts the predicted probabilities of a correct answer on the comment on incomes as a function of information reliability (x-axis) and fact-checking ability (legend). The higher ratings on both variables, the smaller probability of a correct answer. Panel 2 depicts the predicted probabilities of a correct answer for smoking as a function of media literacy and credibility importance. The higher ratings on both variables, the higher probability of a correct answer

For smoking, a higher rating on media literacy, information reliability, and credibility importance were associated with an increased probability of a correct answer, whereas a higher rating on fact-checking ability was associated with a decreased probability of a correct answer (illustrated in Figure 1). For income, a higher rating on media literacy and credibility importance were associated with an increased probability of a correct answer, whereas a higher rating on information reliability and fact-checking ability were associated with a decreased probability of a correct answer (illustrated in Figure 1). For racism, a higher rating on media literacy in school was associated with an increased probability of a correct answer, whereas a higher rating on media literacy, information reliability and credibility importance were associated with a decreased probability of a correct answer. Finally, for Fukushima, a higher rating on media literacy and credibility importance were associated with an increased probability of a correct answer, whereas a higher rating on fact-checking ability and information reliability were associated with a decreased probability of correct answer.

To sum up, a higher rating on credibility importance and media literacy in education were associated with an increased probability of correct answers. The inverse is true for self-reported fact-checking ability and information reliability – here a higher rating was associated with a decreased probability for a correct answer. The picture of a smoking girl and the articles on racism, however, do not follow this pattern: for the smoking girl a higher rating of the reliability of information is associated with an increased probability of a correct answer, and for the articles on racism a higher rating on credibility importance is associated with a decreased probability of a correct answer. Further investigation is needed to understand why the results for these models differ from the others. Finally, speaking Swedish at home was associated with a higher probability for a correct answer on more than half of the items.

4. CONCLUDING DISCUSSION

In this short paper we present three preliminary main results: the performance on all items were relatively poor, less than half of the items were correct; second, the credibility ratings on three articles, one which was fake news, were relatively high and did not differ; finally, regressions with number of correct item/correct answer as outcome variables showed that self-rated importance of credibility of news and media literacy in education were associated with an increased probability of a correct answer, whereas a self-reported higher rating on fact-checking ability and reliability of news on the Internet were associated with a decreased probability of a correct answer. This is indicative of the existence of subgroups in the population, which in turn implies that there is a digital divide between people, who are skilled at determining credibility and others who are not. In one group we find people who rate credibility as very important who do not claim to be vary skilled at fact-checking and finding information online. In the opposite group we find people who do not find it very important with reliable information and see themselves as good critical readers. At present, we do not know what characterises individuals with low digital civic literacy skills and problematic high self-ratings of fact-checking ability and reliability of information on the Internet. A speculative account is that this may be interpreted as a mind-set of ignorance enhancing confirmation bias. People doing well on our test may in contrast have a mind-set with scientific curiosity and an openness to consider biases, also their own (Kahan et. al. 2017). Perhaps our findings also indicate a gap between news-seekers and news-avoiders (Strömbäck, Djerf-Pierre, & Shehata, 2013).

Teaching and learning media literacy seem to be important. Our findings indicate also that digital civic literacy may be linked to appreciating the importance of reliable information and understanding how it is difficult to find and evaluate online information. We need to further investigate this in education and how education may support media literacy and a more humble and curious approach to information.

REFERENCES

Hatlevik, O. E., Guðmundsdóttir, G. B., & Loi, M. (2015). Digital diversity among upper secondary students: A multilevel analysis of the relationship between cultural capital, self-efficacy, strategic use of information and digital competence. Computers & Education, 81, 345-353.

Kahan, D. M., Landrum, A., Carpenter, K., Helft, L., & Hall Jamieson, K. (2017). Science Curiosity and Political Information Processing. *Political Psychology*, 38, 179-199. doi:10.1111/pops.12396

Kahne, J., & Bowyer, B. (2017). Educating for democracy in a partisan age: Confronting the challenges of motivated reasoning and misinformation. *American Educational Research Journal*, *54*(1), 3-34.

Lee, N.-J., Shah, D. V., & McLeod, J. M. (2013). Processes of political socialization: A communication mediation approach to youth civic engagement. *Communication Research, 40*(5), 669-697.

Lewandowsky, S., Ecker, U.K.H, Seifert, C.M., Schwartz, N., & Cook, J. (2012). Misinformation and Its Correction: Continued Influence and Successful Debiasing. *Psychological Science in the Public Interest, 13(3),* 106–131.

McGrew, S., Breakstone, J., Ortega, T., Smith, M., & Wineburg, S. (2018). Can students evaluate online sources? Learning from assessments of civic online reasoning. *Theory & Research in Social Education*, 1-29.

McGrew, S., Ortega, T., Breakstone, J., & Wineburg, S. (2017). The Challenge That's Bigger than Fake News: Civic Reasoning in a Social Media Environment. *American Educator*, *41*(3), 4.

Strömbäck, J., Djerf-Pierre, M., & Shehata, A. (2013). The dynamics of political interest and news media consumption: A longitudinal perspective. *International Journal of Public Opinion Research*, 25(4), 414-435.

Vosoughi, S., Roy, D., & Aral, S. (2018). The spread of true and false news online. *Science*, 359(6380), 1146-1151.

Walraven, A., Brand-Gruwel, S., & Boshuizen, H. P. (2009). How students evaluate information and sources when searching the World Wide Web for information. *Computers & education*, *52*(1), 234-246.

Wineburg, S. & McGrew, S. (2017) *Lateral Reading: Reading Less and Learning More When Evaluating Digital Information*, Working Paper No 2017.A1/Stanford History Education Group, sheg.stanford.edu, September 2017, https://ssrn.com/abstract=3048994

THE USE OF SPACED LEARNING AS A PEDAGOGICAL STRATEGY IN ENHANCING STUDENT LEARNING

Jessnor Elmy Mat-jizat
Universiti Pendidikan Sultan Idris, Malaysia

ABSTRACT

This conceptual paper attempts to explore the use of Spaced Learning technique as a teaching and learning method. Amidst the rapidly changing technological environment, creating long-term memories is still at the core of education. Spaced Learning is a learning method in which highly condensed learning content is repeated three times, with two 10-minute breaks during which distractor activities such as physical activities are performed by the students. It was suggested that spacing learning over time helps people learn more quickly and remember better. This discussion can serve as a starting point for further dialogues and studies among researchers and educators interested in implementing alternative technique in their teaching and learning activities.

KEYWORDS

Pedagogical Strategy, Spaced Learning, Student Learning, Institutes of Higher Learning

1. INTRODUCTION

Creating long-term memories is important in education. Yet it wasn't until 2005 that a key discovery was published in *Scientific American* explaining how long-term memories are formed in the brain (Fields 2005). Fields found that constant stimulation of the brain cell did not make the brain switch on. The length of cell stimulation was not vital for long-term memories, but the gap between stimulation was. This is known as Spaced Learning.

Taking on the findings of this discovery, Kelley and Whatson (2013) had conducted a study on 440 students aged between 13-15 in an urban secondary school in England. The study was conducted in order to identify whether repeated stimuli separated by timed spaces without stimuli can initiate Long-Term Potentiation (LTP) and Long-Term Memory (LTM) encoding. LTP is a persistent strengthening of synapses in the brain based on recent patterns of activity. These are patterns of synaptic activity that produce a long-lasting increase in signal transmission between two neurons (Nicoll 2017). LTM is typically used to make sense of and give meaning to what you are doing now. However, it is also the repository for more permanent knowledge and skills and includes all things in memory that are not currently being used but which are needed to enable understanding (De Bruyckere, Kirschner & Hulshof 2015).

Using a formula of 10-minute breaks between three intensive sessions of 15-20 minutes teaching, Kelley and Whatson (2013) found that Spaced Learning is more efficient in comparison to standard teaching. For each of the three 15-20 minutes intensive sessions, teaching materials were repeated but presented differently, deepening and extending it. During the 10 minute breaks, distracter activities such as juggling, or throwing balls were carried out. When compared between the experiment group who were taught using the Spaced Learning technique for one-hour, with the control group who learned the same topic for four months, the findings showed no significant difference in student achievement. This means that using Spaced Learning, students were able to achieve the same result as the group of students who studied using typical teaching methods for four months.

2. GENERATIONAL LEARNING STYLES

Aside from the different cognitive style and preferences, learning styles are also different based on the year someone is born. Lindsey Pollak (2017), who is one of the leading expert on millennial and multigenerational workplace have categorised the different generations into five category: Traditionalist (born approximately 1922-1945), Baby Boomers (born approximately 1946-1964), Generation X (born approximately 1965-1980), Generation Y (born approximately 1981-1997) and Generation Z (born since 1998). For Baby Boomers, a teacher should value their experience, challenge them to make a difference, and give lots of positive feedbacks (Coates 2007). For Generation X, teachers should put all relevant information up front as Generation X usually will not read the details. They are the tech-pioneers. To communicate with Generation X, one must be direct and be brief as possible to convey what is needed. They are independent and self-reliant thus they do not like to be micro-managed. Generation Y on the other hand are very tech-savvy. They prefer communication through texting and social media. They love multi-tasking, group work and collaborative learning. They have short attention span, so provide a brief change of pace every 20 minutes to assist with processing and assimilation of information (Coates 2007). Finally, Generation Z is a generation whom never experienced life before the Internet. They were accustomed to multimedia and doing everything at the same time. Generation Z youth have become accustomed to interacting and communicating in a world that is connected at all times (Turner 2015).

In their study, Chun, Dudoit, Fujihara, Gerschenson, Kennedy, Koanui, Ogata and Stearns (2016) found that Generation Z usually have a short attention span. These generations have a noticeably low ability to concentrate and focus on longer, more complex or involved problems in learning. They were also used to have easy access to information at the palm of their hand, where they could get results and feedback instantly. They often not want to spend time doing in-depth learning and research. However, they do have an increased development of visual ability in their cognitive functions. Game-based learning, pictures and animations would excite and stimulates them in learning.

Current educational systems must change in response to a new generation of young people. Current students have been variously described as disappointed (Oblinger 2003), dissatisfied (Levin & Arafeh 2002), and disengaged. Brown (2000), contends "today's kids are always "multiprocessing" – they do several things simultaneously – listen to music, talk on the cell phone, and use the computer, all at the same time" (p. 13). It is also argued that the new generations are accustomed to learning at high speed, making random connections, processing visual and dynamic information and learning through game-based activities. It is suggested that because of these factors young people prefer learning styles that provides burst of information in a short period, fun and able to provide them with immediate feedback.

3. SPACED LEARNING

Spaced learning is one of the pedagogical techniques that could provide the suitable learning style for the new generations. Studies of human memory have shown that we remember more when learning is spaced over time rather than crammed together in a single session (Ferguson, Barzilai, Ben-Zvi, Chinn, Herodotou, Hod, Kali, Kukulska-Hulme, Kupermintz, McAndrew, Rienties, Sagy, Scanlon, Sharples, Weller & Whitelock 2017; Rohrer & Pashler 2007). Typically, these studies have focused on learning short items, such as words or phrases in a foreign language, with increasing spaces between attempts to recall the items.

The way this is thought to work is that each recall session stimulates the learner's short-term memory for the item and its new association, until these become fixed in long-term memory. The method is generally successful, providing the student is willing to stick with it. However, the learning takes place over days and has been limited to building connections between words, phrases or images.

A few studies of human brain activity while learning have been carried out. One of these examined magnetic resonance imaging (MRI) brain scans of humans after they had tried to memorise 120 novel pictures of faces (Xue, Mei, Chen, Lu, Poldrack & Dong 2011). Initially, each face was presented to adults multiple times, followed by the next face. Next, the faces were presented in sequence, one after the other. The study showed that spacing out the faces by showing a sequence of different ones produced more activity in the part of the brain linked to face recognition than showing the same pictures multiple times.

In a study on the adaptation of horizontal optokinetic response in mice (Aziz, Wang, Kesaf, Mohamed, Fukazawa & Shigemoto 2014), it was found that 1-hour spacing time produce the highest memory retention, which lasted for one month. Traditional learning do retain memory, however the study showed that it only lasted for one week.

4. SPACED LEARNING FOR EDUCATION

In education, a few studies have shown that, gradually expanding the interval between each teaching sessions could enhance long term memory retention (Pyc & Rawson 2009). However, the results of the studies have shown mixed reviews (Roediger & Karpicke 2010). In Karpicke and Bauernschmidt (2011), they proved that by having a different sets of expanding interval schedules (short spacing, medium spacing and long spacing), it did not translate into gains in long-term retention. Repeated spaced retrieval had powerful effects on retention, but the relative schedule of repeated tests had no discernible impact.

In their study, Kelley and Whatson (2013) have designed a method for spaced teaching of a certain topic in school. The teaching consists of three 20-minute sessions, with 10-minute breaks between them.

- Session 1 (20 minutes) Teacher gives a rapid presentation of a new topic.
- Break (10 minutes) Students engage in physical activity, such as juggling or walking.
- Session 2 (20 minutes) Students actively recall key concepts from the presentation.
- Break (10 minutes) Students engage in physical activity, such as juggling or walking.
- Session 3 (20 minutes) Students apply the knowledge through problem exercises.

Kelley and Whatson ran trials of their teaching method with students aged 13–15 who were learning Biology in a UK school. In one trial, students studied an entire first Biology course through spaced learning over a period of 90 minutes. Their exam performance was compared to a control group of students who studied the course in standard lessons over four months. There was no significant difference in exam scores between students who had done spaced learning in a single day and those who studied over four months.

Spaced learning had also been implemented in medical training. In an experimental study at Hamburg University, the experiment group which had been taught using the spaced learning technique showed improvements in suturing and knot-tying performance, knot quality and knot strength (Boettcher, Boettcher, Mietzsch, Krebs, Bergholz & Reinshagen 2018). Though, there were no significant differences between control group and experiment group in terms of task time and accuracy.

5. IMPLICATIONS AND FUTURE RESEARCH

Schools and universities in some countries are sometimes so overwhelm with a certain set of syllabus that teacher have to teach in limited amount of time. At the same time, the current students have a totally different attitude to learning than the previous generations. A study is currently underway to explore spaced learning in a public university in Malaysia with students consisting of Generation Y and Z. More structured technique, types of suitable break activities and timing will be proposed in this study.

6. CONCLUSION

Spaced learning could be another alternative pedagogical strategy that could be implemented for the current generations. It would be interesting to implement this strategy on student of higher learning institutions, which currently comes from Generation Y. They love multi-tasking, group work and collaborating with each other, have a short attention span and are very tech savvy. It is hope that spaced learning would appeal to their learning needs.

As an educator, we try not discriminate our students. However, there are times that we feel we are at lost in terms of dealing with the new generations. We feel as though we fail to deliver a teaching content when all we could see in front of us are a group of students who are not focus on what is being taught, instead they focus more on their phones. It is hoped that further exploration of this study could proof (or disproof) the potential of spaced learning as a pedagogical tool for the current generations.

REFERENCES

Aziz, W., Wang, W., Kesaf, S., Mohamed, A.A., Fukazawa, Y. and Shigemoto, R. 2014, 'Distinct kinetics of synaptic structural plasticity, memory formation, and memory decay in massed and spaced learning', *Proceedings of the National Academy of Sciences*, vol. 111, no. 1, p. E194.

Boettcher, M., Boettcher, J., Mietzsch, S., Krebs, T., Bergholz, R. and Reinshagen, K. 2018, 'The spaced learning concept significantly improves training for laparoscopic suturing: a pilot randomized controlled study', *Surgical Endoscopy*, vol. 32, no. 1, pp. 154-159.

Brown, J.S. 2000, 'Growing Up: Digital: How the Web Changes Work, Education, and the Ways People Learn', *Change: The Magazine of Higher Learning*, vol. 32, no. 2, pp. 11-20.

Chun, C., Dudoit, K., Fujihara, S., Gerschenson, M., Kennedy, A., Koanui, B., Ogata, V. and Stearns, J. 2016, *Teaching Generation Z at the University of Hawai'i*, 3 April 2018, <https://www.hawaii.edu/ovppp/Leaders/files/2015-2016-Projects/PELP_GenZ_PaperV.6.0-5.4.16.pdf>.

Coates, J. 2007, *Generational Learning Styles*, Learning Resource Network, River Falls, WI.

De Bruyckere, P., Kirschner, P.A. and Hulshof, C.D. 2015, 'Chapter 2 - Myths About Learning Urban Myths About Learning and Education', in, Academic Press, San Diego, pp. 17-92.

Ferguson, R., Barzilai, S., Ben-Zvi, D., Chinn, C.A., Herodotou, C., Hod, Y., Kali, Y., Kukulska-Hulme, A., Kupermintz, H., McAndrew, P., Rienties, B., Sagy, O., Scanlon, E., Sharples, M., Weller, M. and Whitelock, D. 2017, *Innovating Pedagogy 2017: Open University Innovation Report 6*, Milton Keynes, UK.

Fields, R.D. 2005, 'Making memories stick', *Scientific American*, vol. 292, no. 2, pp. 74-81.

Kelley, P. and Whatson, T. 2013, 'Making Long-Term Memories in Minutes: A Spaced Learning Pattern from Memory Research in Education', *Frontiers in Human Neuroscience*, vol. 7, p. 589.

Levin, D. and Arafeh, S. 2002, *The digital disconnect: the widening gap between Internet-savvy students and their schools* Washington DC, <http://www.pewinternet.org/~/media/Files/Reports/2002/PIP_Schools_Internet_Report.pdf.pdf>.

Nicoll, R.A. 2017, 'A Brief History of Long-Term Potentiation', *Neuron*, vol. 93, no. 2, pp. 281-290.

Oblinger, D. 2003, 'Boomers, Gen-Xers and Millennials: Understanding the new students', *EDUCAUSE Review*, vol. no. July/August, pp. 37-47.

Pollak, L. 2017, *What Are The Different Generations In The Workplace? Your Definitive Guide*, viewed 15 April <https://www.lindseypollak.com/different-generations-workplace-definitive-guide/>.

Rohrer, D. and Pashler, H. 2007, 'Increasing retention without increasing study time', *Current Directions in Psychological Science*, vol. 16, no. 4, pp. 183-186.

Turner, A. 2015, 'Generation Z: Technology and Social Interest', *The Journal of Individual Psychology*, vol. 71, no. 2, pp. 103-113.

Xue, G., Mei, L., Chen, C., Lu, Z.-L., Poldrack, R. and Dong, Q. 2011, 'Spaced Learning Enhances Subsequent Recognition Memory by Reducing Neural Repetition Suppression', *Journal of Cognitive Neuroscience*, vol. 23, no. 7, pp. 1624-1633.

EXPLORING THE RELATIONSHIP BETWEEN KINDERGARTENERS' BUDDY READING AND INDIVIDUAL COMPREHENSION OF MULTIMODAL DIGITAL TEXTS*

X. Christine Wang[1,2], Tanya Christ[3] and Ming Ming Chiu[4]
[1]*State University of New York at Buffalo, USA*
[2]*Shandong Yingcai University, China*
[3]*Oakland University, USA*
[4]*The Education University of Hong Kong, Hong Kong*

ABSTRACT

To understand young children's experience with multimodal digital texts, we investigated how 53 kindergarteners' (ages 5-6) buddy reading behaviors (reading mode selection, sequential/non-sequential reading, hotspot use, use of modalities, use of monitoring) were related to their individual comprehension outcomes (prompted retelling, inference/critical- thinking, depth of target vocabulary knowledge) while reading app books. Multivariate mixed response analysis yielded these findings: (1) Buddy monitoring behaviors (e.g., ask questions, draw attention to book content, debate, or negotiate) were associated with higher vocabulary scores as well as higher inferences/critical thinking scores; (2) Triads had lower prompted retelling scores than dyads especially when reading longer app books. The findings highlight the importance to promote these positive buddy reading behaviors and pay attention to group size.

KEYWORDS

Literacy, Early Childhood, Reading

1. PURPOSE OF THE STUDY

The purpose of the study is to understand the relationship between kindergartens' (ages 5-6) buddy reading behaviors and their individual comprehension outcomes while reading multimodal digital texts. The central question is: how are different buddy reading behaviors (reading mode selection, sequential/non-sequential reading, hotspot use, use of modalities, use of monitoring) related to individual reading outcomes (prompted retelling, inference/critical- thinking, depth of target vocabulary knowledge)?

Multimodal digital texts, e.g., app books, are increasingly becoming part of young children's literacy ecosystem (Shuler, 2012; Vandewater, Bickham, & Lee, 2006). Reading app books, which involves the use and interpretation of multiple modes (e.g. images, sounds, animation) to form diverse pathways of reading (Kress, 2010; Wolfe & Flewitt, 2010), is different from reading traditional texts. Unfortunately, we have limited understanding of how young children engage with multimodal digital texts (Authors, under review). In addition, while the issue of how buddy reading processes and behaviors are related to early readers' individual comprehension of traditional texts is well studied; it has rarely been explored with emergent readers (e.g., kindergartners) (Authors, 2012). Thus, our research aims to address these research gaps as well as to offer insights to teachers on how to use buddy reading to promote comprehension.

We explored this issue as part of a broader research project on kindergarteners' app book reading development. The broader study design was modeled on Clay's (1966) seminal concepts about print development research. Likewise, we undertook a school-year-long study to understand and foster kindergartners' children's development of app book reading processes that supported positive reading comprehension outcomes. Using this classroom-based-instruction design of the broader study allowed us to explore the relations between reader processes and outcomes in an ecologically valid setting.

---

*Due to page limit, the full references and tables are not included. But they are available to view via this link: https://docs.google.com/document/d/1uzrFZPM6QIz9ht-zjOXVX0rKwSY6cIc7F3CWNYwnLQw/edit?usp=sharing

2. THEORETICAL FRAMEWORK & RELEVANT LITERATURE

This study is grounded in the sociocultural theories that emphasize the social and cultural nature of learning and development (Cole & Wertsch, 1996). Vygotsky (1978) states: "Every function in the child's cultural development appears twice: first, on the social level, and later, on the individual level; first, between people (interpsychological) and then inside the child (intrapsychological). This applies equally to voluntary attention, to logical memory, and to the formation of concepts. All the higher functions originate as actual relationships between individuals." (p57). In the same vein, we speculate reading in a social context, e.g., app book reading amongst buddies in this case, helps readers extend and transform their knowledge (Cobb, 1996) and externalize their learning, which lead to internalization of these practices (Kozulin, 2003). Two mechanisms may likely contribute to these processes: (1) modelling (showing one another a way to make meaning with the text) and (2) scaffolding (supporting one another to engage in those processes) (Vygotsky, 1978).

Multimodal literacy theories, which deemphasize the centrality of text and language and consider multiple 'modes' of communication, also inform us about the multiple pathways of reading app books that differ from reading traditional print text (e.g., Jewitt & Kress, 2003). The traditional print literacy practices (reading and writing) are privileged in school settings and foreground visual modes (e.g. print) for accessing text (Kress, 1997). In contrast, we hypothesize that reading multimodal text will likely involve both visual and action modes (Wohlwend, 2010), thus resulting in more complex transactions between the reader and text. Our coding of buddy reading behaviors of app books tried to capture such complex transactions.

Finally, our research is informed by existing research on buddy reading. Research has demonstrated that buddy reading facilitates beginning reading (e.g., Flint, 2010; MacGillivray, 1997; MacGillivray & Hawes, 1994; Tharp & Gallimore, 1988). For example, Griffin (2002, p. 773) found that first graders shared reading strategies to "pool their expertise" while buddy reading. Likewise, MacGillvray and Hawes (1994) found that first graders helped one another identify unfamiliar words in text. Additionally, Rubinstein-Avila (2003) identified several scaffolding strategies that second graders used with their buddies to support reading processes. Finally, Flint (2010) found that first graders "used strategies and prior knowledge to scaffold each other's learning" and made connections to construct meaning. While buddy reading has been used fairly widely as a method in which older or more experienced readers help younger or less experienced readers process text (e.g., Lowery, Sabis-Burns, & Anderson-Brown, 2008; Shegar, 2009; Theurer & Schmidt, 2008), a limited body of research has focused on same-age young readers processing text together, especially with multimodal digital texts.

3. METHODS

3.1 Participants

Fifty-three kindergarteners between the ages of 5-6 years old participated from across four classrooms in two schools and two U.S. states. Both schools were suburban and served linguistically, culturally, and socio-economically diverse populations of children.

3.2 Data Collection and Coding

Twelve app books were selected for buddy reading, four for individual reading across the units, and two for pre/post intervention individual reading based on their (1) high interactivity, (2) congruent hotspots that supported children's meaning making, (3) user-friendly features, (4) developmental appropriateness, and (5) good narrative/illustration quality; which are related to children's better comprehension outcomes (Morgan, 2013; Zipke, 2014). App books in each unit had similar design features.

Buddy reading sessions took place after each of 12 30-minute group lessons of reading the 12 app books, which are not the focus of the present study, across four units spanning the school-year. During the buddy reading sessions, children had 15 minutes to read the same app book presented in the lesson with a partner. Child's reading behaviors during buddy reading were coded individually, but there was no assessment of their comprehension outcomes. At the end of each unit, each child was read individually using a novel app book and assessment protocol (15 minutes each; 318 sessions total) and both reading processes and outcomes were coded. All buddy reading and individual test sessions (4 end-of-the-unit sessions plus 2 pre/post sessions) were video-recorded for analysis.

The following four sets of variables were coded. Codes for reading behaviors and outcomes are based on previous work (Authors, under review). Rigorous coder training was undertaken, then two coders separately coded all the data. Differences were discussed to establish consensus, which was used for analyses. Inter-rater reliability was high (see Table 5).

1. Buddy reading behaviors (Table 1, column 2),
2. Individual reading behaviors (Table 1, column 3)
3. Individual reading outcomes (Table 2), and
4. Control variables (these were to avoid uncontrolled variable bias: child demographics, early literacy skills, classroom, time, and basic book attributes – see Table 3).

3.3 Data Analysis

Analyzing the data for this study required addressing outcome and explanatory variable issues (see Table 4). Outcome issues include discrete, infrequent, and multiple types. For discrete outcomes, ordinary least squares regressions can bias the standard errors, so we used a Logit regression to model dichotomous outcomes (Kennedy, 2008). As logistic regression is biased for infrequent events or for small samples, we removed this bias with King and Zeng's (2001) logit correction. Also, multiple types of outcomes can have correlated residuals that underestimate standard errors, which we addressed with a mixed response model (Goldstein, 2011).

Explanatory variable issues include many hypotheses without false positives and robustness procedures. As testing many hypotheses increases the likelihood of a false positive, we controlled for the false discovery rate via the two-stage linear step-up procedure, which outperformed 13 other methods in computer simulations (Benjamini, Krieger & Yekutieli, 2006). To test the robustness of our results, subsets of the data were run separately (Kennedy, 2008).

We modeled kindergarteners' outcomes, *vocabulary knoweldge, inference/critical thinking* and *prompted retelling* (**Outcome**), with a *multivariate, mixed response* model (Goldstein, 2011). An alpha level of .05 was used for all analyses.

$$\mathbf{Outcome}_{iy} = \beta_y + \mathbf{e}_{iy} + \beta_{uy}\mathbf{Control}_{iy} + \beta_{zy}\mathbf{Buddy\ Reading\_Behavior}_{iy} + \beta_{zy}\mathbf{Individual\ Reading\_Behavior}_{iy}$$

The $\mathbf{Outcome}_{iy}$ measure y for each child i has grand mean intercepts β_y with residuals $\mathbf{e}_{iy}$. First, we entered classroom variables for 4 teachers, children's demographics and book affordances: gender, race, English as second language (vs. first language), triad (vs. dyad), concepts about print score, and listening comprehension with traditional text score, total # automatic animations, total # user-activated congruent hotspots, total # user activated non-congruent hotspots, total # pages in app book, readability level, navigation options (p=page turn only), navigation options (m=page turn & menu), text highlights as it reads aloud, ave # lines of text per page, minimum # hotspots per page, and maximum # hotspots per page ($\mathbf{Control}_{iy}$). Next, we entered children's buddy reading behaviors ($\mathbf{Buddy\ Reading\_Behavior}_{iy}$). Lastly, we added each child's individual reading behaviors ($\mathbf{Individual\ Reading\_Behavior}_{iy}$).

4. RESULTS

The summary statistics are listed in Table 5 and the results of the multivariate mixed response model of the three reading comprehension outcomes are available in Table 6.

Related to the central question, one particular kind of buddy reading behaviors was found significantly related to reading comprehension outcomes. Buddy monitoring behaviors (e.g., ask questions, draw attention to app book content, debate, or negotiate) were associated with higher scores of depth of vocabulary knowledge for target words. This buddy reading behavior accounted for 7% of the vocabulary variance. Also, children who asked more questions of their buddy or monitored their comprehension more during buddy reading showed stronger inferences/critical thinking, accounting for 7% of their variance. Buddy monitoring behaviors in our study focused on how buddies interacted regarding the books that they were reading. This finding aligns with existing studies that found young readers "pool their expertise" (Griffin, 2002; p. 773) and scaffold each other's learning (Flint, 2010; Rubinstein-Avila, 2003). The act of monitoring can serve as ways to model good reading behaviors as well as to scaffold each other's reading, the two possible social learning mechanisms (Vygotsky, 1978). This highlights the importance to foster productive buddy reading behaviors as a means to improve individual reading outcomes such as vocabulary and inferences/critical thinking.

Our finding also indirectly revealed the effect of group size. Although most of the buddy-reading sessions were done with two students, sometimes there were three students in a group due to absence of some students in the class. Compared to students in dyads, those in students in triads had lower prompted retelling scores, accounting for 2% of its variance. In addition, students in triads rather than dyads reading app books with more pages had even lower prompted retelling scores, accounting for 2% of its variance. In other words, the reading outcome of a larger group was worsened by the length of the books. Dyads seemed to be a more productive group size in our study, which confirmed the findings of early studies on group size (Webb, 1991; Webb & Palincsar, 1996).

It is worth noting the regressions modeling results also revealed some significant relations between factors such as individual reading behaviors, pre-test listening comprehension, book affordances, and reading outcomes, to name a few: (1) children who listened to the entire page before turning the page had higher target vocabulary scores. Furthermore, students who pressed more hotspots that were relevant had higher target vocabulary scores. Individual reading behaviors accounted for 9% of the vocabulary variance; (2) Pre-test listening comprehension was related to prompted retelling, which accounted for 17% of its variance; and (3) Books with fewer pages, more menu options than only page turning or more lines of text per page were associated with better inferences/critical thinking, accounting for 14% of their variance. These interesting findings are beyond the scope of this paper and will be explored in depth in other papers.

5. SIGNIFICANCE

Our study extends the existing research to uncover the relationship between buddy reading behaviors and reading comprehension outcomes in the context of reading digital multimodal texts. Although we did not find multimodal digital text specific buddy reading behaviors (e.g., use of hotspot) that related to reading outcomes, the effect of productive buddy reading behaviors (e.g., ask questions, draw attention to app book content, debate, or negotiate) on reading outcomes such as depth of target vocabulary knowledge, inference/critical thinking was salient. This highlights the needs for teachers to promote these productive buddy reading behaviors. Also the group size is another factor to consider when arranging buddy reading. Our finding indicates that dyads rather than triads are a more appropriate group size for kindergartners.

REFERENCES

Benjamini, Y., et al, 2006. Adaptive linear step-up procedures that control the false discovery rate. *Biometrika,* Vol. 93,pp. 491-507.

Clay, M. M., 1966. *Emergent reading behaviour* (Doctoral dissertation). University of Auckland, New Zealand.

Cobb, P. (1996). Where is the mind? A coordination of sociocultural and cognitive constructivist perspectives. In C. T. Fosnot (Ed.), *Constructivism: Theory, Perspectives, and Practice.* New York: Teachers College Press, pp. 34–52.

COLLABORATIVE TESTING STRATEGIES IN A COMPUTING COURSE

Juliana de Melo Bezerra
Instituto Tecnológico de Aeronáutica – ITA, São José dos Campos – SP, Brazil

ABSTRACT

Beyond cognitive competence, other abilities are relevant to labor market nowadays, including critical thinking, self confidence, teamwork and communication. It is then important to introduce in the learning process practices that contribute to both the acquirement of knowledge and the development of soft skills. A prominent answer to this challenge is the use of the collaborative learning, where students work together to solve a problem or complete a task. In this paper, we present three strategies to implement collaborative testing in class. We also evaluate the application of such strategies in a computing course in order to provide evidences of their effectiveness compared to traditional tests. We found that collaborative testing contributed not only to improve students' performance in tests, but have a positive impact on perceived learning and students' satisfaction.

KEYWORDS

Education, Computing, Collaboration, Testing, Learning, Satisfaction

1. INTRODUCTION

Technology is increasingly getting into people's lives and becoming one of the keys of economy nowadays. Governments are trying to impulse its economy by developing the industry and using science to aggregate value to its products and services. Besides the importance of technical background, there are other skills that need to be developed during the education process. Wagner (2008) describe seven skills that companies expect students to develop, as follows: critical thinking and problem solving, collaboration across networks and leading by influence, agility and adaptability, initiative and entrepreneurialism, effective oral and written communication, accessing and analyzing information, curiosity and imagination. In other work, Anderson (2014) identified important skills such as flexibility, communication, cooperation, emotional maturity, and initiative.

Education institutions must be prepared for this demand and for the necessary training of students, in order to respond to economic and social developments in the 21st century. According to Henderson and Dancy (2011), a barrier in the education process is the lack of knowledge about how to effectively use the available instructional ideas and strategies. Professors are investigating different ways to improve learning, considering the development of cognitive and non-cognitive skills, by using collaborative activities during the course. Student-centered instructional strategies are proving to be more effective in improving students' conceptual understanding, knowledge retention, and attitudes about learning than traditional methods that do not include student participation (Kober, 2015).

Collaborative testing is a method in which students work together while taking an evaluative exam. Testing is a means to identify whether teaching is effective and how well the student comprehends subjects. Important outcomes, related to enhancement of students' learning, are been generated through investigations of the use of collaborative testing in distinct contexts (Björnsdóttir et al, 2015; Cantwell et al, 2016). For instance, Willey and Gardner (2012) reported the capacity that collaborative frameworks have to develop an effective and integrated learning experience for students. Shen et al (2008) found that collaborative testing enhanced interactions among students and increased the perceived learning. In the present paper, we present three collaborative testing strategies and discuss relevant results associated to their application in a computing course.

2. COLLABORATIVE TESTING: STRATEGIES AND APPLICATION

In this section, we explain the selected collaborative testing, and present the experiment design and results.

2.1 Collaborative Testing Strategies

Three collaborative testing strategies were designed, as follows: "Question Revision", "Question Discussion" and "Pair Work". Figure 1a shows the scheme of the "Question Analysis" strategy. The strategy consists of using knowledge acquired during a test part to help solving other parts of the test. The steps of the strategy are: 1) Each student answer question A individually; 2) Instructor separates students into groups in order to discuss their question and understand their mistakes, without changing their answer; 3) Students separate the groups and solve question B individually, which uses the same idea of question A but in a more complex context. To get the expected result it is important that students discuss question A and try to figure out the answer for it based on what each student wrote and on the discussion itself.

Figure 1b present the scheme of the "Question Discussion" strategy. The strategy tries to use the power of initial discussions to accelerate the reasoning of students. The steps of the strategy are: 1) Instructor forms groups and give them some time to discuss the main idea of Question A; 2) Students separate from the groups and solve question A individually, but using the discussed ideas; 3) Students solve question B individually, which uses the same idea of question A but in a more complex context. The purpose of this strategy is just to accelerate the rationality behind the question, and not have a group question.

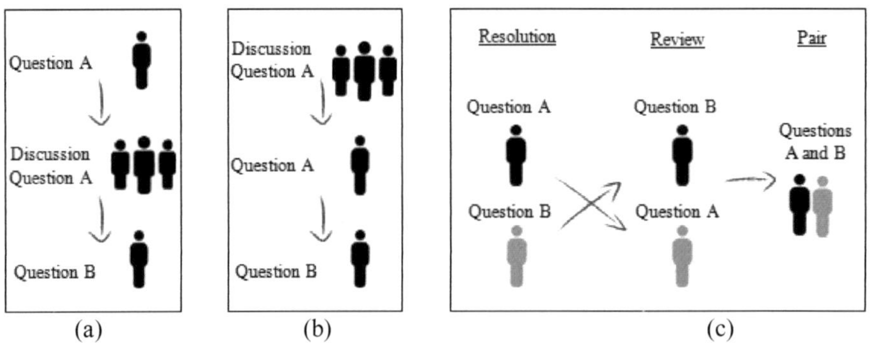

Figure 1. Collaborative testing strategies. a) Question Revision. b) Question Discussion. c) Pair Work

The scheme of the "Question Discussion" strategy is shown in Figure 1c. With this strategy, students have the chance to correct some mistakes during a test. The strategy uses the power of a peer review to give students the possibility to develop their critical thinking and discussion skills. After instructor separates the class into pairs, the steps of the strategy are: 1) Each student of a pair receives one different question and solve it individually; 2) After a stipulated time, students change tests with their pairs and start the review process; 3) Each pair discusses the best answer for each question and hand over the test. This strategy does not require dependences between questions, but it is important to define pairs to avoid them being uneven.

2.2 Experiment Design

The experiment was taken place at an engineering school, during the course of "Data Structure and Algorithms" from the department of Computer Science. We applied the three collaborative tests in a class of 46 students. An important part of the experiment was the selection of subjects for each collaborative strategy. We used "arrays and recursion" topic with "Question Revision" strategy, "linked list" topic with "Question Discussion" strategy, and "queue and stack" topic with "Pair Work" strategy. To evaluate the effectiveness of the proposed strategies, we considered the following aspects: students' performance, perceived learning, and satisfaction of students. The first one was considered to test the concept that students would have better grades if tests involve some collaborative activity. The second one was to understand if students taking collaborative tests would have a better perception of learning than taking traditional exams, whilst the last one is to have a sense if students liked the proposed activities.

In order to evaluate students' performance with "Question Revision" and "Question Discussion" strategies, we divided the class into two random groups, each one with half of the class. One group (called experiment group) used the collaborative strategy, while the other group (called control group) used traditional test format. For the "Pair Work" strategy, the whole class participated in the collaborative activity (configuring the experiment group) and the control group was a class in the previous year that performed a traditional test with the same questions.

The aspects of perceived learning and students' satisfaction were evaluated based on the perception of students who participated in the collaborative activities. Evaluation sentences are shown in Table 2. Sentences L1 to L6 were regarding perceived learning, while sentences S1 and S2 were about students' satisfaction. Students used a 5-point likert scale (with the values: strongly agree, agree, neutral, disagree, and strongly disagree) to assess sentences L1 to S1. The last sentence S2 had "yes" or "no" as possible answers. Sentences L1 to S1 were assesses by all students in the beginning of the course, considering their experience with traditional tests. All sentences were evaluated after each collaborative test but only by students in the experiment group, who really experienced the collaborative strategy.

2.3 Results

Performance results for each collaborative test are shown in Table 1 using the mean of grades (0 to 10.0) of students in experiment group (with collaborative test) and control group (with traditional test). Regarding "Question Revision" strategy, we observed that experiment group had lower performance in Question A compared to control group. It was not a problem, since the strategy include a step to discuss Question A but without changing it. The discussion was expected to positively influence the grades in Question B (more complex than Question A), which was in fact observed with a 10% of performance improvement. Notice that grade mean in Question B was similar in both groups, however the discussion really helped the experiment group to overcome their difficulties and reach better results.

Table 1. Performance of students

Strategy	Group type	Question A	Question B
Question Revision	Experiment group	6.7	7.3
	Control group	8.5	7.1
Question Discussion	Experiment group	9.1	8.3
	Control group	8.2	8.1
Pair Work	Experiment group	8.3	8.1
	Control group	6.4	6.5

Table 2. Sentences and results about perceived learning and students' satisfaction

Id	Sentence	Question Revision	Question Discussion	Pair Work
L1	The test positively contributed to my learning process.	13%	6%	16%
L2	The test made me realize that I know the subject studied.	16%	15%	15%
L3	With the test, it is possible to learn from answers and comments of my peers.	9%	11%	13%
L4	The test contributed to develop my critical thoughts.	39%	11%	35%
L5	The test contributed to develop my analysis capacity.	6%	10%	12%
L6	The test contributed to develop my self confidence.	7%	12%	6%
S1	I feel anxious doing the test.	-13%	-17%	-6%
S2	I would like to do again this kind of test	87%	78%	79%

Regarding "Question Discussion" strategy, the previous discussion about Question A, before solving it, contributed to a better perfomance of experiment group. The performance of experiment group was 11% higher compared to control group. In Question B, the difference of 3% between the two groups was not expressive enough to conclude that it was due to the discussion or if it is just a normal deviation in the class. So it was not clear is if discussing Question A helped them to figure out the solution of Question B. In "Pair work" startegy, we observed a performance improvement of approximately 25% in each question. It was expected since the strategy allowed students to change their answers after using the contribution of their peers. Results of the evaluation of perceived learning and students' satisfaction are presented in Table 2, with the percentage representing how much more the collaborative test is higher than the traditional test (assessed in beginning of the course considering the previous experience of students). The result of S2 sentence is a percentage that represents the amount of students that answered "yes" after performing the collaborative test. Analyzing the results, we noticed that all sentences in all tests had higher scores compared to traditional tests, except in case of S1 sentence. We expected that students would feel more anxious during traditional tests; however students were apprehensive in collaborative test because they had never experience that and they do not know if it could negatively affect their grades. Regarding perceived learning, students acknowledged that collaborative tests were better for their learning, especially for developing critical thinking and for assessing the acquired knowledge. The majority of students, approximately 80%, indicated that they would like to have other opportunities with collaborative testing.

3. CONCLUSION

We presented three collaborative testing strategies and applied them in a computing course. Based on the proposed strategies, adapted versions and even new strategies can emerge, which are extremely valuable for educational community. The application of collaborative testing is possible even in the presence of other forms of evaluation; in our case, we also have traditional tests and practical laboratories. It may be difficult to select the strategy more suitable to the current context, given aspects as definition of questions and organization of class time. The evaluation of strategies is also a challenge, since it depends on several factors including nature and difficulty of questions, time given for each test, context and academic demands of students, and the way the strategy is applied. Considering our results, the approval of the usage of collaborative tests by students, aligned to the students' perception that such tests were more effective than traditional ones in term of learning, are powerful evidences of the potential of collaborative testing. The collaboration itself brings the opportunity to students practice other abilities, such as to expose ideas, to negotiate, and to convince others. Collaborative testing, in turn, contributes not only help students to learn more about technical subjects, but also to improve their non-cognitive skills as communication and teamwork. As future work, we intend to apply distinct collaborative testing strategies and to investigate other kinds of effectiveness evaluation.

ACKNOWLEDGEMENT

A special thanks to Igor Rios for contributing to this research.

REFERENCES

Anderson, R., 2014. Careers 2020: Making Education Work. Pearson.

Björnsdóttir, A. et al, 2015. Evaluating Two Models of Collaborative Tests in an Online Introductory Statistics Course. *In Statistics Education Research Journal*, Vol. 14, No. 1, pp 36-59.

Cantwell et al, 2016. Protocol: Collaborative Testing for Improving Student Learning Outcomes and Test-Taking Performance in Higher Education: A Systematic Review. Campbell Collaboration.

Henderson, C. and Dancy, M., 2011. Increasing the Impact and Diffusion of STEM Education Innovations. A White Paper commissioned for the Characterizing the Impact and Diffusion of Engineering Education Innovations Forum.

Kober, N., 2015. Reaching Students: What Research Says About Effective Instruction in Undergraduate Science and Engineering. The National Academies Press.

Shen, J. et al, 2008. Learning Strategies in Online Collaborative Examinations. *In IEEE Transactions on Professional Communication*, Vol. 51, No. 1,

Willey, K. and Gardner, A., 2012. Collaborative Learning Frameworks to Promote a Positive Learning Culture. *Proceedings of the Frontiers in Education Conference*. IEEE.

Wagner, T., 2008. Rigor Redefines: The Seven Survival Skills for Careers, College, and Citizenship. Advisors Corner.

Reflection Papers

HOLOGRAPHIC REALITY IN EDUCATION: THE FUTURE OF AN INNOVATIVE CLASSROOM

Athanasia Maria Tsiampa [a] and Konstantina Skolariki[b]
[a] *HAU, Hellenic American Union, Athens, Greece*
[b] *Deanery of Biomedical Sciences, University of Edinburgh, UK*

ABSTRACT

Latest research suggests that the most effective methods on education are those which utilize technological tools that provide an interactive approach to learning. Exploratory technology which involves augmented reality applications in the regular school program, gives the opportunity to young learners to become autonomous and active in their thinking, by stimulating multidimensionally their brains. Based upon this claim, this paper aims to present and propose the application, in every classroom, of an exploratory technology (specifically holographic reality), adapted to a new model which emphasizes the personal learning style of every student. This will result in the improvement of the learning process since multidimensional stimuli will create new cognitive paths, affecting the level of assimilation, regardless of any possible special learning needs. This new approach will be supported by the latest research findings in the field of Neuroscience and their implications on the process of learning and memory.

KEYWORDS

Neuroplasticity, Learning Disabilities, Holograms, Holographic Reality, Brain Stimulation, Augmented Environment

1. BACKGROUND INFORMATION

The learning process is highly dependent on neuroplasticity (Zhang and Kourtzi, 2010). Neuroplasticity is the ability of the brain to change and reorganize itself in order to adapt in new situations. During this reorganization, new neural connections are formed (neurogenesis), and the synaptic structures change in response to environmental alterations. However, for the rewiring to be successful, the neurons need to be efficiently stimulated through training. Learning disabilities are primarily neurobiological in origin and are characterised as a group of disorders that affect the acquisition and comprehension of information.

With the concept of neuroplasticity in mind, the Eaton Arrowsmith School (EAS) helps children with learning disabilities such as dyslexia and Attention Deficit Hyperactivity Disorder (ADHD) to overcome educational obstacles by reorganizing their brains. This reformation involves a regimen of cognitive exercises that are founded based on principles of neuroplasticity. Kleim and Jones describe the ten principles of experience-dependent neuroplasticity as: 1) "Use it or Lose it". Neural circuits associated with a certain function begin to degrade if individuals do not perform said function regularly, 2) "Use it and improve it". Training of a particular function could result to enhancement of said function, 3) "Specificity". The type of training determines the type of plasticity, 4) "Repetition Matters". Sufficient repetition is required for plasticity to be induced, 5) "Intensity Matters". Induction of plasticity requires not only sufficient repetition but sufficient intensity as well, 6) "Time Matters". Different types of plasticity occur at different times during training, 7) "Salience Matters". Training must be salient enough to induce plasticity, 8) "Age Matters". Plasticity induction by training, occurs more readily in younger brains, 9) "Transference". In response to one training experience, plasticity can lead to enhanced acquisition of similar behaviours and 10) "Interference". Hence, by creating personalised training exercises that address each individual and disorder separately, EAS managed to help thousands of children with learning disabilities and improve their cognitive functions.

The inclusion of each learner on a regular classroom environment, regardless of any special learning needs, is lacking in the majority of educational systems. New technological approaches can help resolve this problem. Personalized tools, such as assimilation tools, can be used to help learners with disabilities to efficiently transform the information they receive into action, therefore enhancing the development of their higher order cognitive skills. According to De Freitas and Levene, 2004, higher order cognitive skills can be achieved through an "interactive simulation-based learning system", since simulations allow individuals to have repeated trials without risking the loss of valuable information (De Freitas and Levene, 2004).

2. CONSIDERATIONS FOR IMPLEMENTATION

In order to measure the changes that should be induced in the brain during the use of holographic applications, previous literature suggests the use of EEG (electro-encephalograph) (Zhang and Kourtzi, 2010). With EEG we can measure and analyze the power spectra of alpha, beta and theta waves.

It is claimed that learners with special learning needs (SLN) can effectively decode graphic symbols when they can have physical contact and experience with these symbols in space. Hence, by exploring the environment from visual to physical context, learners achieve increased engagement. It is assumed that immersive games such as the virtual representation of the alphabet in space through holographic reality, would help learners to acquire the tasks by physically engaging in the process of learning with the activation of gross motor skills, realizing the meaning and the representation of the symbol in the simulated real-life context. Through this process, we want to demonstrate that when learners have the opportunity to explore the symbol with gross motor skills involvement, synchronicity between brain waves occurs and long term potentiation (LTP) is reached. This way, memory consolidation which depends on LTP, contributing factor of synaptic plasticity, is reached thus affecting brain plasticity. Memory consolidation integrates repetitive reactivation of the memory store (engram) leading to its transformation into long-term memories (Born and Rasch, 2013).

By purposefully planning personalized learning and by following cyclical procedures to ensure impact, the learners ascertain critical skills and a sense of real presence. Simulation tools in education, specifically holograms and their application on school subjects, such as languages and history could bring a breakthrough in teaching methodology. The correspondence between real life experiences and action games can lead to a thorough understanding and intake of information. Evidence propose that visuo-motor and visual attention skills boost specific domains that can make learning faster; empower semantic memory and increase spatial resolution of visual processing (Green and Bavelier, 2007).

Through the targeted use of holographic application in specific classroom activities the visual, auditory and kinesthetic stimuli of learners will be activated by the realistic representation of symbols and contexts in space through holographic reality. Therefore, learners of all learning profiles, will have the opportunity to conceptualize ideas in reality through their unique brain functions.

Future work includes the creation: i) of new three-dimensional interactive contents for targeted learning environments and ii) of prototype contents relevant to specific subjects and their adaptation to the learners' profiles. In addition, further research regarding the applications of holographic reality adapted to personal learning styles, on the augmented environment is required (Koutromanos, Sofos and Avraamidou, 2015).

REFERENCES

Born, J. and Rasch, B. (2013). About sleep's role in memory. *Physiological Reviews*, 93(2), pp.681-766.

De Freitas, S., and Levene, M. (2004). Exercising Your Brain: A Review of Human Brain Plasticity and Training-Induced Learning. IADIS Proceedings, 15-17 December, Lisbon, Portugal

Green, C. and Bavelier, D. (2007). Action-Video-Game Experience Alters the Spatial Resolution of Vision. *Psychological Science*, 18(1), pp.88-94.

Kleim, J. and Jones, T. (2008). Principles of Experience-Dependent Neural Plasticity: Implications for Rehabilitation After Brain Damage. *Journal of Speech Language and Hearing Research*, 51(1), p.S225.

Koutromanos, G., Sofos, A. and Avraamidou, L. (2015). The use of augmented reality games in education: a review of the literature. *Educational Media International*, 52(4), pp.253-271.

Zhang, J. and Kourtzi, Z. (2010). Learning-dependent plasticity with and without training in the human brain. *Proceedings of the National Academy of Sciences*, 107(30), pp.13503-13508.

HOW STUDENTS-MANAGERS USE DESIGN THINKING TO COLLECT IT-PROJECT REQUIREMENTS

Elvira Strakhovich
Graduate School of Management, St.-Petersburg State University
Russia, 199004, Saint-Petersburg, Volkhovsky per., 3., Russia

ABSTRACT

The paper discusses a case of applying the design thinking method in studying one of the key areas of project management - the project requirements gathering. This case is about the study of IT project management on a bachelor program of a business school. The students without special technical background shall understand what characterize the project and product requirements and how to manage the requirements. The results of the experiments with usage of whole cycle of the design thinking process and usage of some of the cycle phases into the different student groups are discussed. The importance of an "empathize" phase in the learning process is highlighted.

KEYWORDS

Design Thinking, Business Case, Project Requirement

1. INTRODUCTION

The requirements management is an important part of every project, especial IT project. Basically, the students-bachelots of the managerial program do not have an experience in IT area and need some additional clarification of the specifics of the product and project requirements. Every project should start with a business case determination. Usually the students get some predefined business case for a training project and collect the requirements using one of the suitable methods. Starting with the suggested predefined business case, the students not always understand its specifics and, as a result, they get a big gap between the proper product requirements and collected ones. To use the design thinking method for the training project, only a problem area is identified and the students shall define a type of IT product and an appropriate business case.

2. USAGE OF THE DESIGN THINKING METHOD FOR EDUCATION

The design thinking method was originally widely used in the technical fields, than it was successfully applied in humanities, including education (Melles G. et al, 2015). The researchers in the education area propose to design curricula on the basis of the design thinking for the different levels of the schools, i.e. the higher education, the secondary school and so one. The special recommendation is to use the design thinking in the business school (Matthews J. and Wrigley C., 2017) because the students in the business school usually study the business case targeted for the result, at the same time the design thinking is a process-oriented that is also very important in management.

The main characteristics of this method are human centered design, integrative thinking, design management and design as strategy. All of these characteristics are important for the manager education. According to the Stanford University design school, the design thinking method composes of the five steps: empathize, define, ideate, prototype and test. The particular attention is paid to the usage of the design thinking method for the project management education (Matthews J. and Wrigley C., 2017), as the steps of the design thinking method are close to project management cycle. Some researchers declare that this method is successfully used for the development of the soft skills, such as communication, negotiation, understanding the other people needs, working in a team, making decisions, etc., what is especially important for the manager's work. Some researchers propose not to implement the whole design thinking cycle into the learning process, but to include some of the steps, arguing that this also benefits the development of soft skills (Ewin N. et al, 2017).

3. USE THE DESIGN THINKING METHOD FOR THE BUSINESS CASE DEVELOPMENT

For the course of IT-project management, the following scenario was chosen: the students should define what a system they would propose for the learning process and what would be a business case for its usage. This scenario used a familiar and understandable situation for the students and they were able to discuss and to collect the system requirements with the full understanding of the system. As pointed in (Wang S. and Wang H., 2008), to better understand the business case it should be based on the previous practice and experience.

Following the design thinking method, the students determined the necessary functionalities of the future system and tested the system design in the student audience. During the discussions about the system, the creators of the business case better understood the main idea and the scope of work for the proposed prototype, what was useful for the next step for the system development – for requirement collection.

The usage of the design thinking method for the development of the business case for the project requirements gathering showed the following benefits:

- the students working on the business case understood the essence of the planned system and well formulated and understood the functional requirements for the system,
- the collaboration for the task execution and the human centered orientation following to the design thinking method allow to develop the soft skills,
- given the different levels of the students familiarity with the information systems, the joint work required the students to exchange knowledge, to learn from each other,
- understanding of the problem area and the business case allows to better execute the next tasks.

4. CONCLUSION

The different scenarios of the design thinking method usage in the learning courses were tested. In the case when the first "empathize" step was skipped and students were given the predefined business case, the solution proposed by the students was limited in comparison with the potential possible solution, the discussed questions were non-specific and did not reflect the features of the business case. In the case when the "empathize" step was included, but the testing step was skipped, the business cases proposed by the students were diverse in topics and functions. Thus, based on this observation, it can be summarized that the inclusion of the "empathize" step opens up the opportunities for the creative approach to the problem solving and allows to get the most interesting cases.

REFERENCES

Ewin N., Luck J., Chugh R., Jarvis J. 2017. Rethinking Project Management Education: A Humanistic Approach based on Design Thinking. *Procedia Computer Science*, 121, 503-510.

Matthews J., Wrigley C. 2017. Design and Design Thinking in Business and Management Higher Education. *Journal of Learning Design*, 10 (1), 41-54.

Melles G., Anderson N., Barrett T., Thompson-Whiteside S. 2015. Problem Finding through Design Thinking in Education. In: *Inquiry-Based Learning for Multidisciplinary Programs: A Conceptual and Practical Resource for Educators (Innovations in Higher Education Teaching and Learning, Volume 3),* ed. Blessinger P., Carfora J.M. Emerald Group Publishing Limited, 191 – 209.

Wang S., Wang H. 2008. A Design Thinking Approach to Teaching Knowledge Management *Journal of Information Systems Education*, 19(2), 137-139.

INTEGRATING TECHNOLOGY AND PEDAGOGY IN UNDERGRADUATE TEACHER EDUCATION

Virginia Rich Lee
Skidmore College, Department of Education Studies , 815 N. Broadway, Saratoga Springs, New York, USA

ABSTRACT

This reflection paper examines the uses and benefits of technology integration into a college course focused on teaching mathematics and provides the foundation for future research. Teacher education course work included technology that included augmentation, modification, and redefinition of learning tasks made possible through technological redesign and creation. Course assignments and classroom activities were enhanced by technological tools and applications to encourage collaborative work, student-centered learning environments, and problem-based learning. Student reflections are included to support observed benefits of integrated technology use during college level pre-service teacher education, and directions for future research are proposed.

KEYWORDS

Technology, Collaboration, Engagement, Student-Centered, Pedagogy

1. INTRODUCTION

The increasing use and applications of information and communication technology (ICT) have impacted the educational, social and work contexts in which we learn and live. The purpose of this paper is to highlight a range of ICT pedagogical practices that have been incorporated into college level mathematics methods education course work in ways that enhance engagement and understanding of mathematical concepts while also modeling technology-rich pedagogy for pre-service teachers.

2. CLASSROOM APPLICATIONS

The use of technology by teachers is motivating to their students and impacts their performance and attitudes. (Ladd & Dinella 2009). Students who are instructed with the use of technology obtain higher scores on mathematics post-tests and demonstrate positive attitudes regarding technology. (Eyyam & Yaratan 2014). The use of a range of technologies provided opportunities for college students to experience applications that could be integrated into elementary classrooms during field placements and future employment as teachers.

2.1 Problem-based, Collaborative, Student-centered Learning

Problem-based learning involves learning through the journey of finding solutions to real-world problems. During this process, students create and revise knowledge while utilizing and expanding their reasoning, communication, critical thinking, and synthesis of information. (Duch, et al. 2001). In this college course, students designed and constructed furnished scale models of "tiny" homes. Students were presented with the problem of designing a blueprint and constructing a scale model of a home measuring less than 350 square feet. This integrated learning project utilized technology in every stage, and involved integration of the mathematical concepts of proportion, ratio, measurement and geometry. Students posed individual design questions designed models that were creative and personally relevant. This technology infused project was integrative and involved research as well as application of a variety of mathematical concepts.

Another technology-infused project in this course involved collaborating in small groups to create online mathematics awareness newsletters to support and encourage parents. The rationale behind this task was that parents of elementary children might be frustrated or unable to help their children with mathematics homework as students are learning mathematics in ways that differ from their parents' learning. Ultimately each group collaborated to compile a family newsletter that included information, templates for making math manipulatives for home use, and online games targeting concept development and mathematical reasoning. The nature of this integrated task served not only practical purposes, but also resulted in a greater depth and breadth of learning as the college students addressed authentic issues in collaborative ways.

2.2 Student Engagement

During this course, each class session incorporated technology and engaged students in collaboration to solve problems and deepen understanding. Engagement and self-directed learning are likely to be enhanced by the integration of technology. (White & Robertson 2015). Below is a sampling of student reflections indicating engagement and learning:

- "My engagement was heightened by the opportunity to use technology and create my own understanding. I will remember the feeling of being truly engaged in an assignment, and the quality of knowledge constructed, and will work to create such an environment in my future classrooms."
- "The group process really helped me to listen and work together to come up with a viable solution and a simplified formula. I think that overall the group worked well together to problem solve, and further one another's ideas."

3. CONCLUSION

Utilizing technology can create dynamic collaboration opportunities as well as creative and problem-based learning. Students claim to be motivated and engaged during these class sessions, and research indicates that students' self-reports of engagement levels are the most valid measures of engagement. (Appleton et al. 2006). This reflection paper identifies that technology-rich pedagogy in teacher education programs can provide motivation and direction for designing research to examine the benefits of technology in this context. These observations have provided a sound basis to justify and design future research to study the impact of technology on student collaboration, problem-solving, motivation, and engagement. The relationship between technology, pedagogy and content is complex. (Harris, et al. 2009). How does technology impact pre-service teachers' motivation, engagement, and collaboration? In turn, how will this impact their teaching in their own classrooms? Technology-rich pedagogy in teacher education has the potential to impact not only these future teachers, but also their future students. Accordingly, future research is being planned to empirically examine these relationships and outcomes in more detail.

REFERENCES

Appleton, J. et al., 2006. Measuring cognitive and psychological engagement: Validation of the Student Engagement Instrument. *Journal of School Psychology,* Vol. 44, No. 5, pp. 427-445.

Duch, B. J., et al., (Eds.), 2001. *The power of problem-based learning.* Sterling, VA: Stylus.

Eyyam, R., & Yaratan, H., 2014. Impact of use of technology in mathematics lessons on student achievement and attitudes. *Social Behavior and Personality,* Vol. 42, pp. 31-42.

Harris, J. et al, 2009. Teachers' Technological Pedagogical Content Knowledge and Learning Activity Types: Curriculum-based Technology Integration Reframed. *Journal of Research on Technology in Education,* Vol. 41, No. 4, pp. 393-416.

Ladd, G.W. & Dinella, L., 2009. Continuity and change in early school engagement: predictive of children's achievement trajectories from first to eighth grade. *Journal of Educational Psychology,* Vol.101, No. 1, pp. 190-206.

White, D. & Robertson, L., 2015. Implementing assistive technologies: a study on co-learning in the Canadian elementary school context. *Computers in Human Behavior,* Vol 51, pp. 1268-1275.

EMPOWERING UNIVERSITY STUDENTS WITH BLOCKCHAIN-BASED TRANSCRIPTS

Timothy Arndt
Department of Information Systems, Cleveland State University, Cleveland, OH, USA

ABSTRACT

Blockchain has emerged as a transformative technology, from its beginning as the basis of cryptocurrencies to wider applications in areas such as property registration and insurance due to its characteristic as a distributed ledger which can remove the need for a trusted third party to facilitate transaction. This spread of the technology to new application areas has been driven by the development of smart contracts – blockchain-based protocols which can automatically enforce a contract. One area where the types of problems being considered for blockchain exists is higher education. Students in higher education are increasingly mobile, and in an ever more agile world, the friction and delays caused by multiple levels of administration in higher education can cause many anxieties and hardships for students. primary platform for higher education promises to open up higher education to a wider range of learners than ever before. In this reflection paper, we give our initial considerations on the use of blockchain technology as a primary platform on which to base university transcripts in order to empower students and better fit today's ever more agile society.

KEYWORDS

Blockchain, Smart Contracts, Higher Education

1. INTRODUCTION

Blockchain burst onto the scene with a paper published by the pseudonymous Satoshi Nakamoto in 2008 and was subsequently incorporated as part of the architecture of the cryptocurrency bitcoin in the following year. Blockchain, which is an open, distributed ledger that can efficiently record transactions between two parties in a verifiable and permanent way and which can also be programmed (via so-called smart contracts) to trigger transactions automatically (Iansiti and Lakhani, 2017). As a foundational technology (like TCP/IP), blockchain has been used or proposed for use in applications far beyond cryptocurrencies, including banking (Peters and Panayi, 2016), land registration – especially in developing countries (Underwood, 2016), insurance (Lamberti, F., et al., 2017), and online voting (Ayed, 2017). In this reflection paper, we give our initial thoughts on another promising area for blockchain technology – higher education records (university transcripts).

2. DISCUSSION

In today's world, learners are more mobile than ever before. University students move from one university to another, both within one country as well as between countries. This may happen within a single degree program (student starts at a community college, moves to 4-year college X and then transfers to university Y where she completes her degree), or when completing one program and moving on to another (student completes his undergraduate degree at institute X in country Y and then starts a graduate program at institute W in country Z). Students today expect to be able to do this with a minimum of difficulty (for instance, credits for courses already taken should be transferred to the new institution so those courses don't have to be repeated).

Governments (at the state level in the USA as well at the national and international level – EU, for instance) have reacted to this new reality by passing laws to facilitate student mobility by mandating transfer of credits, etc. Universities have reacted as well in some cases, streamlining transfer of credit, admissions, transcript requests, and so on, but the record is very uneven and not nearly as frictionless as should be expected in today's agile world.

We posit that a solution (at least partial) to this problem can be achieved through the introduction of blockchain technology for student records. We propose having all of a student's records attached to that student (empowering him or her) rather than have them spread among a myriad of institutions. The student transcript (for all of the institutions attended by the student) will be stored on the distributed ledger which is the blockchain. The trust built into the blockchain means that we no longer need a 3rd party (the university) when, for instance, a potential employer requests an official transcript. Instead, an authenticated electronic transcript can be delivered immediately for a nominal fee (that fraction of a cent needed to fund the distributed infrastructure which makes up the blockchain). Compare that with the situation many students face of paying sometimes significant amounts of money to have a university send their official transcript, sometimes requiring several days time – too long in today's agile world!

There are many significant advantages to this approach to student records, but here we mention just a few. Storing student records in the distributed ledger of the blockchain rather than havimg individual universities storing them will result in cost advantages for those universities which they can pass on to students in the form of lower fees/tuitions as they can eliminate or streamline departments/offices (registrar's office), resulting in a more lean educational entity which can focus on its core mission – educating students. Storing student records in a blockchain will also allow the use of smart contracts – a computation which takes place on a distributed ledger or block chain and enforces a contract. Admissions standards can be coded as a smart contract and students can receive instantaneous admissions decisions, all at a much reduced cost – once again resulting in a leaner educational institution with savings passed on to students. Transfer of credit rules can also be encoded in smart contracts. Since the data in the transcript is itself stored on the blockchain, students will be able to see immediately which classes will transfer for credit at their new institution.

To sum up – there are many advantages to the adoption of blockchain technology for student records (transcripts). Students are empowered since they own their transcript. It is more portable, more readily available, and admissions, transfer of credit, ordering of official transcripts and other services are frictionless. Universities benefit since much of the supporting processes they provide can be outsourced or automated via blockchain allowing them to become more lean and to concentrate on their core competency – educating students – at a lower cost. We will be studying this application more in the immediate future and looking at a platform (possibly Ethereum) for implementation of a prototype system.

REFERENCES

Ayed, A. B., 2017. A conceptual secure Blockchain-based electronic voting system. *International Journal of Network Security & Its Applications*, *93*.

Iansiti, M. and Lakhani, K. R., 2017. The truth about blockchain. *Harvard Business Review*, *95*(1), 118-127.

Lamberti, F., Gatteschi, V., Demartini, C., Pranteda, C., and Santamaria, V., 2017. Blockchain or not blockchain, that is the question of the insurance and other sectors. *IT Professional*.

Peters, G. W. and Panayi, E., 2016. Understanding modern banking ledgers through blockchain technologies: Future of transaction processing and smart contracts on the internet of money. In *Banking Beyond Banks and Money* (pp. 239-278). Springer, Cham.

Underwood, S., 2016. Blockchain beyond bitcoin. *Communications of the ACM*, *59*(11), 15-17.

CHALLENGES FOR RUSSIAN STUDENTS IN COMPUTER-BASED TESTS

Anastasia A. Barsukova and Victoria Y. Aksenova
Ural Federal University named after the first President of Russia B.N. Yeltsin
Ekaterinburg, 620002, 19 Mira street, Ekaterinburg, Russia

ABSTRACT

The article aims to outline and analyze the most demanding parts of computer-based exams for the students of the Ural Federal University named after the first President of Russian B.N. Yeltsin (Ekaterinburg, Russia) during one exam session of spring of 2016-2017. For this research, a quantitative method of mean scores for reading, listening, and use of English (for levels A2, B1, B2 CEFR) was used. The data expressed in mean percentages were processed and several conclusions were drawn, trying to account for the results. The results revealed that at the A2 level there are more difficulties with the Reading part (Reading and identifying appropriate vocabulary) for the first-year students than for the second-year students, 46% and 54% respectively. By contrast, in Listening (Gap-fill) students of the second year showed lower scores (50%) than those of the first one (67%). At B1 level, the greatest challenge was Reading part (Sentence transformation) for students of both years of education (38% for the first and 50% for the second year students). B2 level students demonstrated the most considerable number of issues, among them Use of English (Keyword transformation 0 for both years of education, open cloze, word-formation), Reading (gapped text), Listening (Gap-fill, dialogue/monologue 6 multiple choice questions).

KEYWORDS

English as a Foreign Language, Computer-Based Exams, Assessment

1. INTRODUCTION

Since 2007 in accordance with the Bologna process higher education in Russia has been undergoing significant changes. One of the most important issues has been internationalization, in the broader sense 'to enhance research and knowledge capacity and to increase cultural understanding' (Altbach & Knight, 2007). All of them can be achieved only through better knowledge of English. Thus, in order to ensure graduates' good command of this language, both the process of language learning and its subsequent assessment are of utmost importance.

In the past couple of years, the students of the Ural Federal University named after the first President of Russia B.N. Yeltsin (Ekaterinburg) (hereinafter UrFU) have been learning the target language in the following way. First, students are divided into groups based on their level; Cambridge English placement test is used to determine the incoming level (using the *Cambridge English scale of assessment*). Having studied the language for 2 years, they must attain a higher level than the entrance one. During the first year of education, the test they take is of their incoming level, however, in their second year of education, the difficulty is increased and they are to take a higher level.

To most productively assess students' progress, UrFU has introduced Independent computer-based Test. This system (initially adopted in 2015) is a mock Cambridge English Language Assessment exam, including only receptive skills and use of English. The choice of a computer-based test system is justified since one of the major goals is the impartial assessment of the level of English-language proficiency. These tests, although costly, give instant feedback, reduce the amount of time the staff have to take to check the works, eliminate human-error possibility, ensure higher variability of the test (since the test pool is quite big, several students are unlikely to do the same task at the same time) (Rasskazova, Muzafarova, Daminova, & Okhotnikova, 2017).

Our aim was to analyze the results of the Independent computer-based Test taken by Bachelor degree students of the first and second years of nonlinguistic faculties and departments of UrFU in order to determine the most challenging parts of the exam and observe whether there is any progress from the first year to the second one.

Thus, the novelty of this study consists in the fact that most research dealing with computer-based tests investigate their outcomes as opposed to paper-based tests, aiming to determine whether the former put students under additional pressure. Our main aim, however, was to inform teachers of the most demanding parts of tests with a view to improving the results.

2. RESULTS OF THE RESEARCH

For the research, we chose the results of the exam taken at the end of the second term of the 2016/2017 academic year. The levels and number of students can be seen in table 1. This sample is substantial for the analysis of general trends in success in test completion.

Table 1. Number of test-taking students by level

	A2 (pre-intermediate)	B1 (intermediate)	B2 (upper-intermediate)	Total
1st year	580	259	135	964
2nd year	521	191	135	847
Total	1101	450	270	1821

All the figures here and later are expressed as mean percentage (out of 100%). Speaking about the average test results of students the most successful were the students of the second year at B1 level (71%) and with a minor difference at A2 level (69%). By contrast, the least successful were those at B2 level (62%) (66%) of the first and second year. These results might be predictable since the latter level requires the above average knowledge of the language, which consequently is the most demanding exam among all the others.

Our next stage was to see what types of tasks from what part of the test were the most challenging. We compared the results obtained by the students of the same level but of different years.

2.1 A2-Level Students' Least Successfully Done Tasks

For the students of the second year, the most challenging part was Listening (Gap-fill) 50% while for the first year students this task did not present substantial difficulties and was quite successfully done 67%. What was difficult for them was Reading with the task of reading and identifying appropriate vocabulary 46% as opposed to the second year's 54%.

Gap-fill task tests the ability to extract specific information from a dialogue or monologue. It has always been a problematic type of task for the students learning English as a second language. What is unexpected, though, is the fact that there was a lower rate of success among the second year students who must have had more time to get used to and prepare for the exam than those on their first year of education.

2.2 B1-Level Students' Least Successfully Done Tasks

At this level, there are evident problems with the Reading part (Sentence transformations) 38% for the first year and 50% for the second. This task focuses on grammatical precision and requires students to complete five sentences, all sharing a common theme or topic. However, there is an expected improvement in the score demonstrated by the second year students.

What was most surprising for us was the fact the second least successful task was Reading with the task of understanding of various kinds of short texts: authentic notices and signs, packaging information and communicative messages. The results of students of both years of education are the same 50%. A text is often accompanied by visual information related to its context. Students may either pay not enough attention to this type of task or have real difficulties in understanding the natural English speech from everyday life. We believe this must be further studied and thoroughly investigated.

Listening was challenging for the students of the first year 56% but slightly less than the Reading part. Despite this, the students of the second year did not experience the same problems with the Listening and had a higher average score of 67%.

2.3 B2-Level Students' Least Successfully Done Tasks

At the given level, students demonstrated poor results in the Use of English part in the task that consists of six questions. Each question contains three parts: a lead-in sentence, a keyword, and a second sentence of which only the beginning and end are given. Students have to fill in the gap in the second sentence so that the completed sentence is similar in meaning to the lead-in sentence. The keyword must not be changed in any way. In this part of the paper, the focus is both lexical and grammatical and a range of structures is tested. Students of both years showed insufficient results with 0% success rate.

Use of English (open cloze) presented difficulties as well. Students are required to draw on their knowledge of the structure of the language and understanding of the text in order to fill the gaps. In this part, as there are no sets of words from which to choose the answers, students have to think of a word which will fill the gap correctly. Students' results here are 46% for the first year and 56% for the second.

For the first-year students listening tasks appeared demanding as well as for the students of other levels. Interestingly at this level, not only is Gap-fill task problematic but also the extended monologue/dialogue was of the same difficulty 50%, whereas for the second year it was 73% and 67% respectively. This might be accounted for by the fact that the level presupposes the mastery of a much broader range of vocabulary and grammar, an additional challenge might be the length of the recording which is substantially longer than in the exams of the previous levels.

Moreover, Reading part with the gapped text was similarly challenging for students of both first and second years 57% and 64%. This part is not present in the exams of the previous levels; consequently, the format itself might be foreign to students.

3. CONCLUSION

As a result of our study we determined that in order to improve the results of test-taking students, teachers should be aware of the following peculiarities:

1) At A2 level, more attention should be paid to the Listening Gap-fill tasks, with special emphasis on the way to correctly transfer the answers which might account for these results;

2) At B1 level, writing sentence transformation, reading tasks (short discrete texts, signs and messages, postcards, notes, emails, labels) are particularly challenging. Like first-year students of the A2 level, first-year students of B1 level must improve their performance in Listening Gap-fill;

3) At the B2 level, students tend to experience the greatest number of challenges. In addition, as the data suggest, the year of education only slightly influences the problematic parts of the exam. The main difference is that first-year students perform less successfully in Listening tasks (Gap-fill, multiple choice with a longer dialogue). For both years, Use of English tasks (Keyword transformation, Open cloze, Word formation) and Reading (gapped text) are difficult.

Speaking about some universal challenges, Listening Gap-fill is especially tough. This may occur due to a number of reasons, for example, this task type requires short-term memory activation which does not receive the attention it deserves; students have trouble with authentic pronunciation; students do not know how to write the answers correctly. Thus, students should be taught useful strategies for the completion of these types of tasks; their vocabulary, as well as the knowledge of various accents should be expanded; lastly, work on phonetics is in order since recognizing chunks of words is invaluable for a more complete understanding of a text.

REFERENCES

Altbach, P. G., Knight, J., 2007. The internationalization of higher education: Motivations and realities. *Journal of studies in international education,* Vol.11, №3/4, pp 290-305.

Rasskazova T, Muzafarova A, Daminova J, Okhotnikova A., 2017, Computerised Language Assessment: Limitations And Opportunities. *Proceedings of International Scientific Conference eLearning and Software for Education.* Bucharest, Romania, pp. 173-180.

AUTHOR INDEX

International Association for Development of the Information Society (IADIS)
Rua Sao Sebastiao Da Pedreira
No. 100, 30, 1050-209
Lisbon, Portugal

ISBN 978-1-5108-7539-5

CURRAN ASSOCIATES INC.
proceedings.com

9 781510 875395